THE ZONDERVAN 2017
PASTOR'S
ANNUAL

For a FREE downloadable copy of the book, please visit:
http://downloads.zondervan.com/zpa2017.

THE ZONDERVAN
2017
PASTOR'S
ANNUAL

AN IDEA AND RESOURCE BOOK

T. T. CRABTREE

ZONDERVAN

The Zondervan 2017 Pastor's Annual
Copyright © 1976, 1996, 2016 by Zondervan

Requests for information should be addressed to:
Zondervan, 3900 *Sparks Drive SE, Grand Rapids, Michigan* 49546

Much of the contents of this book was previously published in *Pastor's Annual 1997.*

ISBN 978-0-310-49398-3

Cover Design: Angela Eberlein
Cover Image: Superstock.com

Printed in the United States of America

16 17 18 19 20 21 22 23 24 25 /DHV/ 20 19 18 17 16 15 14 13 12 11 10 9 8 7 6 5 4 3 2 1

CONTENTS

Contributing Authors *10*
Preface. *11*

SERMONS

Jan 1	Sun AM	Be Strong in the Lord *(Eph. 6:10)*	13
Jan 1	Sun PM	The Blessed Poor *(Matt. 5:3)*	16
Jan 4	Wed	Solving Some of Our Prayer Difficulties *(Phil. 4:6)* . . .	19
Jan 8	Sun AM	The Whole Armor of God *(Eph. 6:11)*	21
Jan 8	Sun PM	The Blessed Mourners *(Matt. 5:4)*	23
Jan 11	Wed	For What Shall I Ask? *(Matt. 7:7)*	26
Jan 15	Sun AM	The Belt of Truth *(Eph. 6:14)*	28
Jan 15	Sun PM	The Blessed Meek *(Matt. 5:5)*	31
Jan 18	Wed	Some Things Jesus Taught about Prayer *(Luke 11:1)* . . .	34
Jan 22	Sun AM	The Christian's Bulletproof Vest *(Eph. 6:14)*	35
Jan 22	Sun PM	The Blessed Hungry *(Matt. 5:6)*	38
Jan 25	Wed	A Way of Private Prayer *(Ps. 102:1–2)*	41
Jan 29	Sun AM	The Sandals of Readiness *(Eph. 6:15)*	43
Jan 29	Sun PM	The Blessed Merciful *(Matt. 5:7)*	46
Feb 1	Wed	A Prayer for Spiritual Prosperity *(Col. 1:9)*	49
Feb 5	Sun AM	The Shield of Faith *(Eph. 6:16)*	51
Feb 5	Sun PM	The Blessed Pure *(Matt. 5:8)*	54
Feb 8	Wed	Christ in You, the Hope of Glory *(Col. 1:27)*	57
Feb 12	Sun AM	The Helmet of Salvation *(Eph. 6:17)*	59
Feb 12	Sun PM	The Blessed Peacemakers *(Matt. 5:9)*	62
Feb 15	Wed	Christ and the Barriers That Divide Us *(Col. 3:11)*	65
Feb 19	Sun AM	The Sword of the Spirit *(Eph. 6:17)*	67
Feb 19	Sun PM	The Blessed Persecuted *(Matt. 5:10–12)*	69
Feb 22	Wed	Living for Christ in the Home *(Col. 3:17)*	72
Feb 26	Sun AM	Prayer for Total Spiritual Mobilization *(Eph. 6:18)*	74
Feb 26	Sun PM	The Salt of the Earth *(Matt. 5:13)*	77
Mar 1	Wed	Jesus Visits a Strange Hospital *(John 5:2)*	80
Mar 5	Sun AM	The Church and Jesus *(Matt. 16:18–19)*	82
Mar 5	Sun PM	The Light of the World *(Matt. 5:16)*	85
Mar 8	Wed	The Strategy of Solace *(John 11:35)*	88
Mar 12	Sun AM	The Church and Prayer *(Acts 12:5)*	90
Mar 12	Sun PM	Christ's Standard of Righteousness *(Matt. 5:20)*	93
Mar 15	Wed	Attitudes in a Crisis *(Luke 8:50)*	96
Mar 19	Sun AM	A Church Celebration *(2 Chron. 7:14)*	98
Mar 19	Sun PM	Proper Priorities *(Matt. 5:23–24)*	102

Mar 22 Wed   When It's More Christian Not to Visit the Sick
(John 4:47) 105

Mar 26 Sun AM   A Witnessing Church *(Acts 4:20)* 107

Mar 26 Sun PM   Christ's Standard for the Home *(Matt. 19:4–6)* 110

Mar 29 Wed   A Proper and Orderly Way *(1 Cor. 14:40)* 113

Apr 2 Sun AM   The Joy of the Cross *(Heb. 12:2)* 116

Apr 2 Sun PM   Christ's Standard of Integrity *(Matt. 5:37)* 118

Apr 5 Wed   Three Kinds of Witnessing *(Luke 24:48)* 121

Apr 9 Sun AM   How Will You Treat the King? *(Zech. 9:9)* 123

Apr 9 Sun PM   Second-Mile Religion *(Matt. 5:41)* 125

Apr 12 Wed   The Content of Our Witness *(John 1:32–34)* 128

Apr 16 Sun AM   The Reality of the Resurrection *(Luke 24:11)* 130

Apr 16 Sun PM   Christ's Standard of Love toward Others
(Matt. 6:44–45) 133

Apr 19 Wed   The Manner of Your Testimony *(Acts 10:43)* 136

Apr 23 Sun AM   The Risen Christ Breaks the Blues *(Luke 24:32)* 138

Apr 23 Sun PM   Giving That Glorifies God *(Acts 20:35)* 140

Apr 26 Wed   The Motive for Personal Witnessing *(Acts 8:4)* 143

Apr 30 Sun AM   The Difference a Day Makes *(1 Cor. 15:3–4)* 145

Apr 30 Sun PM   When You Pray Say, "Our Father" *(Matt. 6:9)* 148

May 3 Wed   The Woman Who Made Up Her Mind *(Ruth 1:18)* . . . 151

May 7 Sun AM   The Risen Christ Makes Us Happy *(John 20:20)* 152

May 7 Sun PM   Hallowed Be Thy Name *(Matt. 6:9)* 155

May 10 Wed   A Transformed Enthusiast *(John 4:13–14)* 157

May 14 Sun AM   A Mother Who Prayed *(1 Sam. 1:10–11)* 159

May 14 Sun PM   Thy Kingdom Come *(Matt. 6:10)* 162

May 17 Wed   Two Women Whom Jesus Loved *(John 11:5)* 165

May 21 Sun AM   What Makes a Home Christian? *(Ps. 127:1)* 167

May 21 Sun PM   Thy Will Be Done *(Matt. 6:10)* 170

May 24 Wed   She Went about Doing Good *(Acts 9:36)* 173

May 28 Sun AM   You Will Be What You Choose to Be *(Josh. 24:15)* 174

May 28 Sun PM   Give Us Daily Bread *(Matt. 6:11)* 177

May 31 Wed   The Great Woman of Proverbs *(Prov. 31:30)* 179

Jun 4 Sun AM   Is Premarital Sex Wrong? *(1 Tim. 5:22)* 181

Jun 4 Sun PM   Forgive Us Our Debts *(Matt. 6:12, 14–15)* 184

Jun 7 Wed   Seeing beyond Today *(Gen. 12:1, 9)* 187

Jun 11 Sun AM   Train Up a Child *(Prov. 22:6)* 189

Jun 11 Sun PM   Lead Us Not into Temptation *(Matt. 6:13)* 192

Jun 14 Wed   Knowing Where to Run *(Gen. 35:7)* 195

Jun 18 Sun AM   God Give Us Men *(Jer. 5:1)* 197

Jun 18 Sun PM   Deliver Us from Evil *(Matt. 6:13)* 200

Jun 21 Wed   Loving Those Hard to Love *(Gen. 42:7, 24)* 202

Jun 25 Sun AM   Don't Act Like a Baby *(1 Tim. 4:12)* 204

Jun 25 Sun PM   Fasting That Glorifies God *(Matt. 6:16–18)* 207

Jun 28 Wed   Finding God Unexpectedly *(Exod. 3:2–3)* 210
Jul 2   Sun AM   Boldness in Prayer *(Heb. 4:16)* 213
Jul 2   Sun PM   You Can Take It with You *(Matt. 6:19–21)* 216
Jul 5   Wed   Listening for the Big Noise *(1 Kings 19:12)* 219
Jul 9   Sun AM   The Practice of Forgiveness—How to Handle
                 Mistreatment *(Luke 23:34)*. 221
Jul 9   Sun PM   What Is Important? *(Matt. 6:33)* 223
Jul 12 Wed   Looking in the Mirror *(Isa. 6:5)* 226
Jul 16 Sun AM   The Promise of Paradise *(Luke 23:43)*. 228
Jul 16 Sun PM   Why Worry? *(Matt. 6:31–32)* 230
Jul 19 Wed   In the Shadow of Loneliness *(John 16:32)*. 233
Jul 23 Sun AM   The Christian and Family Concerns *(John 19:25)*. . . . 235
Jul 23 Sun PM   A Judge Who Condemns Himself *(Matt. 7:1)* 238
Jul 26 Wed   Dealing with Despair *(Ps. 22:1)*. 241
Jul 30 Sun AM   The Problem of Loneliness *(Matt. 27:46)* 243
Jul 30 Sun PM   Casting Pearls before Swine *(Matt. 7:6)* 246
Aug 2   Wed   Our Living Savior *(Heb. 7:25)* 250
Aug 6   Sun AM   The Thirst of Our Lord *(John 19:28)*. 252
Aug 6   Sun PM   Encouragement to Prayer *(Matt. 7:11)*. 254
Aug 9   Wed   Christ Lives within His Church *(Matt. 18:20)* 257
Aug 13 Sun AM   Mission Impossible—Accomplished *(John 19:30)*. . . . 259
Aug 13 Sun PM   The Golden Rule *(Matt. 7:12)* 261
Aug 16 Wed   The Living Christ in Your Home *(John 1:11–13)*. 264
Aug 20 Sun AM   The Commitment of Faith *(Luke 23:46)* 266
Aug 20 Sun PM   The Road to Life *(Matt. 7:13–14)*. 268
Aug 23 Wed   Servants to/for the Living Lord *(Matt. 25:45)*. 271
Aug 27 Sun AM   Getting Sinners to the Savior *(Mark 2:3)* 273
Aug 27 Sun PM   The Folly of Hypocrisy *(Matt. 6:5)*. 276
Aug 30 Wed   The Promise of Christ's Abiding Presence
                 (Matt. 18:20). 278
Sep 3   Sun AM   Putting on the Christian's Uniform *(Col. 3:12)*. 281
Sep 3   Sun PM   The Test of Deeds *(Matt. 7:20)* 285
Sep 6   Wed   Anger *(Eph. 4:26–27)*. 287
Sep 10 Sun AM   The Way of Faith *(Ps. 84:12)* 289
Sep 10 Sun PM   Warning against Self-Deception *(Matt. 7:21)* 293
Sep 13 Wed   Backbiting *(1 Peter 2:1–2)*. 296
Sep 17 Sun AM   An Ambassador in Chains *(Eph. 6:19–20)*. 298
Sep 17 Sun PM   Why Be Foolish? *(Matt. 7:24)*. 301
Sep 20 Wed   Boasting *(2 Tim. 3:2)*. 303
Sep 24 Sun AM   The Highest Joy of Living *(Acts 20:35)* 305
Sep 24 Sun PM   Where Is Religious Authority? *(Matt. 7:28–29)*. 309
Sep 27 Wed   Envy *(Prov. 14:30)* 311
Oct 1   Sun AM   Did God Make a Mess? *(Heb. 2:8–9)* 314
Oct 1   Sun PM   Maintaining the Unity of the Spirit *(Eph. 4:3)* 317

Oct 4	Wed	Forgiveness *(Luke 7:47)*	319
Oct 8	Sun AM	God on a Campground *(John 1:14)*	321
Oct 8	Sun PM	Do Not Grieve the Holy Spirit *(Eph. 4:30)*	325
Oct 11	Wed	Rejected Love *(Mark 12:10)*	327
Oct 15	Sun AM	People Need Help *(Mark 1:40–42)*	329
Oct 15	Sun PM	The Command to Be Filled with the Holy Spirit *(Eph. 5:18)*	333
Oct 18	Wed	The Four Who Were Lost *(Luke 15:7)*	335
Oct 22	Sun AM	How to Get Help *(John 4:50)*	338
Oct 22	Sun PM	The Holy Spirit's Use of the Word of God *(Eph. 6:17)* .	342
Oct 25	Wed	The Religion of Resourcefulness *(Luke 16:9)*	344
Oct 29	Sun AM	The Word of God *(Heb. 4:12)*	347
Oct 29	Sun PM	Praying in the Spirit *(Eph. 6:18)*	350
Nov 1	Wed	The Optimism of Jesus *(Matt. 13:31–32)*	352
Nov 5	Sun AM	The Vows of God *(Ps. 116:14)*	354
Nov 5	Sun PM	The Wiles of the Devil *(Gen. 3:4–5)*	357
Nov 8	Wed	God's Wage and Hour Law *(Matt. 20:16)*	360
Nov 12	Sun AM	Channels of God's Grace *(1 Peter 4:10)*	362
Nov 12	Sun PM	Tempted of the Devil *(Matt. 4:1)*	364
Nov 15	Wed	Making the Most of What You Have *(Luke 19:23)*	367
Nov 19	Sun AM	The Shape of Our Thanksgiving *(Ps. 107:1)*	370
Nov 19	Sun PM	The Enemy of the Kingdom—the Devil *(Matt. 13:28, 39)*	373
Nov 22	Wed	Staying Out of God's Business *(Mark 4:28)*	375
Nov 26	Sun AM	What Is Your Heart's Desire? *(Rom. 10:1)*	378
Nov 26	Sun PM	The Tricks of the Devil *(Eph. 6:11)*	381
Nov 29	Wed	When God Throws a Party *(Luke 14:12–14)*	384
Dec 3	Sun AM	The First Christmas *(Matt. 1:23)*	387
Dec 3	Sun PM	Sharing the Good News *(2 Kings 7:9)*	390
Dec 6	Wed	The Danger of Delay *(Matt. 25:11–13)*	391
Dec 10	Sun AM	Is Christmas Too Costly? *(Matt. 2:13)*	394
Dec 10	Sun PM	The Great Commission and You *(Matt. 28:19)*	397
Dec 13	Wed	Make the Most of Your Life *(1 Tim. 4:12)*	398
Dec 17	Sun AM	What to Give for Christmas *(Matt. 2:11)*	401
Dec 17	Sun PM	The Whole Gospel for the Whole World *(Matt. 28:19–20)*	403
Dec 20	Wed	Don't Worry about Tomorrow *(Matt. 6:25)*	405
Dec 24	Sun AM	Why Is Jesus Coming Again? *(John 14:2–3)*	407
Dec 24	Sun PM	The Song the Angels Sang *(Luke 2:10)*	410
Dec 27	Wed	When Life Hands You a Lemon *(Job 2:10)*	412
Dec 31	Sun AM	Retrospective and Perspective *(Matt. 28:20)*	414
Dec 31	Sun PM	You Can Take It from Here *(Matt. 28:19–20)*	417

MISCELLANEOUS HELPS

Messages on the Lord's Supper

The Lord's Supper: Interpretations of It *(Mark 14:22–23)* 421
The Lord's Supper from the Journalistic Point of View *(Luke 22:19–20)* . 422
Taking the Bread and Cup *(Matt. 26:26–27)* 423

Messages for Children and Young People

The Search for Happiness *(Eccl. 12:1, 13)* 425
God Is Looking *(Ezek. 22:30)* 427
An Abundant Life *(John 10:10)* 429

Funeral Meditations

The Lord Provides *(Ps. 23)* 430
Victory over Death *(1 Cor. 15:54)* 432
Quality Living *(Eph. 4:1)* 433

Weddings

Marriage Service 434

Sentence Sermonettes

. . . . 437

Subject Index 439
Index of Scripture Texts 441

Contributing Authors

Harold T. Bryson	AM	April 16, 23, 30
		May 7
T. T. Crabtree		All messages other than those
		attributed to others
T. Hollis Epton	PM	March 1, 8, 15, 22, 29
David T. Grant	AM	December 31

MISCELLANEOUS SECTION

James G. Harris	PM	May 3, 10, 17, 24
		December 3, 10, 17, 24
James E. Heaton		All Sunday Evening messages for
		January 1 through September 24
W. T. Holland	PM	November 5, 12, 19, 26
Joe L. Ingram	PM	January 4, 11, 18, 25
	AM	November 12
David L. Jenkins	PM	June 7, 14, 21, 28
		July 5, 12, 19, 26
Howard S. Kolb	PM	September 6, 13, 10, 27
	AM	December 3, 10, 17, 24
Jerold R. McBride	PM	October 4, 11, 18, 25
		November 1, 8, 15, 22, 29
		December 6, 13, 20, 27
E. Warren Rust	PM	December 31
Leonard Sanderson	AM	March 5, 12, 19, 26
		October 1, 8, 15, 22
Fred M. Wood	AM	May 14, 21, 28
		June 4, 11, 18, 25

PREFACE

Favorable comments from ministers who serve in many different types of churches have encouraged me to believe that the *Pastor's Annual* provides valuable assistance to many busy pastors as they seek to improve the quality, freshness, and variety of their pulpit ministry. To be of service to fellow pastors in their continuing quest to obey our Lord's command to Peter, "Feed my sheep," is a privilege to which I respond with gratitude.

I pray that this issue of the *Pastor's Annual* will be blessed by our Lord in helping pastors to plan and produce a preaching program that will better meet the spiritual needs of the congregation to which they are called to minister.

This issue contains sermons by several contributing authors who have been effective contemporary preachers and successful pastors. Each of these authors is listed with his sermons in Contributing Authors. I accept responsibility for sermons not listed there.

This issue of the *Pastor's Annual* is dedicated to the Lord with a prayer that he will bless these efforts to let the Holy Spirit lead us in preparing "A Planned Preaching Program for the Year."

JANUARY

■ **Sunday Mornings**

Paul's call to victorious Christian living issued to the believers in Ephesus serves as a basis for messages dealing with humankind's problem with Satan and evil. "Putting on the Whole Armor of God" is an appropriate theme for expository messages based on Ephesians 6:10–20.

■ **Sunday Evenings**

Sunday evening messages for the next several months are based on Jesus' Sermon on the Mount. Jesus' sermon contains great principles and ideals by which believers are to live.

■ **Wednesday Evenings**

The apostles asked of Jesus, "Lord, teach us to pray." This is a prayer that we should continue to pray, and it is the theme for this month's Wednesday evening services.

SUNDAY MORNING, JANUARY 1

Title: Be Strong in the Lord

Text: "Finally, be strong in the Lord and in the strength of his might" **(Eph. 6:10 RSV)**.

Scripture Reading: Ephesians 6:10–20

Hymns: "God, Our Father, We Adore Thee," Frazer
                "Breathe on Me," Hatch
                "All the Way My Saviour Leads Me," Crosby

Offertory Prayer: Heavenly Father, we thank you for the privilege of living in a country that has been blessed by the lives and gifts of those who have gone before us. We thank you for the privilege of being members of your family. We are grateful today for all of our brothers and sisters in Christ. Help us now as we bring our tithes and offerings as well as our lives in service to you. We ask that you use our gifts for the building up of your church and for the proclaiming of the good news of your love to people everywhere. In Jesus' name we pray. Amen.

Introduction

Where do you find strength for living?

Some seek for strength in the securing of a good education. These are to be commended. However, a doctorate does not guarantee us the strength we will need when we are threatened by life's pressures. Some seek for strength in the acquiring of great financial resources. Money can solve many of the problems we face but not all of them. Many seek strength for living by developing meaningful friendships. We cannot overestimate the value of strong friendships. True friends are rich blessings from God, but they cannot meet our every need.

The apostle Paul said that strength sufficient for coping with all of life's problems comes only from the Lord. Our text says, "Finally, be strong in the Lord and in the strength of his might." Paul was living in an environment where the strength of the Roman Empire was prominent and evil was well entrenched. From many years of experience, this veteran follower of Jesus Christ encouraged his readers to be strengthened in the Lord, and in the power of his sufficiency. Paul found the strength he needed for all circumstances in Jesus Christ (Phil. 4:13). He had learned how, in the Lord, to live contentedly in the depths of despair as well as on the crest of victory and success.

Paul was aware of Satan's methods, and he knew that our only hope of victory would be found in the strength of the Lord. The immensity of our responsibilities as individuals and as the church demands that we rely on strength that comes from above.

Our Lord had promised his disciples the spiritual vitality they would need to live victorious lives and to render effective service (Acts 1:8). Paul encouraged the believers in Ephesus to be strong in the power of the Holy Spirit (Eph. 5:18). His exhortations about being filled with the Spirit and being strong in the Lord are imperative. Being filled with the Spirit and strong in the Lord are not optional for believers who want to overcome evil and render effective service. They *must* receive God's gift of the Holy Spirit.

I. The Holy Spirit is the Father's personal gift to each believer.

    A. *One of the great promises to each person who repents and confesses his faith in Jesus Christ in believer's baptism is the gift of the Holy Spirit (Acts 2:38).*

    B. *We receive this gift of the Holy Spirit when we put faith in Jesus Christ as Lord and Savior (Gal. 3:14).*

The gifts of God are his personal gifts to us. In the Holy Spirit, God gives to us his personal presence.

II. The Holy Spirit is the Father's present gift to each of his children (1 Cor. 3:16).

Some people think of the Holy Spirit in terms of ancient history. They think of him as having been active on the day of Pentecost and during the days of the church's infancy. They have not responded to his living presence. Are you aware that God has given you this precious gift of the Holy Spirit?

Do not relegate the work of the Spirit to the past or think only in terms of what he might do in the future. He is God's present gift to you.

III. The Holy Spirit is the Father's precious gift to each of his children.

Most of us give birthday gifts to family members and friends. The value and type of gifts we give vary according to our relationship with the persons to whom we give and according to their age and interests. Some gifts will be valuable while others will have little value at all. When God gives us his Holy Spirit, he gives us the most precious gift of all.

    A. *The Holy Spirit helps us to know that we are the children of God (Rom. 8:16).* The Holy Spirit will assist us in our prayer life (Rom. 8:26).

    B. *The Holy Spirit will lead us in the right paths as we try to live godly lives (Rom. 8:14).*

    C. *Through the Holy Spirit God assures us that he will raise us from the dead (Rom. 8:11).*

How do you value this gift of God to you? Do you consider the Holy Spirit a precious gift?

IV. The Holy Spirit is the Father's permanent gift to each of his children.

    A. *The Holy Spirit is the divine seal of God's ownership granted to each believer and serves as a divine guarantee that God will complete the great redemption that was started within each of us in our conversion experience (Eph. 1:13–14).*

    B. *Jesus encouraged his disciples in a time of despondency by assuring them that the Holy Spirit would dwell with them forever (John 14:16).* In comparison with our Lord's brief ministry on earth, the Holy Spirit was bestowed as a permanent gift to do the work of God within each of us.

        It is possible to so grieve and quench the Holy Spirit that we feel that the Holy Spirit has departed from us. Our feelings of emptiness and depression are in reality the work of the Holy Spirit trying to bring us back to a position of faithfulness and responsible discipleship.

V. The Holy Spirit is the Father's powerful gift to each of his children (Rom. 8:26).

When Paul wrote to Timothy, he declared, "The Spirit God gave us does not make us timid, but gives us power, love and self-discipline (2 Tim. 1:7 NIV). God's power becomes available to us in adequate supply when we recognize our weakness and cast ourselves on his grace and sustaining presence (2 Cor. 12:9–10). We are to strengthen ourselves in the power of the Holy Spirit rather than lean on human resources as we try to cope with the stresses, pressures, and dangers of life.

Conclusion

The apostle speaks from personal experience when he says, "I can do all things in him who strengthens me" (Phil. 4:13 RSV). This declaration does not come from the wild imaginations of a fanciful thinker. Rather, Paul was proclaiming the adequacy of Jesus Christ to give him the strength to do what needs to be done in any circumstance. In the strength of the Lord, let us face the fears that threaten us, let us resist Satan and draw close to God, let us face our responsibilities and opportunities. Jesus Christ wants to bring God's strength into your life and will do so as you trust him and follow him.

SUNDAY EVENING, JANUARY 1

Title: The Blessed Poor

Text: "Blessed are the poor in spirit: for theirs is the kingdom of heaven" **(Matt. 5:3).**

Scripture Reading: Matthew 4:23–5:3; Luke 6:12–20

Introduction

The Sermon on the Mount is the greatest sermon ever preached by the greatest preacher who ever preached. The preacher is "the Word of God." Of him the Father God testified, "This is my beloved Son, in whom I am well pleased; hear ye him" (Matt. 17:5). What finer way to enter the New Year than by an extended series of sermons from this greatest of sermons? What did Jesus say? What did his message mean to his first hearers? What is its relevance to us today?

Matthew and Luke preserved the sermon for us in Matthew 5–7 and Luke 6:17–49. Matthew was an eyewitness; Luke claimed to have received his material from eyewitnesses (see Luke 1:1–4). Both accounts are compressed. Matthew's Sermon on the Mount and Luke's Sermon on the Plain seem to be one discourse. Dr. A. T. Robertson, in *A Harmony of the Gospels,* stated the case as follows:

> There is little doubt that the discourses given by Matthew and Luke are the same, Matthew locating it on "the mountain," and Luke "on a level place," which might easily be a level spot on a mountain. Observe that they begin and end alike, and pursue the same general order. Luke omits various matters of special interest to Matthew's Jewish readers (e.g., Matt. 5:17–42), and other matters that he himself will give elsewhere (e.g., Luke 11:1–4; 12:22–31); while Luke has a few sentences (as vv. 24–26, 38–40), which are not given by Matthew (A. T. Robertson, *A Harmony of the Gospels* [New York: Harper and Brothers, 1922], 48).

Luke 6:12–19 recounts that Jesus went up into a mountain to pray. After a night of prayer, he chose from his disciples twelve whom he also named apostles. They came down to a level place where he stood (which probably means that he stopped walking). A multitude gathered, and he healed all who had diseases. Desiring to teach them, "he went up into a mountain: and when he was set, his disciples came unto him: and he opened his mouth, and taught them" (Matt. 5:1–2). As we learn from Matthew 7:28–29, the people also followed and heard the sermon. Jesus probably found a natural amphitheater, a level place in the mountain area, where he could sit down and see the multitudes. The disciples were in the immediate foreground, and the people were behind them.

The rabbis occasionally taught their disciples after the Socratic example, but their formal teaching was done while seated. That Jesus took his seat and that he "opened his mouth" indicates an important discourse. Jesus desired to explain to his disciples the meaning of discipleship. It was in a sense an ordination sermon for the Twelve. Jesus' term "kingdom of heaven," which seems to be synonymous with "kingdom of God," signifies the reign of God. In the kingdom of heaven, Christ is the King. Although the word *Christian* did not come into usage until later at Antioch (see Acts 11:26), it has become the more generally used term to signify a citizen of the kingdom of heaven. The theme, then, of the Sermon on the Mount is the meaning of Christian discipleship, and the purpose was to help the disciples understand the meaning of their Christian faith and service.

The opening section, Matthew 5:3–12, describes the characteristics of a Christian in eight beatitudes (some count seven; others find nine). They are called beatitudes because in the Latin versions the first word of each is the word for "blessed." The first beatitude is the subject of this sermon.

I. The meaning of "blessed."

The Greek used here would literally be translated "happy." It is so translated in some passages: "If ye know these things, happy are ye if ye do them" (John 13:17); "Happy is he that condemneth not himself in that thing which he alloweth" (Rom. 14:22); "If ye suffer for righteousness' sake, happy are ye" (1 Peter 3:14); "Behold, we count them happy which endure" (James 5:11). In several other passages, as in our text, it is translated "blessed." Our English word *happy* etymologically goes back to *hap,* which has the idea of chance, or good luck, as in *haply, hapless, happiness,* etc. No English word quite conveys the Greek. The meaning is happy in the godly sense. It means happy with reference to moral character rather than to outward condition. Perhaps "to be congratulated" conveys the idea. The first hearers must have been startled to hear Jesus say, "Happy are the poor."

II. The meaning of "poor in spirit."

The word for "poor" is the word for "beggar" rather than the more common word for one who works by the day.

A. *The meaning is not:*
1. Poor in this world's goods. Many have so misunderstood and have taken vows of poverty. Poverty is not in itself a blessing, and it is more likely a curse.
2. Poor-spirited cowards, as the ten spies who reported: "And we were in our own sight as grasshoppers, and so were we in their sight" (Num. 13:33). Those who think of themselves as grasshoppers will usually find that others will accept their evaluation.

   In the parable of the talents, the man who was given one talent and failed to invest it, confessed to his master, "I was afraid, and went and hid thy talent in the earth" (Matt. 25:25). His master rebuked him for his cowardice.
3. A mean spirit or a poor spirit who cheats.
B. *Rather, "poor in spirit" means being poor in the realm of the spirit, as when we realize that we are not self-sufficient and that we need God.* When we are conscious of our need, we are humble and contrite rather than proud.

   The publican in Jesus' great parable was "poor in spirit" as he, "standing afar off, would not lift up so much as his eyes unto heaven, but smote upon his breast, saying, God be merciful to me a sinner" (Luke 18:13).

   Isaiah was "poor in spirit" when after a vision of the holy God he saw his own spiritual destitution and cried, "Woe is me! for I am undone; because I am a man of unclean lips, and I dwell in the midst of a people of unclean lips: for mine eyes have seen the King, the LORD of hosts" (Isa. 6:5). Those who are "poor in spirit" are convicted of their sins.

III. The happy condition of the poor in spirit.

A. *"For theirs is the kingdom of heaven" means that those who enter the kingdom of heaven are the "poor in spirit"—that is, people convicted of their sins are the ones who can become Christians.*
B. *Reasons for counting them happy are:*
1. Conviction of sin must precede salvation. David felt that his sin was so great that God would be just to condemn him. You can be happy for a person who is deeply convicted of sin. He or she is not far from the kingdom.
2. Conviction of sin is an evidence of God's love. If God wanted you to be lost, all he would need to do would be to leave you alone. If God did not care, he would not convict you of your poverty in the realm of the spirit.

3. Let the "poor in spirit" be happy, for there is an adequate supply of God's grace. Our guilt may be so great that we think God cannot forgive us, but be happy, friend, "the blood of Jesus Christ his son cleanseth us from all sin" (1 John 1:7). "All we like sheep have gone astray; we have turned every one to his own way; and the LORD hath laid on him the iniquity of us all" (Isa. 53:6).

Conclusion

True happiness does not depend on outward circumstances but on right relationship with God. If you feel no need of God, it is a time to be alarmed. You are in danger of being lost. If you are poor in spirit, rejoice. Christian converts are made from convicted sinners.

WEDNESDAY EVENING, JANUARY 4

Title: Solving Some of Our Prayer Difficulties

Text: "In every thing by prayer and supplication with thanksgiving let your requests be known unto God" **(Phil. 4:6).**

Scripture Reading: Philippians 4:6–8

Introduction

When you pray do you always receive benefit? Do you always feel God's presence? Do you always feel enlightened? Do you always feel strengthened?

If you are normal, the answer is "Sometimes I do and sometimes I don't." Let's face it—we often encounter difficulties when we pray.

I. Identifying some of the difficulties.

Sometimes we are out of fellowship with the Lord. This broken fellowship may be caused by:

Impurity of life. Read Psalm 51 to see how important it is to have a clean moral life.

A vindictive and unchristian spirit. Here is what Jesus said: "Therefore if thou bring thy gift to the altar, and there rememberest that thy brother hath ought against thee; leave there thy gift before the altar, and go thy way; first be reconciled to thy brother, and then come and offer thy gift" (Matt. 5:23–24). He also said, in Matthew 6:14–15: "For if ye forgive men their trespasses, your heavenly Father will also forgive you: But if ye forgive not men their trespasses, neither will your Father forgive your trespasses."

Selfishness and greed. James says that "the effectual fervent prayer of a righteous man availeth much" (5:16). Until the heart is right with God, the life will have no power with God.

Sometimes we try to imitate someone else's prayer life. We must learn not to be a slave to someone else's method. We all have different needs and temperaments. Consider the difference in the lives of Moses, Elijah, Isaiah, Peter, James, John, and Paul. They were different men living at different times with different temperaments and different needs. We get into trouble when we try to pray like someone else.

Sometimes we have the problem of changing moods. Elijah had his good days and his bad days. Likewise, we may become irregular in our prayer lives if we succumb to our moods. Paul urged Timothy to "be instant in season [and] out of season" (2 Tim. 4:2). Make up your mind in advance to keep your course steady. When you can't pray as you would like to, pray as you can. Actually, your prayer life can help you out of a low mood. Many a life is like an old-fashioned well, having latent resources of living water underneath and needing only the experience of prayer to "prime the pump."

II. Solving some of the difficulties.

It surely is impossible to identify all the difficulties or hindrances in your prayer life. Maybe we haven't even touched on one of your prayer problems. Whatever your problem or problems, these statements may help you have a more fruitful prayer life.

Believe the prayer promises of the Bible. Here are a few.

"And Jesus answering saith unto them, Have faith in God. For verily I say unto you, that whosoever shall say unto this mountain, Be thou removed, and be thou cast into the sea; and shall not doubt in his heart, but shall believe that those things which he saith shall come to pass; he shall have whatsoever he saith. Therefore I say unto you, What things soever ye desire, when ye pray, believe that ye receive them, and ye shall have them" (Mark 11:22–24).

"If ye then, being evil, know how to give good gifts unto your children; how much more shall your heavenly Father give the Holy Spirit to them that ask him?" (Luke 11:13).

"Ask, and it shall be given you; seek, and ye shall find; knock, and it shall be opened unto you: For every one that asketh receiveth; and he that seeketh findeth; and to him that knocketh it shall be opened" (Matt. 7:7–8).

"Or what man is there of you, whom if his son ask bread, will he give him a stone? Or if he ask a fish, will he give him a serpent? If ye then, being evil, know how to give good gifts unto your children, how much more shall your Father which is in heaven give good things to them that ask him?" (Matt. 7:9–11).

"If ye abide in me, and my words abide in you, ye shall ask what ye will, and it shall be done unto you" (John 15:7).

There are many other passages concerning prayer, but these should be enough to encourage you.

Think good thoughts. "Be careful for nothing; but in every thing by prayer and supplication with thanksgiving let your requests be made known unto God. And the peace of God, which passeth all understanding, shall keep your hearts and minds through Christ Jesus. Finally, brethren, whatsoever things are true, whatsoever things are honest, whatsoever things are just, whatsoever things are pure, whatsoever things are lovely, whatsoever things are of good report; if there be any virtue, and if there be any praise, think on these things" (Phil. 4:6–8).

Seek to live your life within the will and purpose of God. "Blessed are they which do hunger and thirst after righteousness" (Matt. 5:6).

Conclusion

Remember the words of Paul: "Rejoice evermore. Pray without ceasing. In every thing give thanks" (1 Thess. 5:16–18).

SUNDAY MORNING, JANUARY 8

Title: The Whole Armor of God

Text: "Put on the whole armor of God, that you may be able to stand against the wiles of the devil" **(Eph. 6:11 RSV)**.

Scripture Reading: Ephesians 6:10–20

Hymns: "All Creatures of Our God and King," Francis of Assisi
"The Rock That Is Higher Than I," Johnson
"O God, Our Help in Ages Past," Watts

Offertory Prayer: Father in heaven, we thank you for the beauty of your world. Thank you for all the blessings you send into our hearts and lives. Thank you for friends, family, and brothers and sisters in Christ. Thank you for your Holy Word and for the church and what it means to us. We thank you for every assurance of your love. We come now to express our love for you with tithes and offerings. Add your blessings to these gifts that many more will come to know Jesus Christ's forgiveness of sin and receive the gift of eternal life. In Jesus' name we pray. Amen.

Introduction

The Christian life is warfare, a continuing struggle with evil. If you have not discovered this to be your own personal experience, it is possible that you have already been captured by the enemy and are a prisoner of war without being aware of it.

The apostle Paul spoke to the Ephesian Christians concerning the nature of their enemy and the character of the struggle they must put forth if they would live a victorious Christian life. Our Scripture passage contains relevant truths for each us as we engage in spiritual warfare day by day.

I. As followers of Jesus Christ, we face a wicked enemy in the devil.

Have you ever heard someone say, "I do not have an enemy in the world"? Perhaps you are among those who cannot point to a single human enemy, but all of us have an enemy in the devil (1 Peter 5:8). He is described as a powerful and wicked enemy (Eph. 6:12).

The Bible says little about the devil's origin. It seems to infer that the devil was originally created as a part of God's good creation, an archangel of great power and majesty. Because he became arrogant and greedy for power, he was cast out of heaven.

Jesus was confronted and opposed by the devil but did not yield to the devil's temptations. He repeatedly warned his disciples about their spiritual foe. The devil is described as a roaring lion who walks about seeking whom he may devour (1 Peter 5:8). He is described as the wicked one (Matt. 13:19), as a liar and murderer (John 8:44), as a deceiver (Rev. 20:8), and as the one who blindfolds the minds of people lest the light of the glorious gospel of Christ should illuminate them that they might be saved (2 Cor. 4:4).

II. It is not God's will that his children be defeated, devoured, destroyed, or degraded by the devil.

The devil is God's foe and the enemy of all people. He seeks to bring about our defeat and destruction in both time and eternity. It is difficult for us to comprehend the agony in our heavenly Father's heart when man, the crown of his creation, chooses to follow evil rather than good. God made people free, and that means they are free to do evil and to destroy themselves. People are free to choose the way of faith and faithfulness and to walk in fellowship with God. We can be absolutely assured that God is our ally in the struggle with our evil foe.

III. God offers and provides all the equipment necessary for victory.

God offers to his children his own strength and power for the struggle with evil (Eph. 6:10). The apostle John assured us that greater is he who is within us than he who is in the world (1 John 4:4). God in the Holy Spirit came to dwell within us in the moment of our conversion. The resources of God are available for those who believe and who want to live the victorious Christian life.

Paul was a prisoner for Jesus Christ. He was chained to a Roman soldier. As the days went by, his thoughts were stimulated and the Spirit of God illuminated his meditation as he made a spiritual application of the various pieces of equipment worn by a Roman soldier. He saw in each piece of equipment a part of the provision God makes for his children in their struggle with evil.

We must put on the whole armor of God. It is not enough that God provides the armor. Each believer must put on this armor and utilize it. Paul spoke in the imperative: it is absolutely essential that we use the equipment provided if we are to wage war successfully.

IV. Each of us must use what God provides.

The apostle Paul's message was not just for those who lived in the ancient city of Ephesus; we too must personalize these commands from a veteran soldier of the cross.

God has provided the belt of truth for you.
God has provided a bulletproof vest of righteousness for you.
God has provided the sandals of a ready spirit for you.
God has provided a shield of faith for you.
God has provided a helmet of salvation for you.
God has provided the sword of the Spirit for you.
God has given you the privilege of prayer as a communication system with divine headquarters.

Conclusion

Your success in the struggle with Satan will be dependent on the manner in which you utilize the armor God has provided. You must put on the armor individually and ceaselessly. There is no way by which you can be victorious if you neglect to use the equipment God has provided.

May each of us determine to discover and to utilize that which God has made available for us in the struggle to be what God would have us to be and to do what God wants us to do.

SUNDAY EVENING, JANUARY 8

Title: The Blessed Mourners

Text: "Blessed are they that mourn: for they shall be comforted" (**Matt. 5:4**).

Scripture Reading: 2 Corinthians 7:8–10

Introduction

What would you think of a person who would say to a little girl who was crying, "Little girl, why are you so happy?" You would doubtless consider that person crazy or cruel. No less startling, however, must have been the reception of Jesus' paradox "Happy are they that cry" by the disciples and the multitudes. We also are startled until we realize that the sorrow referred to is limited by the context to sorrow because of poverty in one's spiritual life.

In 2 Corinthians 7:8–10 Paul distinguished between "godly sorrow" and "worldly sorrow." "For godly sorrow worketh repentance to salvation not to be repented of: but the sorrow of the world worketh death" (v. 10).

I. Sorrow without a godly reference has no blessing.

Sorrow because one is caught in a wicked scheme has no blessing. The robber who gets caught or the drug pusher who is apprehended may be sorry because he or she has been caught, but this sorrow has no blessing. Our prisons doubtless hold many who are sorry for their condition but not for their sins.

Sorrow because of the failure of a selfish scheme has no blessing. Sorrow because of envy, jealousy, wounded pride, or frustrated ambition has no divine comfort.

Sorrow for consequences rather than sorrow for sin is sorrow without a godly reference. For example, Simon Magus thought Simon Peter had some magic more powerful than any he knew about, so he offered Peter money, saying:

> Give me also this power, that on whomsoever I lay hands, he may receive the Holy Ghost. But Peter said unto him, Thy money perish with thee, because thou hast thought that the gift of God may be purchased with money. Thou hast neither part nor lot in this matter; for thy heart is not right in the sight of God. Repent therefore of this thy wickedness, and pray God, if perhaps the thought of thine heart may be forgiven thee. For I perceive that thou art in the gall of bitterness, and in the bond of iniquity. Then answered Simon, and said, Pray ye to the Lord for me, that none of these things which ye have spoken come upon me. (Acts 8:19–24)

Simon Magus did not seem to be convicted of the enormity of his sin but rather asked Peter to pray that the consequences of it might be forgiven.

A pastor was counseling with a woman who by her own confession had lost her husband by her own adultery. She was heartbroken. As the counseling developed, however, it became plain that her sorrow was not at all because of her sin but rather because of the consequences of losing her husband.

II. Godly sorrow brings blessing.

Godly sorrow is contrite because of sin, regardless of the consequences. Godly sorrow sees sin as God sees it. One truly contrite does not willfully desire to sin even if he could be assured of personal profit and of complete secrecy.

Blessed are unsaved people who mourn because of their sins. They are poor in spirit, and their conviction issues in contrition.

We can be happy for people who are sorry for their sins, because such people are ready to turn from sin to God. The Bible has many illustrations of this. You are not happy for the prodigal son as he jauntily goes to the far country. But when he is convicted of his sins and is sorry about leaving home, you begin to feel better about him because you hope that his contrition will lead to conversion, as indeed it does.

At Pentecost many who had participated in the death of Jesus were faced with their sin by Peter's words: "Therefore let all the house of Israel know assuredly, that God hath made that same Jesus, whom ye have crucified, both Lord and Christ. Now when they heard this they were pricked in their heart, and said unto Peter and to the rest of the apostles, Men and brethren, what shall we do?" (Acts 2:36–37). It was then that Peter could tell them about salvation and Christian discipleship.

Be happy for mourning sinners, because their sorrow shows spiritual sensitivity. There is no tragedy quite like a hard heart, a tearless eye, a person without tenderness. Father Damien had served the lepers on the island of Molokai for thirteen years when one day he spilled boiling water on his feet yet felt no pain. "Wonderful," you say. No! It was the evidence that he also had leprosy. Likewise, the one whose conscience is numbed by sin is in grave danger.

Some boys were playing baseball when it came time for worship at a Christian camp. Reluctantly they left gloves, ball, and bat to attend the service. During the service one of the boys kept looking out the window toward the ball diamond. He paid no attention to the speaker. Another boy listened intently and tears ran down his cheek. You look at these two boys and are impressed to say, "Is it not sad that a boy should cry? Why cannot this lad be happy as the one whose mind is still on the game?" However, when the invitation was extended, the boy who had listened intently responded to God's invitation. Sorrow that leads one to God is great gain. Conviction, contrition, and conversion mean that God can respond with salvation and all the comforts of right relationship with him. When God sees repentance, he meets it with forgiveness. "For they shall be comforted" is the promise.

Blessed are people who mourn because of their poverty of spirit.

Satan trips believers and causes them to stumble. Saved people are justified and regenerated, and they want to do God's will, but they fall short of being as good as Jesus and may stumble into grievous sin. King David is the outstanding example in the Old Testament. Lust resulted in adultery and then murder in an attempt to cover the adultery. God used Nathan the prophet to convict David of his sin. Psalm 51 records the anguish of David's soul. If God decided to send him to hell, he knew it would be what he deserved. He prayed, "Against thee, thee only, have I sinned, and done this evil in thy sight: that thou mightest be justified when thou speakest, and be clear when thou judgest" (Ps. 51:4). David's godly sorrow led to confession and forgiveness. Rejoice with him as you read again Psalm 32. "Blessed is he whose transgression is forgiven, whose sin is covered" (v. 1).

Peter is the prominent New Testament example of a believer who fell short and repented of his sin. Peter really loved Jesus, but in a time of temptation he denied Jesus. The look of Jesus brought conviction to Peter. "And Peter remembered the word of the Lord, how he had said unto him, Before the cock crow, thou shalt deny me thrice. And Peter went out, and wept bitterly" (Luke 22:61–62). But we can be happy for Peter, for his sorrow was a godly sorrow that led to confession and restoration.

Blessed are Christians who mourn over any of life's providences, because God can use evil for good. God can turn sickness and bereavement for ultimate good. "We know that in everything God works for good with those who love him, who are called according to his purpose" (Rom. 8:28 RSV).

A pastor and his wife had nursed their daughter who had polio through a long illness that ended in death. The pastor testified, "My wife and I would choose to go through it all again if necessary for the experience of the sufficiency of God's grace which we have experienced."

I once assisted the chaplain of a penitentiary at the execution of a convicted murderer. The prisoner admitted his guilt, was truly contrite, and met death with tremendous assurance of God's salvation. He said, "Perhaps it was good that I got caught. If I had not been arrested, I would not have met the chaplain. If I had not met him, I would not have known about Jesus Christ."

Conclusion

The major teaching of Jesus in this beatitude is that sorrow for sin readies one for repentance and salvation. It seems appropriate in conclusion, however, to note that God uses sorrow to build character, compassion, and concern. One cannot reverse the beatitude and say, "Blessed are they who never mourn. Blessed are they who are always happy, lighthearted, and never serious." If there were no pain and no sorrow, there would be no sympathy. If there were no danger, there would be no heroism nor courage. The Arabs have a proverb, "All sunshine makes Sahara." Let us believe the closing words of a great hymn: "Earth hath no sorrow that heaven cannot heal."

WEDNESDAY EVENING, JANUARY 11

Title: For What Shall I Ask?

Text: "Ask, and it shall be given you" **(Matt. 7:7).**

Scripture Reading: Matthew 7:7–11

Introduction

In spite of these invitational words of Jesus, some don't think it is right or wise to petition God. Some people believe that all petitions imply selfishness and a bent toward magic. One commentator said that if prayer means the direct interposition of Providence to favor us in material things, then we can no longer believe in prayer.

The Bible does offer, however, ample evidence that we should petition God. For example, the Lord's Prayer is exclusively petition. Jesus does not propose petitionary prayer as a lazy substitute for work (see Matt. 7:7–11; John 15:7). If it is right for us to "ask," for what shall we ask God?

I. We should pray for forgiveness of sins.

John was writing to Christians when he said, "Again, a new commandment I write unto you, which thing is true in him and in you; because the darkness is past, and the true light now shineth. He that saith he is in the light, and hateth his brother, is in darkness even until now. He that loveth his brother abideth in the light, and there is none occasion of stumbling in him" (1 John 1:8–10). Hebrews 4:15–16 says, "For we have not an high priest which cannot be touched with the feeling of our infirmities; but was in all points tempted like as we are, yet without sin. Let us therefore come boldly unto the throne of grace, that we may obtain mercy, and find grace to help in time of need."

The psalmist cried, "Search me, O God, and know my heart: try me, and know my thoughts: And see if there be any wicked way in me, and lead me in the way everlasting" (Ps. 139:23–24).

II. We should pray to be delivered from temptation and Satan's power.

Jesus said to pray, "Lead us not into temptation, but deliver us from evil: For thine is the kingdom, and the power, and the glory, for ever" (Matt. 6:13).

We are assured, "There hath no temptation taken you but such as is common to man: but God is faithful, who will not suffer you to be tempted above that ye are able; but will with the temptation also make a way to escape, that ye may be able to bear it" (1 Cor. 10:13).

III. We should pray for God to show us the right way.

The psalmist cried, "Teach me to do thy will" (Ps. 143:10). Paul told the Christians at Colossae, "For this cause we also, since the day we heard it, do not cease to pray for you, and to desire that ye might be filled with the knowledge of his will in all wisdom and spiritual understanding; that ye might walk worthy of the Lord unto all pleasing, being fruitful in every good work, and increasing in the knowledge of God" (Col. 1:9–10).

IV. We should pray for strength.

Paul prayed that the Ephesians might "be strengthened with power by his Spirit in the inner man" (Eph. 3:16). He also prayed for the thorn to be removed from his flesh. Here is his answer: "My grace is sufficient for thee: for my strength is made perfect in weakness. Most gladly therefore will I rather glory in my infirmities, that the power of Christ may rest upon me" (2 Cor. 12:9).

V. We should pray that God will help us love one another.

Paul prayed for the Thessalonian Christians with these words: "Now God himself and our Father, and our Lord Jesus Christ, direct our way unto you. And the Lord make you to increase and abound in love one toward another, and toward all men, even as we do toward you" (1 Thess. 3:11–12).

VI. We should pray for daily bread.

Jesus said to pray, "Give us this day our daily bread" (Matt. 6:11).

VII. We should pray for the Lord's help in our sickness.

James said, "Confess your faults one to another, and pray one for another, that ye maybe healed" (James 5:16).

VIII. We should pray for the leadership of the Holy Spirit in our lives.

Acts 8:14–15 tells us, "Now when the apostles which were at Jerusalem heard that Samaria had received the word of God, they sent unto them Peter and John: who, when they were come down, prayed for them, that they might receive the Holy Ghost."

IX. We should pray for anything that is God's will.

In 1 John 5:14–15 the Lord promised, "And this is the confidence that we have in him, that, if we ask any thing according to his will, he heareth us: and if we know that he hear us, whatsoever we ask, we know that we have the petitions that we desired of him."

X. We should pray for anything we need.

Paul advised in Philippians 4:6, 19, "Be careful for nothing; but in every thing by prayer and supplication with thanksgiving let your requests be made known unto God. . . . But my God shall supply all your need according to his riches in glory by Christ Jesus."

Without any doubt, petitionary prayer is as instinctive as a child going to his father for his needs. Dr. C. E. Jefferson testified, "I have noticed that whenever I am in a situation in which no human help is sufficient, I pray spontaneously." When we are in the storm, it is natural to pray: "Lord, save us: we perish!"

Conclusion

Since prayer is offering God the opportunity to speak to us, to give to us, and do through us what he wills, let's pray every day about everything.

SUNDAY MORNING, JANUARY 15

Title: The Belt of Truth

Text: "Stand therefore, having girded your loins with truth" **(Eph. 6:14 RSV)**.

Scripture Reading: Ephesians 6:10–20

Hymns: "Guide Me, O Thou Great Jehovah," Williams
            "This Is My Father's World," Babcock
            "Lead On, O King Eternal," Shurtleff

Offertory Prayer: Our Father, thank you for this day. We rejoice in it because of your goodness and mercy toward us. Thank you for life with all of its privileges. We pray for the grace that we need to face its responsibilities. Today we come bringing tithes and offerings as indications of our gratitude and as tokens of our desire to cooperate with you in ministering to the needs of a world that has gone astray and must find the way back home. Add your blessings to these gifts and multiply them to the end that many will come to know Jesus Christ as Lord and Savior. In his name we pray. Amen.

Introduction

Living a victorious Christian life is not an easy achievement, for one cannot follow a comfortable road and experience victory over evil. The Christian life is a struggle requiring self-discipline and persistent dedication. Jesus' followers are confronted by spiritual foes who seek to destroy our witness and our lives.

Our Father God provides for his children the complete equipment necessary for waging a successful warfare against Satan's attacks. Paul, the missionary evangelist and writer of Scripture, chained to a Roman soldier for three years, was familiar with the soldier's equipment. He makes figurative use of each piece of the Roman soldier's equipment to illustrate great spiritual truths to Christ's followers.

Each disciple has the responsibility to utilize the equipment God has provided. There are some significant imperatives in the Scripture reading. They are "Be strong" (6:10), "Put on" (v. 11), "Take the whole armour of God" (v. 13), and "Stand therefore" (v. 14). "Having girded your loins with truth" is a participle with the force of an imperative.

The first piece of spiritual equipment is the belt of truth. The Roman soldier's belt served three valuable functions. First, the belt provided support for the middle part of the body—the back, stomach, and kidneys. Second, the belt made organization possible. It was used to arrange the various pieces of equipment the soldier carried on his body. This is demonstrated by the uniform of a police officer. His belt supports the holster and holds ammunition, handcuffs, and a billy club. A modern combat soldier would have attached to his belt a knife, perhaps a machete, a bayonet, a canteen, first-aid supplies, and ammunition. Third, the belt made efficiency possible.

Does your life need strong support, better organization, and greater efficiency? Have you ever felt, *I am so weak and helpless*? Have you ever said, "I need to get myself organized"? Are you overwhelmed at times with the impression, "I get so little accomplished"? If this is the case, then you need to buckle on the belt of truth.

I. Jesus Christ is the truth of God (John 14:6).

If you want to know what God is like, then study the life, death, resurrection, and the teachings and activities of Jesus Christ. As you look at him, you will come to an understanding and appreciation of the truth of God.

29

Wrap yourself in all of this great truth about God if you want to provide for yourself support, organization, and efficiency.

II. Great truths from God.

We need to belt ourselves with a number of great truths about God to bring support, organization, and efficiency into our personal experience.

The truth of assurance (John 3:18). This is just one of many verses of Scripture that could be quoted affirming that faith in Jesus Christ is what brings us into a relationship of divine sonship. The only assurance of salvation we can possibly have is that which comes as a result of accepting as truth that which the Bible teaches about God's provisions for us in Jesus Christ. Buckle on this great belt of truth.

The truth of forgiveness and cleansing (1 John 1:7). Through the blood of Jesus Christ, God cleanses us from all sin. We can experience the joy of forgiveness when we sincerely confess our sin and look to God for cleansing. Buckle on this great truth around your heart and life.

The truth of the Golden Rule (Matt. 7:12). Do you worry about how you relate to others? Do you find it difficult to know what to do in many circumstances? Glue the Golden Rule to your mind and heart and let it become your policy in all your relationships with others. Buckle this truth about your whole life.

The truth concerning the way to highest human happiness (Acts 20:35). All of us are seeking the happiness and joy of a fulfilling life, but many of us are missing it because we have the wrong goal. We labor under erroneous ideas about what brings happiness. Jesus taught that if you would experience joy higher than that which comes as a result of getting and having, you must live a life of giving and serving. Accept this great truth from Jesus into your innermost being. Wear it as a belt, and it will help you to organize life's priorities and will bring you support when greed tries to capture your soul.

The truth concerning our Lord's presence (Matt. 28:20). Do you ever feel deserted? Everyone needs a friend. There is never a day when we do not need our Lord's help. He has promised to be with us in all of our ways throughout all of our days. Claim this great promise and wear it as a belt.

The truth concerning the tragedies of life (Rom. 8:28). Many things happen that we cannot explain and find difficult to accept. God is at work in all things to bring about good for those who love him. Believe this with all your heart and trust him for grace and guidance. Wear this truth as a belt.

The truth concerning a hope beyond the grave (John 14:1–3). Comfort yourself with this great promise and wear it as a belt about your innermost being as you contemplate the fate of those who have died in the Lord and your own future.

Conclusion

God has provided us with his belt of truth, and it will strengthen us in times of weakness. Put it on by faith as you read God's Word. Memorize the great truths and claim and trust in God's promises. Believe that God will do what he has promised to do. Let these great truths support you in your times of need and provide a basis for organizing your life, and you will find greater efficiency in your own personal experience. Putting on the belt of truth will enable you to overcome the attacks of the devil.

SUNDAY EVENING, JANUARY 15

Title: The Blessed Meek

Text: "Blessed are the meek: for they shall inherit the earth" **(Matt. 5:5).**

Scripture Reading: Matthew 11:27–30; 1 Timothy 6:10–11; Galatians 5:22–23; Colossians 3:12–14

Introduction

If someone should say that you are a meek person, you would certainly not consider it a compliment. In fact, you would probably consider it an insult. Why? Because meek in our modern usage does not accurately represent the meaning of the Greek word Jesus used. Language is constantly changing so that in our vernacular words do not mean today what they once did. For example, in 1611 when the King James Version of the Bible was completed, homely meant a home-loving person, a spinster was one who spun, and conversation meant the whole manner of one's life and not just speech. In studying the meaning of the Sermon on the Mount, we will discover many instances in which Jesus' meaning must be rescued from the errors caused by a changing language.

I. The meaning of "meek."

Meek *is from an old Scandinavian word meaning "gentle." Merriam-Webster's Eleventh Collegiate Dictionary* defines it: "1: enduring injury with patience and without resentment: mild; 2: deficient in spirit and courage: submissive; 3: not violent or strong: moderate." In modern usage *meek* often is a term of mild contempt. It is invariably associated with weak as in expressions: "meek as a mouse" or "meek as a lamb." A meek little man is represented as a weak, effeminate creature, spineless but sweet tempered—a modern Caspar Milquetoast. This cannot be what Jesus meant.

Meekness is to be:

Like Jesus, who described himself as "meek and lowly in heart" (Matt. 11:29). Paul beseeches the Corinthians, "by the meekness and gentleness of Christ" (2 Cor. 10:1 RSV). If meekness accurately describes Jesus, it must be consistent with tremendous courage, the merciless rebuke of hypocrisy and sham, and abounding vitality. Jesus was in no sense weak in character.

Like Paul, who was courageous. Paul wrote to Timothy, "For God hath not given us the spirit of fear" (2 Tim. 1:7). Christians are not cowards. Yet

Paul admonished Timothy, "Follow after righteousness, godliness, faith, love, patience, meekness" (1 Tim. 6:11). To the Colossians, Paul wrote, "Put on then, as God's chosen ones, holy and beloved, compassion, kindness, lowliness, meekness, and patience" (Col. 3:12 RSV).

If meekness means to be like Jesus and Paul, it cannot mean:

Weakness, apathy, timidity, lack of spirit, or giving in to one's circumstances because one hasn't the spirit to continue the struggle.

Cowardice or lying down before injustice because one has no courage. Absence of anger may be absence of love or of concern.

The Old Testament usage may prove helpful. This beatitude is almost a direct quote from Psalm 37:11, "But the meek shall inherit the earth." In Psalm 37:1–11 the psalmist used the *meek* as a synonym for those who "trust in the LORD and do good," and those who "wait upon the LORD." *Meekness* is an antonym for "workers of iniquity," "evildoers," and "the wicked." The Hebrew words for meek and poor are from the same root, so certainly meekness is akin to poverty of spirit.

Meekness means to be like Jesus in the most characteristic quality of his life: the willingness to do God's will. In the ancient world, *meek* was used of a horse that could be tamed, an animal capable of being taught. A person who is taught of God is meek. Since God's teaching is always good, a meek person and a good person are synonymous. Of himself Jesus testified, "Lo, I come (in the volume of the book it is written of me,) to do thy will, O God" (Heb. 10:7). Again he said, "I do always those things that please him" (John 8:29). Our Lord's prayer at Gethsemane was not just "O my Father, if it be possible, let this cup pass from me" but "nevertheless not as I will, but as thou wilt" (Matt. 26:39).

This meaning is confirmed by the context. People who are "poor in spirit" are convicted of their sin, that is, of their poverty in the realm of the spirit. They mourn because of their sins. Convicted and contrite, they turn to God in faith and trust, willing to dedicate their lives to God. This act requires (1) faith to believe that God's way is best, (2) hope that God will fulfill his promises, and (3) love that is willing to do God's will regardless of personal consequences. This is meekness. It is the essence of Christian experience and equivalent to repentance from sin and faith in the Lord Jesus Christ. Those who have this character, Jesus says, are "blessed," "happy," "to be congratulated."

II. The meaning of "inherit the earth."

Much misinterpretation is avoided if the Hebrew word here is literally translated "land" rather than "earth." "Inherit the land" is used many times in the Old Testament to refer literally to the land promised to Abraham and to his descendants. The Promised Land then became a figurative expression for entering into the divine blessings. In the New Testament the Christian inheritance is spoken of as "eternal life," "salvation," "the kingdom of God," and "the promises," which all are roughly equivalent to "inherit the land."

Today's English Version paraphrases a little but captures the meaning of the text in this translation: "Happy are the meek; they will receive what God has promised!" Stenett's deservedly popular hymn "On Jordan's Stormy Banks" grasps the idea but restricts "the promised land" almost exclusively to heaven. Carter's "Standing on the Promises," another popular hymn, emphasizes the promises fulfilled in the Christian's present life. Both emphases are valid. The meek claim all of the promises of God both for the life that now is and for that which is to come.

We reject as foolish the interpretation that Christians will finally take possession of the whole earth just as we reject the interpretation of *meek* as "weak."

III. The blessedness of the meek.

Happy are the meek, for they have the quiet courage that comes from assured victory. God's will is best. His promises of salvation, of the indwelling of the Holy Spirit, and of heaven are as sure as is his character. As Philip Doddridge wrote in the popular hymn "O Happy Day," "'Tis done—the great transaction's done; I am my Lord's, and he is mine."

Blessed are the meek, for they are willing to die to self and put God and his kingdom first. John the Baptist was meek when he said, "He must increase, but I must decrease" (John 3:30).

Putting God's kingdom first is illustrated in the story of an older preacher who had been popular for many years but found his congregation diminishing as a younger preacher in his city became more popular. The members of the official board spoke with the older pastor and said, "You must do something about it." He replied, "I pray for the young brother daily and for God's continued blessings upon his ministry."

Blessed are the meek, for they have learned to take any place (no matter how humble) if this be God's will. Hear Paul: "But none of these things move me, neither count I my life dear unto myself, so that I might finish my course with joy, and the ministry, which I have received of the Lord Jesus, to testify the gospel of the grace of God" (Acts 20:24).

Conclusion

Do you know this blessedness? Are you happy—really happy? The convicted, the contrite, and the converted are. There is no happiness outside the will of God. In his will there is fullness of joy.

WEDNESDAY EVENING, JANUARY 18

Title: Some Things Jesus Taught about Prayer

Text: "And it came to pass, that, as he was praying in a certain place, when he ceased, one of his disciples said unto him, Lord, teach us to pray, as John also taught his disciples" **(Luke 11:1)**.

Scripture Reading: Luke 11:1–13

Introduction

In immediate response to the disciples' inquiry, Jesus gave them the instruction contained in Luke 11:2–13. However, as you read through the New Testament, you will find that he taught them much more about prayer. I don't purport to give an exhaustive treatment of all that Jesus taught about prayer; I simply want to enumerate some of the things he taught about prayer, especially those things related to unselfishness in prayer.

I. Jesus pointed out that there are times when we need to get alone with God to pray for our need that we might serve God and others better (Matt. 6:6; 14:22–23).

Was it selfish for Jesus to get away from the multitude and pray alone? No! He needed to recover from spiritual exhaustion, gain new insight into God's plans, and gain renewed physical and spiritual strength for the task ahead. Without times like these, we become shallow in our service, superficial in our influence, and ultimately beaten down, discouraged, and frustrated.

II. Jesus encouraged praying for the needs of others.

Luke 11:5–8 is an example of importunate prayer. The one who asked, asked not that his needs be met, but that his friend's needs be met. The need of another had made him feel the poverty of his own life. Jesus taught that even when we pray solitarily, we pray "our" Father, "our" daily bread, "our" debtors. We must see ourselves not simply as a separate thread, but as an inseparable element in the closely woven fabric of human life. We have common needs, common perils, and common tasks—so much so that when we pray we say "our."

III. Jesus taught us to pray for the kingdom of God.

"Thy kingdom come." Surely we need to intercede daily for the whole lost world. We need to pray for those involved in mission strategy, for missionaries and pastors, for the strength of the churches, and for the power of God and the ethical teachings of the Bible to be let loose through those who lead.

IV. Jesus indicated that there are times when we should pray together for others (Matt. 18:18–19).

We often quote the reference "two or three" as a contrast between the few and the many, while Jesus was contrasting solitary praying to group praying. He was emphasizing that he is especially present in a praying group. Praying groups should be established in offices, factories, workshops, businesses, college dormitories, and homes.

V. Jesus set the example in praying:

For children (Matt. 19:13).
For the sick (Mark 7:34).
For his disciples (Luke 22:31–32).
For his enemies (Luke 23:34).
For laborers in the harvest (Luke 10:2).
For all his followers unto the end of time (John 17:20).

Conclusion

The words of Tennyson challenge us:

> *More things are wrought by prayer than this world dreams of.*
> *Wherefore, let thy voice rise like a fountain for me night and day.*
> *For what are men better than sheep or goats that nourish a blind life within the brain,*
> *If, knowing God, they lift not hands of prayer both for themselves and those who call them friends?*
> *For so the whole round earth is every way bound by gold chains about the feet of God.*

SUNDAY MORNING, JANUARY 22

Title: The Christian's Bulletproof Vest

Text: ". . . and having put on the breastplate of righteousness" **(Eph. 6:14 RSV).**

Scripture Reading: Ephesians 6:10–20

Hymns: "Once for All," Bliss
           "Christ Receiveth Sinful Men," Neumeister
           "Though Your Sins Be as Scarlet," Crosby

Offertory Prayer: Father, we come into your presence as children who have been saved by your grace. We thank you for the privilege of coming into the throne room through the death of Jesus Christ for our sins. We thank you for the gift of your Holy Spirit and for the hunger we have for you today. We also thank you for the desire we have to see others come to know Jesus Christ as Lord and Savior. We bring tithes and offerings that we might indicate to you our love and that we might cooperate with you in spreading the gospel here in our own community and to the ends of the earth. Bless these tithes and offerings that they may give honor and glory to your holy name. We pray in Christ's name. Amen.

Introduction

Paul continues to detail the various pieces of armor we must utilize if we are to be victorious in our continuous conflict with Satan and the forces of evil. After emphasizing the belt of truth that supports, organizes, and promotes efficiency, Paul goes on to speak of the breastplate of righteousness. This particular piece of armor gave protection to the breast, the back, the neck, and the hips. It was somewhat similar to a modern vest, and it was made of small metal pieces that were woven together so as to provide protection for the vital organs of the body.

Paul admonishes Christians to put on the breastplate of righteousness. The righteousness of God is the activity of God in setting things aright. Through Jesus Christ, God set things right with man and between men. God's plan is that we should receive to our credit the perfect righteousness of Jesus Christ through faith, and God makes us right with himself on the basis of our faith in Jesus Christ as Lord and Savior (Gal. 3:11–14).

I. The breastplate of righteousness—not a righteousness of our own.

Paul had sought to protect himself from the accusing finger of a guilty conscience and from the weaknesses of the flesh by a righteousness based on perfect obedience to the law. While his performance might not have been perfect, it surpassed that of any of his contemporaries. Romans 7 describes the agony of his heart as he discovered that there was no real protection from sin and guilt through attempting to achieve a righteousness of his own through obedience to the law (Rom. 7:21–25). Paul then proclaimed the message of grace that provided spiritual protection from the assaults of evil through a righteousness offered by God as a gift to those who put faith in Jesus Christ.

Paul was writing to those who were threatened by evil and were in danger of being defeated. He declared that they must put on this breastplate of righteousness that comes through faith in order that they might not be destroyed by the enemy.

They were threatened by their own weaknesses and helplessness.

They were threatened by the strength of evil inclinations and degrading habits formed in the past.

They were oppressed by the devil who was continually seeking to destroy them.

They were threatened and confronted with an evil environment that was not conducive to spiritual growth. Facing inward as well as external foes, they needed every means of support they could muster. Paul urges them to recognize that their standing before God, justified, declared righteous and acceptable, was on the basis of their faith in Jesus Christ and not on the basis of their own obedience to the law.

II. The breastplate of righteousness—"the righteousness from God that depends on faith" (Phil. 3:9).

Paul found security in the position that was granted to him by the grace of God on the condition of his faith response to Jesus Christ. When Paul recognized that he was clothed in this perfect righteousness of Jesus Christ, it served as a bulletproof vest to protect the vital organs of his spiritual nature against all assaults and accusations.

Dressed in the righteousness of God through faith in Jesus Christ, Paul was persuaded that nothing could separate him or other believers from the love of God in Christ Jesus. Paul responded to the certain salvation that is provided through Jesus Christ with some significant questions as he contemplated the time when we all will appear before our Creator God.

"Who shall bring any charge against God's elect? It is God who justifies" (Rom. 8:33). Justification is an act of God in which he declares believing sinners righteous and acceptable in his sight on the basis of their faith in Jesus Christ (Rom. 5:1).

"Who is to condemn? Is it Christ Jesus, who died, yes, who was raised from the dead, who is at the right hand of God, who indeed intercedes for us?" (Rom. 8:34). Paul affirmed that believers will not be condemned by Jesus Christ on that day because Jesus Christ loved them to the extent that he died for them and conquered death and the grave. And he presently renders a ministry of intercession on their behalf.

"Who shall separate us from the love of Christ? Shall tribulation, or distress, or persecution, or famine, or nakedness, or peril, or sword? . . . No, in all these things we are more than conquerors through him who loved us" (Rom. 8:35–37). Paul is encouraging believers to recognize and respond to the truth that the great crises and tragedies that befall them are not to be interpreted as indications that they have been separated from the love of God and that God is no longer concerned about them. Unless we dress ourselves in the bulletproof vest of God's righteousness and recognize that our relationship to him has been assured on the basis of our faith in Christ, the devil will use tragedies that befall us to deal a death blow to us.

These may be considered to be deep theological truths and doctrinal statements, but the truth is that unless you are strengthened by a grasp of the great truths of God, you will become a victim instead of a victor when Satan brings his assaults against you.

III. The breastplate of righteousness—the protection it provides.

Someone has declared that one cannot go to heaven without a perfect righteousness. In view of the fact that all people are lawbreakers and sinners, this leaves us in a hopeless condition unless somehow we can receive a righteousness from God. To illustrate this truth, someone has said, "In order to go to heaven, you must have a perfect record." We do not go to heaven on our own record. Instead, through faith in Jesus Christ, we are given his perfect record, and we go to heaven on the record of the one who lived a sinless life and then died on a cross as a substitute for sinners.

The breastplate of righteousness, a Christian's bulletproof vest, will protect us from the guilt and the sins and the imperfections of the past. God does not want us to spend our lives in melancholy meditation on our failures, mistakes, and sins. He wants us to be able to face the future with joy, assurance, and confidence that our sins have been forgiven.

The breastplate of righteousness, the Christian's bulletproof vest, will protect us in all our future days. We can face temptation with greater strength because we are assured of the strength and the resources of our God who loves us and who has high hopes for our living a victorious Christian life.

We can endure suffering and disappointments in the awareness that these do not necessarily indicate the withdrawal of God's love for us. At no point does the Bible promise us that if we will live a life of obedient faithfulness we will be given an immunity from hardships, disappointments, and tragedies. We are assured that God will be at work in all of these things to bring about good for those who love him (Rom. 8:28).

The breastplate of righteousness, the Christian's bulletproof vest, can protect us from fear as we face the fact that one day we will meet God before the judgment seat of Christ (Rom. 8:1). It is through faith in Jesus Christ as Savior and Lord that we move into a position with God that removes the possibility of our being utterly condemned and rejected on the day of judgment (John 3:17–18). Instead of dreading the day when we stand before God, we can look forward to it with anticipation because of the breastplate of righteousness that comes to us through faith (John 5:24).

Conclusion

It is one thing to have a piece of armor set aside to put on for protection when battle comes. It is another thing to clothe oneself in that armor and go out to face his enemy. If we want to overcome Satan, we need to dress up in this breastplate of armor, this bulletproof vest, that will sustain us and strengthen us in our every moment of conflict with evil.

SUNDAY EVENING, JANUARY 22

Title: The Blessed Hungry

Text: "Blessed are they which do hunger and thirst after righteousness: for they shall be filled" **(Matt. 5:6).**

Scripture Reading: Isaiah 55:1–7

Introduction

Have you ever been really hungry? Or thirsty? Not many of us have been so hungry or thirsty as to despair of life. Feeding the people of the world is a tremendous task. In spite of modern technology, myriads of people go hungry each day. Food and water are essential. We cannot think or work or enjoy life unless we have had something to eat. In fact, we must eat and drink or die. Hunger and thirst, then, are two of the basic drives that sustain life. One who does not hunger or thirst is dead or dying.

I. Hunger and thirst are apt words to express intense desire.

They are figures often used in the Bible for spiritual hunger. For example: "As the hart panteth after the water brooks, so panteth my soul after thee, O God. My soul thirsteth for God, for the living God: when shall I come and appear before God?" (Ps. 42:1–2). "O God, thou art my God; early will I seek thee: my soul thirsteth for thee, my flesh longeth for thee in a dry and thirsty land, where no water is" (Ps. 63:1). "For he satisfieth the longing soul, and filleth the hungry soul with goodness" (Ps. 107:9). "Neither have I gone back from the commandment of his lips; I have esteemed the words of his mouth more than my necessary food" (Job 23:12). "Ho, every one that thirsteth, come ye to the waters" (Isa. 55:1).

Spiritual satisfaction is likened to feasting. Jesus said: "Many shall come from the east and west, and shall sit down with Abraham, and Isaac, and Jacob, in the kingdom of heaven" (Matt. 8:11). "The kingdom of heaven is like unto a certain king, which made a marriage for his son" (Matt. 22:1). "I am the bread of life: he that cometh to me shall never hunger; and he that believeth on me shall never thirst" (John 6:35). "If any man thirst, let him come unto me, and drink" (John 7:37). In our text Jesus congratulated those who "hunger and thirst after righteousness."

II. What is the righteousness one is to seek?

Righteousness is whatever is right in the eyes of God. Later in the sermon, Jesus commanded, "But seek first the kingdom of God, and his righteousness" (Matt. 6:33). The kingdom, or reign, of God is a synonym for God's will.

What did Jesus say righteousness is? His revelation gave us the final word about God's righteousness.

The heart of Jesus' ideal of righteousness is that one shall love. Righteousness is the right deed accompanied by the right motive. The right motive is love. If a deed is not motivated by love, it cannot be right. Love is the attitude of compassionate goodwill that God in Christ has toward humankind. God is love. All that he does he does in love. Any specific act must be in love or it ceases to be right.

Mark 12:28–31 records the well-known incident in which Jesus answered a scribe's question about which was the most important commandment by combining Deuteronomy 6:4 and Leviticus 19:18 as follows: "And Jesus answered him, The first of all the commandments is, Hear, O Israel; the Lord our God is one Lord: and thou shalt love the Lord thy God with all thy heart, and with all thy soul, and with all thy mind, and with all thy strength: this is the first commandment. And the second is like, namely this, Thou shalt love thy neighbour as thyself. There is none other commandment greater than these" (Mark 12:29–31).

Jesus said to his disciples, "That except your righteousness shall exceed the righteousness of the scribes and Pharisees, ye shall in no case enter into the kingdom of heaven" (Matt. 5:20). The Pharisees had the idea that certain deeds had merit in them. "Do this," they said, "and you will be righteous." "Not so," replied Jesus in effect. "No deed is righteous unless the motive is right." Later in the sermon, as recorded in Matthew 6:1–18, Jesus emphasized that deeds of righteousness such as almsgiving, prayer, and fasting are not approved of God when the motive is wrong.

The scribe who had asked Jesus about the greatest commandment was very perceptive when he replied, "Well, Master, thou hast said the truth: for there is one God; and there is none other but he: and to love him with all the heart, and with all the understanding, and with all the soul, and with all the strength, and to love his neighbour as himself, is more than all whole burnt offerings and sacrifices" (Mark 12:32–33). The scribe had come a long way from the ritualistic concept of righteousness of the Pharisee to the spiritual concept of righteousness of Jesus.

A corollary of the basic idea of love is that personal values are supreme. No rite, nor ceremony, nor sacred day is to be used to harm a person. "The sabbath was made for man, and not man for the sabbath" (Mark 2:27). Of course, it was proper to heal a man on the Sabbath. One would pull a sheep out of the ditch on the Sabbath. "How much then is a man better than a sheep? Wherefore it is lawful to do well on the sabbath days" (Matt. 12:12).

Righteousness then is to choose, reverence, and obey God as revealed in Jesus Christ. Righteousness is love in action. It means to love what he loves; to desire for others what he would have us to desire for others; to desire for ourselves what he would have us to desire for ourselves. To be what he would have us to be; to do what he would have us to do; to say what he would have us to say, all with the motive of love, is the righteousness Jesus bids us to seek.

III. Why the blessing on the one hungering and thirsting after righteousness?

God judges by the heart rather than by the deed. "For as [man] thinketh in his heart, so is he" (Prov. 23:7). "For the LORD seeth not as man seeth; for man looketh on the outward appearance, but the LORD looketh on the heart" (1 Sam. 16:7). "And the LORD said unto David my father, Whereas it was in thine heart to build an house unto my name, thou didst well that it was in thine heart" (1 Kings 8:18).

It is spiritually healthy for one to hunger and thirst. God made us in his own image. Spiritual hunger is an evidence of God's work in one's heart. The blessing, however, is not on the basic need in every heart for God but on one who actively hungers and thirsts for God.

"For they shall be satisfied" is the promise. The figure is that of contented cattle. One who does not hunger and thirst for God can never be satisfied, because one is doomed to unhappiness who does not know God. The father could not forgive and restore the prodigal son until he came home. Even God cannot forgive one who is unwilling to be forgiven. He cannot further reveal himself except to the receptive person.

Note progression in the Beatitudes. Those poor in spirit are convicted of their sin. Conviction issues in contrition. They mourn because of their spiritual poverty. Conviction and contrition lead to conversion as they turn in meekness to be taught of God. Now that they belong to God (sanctification in the primary meaning), they continue to desire to be more like Christ (sanctification in the secondary meaning).

Conclusion

The promise is only to the one who is in earnest. One who hungers and thirsts will find. There is no promise to the one who is indifferent. "And ye shall seek me, and find me, when ye shall search for me with all your heart" (Jer. 29:13). Claim Jesus' promises, "If any man will do his will, he shall know of the doctrine, whether it be of God, or whether I speak of myself" (John 7:17). Do God's will insofar as you know it. Seek for his righteousness with the intensity of a hungry man after food. You will find spiritual satisfaction. The Lord promises it to you.

WEDNESDAY EVENING, JANUARY 25

Title: A Way of Private Prayer

Text: "Hear my prayer, O Lord, and let my cry come unto thee. Hide not thy face from me in the day when I am in trouble; incline thine ear unto me; in the day when I call answer me speedily" **(Ps. 102:1–2).**

Scripture Reading: Psalm 102

Introduction

A big truck stalled on an expressway, and a man stopped to help. Upon inquiring about the problem, he found that the truck's wheel bearings had "frozen" for lack of grease. What's so peculiar about that? The truck was an oil company truck—and it was hauling grease.

Is not the story a parable applicable to many of us who serve the Lord? Is it not true that often we get so busy carrying the grease of the gospel that we neglect greasing our own spiritual bearings? Many Christian workers are stalled on the roadside because they fail to take the time to be alone with God in prayer.

If we are too busy to pray, we are just too busy. The Gospels tell us that Jesus rose a great while before day to talk with the Father. It is imperative that we follow his example. I do not walk with the presumptuous steps of a "know it all" when it comes to prayer, but I share with you some basic steps that should be included in your private prayer life.

I. Adoration.

Prayerfully read Isaiah 6 and you will find that Isaiah had a strange awareness of the presence of a holy, omnipotent, and transcendent God. If prayer is a conscious and personal experience with God, it is obvious that a consciousness of God's presence is essential to prayer. Take the time to close your eyes and think about God—he is your Father, and he is almighty, personal, kind, merciful, gracious, and concerned about you. "He sitteth upon the circle of the earth." "He giveth power to the faint; and to them that have no might he increaseth strength. . . . They that wait upon the LORD shall renew their strength" (Isa. 40:29–31).

II. Confession.

First John 1:9 was written to Christians: "If we confess our sins, he is faithful and just to forgive us our sins, and to cleanse us from all unrighteousness." Every day we need to be honest with God—to confess and repent of every sin. We also need to pray for strength to overcome the day's new temptations. Pray the prayer of the psalmist: "Search me, O God, and know my heart: try me, and know my thoughts: and see if there be any wicked way in me, and lead me in the way everlasting" (Ps. 139:23–24). Reading Psalms 32 and 51 will be helpful.

III. Thanksgiving.

We have so much to thank God for—our spouse, our children, our church, our pastor, our health, and the opportunity of Christian service. The very breath we breathe is by the grace of God. Too often we unthoughtfully say, "We thank you for all your blessings," but we fail to name them one by one. Read Psalm 103 to rediscover how to express thanksgiving.

On a day when everything seems to be going wrong, try drawing a line down the middle of a sheet of paper. On the left side, write the bad things that have happened to you—you probably can think of a few. Then on the right side, write the good things—you will write until you run out of space. Take time to thank the Lord for his blessings—one by one.

IV. Supplication or Intercession.

James 5:16 says, "The effectual fervent prayer of a righteous man availeth much." Intercession should always follow confession and repentance. Only when we have confessed our own sins and experienced cleansing and dedicated ourselves afresh to do the will of God in our own lives can we effectively pray for others. A prayerful reading of Romans 9:1–3 and 10:1 will help us see the need for being in "dead earnest" about praying for others.

I will never forget how earnestly I prayed for my daughter when we thought she was bleeding to death, or for my son when he was in battle. I have often felt that my intercessory prayer life would be more effective if I could care as deeply for others as I did for my children. Take time to pray compassionately for the lost, the sick, the bereaved, and the troubled.

V. Petition.

Jesus said, "Ask, and it shall be given you; seek, and ye shall find; knock, and it shall be opened unto you" (Luke 11:9). Bring your needs before him. I am convinced that if we adore him, confess our sins to him, thank him for his blessings, and intercede on behalf of others, as we bring our needs to him, we will pray with Jesus, "Nevertheless not my will, but thine be done" (Luke 22:42).

Conclusion

Take time today—and every day—to pray!

SUNDAY MORNING, JANUARY 29

Title: The Sandals of Readiness

Text: ". . . and having shod your feet with the equipment of the gospel of peace" **(Eph. 6:15 RSV)**.

Scripture Reading: Ephesians 6:10–20

Hymns: "All Things Bright and Beautiful," Alexander
"Sweet Peace, the Gift of God's Love," Bilhorn
"Rescue the Perishing," Crosby

Offertory Prayer: Heavenly Father, we come to you as the great giver of life and joy and peace. We thank you for food for the body as well as food for the soul. Thank you for our country and for the good citizens of our community who make it a better place to live. We recognize you as the divine giver of every good and perfect gift. We want to be like you, and so we come today bringing tithes and offerings. We give ourselves afresh to you, and we express this in ministries of mercy to others. Help us to live to be givers rather than merely to get and to have. In Jesus' name we pray. Amen.

Introduction

Every Christian has a malicious enemy in the devil, for he will do all within the powers of hell to disappoint us, defeat us, and destroy our witness for Jesus Christ. If you live under the illusion that you do not have an enemy in the world, you need to cause that illusion to evaporate. The devil is out to get you and will do so unless you commit yourself without reservation to the lordship of Jesus Christ. The Christian life is a struggle. It is like running uphill, like swimming upstream. Followers of Jesus Christ are not to float through life.

Paul sought to strengthen the believers in Ephesus, as well as those of us who live in the present, by detailing the various pieces of armor that God has provided for the protection of his children, his servants, as they engage in spiritual conflict. He pointed out the absolute necessity of our putting on the whole armor of God if we would withstand in the evil day and having done all, to stand.

Paul pointed out the necessity of our buckling the belt of truth about our midsection that we might have protection, organization, and efficiency in our lives. He also emphasized that we must wear the breastplate of righteousness, the Christian's bulletproof vest, if we are to withstand the satanic taunts against our spirit. In today's passage, Paul called attention to the fact that a good soldier must provide proper care and protection for his feet since his feet are his means of locomotion, the limbs that make for progress in life and in service.

The Roman soldier wore a rugged type of hobnailed sandals that enabled him to establish a firm footing even on slippery ground while in hand-to-hand conflict with the enemy. Paul declared that our Father God provides the necessary and proper sandals for Christians in their conflict with evil and in their service in the world.

We should not be dogmatic about the meaning of our text. It definitely has to do with the gospel that brings the peace of God into the hearts of people, and it specifically emphasizes an attitude of readiness and eagerness. Perhaps what Paul was trying to communicate is that if we are to overcome evil, we must respond to God's goodness and let peace fill our hearts. We must then have a deep inward eagerness to share the message that brings peace and joy to the hearts and lives of others.

I. The believer enjoys peace with God (Rom. 5:1).

Isaiah described the Messiah with a number of beautiful titles that told of the ministry that he would render. Isaiah's list of titles came to its apex when he declared that the Messiah would be the "Prince of Peace" (Isa. 9:6).

When the birth of the Savior was announced, the angelic choir sang of the peace he would bring on earth among people who would seek to do God's will (Luke 2:13–14). Following our Lord's resurrection from the dead, he greeted his disciples with a benediction of peace on them (John 20:21).

44

Our Lord came to bring peace to people and among people. The peace that he seeks to give is not that which is won on the battlefield but at the depths of the human heart. His peace is not the peace of stagnation or inactivity. His peace is not a spiritual narcotic to keep one from facing reality. The Prince of Peace gives believers peace with God through a right relationship with him.

This relationship allows believers to form right relationships with themselves and others and results in the furthering of peace.

II. The believer is to share the message of peace.

One reason why the average follower of Christ is not an enthusiastic sharer of the good news of God's love is the confusion concerning the nature of the message we have to proclaim. The gospel is not mere good advice. Our primary function is not to call for a reformation of conduct; it is to share the good news of God's grace in and through Jesus Christ. Isaiah described our function as peace bringers to those who are captives:

> *How beautiful upon the mountains*
> *are the feet of him who brings good tidings,*
> *who publishes peace, who brings good tidings of good,*
> *who publishes salvation. (Isa. 52:7 RSV)*

Paul quoted this passage from Isaiah as he sought to encourage believers to share the gospel with an unbelieving world (Rom. 10:14–15).

Using the sandals of a Roman soldier as a metaphor, Paul declared that if we are to overcome evil, we must have our feet prepared—that is, we must be eager and ready—to carry Christ's message of peace to all who are in spiritual darkness.

Are you ready at all times and under all circumstances to share with others the great truth of God's love for them as it is revealed in Jesus Christ? This attitude of readiness and eagerness will not only provide protection for us but will also be the means of communicating God's love to those who are in great need. An extreme illustration of this is demonstrated by a missionary's account of an incident in which a drunken soldier in a war-torn country came into the missionary's home at night with an automatic rifle and threatened to kill the missionary if he hindered the soldier's plans to rape the missionary's wife. The missionary told how he prayed as he had never prayed before, and through the wall he could hear his wife praying and then pleading with the soldier not to carry out his evil purpose. She began to declare to him that God loved him and that God was concerned about him and would be displeased with his actions. She pleaded with him to give his life to God rather than to a life of evil. Shortly, with a curse, the soldier left without harming the woman. God's message had gone forth with power.

Paul often expressed his eagerness and readiness to share the good news of God's love with a needy world (Rom. 1:14–15). He considered himself a debtor to God and a debtor to the unsaved world. He was filled with an eagerness to share the good news of God's love with the people in Rome. Further, he encouraged the believers in Corinth to have this attitude of eager readiness to share the good news by assuring them that God was in the business of saving those who would come to him (2 Cor. 6:1–2).

Conclusion

If you do not rejoice in the peace that passes all understanding that comes through faith in Jesus Christ, and if you are not eager to share this message that brings peace with others, you are in danger of being overcome by evil and defeated by the devil.

The primary emphasis of this passage is on the proclamation of the good news of God's love to a needy world. The subjective effect of this attitude of readiness will provide for us as individuals the protection we need from the assaults of Satan.

We need to respond to the call of God as did Isaiah when he said, "Here am I! Send me" (Isa. 6:8). Like the early disciples of our Lord, we need to go everywhere announcing the good news of God's love (Acts 8:4).

SUNDAY EVENING, JANUARY 29

Title: The Blessed Merciful

Text: "Blessed are the merciful; for they shall obtain mercy" **(Matt. 5:7).**

Scripture Reading: Psalm 103

Introduction

The Beatitudes have a logical and natural progression. Happy are those who are convicted of their sins. They realize their spiritual poverty. Of such people Christians come. Happy are those who are contrite because of their sins. Godly sorrow for sin leads to repentance. Happy are those who are willing to be taught of God. They are meek as was Jesus in his willingness to yield to God's will. They will inherit their portion of the promised land— that is, all that God has promised believers. Blessed are those disciples who seek after God's righteousness as eagerly as a hungry person seeks food or a thirsty person seeks drink. God will reward such earnestness with spiritual satisfaction. The four remaining beatitudes present qualities of the redeemed that alliteratively may be called pity, purity, peacemaking, and persecution. We come now to the fifth beatitude, "Blessed are the merciful."

I. What does it mean to be merciful?

Mercy is a godlike quality. Many wonderful Bible passages emphasize this truth. "The LORD is merciful and gracious, slow to anger, and plenteous in mercy" (Ps. 103:8). "Not because of righteous things we had done, but because of his mercy. He saved us through the washing of rebirth and renewal by the Holy Spirit" (Titus 3:5 NIV). "Grace, mercy, and peace, from God our Father and Jesus Christ our Lord" (1 Tim. 1:2). "But God, who is rich in mercy, for his great love wherewith he loved us, even when we were dead in sins, hath quickened us together with Christ, (by grace ye are saved;) and hath raised us up together, and made us sit together in heavenly places in Christ Jesus" (Eph. 2:4–6). "Blessed be the God and Father of our Lord Jesus Christ, which according to his abundant mercy hath begotten us again unto a lively hope by the resurrection of Jesus Christ from the dead" (1 Peter 1:3).

Mercy is a Christlike quality. "Keep yourselves in the love of God, looking for the mercy of our Lord Jesus Christ unto eternal life" (Jude 21). "Wherefore in all things it behooved him to be made like unto his brethren, that he might be a merciful and faithful high priest in things pertaining to God, to make reconciliation for the sins of the people" (Heb. 2:17).

Mercy is love in action. It is to have Christ's way of looking at people with a heart of pity and compassion, and it is the result of the regenerating power of the Spirit of God. It is desiring to give as God gave when he sacrificed his only begotten Son.

II. A merciful person will be merciful.

Kind, considerate, compassionate.

Merciful people consider others as objects of God's love and concern, souls for whom Christ died. They desire the salvation and restoration of others, never damnation. Jesus is the perfect example of his own teaching. Note his merciful attitude toward the woman taken in adultery (John 8:1–10), to the woman in Simon's house (Luke 7:36–50), and to the repentant robber on the cross (Luke 23:42–43).

Merciful people believe the best until the worst is proved. They have the qualities ascribed to love by Paul: "Love is patient and kind; love is not jealous or boastful; it is not arrogant or rude. Love does not insist on its own way; it is not irritable or resentful; it does not rejoice at wrong, but rejoices in the right" (1 Cor. 13:4–6 RSV).

Barnabas gave Paul two good lessons in mercy—the first when he sponsored Paul to the brothers in Jerusalem and the second when he gave John Mark a second chance.

Jesus pictured a hypocrite as a man with a post in his eye trying to find a speck of dust in another's eye. The merciful man is just the opposite type. He is not looking for flaws; he is looking for the praiseworthy in others.

Forgiving.

Merciful people have goodwill even to their enemies. Later in this sermon in Matthew 5:43–48, Jesus affirmed God's love to all and his desire that all people be saved. Jesus prayed from the cross, "Father, forgive them; for they know not what they do" (Luke 23:34). Similarly merciful people desire reconciliation.

Merciful people will ask forgiveness if they have sinned against another Christian. They will follow the Lord's instruction in Matthew 5:23–24.

Merciful people, in accord with Jesus' instruction in Luke 17:3 and Matthew 18:15–18, seek reconciliation with those who have sinned against them. The parable of the unmerciful servant in Matthew 18:21–35 teaches that one who refuses to forgive has never been forgiven of God. Paul pleaded, "Be ye kind one to another, tenderhearted, forgiving one another, even as God for Christ's sake hath forgiven you" (Eph. 4:32).

Even God, however, cannot forgive a person who will not be forgiven; but he wants to do so. This should be the attitude of the merciful person. Paul recognized that peace is not always possible with one who will not be peaceable when he wrote, "Recompense to no man evil for evil. Provide things honest in the sight of all men. If it be possible, as much as lieth in you, live peaceably with all men" (Rom. 12:17–18).

Helpful, serving. The good Samaritan is an example of a merciful man. He came where the wounded man was, had compassion on him, cared for his wounds, and took him to a hospital. He even arranged to pay his bill. Mercy is more than pity; it is love in action.

III. What is the blessing? "They shall obtain mercy."

From people? Perhaps, but not certainly. A young minister was shot to death by a criminal who had kidnapped him and stolen his car when the minister tried to witness to him about Christ. Jesus was merciful. He received unmerciful treatment from people.

From God? Yes. The merciful attitude is evidence of a right heart attitude. No more can God make two times two equal eight than he can bestow forgiveness on an unrepentant person. The merciful are already justified and regenerated, and they will receive mercy at the judgment.

The late Max Stanfield told this personal experience. As a youth he was cited to appear in court on a minor traffic charge. He was in court at the appointed time and waited through case after case. Finally, with fear he approached the judge and said, 'Your Honor, I really ought to be in school. When will my case be called?" The judge was very perceptive. He thumbed through some papers and then said, "Son, there is no charge against you here. Go on back to school." How sweet were those words, "There is no charge against you here." And how sweet it will be for merciful people to know that at the judgment the Judge will say, "There is no charge against you here."

Conclusion

Blessed, happy, to be congratulated are the merciful. Sing the doxology! Shout for joy! They are forgiven of God and have God's merciful attitude toward others. They are full of love, generosity, and goodwill. They have overcome hate, jealousy, and envy, and have become rich with the blessings of God.

FEBRUARY

■ **Sunday Mornings**

Continue with the theme "Putting on the Whole Armor of God."

■ **Sunday Evenings**

Continue with expository messages from Jesus' Sermon on the Mount.

■ **Wednesday Evenings**

"Christ and Our Pressing Problems" is the theme for Wednesday evening meditations based on passages from Paul's epistle to the Colossians.

WEDNESDAY EVENING, FEBRUARY 1

Title: A Prayer for Spiritual Prosperity

Text: "We have not ceased to pray for you" **(Col. 1:9 RSV)**.

Scripture Reading: Colossians 1:9–14

Introduction

The epistle to the Colossians holds many words of encouragement for God's children. Tonight let us look at Paul's prayer for the faithful saints at Colossae.

I. Paul prayed that the Colossians might be filled with the knowledge of God's will (1:9).

The message of the Word of God from the beginning to the end is that God has a program for humankind. He seeks to reveal this will to his people collectively and to individuals personally.

Paul believed that God had a universal will for all people and a personal will for each person. He did not consider God's will as something that a blind fatalistic fate imposed on us. He saw it as God's good plan to enable us to live abundant lives. We must believe that God wants us to have a clear, personal knowledge of his plan for our lives.

II. Paul prayed that the Colossians might walk worthy of the Lord in a pleasing manner (1:10).

It is possible for us to walk through a wicked world in a manner pleasing to our heavenly Father. We read in the Old Testament that "Enoch walked with God; and he was not, for God took him" (Gen. 5:24). We also read that Abraham was the friend of God and walked and talked with him. So did Moses. Paul would not have prayed this prayer if the fulfillment of the prayer was an impossibility (2 Cor. 5:9).

III. Paul prayed that the Colossians' lives might be fruitful in every good work (1:10).

God's original commission to man was to "be fruitful and multiply, and fill the earth and subdue it; and have dominion over the fish of the sea and over the birds of the air and over every living thing that moves upon the earth" (Gen. 1:28 RSV). It has always been God's will for people to live fruitful, productive, and happy lives.

Our Lord was eager for his disciples to live fruitful lives (John 15:8). He gives specific instructions concerning what we must do to be productive (John 15:1–5).

Our Father God has given us the Holy Spirit to dwell within us, and he proposes to produce within us the fruit of the Spirit (Gal. 5:22–23).

IV. Paul prayed for the Colossians that they might constantly increase in their knowledge of God (1:10).

Paul was eager that they have something more than knowledge *about God.* He was eager that the church in Colossae have experiential knowledge *of God*—that they come to know God in a deeper, richer, more wonderful way (cf. Phil. 3:10).

We should know God at a deeper level and in a richer dimension with the passing of time. God is personal, and our faith in him and our relationship to him should grow and develop with the passing of time.

V. Paul prayed for the Colossians that they might be strengthened with the power of God (1:11).

The people of that day faced the difficulties and hardships of life without many of the benefits we enjoy as a result of modern technology, yet they were able to live in a difficult world with patience and with joy because they equipped themselves with the strength of God (cf. Eph. 6:10).

VI. Paul prayed for the Colossians that they might have an attitude of gratitude (1:12).

Developing the habit of being thankful helps one to overcome the tendency toward negativism and pessimism. When we focus on our blessings and benefits and concentrate our attention on good things, it adds beauty to our lives and enables us to give praises to God and helpfulness to others.

Conclusion

Paul's prayer is a great encouragement and challenge to us as we face life's difficult times.

SUNDAY MORNING, FEBRUARY 5

Title: The Shield of Faith

Text: ". . . besides all these, taking the shield of faith, with which you can quench all the flaming darts of the evil one" **(Eph. 6:16 RSV)**.

Scripture Reading: Ephesians 6:10–20

Hymns: "God, Our Father, We Adore Thee," Frazer
           "O God, Our Help in Ages Past," Watts
           "Faith Is the Victory," Yates

Offertory Prayer: Our heavenly Father, for beautiful days, for the warmth of the summer, for growing crops, and for all the beauties of nature, we thank you. We rejoice in the beauty of your creation, and we pray that you will help us to be as beautiful in our lives as you have made the world in which we live.

Today we are eager to give ourselves afresh to you. We reaffirm our faith in your precious promises. We bring tithes and offerings, acknowledging your ownership of all we are and have. Help us as we work for our daily bread. Help us that we might labor in order to share and give. We desire to experience the joy of giving. Use our gifts that we might share in your kingdom's work in this community and to the ends of the earth. In Jesus' name we pray. Amen.

Introduction

Do we need to be reminded that as Christians we have an enemy in the devil who is seeking to defeat us in our worship and in our work for our Lord? All about us we see evidence of the work of Satan's forces. Day by day he seeks to invade our innermost being to cast doubts and fears into our hearts.

In the great passage of Scripture we are considering, Paul spiritualized the various pieces of armor worn by a Roman soldier in battle. The apostle asserted that we need to do more than merely profess faith in Jesus Christ if we want to live victoriously in a world dominated by evil. We need to put on the equipment with which our Father God provides us for achieving victory. It is not our Father's will that we live in failure and go down in defeat. Above all, we must put on and utilize the shield of faith to quench Satan's fiery darts.

The Roman soldier's shield was rectangular and formed of thin pieces of brass laced together with leather. It served to protect against arrows whether the soldier was advancing or retreating. In warfare those who were defending a position would often dip arrows in pitch and set them afire before launching them toward the enemy. To be struck by an arrow that had been dipped in pitch and set on fire was to experience an injury that was almost always fatal. Survival depended on the use of a shield.

What are some of the fiery darts the devil launches against us today? What is the shield of faith we can use today to protect us from these flaming arrows that would destroy us?

I. All of us are seeking shields.

The trouble in our seeking of shields is that we often concentrate on those that do not provide ultimate protection.

Property is a shield of great value. To own property provides one with a degree of economic security and protection against poverty and need.

We live in a world where cash is needed. Some depend on the government to provide them with cash. Others work and save. Others invest and try to increase their net worth.

Insurance serves as a shield against catastrophe. It is one of the largest industries in the Western world because people feel the need for a shield against that which threatens them.

When we study the life of the apostle Paul, we have to come to the conclusion that he was talking about a different kind of shield than those mentioned above. He was not thinking primarily in terms of physical protection but in terms of spiritual protection from that which was destructive to one's spiritual life. We come to this conclusion because Paul was not primarily concerned about protecting himself from physical harm (2 Cor. 11:24–33).

II. The flaming arrows of Satan.

The flaming arrows against which we need spiritual protection are those that would destroy us as far as our spiritual life is concerned. We can be certain that the devil is going to shoot his fiery arrows at us.

We will face the fiery arrow of temptation to do evil. It is within the power and the practice of the devil to tempt us in such a manner as to lead us astray unless we are on guard.

We will be tempted to live an immoral life.

We will be tempted to live for secular materialistic values.

We will be tempted to live only for the pleasure of the moment.

We will face the fiery arrow of doubt that leads to disappointment and despair. Since the beginning of time, Satan's strategy has been to raise questions concerning God's goodness. He will cast doubts into our mind concerning our own integrity and motivations as well as concerning the intentions and abilities of others. Satan will seek to destroy our faith in God, self, and others.

We face the fiery arrow of discouragement. Satan means "accuser." The devil will accuse God of things for which he is not responsible, and he will accuse us of not being all that we ought to be. He will slander our character to our faces. He will cast aspersions on our personal ability and remind us of our past failures and mistakes.

We face the fiery arrows of personal disappointment that will numb us and destroy us. Satan will be certain to bring across our pathway that which will disappoint us and hinder us in our forward thrust in doing God's will.

We face the fiery darts of disease and disability. Paul speaks of having a thorn in the flesh that seemingly was a gift of God to keep him humble, and yet he refers to it as a messenger of Satan that harassed him (2 Cor. 12:7–8). The devil will give us a false interpretation or explanation of the circumstances that life brings to us.

We face the fiery arrow of personal injury. We all are subject to injury because of our own errors in judgment and because of the cruelty or thoughtlessness of others. To be injured gives us an occasion to feel hostile, to develop hate, and to begin carrying a grudge. The devil will slip up on our blind side and shoot some arrow that is destructive and hurtful into us to destroy our spirituality and to deprive us of being the persons we ought to be.

What kind of a flaming arrow is Satan using on you? Could it be that he is making you wealthy or successful in order to lure you away from God? Wealth is not always the blessing of God. It may be a gift from the underworld of evil to lure you away from the pathway of righteousness and faithfulness.

III. Above all taking the shield of faith.

The apostle declared that there is no possibility of victory in the struggle with evil unless we utilize the shield of faith. It was through faith that the saints of old accomplished great things in God's name and for the people of their time (Heb. 11:32–40).

Jesus, our Lord, is the pioneer and perfecter of our faith (Heb. 12:2). If it was necessary for our Lord to face life with all its struggles with a great faith in God, we can be absolutely certain that we must face life with faith and not give way to fear. Without faith it is absolutely impossible to please God (Heb. 11:6). To not trust in the truthfulness and in the faithfulness of God is an insult to the divine Creator.

Jesus told his apostles that under all circumstances they should "Have faith in God" (Mark 11:22). How can one develop great faith that will sustain and strengthen in the time of trial?

Born-again believers should trust in the Word of God and believe with all their hearts that it is through faith that God will give them the victory over the world system in which we live (1 John 5:4).

Each of us needs to use the faith he or she has. Jesus emphasized the necessity of utilizing the faith we have even though it may be small (Matt. 17:19–20).

Faith comes by hearing and heeding the Word of the Lord (Rom. 10:17). We need to read the Scriptures to nourish our faith. We need to see the great redemptive acts of God in the past as pictures of what he wants to do in the present in the lives of those who will trust and obey him. We need to search for his promises and listen to the still small voice of the Spirit as God speaks to us through the pages of the Bible.

If we are to utilize the shield of faith and develop a greater faith in God, we need to be obedient to God's will as we know it in the present. God's promise of his blessings on the tither is a case in point (Mal. 3:10–12). Those who do not bring their tithes into God's storehouse in the present deprive themselves of the blessings that God has promised to those who in faith obey his command.

If we are to utilize the shield of faith and develop a greater faith, we need to get acquainted with those whose experiences can strengthen our faith and cheer our spirit. Hebrews 11 has been called "Faith's Hall of Fame." This chapter gives us a list of the great heroes of God who through faith overcame evil and accomplished much in the kingdom of God.

Conclusion

What have you done with the faith you have? Have faith in God and in yourself and face the future without fear.

SUNDAY EVENING, FEBRUARY 5

Title: The Blessed Pure

Text: "Blessed are the pure in heart, for they shall see God" **(Matt. 5:8).**

Scripture Reading: John 14:1–11

Introduction

A little boy said to the Christian woman who was caring for him, "How can I ever see God if you make me shut my eyes every time you talk to him?" His logic was perfect, but his conclusion was false because "no man hath seen God at any time" (John 1:18). One does not see God with physical eyes. A little girl said to her preacher father, "Daddy, I want you to show me God sometime." The father assured her that he earnestly would try to do so. Philip was making a request for us all when he said, "Lord, show us the Father and that will be enough for us" (John 14:8 NIV). In the sixth beatitude, which is our text, Jesus affirmed that the eye by which one sees God is a pure heart.

I. Who are the pure in heart?

Pure means to be clean and separated from the adhesion or the admixture of anything that soils or adulterates. For example, pure linen is linen cleansed by washing. Pure gold is gold separated by the refining fires from baser metals and dross. The vine in John 15:1–3 is purged (that is, purified or cleansed) by pruning away the dead branches so that it is ready to bear fruit.

In an ethical sense, the word *pure* means free from the admixture of the false; hence genuine and sincere. We have many examples: "Whereas the aim of our charge is love that issues from a pure heart and a good conscience and sincere faith" (1 Tim. 1:5 RSV). "So shun youthful passions and aim at righteousness, faith, love, and peace, along with those who call upon the Lord from a pure heart" (2 Tim. 2:22 RSV). "I thank God, whom I serve from my forefathers with pure conscience" (2 Tim. 1:3). "Holding the mystery of the faith in a pure conscience" (1 Tim. 3:9). To the Jews at Corinth Paul said, "Your blood be upon your own heads; I am clean" (Acts 18:6)—that is pure, innocent, blameless, with no admixture of guilt.

The heart is the central organ of the physical body. In the Bible it is the symbol of the spiritual life; the soul; the seat or fountain of thoughts, desires, appetites, and motives. In modern usage we think of the mind as the seat of thought, but in scriptural usage the heart is the seat of thought as well as of feeling. Heart means the entire personality, the inner man.

"Pure in heart," then, means pure or clean in the realm of the inner life; sincere in one's innermost purpose and motive. Those who are pure in heart truly love God. They are regenerated people who have God's glory as their main focus. Some passages from the Psalms help illustrate the meaning: "Who shall ascend into the hill of the LORD? or who shall stand in his holy place? He that hath clean hands, and a pure heart; who hath not lifted up his soul unto vanity, nor sworn deceitfully" (24:3–4). "Create in me a clean heart, O God" (51:10). "Truly God is good to Israel, even to such as are of a clean heart" (73:1).

Note that "pure in heart" is not used to indicate a morally perfect person—for no one is—but a regenerated person who sincerely purposes to do God's will. Again, we have many scriptural examples: "[God] put no difference between us and them, purifying their hearts by faith" (Acts 15:9). "And the blood of Jesus Christ his Son cleanseth us from all sin" (1 John 1:7). "If we confess our sins, he is faithful and just to forgive us our sins, and to cleanse us from all unrighteousness" (1 John 1:9). Those who are "pure in heart" then, are redeemed people who with singleness of mind are yielded to God. With all on the altar, without reservation, without double-mindedness, their purpose in life is to glorify God.

II. The promise: "For they shall see God."

What does this mean? The expression is derived from the practice of ancient Eastern monarchs who lived in great seclusion. They were seen by only a relatively few trusted members of the court. Seeing the face of the king was considered a rare privilege. The book of Esther illustrates. Esther 1:14 names "the seven princes of Persia and Media, which saw the king's face, and which sat the first in the kingdom." Even after Esther became queen she could not go uninvited into the presence of her husband, the king, upon penalty of death (see Est. 4:11–17).

The promise that the pure in heart shall see God is not a promise that they will see him with their physical eyes while on this earth, but that they will experience the reality of God. In John 3:3 Jesus said to Nicodemus, "Except a man be born again, he cannot see the kingdom of God"—that is, enter therein, experience the reality of it.

The pure in heart shall see God.

In heaven. This is certainly part of the promise, although not the whole of it. Jesus promised that his disciples (the pure in heart) will be with him in the heavenly home forever (see John 14:1–3). David expressed his faith, "As for me, I will behold thy face in righteousness: I shall be satisfied, when I awake, with thy likeness" (Ps. 17:15), and again, "Surely goodness and mercy shall follow me all the days of my life: and I will dwell in the house of the LORD for ever" (Ps. 23:6). The apostle John wrote, "Beloved, now are we the sons of God, and it doth not yet appear what we shall be: but we know that, when he shall appear, we shall be like him; for we shall see him as he is" (1 John 3:2). Revelation 22:4 assures, "And they shall see his face; and his name shall be in their foreheads." Paul was sure that "eye hath not seen, nor ear heard, neither have entered into the heart of man, the things which God hath prepared for them that love him" (1 Cor. 2:9).

John Jasper, a slave who preached with great eloquence, was reported to have said that all he wanted in heaven was to slip in a side door and look at Jesus for ten thousand years. But Scripture promises more: "I heard a great voice out of heaven saying, Behold, the tabernacle of God is with men, and he will dwell with them, and they shall be his people, and God himself shall be with them, and be their God" (Rev. 21:3). Only the redeemed will go to heaven, but all of them will go. The pure in heart shall see God.

Those who will see God are those who now see him—that is, experience him by faith. The idea is that they will keep on experiencing God. The pure in heart see God in Christian experience. God is known by his works. "The heavens declare the glory of God" (Ps. 19:1). "For the invisible things of him from the creation of the world are clearly seen, being understood by the things that are made, even his eternal power and Godhead" (Rom. 1:20). "No man hath seen God at any time; the only begotten Son, which is in the bosom of the Father, he hath declared him" (John 1:18).

The normal experience of the "pure in heart" is that they just know in their hearts the reality of God. Jesus' promise, "Lo, I am with you alway, even unto the end of the world" (Matt. 28:20) is a present experience. "When we cry, 'Abba! Father!' it is the Spirit himself bearing witness with our spirit that we are the children of God" (Rom. 8:15–16 RSV). A dear saint testified, "I have not seen God with these eyes (pointing to his physical eyes); but God is as real to me as my wife and children. I would no more think of sinning in his sight than in theirs."

Conclusion

Seeing God changes life wonderfully.

Seeing God humbles us. Witness Isaiah: "Then said I, Woe is me! for I am undone; because I am a man of unclean lips, and I dwell in the midst of a people of unclean lips: for mine eyes have seen the King, the LORD of hosts" (Isa. 6:5). Witness Job: "I have heard of thee by the hearing of the ear: but now mine eye seeth thee. Wherefore I abhor myself, and repent in dust and ashes" (Job 42:5–6).

Seeing God motivates to service. Witness Isaiah: "Also I heard the voice of the Lord, saying, Whom shall I send, and who will go for us? Then said I, "Here am I; send me" (Isa. 6:8). Witness Paul: "He trembling and astonished said, Lord, what wilt thou have me to do?" (Acts 9:6).

Seeing God changes life's priorides. Affections are now set on heavenly rather than earthly goals. "Therefore if any man be in Christ, he is a new creature: old things are passed away; behold, all things are become new" (2 Cor. 5:17).

Seeing God takes the fear out of death and judgment. Hear Paul: "For to me to live is Christ, and to die is gain" (Phil. 1:21).

Dr. John R. Sampey, a noted scholar, told about a time when a little boy climbed on his lap and said, "When I get to heaven I'm going to sit in God's lap and kiss him." The noted scholar said, "Did I turn theologian and explain to that boy that he was thinking in anthropomorphic terms? I did not. I said, 'Son, I think that is exactly what God would want you to do.'" The pure in heart are to be congratulated, for they shall keep on seeing God.

WEDNESDAY EVENING, FEBRUARY 8

Title: Christ in You, the Hope of Glory

Text: "To them God chose to make known how great among the Gentiles are the riches of the glory of this mystery, which is Christ in you, the hope of glory" **(Col. 1:27 RSV)**.

Scripture Reading: Colossians 1:24–29

Introduction

We can sense a spirit of despair in the world today among all cultures and among all age groups. How can we change from having an attitude of despair to an attitude of hope? How can we cease being pessimists and become optimists? How can we live triumphant lives rather than being conquered by the events that threaten us? How much hope do you have as you face the future?

If you would have hope instead of despair, you must find and receive the gift of faith. Real faith and a spirit of hope are inseparable: "Faith is confidence in what we hope for and assurance about what we do not see" (Heb. 11:1 NIV). Paul sought to challenge, encourage, and motivate the believers in Colossae with the tremendous truth that the living Christ has come to dwell within the heart of each believer.

I. The indwelling Christ is a basis for hope.

The indwelling Christ is the Christ of eternity (John 1:1–3).
The indwelling Christ is the Christ who entered time (John 1:14).

The indwelling Christ is our contemporary. He is the living Christ who has conquered death and hell (Rev. 1:18).

The exalted Lord comes to fill our total being (Rev. 3:20).

This living Christ comes to us individually.

This living Christ comes to us collectively as we meet together for worship.

II. The indwelling Christ is the basis of God's hope for us.

The living Christ has given to each of his disciples the gift of his spiritual presence (Matt. 28:20).

The living Christ is at work within us to accomplish God's good purpose within us (Gal. 2:20; Phil. 2:13).

The indwelling Christ is the basis of God's hope for something significant from each of us. God sent his Son not only into the world but into our hearts as well.

III. The indwelling Christ is the basis of our hope for fulfilling God's plan for our lives.

Paul expressed this hope in his letter to the Galatians when he declared that the living Christ lived within him and that he lived his life through faith in this living Christ. Paul had faith to believe that he would be able to meet any circumstance in life through the strength that the indwelling Christ provided (Phil. 4:13).

The indwelling Christ is the basis of our hope for the forgiveness of all our sin.

The indwelling Christ is the basis of our hope for victory over evil in the present and in the future.

The indwelling Christ is the basis of our hope for significant service.

The indwelling Christ is the basis for our hope of heaven at the end of the way (John 6:40).

IV. The indwelling Christ is the basis of our hope for others.

Christ came not only to be the Savior of individuals, but also to create a spiritual family for the Father God. The indwelling presence of Christ in the heart of other believers can give us assurance of acceptance and assistance as we seek to live faithfully for God.

The indwelling Christ creates a disposition of love within individual believers that expresses itself toward other members of God's family.

The indwelling Christ through the gift of his precious Holy Spirit is at work in all believers. He works not only in the hearts of the faithful, but also in those who have drifted and who at the moment are unfaithful. Thus we should not despair over them. He who began a good work in them will be faithful to complete it (see Phil. 1:6). We should have faith to believe in the lifting and reclaiming power of the indwelling Christ.

Conclusion

When you are inclined to be discouraged, remember that Christ has come to live within you. He wants to accomplish God's good work in you and through you. Cling to the precious promise of his abiding presence to find the courage you need to live victoriously this week.

SUNDAY MORNING, FEBRUARY 12

Title: The Helmet of Salvation

Text: "And take the helmet of salvation . . ." (**Eph. 6:17 RSV**).

Scripture Reading: Ephesians 6:10–20

Hymns: "What a Wonderful Savior!" Hoffman
"He Is Able to Deliver Thee," Ogden
"Grace Greater Than Our Sin," Johnston

Offertory Prayer: Heavenly Father, thank you for all the rich gifts you have bestowed on us. Thank you for the gift of your gracious person to us. Thank you for forgiveness and for eternal life. Thank you for your Spirit who comes to work within us and to bring us into conformity to the character of your Son and our Savior. We thank you for the opportunity to work and earn a livelihood and for the opportunity to serve, to give, to share, to minister, and to help. Bless these tithes and offerings as they are brought into the treasury of your church. Add your blessings to them and multiply them to the end that your rule might become real in the hearts of people. We pray in Jesus' name. Amen.

Introduction

Are you wearing all the armor our Father God has provided for you as you face the assaults of Satan and struggle to win the battle of life?

Football players are required to wear helmets to protect their heads while playing. In some states motorcyclists are required to wear helmets so as to lessen the danger of damaging the brain in an accident. Construction workers are required to wear hard hats to protect themselves from falling objects. What is the purpose of the helmet of salvation to which the apostle Paul refers? Surely it has to do with the head, the seat of our intellect, the fountain of our personality, and the source of our actions. "The helmet of salvation" emphasizes that genuine religion involves the intellect as well as the emotions. Jesus said that the greatest commandment is to "love the Lord your God with all your heart, and with all your soul, and with all your mind" (Matt. 22:37). We respond to God's will with our emotions and our mind. Only as we respond totally can we overcome the evil that would destroy us.

I. The helmet of salvation emphasizes the role of our head in the conflict with evil.

It is God's will that we be delivered from the tyranny of evil in our rational or intellectual life. God spoke through Isaiah, urging the people of that day to seek the Lord with all their being and to turn from their wicked ways. Their wicked ways are explained as being a result of their thoughts not conforming to God's thoughts (Isa. 55:6–9). People will be delivered from the tyranny and destructiveness of evil only when they direct their minds toward the mind of God and let the thoughts of God become their way of thinking.

The call to repentance is basically the call for a deep, sincere, and continuous turning from the mind of the flesh to the mind of God. John the Baptist appeared as the forerunner of Jesus calling on people to repent. His message of repentance was not so much a threat as it was an invitation for them to change their thought patterns with reference to the nature of God and the program of God in the world. Only as they changed their attitude could they experience forgiveness and be prepared for the coming of the Messiah (Mark 1:4). Jesus opened and closed his ministry by calling for repentance (Mark 1:14–15; Luke 24:46–47). Jesus called on people to make a basic and fundamental change of direction in their lives. They were to stop rebelling and come to God in an attitude of recognition, submission, and trust.

The apostle Paul urged Roman Christians to forsake their natural, fleshly, earthly way of thinking and experience spiritual transformation that could come about only as they experienced a "renewal of [their] mind" (Rom. 12:1–2).

Paul encouraged the believers in Corinth to bring every thought into captivity to the lordship of Jesus Christ (2 Cor. 10:3–5). He reminded them that they were engaged in spiritual warfare, and in order to overcome, they must let Jesus Christ have control of their thoughts and attitudes.

The mind of Jesus Christ is said to be the goal for which all of us should seek if we would be true followers of our Lord (Phil. 2:5). We will never be able to reflect and manifest true Christianity until we bring our intellect, our thought processes, and our scale of values into conformity to the mind and the Spirit of Jesus Christ.

If we would truly put on the helmet of salvation, we must let Jesus Christ be the Lord of our intellect. We must not live our lives subject to the moods and impulses of our emotions. We must bring our emotions under the control of an intellect that has been fashioned after the mind of Jesus Christ.

II. The helmet of salvation emphasizes full salvation.

One of the major reasons why so many of us are defeated in the struggle with evil is that we are uninformed concerning the nature of God's great salvation, which is offered to us through Jesus Christ. We need to fill our intellect with an understanding of what God has done, what God is doing, and what God will do to accomplish his salvation within us. If we do not understand what God is doing with our intellect, then we will be open to many assaults by the devil as he tries to defeat us.

Ours is indeed a great salvation including justification, sanctification, and glorification.

Justification—salvation as a past accomplishment (Eph. 2:8–9). Paul wrote to the Ephesian Christians on the basis that they were followers of Jesus Christ. They had experienced a spiritual resurrection from the deadness of sin and were now seated in heaven with Jesus Christ as far as their position with God was concerned. Paul saw their salvation from the penalty of sin as a past accomplishment of God.

Sanctification—salvation as a present process (Phil. 2:12–13). Paul wrote to the Philippian Christians about their persistent participation in the process of being saved from the power and practice of sin in their daily lives as the children of God. He was not inferring at all that they must work their way to heaven or that they must earn the right to be the disciples of Jesus Christ. Paul considered eternal life to be the free gift of God's grace through faith in Jesus Christ (Rom. 6:23). With great enthusiasm, Paul urged all believers to work diligently with the Holy Spirit, whom God gave to them in the conversion experience (Gal. 4:6) so that they might experience the fruit of the Spirit (Gal. 5:22–23). The various expressions of the fruit of the Spirit are not stages of progress that one must achieve in order to make it to heaven at death. They are the natural expressions of the work of the indwelling Spirit in the hearts of believers as they cooperate with God who is seeking to deliver them from the evil of this present world.

Glorification—salvation as a future prospect (Phil. 3:20–21; Heb. 9:28). Children of God who are saved from the penalty of sin because of their initial faith commitment to Jesus Christ, and who are in a process of being saved from the power and practice of sin through cooperation with the Holy Spirit, will not be saved from the presence of sin until the Lord Jesus Christ returns or until he calls them to heaven.

If we would truly put on the helmet of salvation, we must understand and appreciate what God has done for us in the past. We must remind ourselves that when we trusted Jesus Christ as Lord and Savior, God accepted us and received us into his family, declaring us acceptable to him on the basis of our faith commitment to Jesus Christ (Rom. 5:1). We need to understand and respond to the present work of God as he works from the moment of conversion to the consummation of our life by means of the Holy Spirit who is seeking to reproduce within us the character and personality of Jesus Christ. The Holy Spirit is engaged in an unending conflict with the evil that is within us and the evil that is about us. The Holy Spirit will deliver us from every assault of Satan. When we experience failure and defeat, the Holy Spirit comes to rescue us and to cheer us in a continuing struggle to become all that God desires for us to be.

We need to understand with our minds and hearts that we will never completely conquer evil in this life. While we must continue to strive, we must not let the devil fill us with despair when we discover that there are areas in our lives that still need redemption. We must not let him slander us and discourage us by trying to convince us that we do not belong to God because we continue to be imperfect human beings.

Conclusion

God wants to save everyone from the penalty of sin, which is spiritual death. He has made this possible for everyone through the life, death, and resurrection of Jesus Christ. To experience this salvation, we need to put faith in Jesus Christ.

God, by means of the gift of his Spirit, is seeking to deliver us from the tyranny of sin in our day-to-day existence. He will continue this struggle within us and desperately needs our constant cooperation in order to deliver us from the power of sin.

Our complete salvation will come at the end of the way. It will be salvation from the presence of sin, and we shall be like Jesus, for we shall see him as he is. Put on the helmet of salvation.

SUNDAY EVENING, FEBRUARY 12

Title: The Blessed Peacemakers

Text: "Blessed are the peacemakers, for they shall be called sons of God" **(Matt. 5:9 RSV)**.

Scripture Reading: 2 Corinthians 5:14–6:2

Introduction

"Sons of God" in the Revised Standard Version is the correct translation in Matthew 5:9, and Jesus certainly did not mean to exclude daughters. "Children" is an improper translation, because a child, son or daughter, is one begotten by a father and born of a mother, and this is not the usage in the seventh beatitude. A child may also become a son or daughter by adoption, yet neither is this the usage here. Sons and daughters are direct descendants of someone, for example, sons of Abraham, daughters of Israel, or children of Israel. But this is not the usage here.

Rather *son* is a Hebrew idiom for one who is a disciple or follower of another in close relationship, as the sons of the prophets are their pupils or disciples. In the parable of the tares in Matthew 13:37–38, "The good seed means the sons of the kingdom; the weeds are the sons of the evil one" (RSV). In the parable of the wicked steward in Luke 16:8, Jesus said, "For the sons of this world are more shrewd in dealing with their own generation than the sons of light" (RSV). In Acts 13:10 Paul called Elymas, "You son of the devil" (RSV). On the contrary, Jesus said to Zacchaeus,

"Today salvation has come to this house, because this man, too, is a son of Abraham" (Luke 19:9 NIV). This is not the usage in the seventh beatitude, but it is close.

Son of God is used as a synonym for saved persons, as in John 1:12: "But as many as received him, to them gave he power to become the sons of God, even to them that believe on his name."

Jesus is the Son of God in a unique sense. "Only begotten Son of God" (John 3:16) describes the unique relationship of Jesus and the Father that can be true of no one else.

Sons of God is also a term used in an ethical sense of those who in character and life resemble God. Later in Matthew 5 Jesus says, "Love your enemies and pray for those who persecute you, so that you may be sons of your Father who is in heaven; for he makes his sun rise on the evil and on the good, and sends rain on the just and on the unjust" (Matt. 5:44–45 RSV; cf. Luke 6:35). This seems to be the meaning of our text, "They shall be called the sons of God." They are sons of God by the new birth. They will be recognized as such by their character as peacemakers for the following reasons.

I. God is a peacemaker.

The entire Bible tells the story of the lengths to which divine love will go to make peace with sinful persons. The passage chosen for the Scripture reading speaks eloquently of God's peacemaking mission. Note especially these verses: "And all things are of God, who hath reconciled us to himself by Jesus Christ, and hath given to us the ministry of reconciliation; to wit, that God was in Christ, reconciling the world unto himself, not imputing their trespasses unto them; and hath committed unto us the word of reconciliation" (2 Cor. 5:18–19).

God, speaking through the prophet Isaiah, called the Messiah "the Prince of Peace" (Isa. 9:7). He foretold Christ's reconciling ministry: "He was wounded for our transgressions, he was bruised for our iniquities: the chastisement of our peace was upon him; and with his stripes we are healed" (Isa. 53:5). Zechariah predicted the mission of Jesus: "To give light to them that sit in darkness and in the shadow of death, to guide our feet into the way of peace" (Luke 1:79). The angelic chorus at Jesus' birth praised God, saying, "Glory to God in the highest, and on earth peace, good will toward men" (Luke 2:14).

Jesus preached peace in the upper room: "Peace I leave with you, my peace I give unto you: not as the world giveth, give I unto you. Let not your heart be troubled, neither let it be afraid" (John 14:27). "These things have I spoken unto you, that in me ye might have peace" (John 16:33). Jesus appeared to the disciples on that first resurrection evening with the words "Peace be unto you" (Luke 24:36). Peter characterized the gospel to Cornelius as "the word which God sent unto the children of Israel, preaching peace by Jesus Christ" (Acts 10:36).

God will not make peace at any price. He is not an appeaser. He does not compromise. He offers peace on the terms of absolute surrender. "There is no peace, saith my God, to the wicked" (Isa. 57:21). "Except ye repent, ye shall all likewise perish" (Luke 13:3). The gospel which Jesus commanded us to preach to all nations is a gospel of "repentance and remission of sins . . . in his name" (Luke 24:47). The remission of sins is conditioned on repentance. James wrote, "But the wisdom that is from above is first pure, then peaceable, gentle, and easy to be entreated, full of mercy and good fruits, without partiality, and without hypocrisy. And the fruit of righteousness is sown in peace of them that make peace" (James 3:17–18). God insists on salvation before peace of conscience.

God does make peace with those who repent of sin and believe on Jesus. This is the very heart of the gospel. "For he is our peace, who hath made both one, and hath broken down the middle wall of partition between us; having abolished in his flesh the enmity, even the law of commandments contained in ordinances; for to make in himself of twain one new man, so making peace; and that he might reconcile both unto God in one body by the cross, having slain the enmity thereby; and came and preached peace to you which were afar off, and to them that were nigh" (Eph. 2:14–17; cf. also John 3:16, 36; 5:24; Rom. 5:1–10; Gal. 3:24–29).

II. Sons of God are to be peacemakers.

God has given to the redeemed that ministry. "And all things are of God, who hath reconciled us to himself by Jesus Christ, and hath given to us the ministry of reconciliation; to wit, that God was in Christ, reconciling the world unto himself, not imputing their trespasses unto them; and hath committed unto us the word of reconciliation. Now then we are ambassadors for Christ, as though God did beseech you by us: we pray you in Christ's stead, be ye reconciled to God" (2 Cor. 5:18–20).

As the ambassadors of Christ, the redeemed have full authority to proclaim the gospel but no authority to change the gospel. We call people to peace with God on God's terms.

III. God blesses this ministry of peacemaking between God and people.

Blessedness of doing God's will. His commands to his disciples until he comes again are clear: "All authority in heaven and on earth has been given to me. Go therefore and make disciples of all nations, baptizing them in the name of the Father and of the Son and of the Holy Spirit, teaching them to observe all that I have commanded you; and lo, I am with you always, to the close of the age" (Matt. 28:18–20 RSV). "But you shall receive power when the Holy Spirit has come upon you; and you shall be my witnesses in Jerusalem and in all Judea and Samaria, and to the end of the earth" (Acts 1:8 RSV). "If ye love me, keep my commandments" (John 14:15). "If ye know these things, happy are ye if ye do them" (John 13:17).

Joy of seeing souls saved. John wrote: "That which we have seen and heard declare we unto you, that ye also may have fellowship with us: and truly our fellowship is with the Father, and his Son Jesus Christ. And these things write we unto you, that your joy may be full" (1 John 1:3–4). The Revised Standard Version has "that our joy may be complete." Translators are uncertain whether this should be "your joy" or "our joy." In this instance, this is good, for when one comes to fellowship with God through Christ, both that person and the one who helps that one come to Christ are glad. Have you ever had anyone tell you that he or she is sorry that you helped him or her to become a Christian? You have probably had many tell you of their joy in Christ and thank you for helping them to become Christians.

A seminary student had been teaching a Sunday school class at a children's home for several Sundays. One Sunday his efforts were rewarded when several of the girls made professions of faith. As he was leaving the grounds, one of the new Christians placed a hastily written note in his hand. It read, "Isn't it good to be a Christian? I just had to write and tell you." The soul winner was happy. The soul won was happy. And God was happy, for "there is rejoicing in the presence of the angels of God over one sinner who repents" (Luke 15:10 NIV).

Conclusion

This beatitude builds on the six that precede it. People are not equipped to be peacemakers until they are convicted of sin—poor in spirit; contrite for sin; converted to God's will in full surrender, which is the meekness of Christ; dedicated to hungering and thirsting for what is right; compassionate and merciful like Jesus; and sincere in motive and purpose.

Happy, to be congratulated, blessed are the peacemakers, for they are cooperating with God in his glorious mission. Do you know this joy? Are you at peace with God? Are you at peace with yourself? Are you a peacemaker? Jesus says that this is the way to be happy.

WEDNESDAY EVENING, FEBRUARY 15

Title: Christ and the Barriers That Divide Us

Text: "Here there cannot be Greek and Jew, circumcised and uncircumcised, barbarian, Scythian, slave, free man, but Christ is all, and in all" **(Col. 3:11 RSV)**.

Scripture Reading: Colossians 3:1–11

Introduction

Christ came into the world to minister to the deepest problems that disturb human hearts. He came to reveal the way of love for all people. In this passage from Colossians, Paul is speaking to believers concerning their position in and relationship to Jesus Christ. Paul deals with the painful problems that distress and divide people by first of all emphasizing our relationship to God from God's perspective. He points out that we died to sin through Christ (Col. 2:20) and that we have been raised with Christ to new life (3:1). Further, he asserts that when our Lord appears in his glory, we will appear with him (3:4). In view of these great spiritual realities, Paul encourages us to cooperate with our Lord as we seek to live out our union with him. The apostle provides spiritual encouragement in the form of some great imperatives.

I. We are encouraged to focus our lives on Christ (Col. 3:1).

Paul had defined his purpose for being in terms of relating himself to Jesus Christ and letting Christ live in him (Phil. 1:21).

II. We are encouraged to focus our minds on Christ (Col. 3:2).

Our affections, our dispositions, and our wills—our entire personalities are to be affected by our desire to let Jesus Christ have his way with us.

III. We are encouraged to focus our hope on Christ (Col. 3:4).

Our great hope for the future and beyond time is to be united with Christ and with the people of God throughout all eternity. Thus Paul encourages us to remove barriers to Christian fellowship (Col. 3:5–17).

We are to put to death all destructive impulses and drives (Col. 3:5–6).

We are to put away a disposition that is evil, mean, and hurtful (Col. 3:8).

We are to put away falsehood and dishonesty from every area of life (Col. 3:9—10).

We are to recognize that in Jesus Christ there can be no destructive discrimination (Col. 3:11).

In Christ there can be no racial discrimination: "Here there cannot be Greek and Jew."

In Christ there can be no spiritual discrimination: "Here there cannot be . . . circumcised and uncircumcised."

In Christ there can be no cultural discrimination: "Here there cannot be . . . barbarian, Scythian." In the Greek world *barbarian was* a word of contempt for the uncultured, while "Scythian" was a synonym for *savage.*

In Christ there can be no social or economic discrimination: "Here there cannot be . . . slave, free." In Christ the rich and the poor are on level ground.

In Christ there can be no sexual discrimination. "There is neither male nor female; for you are all one in Christ Jesus" (Gal. 3:28 RSV). In Christ womanhood was exalted, reaching the highest position of status and dignity.

We are to put on the tender graces of Jesus Christ that are associated with love and mercy (Col. 3:12–14).

We are to let the peace of Christ rule in all our relationships (Col. 3:15).

66

We are to let the Word of Christ dwell in us richly to guide us and to instruct us (Col. 3:16).

We are to do all that we do under the authority and for the glory of our precious Lord, being thankful for every blessing and every opportunity to serve (Col. 3:17).

Conclusion

Christ came and died for our sins, conquering death and the grave so that eternal life might be a reality for us. Christ came to dwell within each of us when we trusted him as Savior. He wants to help us live the heavenly life even as we continue to live in the flesh on the earth. For Christ to help us with our pressing, painful problems, we must recognize and respond to him continuously. It was faith in Christ that established us in a loving relationship with him, and it is obedience to him that will bring satisfaction and joy to our hearts.

SUNDAY MORNING, FEBRUARY 19

Title: The Sword of the Spirit

Text: ". . . and the sword of the Spirit, which is the word of God" **(Eph. 6:17 RSV).**

Scripture Reading: Ephesians 6:10–20

Hymns: "Glorious Is Thy Name," McKinney
  "Break Thou the Bread of Life," Lathbury
  "Wonderful Words of Life," Bliss

Offertory Prayer: Holy Father, we rejoice in the privilege of being the receivers of the many gifts you have bestowed on us. Help us to see how generously you have blessed us. We rejoice with the joy that comes as a result of receiving. We come now with the joy of those who give, bringing tithes and offerings to indicate our love for you and our desire to see others come to know Jesus Christ as Lord and Savior. As we give our tithes, help us also to give ourselves into your service. Through Jesus Christ we pray. Amen.

Introduction

The Christian life is a struggle from beginning to end. We have a battle to fight with evil. If we are not involved in the struggle against evil and for good, it may mean that we have been neutralized by the seductive powers of Satan. We should be disturbed about our apathy and our lack of effort to achieve all that the Holy Spirit would lead us to do in the service of our Lord. We recognize our need to give heed to Paul's warning, "Give no opportunity to the devil" (Eph. 4:27 RSV).

We have been looking at the various pieces of armor that we must utilize in the battle against evil and for good. Paul uses the pieces of armor to make a spiritual application to the life and ministry of Jesus' followers and points out the necessity of putting on the whole armor of God. It is vital that we wear the belt of truth, the breastplate of righteousness, the sandals of readiness to do God's will, and the helmet of salvation. We must also carry the sword of the Spirit, which is the Word of God. The Roman soldier used a short, double-edged sword in battle. He could use it to jab or to cut the enemy. It was used for both offensive and defensive conflict. Paul declares that the Word of God performs this same function for the Christian soldier.

God has given his children what they need for successfully waging spiritual warfare. The first great truth Paul emphasizes in this text is that God has given us the Holy Spirit to dwell within us. The tool the Holy Spirit uses to accomplish God's purposes is God's Word. For us to neglect or to ignore the teachings of the Word of God in our daily life would be as foolish as it would be for a soldier to depart for battle without taking his weapons with him.

I. Joshua and the way to success (Josh. 1:8).

When Joshua took over the leadership of the twelve tribes of Israel, he was informed that he would find the way of success and that his leadership would prosper only as he gave daily attention to God's law. He was to meditate on the book of the law both day and night and follow its teachings carefully. He was promised prosperity and success as he gave attention to God's Word. God's counsel to Joshua is still meaningful and true for the present.

II. The psalmist points the way to happiness (Ps. 1:1–3).

The psalmist describes the man who is both happy and successful as one who avoids the ways of the wicked and who delights in the law of the Lord both day and night. The man who so fills his mind and heart with the great truths of God is likened to a tree planted by a river. Its leaf never withers, and it prospers in its way. There is no way a Christian can experience happiness and success if he or she neglects the clear teachings of God's Word.

III. Our Lord and his victory over Satan (Matt. 4:1–11).

In the great temptations our Lord experienced at the beginning of his public ministry, he used the sword of the Spirit to defeat Satan. In each instance, great scriptural truths rose up from his memory to strengthen, sustain, warn, and guide him. The psalmist had said, "I have laid up thy word in my heart, that I might not sin against thee" (Ps. 119:11 RSV). In the great crises in Jesus' life, his knowledge of the great truths of the Old Testament gave him the strength and help he needed. In the midst of his sufferings on the cross, he quoted from the Scriptures.

Our Lord had studied the Scriptures in the synagogue as a child and had memorized many great scriptural truths. We too can memorize Scripture so that we have resources to draw on when we face crises or opportunities. Like computers, which are limited to recalling information that is fed into them, our minds can recall only the spiritual truths that we store up.

IV. The function of Holy Scriptures.

The sacred writings reveal the nature of God and the way of salvation through Christ (2 Tim. 3:15).

The sacred Scriptures provide authoritative guidance for conduct that is pleasing to God (2 Tim. 3:16).

Profitable for teaching.

Profitable for reproof.

Profitable for correction.

Profitable for instruction in righteousness.

The sacred Scriptures equip the receptive and responsive believer for fruitful service (2 Tim. 3:17).

Conclusion

Here are some suggestions for how you might use the sword of the Spirit for God's glory.

Read the Word of God daily. Set aside time in your schedule to read the Word.

As you read listen intently for God speaking to you.

Pray the Word of God into your heart. Ask God for guidance and help that you might understand it.

Obey the great truths of the Word of God reverently and regularly.

Communicate the great truths of the Word of God to others.

Look for promises to claim in the Word of God.

Look for commandments to obey.

Look for examples to follow.

Look for sins to forsake and to avoid.

Look for solutions to the problems you face in your daily living. "Take the sword of the Spirit, which is the word of God."

SUNDAY EVENING, FEBRUARY 19

Title: The Blessed Persecuted

Text: "Blessed are they which are persecuted for righteousness' sake: for theirs is the kingdom of heaven. Blessed are ye, when men shall revile you, and persecute you, and shall say all manner of evil against you falsely, for my sake. Rejoice, and be exceeding glad: for great is your reward in heaven: for so persecuted they the prophets which were before you" **(Matt. 5:10–12).**

Scripture Reading: 1 Peter 2:19–25; 3:14–18

Introduction

This beatitude is the most paradoxical of all. It seems incredible that one should be happy when persecuted, reviled, and lied about. Let us note carefully the conditions of the beatitude.

I. No blessing is promised to those who persecute.

A. *Jesus puts himself on the side of persecution, no reviling, no false accusation.*

In the parable of the tares, recorded in Matthew 13:24–30, 36–43, the workers ask the householder with reference to the tares, "Wilt thou then that we go and gather them up? But he said, Nay, lest while ye gather up the tares, ye root up also the wheat with them" (Matt. 13:28–29). The business of Christians is not to persecute heretics. Judgment belongs to God. When in the dark annals of history Christians have tried to weed out the tares, they have just as often rooted up the wheat. Persecution is a miserable business. When Paul thought he was serving God by persecuting Christians, he had inner revulsion and pain about it like the pain of the ox who kicks against the sharp goad that is used to prod him.

Luke 8:49–56 offers further proof that persecution is not part of Jesus' plan.

B. *The competency of each person to come to God without any intermediary is at the heart of the gospel.* "For God so loved the world, that he gave his only begotten Son, that whosoever believeth in him should not perish, but have everlasting life" (John 3:16). Each person is invited to come to God for himself or herself. Each one is responsible for his or her own response. "So then every one of us shall give account of himself to God" (Rom. 14:12). No person can give account for another. Further, each person has the right to worship God according to the dictates of his or her own conscience. Christians are not to use any force—physical, political, economic, or social—to compel others to their belief. Speaking the truth in love and a Christlike life are the legitimate weapons of Christian conquest.

II. No blessing is promised to the one who is persecuted for folly or wickedness.

A. *The meaning of being persecuted for righteousness' sake.*

To persecute means to follow after another in order to do harm. Sometimes people think they are persecuted when they are not. We are not being persecuted if someone in good faith and in good spirit challenges our doctrinal position. Truth is under eternal obligation to expose error. "Be ready always to give an answer to every man that asketh you a reason of the hope that is in you with meekness and fear" (1 Peter 3:15).

Persecution is when one is physically molested, denied the economic freedom accorded other citizens, denied public rights, is taxed to support religion, and the like because of one's faith.

B. *To revile is to treat as vile.* We ought to be willing to defend our faith in the arena of truth and conscience. We accord that right to others. We do not have the right to treat others' beliefs as vile by ridiculing them.

III. Conditions of the blessing.

A. *Falsely.* There is no blessing if the charge for which one suffers is just, but when one is lied about and charged unjustly, that person is blessed.

B. *For righteousness' sake and for my sake.* Note that Jesus equates loyalty to right with loyalty to himself. This is one of many claims to deity that Jesus makes in the Sermon on the Mount.

IV. Why the blessing?

Persecution, reviling, and false accusation for Jesus' sake indicate that one is a citizen of the kingdom of heaven (a Christian) and in the good company of the prophets.

Genuine Christians stir up opposition because they are a constant rebuke to selfishness and sin. Jesus lived the perfect life. He had all the qualities of goodness, yet he was reviled. They called him Beelzebub, a bastard, a winebibber, a sinner. They lied about him and even paid false witnesses to lie about him. They persecuted him even unto death. Jesus warned his disciples, "If the world hate you, ye know that it hated me before it hated you. If ye were of the world, the world would love his own: but because ye are not of the world, but I have chosen you out of the world, therefore the world hateth you. Remember the word that I said unto you, The servant is not greater than his lord. If they have persecuted me, they will also persecute you; if they have kept my saying, they will keep yours also" (John 15:18–20).

Genuine Christians stir up opposition because they interfere. Jesus said, "Think not that I am come to send peace on earth: I come not to send peace, but a sword" (Matt. 10:34). Loyalty to Jesus divides households. Jesus dared to interfere with the corrupt racket the chief priests were operating in the temple in the name of religion (see Mark 11:15–18). John the Baptist dared to say to King Herod of Herodias, his brother's wife, "It is not lawful for thee to have her" (Matt. 14:4). Peter and John were in prison preaching the truth about Jesus. From the viewpoint of the Sadducees, they were meddling with established religion (see Acts 5:28–29). Paul and Silas were beaten and cast into jail in Philippi. The charge was: "These men, being Jews, do exceedingly trouble our city, and teach customs, which are not lawful for us to receive, neither to observe, being Romans" (Acts 16:20–21). The offense behind their arrest was delivering a girl from slavery. The mob in the theater at Ephesus was aroused because Paul's preaching was hurting their idol-making business. Criminals, drug dealers, racists, and all who profit by the weakness of others hate the gospel because it interferes with their agendas.

V. In what does the blessing consist?

A. *Persecution, reviling, and false accusation for righteousness' sake indicates that one is a citizen of the kingdom of heaven and in the good company of the prophets.* Are you loyal enough to Jesus to have some enemies because of your loyalty? Jesus said, "Woe unto you, when all men speak well of you! for so did their fathers to the false prophets" (Luke 6:26). If it was lawful to arrest Christians, would there be enough evidence against you to convict you? The true prophets of God have suffered persecution. Rejoice when you are loyal enough to God to be counted with them.

B. *Rejoice also in the assurance that your Father in heaven knows all about it and understands.* "For great is your reward in heaven" (v. 12). Through loyalty to Jesus, you have been laying up heavenly treasure (see Matt. 6:19–21; 25:31–40).

Conclusion

Christianity is not a call to do the conventional. It is a call to the heroic, to do right regardless of consequences. Let Jesus be Lord (see Rom. 14:8–9). Our business is to live for righteousness, for Jesus' sake, for God's glory.

We are not to seek persecution, but if it comes, we should not be surprised. While not pleasant, it is something to rejoice about. Continue to be loyal to the message and spirit of Jesus Christ. You may win your enemy by love. In any case, you will be a better person for the experience.

WEDNESDAY EVENING, FEBRUARY 22

Title: Living for Christ in the Home

Text: "And whatever you do, in word or deed, do everything in the name of the Lord Jesus, giving thanks to God the Father through him" **(Col. 3:17 RSV)**.

Scripture Reading: Colossians 3:17–21

Introduction

The most important place of Christian service may be your own home. An earnest effort should be put forth to demonstrate the Spirit of Christ and to show forth the graces of a Christian disposition within the home.

We will fail miserably if we practice our Christianity only within the fellowship of the church or out in the midst of a wicked world. We need to put forth a persistent effort to show genuine piety and all that it means to be followers of Jesus Christ within the home.

The passage of Scripture under consideration emphasizes the reciprocal obligations of those who make up family life.

I. Wives are encouraged to subject themselves to their husbands (Col. 3:18; Eph. 5:22).

Some women, misunderstanding Paul's teaching about submission, have rebelled against it. But he is not emphasizing a superiority of husbands over wives. Instead, he is encouraging wives to accept their proper role in relationship to their husbands being head of the household. Likewise, Paul is encouraging husbands to take their position of leadership in the home. Someone must assume a position of leadership if a home is to be well ordered, productive, and happy.

Wives are to have an attitude of reverence and loyalty toward their husbands. If a wife has resistance to the idea of being in subjection to her husband, she should remember that it is a subjection in which love is the very soul and animating principle of the relationship.

II. Husbands are encouraged to love their wives.

Paul is giving husbands a present, active imperative. Husbands are to keep on loving their wives and not be bitter, harsh, and unkind in words or deeds. They are to practice patience, gratefulness, and generosity and are to help their wives. This is not sentimental love. It is a spirit of sacrificial, unselfish giving for the well-being of one's wife and the mother of one's children.

Paul describes the love husbands are to have for their wives as comparable to the love that Christ had for the church when he sacrificed himself for her, his bride (Eph. 5:25). Husbands are to love their wives as they love their own bodies (vv. 28–31). The union of husband and wife in a one-flesh relationship makes this kind of love reasonable and responsible.

III. Children are to be obedient to their parents if they would please the Lord (Col. 3:20).

This obedience is to be continuous rather than just occasional.

Parents must assume the responsibility for teaching their children to be obedient. This is not easy in an age that encourages revolt and irreverence.

Parents do their children no favor if they permit them to practice disobedience.

Children need to recognize and respond to the fact that God has appointed their parents to be their teachers. God's will is that they be obedient to their parents.

IV. Fathers (parents) are responsible for the manner in which they treat their children.

The apostle encourages parents to practice a spirit of gentle consideration toward their children. They are to avoid provoking their children to anger and wrath.

Parents should avoid issuing unreasonable commands to their children.

Parents need to avoid undue harshness toward their children.

Parents need to avoid cutting, critical comments that destroy the personhood of their children.

Parents need to avoid "capricious jerks on the bridle" by which they would guide their children.

Parents need to control the tone of their voice and avoid harshness in correcting their children.

Parents must recognize that they cannot enforce perpetual restrictions on their children.

Being a wise and gracious parent is no easy task. Parents need all of the grace and wisdom that God makes available to them.

Conclusion

Paul emphasizes reciprocal responsibilities and obligations rather than rights and privileges of those who make up the Christian household. If each member of the household will respond to his or her duty, all will experience a beauty and a joy in relationships.

SUNDAY MORNING, FEBRUARY 26

Title: Prayer for Total Spiritual Mobilization

Text: "Pray at all times in the Spirit, with all prayer and supplication" **(Eph. 6:18 RSV)**.

Scripture Reading: Ephesians 6:18–20

Hymns: "O God, Our Help in Ages Past," Watts
"Take the Name of Jesus with You," Baxter
"Lead On, O King Eternal," Shurtleff

Offertory Prayer: Loving Father, we come to thank you for this privilege of communicating with you in prayer. We thank you for the promise of our Lord to always be present with your people when we meet for prayer and worship. We thank you for the privilege of being able to bring to you our tithes and offerings as indications of our desire to give you every part of our lives. Bless the work of our hands. Bless the testimony of our lips. Bless the gifts that come from our hearts, and use them to bring glory to your holy name and blessings into the hearts and lives of people. We pray in Jesus' name. Amen.

Introduction

Those who profess to be followers of Christ have a battle to fight and an enemy to overcome. The devil is always seeking to bring about the disgrace and defeat of each one who professes faith in Jesus Christ and who seeks to do God's will. Christians must put on the whole armor of God if they would stand against the evil that assaults them from all points. Each portion of the armor is of great significance and must not be neglected.

The apostle Paul, a veteran of many conflicts with Satan, brought his teaching to a close by emphasizing the importance of always being in a spirit of prayer so that we will be totally mobilized to do God's will and to resist the ever-present evil. Prayer is not so much another piece of armor as it is the means of communication between soldiers and their Commanding Officer.

Through the Word of God, the General speaks to his soldiers. By prayer soldiers stay in contact with their General.

I. The necessity of prayer.

In any military campaign, good communication between headquarters and the foot soldiers who are to fight the battle is absolutely essential. This truth can be paralleled in the spiritual realm. Paul emphasizes the necessity of prayer because of the essential nature of prayer. Prayer is not merely the means by which we requisition supplies for the conflict. It is a dialogue between the Father God and his needy children, between the Commanding Officer and the soldiers on the field. It is while we pray that the Father God reveals his will and speaks the words of encouragement and guidance we need. It is also in prayer that we have the opportunity to speak personally to our Father God concerning our fears, doubts, hurts, and aspirations.

A person who seeks to live even one day without prayer is like a soldier who would depart for battle without any communications from the commanding officer. There is no way by which we can resist our enemy, the devil, and overcome the evil within us and about us if we neglect the privilege of prayer.

II. The variety of prayer.

"With all prayer and supplication." We should pray on a variety of occasions and offer up a number of different kinds of prayers. Every experience of life calls for appropriate prayers. That we are to "pray at all times" means that we can pray in childhood or adulthood, in weakness or strength, in success or failure—at any time. Prayer must not be limited to particular seasons or moods that may come to us.

When Paul wrote to Timothy, he spoke of four different forms of prayer.

Supplications. We should humbly entreat the mercy and the grace of our God.

Prayers of confession and of petition concerning our personal needs are always of primary importance when we pray.

Intercessions. Our Lord instructed his disciples to address "Our Father" when offering prayer. Through the model prayer, the plural pronoun is used, implying that others are to be remembered in our prayers of intercession.

Thanksgivings. Thanksgiving is always appropriate on every occasion when we pray (Phil. 4:6–7). We can thank God for his goodness in the past, his blessings in the present, and his unchanging nature and purpose in the future.

In speaking of the variety of prayer (1 Tim. 2:1), Paul urged Timothy and those with him to be in prayer for all people and particularly for those in positions of authority and responsibility.

III. The occasion for prayer.

"Pray at all times in the Spirit." Prayer is always appropriate and should be practiced with the assistance of the Holy Spirit. Although there is never a time when prayer is inappropriate, we must recognize that the apostle is not suggesting that we spend all day on our knees. Rather, he is suggesting that we always be on speaking terms with God and that we always have our "receiving set" turned on so as to receive a communication from God. We are to keep ourselves in such harmony with God's will that we have immediate access to the throne room to express our needs or to give voice to our thanksgiving.

Prayer brings us into contact with God and opens the gate so that the river of God's blessings can flow into our hearts and lives. It brings us into contact with the power of God as throwing an electric switch completes a circuit and lets the power flow into a lightbulb. In every circumstance of life, in every time of need, we are to utilize the privilege of prayer, and we are to do it in the power of the Holy Spirit.

The Holy Spirit creates within us a prayerful heart (Gal. 4:6). The Holy Spirit seeks to lead each child into communion with the heavenly Father.

The Holy Spirit gives us guidance concerning the substance of our prayers (Rom. 8:26).

The Holy Spirit identifies with us to the extent that he makes intercession for us according to the Father's will (Rom. 8:27).

IV. The purpose of prayer.

"That utterance may be given me in opening my mouth boldly to proclaim the mystery of the gospel" (Eph. 6:19 RSV). The purpose for prayer is not to give us some special status with God by which we may receive "goodies" from him, for each of us has equal access into his presence. The purpose for prayer is that we might grow and become all that we ought to be as God's children and as his servants. Prayer is the divinely appointed means by which we requisition that which is needed for doing God's will and accomplishing his work in the world.

It is appropriate that we pray for ourselves that we might be used by God to build up the church and extend the kingdom.

We are always to remember to pray for others as they serve God and seek to do God's will.

We are to pray particularly for leaders who occupy positions of responsibility and whose decisions affect the destiny and the well-being of all of us (1 Tim. 2:2).

V. Persistence in prayer.

We are instructed to "keep alert with all perseverance" in our offering of prayer on behalf of the saints. This means that we are to have the habit of prayer and not to break it. It also means that we are to be alert moment by moment concerning the needs of others in order that we might continuously hold them up before God's throne of grace.

We should remember the various members of our family day by day before God's throne of grace.

We should remember the officials of our country before God's throne of grace. All elected and appointed officials are involved in a manner that affects the well-being of us all. Each of them is subject to the perils of errors in judgment. We need to pray for them to have genuine faith in God and integrity of character (1 Tim. 2:2).

We need to remember our spiritual leaders (Phil. 1:19; Eph. 6:19).

We need to hold ourselves up before God's throne of grace and bring our lives under the searchlight of his personal presence day by day (Matt. 6:6). The greatest effects produced by prayer are inward and spiritual. When we let God do something in us, we are letting his kingdom come within our own lives.

Conclusion

Individually there is no way we can be victorious over evil if we neglect to pray. Collectively the congregation needs to pray so that our united efforts might not be defeated by Satan. The Holy Spirit is our leader when we pray. Let us allow him to guide us in our dialogue with God as we work with him to overcome evil and to be the godly people God wants us to be.

SUNDAY EVENING, FEBRUARY 26

Title: The Salt of the Earth

Text: "You are the salt of the earth. But if the salt loses its saltiness, how can it be made salty again? It is no longer good for anything, except to be thrown out and trampled by men" **(Matt. 5:13 NIV).**

Scripture Reading: Romans 14:7–13

Introduction

Like sunrises and sunsets—common events that are never commonplace—there are familiar truths that are always fascinating and interesting. One of these is the fact of influence. How significant that others will be better or worse because of you!

Having described in the Beatitudes the character of Christians, our Lord then described the influence of Christians under the figures of salt and light.

I. You are the salt of the earth.

Who? *You* is emphatic and refers to those spoken of in the Beatitudes. You who are poor in spirit, contrite, meek, hungering and thirsting after righteousness, merciful, pure in heart, and peacemakers, are salt. You who are persecuted, reviled, and lied about are salt. You who are citizens of the kingdom of God have the responsibility of being salt in the world.

What is salt?

"Salt is what makes food taste bad when you leave it out," according to a child's definition. Salt gives zest and flavor to food just as Christians give zest and flavor to life. The Christian life is the happy life, as Jesus described in the Beatitudes. "If ye know these things, happy are ye if ye do them," Jesus said (John 13:17). And "I am come that they might have life, and that they might have it more abundantly" (John 10:10).

Paul said so: "If you have any encouragement from being united with Christ, if any comfort from his love, if any common sharing in the Spirit, if any tenderness and compassion, then make my joy complete by being like-minded, having the same love, being one in spirit and of one mind" (Phil. 2:1–2 NIV). "Yea, and if I be offered upon the sacrifice and service of your faith, I joy, and rejoice with you all" (vv. 17–18). "Finally, my brethren, rejoice in the Lord" (3:1).

Devout Christians say so. Think of the most consecrated Christians you know. The nearer they are to Jesus, the happier they are. Missionaries seem to know the peace that passes understanding. Joy is Jesus and you with nothing between.

Salt is a preservative. Even today, with modern refrigeration, salt is used to preserve meat and fish. For the fishermen, shepherds, and farmers to whom Jesus spoke, salt was essential for preserving fish and meat. They cut blocks of salt from the Dead Sea for this purpose. Christians are the means God has chosen to keep the world from going bad. Our Lord's last words before his ascension were, "It is not for you to know the times or the seasons, which the Father put in his own power. But ye shall receive power, after that the Holy Ghost is come upon you: and ye shall be witnesses unto me both in Jerusalem, and in all Judaea, and in Samaria, and unto the uttermost part of the earth" (Acts 1:7–8). We cannot know the time schedule, but we do know that the Lord's plan for saving the world is that Christians guided and empowered by the Holy Spirit bear witness to Jesus Christ.

II. But if the salt loses its saltiness, how can it be made salty again?

These Galilean fisherman who heard Jesus speak these words had no difficulty understanding the illustration. A block of salt cut from the edge of the Dead Sea contained in addition to the soluble sodium chloride (common salt) many insoluble salts, some dirt, and other impurities. If exposed to rain or a season of prolonged dampness, the soluble salt would run off, leaving the other minerals and dirt. That which remained was incapable of doing what salt is to do—namely, give flavor and preserve.

What could the farmer or fisherman do with this salt? If put on the field, it would render the ground infertile. It was useless. He cast it out on the path or road where it would do the least harm.

The application as determined by the context is not that Christians could lose their salvation, but rather their witness, their testimony, their spirituality, their good influence on others. What good are Christians who do not Christianize? What can God do with Christians who backslide into an unworthy life? Sinners will call them hypocrites and will use their bad example as an excuse for their wickedness. David was a saved man. By his sin, however, he did great harm. The courageous prophet Nathan dared to tell the king that by his wicked deed he had given great occasion to the enemies of the Lord to blaspheme. Read Paul's indictment of the religious Jews who professed but did not practice in Romans 2:17–24, ending with the indictment, "For the name of God is blasphemed among the Gentiles through you" (Rom. 2:24).

Conclusion

There is no substitute for salt. "But if the salt loses its saltiness, how can it be made salty again?" (Matt. 5:13 NIV). God has no alternate plan. He depends entirely on Christians to be the instruments of his purpose to Christianize the world.

Happily the illustrations of nature, when pushed to rigorous conclusions, do not fully illustrate the grace of God. Salt that has lost its savor cannot be recovered. A backsliding Christian who has been useless—even harmful—to the cause of Christ, can return to the Lord and become useful.

Hear the invitation extended by Isaiah, "Seek ye the LORD while he may be found, call ye upon him while he is near: let the wicked forsake his way, and the unrighteous man his thoughts: and let him return unto the LORD, and he will have mercy upon him; and to our God, for he will abundantly pardon" (Isa. 55:6–7).

MARCH

■ **Sunday Mornings**

"The Church and Its Primary Ministry" is the theme for Sunday mornings this month. While the church has many functions to fill and services to render, its primary task is to evangelize.

■ **Sunday Evenings**

Continue with expository messages from Jesus' Sermon on the Mount.

■ **Wednesday Evenings**

The theme for this month's Wednesday evening services is "The Christian's Ministry to the Sick." Our Lord ministered to the sick, the sorrowing, and the troubled. If we want to properly manifest Christian love, we must not neglect a ministry to those who suffer. These messages come from the heart and pen of a vocational hospital chaplain.

WEDNESDAY EVENING, MARCH 1

Title: Jesus Visits a Strange Hospital

Text: "Now there is at Jerusalem by the sheep market a pool, which is called in the Hebrew tongue Bethesda, having five porches" **(John 5:2).**

Scripture Reading: John 5:1–16

Introduction

The pool of Bethesda was frequented by many people with different ailments, for, right or wrong, many believed that the waters of the pool had healing qualities. Without arguing the validity of such contentions, the important thing to note is that Jesus started where the people were, both geographically and spiritually. He still does today.

I. The designation is justified (5:3).

"A great multitude" with a variety of ailments came to the pool hoping for a miracle. They included people who were lame, blind, and paralyzed. The size of the crowd was matched by the magnitude of their ailments.

II. A desire is important (5:6).

Those who care for the sick will be the first to agree that a desire to get well is highly essential to a patient's recovery. The Great Physician asked the ailing man, "Do you really desire to be cured?" Such a question is basic in our own illness and in our ministry to those who are sick.

III. A difficulty is presented (5:7).

The sick man declared that because he had no one to place him in the pool when the waters were disturbed, others who could move their bodies would rush in and claim the therapy of the moving waters, leaving him merely a spectator. The fact that the man could not move was a difficulty, but it was not his chief difficulty. He needed to rearrange his priorities, and in doing so he would have rearranged his difficulties.

IV. A directive is given (5:8).

"Rise, take up thy bed and walk" is as clear as it is radical. But it worked because the man worked. To hear by faith the incredible and attempt the impossible is to experience the inexplicable. Thomas Carlyle said, "Every noble work is at first impossible." The impossible becomes possible when Christ is in the picture.

V. A deliverance is recorded (5:9).

"And at once the man was healed" (RSV). It was as clear and sharp and simple as that. And the man's future biographical data indicated that he was healed.

VI. The directions are followed (5:9).

Jesus told the man to rise, take up his bed, and walk. He did just that, no more and no less, at the moment. Jesus would require more of the man along the way, but the man's immediate response was obedience to the word from the Lord.

VII. A deed is observed (5:14).

No attendance campaign is reported. No pressures were placed on the healed man. Yet his grateful heart was drawn to worship in the temple of the living God. Gratitude is a sufficient motive for all of us to be in the Lord's house at every opportunity.

VIII. A depth is plumbed (5:14).

Jesus warns about the consequences of sin. Sin is the taproot of every bad tree. We cannot afford to enjoy the external blessings of Christ's grace without heeding the spiritual condition of the inner person.

IX. A departure is made (5:15).

No one lives in the spiritual parking lot after he or she has met Jesus.

X. A declaration is delivered (5:15).

Our text talks of an ancient version of "show and tell." Today we still have convincing evidence of what Christ can do and does do in people's lives. There is still no more effective tool for carving out the kingdom than such a personal testimony as is seen here.

XI. A determination is accelerated (5:16).

The Jews intensified their efforts against our Lord. Let it be noted that their major immediate objection was really a minor consideration—it was on the technicality that these things were done on the Sabbath. A great leader said he would prefer to be swallowed by a whale than to be nibbled to death by minnows. These religious minnows continued to nibble at the character and life of Jesus.

Conclusion

Let us remember that the sick and the sinful are always about us. Let us never forget that Jesus is their greatest need and supreme help. Let us be sensitive to their needs and responsive to Christ's call as we minister to them in his name. Hundreds of such people need us—now!

SUNDAY MORNING, MARCH 5

Title: The Church and Jesus

Text: "I will build my church, and the powers of death shall not prevail against it. I will give you the keys of the kingdom of heaven, and whatever you bind on earth shall be bound in heaven, and whatever you loose on earth shall be loosed in heaven" (**Matt. 16:18–19 RSV**).

Scripture Reading: Matthew 16:13–19

Hymns: "The Church's One Foundation," Stone
"Onward Christian Soldiers," Baring-Gould
"All the Way My Saviour Leads Me," Crosby

Offertory Prayer: Father, we praise you for your presence in the church and that we can be a part of your church. Now we thank you that we can worship by bringing that with which you have blessed us so that your church may function effectively in the world. We express our love and demonstrate our commitment with our tithes and offerings. In Jesus' name. Amen.

Introduction

On a recent Sunday I preached in a church with a membership of four thousand and a Sunday school enrollment of just above two thousand. Attendance was less than one thousand. The next Sunday I conducted a service in a campground for recreational vehicles. Conversation with campers indicated that 90 percent of those above twelve years of age were members of some church although only half had a vital relationship with Christ. My question is, "What does church membership have to do with being a Christian?"

Recently a man told me in his home, "Yes, I certainly consider myself a Christian, but I am not presently a member of any church." He then proceeded to catalog the weaknesses and failures of the church.

I have said two things: (1) Many people are on church rolls yet have no vital relationship with Jesus. (2) Some people say they love and serve Jesus but have no appreciation for the church. Now I would like for us to look at these questions.

I. Can I take Jesus without the church?

A pastor recently told me, "We have found that people will make a commitment to Christ as we visit them in their homes, but a large percentage will not come to the church and make a public commitment." You could certainly raise some question as to the genuineness of their conversion.

What was the attitude of Jesus toward the religious establishment of his day? For one thing, he saw the cold, empty, perfunctory deadness of the temple and synagogue and sharply rebuked the religious leaders. Nevertheless, when in Jerusalem, he went to the temple. When in the cities and villages, he worshiped and taught in the synagogue.

Have you ever heard someone say, "I used to go to church, but I became so disillusioned I quit"? That person has never attended a church as weak, heretical, hypocritical, cold, or unfriendly as the synagogues Jesus attended every week, but he continued going. He pointed out their weaknesses, but he kept attending. He offered something better, but he never quit.

A man said to me recently, "My father was a preacher. I became so sick and disgusted with the way they treated him that I quit the whole thing." Jesus must have been very upset about the way they treated his Father, but he didn't quit.

Jesus went into the church business. Following the confession and commitment of his own disciples, Jesus promised continued success for his church. Whatever else may be said about that conversation between Jesus and his disciples, he clearly was building a church that was inseparable from a confession of him as Savior.

Jesus established his church to do more effectively what he came into the world to do. "I came that they may have life, and have it abundantly," he said. Everything he said and did was related to this life-giving commitment. He knew our need and answered it.

Because people are spiritual creatures, they have a hungering and thirsting for that which is spiritual. With billions of people in this world, this thirst has never been satisfied. People are always searching, but sometimes in the wrong places. God said through Jeremiah, "For my people have committed two evils; they have forsaken me, the fountain of living waters, and hewed out cisterns for themselves, broken cisterns, that can hold no water" (Jer. 2:13 RSV).

People sincerely believe that if they can just make enough money, buy enough gadgets, and have enough fun, they will be happy. But you cannot swap God for gadgets. Gather about you every convenience in the world, and you will still be thirsty. Crises inevitably come into all our lives. We have learned that the happiness ratio is no higher with affluence and education than without it. This is not to speak against education, economic security, or even gadgets and expensive cars. It is to say that we are made for something that these will not satisfy.

Recently I spent an hour and a half walking with a man through his manufacturing plant. He proudly told me how he had invented most of the machinery in it and built it from almost nothing. Before he finished, however, he began to tell me how bad his life was. He had some of the most expensive hobbies a person could have, yet they did not bring him happiness.

Another man told me how he had nearly lost his mind because his dreams had not come true and his ambitions for his son had not been realized. He had lost everything he had just about the time he was expecting his son to take over. He was shocked and surprised when his son said, "Dad, I regret this has happened to you, but I want you to know that it is perhaps the best thing that could have happened to me, because God has a different plan for my life. I guess I would have followed your plan rather than hurt you, but if I had I would not have followed God's plan for my life." Jesus is not opposed to property, but he makes it clear that life does not consist of the abundance of things we possess. His plan for us is always best.

Jesus gave us the church as a means of keeping the Good News alive. He commits this function to his churches, and we are unfaithful if we do not keep the proclamation of the Good News in the forefront.

Another advantage of church membership is fellowship. We are social beings who benefit from corporate worship. We need to share with others, confess our sins to others, and serve with others. You could be a Christian on a lonely island, but your Christian life would be as incomplete and perverted as all other facets of your life would be. As members of Christ's body, we are dependent on all the other members. The Lord gave us the church because we need the church.

A woman told me, "I used to say I could be as good a Christian outside the church as I could be in it. For the sake of my children, I began attending on Sunday morning. I began to discover the value of the church. The more I became involved the more I saw I needed it. I don't see how I ever got along without it."

II. Can I take the church without Jesus?

Perhaps you have never heard anyone ask that question. I raised it, not because of what I hear, but because of what I see.

Most of the four thousand members of the church I mentioned at the outset attach some value to their church membership. Most of them would confess that they do not have a vital relationship with Jesus, but they are proud that they have some kind of church connection.

You too can attend church regularly and participate in its programs yet have a poor relationship with Jesus. You can do the job you have been elected to do, faithfully pay your tithes, usher, teach Sunday school classes, sing in the choir, lead in public prayers, and even go out for church visitation, yet still go days and days without any personal relationship with the Lord. So is it possible to take the church without taking Jesus?

Conclusion

I thank God for the hundreds of happy, wholesome, growing, maturing, vibrant Christians who have learned and are learning what it means to be a Christian. Thank God this number has been increasing in recent years.

During the last five years, I have had the privilege of associating with hundreds who tell me the Lord means more to them than ever before. Some of them testify of how they had once been active in the church, doing their jobs perfunctorily, feeling hurt if they were not elected to places of leadership and feeling disgusted with their fellow members for not being "active." Then they relate how they began to become aware of their own emptiness, how church work was done out of a sense of duty or respectability. In some cases, they relate how they were actually "hiding" in the church. Many relate how that because of their own self-conscious and self-centered activity they had been critical of pastors and other church leaders. Now, in their renewed relationship with God, they find themselves loving their neighbors and enjoying the church even when someone else gets the recognition.

Christians trying to follow Jesus without the church are like workers working without tools or soldiers fighting without weapons. Trying to find meaning in life by serving in the church without commitment to Jesus is useless.

SUNDAY EVENING, MARCH 5

Title: The Light of the World

Text: "Let your light so shine before men, that they may see your good works, and glorify your Father which is in heaven" (**Matt. 5:16**).

Scripture Reading: Matthew 5:14–16

Introduction

To extend his teaching on the Christian's influence, Jesus moved from the salt metaphor to a light metaphor. He said to Christians, "Ye are the light of the world" (Matt. 5:14).

I. Every person has an influence.

One can no more escape having an influence than a city set on a hill can be hidden. By day one can see it; by night lights reveal its location. Jesus is not urging Christians to be light. He affirms, "You are light for all the world" (Matt. 5:14 NEB). He does not exhort, "Let your light shine" but rather, "Let your light *so* shine" (italics mine). His emphasis is on the manner of the shining.

The reference in verse 15 is almost certainly to a lamp or lampstand, as in the Revised Standard Version and almost all modern versions, rather than to candle and candlestick of the King James Version. In every Palestinian home, one could find an oil lamp with a wick and an earthenware vessel called a "bushel" (KJV; "bowl," NIV). No one would light a lamp and put it under the bushel, for the lamp would promptly go out. As long as a lamp is burning, it sheds light; as long as a person is alive, he or she has influence. "For none of us liveth to himself and no man dieth to himself" (Rom. 14:7).

II. The manner of this shining.

Jesus in this text is exhorting his disciples to shine the light of their influence in such a manner that people will see their good works and glorify the heavenly Father. How can one do this?

To have a Christian witness, one must be Christian. A lamp must be burning to give light, and it must be burning brightly and steadily to give a good light. One who is not a genuine Christian may fool some of the people part of the time but not all of the people all of the time. He or she will not fool God at any time. A hypocrite cannot obey this command.

The Christian is to confess Christ before others. "Let your light so shine before men" is Jesus' exhortation. He is not satisfied with secret discipleship. He calls for public confession. "Whosoever therefore shall confess me before men, him will I confess also before my Father which is in heaven. But whosoever shall deny me before men, him will I also deny before my Father which is in heaven" (Matt. 10:32–33).

Have you ever considered that people who allow others to think that they are worse than they are for applause are hypocrites just as surely as are those who, for the same purpose, represent themselves as better than they actually are? All of us are familiar with the hypocrisy of the Pharisee who ostentatiously performed his religious acts so that people would think he was pious. How about Simon Peter, a genuine believer, who in a moment of weakness denied that he was a disciple of Jesus to gain the favor of the hostile crowd? Wasn't he also playing the hypocrite?

A pastor went to the office of a prominent state official to talk with him about becoming a Christian. The official was known as a good moral man and a competent public servant. His wife was an active member of the church, but he was not a member. The man replied, "I am a Christian. I have trusted Jesus as my Savior." The pastor said, "Have you ever confessed your faith publicly? Have you been baptized? Have you joined a church?" His answer was no to all of these questions. The pastor continued, "How glad I am to know that you are a Christian. The people of this state hold you in high esteem, but the universal opinion is that you are not a Christian. Would you not now like to come out into the open by confessing Christ publicly and obeying his command to be baptized?"

He replied, "No, I am afraid that if I did that I would be a hypocrite." The pastor tried to show him that if he was a Christian and let people think that he wasn't, he was a hypocrite. He was unsuccessful at that time, but later the official did publicly profess his faith. Jesus does not want people to profess a faith they do not have, but he does call believers to confess him before others.

So shine your light as to glorify God. A lamp does not call attention to itself. It is simply placed on a lampstand from which it will give the best illumination. It is not always easy for Christians to do good works in such unostentatious ways that people will praise God rather than the Christians, but this is exactly what is commanded. Believers can, however, make public confession, be baptized, join the church, and be cooperative members by wholeheartedly participating in the worship and witness of the church. Christians should strive personally and as church members to do all Jesus has commanded.

III. Conscious and unconscious influence.

Many years ago Dr. Horace Bushnell preached a wonderful sermon titled "The Power of Unconscious Influence." By unconscious influence he meant influence that is exerted when we are not aware that we are influencing others. Conscious influence is that which is sensibly exerted, as by preaching or teaching. When conscious and unconscious influence pull together, they are very strong. When they pull against each other, unconscious influence is almost always the stronger.

Example is more persuasive than precept. Dr. Bushnell used as his Scripture John 20:1–10. Simon Peter and John learned from Mary Magdalene of the empty tomb. They ran to see about it. John outran Peter. He timidly waited at the door of the tomb, content to peep in. When Peter arrived he did not hesitate but went right into the tomb. "Then went in also that other disciple [John], which came first to the sepulcher, and he saw and believed" (John 20:8). Would John have gone in had Peter not done so? Did Peter ever know that he had influenced John to enter? Such is the power of example.

A young lady who had been serving as a Baptist Student Union director boarded a public bus. She gave her money to the young driver and received her bus token and change. On reaching her seat, she counted her change and found that she had a dime too much. At the first convenient opportunity, she took the dime to the driver and explained, "You gave me a dime too much change." He smiled and said, "I know it, Miss. I have been hearing you make some speeches, and I wanted to see if you practice what you preach." She returned to her seat and thought, *How easily I could have crucified my Lord afresh for a dime!*

A coed accepted a date with one of the campus football heroes. He pushed her to do wrong. She refused but explained why and bore witness to her faith in Christ. The young man was convicted. That night he found Christ with the help of the chaplain. She let her light so shine as to glorify God.

A visiting preacher was extending the invitation. One man spoke to another; then both came forward and the second man confessed faith. After the service, one of the church staff explained. The man who came forward had embezzled from his employer. While he was in prison his employer was good to his family, visited him, and witnessed to him about Christ. It was his employer who that night brought him to the front. He let his light so shine as to glorify God.

Conclusion

No one can bear a Christian witness unless he or she is a Christian. Genuine Christians need have no fear; their influence will always be good because they *are* light. "Let your light so shine before men, that they may see your good works, and glorify your Father which is in heaven" (Matt. 5:16). The Holy Spirit promises to help Christians with this difficult responsibility.

WEDNESDAY EVENING, MARCH 8

Title: The Strategy of Solace

Text: "Jesus wept" **(John 11:35).**

Scripture Reading: John 11:1–46

Introduction

This is the story of the sickness, death, and resurrection of Lazarus. That Jesus was the key to victory is without dispute, and that we have Jesus' help in comparable circumstances is a cheerful reality for all Christians. This story has profitable insights for us as we look at our Lord's methodology in what we consider a crisis situation.

I. What Jesus did not do.

Jesus did not wait until the crisis hour to fortify his people. His previous relationship with the home had reinforced the sorrowing for just this hour.

The wise Christian leader does not wait until a crisis occurs to help instill in people the resources they need to meet the inevitable. One does not wait until a tire is flat to purchase a spare. And one does not wait until the house is on fire to take out an insurance policy. The wise leader will help instill in people spiritual shock absorbers that come from knowing and trusting God's Word.

Jesus did not let haste make waste when he heard of the crisis. "He abode two days in the house where he was." Jesus beautifully demonstrated that the tempo with which one moves can never take the place of the cargo with which he or she finally arrives.

A man was asked what he did when he discovered that his house was on fire. He replied, "I ran downstairs, jumped in my car, and drove off in every direction as fast as I could." No such frantic hysteria marks the path of the Savior. Jesus never seems to be in a hurry, yet always gets where he needs to be on time.

Jesus sincerely avoided a cold and competent professionalism. Medical doctors sometimes shed tears as they recall the death of a patient. One cannot help being moved by such genuine expressions of grief. It was also reported of the Great Physician, "Jesus wept."

Jesus did not evade the facts or cloud the issue with pseudo-sacred synonyms. "Then said Jesus unto them plainly, Lazarus is dead" (11:14). What a beautiful example for us!

II. What Jesus did.

Jesus went to be with Mary and Martha. Nothing speaks so eloquently as the bodily presence of a friend. The presence felt may be of more comfort than any sentence spoken.

Jesus sincerely shared their sorrow. "Jesus wept" (11:35). We, too, can do this.

Jesus spoke simply, kindly, and briefly. In his terse and measured words, we have our pattern.

Jesus prayed, invoking the available presence and power of God. Within our limits we have this opportunity, and there is nothing greater we can do for people in sorrow than to pray for them.

Jesus employed the therapy of work. Hear him say, "Take away the stone" and "Loose him, and let him go." Oh, the blessed therapy of active engagement for those who stay busy rolling away stones and removing the garments of grief!

Jesus directed and matured their faith. We really help others when we nourish their deep Christian faith. It is so much more constructive than spending time applying sentimental Band-Aids.

Jesus engaged their help in the business of miracle making. He often used people in miracle making: people to fill pots with water so that he could make wine, people to make the multitude sit on the grass and distribute the loaves and fishes, a lad to provide a lunch basket, and four men to bring a sick man to him. Perhaps if we would get busy rolling away stones and untying grave clothes, we too could witness fresh new miracles among us.

Conclusion

Jesus' methodology can be our pattern, but let us temper our imitation of him with one caution: He was Christ the Lord and we are but fellow pilgrims. As such, however, we can be better bearers of burdens by an awareness of his strategy and a demonstration of his spirit. There are many Marys and Marthas who need us!

SUNDAY MORNING, MARCH 12

Title: The Church and Prayer

Text: "So Peter was kept in prison; but earnest prayer for him was made to God by the church" (**Acts 12:5 RSV**).

Scripture Reading: Acts 12:1–5

Hymns: "Come Thou Almighty King," Anonymous
         "I Need Thee Every Hour," Hawks
         "Rock of Ages," Toplady

Offertory Prayer: Father, we thank you for promising to hear and answer our prayers. We thank you for receiving our gifts of love. May they be useful in your kingdom. Help us to give the greatest gift, ourselves, O Lord, to you. Amen.

Introduction

What one thing above all others would you like for your church to be or do? For most of you, your church is a vital part of your lives. Aside from your homes and work, your church receives more time, thought, and energy from you than any other one thing. Now what would you like to have characterize your church above every other thing?

I read an interesting and exciting story in our Scripture lesson. The church was in trouble. That usually means personality clashes within the church that are spawned by people who have self-serving interests. In this case, the problem was Herod Agrippa I. Though he was outside the church, his kind are sometimes inside. Herod was a phony. One characteristic of a phony is the tendency to oversell. Phony people often are overbearing, dogmatic, and given to extremes because they don't have genuine convictions and abilities. They must fake them. Pretending to be a sincere Jew, Herod began persecuting Christians. He killed James, and because this seemed to be good politics, he apprehended Peter with plans to kill him too. In doing this he thought he might stand a better than even chance of splitting the church, because some members had quarreled with Peter on some racial issues.

But there was a source of strength in the church of which Herod was unaware: prayer. What is the best thing a church can do for its members? What is the most significant contribution the church can make to the community or the world? There are many things a church can and should do. Sometimes church members should sell their property and give the money to feed the hungry. Barnabas, one of the members of the church we are talking about, did that. Sometimes they should visit the sick and those in prison. Jesus taught that. The church should always be busy telling others about Jesus. Jesus commanded this. But what one thing would you rather have your church do than anything else in the world? This church did it! They prayed!

I. The early church prayed all the time.

An unfortunate translation of our text in the King James Version says that prayer was made "without ceasing." Most Bibles correct this in the margin to read that they prayed "earnestly." We will come back to that later, but this church had been born in prayer and had prayed unceasingly since Jesus' resurrection and ascension. The book of Acts is full of instances.

After the Eleven saw Jesus ascend into heaven, they returned to the upper room in Jerusalem and prayed. They prayed about the selection of a successor to Judas. Following the baptism of three thousand, they prayed. When Peter and John were released from prison, they met with their friends and prayed. They prayed about the selection of the first deacons, for the healing of the sick, for the raising of the dead, and for all their bold evangelistic ministries.

I am not saying that all the members of the early church prayed like they should all the time or any of the time. In Acts 12 we find that some of the members were very surprised when their prayers were answered. If we have to wait for every member of any church to pray, we will have waited too long. What I am saying is that enough of them were praying that it changed their church and changed the world.

I found this characteristic among South Korean Christians. Preceding an evangelistic crusade there in 1970 I had the privilege of traveling over the country and meeting with Christians in most of their cities. A big part of every planning meeting was a prayer meeting. I think their prayer meetings did more to change my life than anything I did to change theirs. We had crusades in twenty of their largest cities simultaneously. Because they had already had a year of revivals in their churches, their spiritual lives were "in shape."

We were having outdoor meetings in Seoul. One afternoon it was pouring rain, and I attended a meeting at which we were to discuss what we would do if the rains continued. Since there seemed to be no answer, the meeting turned into a prayer meeting. The rains stopped. Thousands came to the services, and hundreds were saved.

On another night the authorities canceled our arrangements in favor of another meeting. When all the wire-pulling and other pressures failed in the mayor's office, someone said, "Let's pray about it." Right there in the mayor's office the praying began. Right there the prayers were answered. An arrangement was made so that we not only could have our meeting but could also have the fifteen or twenty thousand people attending the other meeting. More than five hundred professions of faith were registered that night.

II. The early church prayed earnestly.

The same root word translated *"earnest"* in our text is the one used to describe the praying of Jesus in the garden of Gethsemane when his sweat was like blood (Luke 22:44). It was the kind of praying Paul requested of the Roman Christians: "Strive together with me in your prayers to God on my behalf" (Rom. 15:30). It was the kind of praying I witnessed among Chinese missionaries for an evangelistic meeting in Taiwan that resulted in more than five hundred people coming to know the Lord in a single service.

Charles G. Finney tells the story of a pastor who was having constant revival in his church year after year. He kept wondering what the secret was. One day he was in a prayer meeting when a lay member of that church made a confession. He confessed that for a long time he had been praying on a regular basis for his pastor but that lately he had been delinquent in his praying. Finney said he had learned the answer. The pastor had power because his people were praying.

III. The early church prayed specifically.

The church in our text was praying "for him"—Peter. The church was in a crisis. Their leader was in prison and would be put to death unless God intervened. So the people prayed directly and specifically.

In a Nashville church I referred to Jesus' promise to answer two people who were praying at the same time with the same earnestness about the same thing (Matt. 18:19). A woman went to her Sunday school teacher and requested her as a prayer partner for her husband to become a Christian during that week. They prayed together in their Sunday school classroom three times and together by telephone several times. Two days later her husband received Jesus as Savior.

The pastor related this story to the congregation, whereupon a man went to his Sunday school teacher and said, "If the lady and her teacher can pray and their prayers be answered, do you suppose if you and I met this condition of prayer for my father, who has not been to church in twenty-five years, he might become a Christian this week?" His teacher joined him in prayer. They prayed that night after the service. They met the next morning and prayed together at breakfast. They prayed before and after the services the next night. The following night the man did not know his father was in the service until he saw him coming forward to announce that Jesus had saved him.

In the opening chapter of Acts, Luke writes that in his former book he had told all that Jesus began to do and teach, suggesting that in the book of Acts he was telling what Jesus continues to do and teach through his church. Jesus continues to do many mighty works just as he did during his life on the earth. Nothing more nearly characterized his life than his prayer life. There are many things our churches must be and do, but I would rather my church pray for me than anything else in the world.

Conclusion

Of course, the only way a church can pray all the time is for its members to pray individually and together all the time. The power of God is available today in this community and in the world. Shall we pray?

SUNDAY EVENING, MARCH 12

Title: Christ's Standard of Righteousness

Text: "For I say unto you, That except your righteousness shall exceed the righteousness of the scribes and Pharisees, ye shall in no case enter the kingdom of heaven" **(Matt. 5:20)**.

Scripture Reading: Matthew 5:17–20

Introduction

In the Beatitudes Jesus describes the characteristics of the happy Christian. By using illustrations of salt and light, he impresses on his disciples the responsibility of their influence. Jesus now comes to the first major division of the sermon on the superiority of Christian righteousness to the righteousness of the scribes and Pharisees. The truth is stated in Matthew 5:17–20 and is illustrated in a half dozen ways in the remaining verses of chapter 5.

I. The relationship of Christianity to the Old Testament is important.

A pastor was explaining to an inquirer that his church accepted the New Testament as the sufficient, authoritative guide to faith and practice. The young man quickly asked, "Then you do not accept the Old Testament?" That question is hard to answer with a yes or no. If the answer is, "Yes, we do accept the Old Testament," then the inquirer might ask, "Why then do you not observe it? Do you keep the seventh day as the Sabbath? Do you make a distinction between clean and unclean foods? Do you insist on circumcision? Do you observe the Year of Jubilee and Old Testament feast days?" If the pastor had answered, "No, we do not accept the Old Testament," the inquirer might have asked, "Why then in vacation Bible school did you teach my child to sing this song?

> *"I know the Bible was sent from God,*
> *The Old, as well as the New;*
> *Inspired and holy, the Living Word,*
> *I know the Bible is true."*
> (Baptist Hymnal *[Nashville: Convention Press, 1956], 184)*

What are the claims of the Old Testament on Christians today? Are the Ten Commandments binding? What about the Sabbath, circumcision, tithes, distinctions of clean and unclean foods? The usual answer is that whatever commands were local, temporary, or ceremonial have passed away, but the commands of moral value abide. One will look in vain, however, for this distinction. Let us look carefully at the Scripture reading to see what Jesus said.

II. What did Jesus say?

Not an iconoclast. Jesus did not come to destroy the Law and the Prophets. The religious leaders of his day, however, may have thought so. Jesus did not keep the Sabbath as they understood it. Nor did he observe the ceremonial laws about clean and unclean foods. Jesus did not say, "Think not that I am come to destroy the law, or the prophets: I am not come to destroy"—period. He added, "but to fulfil." Jesus did not say, "Till heaven and earth pass, one jot or one tittle shall in no wise pass from the law"—period. He added, "till all be fulfilled." Dr. George Barker Stevens of Yale stated the meaning accurately:

> But the question now arises, Did Jesus intend to abrogate the whole Old Testament religious system, and if so, by what means? This question also involves another: If he did do away with this system, how is the fact to be reconciled with his frequent assertion of its divineness? The most important passage, in its bearing on these problems is Matthew 5:17: "Think not that I am come to destroy the law or the prophets: I came not to destroy, but to fulfil." This passage must be read in the light of the explanations and applications which follow it. Jesus proceeds to say that not a jot or tittle shall pass away from the law—a statement which, if read by itself, would seem to indicate the perpetual validity of the whole Old Testament system, ritual, sacrifices, and all. But to the statement in question he immediately adds: "till all things be fulfilled, or accomplished." He does not, therefore, say that no part of this system shall ever pass away (as it has done, and that, too, in consequence of his own teaching),

but only that no part of it shall escape the process of fulfillment; that it shall not pass away till, having served its providential purpose, it is fulfilled in the gospel. (George Barker Stevens, *The Theology of the New Testament* [New York: Scribner, 1927], 19)

Christ fulfills the Old Testament. Nothing valid and useful will be lost. It will all be taken up in the process of fulfillment.

The prophecies are fulfilled in Jesus Christ. That which God spoke before about the Messiah through the Law and the Prophets, God fulfilled in Jesus. Read carefully Luke 24:44–48 in this connection.

The ceremonial system was fulfilled in Jesus. Sacrifices are no longer necessary. "Behold the Lamb of God, which taketh away the sin of the world" (John 1:29). Priests are no longer necessary (see 1 Tim. 2:5–6; Heb. 4:14–16; 7:17–28). Worship is not confined to the temple nor to special places (see John 4:21–24).

The ethical teaching is fulfilled in the teaching of Jesus. Christ's standard of righteousness will in every case be higher than the Old Testament standard. The scribes and Pharisees insisted on the letter of the law, while Jesus emphasized the intent of the heart. The superiority of the righteousness that Christ teaches is illustrated as follows:

Murder (Matt. 5:25–26).
Adultery (Matt. 5:27–30).
Divorce (Matt. 5:31–32).
Oaths (Matt. 5:33–37).
Retaliation (Matt. 5:38–42).
Attitude toward enemies (Matt. 5:43–47).

III. Is the Old Testament destroyed by fulfillment in Jesus?

Yes, in the sense that it has no binding authority except as fulfilled in Jesus. No, in the sense that not a jot nor a tittle of value has been lost. All of the ethical teaching of the Law and the Prophets is fulfilled in the two great commandments (see Matt. 22:35–40; Mark 12:28–35). The commands about the Sabbath in the Law are not binding on Christians except as they are fulfilled in the teaching and practice of Jesus. "Therefore the Son of man is Lord also of the sabbath" (Mark 2:28). Every value of the Sabbath as a day of worship and for doing good is fulfilled in the teaching of Jesus. The commands about tithes are not binding as such but are included in Jesus' teaching about total stewardship.

Is the preliminary sketch destroyed now that the artist has finished the picture? Yes, in the sense that it cannot be found. No, in the sense that having fulfilled its appointed purpose it is embodied in the completed picture.

Is the bud destroyed now that it has become a rose? Yes, in the sense that there is no more bud. No, in the sense that it has fulfilled its appointed purpose.

Is the baby destroyed now that the infant has become an adult? Yes, in the sense that the baby exists no more. No, in the sense that the baby has grown to maturity.

Is the Old Testament destroyed? Yes, in the sense that it has no independent authority. No, in the sense that having fulfilled its appointed purpose, it has been completed in the new covenant in Christ. "For Christ is the end of the law of righteousness to every one that believeth" (Rom. 10:4).

Conclusion

Jesus Christ is the final authority. At his transfiguration the voice from heaven proclaimed, "This is my beloved Son, in whom I am well pleased; hear ye him" (Matt. 17:5). Jesus said, "I am the way, the truth, and the life" (John 14:6). "All authority in heaven and on earth has been given to me" (Matt. 28:18 RSV).

Do not bind the Christian's conscience by anything in the Old Testament nor in the New Testament nor anywhere else that is not in accord with the truth as it is in Christ Jesus. All truth is fulfilled in him.

For the Christian teaching on race, let us not go to drunken Noah, nor to Moses who married an Egyptian wife, nor to Ezra who separated families of those who had married foreigners, but rather to Jesus.

For the Christian teaching on capital punishment, let us not go to the laws of Israel, but rather to Jesus.

For the Christian teaching on the personhood of women, let us not be content with the teaching of the Old Testament, nor of the New Testament except as fulfilled in Jesus. For the final authority, do not stop with Paul, but go on to Jesus.

Since Jesus spoke in principles rather than in rules, Christians must use their own minds to interpret both the actions and the teachings of our Lord. The Holy Spirit will help. Yielding your life to Jesus Christ and asking the leadership of the Holy Spirit are essential.

WEDNESDAY EVENING, MARCH 15

Title: Attitudes in a Crisis

Text: "But when Jesus heard it, he answered him, saying, Fear not: believe only, and she shall be made whole" **(Luke 8:50).**

Scripture Reading: Luke 8:41–42, 49–56

Introduction

Someone has observed that the mortality rate is the same the world over: one death per person. In our Scripture lesson we read of a young woman who died. To her father it was a crisis. In spite of all we think we know about death and all we think we can do about it, the death of a loved one continues to be a critical experience. As we review the story of the young woman's death, we can learn lessons that will help us in crises that come our way. At least four attitudes are reflected in the narrative.

I. The attitude of the fatalist.

One hears the hollow ring of it in the message, "Thy daughter is dead, trouble not the Master." No use bothering anyone: what is done is done. There is no hope. Her fate has been sealed.

One hears the coarse laughter of their scorn (8:53). Any affirmation of optimism on Jesus' part is met not only with disbelief but also with ridicule.

Let it be said to the credit of Jairus's servant and the ones who laughed at him that they at least verbalized their doubts. Perhaps not so much danger may come from those who speak their piece as from those who say nothing but whose silence betrays their cynicism. An unsaved man who had lost a member of his family was heard to say, "There's not a thing in the world that anyone can do but grit his teeth and bear it." Many are saying by their attitude and pessimistic spirit that there is no hope left in our world.

II. The attitude of the father.

The girl's father had the right attitude that life must go on. His grief did not extinguish his hope. Faced with the loss of his only child, he did not panic nor was he the victim of despair.

He remained open for help. The doors are not closed and the lines of communication and compassion are not cut. People can always be helped except when they refuse to be helped. Open minds and hearts give God an opportunity to enter and to help.

He worshiped the Master even in his personal grief. How beautifully does the story say, "He fell down at Jesus' feet" and invited him into his home. Such a spirit and attitude in the midst of sorrow is hard to beat. Christ can both use and help such a person.

III. The attitude of the friends.

Peter, James, and John are taken into the intimate confidences of the home. It cannot be denied that they had their doubts. Yet they were present and sympathetic. Their close circle always brought help when the load was heavy.

Let it be noted that it was Jesus' will that they be in the inner circle, and it is still his will that we rally around in prayerful support when the clock strikes midnight.

IV. The attitude of the Friend.

This Friend is Jesus, and his attitude is the best of all. He said of the girl, "Weep not; she is not dead, but sleepeth" (Luke 8:52). Theologians have used much paper and ink contending for positions. Some insist that she was not dead but in a coma. Others insist that it is figurative language. The weight of evidence seems to be with the latter. At any rate, over and over in the New Testament death is spoken of as sleep.

Sleep means relief. As Longfellow wrote, in "the cares that infest the day fold their tents like the Arabs and silently steal away."

Sleep means rest. The dead shall rest from their labor. The body, mind, and soul will rest.

Sleep means refreshment. Who among us has not felt a different world greeting us after a good night of sleep?

Sleep means resurrection. We lie down to rise up. Life is always better after the sleep of the night. It will be so in the resurrection.

Conclusion

Much of life is attitude. Let us strive for the mind of Christ that we may have his attitude, even in the crises that punctuate the way for us.

SUNDAY MORNING, MARCH 19

Title: A Church Celebration
(May be used as a dedication service for a new building)

Text: "If my people who are called by my name humble themselves, and pray and seek my face, and turn from their wicked ways, then I will hear from heaven, and will forgive their sin and heal their land" **(2 Chron. 7:14 RSV)**.

Scripture Reading: 2 Chronicles 7:11–16

Hymns: "A Mighty Fortress," Luther
"I Love Thy Kingdom, Lord," Dwight
"Onward Christian Soldiers," Baring-Gould

Offertory Prayer: Father, today is a special day for us. We pray that it may be a day of special and permanent commitment to you. We bring our tithes and offerings in the same spirit and for the same purpose as we dedicate this building: to glorify God and share his love with others. In Jesus' name. Amen.

Introduction

Susan went to her grandfather while he was shaving and said, "Granddaddy, what is salivate?" When he thought he understood what she was saying, he said, "Why do you ask?"

"Oh, I just need to know," she said.

He said, "Well, I guess to salivate is to slobber like a horse. Now tell me why you ask."

She said, "Well, Mommy said we were coming down here to salivate your birthday."

We are gathered together today for a great celebration and perhaps some salivation. I believe the early New Testament churches celebrated more than most of our churches do now, even though they did not have beautiful new buildings to celebrate and dedicate as we do today. This is both a celebration and a dedication because we could not possibly come together today without celebrating. We have a magnificent building, well appointed and functional. We have been looking forward to this time, and to restrain our emotions would be sinful. It is a time of dedication because we very much desire to commit all of this to the Lord's use.

I would like to begin this message with a question. It is not a new question, for you discussed it several years ago when you began to make plans for this day. I do feel it is a relevant question today because it helps us find just where we are and why we are here. This is the question: Why have you erected this building? If I were to give you the opportunity, I would hear a hundred voices answering in harmony and you would be very convincing. You would be convincing because you are convinced. But there are some other questions first.

Why do you have this church? Why do you have a pastor? Why do you have a Bible school? Why do you have a choir? Why do you have a church staff with all of the organizations in the life of the church? Why do you have prayer meetings? Why do you go out ringing doorbells and inviting people to come to church? Do you know you can answer every one of these questions with one word: People!

God so loved people that he gave Jesus. Jesus came to seek and save people. He had people in mind when he said, "I will build my church." People, made in the image of God and just a little less than divine, explain the whole purpose of the church—its organization, leadership, buildings, programs, and all the rest. This building is a place for people to worship, to enjoy together the community and fellowship of a New Testament church. We are using this building today to worship. We will use it to study God's Word and to train people in Christian service. We will use it to share together our joys, our sorrows, our burdens, and our prayers. Here we will confess our sins and worship God. Here we will grow in the grace and knowledge of the Savior as we pray together, play together, and worship together. This building is for people.

Dedication means to set something apart for some special use. Many dedications and celebrations are recorded in the Word of God. As I thought of this dedication, one passage seemed to emerge above all the others. It is the most familiar building dedication in the Bible and possibly one of the most exciting moments recorded in biblical history. You cannot read about the building and dedication of the temple without excitement. It is the most extraordinary building you have ever read about and was erected under the most extraordinary conditions. We read about this celebration in 2 Chronicles 6 and 7 and in 1 Kings 8 and 9. Let's pull back the curtain and look in on this happy dedication celebration.

I. It was a time of prayer.

Solomon prayed one of the great prayers of the Bible at the dedication of the temple. If Solomon, the wisest of men, had always acted as wisely as he did at this time, he would have lived and died a much happier man, having made a far greater contribution to the world. Here we see the king, the wisest and wealthiest of men, the leader of the most prominent nation of the earth, getting down on his knees in prayer to God and calling himself a servant.

Solomon praised God. If the people of this church were to allow this day to pass by without being lifted to a high moment of ecstasy, praise, and worship, your lives would be forever poorer. Any day is a good day to worship and praise God, but he gives us these extraspecial times when the fountains can be opened wide and we can bathe in the beauty and freshness of his grace. Even as we recognize the talents and crafts that were involved in the erection of this magnificent building, we are recognizing that God gives gifts to people, and all of them can be used for his glory and for the building of his church. Every participant on every committee, as well as every worker, allowed his or her brain to become God's brain and his or her hands to become God's hands.

Solomon's prayer was a prayer of intercession. If this building is for people, then this day is a time and this building is a place in which to pray to God on behalf of his people. It is a time of intercession for those who have contributed to this day. It is a time of prayer for those of this community to whom this church shall reach out in the future. This building is a place of intercessory prayer, one of the most important ministries among you.

II. It was an occasion of answered prayer.

God answered the Israelites by letting them know he was aware of them. His eyes were on them and his ears were attentive to them. I admit I would be a little scared of the awareness that the eyes of God are on me if it were not for the fact that I know he understands me, and in spite of all my failures, foibles, sins, and blunders, he loves and desires to bless me. I assure you, if you are praying today, God is in the process of answering. This truth is almost beyond our ability to comprehend. The God of glory stands ready to answer every prayer that goes up from any heart or mind in this building.

III. It was a time of promised forgiveness.

"If my people who are called by my name humble themselves, and pray and seek my face, and turn from their wicked ways, then I will hear from heaven, and will forgive their sin and heal their land" (2 Chron. 7:14 RSV). God was addressing his people, and he is addressing us today. He is not promising blessings on the basis of the way someone else acts, but on the way his own people act. God didn't promise to bless Israel on the basis of the response of the Amorites, Hittites, Jebusites, or Canaanites. He promised to answer their prayers and bless them on the basis of their own humility and confession.

Naturally, I would rather confess another person's sins. I remember a deacon one time suggesting that I preach more on sin. He surprised me. I thought I preached the Bible, and you really can't preach the Bible without preaching about sin. I said, "I'm not making excuses, but I thought I had been preaching on sin all along. I have just finished preaching a series of sermons on the Sermon on the Mount. I have preached on covetousness, selfishness, gossiping, hypocrisy, and the numerous other sins mentioned in the Sermon on the Mount."

The deacon said, "That's not what I'm talking about."

I said, "Okay, what are you talking about?"

He said, "I wish you would preach more often on drinking, adultery, and gambling."

I think I recalled what I had read somewhere, because I couldn't have thought of this all by myself. I said, "You want me to preach on other people's sins, don't you? You know, as I looked out over our congregation last Sunday morning, I don't think I saw over two or three drunks in the crowd. I do not believe there were more than a half dozen people who had been overtly guilty of adultery during the past week, and I do not believe gambling is a big deal among our people. However, I did see people who had gossiped about their neighbors, criticized their fellow church members, and reacted with jealousy and envy. I saw some kids who had cheated on school examinations and some parents who had cheated on their income tax. I just figured I ought to preach about the sins of which we are guilty rather than those of people who never know what I preach about."

We would prefer not to confess our sins. But if I can come close enough to God, feel his presence warmly enough and his love deeply enough, I will begin to confess my sins and feel the presence and power of his Spirit as he forgives me.

Conclusion

Today can be one of the greatest days of your life, not only because of the joy and ecstasy you feel in celebrating your triumphs and God's blessings, but also because his Spirit can come to cleanse and fill you.

On what basis does God forgive sin? On the basis of our humility. If we humble ourselves, pray, seek his face, and turn from our wicked ways, he will hear from heaven and forgive our sin. He is asking us to surrender.

SUNDAY EVENING, MARCH 19

Title: Proper Priorities

Text: "Therefore if thou bring thy gift to the altar, and there rememberest that thy brother hath ought against thee; leave there thy gift before the altar, and go thy way; first be reconciled to thy brother, and then come and offer thy gift" (**Matt. 5:23–24**).

Scripture Reading: Matthew 5:21–26

Introduction

"God, who at sundry times and in divers manners spake in time past unto the fathers by the prophets, hath in these last days spoken unto us by his Son, whom he hath appointed heir of all things, by whom also he made the worlds; who being the brightness of his glory, and the express image of his person, and upholding all things by the word of his power, when he had by himself purged our sins, sat down on the right hand of the Majesty on high" (Heb. 1:1–3).

This inspired evaluation of Jesus Christ, the Son of God, as the supreme authority is the reflection of Jesus' own teaching about himself. In Matthew 5:17–20 Jesus proclaims that the Law and the Prophets are fulfilled in himself. Christianity is whatever he reveals it to be. All that is true he brings to fulfillment. All that is false, he judges. Not a jot nor a tittle (smallest part of a letter, like the dotting of an *i* or the crossing of a *t*) of truth will be lost or fail to be fulfilled. Jesus' call is to a standard of righteousness higher than that of the scribes and Pharisees. He will be content with nothing short of truth, love, and God's will.

Matthew 5:21–26 contains the first of six illustrations that our Lord used to clarify his meaning.

I. The Law said, "Thou shalt not kill."

"Ye have heard that it was said by them of old time, Thou shalt not kill; and whosoever shall kill shall be in danger of the judgment" (Matt. 5:21). The reference is to the sixth commandment recorded in Exodus 20:13, which the people heard as it was read in the synagogue. The better translation is 'You shall not murder" (NIV). The context in the Decalogue clearly shows that Moses' command says nothing about the slaying of animals. The Law provided for the taking of human life by the authorities. It provided for the taking of human life without guilt under certain circumstances by an individual, as in self-defense, accidental death, and in war approved by the state. Jesus was obviously thinking of murder—that is, the taking of another's life in anger or for personal advantage.

II. Jesus said, "I say unto you."

Jesus spoke as an independent authority above the Mosaic law. He did not cancel the law that said, 'You shall not murder." He did not lower the standard a jot or a tittle. He did fulfill it by emphasizing its inner content and purpose.

A. *A disciple will not provoke anger that leads to murder.*

Unjust anger is sin. For such an offense a person was liable to appear before the local Jewish court (see Deut. 16:18; 2 Chron. 19:5). Name calling that leads to anger is wrong. One who called another a "simpleton" or a "blockhead" or a "moron" could be called before the Sanhedrin, and one who called another a "scoundrel" could be in danger of God's judgment in the fire of Gehenna. The Valley of Hinnom near Jerusalem had been defiled in earlier years as the place in which the heathen sacrificed their children to the fire god, Molech, as you can read in 2 Kings 23:10. In New Testament times, it was the garbage heap for Jerusalem. The fires continued to burn day and night, and the maggots never ceased eating the carcasses of dead animals deposited there. Gehenna, Valley of Hinnom, was an illustration of hell, which is God's garbage heap.

Words spoken in anger can cause great damage. One person said, "I say what I think," to which another replied, "Even a furnace has a filter." Another said, "I have a quick temper, but I cool off fast," to which another responded, "A gun cools off fast too, but it can do a lot of damage in a short time."

Any wrong done to one's fellowman is a serious offense. Second only to love for God is love for one's neighbors.

B. *Reconciliation to one's fellowman is a first priority after reconciliation to God.*

Reconciliation to God is the first priority for every person. "But seek ye first the kingdom of God, and his righteousness" (Matt. 6:33), said Jesus. To the lawyer who asked, "Which is the great commandment in the law?" Jesus replied, "Thou shalt love the Lord thy God with all thy heart, and with all thy soul, and with all thy mind. This is the first and great commandment" (Matt. 22:37–38).

Reconciliation to one's fellowman is second only to a right relationship with God. After the first and great commandment, Jesus added, "And the second is like unto it, Thou shalt love thy neighbour as thyself" (Matt. 22:39).

In our text Jesus illustrates the importance of reconciliation. A man comes to worship. He seems to be a disciple as he brings a gift and is called a brother. The wait before the service gives him time for reflection. His conscience begins to trouble him because a brother has something against him. The man who has been wronged has a right to be upset. Maybe the man coming to worship has slandered the other man or spread gossip about him. Or maybe he misrepresented some goods he sold to the man. Or perhaps he promised delivery of goods at an impossibly early date to get ahead of other salespeople. He thinks, "As soon as church is over, I'll straighten it out." But

Jesus said, "Leave there thy gift before the altar, and go thy way; first be reconciled to thy brother" (Matt. 5:24).

According to God's priorities, right personal relationships are more important than worship, giving, or any external expression. Songs, worship, and gifts are to no avail without justice, mercy, and kindness. Note Jesus' emphasis in Matthew 23:23. He is fulfilling the words of the Old Testament prophets at this point as, for example, Isaiah 1:11–18; Amos 5:11–15; and Micah 6:6–11.

Go and right wrong, Jesus insists. Make a sincere effort. Confess your sin. Ask your brother or sister's forgiveness. Earnestly desire reconciliation. If the person who holds something against you is truly a Christian, he or she will forgive. If not, you will have done all you could do.

If the case be that a brother or sister has wronged you, the Lord has given instruction in Matthew 18:15–18 and in Luke 17:3. Whether you are the offended or the offender, as a Christian you should be eager for reconciliation. "And be ye kind one to another, tenderhearted, forgiving one another, even as God for Christ's sake hath forgiven you" (Eph. 4:32).

"And then come offer thy gift." Do not let another's response or lack of it keep you from worship and service. Having a heart that is right with God and with one's fellow Christians brings joy to service in Christ's name.

One is not to stop short of the offering. Justice, mercy, and faith are more important than tithes. "These ought ye to have done, and not to leave the other undone" (Matt. 23:23). God cannot be bought with tithes. Gifts do not make wrong practices right. A Christian who is right with God will, however, delight to bring gifts of self and of substance.

C. *Reconciliation is not only right, but it is also reasonable.* Verses 25–26 reflect the practice current in Jesus' day of delivering the debtor to prison. The assumption is that he is guilty. Better to make terms even with an adversary while one can.

Conclusion

Divine priorities are clear. First, seek God's righteousness. Second, be reconciled to others. "If it be possible, as much as lieth in you, live peaceably with all men" (Rom. 12:18). Third, bring your gift to God's altar. "I beseech you therefore, brethren, by the mercies of God, that ye present your bodies a living sacrifice, holy, acceptable unto God, which is your reasonable service. And be not conformed to this world: but be ye transformed by the renewing of your mind, that ye may prove what is that good, and acceptable, and perfect, will of God" (Rom. 12:1–2).

WEDNESDAY EVENING, MARCH 22

Title: When It's More Christian Not to Visit the Sick

Text: "When he heard that Jesus was come out of Judaea into Galilee, he went unto him, and besought him that he would come down, and heal his son, for he was at the point of death" **(John 4:47).**

Scripture Reading: John 4:46–54

Introduction

Our Lord taught us by precept and example to visit the sick, but the coin has another side: there is a wrong time for what is otherwise the right thing to do. There is a time when it is more Christian *not to* visit the sick.

A second-string quarterback who was noted more for his brawn than for his brain was sent in by the coach in a desperate fourth quarter. The coach reviewed the plays and their sequence with him. Number one was over right guard; number two, around left end; number three, a pass; and number four, to punt. "Old Brute" went in and called number one, resulting in a fifteen-yard gain. Number two brought eleven more. Number three put the crowd on its feet with a thirty-five-yard run to the three-yard line. You guessed it: he punted!

The obvious point is that you can execute the play perfectly—at the wrong time. Visiting the sick is like that. Let us remember that our Lord performed his first recorded healing miracle when he did not visit the sick one. It is more Christian not to visit the sick:

I. When the sick one does not need your physical presence.

A hospital patient was recovering from a brain operation. He was not to move or have visitors. A visitor came to his room, stayed two hours, talking and tapping the bed lightly with the toe of his shoe. The patient was so upset that he relapsed and spent extra time in the hospital, all because a well-meaning guest visited when the patient did not heed him.

II. When the family needs your time and ministry more than the patient does.

The husband of a surgery patient sat all day alone in a large city hospital while his wife was in serious surgery and recovery. The husband himself had a seizure in the evening, triggered by stress and loneliness, and became quite ill. While all the attention was given to the patient, the husband needed someone to help him sit out the day.

Frequently the family needs a visit more than the patient does. After all, when there is illness in one member of a family, there is illness in the family. When we help a family, we help the patient of that family to recover.

It does not lessen the glory of our divine Lord to suggest that Jesus filled

105

a supportive role to a family when he said to the father, "Go thy way; thy son liveth" (4:50). Belief did not stop with the father; he believed, and so did "his whole house" (v. 53). The Great Physician did not forget the family.

III. When you can do just as much good by not visiting the sick one.

Jesus did as much for the son in absentia as he could have done in person. Let us be reminded that we too may sometimes do as much for the patient by not visiting in person. Other ways to show concern and give encouragement are by sending flowers or a note or card, by delivering a meal to the family, by calling on the phone, or by running an errand for the family.

IV. When priority puts you elsewhere.

It may be more important that we attend one with a broken heart than one with a broken limb. There are sorrows more demanding than surgery. Being with those who need us most may make it impossible for us to visit the sick at a given time.

V. When your prayer can bring power for healing that is not otherwise available.

We may do more good in our private prayer room than in someone's hospital room. Calling on the Almighty in prayer may be better than calling on an acquaintance in person. It may not be as glamorous nor feed the ego as much, but it can be more productive.

Let us remember that the nobleman, the child's father, was absent from his sick son, praying, when healing came. Surely if the father absented himself in person in order to appeal to our Lord in bold personal request, there must be times when we too ought to follow his example.

VI. When the visitor is not qualified to visit.

At the risk of being called harshly judgmental, let me say that there are some people who are not qualified visitors. In our churches we have standards for various workers. Only those who are qualified for a position are asked to serve. A person may have an intense desire to play the organ and still not be qualified to play it. Likewise, not everyone makes a good visitor.

Conclusion

People need training in visiting, just as they do for any other ministry in the church. Our ministry to the sick should also be Spirit led. Ask the Lord for wisdom concerning what you can do for the sick and for their families.

(Pastor: You may want to invite a hospital chaplain or other qualified resource person to speak to your congregation about the ministry of visiting the sick.)

SUNDAY MORNING, MARCH 26

Title: A Witnessing Church

Text: "For we cannot but speak of what we have seen and heard" **(Acts 4:20 RSV).**

Scripture Reading: Acts 1:1–8

Hymns: "O Worship the King," Grant
           "I Love to Tell the Story," Hankey
           "Lord, Lay Some Soul upon My Heart," McKinney

Offertory Prayer: Father, we gather today as a part of the body of Christ to worship and to reflect on the church's mission. A part of this worship is bringing our tithes and offerings. We do so out of love and devotion to you and with a desire to be a church performing its mission in the world. Help us to give in the awareness that we obey your commission and help people to recognize your presence in the world today. May these gifts be used of your Spirit to help people know the Lord. We pray in Jesus' name. Amen.

Introduction

Recenty I spoke in a church with about 500 people present in Sunday school and perhaps 600 in the morning worship service. A large, excited, enthusiastic crowd attended the evening service. The very atmosphere of the services was evangelistic. Evidence of their evangelistic emphasis was the baptism of 140 people during the previous year.

Throughout that Lord's Day I kept remembering that just a few years ago this little struggling church had fears it would lose its property and have to close its doors. I kept reminding myself that in this city of a million people, most of the churches were actually struggling to maintain the status quo and constantly making excuses about how difficult it was to maintain, much less enlarge, their church. I kept looking for the key to the recent transformation in this church and the distinguishing marks between it and surrounding churches. Was there some formula they had discovered that might be applied in other places?

Most pastors and churches would enjoy the kind of experience this church was so obviously enjoying. The question is how? Do we struggle along hand to mouth trying to survive until one day via some magical formula or person everything is suddenly changed? Let us look at the New Testament for parallels as to what motivated this church under the leadership of the Holy Spirit.

During Jesus' early ministry he went to the cities and villages. As he came back into the presence of his disciples to plan the strategy for his future ministry, he still had the multitudes of people on his mind. They represented all kinds of people. It is easy for us to think that his statement of compassion had to do only with the poor, the hungry, and the sick. This is not true. He spent much of his time ministering to the privileged and successful of his day. Many of them were successful in their careers and healthy in their bodies. Nevertheless, Jesus saw them in need of a full, meaningful, and complete life. Of course, he also saw the poor, the hungry, the deprived, the sick, and the afflicted. He saw them as harassed and helpless, like sheep without a shepherd. He had come to give life, and he recognized that these people had not found life. Therefore his heart went out to them in compassion and concern. He said to his disciples, "The harvest is plentiful but the laborers are few; pray therefore the Lord of the harvest to send out laborers into his harvest" (Matt. 9:31, 38 RSV).

All church planning must begin by looking at who we are and where we are. We must then recognize that we cannot be a church and meet the needs of the world without divine power and direction. Our church needs to spend much time in prayer. When we really pray, the church begins to take shape. All organizational structure must be planned on the basis of our having prayed. The church is not to decide its direction and then ask God to bless it. A church is a church when it recognizes its relationship to God and prays for his guidance in making decisions as well as praying for his power in following his directions.

Following this summary statement of what he saw and felt, Jesus began to reach out to the people with the Good News, and he followed up with his announcement concerning the building of the church. As Jesus moved steadfastly toward Jerusalem and his death on the cross for our sins, he prepared his followers for his continued Holy Spirit ministry after he ascended to the Father. Following his death and resurrection and preceding his glorious ascension, he said to his disciples, "You shall receive power when the Holy Spirit has come upon you; and you shall be my witnesses in Jerusalem and in all Judea and Samaria and to the end of the earth" (Acts 1:8 RSV).

As we prayerfully plan our own church strategy in being a witnessing church, let us look at the early church for some things that characterized their life and ministry.

I. They believed that people needed Jesus.

We do not see evidence that the early church ever asked, "What can we do to help our church?" They looked at the world around them and asked, "What can our church do to meet the needs of people?" They knew that Jesus came to give life and that he desired that they be the messengers of this new life.

They believed the claims of Jesus. He had said he was the Son of God and Savior. They believed that he and the Father were one. They believed that he would keep the promise of the Father in providing the Holy Spirit's direction for their lives. They believed that because Jesus lived in them, they could continue what he had begun to do and teach. They believed he was now at the right hand of the Father and would return in glory for a final consummation at which time all believers would be with God forever.

They knew what Jesus had done for them. They had received new life. They had been changed from proud, self-centered seekers of personal glory into selfless, Spirit-filled men and women. Their sins had been forgiven, and they considered themselves new creations in Christ Jesus.

They had no illusions about an easy, passive life without frustrations and problems. They had accepted the fact that as Jesus suffered they must suffer. Even though their Master had healed all manner of diseases, they did not for one moment think they would have perfect health and live forever in this world. Even though he had taught them that love is the greatest commandment of all, they understood that they would have to spend their lives in a hate-filled world. Though Jesus taught the highest morality ever imagined and they were committed to this kind of life, they understood they would have to live among immoral people.

They believed that even the people who crucified Jesus could be redeemed from their sins and that the best people in the world needed this same redeeming power.

II. They communicated the Good News with boldness and consistency.

Simon Peter, who earlier had fearfully denied the Lord, was now willing to preach to the very people who crucified Jesus. He spoke with such boldness that the enemies of Christ recognized he had been with Jesus. When his life was threatened because of his preaching, he went back to the church and prayed for boldness to speak the Word of God. And *boldness* is the word that characterized the ministry of Paul after his conversion. We must not confuse the word *boldness* with *arrogance*. It was just the reverse—the boldness that possessed these early Christians was born of humility. Self had died in their surrender to Jesus. Jesus had been crucified, and they had been crucified in their surrender to him. They were willing to risk their lives for the sake of spreading the Good News.

When the laypeople were driven out of Jerusalem because of their convictions, they went everywhere preaching the Word. Wherever they went, their testimony was so clearly born of the Spirit of God that believers were added to their numbers and churches were begun. Their lives were so consistently bold and dedicated that people knew they had been with Jesus.

One night in South Korea I sat in a missionary's home and talked with a group of Korean pastors. I asked them each to relate the conditions surrounding their own conversion. One of them told how he was a prisoner taken from the North Korean army when he came under the influence of a Christian chaplain and some Christian military men. He said their lives were so different that he immediately desired this kind of life and became a Christian while he was a prisoner. Another told of how he kept watching a small group of people gather around a bonfire singing and praying. He said that night by night he moved closer and closer to them until finally he knew he just had to have what they had. He proceeded into their group, and they shared the Good News with him. He served for many years as a pastor of a fine church in South Korea.

III. They were possessed with the love of Jesus and shared it with everyone.

Jesus made it clear that the greatest commandments are to love God with all of one's life and to love one's neighbor as oneself. The disciples had sensed the consistency of the Great Commission growing out of the Great Commandment. God loved people and sent Jesus into the world to die for their sins. Jesus loved people to the extent that he was willing to pay the price for their sins. If the disciples loved people, they would share the Good News with them.

Conclusion

A witnessing church is not a church merely trying to survive or even trying to build a great institution. It is a group of people bound together by the power of the love of Christ, who are possessed by a divine compulsion to share this Good News with as many people as they can as fast as they can.

SUNDAY EVENING, MARCH 26

Title: Christ's Standard for the Home

Text: "And he answered and said unto them, Have ye not read, that he which made them at the beginning made them male and female, and said, For this cause shall a man leave father and mother, and shall cleave to his wife: they twain shall be one flesh? Wherefore they are no more twain, but one flesh. What therefore God hath joined together, let not man put asunder" (**Matt. 19:4–6**).

Scripture Reading: Matthew 5:27–32

Introduction

Matthew 5:27–32 contains the second and third illustrations of the theme in Matthew 5:17–20 that Jesus fulfills the Law. Today's topics—adultery and divorce—are not easy to preach on. Earnest ministers, including myself, have agonized over these topics and have come to different conclusions involving the gray areas of divorce.

I. The problem of adultery (Matt. 5:27).

"Thou shalt not commit adultery" (Ex. 20:14) is the seventh commandment. Those to whom Jesus preached were familiar with it, for they had heard it quoted often in synagogue worship.

Jesus fulfilled the commandment. "But I say unto you, that whosoever looketh on a woman to lust after her hath committed adultery with her already in his heart" (Matt. 5:28).

Jesus asserted independent authority over the law. He did not destroy it. He built on it and fulfilled it. Not only is the act of adultery wrong, but the heart attitude that prompts it is sin.

It is a matter of heart, of motive. "To lust after her" means that one looks on a woman with the purpose of lusting after her. Surely our Lord did not mean to condemn every man as an adulterer who notices that a woman is attractive. Nor would he agree with the young man who rationalized his desire to commit adultery by saying, "To think it is as bad as to do it. Since I have thought it, I might just as well do it." One who purposes to commit sexual sin is an adulterer at heart, even though thwarted in his efforts to complete the act.

Jesus would condemn anything that intensifies lustful, illicit sexual desire. This would certainly include pornography, erotic books and pictures, and nudity outside the marriage relationship for the purpose of stimulating immoral lust.

One should practice self-denial rather than sin. Matthew 5:29–30 is not to be taken literally, but it is to be taken seriously. If sin be as dear to one as hand or foot, repent of it (almost like our slang, "Cut it out"), for one cannot hold on to sin and hold on to God. The word translated "offend" means to "spring the trap." Better that man should pluck out his eye than allow that eye to ensnare him in adultery.

II. The problem of divorce (Matt. 5:31–32).

Marriage in Jesus' day usually was arranged by the parents, often when the prospective bride and groom were quite young. The father of the bride paid a dowry. The husband could divorce; but if he did he must return the dowry unless he could prove that his bride was not a virgin. The betrothal took place about one year before the marriage. If unfaithful after betrothal, the woman could be stoned to death.

The Mosaic law provided for divorce in these words: "When a man hath taken a wife, and married her, and it come to pass that she find no favour in his eyes, because he hath found some uncleanness in her: then let him write her a bill of divorcement, and give it in her hand, and send, her out of his house" (Deut. 24:1). The rabbis had much debate over the phrase "some uncleanness in her." Rabbis interpreted it literally, making, for example, the spoiling of her husband's dinner a cause for divorce. It was concerning this that "the Pharisees also came unto [Jesus], tempting him, and saying unto him, Is it lawful for a man to put away his wife for every cause?" (Matt. 19:3).

God does not intend for marriage to end in divorce. "He answered and said unto them, Have ye not read, that he which made them at the beginning made them male and female, and said, For this cause shall a man leave father and mother, and shall cleave to his wife: and they twain shall be one flesh? Wherefore they are no more twain, but one flesh. What therefore God hath joined together let not man put asunder" (Matt. 19:4–6). God's high ideal is that a man and a woman who have kept themselves for each other leave their parents, give themselves to each other as one flesh and to none other for as long as they shall live.

"Why then did Moses command to give a writing of divorcement?" (Matt. 19:7). Jesus replied that it was a concession to the Israelites' hardness of heart. Moses' command was an advance on the previous practice when a man could divorce his wife by oral command. It assured a hearing before the priest, who could write. And it certified that the woman was not an adulteress. But this practice was not in accord with God's actual will.

Jesus' high standard. "And I say unto you, Whosoever shall put away his wife, except it be for fornication, and shall marry another, committeth adultery: and whoso marrieth her which is put away doth commit adultery" (Matt. 19:9). In the parallel passages, Mark (10:11–12) and Luke (16:18) do not have the exception, "except it be for fornication." In this case, fornication (which is strictly sexual sin of the unmarried) seems to cover also adultery (which is strictly sexual sin of the married). Adultery (or fornication) is a sin that by its very nature breaks the bond of "one flesh." When two are "one flesh," adultery is unthinkable. No one listening to Jesus would have questioned this exception. Mark and Luke apparently accepted it so naturally that they did not think it was necessary to mention this exception.

There seems to be no real difficulty about the innocent party being allowed to divorce and remarry if the spouse had committed adultery.

Is Jesus' statement in Matthew 5:31–32 a statement of principle or a legalistic ruling?

A man thirty-five years of age requested his pastor to marry him to a fine woman. The conversation went like this: "Have you been married before?" "Yes." "Broken by divorce?" "Yes, over ten years ago." "Broken by adultery?" "No, my wife became a religious fanatic. She lost all interest in me. She asked for a divorce." "Has she married again?" "I don't know. I haven't seen her in ten years. Would it be right to snoop about to see?" The pastor asked to be excused. But the young man was persistent. He said, "Pastor, I'm only thirty-five years old. That marriage is dead. There is nothing I can do about it. Do you think that God wants me to live as a eunuch the rest of my life?" The pastor asked for time. He paced the floor; he prayed in anguish; he read all he could find; and finally he married the couple because he believed that the Spirit of Christ took precedence over the letter of the Word.

Another pastor had persuaded a young wife to go back to her husband. A few hours later, the young wife came running to the pastor. Her head was bloody because her husband had broken a beer bottle on it. Some would say that a literal reading of Jesus' words means that she must continue to live with him. Others would say that she is free to separate but with no right to marry another. She should try to win her husband to the Lord, hoping for his salvation and restoration of their marriage. This is wonderful! However, it would be a strict legalist indeed, who would say that the Lord wills that this young woman ought never to have a husband and a family because in good faith she married a man who beats her over the head with a beer bottle.

Conclusion

In conclusion, let's take a look at some important principles that apply to today's message:

The whole teaching of Christ overrules any single statement that if applied as law contradicts his Spirit. For example, take John 3:36: "He that believeth on the Son hath everlasting life: and he that believeth not the Son shall not see life." Taken as a rule without qualification, this would say that no babies can go to heaven, for no babies believe in Jesus; that no one who lived before Jesus' birth could be saved; and that no one who has never heard of Jesus can be saved. These conclusions are obviously contrary to the Spirit of Christ.

One's sexuality is properly expressed in monogamy. Sex apart from a loving life commitment is wrong. It adulterates God's purpose. In the context of a life commitment, it is wonderful.

We are to cultivate purity of thought and of life. If you have sinned, repent. Ask God's forgiveness. Do what you can to make matters right. Forgive yourself as God has forgiven you, and do your best to be the most winsome Christian person you can be.

WEDNESDAY EVENING, MARCH 29

Title: A Proper and Orderly Way

Text: "Let all things be done decently and in order" **(1 Cor. 14:40).**

Scripture Reading: 1 Corinthians 14:40; James 5:13–16

Introduction

It goes without challenge that Jesus gave much attention to the sick. The disciples were faced with ministering to the sick, and so was the early church. And we are today. Perhaps of all the practical New Testament precepts, none is more simply stated nor more desperately needed than Paul's word to the Corinthians: "Everything should be done in a fitting and orderly way" (1 Cor. 14:40 NIV).

Many people who visit hospital patients are helpful and contribute substantially to the healing process. However, some hospital visits do more harm than good. Visiting hours are often ignored. Too many people crowd into a room. The halls can be filled to the point where nurses and other hospital personnel find it difficult to do their work effectively. Even when the behavior of some hospital visitors is not detrimental to the healing of the patient they have come to see, it can be harmful to other patients whose proximity and condition make them helpless victims of the conduct of people they do not know.

The following "Ten Commandments for Hospital Visitors" are offered in a spirit of helpfulness.

I. Thou shalt decide for whose good the visit is made—the patient's or the visitor's.

Unselfish concern must prompt the helpful visit. Sometimes we visit the sick, motivated by a sense of our own guilt. We have neglected friends or family, so we go to the hospital in a subconscious effort to effect a sort of atonement for our own neglect. The welfare of the patient must not be sacrificed on the altar of the visitor's bad conscience.

II. Thou shalt observe visiting hours as far as possible.

These hours are set for the patient's good and do not indicate that the people who set them are necessarily mean. Bathing, cleaning, changing of linens, and personal hygiene require time—time best utilized when visitors are not present. Physicians also need the privacy afforded by the absence of others.

III. Thou shalt keep thy voice down.

One sure way to keep the patient down is to keep the voice up. A hospital hall is not a recreation hall. Speak softly and move quietly.

IV. Thou shalt not get in the way of the doctors and hospital staff.

Let visiting in the halls be cut to a minimum. You can't do your best work with someone in your way. Neither can the members of the professional healing team.

V. Thou shalt arrive quietly, stay briefly, and leave graciously.

If a patient is hospitalized for a considerable period of time, several short visits are more helpful than one long one. When well, the patient may enjoy your "spending the day," but remember that sick people tire easily. It is better to leave while the patient wants you to stay than to stay when the patient wants you to leave.

VI. Thou shalt cultivate a cheerful spirit.

Do not make the patient's ear a conversational garbage disposal by repeating bad news. Don't tell of all the people you know who have died with the same symptoms. Don't give an "organ recital" about your own ailments. Optimism is contagious, and it is necessary.

VII. Thou shalt not lean on the bed or bump or shake the resting place of the patient in any way.

Things that well people don't notice at all can be very annoying to sick people. Thoughtless little habits on the visitor's part can make the patient tense. The patient's senses of motion, sound, and light may be heightened due to his or her illness.

VIII. Thou shalt learn to listen eloquently.

Sometimes the nicest thing we can do for people is to listen to them. Give them a chance to say whatever they want to say, but do not urge them to talk. They will likely need your advice much less than they will need your audience.

IX. Thou shalt inspire confidence.

The patient needs genuine assurance. Confidence in self, in the doctors, nurses, technicians, and in God are highly essential to the patient's quickest recovery.

X. Thou shalt magnify the Great Physician by a good example of quiet, thoughtful, friendly concern for the welfare of others.

Remember, we are all channels, not sources. Ultimately all healing is divine healing. We are privileged to be instruments in God's hand to help effect this healing.

APRIL

■ **Sunday Mornings**

"Living Life in the Light of the Resurrection" is the theme for messages that emphasize the difference Jesus Christ makes for believers today.

■ **Sunday Evenings**

Continue with expository messages from Jesus' Sermon on the Mount.

■ **Wednesday Evenings**

The theme for the Wednesday evening messages is "The Christian as a Witness for Our Lord." It is the opportunity and responsibility of every believer to be a witness for the Lord.

SUNDAY MORNING, APRIL 2

Title: The Joy of the Cross

Text: "Jesus . . . who for the joy that was set before him endured the cross, despising the shame" **(Heb. 12:2).**

Hymns: "Hallelujah, What a Saviour," Bliss
"At Calvary," Newell
"Glory to His Name," Hoffman
"Must Jesus Bear the Cross Alone?" Shepherd

Offertory Prayer: Our heavenly Father, we offer to you the gratitude of our hearts for your unspeakable gift to us in Jesus Christ, our Savior. We offer to you the praise of our life. We come in worship, bringing the fruit of our labors, the results of the thoughts of our minds, and the efforts of our hands in the form of tithes and offerings. Help us to bring these gifts in an attitude of reverent worship. As you have given yourself for us, we give ourselves to you for Christ's sake. Amen.

Introduction

We have heard many sermons on Christ's suffering on the cross. Words do not have the capacity to communicate the suffering he experienced as he died for our sins. The loneliness of the cross was terrible. Jesus was forsaken by his friends. In the midst of his agony, he felt forsaken by God and cried out, "My God, my God, why have you forsaken me?"

The shame of the cross is frequently forgotten by modern-day Christians.

Crucifixion was the ultimate in insult and public contempt for a criminal. We cannot even begin to understand the horror of the cross to the sinless, innocent Son of God.

The writer of Hebrews injects into our thinking an idea that appears to be contradictory. He makes much of the fact that a part of our Lord's motive for enduring the agony of the cross was because of "the joy that was set before him" (12:2). Is it possible that one could endure such agony, such loneliness, such shame, such horror and yet experience joy in doing so? The writer of Hebrews said yes. There were at least three joys that led Jesus Christ to the cross.

I. The joy of glorifying God.

In his great prayer, Jesus prayed, "Father, the hour is come; glorify thy Son, that thy Son also may glorify thee" (John 17:1). To glorify means to "make known." Jesus came to the earth to make known God's nature, character, and purpose. In this petition Jesus prays that God might reveal the nature and the divine purpose of Jesus of Nazareth who was to be manifested as the Son of God in the resurrection. He is also affirming his purpose to make known the nature and character of God by his death on the cross.

What is God like? He is the eternal Creator. He is the almighty Sovereign. He is majestic and holy, righteous and just.

The supreme revelation of God's love, mercy, and grace is revealed by the substitutionary death of Jesus Christ on the cross. Jesus was eager to reveal once and for all that love and grace are at the very heart of God. He was seeking to repudiate in a manner that could not be disputed that God was totally different from that which he had been reported to be by the serpent in the garden and through all succeeding generations.

The devil has misrepresented the nature and character of God from the beginning of time. People resent God and try to evade him because Satan has slandered his character with malicious falsehoods. By Jesus' death on the cross, he refuted Satan's lies and glorified God, revealing him as the God of love, mercy, and grace.

II. The joy of the highest possible personal achievement.

Could Jesus have escaped the cross? Perhaps this question is idle speculation, but it is evident that Satan thought that Jesus could avoid the cross. Satan offered him the kingdoms of this world if he would but fall down and worship him. The heart of this temptation was a suggestion on how to avoid the cross and employ a convenient, inexpensive way to win the kingdoms of this world for God. Jesus rejected this suggestion and endured the cross because there was no other way to save people. In doing so he was to achieve the highest possible destiny for his life.

Apart from the sufferings of the cross there could be no resurrection from the tomb and demonstration of the reality of eternal life.

Apart from the sufferings of the cross there could be no crusade of love by gospel teams carrying the message of redemption to a lost world.

Apart from the sufferings of the cross there could be for Christ no divine approval and exaltation at the end of the way.

Jesus' first recorded words were "Wist ye not that I must be about my Father's business?" From the cross he cried, "It is finished!" This was not the last gasp of a defeated idealist. It was the triumphant shout of one who had fully achieved his unique and divinely ordained destiny. It was, in a profoundly sober way, a shout of joy.

III. The joy of saving souls.

Jesus endured the cross to experience the joy of saving you and me from sin. We were slaves, and he came to set us free. We were guilty, and he came to cleanse us. We were helpless, and he came to rescue us. We were in a hopeless condition, and he came and gave us life.

Jesus died for our sins. He makes forgiveness possible. He gives new, divine, and eternal life.

The joy of rendering the highest possible service to you and meeting the deepest need of your heart and life was a part of the joy that led Jesus to suffer the agony of the cross.

Conclusion

Was the death of Christ on the cross a waste as far as you are concerned? If you have rejected him, then as far as you are concerned, he died in vain. Let his death on the cross be your death to sin. Let the life he revealed on the first Easter morning be your life.

Let Jesus' example challenge you to give your life completely to God's plan for you. Determine to live so as to glorify God in your daily life that others might come to your Savior and be saved by his death on the cross and be transformed by his living presence.

SUNDAY EVENING, APRIL 2

Title: Christ's Standard of Integrity

Text: "But let your communication be, Yea, yea; Nay, nay; for whatsoever is more than these cometh of evil" **(Matt. 5:37)**.

Scripture Reading: Matthew 5:33–37

Introduction

Jesus Christ fulfills the Law and the Prophets. His standard of righteousness is higher than that of the scribes and Pharisees. This theme, which was stated in Matthew 5:17–20, has been illustrated by murder (Matt. 5:21–26), by adultery (vv. 27–30), and by divorce (vv. 31–32). The fourth illustration, oaths, is the subject of this message.

I. The law.

Jesus' statement in verse 33, "Thou shalt not forswear [perjure] thyself, but shall perform unto the Lord thine oaths" probably refers to Leviticus 19:12, "Ye shall not swear by my name falsely, neither shalt thou profane the name of thy God: I am the LORD," and to Deuteronomy 23:23, "You shall be careful to perform what has passed your lips, for you have voluntarily vowed to the LORD your God what you have promised with your mouth" (RSV). The third commandment, "Thou shalt not take the name of the LORD thy God in vain" (Ex 20:7) prohibits using God's name to bolster a falsehood.

The commandments in the Law prohibited false swearing, but they did not forbid using God's name to affirm the truth. Numerous examples abound in the Old Testament of vows both to God and to men, as in Numbers 30:1–2; Deuteronomy 6:13; 23:21–32; Ecclesiastes 5:4–5.

The Jews to whom Jesus spoke had developed a system of gradation of oaths so that one's obligation to abide by a vow or to tell the truth was in proportion to the value of that by which one swore. Some rabbis held that only oaths that referred to God were binding. Swearing by Moses, by the Law, by the temple, by one's life, and so on had become common and really meant nothing with reference to the integrity and truthfulness of the one using such oaths. A whole system of casuistry had developed.

II. Jesus replied: "Swear not at all" (Matt. 5:34–37).

This was a principle rather than a rule.

Jesus was not forbidding a Christian to be placed on oath in court. This is clear if we interpret what he said by what he did. Jesus allowed himself to be put on oath before Caiaphas the high priest as you will read in Matthew 26:63–65.

Paul did not understand Jesus to prohibit sincere oaths. He frequently appealed to God as in Romans 1:9, "God is my witness," or in Galatians 1:20, "Before God, I lie not," or in 1 Thessalonians 5:27, "I charge you by the Lord that this epistle be read unto all the holy brethren."

A Christian will not need to be put on oath. His yes is yes; his no is no. He is a person of integrity. The Christian will not rely on any system of casuistry. Jesus said in effect that since God is the Creator of everything, one cannot swear by anything that does not refer to God. Heaven is his throne; earth is his footstool; Jerusalem is his city; you are his creation. When one swears by anything to bolster a falsehood, that one is in effect taking God's name in vain (i.e., a falsehood). There is no need for a Christian to swear by anything.

III. Application.

A Christian is truthful.

Truthful with God. God is not mocked. No person can fool God. He knows the motives, the intent of the heart out of which the mouth speaks.

Truthful with fellow humans. Words are a medium of communication, signals to others. If the signals are false, one deceives one's neighbor.

Earlier Jesus had condemned the use of such words as *stupid, blockhead,* and *scoundrel* to stir up anger. He here affirms that words are useful to convey information, but lying by any means in order to get an advantage over another is wrong and stands condemned.

"Thou shalt not bear false witness against thy neighbor" (Ex. 20:16) is the ninth commandment. The immediate reference seems to be to perjury in court. It has, however, a much wider application. Christians will not harm their fellow humans by lying. Their yes is yes; their no is no. They will not dishonor God by adding his name to a lie.

Christian businesspeople are expected to represent their products accurately. They will state the guarantee in clear language and will fulfill it without resorting to fine-print exclusions.

A man in Tulsa promised to sell a herd of cattle at a certain price if the offer was accepted within two weeks. During those days the price of cattle rose sharply. Other buyers offered to buy the cattle at a higher price. Although he had made no written agreement and received no earnest money, his word was as good as his bond. He lost several hundred dollars but retained the respect of everyone.

Christians are also expected to be true to their marriage vows and baptismal vows, for Christ calls his disciples to integrity and truthfulness.

Are there times when one can obey the principle of integrity and not tell the truth? Yes, there are such times:

When people are acting in a dramatic presentation such as a play, they speak lines that are not true. Since everyone knows they are acting, no real deception is involved.

There are some general customs and occasions when no one is fooled by one's insincerity. When someone greets you with "How are you?" that person probably does not want your fever chart or a list of the medicines you have taken recently. Even though you have a splitting headache and reply, "Fine," no real deception is involved.

Some emergencies seem to require that the principle "Thou shalt love" takes precedence over "Tell the truth."

I was one of a small group of navy chaplains sitting in an office when a distraught woman burst into the room crying, "Help me, my husband is going to kill me." We had barely gotten her to the next room when a wild-eyed man with a knife in his hand asked about the woman. We lied like heathens rather than telling the truth like preachers, and we detained the man until the authorities from the floor below could restrain him. My conscience has never hurt me for that forthright lie.

Conclusion

It is refreshing to note that while misunderstandings may result between people of integrity, the Lord never misunderstands. He knows the heart. One can never be right with one's fellow humans unless he or she is first right with God.

WEDNESDAY EVENING, APRIL 5

Title: Three Kinds of Witnessing

Text: "You are witnesses of these things" **(Luke 24:48 RSV).**

Scripture Reading: Luke 24:36–50

Introduction

Among the several terms the risen Christ used to define the major task he was committing to his church was that of serving as a *witness.* He defined his strategy for winning the world to faith through the witness of his disciples (Acts 1:8). We find the activity of the apostles described in terms of giving a personal witness: "And with great power the apostles gave their testimony to the resurrection of the Lord Jesus, and great grace was upon them all" (Acts 4:33 RSV).

Many Christians are confused about being a witness. It is interesting to note what our Lord did not mean by this commission. He did not mean that we are to be his "debaters." While the dialogue of the apostles did take the form of a debate at times, they were not primarily debaters.

Jesus did not mean that we are to go out and be his "complainers." Although at times the apostles were critics of the status quo, their fundamental message was not that of giving voice to a complaint.

Our Lord did not mean that we should go out and be his "condemners." Some self-righteous people like to condemn others and find fault. While our Lord and the early church did not approve of everything, their major emphasis was not condemnation. God did not send Christ into the world to condemn but to save (John 3:17).

Our Lord did not mean that his disciples should go out and serve as his "advisers." Many people think of the gospel as being good advice when in reality it is good news. Witnesses for Jesus Christ share the good news of what God did through him and what God is doing in their personal lives.

I. The apostles were eyewitnesses.

The major impact of our text is that Jesus' apostles were eyewitnesses of his ministry. With their ears they had heard his words. With their hands they had actually touched him. With their eyes they had beheld his sacrificial death on the cross, seen the empty tomb, and witnessed his living presence after his resurrection. They were eyewitnesses to the great redemptive acts of God in Jesus Christ. In this sense they occupied a unique place in God's program.

II. The apostles were to be voice witnesses.

The basic concept in Acts 1:8 is that the apostles were to verbalize that which they had seen and heard in the life of Jesus Christ. It was not enough that they be good eyewitnesses; they were also to be voice witnesses.

If you and I are to be good witnesses to Jesus Christ today, we must recognize that we do not have the opportunity of being eyewitnesses, but we can be voice witnesses. It is not enough that we live a good life; we must also verbalize the good news of what God is doing in us through faith in Jesus Christ and through the work of the Holy Spirit.

III. The apostles were life witnesses.

With their lives the apostles bore testimony to the presence of Jesus Christ within them (Acts 4:13). The unmistakable transformation in their lives that came by faith in a living Lord gave authenticity to the message from their lips. Had it not been for this evidence of the living Christ within them, the testimony of their lips would not have been acceptable and would not have produced the dramatic results that came about as a result of their devotion and loyalty to Christ.

Conclusion

Today's Christians do not have the opportunity of giving exactly the same kind of witness as did the apostles. There are, however, three ways people today can give testimony to Christ. First, some people can give the testimony of a spectator who relates what God is doing in others' lives. If this is the only testimony one can give, it will not have great weight.

Second, others can give the testimony of a participator. Each of us should so relate to Jesus Christ and so cooperate with the Holy Spirit that we can give our Christian testimony from the viewpoint of a participator in what God is doing in the here and now. While it is wonderful to be able to relate our past conversion experience, we need to keep our experience with the Lord current. It is not enough to live a good life and demonstrate the difference Jesus Christ makes. We must verbally communicate to those about us the great things he does for us every day. God wants to use your personal statement of what he is doing in your life to assist others to have faith. We need to recognize that the church would be nonexistent two generations from now if all of Jesus' followers were to suddenly stop verbalizing what God was doing in them.

Third, all of us can give our witness as commentators. Television news programs employ analysts and commentators to interpret what is happening in the world. While guarding against the peril of speculating, we should not hesitate to venture our opinion concerning what God is doing in our community and in the world.

It is the Lord's will that each of us be a good witness. We do not have a choice about whether we will be a witness; our only choice involves whether we will be a poor one or a good one.

SUNDAY MORNING, APRIL 9

Title: How Will You Treat the King?

Text: "Rejoice greatly, O daughter of Zion! Shout aloud, O daughter of Jerusalem! Lo, your king comes to you; triumphant and victorious is he, humble and riding on an ass, on a colt the foal of an ass" (**Zech. 9:9 RSV**).

Scripture Reading: Matthew 21:1–11

Hymns: "Crown Him with Many Crowns," Bridges
"I Will Sing of My Redeemer," Bliss
"I Love to Tell the Story," Hankey

Offertory Prayer: Our Father, we come to thank you today for offering so much to us in the person of Jesus Christ. We thank you for the gift of salvation through him. We thank you for our great salvation, past, present, and future. We thank you for Christ as our Redeemer, Teacher, Guide, and Friend. We thank you for the privilege of being able to share with you in ministries of love and mercy to the needy, the unfortunate, and the unsaved. Bless these tithes and offerings to the end that suffering will be relieved, that life will be uplifted, and that souls will be saved through Jesus Christ. Amen.

Introduction

On this Sunday before Easter, we see our Lord making his triumphal entry into Jerusalem, offering himself as the fulfillment of Old Testament prophecy and as the King who alone can bring peace and harmony to human hearts. How have you treated the King of Kings and Lord of Lords? Matthew's gospel presents Jesus Christ, the Savior, as the King whom the people of God had been expecting as the fulfillment of messianic prophecy.

I. Christ was born to be a king (Matt. 2:2).

The magi from the East came seeking a mysterious baby "born king of the Jews." In his infancy our Lord was recognized as a king by these mysterious magi, and he was treated as a king by the wicked Herod. Herod saw him as a rival for the throne and plotted to bring about his death (Matt. 2:13).

II. Christ was anointed to be a king.

At his baptism the heavens opened, revealing the King's realm of authority (Matt. 3:16).

The Holy Spirit descended as a dove, indicating the spiritual nature of Christ's reign.

The voice from heaven was the voice of the eternal God revealing the divine favor of the Almighty on this King and his kingly program.

III. Christ explained the principles and the program of his kingdom in the Sermon on the Mount (Matt. 5–7).

IV. Christ demonstrated his kingship in many areas of authority.

Our Lord exercised kingly authority over nature. The winds obeyed his command, and the waves of the sea granted his wishes.

Our Lord exercised kingly authority over disease. At his word or at his touch, healing came to those who suffered.

Our Lord exercised kingly authority over the demonic world. He resisted and overcame the temptations of the devil. He exercised authority over demons, commanding them to depart from those who were demon possessed.

Our Lord exercised kingly authority over death. He restored life to the daughter of Jairus (Mark 5:35–43). He raised to life the son of a widow (Luke 7:11–17): He raised Lazarus back to life (John 11:38–44). Our Lord was later to conquer death and the grave, coming forth triumphant and victorious.

V. Christ died as a king.

In satire and cruelty, the Roman soldiers arrayed our Lord in a purple robe and bowed before him, saying, "Hail, King of the Jews!" (John 19:3). Pilate instructed those who crucified Jesus to put the superscription "Jesus of Nazareth, the King of the Jews" (John 19:19) on his cross to indicate the crime of which he was accused and for which he was dying. Ironically, never did Pilate speak words of greater truth than when he recognized Jesus Christ as "the King of the Jews."

VI. Christ conquered death as a king.

Christ's death at the hands of wicked men appeared to be a great triumph for the forces of evil, but in reality it was a conquest of evil by the powerful King of love and grace. Death could not hold him, and the grave could not conceal him.

VII. Following his resurrection, our Lord assumed kingly authority on a universal scale (Matt. 28:18–20).

Jesus said that all authority in heaven and earth had been given to him. We need to recognize and respond to his authority. As believers in Jesus Christ, as followers of the Lord, and as children of the King, we need to treat him as the King who alone can bring about peace, purpose, power, and plenty in our lives.

Conclusion

How have you treated the King? We can be grateful that we have not treated him as did Herod. We can rejoice that we have not treated him as did the soldiers. We can find peace in the fact that we have not mistreated the King as did Pilate.

One day the King will return in all his glory and power for those who have trusted him and who love him. Today we would be wise to receive him as the King and treat him as an honored guest in our hearts and lives. We would be wise to listen to him and to heed his teachings and follow his commandments. We should trust him as our dearest and most precious friend. We should obey him as the Lord of unquestioned and immeasurable love. We should follow him as our divine and infallible leader. He can bring peace and joy into our hearts only when we make him sovereign Lord and King in every area of our lives.

SUNDAY EVENING, APRIL 9

Title: Second-Mile Religion

Text: "And whosoever shall compel thee to go a mile, go with him twain" **(Matt. 5:41).**

Scripture Reading: Matthew 5:38–42

Introduction

Matthew 5:38–42 has been subject to misinterpretation and misapplication by both the friends and enemies of our Lord. Jesus spoke in principles rather than in rules. What he meant must be interpreted by what he did, as well as by what he said. Four separate illustrations with reference to the law of retaliation combine to form the fifth illustration of the theme in Matthew 5:17–20 that Jesus fulfills the Law and the Prophets. He calls for a higher and more inward righteousness than that of the scribes and Pharisees.

I. The Law.

"Ye have heard that it hath been said, an eye for an eye, and a tooth for a tooth" *(Matt. 5:38).* This was indeed the Mosaic law, which read, "Life for life, eye for eye, tooth for tooth, hand for hand, foot for foot, burn for burn, wound for wound, stripe for stripe" (Ex. 21:23–25 RSV). With reference to a false witness, the Law reads, "Then shall ye do unto him, as he had thought to have done unto his brother; so shalt thou put the evil away from among you. And those which remain shall hear, and fear, and shall henceforth commit no more any such evil among you. And thine eye shall not pity; but life shall

go for life, eye for eye, tooth for tooth, hand for hand, foot for foot" (Deut. 19:19–21). In Leviticus it is stated this way: "If a man cause a blemish in his neighbour; as he hath done, so shall it be done to him; breach for breach, eye for eye, tooth for tooth: as he hath caused a blemish in a man, so shall it be done to him again. And he that killeth a beast, he shall restore it: and he that killeth a man, he shall be put to death" (Lev. 24:19–21). This was the *lex talionis*, law of kind, or law of retaliation, found in many ancient law codes.

The Mosaic law was an advance on the preceding practice.

It limited revenge and fixed compensation. This was better than family feuds and clan warfare.

The execution of the law was left to the authorities. Personal revenge of private injuries was forbidden. "Thou shalt not avenge, nor bear any grudge against the children of thy people, but thou shalt love thy neighbour as thyself: I am the LORD" (Lev. 19:18). The general practice of the Jews, however, was to justify personal retaliation on the basis of the law of kind.

One observes this practice in operation today. Both Israel and the Arab nations seem to operate on the principle of retaliation. They kill persons of the other nation apparently on the assumption that the whole nation stands guilty for what some persons of the nations do.

II. Jesus calls to a higher standard.

"But I say unto you, that ye resist not evil: but whosoever shall smite thee on thy right cheek, turn to him the other also" (Matt. 5:39). Today's English Version rightly translates this verse, "But now I tell you: do not take revenge on someone who does you wrong. If anyone slaps you on the right cheek, let him slap your left cheek too." William Barclay notes that to slap the right cheek implies a slap with the back of the hand. It was an insult. Jesus is not speaking about defending oneself from aggression, but rather about not taking revenge for an insult. "Vengeance is mine; I will repay, saith the Lord" (Rom. 12:19). Vengeance is God's responsibility.

We may judge what Jesus meant by what he did. He certainly resisted evil. He denounced the scribes and Pharisees and fought the devil. He did not match this with this, that with that. When one of the officers of the high priest insulted him by slapping him, Jesus did not literally turn the other cheek, nor did he retaliate; but he made a dignified protest, "If I have spoken evil, bear witness of the evil: but if well, why smitest thou me?" (John 18:23).

How then are we to understand? Jesus is speaking against retaliation in revenge. His statement is like a word picture cartoon rather than like a photograph. Over against the evil of revenge, it would be better to allow oneself to be imposed on, if that were the alternative. We are to resist evil but not retaliate for evil done to us.

"And if any man will sue thee at the law, and take away thy coat, let him have thy cloak also" (Matt. 5:40). The coat was an undergarment much like a long

shirt. Even a poor man would have more than one. It corresponded to the robe of Jesus that was woven without seam for which the soldiers gambled. The cloak was the outer garment that doubled for a cover at night. The interpretation seems to be similar to that given above. Rather than have a spirit of vengeance, it would be better to allow oneself to be imposed on.

"And whosoever shall compel thee to go a mile, go with him twain" (Matt. 5:41). The Jews were a subject nation. The Romans could impress their subjects for menial tasks. Simon of Cyrene was impressed to carry the cross for Jesus (see Matt. 27:22). The meaning seems to be that it would be better to go an extra mile than to have a spirit of hatred and vengeance.

"Give to him that asketh thee, and from him that would borrow of thee turn not thou away" (Matt. 5:42). Some have noted that Jesus does not command his disciples to give the beggar what he asks, but rather tells them not to turn away from his plea.

The late Dr. W. Hersey Davis told the story of Henry Richardson, a missionary to Africa in the late nineteenth century, who literally followed this command. The natives carried off everything of value that he had. Their consciences caused them to return the goods they had taken, which opened the door to their evangelization.

Critics have taken these words literally to poke fun at Christianity. In my judgment, both the good missionary and the critics have failed to interpret Jesus rightly. Jesus seems to be saying that rather than be callous, hardhearted, unfeeling, and rebellious, it would be better to allow yourself to be imposed on.

Conclusion

The natural man thinks, "How can I get even? If he harms me, I'll harm him. If he curses me, I'll curse him. If he kicks my shins, I'll kick his shins. If he knocks out my tooth, I'll make him pay." The late Soviet premier Nikita S. Khrushchev said, "I agree with Christ in most of his teachings. There is much in Christianity that is common to us Communists. There is only one point where I do not agree: when Christ says one has to turn the other cheek. For me, if a man strikes me on the cheek, I knock his head off."

When the Spirit of Christ changes a person, all things become new. He or she has faith in God and believes that God will balance the books. Rather than asking, "How can I make this person pay for what he has done?" the Christian asks, "How can I help this person to be a Christian?"

When you follow the natural law of retaliation, you are reacting to someone else. The offender determines your action. When you follow the way Jesus recommends, you are free from the poison of revenge and have goodwill toward others. This does not mean that you like their ways; it means that you have goodwill toward them.

A young preacher had begun to draw the crowds that for years had attended the ministry of an older man in another church. The elder minister's church board said, "Pastor, we must do something about it." The pastor replied, "I am doing something. I pray for God's blessings on his ministry every day."

Jesus calls us to go beyond duty, beyond the expected. He calls us to go the second mile of privilege, of love, of service.

WEDNESDAY EVENING, APRIL 12

Title: The Content of Our Witness

Text: "John bore witness, 'I saw the Spirit descend as a dove from heaven, and it remained on him.' I myself did not know him; but he who sent me to baptize with water said to me, 'He on whom you see the Spirit descend and remain, this is he who baptizes with the Holy Spirit.' And I have seen and have borne witness that this is the Son of God" **(John 1:32–34 RSV)**.

Scripture Reading: John 1:6–8

Introduction

Jesus wants his disciples to be his witnesses. We can discover the nature of the function we are to fulfill by looking at the example of John the Baptist. Scripture clearly states that John the Baptist came from God that he might be a communicator, a testator, concerning Jesus Christ.

The personal, experiential, firsthand nature of witnessing is revealed in John's statement concerning what he saw and what he heard on the occasion of Jesus' baptism. His was a unique witness. It appears that he alone saw the Holy Spirit descend as a dove and that he alone heard the voice from heaven identifying Jesus of Nazareth as the Lamb of God who was to take away the sin of the world.

It is impossible for our witness to have the same content as the witness of John the Baptist. In fact, each disciple has a unique witness. In the final analysis, we can only give as our testimony that which we have seen, heard, and experienced in our own life concerning who Jesus Christ is, what he has done, and what he is doing in our lives. We must not even attempt to give the testimony John gave or the testimony of anyone else.

What is your witness? What testimony can you give? It all depends on your personal experience with Jesus Christ.

I. Testify of the joy of forgiveness.

A sense of sin, a feeling of guilt, an awareness of incompleteness, a hunger for God may be the primary factors that lead one to put faith in Jesus Christ who came to solve our sin problem. The assurance that through faith in him things are now right between the believer and the Creator God is a source of joy. Every person is a sinner in need of forgiveness. To give testimony concerning the joy that comes as a result of forgiveness can encourage others to have faith in the God of grace who is in the business of forgiving sinners (Ps. 32:1–2).

II. Testify of the joy of eternal life (John 3:16, 36).

Eternal life does not come to us at the end of our earthly pilgrimage. It is the gift of God as a present possession to those who receive Jesus Christ as the Lord of life and as the Lord over death. To rest in the assurance that one has an eternal and abiding relationship with God makes a contribution toward a joyous life. Give testimony concerning this to others, and you will assist them to come to the decision to receive Jesus Christ as Lord and Savior.

III. Testify of the friendship of Jesus Christ (John 15:15).

Most of us do not hesitate to speak to others concerning our friends. We will often describe the nature of this friendship and the importance of a certain friendship.

One of the joys of being a follower of Christ is to enjoy his friendship. Everyone needs Jesus Christ not only as Savior, but also as a friend. He is the Friend who sticks closer than a brother.

IV. Testify of the Holy Spirit's help.

God gives to each believer the Holy Spirit as a permanent indwelling guest (John 14:16–17). The Holy Spirit comes to us in the moment of our spiritual birth to assure us of our relationship with God and to produce within us the fruit of the Spirit—the very mind, spirit, and personality of Jesus Christ (Gal. 5:22–23).

The Holy Spirit struggles within us to deliver us from evil and to lift us to the higher level of walking in the Spirit in the here and now. As the Spirit of God does his work in you and to you, do not hesitate to tell others of God's gracious work within you.

V. Testify of the privilege of prayer (Matt. 6:6).

One of the most rewarding and delightful experiences one can have is to enter into the throne room of the eternal God and into dialogue with him as the heavenly Father (Matt. 6:9–13). We come into his presence not as delinquent beggars, but as the children of his grace and love. We come not so much to beg as to be blessed. Glorify God and praise him and exalt him by telling others of his goodness to you during this dialogue that we call prayer.

VI. Testify of God's leadership during times of uncertainty.

Life is made up of decisions. We face many paths. At times it is exceedingly difficult to know what to do. In such times we can study God's Word, give ourselves to prayer, follow the deep impulses that come from the Holy Spirit, and listen to the counsel of friends. The main thing to do is to look to

God for guidance and leadership, for we walk not by sight but by faith. There is always a risk involved in the decisions we make. In some instances we can know that we have had the leadership of our God only as we look back on those decisions we have made.

If you have had the guidance of God in his providential care in your times of uncertainty, share this with others in order to strengthen their faith and to encourage them to have faith.

VII. Testify of God's comfort during times of grief.

Some of you have never been touched by the agony of grief. The family circle is still complete. And for that you can be grateful. Others of us have been touched by the agony of having one very dear to us pass on. It is comforting, strengthening, and helpful to know that our dear one has gone to be with our Lord. It can also be strengthening to know that through faith in Jesus Christ the pain of our separation is temporary, that there will come a time when we shall be reunited with these in the home where there will be no more sickness, sorrow, suffering, separation, pain, and death (Rev. 21:3–5).

Conclusion

The content of your witness, your personal testimony, will be determined by your personal experiences in the Lord. Do not deprive others of the blessing your testimony can bring to them. Do not rob yourself of the joy of speaking a good word concerning God's grace in your life.

SUNDAY MORNING, APRIL 16

Title: The Reality of the Resurrection

Text: "And their words seemed to them as idle tales, and they believed them not" (**Luke 24:11**).

Scripture Reading: Luke 24:1–11

Hymns: "Christ the Lord Is Risen Today," Wesley

"I Know That My Redeemer Liveth," Pounds

"He Lives," Ackley

Offertory Prayer: Our heavenly Father, we acknowledge that life and its numerous blessings are gifts from you. We acknowledge that you give wonderful and precious gifts. Help us to discover and to discern these many material and spiritual blessings. We ask that you would teach us to be good stewards of these gifts. Help us to see that they are not to be enjoyed selfishly but are to be used selflessly for others. As we bring our tithes and offerings, we ask the Great Teacher to guide us as we give and to lead us as we distribute these offerings. Through Jesus Christ our Lord. Amen.

Introduction

Roman soldiers nailed Jesus to the cross at 9:00 one Friday morning. By 3:00 in the afternoon of the same day, he was dead. Friends came to take Jesus' body. They wrapped it in burial linens and laid it in a tomb, but there was no time for the usual burial ritual. The Jewish Sabbath was only a few hours away, and no Jew would touch a dead body on the Sabbath, for it would make that person ceremonially unclean and prohibit him or her from participating in the Sabbath observance.

When the Sabbath day was over, early on Sunday morning, devout women went to Jesus' tomb with spices and ointment. Out of respect, love, and honor they wanted to perform the formal rites associated with burial. When they arrived at the tomb, they found that the massive stone had been rolled away from the entrance. And when they entered the tomb, they did not find Jesus' body. Two angelic messengers informed them that Jesus Christ had risen. They were the first to discover the reality of the resurrection.

The women rushed back to where the disciples were meeting and told them about the reality of the resurrection. The disciples had a strange response to the women's message. "Their words seemed to them as idle tales, and they believed them not" (Luke 24:11). The expression "idle tales" comes from Greek medical writers who used it to describe the babbling of a fevered and insane mind. The disciples were not convinced of the resurrection.

Still today many people do not believe in the resurrection. The gospel account seems to many as an "idle tale." But Christians know that Jesus is alive, for his Spirit lives in them. Therefore they can be bold about affirming the reality of Christ's resurrection.

I. The touch of personal experience.

Nothing can be more convincing than a personal experience. Seeing the empty tomb and hearing the angelic messengers convinced the women visitors of the reality of the resurrection. They needed no apologetic proof to convince them or to persuade others that Jesus was alive.

The Romans sought to nullify the Lord's resurrection. Matthew wrote, "And when they were assembled with the elders, and had taken counsel, they gave large money unto the soldiers, saying, Say ye, His disciples came by night, and stole him away while we slept" (28:12–13). The Jews used treachery to arrest Jesus. Then they tried him illegally on false charges. Now Jesus' enemies used bribery to silence the news of his resurrection.

Yet not any of the machinations of malicious people could suppress the risen Lord. Bribery could not silence the news about him. Roman guards could not contain him in a cave. Jesus presented himself alive to people. They experienced him personally. He met with them, ate with them, and taught them. These personal experiences of the risen Lord furnish conclusive evidence of his resurrection from the dead. Further, Christians today are convinced of the reality of Jesus' resurrection by having a personal experience with him. When we open our lives to the risen Christ, we can testify of his living presence.

II. The testimony of Scripture.

Another convincing factor of Jesus' resurrection is the testimony of Scripture. When the women came to the tomb, the angelic messengers reminded them of Jesus' promise of resurrection. Throughout the New Testament there are numerous references to it.

The New Testament gives a unified testimony. The Gospels relate in simple narrative the events of Jesus' resurrection. Some critical scholars want to emphasize the differences evident in the four narratives, but upon close examination, one can explain these variations. The book of Acts frequently mentions Jesus' resurrection. When Peter preached at the feast of Pentecost, he said, "This Jesus hath God raised up, whereof we all are witnesses" (Acts 2:32). Later the risen Christ appeared to Saul, whom he renamed Paul. He said to Saul, "I am Jesus" (Acts 9:5). As we read Acts we notice numerous testimonies regarding the risen Christ.

The various New Testament letters give a unified witness of Jesus' resurrection. Paul said, "I delivered unto you first of all that which I also received, how that Christ died for our sins according to the scriptures; and that he was buried, and that he rose again the third day according to the scriptures" (1 Cor. 15:3–5). Peter mentioned the "resurrection of Jesus Christ from the dead" (1 Peter 1:3). John recorded the words of the risen Lord, "I am he that liveth, and was dead" (Rev. 1:18).

The New Testament references to Jesus' resurrection are straightforward. There is no elaborate language and there are no adornments to the story, no visionary experiences. Another unique factor of the New Testament accounts is the verb tense. The biblical writers speak of Jesus after his death in the present tense. One notable example is Paul's testimony of Jesus: "He is the head of the body, the church: who is the beginning, the firstborn from the dead" (Col. 1:18).

Several other unique factors can be seen in the New Testament accounts of Jesus' resurrection. The folded grave clothes prove that Jesus' body had not been stolen. Scripture also carefully records that Jesus had scars on his body where he had been nailed to the cross. This clearly establishes evidence of his identity. Furthermore, his words and actions are recorded by Scripture, testifying that the Christ who died on the cross was truly alive.

If you desire to learn of the reality of Jesus' resurrection, make a serious study of Scripture. The Bible will convince you of the reality of the risen Lord. He is alive! The Bible tells us so.

III. The transformation of people.

When we observe how the risen Christ transformed people, we do not doubt the reality of the resurrection. Jesus made a difference in the lives of first-century disciples. The news of Jesus' resurrection changed the attitudes of Mary Magdalene, Joanna, and Mary.

Jesus changes temperaments. Before the resurrection, the disciples were fearful, disillusioned, disappointed, and depressed, but the risen Christ transformed their temperaments. Jesus can also transform the feelings of modern disciples, helping them to overcome disappointment and fear.

Jesus also dispels doubts. When Jesus appeared to the disciples, Thomas was absent. They told him of Jesus' appearance to them, but Thomas doubted the resurrection. It seemed incredible to him. After seven days Jesus ministered especially to Thomas, dispelling Thomas's doubts. In today's world numerous people find the news of a risen Christ incredible. Yet Christ is able to minister to them by his Holy Spirit and by his Word, dispelling their doubts as he did for Thomas.

The risen Christ gives meaning and purpose to life. The apostles thought Jesus was the Old Testament Messiah. Basically their messianic concept was political. When Jesus did not restore Israel as in the days of David and reign as an earthly king, they lost their direction in life. But after his resurrection, Jesus taught them the real meaning of following him. No greater malady affects our world today than meaninglessness. Only the risen Christ can give our generation meaning and purpose.

Conclusion

Jesus' resurrection is a reality, not an idle tale. The greatest proof of its authenticity is for you to open your life to the risen Lord and let him begin the process of changing your life.

SUNDAY EVENING, APRIL 16

Title: Christ's Standard of Love toward Others

Text: "But I say unto you, Love your enemies, bless them that curse you, do good to them that hate you, and pray for them which despitefully use you, and persecute you; that ye may be the children of your Father which is in heaven" **(Matt. 6:44–45).**

Scripture Reading: Matthew 6:43–48

Introduction

An uneducated but devout woman was reading a portion of Scripture during a meeting of the Women's Missionary Society. She came to a difficult word and began to spell it. One of the women, somewhat irritated by the slowness of her reading, said, "Skip it." The one reading replied, "It doesn't spell skip it." In this message we come to one of the noblest and most difficult passages from the lips of our Lord, and "it doesn't spell skip it."

This is the sixth and final illustration of the theme presented in

Matthew 5:17–20, that the Law and the Prophets are fulfilled in Jesus. God's revelation in the Old Testament was partial. It was better than the prevailing ethical standards, but it needed completion, fulfillment. Jesus called people to a higher standard. Christian disciples are not to be content to live down to the law. Jesus calls them to come up higher. "Except your righteousness shall exceed the righteousness of the scribes and Pharisees," he said, "ye shall in no case enter into the kingdom of heaven" (Matt. 5:20). The previous illustrations had been murder, adultery, divorce, oaths, retaliation, and now attitude toward others, especially attitude toward enemies.

I. The law.

"Ye have heard that it hath been said, Thou shalt love thy neighbour, and hate thine enemy" (Matt. 5:43). "Thou shalt love thy neighbour as thyself is indeed a part of the law. "And hate thine enemy" was not a part of the law. "Neighbor" was usually interpreted to mean fellow Jew, while "foreigner" meant Gentile. Moses in Leviticus 19:33–34 expanded neighbor to strangers living in Israel. In general practice, however, "foreigner" became synonymous with "enemy," and "hate thine enemy" became an accepted addition—not commanded but permitted. The hatred of the Jews and the Samaritans as illustrated in John 4:1–42 is an example.

II. What Jesus said.

A. *Jesus made Leviticus 19:18 second only to Deuteronomy 6:4–5.* In answer to a lawyer's question, "Master, which is the great commandment in the law? Jesus said unto him, Thou shalt love the Lord thy God with all thy heart, and with all thy soul, and with all thy mind. This is the first and great commandment. And the second is like unto it. Thou shalt love thy neighbour as thyself. On these two commandments hang all the law and the prophets" (Matt. 22:36–40).

It is important to know what love means in these commandments. The word is not *eros,* which means the attraction of the sexes. The word is not *philos,* which means attraction to a pleasing person or object. The word is *agape.* It means the right motive accompanied by the right action. Christ's attitude toward humankind is love, so *love* means "Christlike in motive." His attitude is one of goodwill.

To love God is to have toward God the attitude of goodwill that he desires, accompanied by the right actions. To love self is to have toward oneself the attitude of goodwill that God desires one to have, accompanied by the right actions. To love one's neighbor is to have toward him or her the attitude of goodwill that accords with God's will, plus appropriate actions.

It is important to understand who one's neighbor is. In the parable of the good Samaritan in Luke 10:30–37, Jesus made it clear that any human being is our neighbor.

B. *Jesus made the command explicit in Matthew 5:24:*

134

"Love your enemies." Jesus did not command us to like our enemies but to love them. Jesus did not command us to love their *evil ways* but to love *them*.

"Bless them that curse you." Christians pray for their enemies, "God forgive them" rather than "God damn them." Jesus is the supreme example of his own preaching when from the cross he prayed for those who were crucifying him, "Father, forgive them; for they know not what they do" (Luke 23:34).

"Do good to them that hate you." God wants all people to be saved. The purpose of Christ's command here is their salvation. The only way to get rid of enemies without killing them is to make them friends. We do not convert enemies to friends by retaliation in kind. When bereavement comes to someone who has wronged you, take that person a nice dish of food or send flowers. He or she will burn with remorse, which may lead to repentance. The apostle Paul in Romans 12:17–21 quotes Proverbs 25:21–22 and reflects the spirit of Christ.

"Pray for them that despitefully use you and persecute you." We are to pray for their salvation rather than for their success in evil.

C. *These attitudes are appropriate for children of the heavenly Father.*

Jesus was speaking to saved people. Christians are not to live down to the prevailing standards. "What do ye more than others?" (Matt. 6:47) implies that Christians are not to be ordinary persons. "If any man be in Christ, he is a new creature: old things are passed away; behold, all things are become new" (2 Cor. 5:17).

Disciples are to follow God's perfect example. "For he maketh his sun to rise on the evil and on the good, and sendeth rain on the just and on the unjust" (Matt. 5:45).

"For when we were yet without strength, in due time Christ died for the ungodly. For scarcely for a righteous man will one die: yet per-adventure for a good man some would even dare to die. But God commendeth his love toward us, in that, while we were yet sinners, Christ died for us" (Rom. 5:6–8).

D. *"Be ye therefore perfect, even as your Father which is in heaven is perfect"* (Matt. 5:48). Any person or anything that has attained the end for which it was created is said to be perfect. Perfect means full grown, mature, complete in body and mind as an adult is a child become perfect. It is sometimes used with reference to moral perfection in general, but here it is used specifically with respect to love—that is, goodwill to persons. Let God's perfect example and standard be ours. As God is the perfect Father, let us be perfect sons and daughters.

Conclusion

We would know that there was something wrong with a Savior who would be content with a lower standard. And we would know that something was wrong with a saved person who was content to fall short of God's high standard.

The Christian's application of the principle of love presents many problems. Does love for wicked persons mean that disciples fail to protest that wickedness? Can one have goodwill for a person and yet have that person confined in prison for the protection of others? Does goodwill prohibit defense of one's person, one's family, one's possessions, one's country? Does Jesus' willingness to be put to death without resistance mean that his followers should not resist?

Refusal to hate; refusal to return insult for insult and evil for evil is a great step forward. Earnestly pray for the salvation of others. Press on to be like Jesus. Remember, when we fall short of perfection, God for Christ's sake forgives the repentant sinner and calls to us, "Come, follow me."

WEDNESDAY EVENING, APRIL 19

Title: The Manner of Your Testimony

Text: "To him all the prophets bear witness that every one who believes in him receives forgiveness of sins through his name" **(Acts 10:43 RSV)**.

Scripture Reading: Acts 2:5–11

Introduction

Luke declares that the Old Testament prophets testified of their faith that God would provide a Savior. These words of testimony were recorded in scrolls that became recognized as Holy Scripture among the Jews.

On the day of Pentecost, the devout believers in Jerusalem described the wonderful works of God, and people from throughout the whole world who were present heard them in their own dialects. One of the characteristics of a good testimony is that it is given in language that can be understood by the hearers.

In what form or in what manner will you give your testimony for Jesus Christ? There is no limit to the number of different forms in which one can give his or her testimony for Christ.

I. You can give your testimony in believer's baptism.

We proclaim through the symbolism of baptism that Jesus Christ died for our sins and was buried, that he conquered death and arose triumphant, and that he has come to live within our hearts. To be baptized without faith would be to proclaim a falsehood to self, to others, and to God.

II. You can give your testimony in active, meaningful church membership.

To claim to know Jesus Christ and to profess faith in him without being vitally involved in the life and ministry of the church is a contradiction. Those who claim to be Christians yet omit the church from their lives are fooling no one but themselves.

III. You can give your testimony in a sermon.

The pastor who preaches effectively speaks out of a personal experience with God from service to service. He must be a testator, an articulator of what God is doing in his life as well as being a commentator concerning what God has done in the past and what God is doing in the lives of others in the present.

IV. You can give your testimony by teaching a lesson.

The church grants to many the priceless privilege of being Bible school teachers. The good teacher will do something more than discuss the content of a biblical passage. The effective teacher will not only draw out the truth and apply it to the lives of students, but will also bear personal testimony concerning how this truth works in a life.

V. You can give your testimony in a song.

It is one thing to be a musician, and it is something more to be a Christian with musical talent dedicated to the glory of God. There is a difference between knowing the tune and the timing of a piece of music and singing that song as the testimony of your personal experience with Jesus Christ. If God has given you the ability to sing, you should be a part of the church choir, a choral group, or a worship team dedicated to singing the praises of our Lord.

VI. You can give your testimony in a personal conversation.

This type of personal testimony can be most effective. In this type of testimony you can exercise more freedom discussing your own experience with God and helping the other individual with his or her problems, questions, and personal needs.

VII. You can give your testimony in a comment along the way.

Sometimes just a word or phrase or an observation growing out of your own experience with God will be much more powerful than a sermon proclaimed from the pulpit.

VIII. You can give your testimony by taking a position on some public moral issue.

Not all laws are good. Not all conditions that prevail in the community are wholesome. Not all things proposed will build the community or the country into a better place in which to live. Christians are supposed to be the salt of the earth that preserves from decay. There comes a time when Christians should stand up and be counted for against the forces of evil and for the forces of good.

IX. You can give your testimony in a telephone conversation.

Have you ever used the telephone to encourage someone? To strengthen someone? To comfort someone? To invite someone to your Bible study class or to your church worship service?

X. You can give your testimony in a letter, birthday card, or Christmas card.

To use the mail as a medium for communicating your concern and your desire to see others come to know God's grace and mercy can be most helpful.

XI. You can give your testimony in the investments you make or in the investments you refuse to make.

There are some things in which Christians should not be involved. Christians should be very careful about the investments they make and the businesses they support.

XII. You can give your testimony in the clothes or emblems you wear.

Most service clubs have an identification pin by which a member proclaims his or her affiliation. These usually are worn with a sense of honor and joy. Some have chosen to wear a cross on a chain around their neck. Others wear some kind of a religious symbol on the lapel of their coat. Christian businessmen sometimes have a Bible on their desk or on a shelf in their office as a silent but bold witness to the fact that they belong to Jesus Christ and want to do his will.

Conclusion

The time for giving your witness is at any time and at all times when there is a need—in your home or on the job, in times of joy and happiness, trouble and disappointment, and grief and sorrow. There is no limit to either the form or the manner in which you may give your testimony for Jesus Christ.

SUNDAY MORNING, APRIL 23

Title: The Risen Christ Breaks the Blues

Text: "And they said one to another, Did not our heart burn within us, while he talked with us by the way, and while he opened to us the scriptures?" (**Luke 24:32**).

Scripture Reading: Luke 24:13–35

Hymns: "Because He Lives," Gaither
              "Rejoice, All Ye People," Bergen
              "Since Jesus Came into My Heart," McDaniel

Offertory Prayer: Eternal Father, we acknowledge your presence with us this morning. Because of Christ's resurrection from the grave, we praise your name. Knowing that Jesus is alive and with us prompts us to bow before you in worship. We thank you that the risen Christ can meet our various needs this day. As we bring our tithes and offerings, we earnestly ask that they will extend the gospel message. We pray in the name of the living Lord. Amen.

Introduction

Depression is one of the world's most prominent illnesses. Thousands in the United States are hospitalized annually with depression, and even more go untreated. Most people suffer at some time with some form of depression, ranging from a minor case of the blues to a severe case of psychosis.

Two of Jesus' disciples had a case of the blues. They had followed Jesus thinking that he was the Messiah promised in the Old Testament. But the crucifixion in Jerusalem shattered their idea of the Messiah. They traveled from Jerusalem to Emmaus, and as they traveled they vented their disappointments. Their countenance was extremely sad. During the course of their travel, the risen Christ joined them, but they did not recognize him. In a post-resurrection appearance, Jesus ministered to the mood of these disciples.

I. Instruction from the Scripture.

Jesus dealt with the disciples' depression by explaining the Scriptures. "And beginning at Moses and all the prophets, he expounded unto them in all the scriptures the things concerning himself (Luke 24:27). A clue to overcoming the blues is learning what God says in his Word.

The disciples failed to know the Scriptures. An explanation of the events was readily accessible to them in the Old Testament, but their personal prejudices prevented them from understanding God's Word. Often our despair of life comes from a failure to understand and apply the Scriptures.

Jesus explained the Scriptures to these two sad disciples. He related Old Testament passages to himself, showing them that he is the theme of Scripture, that the Old Testament portrays and anticipates the Messiah. Finding Jesus in the Scriptures is the secret to the Bible's meaning. Through reading the Bible, we encounter the living Christ. He causes life to make sense. And he can dispel the blues if we trust his Word.

II. Intimacy with Christ.

Upon closer examination of Jesus' appearance to the two disciples on the road to Emmaus, we learn another clue about overcoming the blues. Their despondency did not improve as long as they majored on the problem of reconciling the crucifixion with their expectations of the Christ. But as the disciples walked and talked, Jesus joined them and contributed to the conversation. His presence changed their mood. Once they asked the Lord to abide with them, he broke their despondency by having intimate fellowship with them.

Deep despondency can result when we major on the negative part of life. Rehearsing disappointments over and over causes us continual disturbance. Morbid preoccupation with our problems and disappointments will do us no good. But if we spend time in conversation with Christ and focus on the truth of the Scriptures, he will lift us up.

III. Involvement for Christ.

Jesus dealt with the disciples' depression by getting them involved. Instead of turning away from Jerusalem as they had at first, they now returned and told the apostles that the Lord had risen from the dead. We can only guess why their first inclination was to go to the small village of Emmaus. Perhaps they were so disappointed that they were going to get involved in another vocation. But the risen Christ kept them involved for him.

A person's mood can be sad because of extreme concern over self. These disciples were sad because their hopes had been frustrated. Their vocation seemingly had been eliminated. They became extremely blue because their selfish desires had been thwarted. Modern disciples often get depressed because of a preoccupation with themselves.

Jesus challenged these men to be involved with his ministry by serving others. Psychologists attest that our minds are helped when we get beyond ourselves and help others. Getting involved with the needs of others helps to break the blues.

Conclusion

Perhaps you have some problems in your life today. Maybe you are frustrated because your dreams have been shattered. You can identify with the sadness of the two disciples traveling to Emmaus. The remedy to their problem was the risen Christ, and he is also the remedy for your problems. He can break the blues of modern disciples.

SUNDAY EVENING, APRIL 23

Title: Giving That Glorifies God

Text: "Remember the words of the Lord Jesus, how he said, It is more blessed to give than to receive" (**Acts 20:35**).

Scripture Reading: Matthew 6:1–4

Introduction

This message is the first from the second major division of the Sermon on the Mount. The opening section, Matthew 5:3–12, described the characteristics of Christians in eight Beatitudes and the influence and responsibilities of Christians under the figures of salt and light in Matthew 5:14–16. The first major division in Matthew 5:17–48 discussed the superiority of Christian righteousness to the righteousness of the scribes and Pharisees. This division in Matthew 6:1–18 discusses Christian motives for worship and service.

Verse 1 emphasizes the importance of right motives. This is illustrated in three areas of doing righteousness: (1) giving that glorifies God (Matt. 6:2–4); (2) prayer that glorifies God (Matt. 6:5–14); and (3) fasting that glorifies God (Matt. 6:16–18).

I. The importance of right motives.

Matthew 6:1 introduces the whole section. Jesus said, "Take heed that ye do not your alms before men, to be seen of them: otherwise ye have no reward of your Father which is in heaven." "Take heed" means hold your mind on this matter; consider it. It is a red light warning: "Be alert to the danger." Right motive is important. "Alms" is a poor translation. The New International Version translates it literally, "Be careful not to practice your righteousness in front of others to be seen by them." "To do righteousness" is a phrase of frequent occurrence in the Bible, as, for example, "Blessed are they that keep judgment, and he that doeth righteousness at all times" (Ps. 106:3). "If ye know that he is righteous, ye know that no man deceive you: he that doeth righteousness is righteous, even as he is righteous" (1 John 3:7). Doing righteousness seems to be illustrated in duties to others, such as giving and good deeds; duties to God, such as prayer and worship; and duties to self, such as fasting and self-denial.

Warning about wrong motives. "To do righteousness" before people for the purpose of gaining their approval rather than God's approval is wrong. There is no conflict between Matthew 5:16 and 6:1. The prohibition is not against doing one's righteousness before people but against the improper motive for doing so. If the motive is "to glorify your Father which is in heaven," then neither doing righteousness secretly nor before others is prohibited.

Right motive is everything.

No reward, praise, or approval can be expected from the heavenly Father when the motive is wrong. "God is a Spirit: and they that worship him must worship him in spirit and truth" (John 4:24).

People judge by deeds. "Ye shall know them by their fruits" (Matt. 7:16). "For man looketh on the outward appearance, but the LORD looketh on the heart" (1 Sam. 16:7). God judges righteous judgment because he knows the motive.

Outward acts may seem the same but be completely different when one knows the motives. Judas kissed Jesus, an act that normally would be considered a display of affection. His motive made it a tragic betrayal. Two men professed faith and were baptized. Outwardly their actions were similar. One did it from good motive. The other did it to influence a girl in the church. Their actions, which looked so similar, were as different as were the motives.

II. Right motive in deeds of mercy (Matt. 6:2–4).

"Therefore when thou doest thine alms" in verse 2 is a poor translation. The word translated "alms" means more than gifts of money. It includes deeds of mercy and kindness, services rendered to the aged, poor, and needy as that rendered by the good Samaritan to the victim of robbers in Jesus' parable. It would apply to the missions and benevolent program of your church.

"Be not . . . as the hypocrites" assumes that you are a Christian and not a hypocrite. If not a hypocrite, don't act like one. The word *hypocrite* means play actor, one who is not what his face says he is. The hypocrite sounds a trumpet before him in the synagogue and public places to call attention to his generosity. This is probably a figurative expression for ostentatious giving, much like our colloquial expression "He blows his own horn."

Doing their deeds of righteousness for the purpose of being seen by others resulted in their not being seen with approval by God. "They have their reward." They did their deeds for praise of men, and they received praise of men. "They have their reward" is literally "paid in full." They can write "paid in full" on that deed, for praise of men is all they will receive.

The Christian doing good deeds is to have an ignorant left hand. "Let not thy left hand know what thy right hand doeth," verse 3, is a figure of speech for lack of ostentation. The picture is of one giving alms with so little fanfare, as it were, that one hand does not know what the other is doing. Verse 4 is also to be interpreted figuratively in the light of Jesus' example and in the light of his admonition in Matthew 5:16, "Let your light shine before others, that they may see your good deeds and glorify your Father in heaven" (NIV).

The heavenly Father who sees what is done in secret will recompense according to the motive. "Openly" in verse 4 is a gloss and not a part of the true text.

Conclusion

Giving glorifies God. Only those whose hearts are right with God can give gifts that are wholly pleasing to him. We cannot give God anything until we first give ourselves. The Macedonians of whom Paul wrote to Corinth set a good example. "And this [giving liberally] they did, not as we hoped, but first gave their own selves to the Lord" (2 Cor. 8:5).

The right motive for giving of self or of substance is to glorify God rather than to glorify oneself. The purpose is to get God's approval rather than human approval. The secondary motive for doing good to others is one that gives glory to God and meets his approval: "Inasmuch as ye have done it unto one of the least of these my brethren, ye have done it unto me" (Matt. 25:40).

The church program should be such that Christians can serve with their time and money in the full confidence that God will be glorified by the salvation of souls, by the growth of Christians, and by support of missions and benevolences. The church plan of giving should not appeal to wrong motives. This story illustrates: All of the employees of a company had pledged to the United Fund except one. The boss was very eager to have 100 percent participation. He was irate when he heard that an employee was not planning to give. He called the employee into his office and said, "Give or you're fired." The employee replied, "Yes, sir, I'll give. No one explained it to me like that before."

The church has no such leverage as this. It would be unworthy for the church to use such if it had it. We are to serve and give for God's glory and not for the glory of self or for the glory of others. If we are sure of God's approval, we deserve no censure from church, pastor, or peers.

WEDNESDAY EVENING, APRIL 26

Title: The Motive for Personal Witnessing

Text: "Now those who were scattered went about preaching the word" **(Acts 8:4 RSV).**

Scripture Reading: Acts 8:4–8

Introduction

Jesus had much to say about motives. A motive is that which moves one toward some gratification, physically, socially, mentally, or spiritually. Motives are inward forces that impel life upward or downward. In the Sermon on the Mount, Jesus spoke of the motives behind the acts of giving, praying, and fasting (Matt. 6:1–18). He warned his disciples against the peril of being motivated to religious acts out of a desire for applause. Present-day followers of Jesus Christ need to give careful attention to their motivation for worship and service. We must be careful lest we let the motive of self-importance, self-gratification, or self-interest be primary.

Christ followers must be constantly on guard lest their kingdom activity be prompted by a disguised selfishness. Is it possible that some of our visitation programs, efforts to increase enrollments, and attendance campaigns are motivated by a desire to build up our church so that we can have the satisfaction of being successful? Many unbelievers get the impression that our efforts in their direction are attempts to exploit rather than to bring God's blessings into their lives. A worthy motivation is of supreme importance if we are to become consistently effective witnesses to the saving power of the gospel.

When we study the New Testament, we cannot help but discover that even the apostles witnessed for mixed motives. Their motives were not always the highest and the purest.

I. The devastating shock of persecution moved the disciples to depart from Jerusalem and to enter other areas with the good news of God's love (Acts 8:4).

We would like to think that Jesus' early followers were so overwhelmed with the love of God and with the love of lost people that they rushed out to the four corners of the earth giving their Christian testimony. Such was not the case. Until persecution caused them to flee, they were a satisfied, nationalistic, prejudiced group of Jewish followers of Christ who indicated no great concern for responding to the claims of the Great Commission. Later their motives for witnessing were lifted to a higher level.

II. The pure joy of being a bearer of good news about Christ moved the early church to witness.

Personal gratification in seeing someone else come to know Christ is one of the motives that should move us to share our testimony and to tell others what God has done for us in Jesus Christ. This is not an unworthy motive.

III. Recognizing and responding to the authority of the crucified and risen Lord should move us to witness (Matt. 28:18–20).

The Christ who died for us has been given the position of highest authority in the economy of God. To him has been given the right and the authority to command our person and our resources for redemptive activity. It is his will that his disciples literally permeate every area of human activity with the good news of God's grace and mercy revealed in his sacrificial death and his triumphant resurrection from the dead. The real motive for witnessing is the presence of Jesus Christ within the heart of believers.

IV. The gift of the Holy Spirit as an abiding presence moved the disciples and should move us to give our Christian testimony.

Following Pentecost the early disciples discovered that the divine presence of which they had become aware while their Master was with them in the flesh had come back to them in the Spirit. The Holy Spirit had come on them to equip them to be spokespersons for the Lord (Acts 2:17–18). As the prophets had been speakers for God, now all believers were equipped by the Spirit to speak of God's wonderful works.

V. A deep conviction that all people apart and away from Christ were lost from God and did not know the way home moved the early disciples to witness (Acts 4:12).

People are sinners, and because they are spiritually dead until they believe on Jesus as Savior and Lord, they walk in darkness. People are lonely and lost and do not know the way home until they are introduced to Christ.

The early disciples believed that Jesus Christ came seeking lost humanity.

They were overwhelmed with the compassion of the divine heart for people in their helpless condition. They believed that by giving their testimony of God's grace and love in Jesus Christ, the Holy Spirit would be able to bring conviction and conversion to the hearts of those who did not know God.

Conclusion

What is your motive for giving your testimony? Will you give your testimony because of love for God and gratitude in your heart? Will you give your testimony because of a personal response to the lordship of Jesus Christ? Will you give your testimony because of an inward impulse of the Holy Spirit? Will you give your Christian testimony because of the desperate need of others for that which you have to offer them? Whatever your motive, be sure to speak a good word for Jesus Christ this week.

SUNDAY MORNING, APRIL 30

Title: The Difference a Day Makes

Text: "For I delivered unto you first of all that which I also received, how that Christ died for our sins according to the scriptures; and that he was buried, and that he rose again the third day according to the scriptures" **(1 Cor. 15:3–4)**.

Scripture Reading: 1 Corinthians 15:1–22

Hymns: "Christ the Lord Is Risen," Wesley
"The First Lord's Day," McElrath
"This Joyful Eastertide," Green

Offertory Prayer: Our Father, we have come into this place to worship you. We acknowledge that you are a God worthy of worship. We give thanks that you have granted us the privilege of praising you. We give thanks that you have given us the opportunity to share in Christ's ministry. We bring our tithes and offerings that others may share the joy we possess. May we continue to look beyond ourselves to the people who need the gospel of Christ. In the spirit of humility we give joyfully and generously. We pray in Jesus' name. Amen.

Introduction

Many significant days have occurred in the history of humanity. Just to think about the important days in American history causes us to realize the difference that one day can make. On July 4, 1776, the course of American history was changed when thirteen colonies declared their independence from British rule. On April 12, 1861, the internal disunity of America began with the firing on Fort Sumter. On December 7, 1941, Japanese planes bombed Pearl Harbor, marking a decisive day in international affairs. On July 20, 1969, another significant day was recorded when an American walked on the moon. And then on September 11, 2001, terrorists flew planes into the World Trade Towers in New York City and into the Pentagon in Washington, DC, killing thousands and sparking a "war on terror." These days as well as numerous other days have made a difference.

Many significant days occurred in Jesus' life as well. It was a monumental day when Jesus came to Bethlehem as a baby. It was a significant day when Jesus was baptized by John. The day Jesus set out for Jerusalem to die for sinful humanity was a meaningful day. The Friday of Jesus' crucifixion has been a day analyzed and discussed through the years. It was a day that uniquely affected Christianity.

Paul and various other New Testament writers carefully record the account of Jesus' resurrection day. "He rose again the third day" (1 Cor. 15:4). That third day made a difference for all of humankind for all of eternity. It changed the bad news of Jesus' crucifixion to the good news of deliverance. Using the ideas of Paul, let us notice the distinct differences the day of resurrection makes.

I. A historical reality.

The third day authenticated the resurrection of Jesus Christ as a historical event. This day removed the resurrection from the realm of philosophical speculation and put it in the realm of historical fact. The third day is celebrated every Sunday as a reality.

Paul speculated on the possibility that Christ did not rise: "If Christ be not risen." If this day had not happened, there would be no gospel story. The gospel simply stated is that "Christ died for our sins, was buried, and rose again the third day." The first two facts—namely, Jesus' death and burial—do not complete the story. His resurrection on the third day completes the story.

If Christ had not risen, there would be nothing to our faith. Christianity would be futile and ineffectual. But Jesus did rise! Christianity is trustworthy and reliable. The Bible is true. The third day is a historical reality. "Now is Christ risen from the dead" (1 Cor. 15:20).

Jesus' resurrection on the third day makes a difference. It is a recorded historical fact that no other religion can claim. The annual celebration of Easter is not the only way Christians experience Christ's resurrection. Rather, they experience Christ's living presence every moment of every day. He promises always to be with his people, guiding them and keeping them in his care until they leave this earth to join him in resurrected bodies in heaven.

II. A theological necessity.

The third day, the day of Jesus' resurrection, makes a tremendous difference in humanity's redemption. For a person to have full assurance of salvation, the resurrection of Jesus is a necessity. "If Christ be not raised, your faith is vain; ye are yet in your sins" (1 Cor. 15:17). When Jesus rose from the grave, an entirely new perspective was put on the crucifixion.

Paul supposed that if Christ had not risen, we would still be in our sins. This would mean that Jesus died but was powerless to defeat the final enemy of humankind, death. If Christ would have remained in a Palestinian tomb, humankind would not have salvation from the ultimate penalty of sin.

Jesus did rise from the grave, which guarantees to the world that salvation is complete. The life and ministry of Jesus comprised one phase of Jesus' work for sinful humanity. His death involved another phase. But his resurrection was essential for the other phases to have their full meaning.

If the decayed body of Jesus still lies in a Palestinian tomb, we should forget salvation and disregard the Bible, for we have no Good News. But we know that Jesus did rise from the dead on the third day, and we have assurance of the forgiveness of sin. Jesus triumphed over every foe on that day as a testimony to his lordship. The third day was a theological necessity in the gospel story.

III. An eschatological certainty.

The third day assures every believer that there will be an eternity with the Lord. The resurrection of Jesus makes the difference between dismal despair about life beyond the grave and glorious hope. Because Jesus rose from the dead, Christians know they will be raised from the dead and will possess resurrected bodies. Paul said, "And if Christ be not raised, your faith is vain; ye are yet in your sins. They also which are fallen asleep in Christ are perished" (1 Cor. 15:17–18). This is a dismal picture. Without Jesus' resurrection, Christians would have no hope for a future life. If they have hope only in this life, they are miserable people.

Eugene O'Neill portrayed the truth of Christ's victory over death in the play *Lazarus Laughed.* He created a story of how Lazarus, the brother of Mary and Martha, left Bethany and journeyed to Greece. In Athens, Lazarus met Gaius Caligula, who had been chosen by the emperor as his successor. Caligula was a tyrannical emperor. On one occasion he reprimanded Lazarus and threatened to kill him for teaching people to laugh about death. Lazarus looked into his face and answered, "Death is dead, Caligula. Death is dead." When Jesus rose from the dead, he defeated death.

Conclusion

"He rose again the third day." That day made the difference. The Christ who rose wants to come into your life today. This day can be the beginning of many glorious days in your life. Allow the risen Christ to enter your life today.

SUNDAY EVENING, APRIL 30

Title: When You Pray Say, "Our Father"

Text: "After this manner therefore pray ye: Our Father which art in heaven . . ." **(Matt. 6:9)**.

Scripture Reading: Matthew 6:5–15

Introduction

The petitions of the "model prayer" reveal what Jesus considered to be people's most vital needs. What a privilege we have to learn from Jesus how to pray.

Jesus was a person who prayed. At his baptism, while he was "praying, the heaven was opened, and the Holy Ghost descended in a bodily shape like a dove upon him, and a voice came from heaven, which said, Thou art my beloved Son; in thee I am well pleased" (Luke 3:21–22). "He went out into a mountain to pray, and continued all night in prayer to God" (Luke 6:12) on the night before he chose his twelve disciples. After the feeding of the five thousand, the multitude wanted to make him king. "And when he had sent the multitudes away, he went up into a mountain apart to pray" (Matt. 14:22).

At the transfiguration, "as he prayed, the fashion of his countenance was altered, and his raiment was white and glistening" (Luke 9:29). He thanked God for daily bread (see Luke 24:30), for hearing and answering prayers (see John 11:41–42), for the simplicity of the gospel (see Matt. 11:25), and for the privilege of shedding his blood on the cross for humankind's sins (see Matt. 26:26–28). In the anguish of Gethsemane, he "fell on his face, and prayed, saying, O my Father, if it be possible, let this cup pass from me: nevertheless not as I will, but as thou wilt" (Matt. 26:39).

Calvary was a series of prayers beginning with, "Father, forgive them; for they know not what they do" (Luke 23:34) and concluding with, "Father, into thy hands I commend my spirit" (Luke 23:46). We are not surprised then that "as he was praying in a certain place, when he ceased, one of his disciples said unto him, Lord, teach us to pray, as John also taught his disciples" (Luke 11:1). On this occasion Jesus repeated the prayer that he had given earlier in the Sermon on the Mount with some added instruction. The two accounts are not verbally the same, which should warn us that the "model prayer" was not given as a liturgy.

Recognizing our own poverty in prayer, we join the disciples in their request, "Lord, teach us to pray."

I. Jesus warns of dangers in the approach to prayer.

The hypocrisy of the Pharisees (Matt. 6:5–6). The emphasis of this division of the Sermon on the Mount, Matthew 6:1–18, is on doing one's righteousness for God's approval rather than for human approval. The Pharisees often managed to be in the most prominent places at the hour of prayer so that their piety might be clear to all. They received praise of men but could write "paid in full" on their prayers, for they did not receive God's approval. Prayer for show is no prayer at all. People who think they can fool God are deluded. Jesus never asks anyone to be insincere. Nor should we as his followers desire for anyone to pray, to be baptized, to join the church, nor do anything that is not from the heart.

Inasmuch as Jesus prayed before his disciples and encouraged them to do so, it is clear that verse 6 should not be interpreted so literally as forbidding public prayer. We can imagine a person saying, "Now while I go to my closet for prayer, you be very quiet so as not to disturb me." We would literally apply the teaching but would miss the intent of Jesus that prayer is personal communication with the heavenly Father.

Dr. Frank Leavell, a student leader among Southern Baptists years ago, suggested a splendid acrostic on Matthew 6:6. Let P stand for:

Period of prayer—"But thou when thou prayest"
Place of prayer—"enter into thy closet"
Privacy of prayer—"and when thou hast shut thy door"
Personal in prayer—"pray to thy Father which is in secret"
Promise of prayer—"and thy Father which seeth in secret shall
    reward thee."

The ignorance of the heathen (Matt. 6:7–8). Hoping to win their god's favor, the prophets of Baal with whom Elijah faced off on Mount Carmel "cried aloud, and cut themselves after their manner with knives and lancets, till the blood gushed out upon them" (1 Kings 18:28). This is an example of the heathens' ignorance. Our God is not to be wearied by ceaseless beseeching, convinced by argument, influenced by threats, or bribed by gifts or promises.

Since God is "our heavenly Father," he does not need to be informed. He knows "what things ye have need of before ye ask him." Prayer is primarily an expression of fellowship between God and his child. Prayer is much like the relationship of husband and wife where love abides. They have understanding. Words may be helpful, but they are not always essential. The desire of your soul is your prayer, whether expressed or not. You are to be in the attitude of prayer always. At times it will overflow in words of adoration, confession, thanksgiving, petition, and intercession. Is this not what Paul meant when he admonished, "Pray without ceasing" (1 Thess. 5:17)?

II. The right approach to prayer.

"After this manner therefore pray ye: Our Father which art in heaven . . ." (Matt. 6:9).

To approach God as Father gives meaning to worship.

149

Since God is our Father, we can approach him boldly, knowing that he wants to give us his best (see Matt. 7:7–11).

"Who art in heaven" indicates that God is a spiritual person. Jesus means here just what he meant in John 4:21–24. One does not have to be on Mount Gerizim or Mount Zion to worship God. The Russian cosmonauts reported that they did not see God in space. Some cynics laugh at the idea that God is "out there." But God is spirit. He is not seen by physical eyes; he is both transcendent and immanent. He is both "out there" and "right here." Sincere worshipers can pray to him from any place.

"Our Father" gives new meaning to brotherhood. One's relationship to God is personal but not exclusive. We are brothers and sisters to all the sons and daughters of God.

"Our Father" gives meaning to the concept of duty. The slave serves out of fear. The servant serves for wages. The son serves because of love. "For the love of Christ constraineth us" (2 Cor. 5:14). For Christians, what we ought to do becomes what we want to do. The will of a righteous, loving heavenly Father is the desire of his children.

"Our Father" gives new understanding of the trials of life. God the Father knows what we are; he also knows what we ought to be. In love he seeks to shape us. The pain of chastening may be necessary. "Whom the Lord loveth he chasteneth." Read thoughtfully Hebrews 12:1–13.

"Our Father" brings a new appreciation of heaven. Heaven is more than streets of gold and gates of pearl. Heaven is to be with the Father and the heavenly family. Heaven will be home (see John 14:1–3).

Conclusion

Because God is a loving Father, there is hope for everyone. "The Lord is not slack concerning his promise, as some men count slackness; but is longsuffering to us-ward, not willing that any should perish, but that all should come to repentance" (2 Peter 3:9). Like the loving father in Jesus' famous parable (Luke 15:11–24), who yearned for his wayward son and was more forgiving than the son expected, so the heavenly Father yearns for every one of us to repent and receive forgiveness and adoption into his family. The best we can imagine will fall far short of his fatherly plans for us.

MAY

- ### Sunday Mornings

    "The Living Christ and Our Home Life" is the theme for Sunday mornings this month. The foundations and the superstructures of home life need to be strengthened.

- ### Sunday Evenings

    Continue with expository messages from Jesus' Sermon on the Mount.

- ### Wednesday Evenings

    "Great Women of the Bible" is the theme for Wednesday evenings this month.

WEDNESDAY EVENING, MAY 3

Title: The Woman Who Made Up Her Mind

Text: "When she saw that she was stedfastly minded to go with her, then she left speaking unto her" (**Ruth 1:18**).

Scripture Reading: Ruth 1

Introduction

A large church in New England polled the members to see who they believed were the ten greatest women in the Bible. To the pastor's surprise, Ruth was first and Eve was last. With Mary, Sarah, Hannah, Deborah, and many other great women, he did not expect Ruth to place first.

Why was she rated at the top? Was it because she was the great-grandmother of David and the ancestress of our Lord? Was it because of her unusual loyalty to her mother-in-law, Naomi? Was it her positive choice of God and his people? No single factor merits her this position, but when these factors are added together, Ruth stands out as a truly great and godly woman.

The book of Ruth is a choice gem in the library of inspired books. We cannot find in it a single instance of cruelty or wickedness. No one is the victim of vengeance and violence. The book is filled with examples of virtue, courage, faith, industry, love, sorrow, and loyalty.

The book of Ruth is the story of two widows. It tells of famine, prosperity, and separation in the strange land of Moab. It tells of homesickness and Naomi's decision to return to her native land of Israel.

This book is loved because it records the most beautiful confession of human love in all literature. It also tells of a beautiful commitment to God by a pagan woman. The book has a happy ending as Ruth is welcomed into the heritage of Israel and the genealogy of Jesus.

I. God has a plan for each life.

On every page of the book of Ruth we see the providence of God. What if Elimelech and Naomi had not gone to Moab? What if the father and sons had not died? What if Naomi had not returned to Bethlehem? What if Ruth had turned back from Naomi, as Orpah did? What if Ruth had not gleaned in Boaz's field? We see God's hand in every development. If Ruth had not been submissive to God, she would have lived and died in a land where people did not serve Jehovah. When we place ourselves in God's hands, he will bring his plan to fruition in our lives. Young women today would do well to emulate Ruth's example.

II. The power of human choice.

We find a contrast between Orpah's decision and Ruth's decision. Let us not be too hard on Orpah. She had been cradled in a pagan home. Her past was against her leaving her native land. Her teaching was against her rejecting her national gods. Even her gracious mother-in-law, Naomi, urged her to turn back. She came to the brink of decision and could not bring herself to break with the world she knew. Her heart was still in Moab. She turned her back on Ruth and Naomi and cast her lot and destiny forever with the Moabites.

Ruth made the decision to cast her lot with Naomi and to commit herself to Naomi's God. She did not look back. Her decision was final and irrevocable. What a tribute Ruth's decision was to Naomi. It had been her life and love for God that had commended God to Ruth. Does our life draw people to our Lord? Do we make our faith attractive and contagious to others?

Conclusion

As in the life of Ruth, the time of decision comes to each of us. Choosing the right is never easy. The world is slow to let us go. But the happy ending of the book of Ruth can come true in our lives also if we turn our backs on the old country and commit ourselves to Christ with conviction and devotion.

SUNDAY MORNING, MAY 7

Title: The Risen Christ Makes Us Happy

Text: "And when he had so said, he shewed unto them his hands and his side. Then were the disciples glad, when they saw the Lord" **(John 20:20)**.

Scripture Reading: John 20:19–29

Hymns: "Great Redeemer, We Adore Thee," Harris
"Jesus Lives and Jesus Leads," Hood
"Crown Him with Many Crowns," Bridges

Offertory Prayer: Our heavenly Father, help us to worship you in spirit and in truth this day. Keep our minds concentrated on the many bountiful blessings of life that we might not complain about our circumstances. Help us to remember how you endured hardships and discomforts, perils and dangers, ultimately giving your life that every person who believes in you may have abundant life.

We ask today that you will lead us as we give our money. We acknowledge that you have given us health and strength to earn these material goods. With our tithes we acknowledge that everything we have belongs to you. We adore your name and earnestly desire that through the use of this offering people all over the world will learn of you. We pray this in the name of him who is Lord of all, Jesus Christ. Amen.

Introduction

In the third year of Jesus' ministry, there came a fateful Friday. For three years Jesus ministered to humankind, and during this time the Jewish leaders sought to put him to death. They finally accomplished their intentions by using unjust accusations. The Jews conspired with the Roman authorities to have Jesus crucified.

After Jesus' death, few people were happy. Pilate, the Roman governor, suffered miserable flashbacks. He knew that he had allowed an innocent man to be crucified. Roman soldiers knew before breath had left Jesus' body that someone more than a man died that Friday. Perhaps Herod tried to erase the memory of Jesus through a night of carousing, but Jesus lingered on his conscience to make him miserable. Each member of the Sanhedrin undoubtedly suffered from guilt. Tired and irritable travelers returned to their homes after the close of the Passover festival. But probably the saddest people in Jerusalem were Jesus' disciples. Their Messiah had died on a cross.

On Sunday evening following that Friday, the risen Christ came to these dejected, disillusioned, and miserable followers. After the visit, "then were the disciples glad, when they saw the Lord" (John 20:20). They were glad because the same Jesus who died now visited with them. Their dearest Friend had returned from the grave.

The sad disciples' experience with the risen Lord could mean much to contemporary followers of Jesus. Often the circumstances of life make us unhappy, but when we come into Christ's presence, we can rejoice, for in his presence there is fullness of joy. What really made the difference with the first-century disciples was not an announcement of the resurrection but the appearance of Jesus. Let us learn some ways that Jesus can make modern disciples happy.

I. The risen Lord deals with our fears.

The circumstances of life bring fear. The disciples assembled in an upper room after Jesus' crucifixion. They feared for their future. Various happenings in life cause Christians to be afraid, and fear takes many forms. We fear losing our job, getting sick, being criticized, growing old, facing death, as well as numerous others things.

Fear brings negative consequences. The disciples could not do what Christ wanted them to do with their raging fear, for fear filled them with negative thoughts and robbed them of maximum efficiency. Fear leads to greater fear. It weakens us and puts us in a position that makes us susceptible to the very thing we fear. But the risen Christ can deal with our fears. To a panic-stricken group, Jesus said, "Peace be unto you" (John 20:19). Jesus provides courage to face fear.

II. The risen Lord develops our faith.

Even though these men had lived intimately with Jesus for three years, their faith was not yet perfect. Jesus had taught them on numerous occasions about his resurrection, but they did not believe. Likewise, our faith is immature. We need to be continuously developing the character of the Master. Modern disciples often fail to claim Jesus' promises. Such neglect robs us of growth experiences in the Lord. Our faith grows as we read the Word and hide God's promises in our hearts. To develop our faith, we must encounter the risen Lord daily.

III. The risen Lord discloses the future.

Many people live in despair over the future. Perhaps the disciples in the upper room talked despairingly of what the future would bring and surrendered to the finality of physical death. Several years ago when archaeologists excavated Roman cemeteries, they noticed that almost all grave markers had seven letters carved on them—NFF NS NC. These are the first letters of the words in four brief sentences familiar to the Roman world—Non fui. Fui. Non sum. Non curo—which means, "I was not. I was. I am not. I do not care." Something akin to their feeling may have filled the disciples.

The risen Lord disclosed a glorious future by showing himself alive. He had been crushed to death, but now he stood before the disciples with nail-pierced hands and feet. He arose the Victor from the "dark domain" of death. Because he lives, every one of his followers will live also.

Conclusion

Have you found joy amid the troubled conditions of today's world? You cannot find happiness apart from the risen Lord. Seek Jesus' presence today and let him bring happiness to your life. Christ is here! He waits for your openness. As he did for the disciples on that Sunday evening, he can dispel your fears, develop your faith, and disclose a glorious, victorious future after death.

SUNDAY EVENING, MAY 7

Title: Hallowed Be Thy Name

Text: "Hallowed be thy name" (**Matt. 6:9**).

Scripture Reading: John 12:20–32

Introduction

The title of tonight's sermon is the first petition in the model prayer that Jesus, the Master of prayer, gave to his disciples. It is popularly called the Lord's Prayer. It is not the Lord's prayer in the sense that he would pray it. Some of the petitions in this prayer, as, for example, the petition for forgiveness, would not be appropriate for our Lord, for he was without sin. It is the Lord's prayer in the sense that he has given to his disciples a marvelously comprehensive, concise model for their praying.

Before giving the model of correct practice, Jesus warned of the hypocrisy of those who pray to be seen of men and of the error of the heathen who think they will be heard for their much speaking. "Be not ye therefore like unto them: for your Father knoweth what things ye have need of, before ye ask him. After this manner therefore pray ye: Our Father which art in heaven, hallowed be thy name" (Matt. 6:8–9). The fatherly nature of God is ground for confidence so that we come to him with boldness. Since he is the heavenly Father, we come with reverence. He is not only my heavenly Father, but the heavenly Father of all who love him in sincerity so that we address him as "Our Father" rather than "My Father." Especially when we come to pray are we conscious that we are brothers to those of whom God is Father.

I. The first petition is "Hallowed be thy name."

The true prayer starts here. It is a petition not for self nor for others but for God to be glorified. "Let thy name be hallowed."

What is the meaning of this petition?

The meaning of "name." Among ancient people a name was not a mere appellation but was expressive of the character of the person so named. When one's character changed, that person often was given a new name, as, for example, Abram, "father," became Abraham, "father of people"; and Jacob, "supplanter," became Israel, "prince of God."

The name Jehovah as revealed in Exodus 3:13–15 characterizes God as the great, eternal, covenant-keeping God, the great "I AM." It means "I am that I am" or "I will be that I will be." It names God as the one who is the same yesterday, today, and forever.

The name stands for the person. When we sign a check, our name stands for our person, so to pray in the name of Jesus is to pray a prayer to which he could sign his name. When in 3 John 7 we read of the missionaries that "for his name's sake . . . went forth, taking nothing of the Gentiles," it is the same as saying, "for Jesus' sake," for the name stands for the person.

In Philippians 2:9–11 Paul wrote of Jesus, "Wherefore God also hath highly exalted him, and given him a name which is above every name: that at the name of Jesus every knee should bow, of things in heaven, and things in earth, and things under the earth; and that every tongue should confess that Jesus Christ is Lord, to the glory of God the Father." The name Jesus expresses our Lord's true character as Savior. When we pray, "Hallowed be thy name," we are praying that God himself shall be hallowed.

The meaning of *hallowed*. It is the word often translated "sanctified," which means "set apart," "dedicated," "holy." God's name—that is, his true character, his person—is to be hallowed—that is, set apart, reverenced—above all others. What can we do to make God any more or less holy than he by nature already is and always will be? The import of the prayer is that the name of God will be held holy by all persons.

How do persons hallow God's name?

Negatively it means, "Thou shalt not take the name of the LORD thy God in vain" (Ex. 20:7).

The primary reference is not to swear to a falsehood and use the name of God to bolster a false oath.

Hallowing God's name would also forbid the evil, senseless sin of profanity—a sin that is most foolish and useless. One may as well say, "I can't quit murder, or adultery, or theft," as to say, "I can't quit profanity."

When a man cursed in the presence of Woodrow Wilson's father, he asked the elder Wilson's apology when he heard that he was a minister. Mr. Wilson replied, "Sir, it is not to me but to God you owe your apology."

God's name is dishonored by vain worship. Through the prophet Malachi, he spoke to the priests: "A son honoureth his father, and a servant his master: if then I be a father, where is mine honour? and if I be a master, where is my fear? saith the LORD of hosts unto you, O priests, that despise my name. And ye say, Wherein have we despised thy name? Ye offer polluted bread upon mine altar; and ye say, Wherein have we polluted thee? In that ye say, The table of the LORD is contemptible. And if ye offer the blind for sacrifice, is it not evil? and if ye offer the lame and sick, is it not evil? offer it now unto thy governor; will he be pleased with thee, or accept thy person? saith the LORD of hosts" (Mal. 1:6–8). God's name is dishonored when we give him less than the best.

Lip worship without heart content dishonors God. Later in this sermon, Jesus solemnly warns some who called him Lord and preached in his name yet had no relationship with him. "Not every one that saith unto me, Lord, Lord, shall enter into the kingdom of heaven; but he that doeth the will of my Father which is in heaven. Many will say to me in that day, Lord, Lord, have we not prophesied in thy name? and in thy name have cast out devils? and in thy name done many wonderful works? And then will I profess unto them, I never knew you: depart from me, ye that work iniquity" (Matt. 7:21–23).

Positively, "Hallowed be thy name" is a great missionary petition that God may have his rightful place, the first and highest place, in the hearts of all the peoples of the earth. It is to pray with the psalmist, "Oh that men would praise the LORD for his goodness, and for his wonderful works to the children of men" (Ps. 107:8). The missionary enterprise is, "To the praise of the glory of his grace, wherein he hath made us accepted in the beloved" (Eph. 1:6).

II. Jesus prays this petition.

Jesus does not pray with us every petition of the model prayer, but this first petition is certainly one he does pray. His word is *glorify*. John 12:20–32 is a very significant portion of Scripture. The Greeks seeking Jesus had caused him to see them as the vanguard of that great group of all nations who would come to God by him. But Jesus must be lifted up on the cross if sinners are to be saved. The temptation to avoid the cross was renewed. Hear Jesus: "Now is my soul troubled; and what shall I say? Father, save me from this hour?" (John 12:27). Would this be his prayer? No, rather, "but for this cause came I unto this hour. Father, glorify thy name" (John 12:27–28). Jesus prayed this knowing that the means of such glorification would be the cross.

Conclusion

It is no light matter to pray, "Hallowed be thy name." When we pray, "Hallowed be thy name," we are praying, "By life or by death, by sickness or by health, now and always, let your will be done. All that is false and dishonoring to God take away; all that honors God let me be and do."

Dare we pray this first petition of the model prayer? Can we qualify in this first filial act of sonship? Is our faith sufficient to let God be all and in all? O heavenly Father, help us now as we pray, "Hallowed be thy name."

WEDNESDAY EVENING, MAY 10

Title: A Transformed Enthusiast

Text: "Jesus answered and said unto her, Whosoever drinketh of this water shall thirst again: But whosoever drinketh of the water that I shall give him shall never thirst; but the water that I shall give him shall be in him a well of water springing up into everlasting life" **(John 4:13–14)**.

Scripture Reading: John 4:1–30

Introduction

In John 3 and 4 we see a dramatic contrast in the persons Jesus confronted with the claims of God on their lives. Nicodemus was a respectable, influential religious leader. The woman at the well had a bad reputation. She was trapped in a sordid affair that was offensive both to God and society.

Jesus treated both of these persons with equal courtesy, patience, and kindness. He accepted the respectable and the disreputable as persons made in God's image. You, too, can accept a person without accepting that person's lifestyle.

I. Meeting Jesus at the well.

If ever there seemed to be a hopeless case for Jesus, this was the one. This woman was a Samaritan, a religious and social outcast to the Jews. She came to the well at noon, the hottest time of the day. Jesus spoke to her there even though a Jewish man and a Samaritan woman did not normally engage in conversation.

We can piece together something of her story. She probably was quite attractive in her youth. As was the custom of the day, she had married young. Perhaps she was more in love with love than with a person. The marriage ended on the rocks.

Before her second marriage, she hoped for better days, for she now knew the heartaches of a broken home. Her second marriage also ended in failure, making her a two-time loser.

Her third marriage did not have a chance. She tired of her husband quickly. It may be that she had an extramarital affair with the man who was to be her fourth husband.

Now marriage had become a habit and a matter of convenience and security. Love for her had turned to lust. Dreams and hopes had ended in disillusionment. After her fifth marriage, we hear her saying, "Why go through the formality of a ceremony anymore? It just makes me a liar to say, 'Until death do us part.' I shall take a man where I find him, live with him as long as I please, and move out when I choose."

II. Meeting the woman in her needs.

But Jesus saw more than this woman's sins. He saw more than what she was; he saw what she could become. He saw her needs, discerning her thirst for satisfaction and fulfillment in life. She had been exploited for the pleasure of others and was disgusted with the mess she had made of her life. She hated herself. She hated the women who looked down on her. Beneath her brazen, flippant exterior was a longing to be different.

In a skillful confrontation, Jesus revealed to the woman that it was the Water of Life that would satisfy her thirst for a better life. "I shall install within you a spring that is perennially fresh," he said. "Life will never be stagnant again. This water will be bubbling up in buoyant joy and excitement."

The woman tried to start an argument, but Jesus kept her on the main track. He was not interested in winning an argument; he was interested in winning the person.

The Samaritan woman became an enthusiast. She left her waterpot and rushed to the village to share her new faith. This reminds us of the disciples who left their boats and their nets and of Matthew who left his tax office to follow Christ. Most important of all, these people left their old lives, their old ways, their old attitudes, and their former loyalties. What have you left to follow Jesus?

When we drink of the water of the earth, we thirst again and again. People have drunk of the wells of power, fame, knowledge, riches, ambition, and sensual pleasure—always to thirst again. The world does not satisfy.

Conclusion

Jesus says to us as he said to the woman at the well, "Everyone that drinketh of this well shall thirst again. But whosoever drinketh of the water that I shall give him shall never thirst. But the water that I shall give him shall become in him a well of water springing up unto eternal life."

The woman responded, "Sir, give me this water." Would you pray that same prayer? And then, like this transformed, excited believer, God will help you share your faith with those who also thirst for him.

SUNDAY MORNING, MAY 14

Title: A Mother Who Prayed

Text: "And she . . . prayed unto the LORD . . . and she vowed a vow" **(1 Sam. 1:10–11).**

Scripture Reading: 1 Samuel 1:1–11

Hymns: "Faith of Our Mothers," Patten
"Did You Think to Pray?" Kidder
"Near to the Heart of God," McAfee

Offertory Prayer: Our Father, create within us the consciousness that in Christ we are members one of another. May we realize also that there are many who do not know the redeeming love of Christ and hence are not a part of his twice-born family. May the offering we bring this morning be used to bring people into a personal relationship with God through Jesus Christ his Son and our Savior. May the bringing of our gifts, however, never be a substitute for the giving of ourselves in dedicated service to you. Help us always to remember that our Lord said, "It is more blessed to give than to receive." Help us to give both ourselves and our money lovingly and generously. We pray in Jesus' name. Amen.

Introduction

A prominent American once declared that he did not know of a single institution working for the betterment of humankind that was not founded by a person who had a praying mother. This is a strong statement, perhaps slightly exaggerated, but there is certainly a relationship between the prayers of a mother and the spiritual life of her children. No greater calamity could befall a nation than for godly motherhood to vanish.

I. Hannah prayed.

The desire to bring children into the world and rear them is normal. Perhaps this longing is even greater for a woman. In ancient Israel the feeling was especially strong. The Hebrew male found his need for earthly immortality fulfilled in his offspring, especially his male children. For a woman to disappoint her husband by failing to bear children was virtually a disgrace. Hannah was fortunate, however, that her husband understood her plight and loved her in spite of her seeming inability to perform this function. Because of her husband's affections, Hannah was even more eager to please him by producing a child.

Although we do not have Scripture to prove the fact irrefutably, Hannah must have prayed many times before the prayer recorded in the account of her visit to the temple. Everything about this story and Hannah's subsequent actions seems to say that she was a godly woman who maintained intimate fellowship with the Lord.

II. Hannah prayed with persistence.

Too often our requests of God are shallow and lacking in deep fervor. Hannah's prayer was more than a Polly-want-a-cracker type of petition. The thing for which she was asking was of vital importance. She poured out her heart. In fact, the Bible says she "spake in her heart; only her lips moved," which indicates that she had strong feelings as she petitioned God for a child. The priest, seeing her utter sincerity, misinterpreted it as the stimulus of intoxication.

Throughout the New Testament, emphasis is placed on persistence in prayer. When Jesus said, "Ask, and it shall be given you; seek, and ye shall find; knock, and it shall be opened unto you" (Matt. 7:7), he used verb forms that indicate continuous action. A literal translation of the verse is, "Keep on asking and you will receive; keep on seeking and you will find; keep on knocking and it will be opened to you." Jacob, while wrestling with the Lord, held on and would not let go until he was promised a blessing. The history of Christianity is filled with devout men and women who refused to cease praying until they were certain of victory.

III. Hannah prayed though persecuted.

In that day God allowed men to have more than one wife. It was never a part of his original plan, but he permitted it because of their spiritual immaturity. This Scripture must never be taken as justification for polygamy today. In fact, some terrible lessons can be learned from Old Testament accounts of men who had more than one wife and families by two different women.

The other wife of Elkanah, Hannah's husband, mocked her so much that she caused great stress in Hannah's life. Yet Hannah refused to grow bitter. Instead, she developed a deep prayer life. This is always the best thing to do when we are persecuted. It is never easy to turn the other cheek, but great rewards come for those who learn that vengeance belongs to God.

Eli's accusation that Hannah was drunk should certainly be considered a form of persecution. Notice how tenderly Hannah answered him. She told him that she had poured out her soul before the Lord and pleaded with Eli not to count her as an unworthy woman. She explained that it was because of her great grief that she had prayed so insistently. So sweet was her spirit that Eli immediately believed her and sent her on her way in peace with a promise that he would join in prayer with her that God would grant her petition.

Again, we should remember that history is filled with martyrs who prayed even though mistreated. Stephen may have seen Jesus die, for he repeated similar words to Jesus' cry at his death. Both cried to God to forgive those who were their antagonists.

IV. Hannah prayed with a pledge.

There is need for caution at this point. To wring promises from a person when he or she has a serious, and even urgent, need may be a dangerous thing. One cannot bargain with God. If we need to make a decision concerning our spiritual life, we should do it regardless of whether God grants us the favor we wish. Promises made under pressure are seldom kept.

This was not that kind of promise. Hannah had no child. She promised the Lord that if he were to give her a child, she would dedicate that child to the Lord's service. This is different from the man who promises that if the Lord will grant him some desire he will begin to go to church, tithe his income, or quit "running around" with some woman whom he has no business being with in the first place. Hannah's pledge was one of dedication for the good of God's kingdom. This kind of pledge is worthy, and God takes delight in honoring it.

V. Hannah performed that which she promised.

Everything about the biblical account indicates that Hannah was a woman of integrity. She named her child Samuel, for which the Hebrew sounds like "heard by God," because she asked him of the Lord. After the child was born, she resolved that as soon as he was weaned, she would bring him to God's house and let him "abide there forever."

When Hannah brought Samuel to Eli, she identified herself, acknowledged her debt to God, and agreed to "lend him to the Lord" as long as he lived. Making a promise to the Lord is a serious thing. On one hand, if we obligate ourselves and then do not perform that which we promised, we build up feelings of guilt that will haunt us in the days to come. On the other hand, many testify that they vowed a vow, the Lord granted their request, and they faithfully did that which they said they would do. The psalmist raised the question, "What shall I render unto the LORD in exchange for all his benefits toward me" (Ps. 116:12). He then answered with a series of things he said he would do. One of those was, "I will pay my vows unto the LORD" (v. 14).

Conclusion

Some great lessons come to us from this story. For one thing, *we should never despair when we are discouraged.* God knows our plight and has sufficient resources to meet our need. Another truth is that *the continuous prayer of a godly person will not go unheeded.* A third truth is that *our prayers must be such that if they are answered, God's kingdom will be advanced.* No one has a right to pray for anything that will not, if granted, extend God's rule in the hearts of the people. A fourth lesson we learn from this story is that *noble people find joy in producing what they promise.* To do God's will is the highest achievement of one's life.

SUNDAY EVENING, MAY 14

Title: Thy Kingdom Come

Text: "Thy kingdom come" (**Matt. 6:10**).

Scripture Reading: Psalm 103:19; Isaiah 9:6; Luke 1:33; 17:20–21; John 18:36–37

Introduction

The second petition of Jesus' model prayer is the title of this message. The word *kingdom* was often on Jesus' lips. More than one hundred times the Gospels record his use of the word. Counting the total times used by Jesus and by others, the term "kingdom of heaven" is used 112 times; the term "kingdom of God" is used 32 times, and simply "kingdom" or "my kingdom" 10 times. The terms "kingdom of heaven" and "kingdom of God" are used so frequently in parallel passages in the Gospels that we believe the terms to be synonymous. The ancient Jews so reverenced the name of God that they would not pronounce it lest they should profane it. Matthew, who is writing for Jewish readers, usually uses the term "kingdom of heaven," while Luke, himself a Gentile writing for Gentile readers, has no such scruples and uses the term "kingdom of God." Sometimes today we hear devout people pray, "May heaven grant this petition" when they mean, "May God who is in heaven grant this petition."

I. The meaning of "thy kingdom."

The meaning of kingdom in this petition is not a nation of people or a political identity, but the reign or domain over which God rules. The term is used for God's providential reign over the universe, as when the psalmist exclaims, "His kingdom ruleth over all" (Ps. 103:19). Obviously, Jesus is not commanding us to pray for that, for God's providential rule already exists now and always will. He is God; he has not nor will he abdicate his rightful place on the throne of the universe.

The kingdom here referred to in the petition "Thy kingdom come" is the kingdom of which Christ is King. It is the kingdom foretold by the Holy Spirit speaking through the prophet Isaiah, "For unto us a child is born, unto us a son is given: and the government shall be upon his shoulder: and his name shall be called Wonderful, Counsellor, The mighty God, The everlasting Father, The Prince of Peace. Of the increase of his government and peace there shall be no end" (Isa. 9:6–7).

Wherever Jesus reigns, there the kingdom of God is. The kingdom of God is not defined geographically but by the new birth. It is not material but spiritual, although the person yielded to God's will and hence in the kingdom of God will use material things to further spiritual ends. Hear our Lord's own explanation: "The kingdom of God cometh not with observation: Neither shall they say, Lo here! or, lo there! for, behold, the kingdom of God is within you" (Luke 17:20–21). He also affirms, "My kingdom is not of this world: if my kingdom were of this world, then would my servants fight, that I should not be delivered to the Jews: but now is my kingdom not from hence" (John 18:36) Jesus instructed the scholar Nicodemus, "Verily, verily, I say unto thee, Except a man be born again, he cannot see the kingdom of God" (John 3:3). Paul understood the spiritual nature of the kingdom of God and so said, "For the kingdom of God is not meat and drink; but righteousness, and peace, and joy in the Holy Ghost" (Rom. 14:17).

The kingdom of God exists wherever God reigns in a person's heart. It has come insofar as God has come into people's hearts; it is coming as he is allowed by the transforming experience of the new birth to reign in people's hearts.

II. Our Lord certainly treated the kingdom of God as a present reality.

He said, "The time is fulfilled, and the kingdom of God is at hand; repent ye, and believe the gospel" (Mark 1:15).

In the Beatitudes in Matthew 5 Jesus describes the characteristics of the Christian and adds, "for of such is the kingdom of heaven."

To the scribes and Pharisees who refused to believe, as recorded in Matthew 21:31–32, Jesus affirmed, "The publicans and the harlots go into the kingdom of God before you." You will note that it was a present kingdom into which they were entering. So also is the testimony of Jesus in Matthew 12:28: "But if I cast out devils by the Spirit of God, then the kingdom of God is come unto you," and again as in Luke 4:43: "And he said unto them, I must preach the kingdom of God to other cities also; for therefore am I sent."

Other passages also confirm that the kingdom of God is a present reality, as for instance, Acts 8:12: "When they believed Philip preaching the things concerning the kingdom of God, and the name of Jesus Christ, they were baptized." Paul at Ephesus was "arguing persuasively about the kingdom of God" (Acts 19:8 NIV), and later at Rome "he witnessed to them from morning till evening, explaining about the kingdom of God, and from the Law of Moses and from the Prophets he tried to persuade them about Jesus" (Acts 28:23 NIV).

III. This kingdom of which Christ is King will last forever.

"Of the increase of his government and peace there shall be no end" (Isa. 9:7). Matthew 25 details the consummation of the kingdom at the end of this gospel age when the Lord shall return in great glory with all his holy angels and sit on the throne of judgment to separate those who are his, who are destined for eternal life, from those who are not and are destined for everlasting punishment. Of this consummation Paul wrote:

> Then cometh the end, when he shall have delivered up the kingdom to God, even the Father; when he shall have put down all rule and all authority and power. For he must reign, till he hath put all enemies under his feet. The last enemy that shall be destroyed is death. For he hath put all things under his feet. But when he saith all things are put under him, it is manifest that he is excepted, which did put all things under him. And when all things shall be subdued unto him, then shall the Son also himself be subject unto him that put all things under him, that God may be all in all. (1 Cor. 15:24–28)

IV. The parables of Jesus throw great light on the nature of the kingdom of God and on its growth.

The parable of the seed growing by itself attests the vitality of the gospel. As the soil was made for the seed and the seed for the soil, our hearts have been made for the gospel. The parable of the sower teaches that the field is the world in which the gospel seed is sown. Some seed will be lost, but some will bring forth good fruit.

The growth of the kingdom will be so phenomenal as to be likened to the tree that grows from the small mustard seed. As one particle of leaven or yeast touches another and leavens it until all the dough is leavened, so the kingdom grows as one life touches another.

The parables of the pearl of great price and of the hidden treasure teach that the kingdom of God is more valuable than all other considerations. The man who found the treasure "hid it again, and then in his joy went and sold all he had and bought that field" (Matt. 13:44 NIV), and likewise, when the merchant found a pearl "of great value, he went away and sold everything he had and bought it" (Matt. 13:46 NIV). Christ must be valued above all or he is not valued at all.

The parables of the dragnet, the wheat and the tares, and of the sheep and the goats indicate that the Lord will do the separating of those who are his from those who are not, and that he will do it thoroughly.

The parable of the great banquet extends the Lord's invitation, "Come for all things are now ready," but the parable of the wedding garment warns that we must not try to enter the kingdom except on the Lord's terms.

The parable of the good Samaritan, the acted parable of our Lord's washing of the disciples' feet, and his express teaching all confirm that greatness in the kingdom of God depends on service.

Conclusion

What then are we asking for when we pray, "Thy kingdom come"? In the first petition we prayed that God's name might be hallowed, that is, that his person or character would be set apart and reverenced. This petition reinforces the first by praying that God's name will be hallowed specifically as people accept Jesus and by the new birth enter into the eternal kingdom of God's dear Son.

To pray "Thy kingdom come" is to pray for the salvation of the lost that by salvation they may enter the kingdom of God and live with the King forever. To pray "Thy kingdom come" prepares one for the next petition, "Thy will be done on earth, as it is in heaven." Let us be sure that we are in the kingdom of God and that the King reigns in our hearts.

WEDNESDAY EVENING, MAY 17

Title: Two Women Whom Jesus Loved

Text: "Now Jesus loved Martha, and her sister, and Lazarus" **(John 11:5).**

Scripture Reading: Luke 10:38–42

Introduction

If Jesus was a normal person, and we know that he was, he longed for a home. In his strenuous ministry, he needed privacy, quietness, peace, love, and fellowship like everyone else. Yet he said, "Foxes have holes and birds of the air have nests, but the Son of Man has no place to lay his head" (Matt: 8:20 NIV). He was a wanderer in his native land. He never married. He was betrothed to his church, his bride.

Jesus was welcome in the homes of his friends. He was entertained in the home of Simon Peter. He was the honored guest in the home of Zacchaeus. He broke bread with two disciples in their home in Emmaus. But the home where he felt most welcome was the home of Martha, Mary, and Lazarus in Bethany. When Jerusalem was hostile, he felt at home in their house. When other doors were shut, their door was always open. When tumultuous opposition raged, he found a refuge there from the storm. When the fickle crowd turned from him, he could count on the love, loyalty, and hospitality of this gracious home.

Jesus had a standing invitation to visit Martha, Mary, and Lazarus at any time. One day he arrived unannounced and was warmly greeted by the two sisters. Both became his hostesses. One cared for his bodily needs, the other entered into his plans and thoughts. Both were important to his comfort and fulfillment.

Martha was the practical, energetic manager of the household. She excused herself and busied herself in the kitchen preparing a big meal. Mary, who was contemplative in nature, sat at Jesus' feet and listened to his teaching.

Martha was annoyed that Mary wouldn't help her. She felt mistreated and thought that Mary should be in the kitchen helping her prepare a sumptuous dinner. Finally, her volcanic temperament erupted and she became like a fretful child. "Make Mary come help me," she said.

Jesus took Mary's side. It was not that there were no times for Mary to be in the kitchen. Apparently she normally helped with the chores, or Martha would not have expected her assistance. But Mary's place at this time was with Jesus. He needed quiet, and Martha started a wrangle. He needed peace, and she was bickering. The cross was just ahead. The hostile enemy was closing in, and Jesus needed understanding. But all Martha was concerned about was an elaborate meal.

Why did Jesus take Mary's side?

I. Martha was unduly worried by things.

Martha did not take the time to enjoy Jesus. She had the privilege of sitting at his feet, yet she was wrapped up in the mechanics of kitchen drudgery.

Jesus normally enjoyed a good meal. His enemies accused him of being "a glutton." But an elaborate dinner was not important to Jesus on this occasion. His needs were simple. He wanted Martha's attention, not a big meal.

Martha meant to be kind, but she was unkind. She meant to be helpful, but she was hurtful. She decided what Jesus needed and proceeded to give it to him, even when he didn't want it. She spoiled Jesus' visit by being fretful and flustered and peevish.

It is possible for us to attempt too much and miss Jesus. We get so busy that we do not have time to pray. We become tired and complaining. We bog down in details. A church usher can become so involved in providing comfort for others that he does not worship. A finance committee member can become so concerned about the offering meeting the budget that he overlooks other vital phases of church life. It is possible for a mother to so give herself to the physical care of her children that she becomes a slave. She loses all joy in creative motherhood.

II. Martha was critical of Mary's role.

Martha's place was in the kitchen. She was a good housekeeper and a good cook. Many homes today would be better off if they had a Martha presiding over the household. But Martha's mistake was in trying to determine Mary's role. She tried to force Mary into the kitchen at a time when her place was at Jesus' feet.

Sometimes a missionary resigns and comes home to serve. Occasionally a minister leaves the vocational ministry to engage in some other work. Do you sit in judgment on those who make such decisions? Do you criticize them or hold them in disdain? Each of us must find his or her own vocation and let others mind their work.

"Now Jesus loved Martha and Mary" (John 11:5). Jesus loved both women. They were different. Martha was a dynamo of energy, a practical person. Mary was quiet and imaginative, a good listener. We need women who are a combination of the two. In fact, we all need both of these attributes. We need to pray and work. We must not try to practice the one and not the other. We must not withdraw from the world and give ourselves wholly to prayer. There is spiritual barrenness in the monastery. On the other hand, our religious practice must not be a continual round of meetings and conferences and visits, with no time for meditation and waiting on God. Faith without works is dead. Works without faith also are dead. Activism can make us anxious and fretful. Without sitting at Jesus' feet, we will lack power, joy, and fulfillment.

Conclusion

Jesus sat at Martha's table. Mary sat at Jesus' feet. God grant that we may both give and receive from him who is God's gracious gift to humankind.

SUNDAY MORNING, MAY 21

Title: What Makes a Home Christian?

Text: "Except the LORD build the house, they labour in vain that build it" **(Ps. 127:1).**

Scripture Reading: Ephesians 5:22–6:4

Hymns: "Footsteps of Jesus," Slade
"He Leadeth Me," Gilmore
"Take Time to Be Holy," Longstaff

Offertory Prayer: Our Father, we are grateful for those who have learned the joy of bringing the tithe into the storehouse regularly. They know the delights of obedience. We pray that more of our people will learn the truth that happiness comes in being faithful to God in every area of life—including the stewardship of money. Make this part of the service meaningful in the lives of all who participate. We pray in Jesus' name. Amen.

Introduction

Both the Old and New Testaments emphasize the value of a godly home. We who know Jesus as Savior and Lord use the expression "Christian home" to express our ideal for family relationships. The psalmist realized the absolute necessity for spiritual influence in every area of life. His emphasis on "the Lord building the house" in today's text reveals to us that Christian goals in family living have their roots deep in Old Testament soil. The psalmist used the word "Jehovah" (KJV "LORD") in our text, which is the name that was so dear to the heart of every Jew because it was the name by which God had revealed himself to his people. Since the early Christians used the phrase "Christ is Lord" as their confession of faith, we can almost equate Jehovah of the Old Testament with Jesus of the New Testament. The psalmist came as near as an Old Testament writer could to saying a home must be Christian in order for it to be effective and meaningful in everyday living.

I. More than an influence.

A Christian home is more than one in which people say kind things to each other and seek to live unselfishly. Someone said recently that America's problem is that we are trying to practice Christianity without believing it. This is the problem in many homes. People try to have a Christian home without believing in Jesus and committing their lives to him.

One cannot have the fruits of Christianity without also having its roots. During World War II an outstanding seminary president was invited to speak on a nationwide religious program. The network insisted on seeing his manuscript in advance. One of the program planners called him to ask him to change one word in it. The seminary president had written in the manuscript for broadcast that he "hoped every person who sat at the peace table when World War II was concluded would be a Christian." The network executive asked him if he would eliminate the word "a" and say that he "hoped every person who sat at the peace table would be Christian." The seminary president said in chapel to several hundred students, "I spent twenty minutes explaining to that executive why I could not, in good conscience, make that slight change."

The word *Christian* must be a noun before it becomes an adjective. There is a subtle philosophy existent in our nation that many people who do not profess to be Christians in the orthodox sense actually have more of the spirit of Christ than some who are openly committed to Christ as Savior. This simply is not true! Although one may occasionally find a person whose personal living standards do not conform to his or her profession, the greatest Christian deeds are being done by Christians who have openly committed themselves to Jesus as Savior and Lord. The same is true with reference to our homes. It is not enough to say vaguely that we should be Christian in attitude and minimize the importance of personally accepting Jesus as Savior.

II. Every member should be born again.

Just as every member of a church should be a born-again Christian, so every member of a Christian home should be a born-again person. There are, to be sure, an overwhelming number of mothers who have held a home together when Daddy would not bear his share of the load. Some such mothers have reared children who have gone out to bless the world. To say those homes were not Christian homes seems cruel and overbearing, but one must be honest. A home can be genuinely and thoroughly Christian only if every member of the household is an openly committed Christian.

What about the children? Surveys have shown over and over that where mother and father are both committed to Christ as Savior, the children often come to Jesus at an early age. A number of years ago, the foreign mission board of a major denomination in America ran a survey on the "conversion age" of the missionaries appointed that year. The average age of the group was less than eight years. The children of homes that are Christian in the fullest sense are those who go out to bless the world with strong Christian convictions, sweet spirits, and stable emotional lives.

III. Every member should practice his or her religion.

An outstanding marriage counselor told of a survey he conducted among married couples. He asked, "What, in your opinion, contributes most to a happy, successful marriage?" A large percentage of the group replied, "Religion lived daily in the home." Paul's letter to the Ephesians gives some practical rules for family relationships. Women are to "submit [them] selves unto [their] own husbands as unto the Lord" (Eph. 5:22), and husbands are to "love [their] wives, even as Christ also loved the church, and gave himself for it" (v. 25). Any woman is safe who submits herself to a man who loves her in the same way that Christ loves his church. Paul continued, "For no man ever yet hated his own flesh; but nourisheth and cherisheth it, even as the Lord the church" (v. 29).

Children are to obey their parents, and they are to do it "in the Lord" (Eph. 6:1). Both in the Old Testament and in the New Testament, children are told to honor their fathers and mothers. Likewise, fathers are told that they are not to provoke their children to wrath but rather to "bring them up in the nurture and admonition of the Lord" (v. 4).

The important matter in family life is relationships. If we practice our religion faithfully, we will keep the right attitude toward the other members of our family, and we can live together in Christian love. This is the thing that makes a home Christian.

Conclusion

A hymn writer of yesteryear said, "A happy home is an early heaven." Charles Spurgeon once said that when home is ruled according to the principles of God's Word, angels might visit and not find themselves out of their habitation.

Is your home genuinely Christian? Has everyone in it made public profession of faith in Christ and committed himself or herself openly to following Jesus as Lord of life? If not, today would be a good day to bring the family circle together and decide in the words of Joshua that "as for me and my house, we will serve the LORD" (Josh. 24:15).

SUNDAY EVENING, MAY 21

Title: Thy Will Be Done

Text: "Thy will be done in earth, as it is in heaven" **(Matt. 6:10)**.

Scripture Reading: Matthew 26:36–46

Introduction

"Thy will be done in earth, as it is in heaven," is the third petition in Jesus' model prayer. Is this prayer necessary? Won't God's will be done anyway? Who is puny man to thwart the will of Almighty God?

There is a sense in which God's will is done. We do not believe that anything can happen outside the permissive will of God. But since God, with the courage of love, has created people in his own image and has endowed us with the power of choice, it is possible that much practiced by sinful people within the limits of God's permissive will is not in accord with his actual will. Surely war, hate, poverty, alcoholism, greed, and lust cannot be in accord with God's actual will. It is not the will of God that any should perish—and yet many are perishing.

It is refreshing to note that the petition "Thy will be done in earth, as it is in heaven" assures us that heaven is a place where God's will is done. That is what makes heaven really heaven. If heaven were filled with liars, thieves, whoremongers, fornicators, and those who love iniquity, it would cease to be heaven. John wrote, "We shall be like him, for we shall see him as he is" (1 John 3:2). Wherever people do the will of God, 'tis heaven there.

I. This petition climaxes and personalizes the two preceding ones.

"Hallowed be thy name." Let God be held in reverence. How? By doing his will. "Thy kingdom come" refers to the kingdom of which Christ is King. How do we let the kingdom come? By doing God's will on earth and hence letting God reign in one's heart.

"Thy will be done on earth" is an active rather than passive prayer. It is not a prayer for the will of God to be suffered but for the will of God to be done.

The prayer "Thy will be done in earth, as it is in heaven" is present rather than future. God's will is to be done in earth, here and now.

The petition "Thy will be done in earth, as it is in heaven" is practical rather than speculative. It is a petition for God's will to be done in practical day-to-day events. For people in relation to their fellow humans, within their family circles, in their communities, in their worship, in their business affairs, and in all things, the prayer is "Thy will be done."

II. To pray this prayer one must have faith in God and in his purposes.

One must believe that God is good and that he purposes the best for all his children. One must believe that God's will is always best, that he has a plan for every life. One who prays this prayer must not simply have the concept that God is the divine potter with his hands in the clay of our human experience, but that he also is the Father God.

This faith was demonstrated by Jesus. He never had any doubt about God. He did not speculate about him. He affirmed absolutely that God is the God of the loving heart. Jesus went to the cross believing it to be the Father's will; but he had faith enough in God to believe that if the heavenly Father should will death on a cruel cross for the innocent, he would have purpose in it, because God's will is always best. Indeed, God did have purpose in the cross; what once was the emblem of ignominious death has become the symbol of victory. Of our Lord we read that he "endured the cross, despising the shame, and is set down at the right hand of the throne of God" (Heb. 12:2). In the cross he fulfilled the word of Isaiah: "Yet it pleased the LORD to bruise him; he hath put him to grief" (Isa. 53:20); but because God's will was best, Jesus also fulfilled the word "He shall see of the travail of his soul, and shall be satisfied" (Isa. 53:11).

III. To pray, "Thy will be done in earth as in heaven," not only demands faith that God's will is best, but it also demands full surrender and obedience.

Here again Jesus is the best example of his own teaching. He said, "Lo, I come to do thy will, O God" (Heb. 10:9). At his baptism he submitted to the rite that prefigured his death, burial, and resurrection with this prayer of dedication on his lips, "Suffer it to be so now: for thus it becometh us to fulfil all righteousness" (Matt. 3:15).

John 12 records Jesus' struggle as he faced the cross. He cried, "Now is my soul troubled; and what shall I say? Father, save me from this hour: but for this cause came I unto this hour. Father, glorify thy name. Then came there a voice from heaven, saying, I have both glorified it, and will glorify it again" (vv. 27–28).

As the final illustration of our Lord's complete submission to God's will, note his prayer in Gethsemane, "O my Father, if it be possible, let this cup pass from me: nevertheless not as I will, but as thou wilt" (Matt. 26:39).

Jesus is the one who has earned the right to instruct us to pray, "Thy will be done in earth, as in heaven." He alone could say, "[Father] I have finished the work which thou gavest me to do" (John 17:4), and "I do always those things that please him" (John 8:29).

IV. Many are the promises to one who does the will of God from the heart.

He has assurance of salvation. "Hereby we do know that we know him, if we keep his commandments" (1 John 2:3). "Not every one that saith unto me Lord, Lord, shall enter the kingdom of heaven: but he that doeth the will of my Father which is in heaven" (Matt. 7:21). "If we say that we have fellowship with him, and walk in darkness, we lie, and do not the truth: but if we walk in the light, as he is in the light, we have fellowship one with another, and the blood of Jesus Christ his Son cleanseth us from all sin" (1 John 1:6–7). One who sincerely does God's will can claim Jesus' promise of assurance, "If any man will do his will, he shall know of the doctrine, whether it be of God, or whether I speak of myself" (John 7:17).

One who does the Lord's will is assured also of hearing the Father's "Well done, thou good and faithful servant: thou hast been faithful over a few things, I will make thee ruler over many things: enter thou into the joy of the Lord" (Matt. 24:21). There is no substitute for obedience. As Samuel said to Saul, "To obey is better than sacrifice, and to hearken than the fat of rams" (1 Sam. 15:22).

"Who is my mother? and who are my brethren?" asked Jesus; then he proceeded to answer, "Behold my mother and my brethren! For whosoever shall do the will of my Father which is in heaven, the same is my brother, and sister, and mother" (Matt. 12:48–50).

One who sincerely does God's will can claim God's promise to supply all that is needful. Here is the promise: "But seek ye first the kingdom of God, and his righteousness; and all these things shall be added to you" (Matt. 6:33).

Conclusion

No one who does God's will is ever a failure. As a soldier is to obey orders, so a Christian is to do the will of God. One who does God's will from the heart will prove that God's will is best even as Paul exhorted in Romans 12:1–2: "I beseech you therefore, brethren, by the mercies of God, that ye present your bodies a living sacrifice, holy, acceptable unto God, which is your reasonable service. And be not conformed to this world: but be ye transformed by the renewing of your mind, that ye may prove what is that good, and acceptable, and perfect, will of God."

May God give to you the faith and the dedication to pray this great petition: "Thy will be done in earth, as it is in heaven."

WEDNESDAY EVENING, MAY 24

Title: She Went about Doing Good

Text: "She was full of good works and acts of charity" (**Acts 9:36 RSV**).

Scripture Reading: Acts 9:36–42

Introduction

In today's brief Scripture reading, we have a portrait of a woman who, like our Lord, "went about doing good." The New English Bible says, "She filled her days with acts of kindness." We have no record that she ever made a speech or prayed in public. She probably held no office. But her name was synonymous with charity. She was "full of good works." She lived her faith and acted out her love.

Her name gives us an insight into her character. Actually, she is known by two names. Dorcas was her Greek name and means "antelope," suggesting grace and beauty. Her Aramaic name was Tabitha, which means "elegance."

Dorcas was also called a disciple. The word *disciple* means "learner." She was humble and teachable, benevolent and compassionate. No human words, regardless of their eloquence, can match the eloquence of a beautiful life of caring and service.

In all likelihood, Dorcas had been left a widow in a harsh and demanding world. Yet she showed no spirit of bitterness. She did not question God's wisdom or his goodness. She became known as a disciple, and she took her place among the other widows of the church.

God seemed to say to Dorcas, as he did to Moses, "What is that in thine hand?" It was a rod, but a very tiny one in the shape of a needle. Her gift was not using her lips to teach or her vocabulary to write. Her gift was a sewing needle, applied with deft and disciplined hands. Her home was her workshop. She had no sewing machine, but she had willing hands and heart.

I. Dorcas gave of herself.

When the spirit of Jesus prevailed in Dorcas's life, her needle became an instrument of loving service. Her time was God's time, and long hours of work for others brought her great joy. Perhaps she had heard the saying of Jesus, "I was naked and you clothed me. . . . Truly, I say to you, as you did it to one of the least of these my brethren, you did it to me."

II. Dorcas saw a chance to do good on the street where she lived.

The widows whom Dorcas loved and served wept profusely when she died. They showed Peter the "tunics and other garments which Dorcas made while she was with them." Dorcas was missed and mourned after she died. It is sad when one has lived such a barren and selfish life that he or she is not missed when gone.

173

Dorcas reminds us of the godly woman featured in the book of Proverbs. "She seeketh wool, and flax, and worketh willingly with her hands. . . . She stretcheth out her hand to the poor; yea, she reacheth forth her hands to the needy" (Prov. 31:13, 20). We need to remember that "charm is deceptive, and beauty is fleeting; but a woman who fears the LORD is to be praised" (Prov. 31:30 NIV).

When Dorcas died, her friends wept and displayed the work of her skillful hands. But she entered into the promise of the voice from heaven, "Blessed are the dead which die in the Lord . . . they rest from their labours; and their works do follow them" (Rev. 14:13).

Conclusion

Are you engaged in good works in the name of Jesus that will endure after you are gone? Then may God in his time give you a deserved rest in him.

SUNDAY MORNING, MAY 28

Title: You Will Be What You Choose to Be

Text: "Choose you this day whom ye will serve" **(Josh. 24:15)**.

Scripture Reading: Joshua 24:1–15

Hymns: "I Would Be True," Walter
           "Jesus Calls Us," Alexander
           "Our Best," Kirk

Offertory Prayer: Our Father, we know that where there is no vision, the people perish. Likewise, where there is no Savior, the people are lost both in this world and in the world to come. We bring our offerings that the message of Christ can be preached. Here in our own church this money will be used to carry on your work. Some of this money will be sent to various places to carry the name of Jesus to those who need to know him. May we give sacrificially and cheerfully. Most of all, may we give with a prayer in our hearts that our money will be used wisely and efficiently in proclaiming the good tidings of redemption to those who have never surrendered to the lordship of Christ. We pray in Jesus' name. Amen.

Introduction

At the close of an illustrious career, Joshua gathered the people together to bring them a final message. He stressed the providential hand of God in the nation's history. How good God had been! Under Moses he had led them from the house of bondage to the edge of the Promised Land. During Joshua's days of leadership, the Israelites had entered Canaan and had defeated the enemy. Israel was now in the land God intended for them to possess. Joshua realized, however, that the people faced many choices.

Moses had warned them that they should not become self-satisfied and complacent once they had taken over the cities of the pagan tribes. He insisted that they thoroughly exterminate the enemy and have nothing to do with pagan religions. Joshua echoed many of the warnings that Moses had given. God had blessed the nation, and the people were to remain true to him.

I. Goals are important.

A commencement speaker once said to a group of students, "Be careful what you set as your goal in life. Whatever you make up your mind to be, you probably will become. Therefore, be sure it is a worthy goal." No person ever drifted into success. One must plan for it, and part of that planning is the setting of goals. Your key for personal success is in establishing some long-range aims in life. Nothing is lost on people who are always bent on moving forward. They never waste time because they are always preparing for their work and their lives by keeping their eyes, minds, and hearts open to experiences that will enrich them personally and bring them nearer completion of their dreams. Persons such as this find that everything ministers to their education and that all things cooperate with them in their passion for growth.

There is a difference between one's goal in life and one's purpose for living. Purpose is long range. It is like the pot of gold at the end of the rainbow. You never quite reach it. It is always ahead of you. Goals, however, are clearly defined and may be attained. They are specific actions that we intend to and do carry out. Also we can measure goals and thereby judge our progress. Often they are quantitative and involve how much we intend to do and how often we intend to do it. They may be related closely to time and include how soon we plan to accomplish an objective.

II. Goals mean hard work.

There is nothing wrong with building "castles in the air." Every accomplishment that is worthwhile once began as a dream in the heart of the one who brought it to reality. A guide was showing a group through a large university where there were statues of Socrates, Aristotle, and Plato. To the side was a dreamy-eyed boy who represented Alexander the Great. When a member of the party said the artist's conception of Alexander the Great was false, the guide replied, "No, the artist was exactly correct. He who conquers a world must first of all dream that he has done so."

But to make these dreams come true requires work—hard work. Moreover, it requires patience. Someone asked Mr. William Pitt, "What is the chief characteristic necessary to be prime minister of England?" He replied, "Patience." The speaker said, "What is the second requirement?" He replied, "Patience." The speaker continued, "What is the third?" Mr. Pitt replied, "Patience." Too many people fail to realize their goals because they have not learned both "to labor and to wait."

The apostle Paul kept his life goal constantly before him. He knew that he had not yet attained to the fullest that which Christ had for him when he confronted him on the Damascus road and changed the direction of his life.

Paul was, however, constantly seeking to know more of Christ's will for his life. His statement, "This one thing I do, forgetting those things which are behind, and reaching forth unto those things which are before, I press toward the mark for the prize of the high calling of God in Christ Jesus" (Phil. 3:13–14), was the secret of his Christian growth. To continue day by day striving toward a goal is hard work, but it is the only way goals can be reached. Thomas Edison once said:

> One must fix his mind . . . with persistence and begin searching for that which he seeks, making use of all the accumulated knowledge of the subject which he has or can acquire from others. He must keep on searching no matter how many times he may meet with disappointment. He must refuse to be influenced by the fact that somebody else may have tried the same idea without success. He must keep himself sold on the idea that the solution of his problem exists somewhere and that he will find it.

Someone has wisely said that the trouble with most people is that they "quit before they start."

III. Most important, choose Jesus.

Whatever you are seeking to be in life, first of all evaluate it under the searchlight of Jesus Christ. Even goals that seem mainly secular and nonspiritually oriented must be in harmony with the will of God in Christ or they are futile and may even be dangerous. Look at each your goals and ask yourself, "Is this goal pleasing to Jesus Christ?"

If you have not yet made the choice of Jesus Christ as Savior, settle that matter before you choose any career goals. When you receive Jesus as Savior and Lord, you will automatically reevaluate all your other goals. Some of them may be worthwhile but need the refining touch of the Master's hand.

When Jesus comes into your heart, you will receive not only personal salvation but also a new power for achieving your aims. Paul said, "I can do all things through Christ which strengtheneth me" (Phil. 4:13). Someone has translated this, "In him who pours power into me, I am able for anything." One distinguished preacher said, "Every human soul has a complete and perfect plan cherished for it in the heart of God—a divine biography marked out, which it enters into life to live." Such an attitude toward life gives it a sacred dignity and importance. Someone else said, "I would rather be what God chose to make me than the most glorious creature that I could think of; for to have been thought about, born in God's thought, and then made by God, is the dearest, grandest, and most precious thing in all thinking."

Conclusion

You are standing today at a crossroads in your life. What you will or will not be is determined largely by the choices you make. You may not be able to achieve everything that you think, at this moment, you wish for your life. With God's help, however, you can properly evaluate those things that are important. The words of Joshua come echoing down the corridors of the centuries. They are as true today as they were when he spoke them to ancient Israel. Let God have his way in your life, and you will become all that he wants you to be. Pray, "Lord, help me to make your will my will in order that my will may be your will."

SUNDAY EVENING, MAY 28

Title: Give Us Daily Bread

Text: "Give us this day our daily bread" **(Matt. 6:11)**.

Scripture Reading: Isaiah 55:1–11

Introduction

The first three petitions of Jesus' model prayer have to do with God's glory: "Hallowed be thy name. Thy kingdom come. Thy will be done in earth, as it is in heaven" (Matt. 6:9–10). This is the right order: God comes first. Then after one has prayed for God's glory, it seems that the heavenly Father looks down and says, "And now, my child, what are your personal requests?"

So many things that we might have asked for now seem so selfish or unimportant that we decline to request them. God's fatherly nature, however, encourages us to bring to him anything that causes us concern. Every father can understand this. The broken toy or the death of a pet may have no real concern for a parent, but because we are concerned about our children, we care. God invites us to pray about anything that is of concern to us.

The first personal petition is, "Give us this day our daily bread" (Matt. 6:11).

I. Bread.

A. *Bread means food, and by a legitimate extension of the idea means employment, the strength to work, health—all that pertains to this life.* According to Jesus, God is interested in our temporal needs. "Your Father knoweth what things ye have need of, before ye ask him" (Matt. 6:8). The passage that says, "Man shall not live by bread alone, but by every word that proceeded out of the mouth of God" (Matt. 4:4), assumes that bread is essential to life.

B. *Daily bread.* Disciples do not pray for luxuries but for necessities such as bodily strength for the day, for jobs, and for good health. The key is to always pray in God's will.

II. Give us this day.

A. *"Give us" emphasizes humility, dependence, and trust in God.* A little girl asked, "Daddy, why do we have to thank God for the food if you paid the grocery store for it?" The answer, of course, is that the father was thanking God for the health and strength to earn the money to buy the food. "The earth is the LORD's and the fulness thereof; the world, and they that dwell therein" (Ps. 24:1). "Every good gift and every perfect gift is from above, and cometh down from the Father of lights, with whom is no variableness, neither shadow of turning" (James 1:17).

B. *"This day" emphasizes trust in God for the day that now is rather than worry about those that will come.* "All creatures look to you to give them their food at the proper time. When you give it to them, they gather it up; when you open your hand, they are satisfied with good things. When you hide your face, they are terrified; when you take away their breath, they die and return to the dust" (Ps. 104:27–29 NIV). Cardinal Newman's great hymn "Lead Kindly Light" is a commentary on trusting God for today.

III. "Our" emphasizes that this is an unselfish petition.

A. *It would be sheer hypocrisy for one to pray this prayer and then deny another the right to earn daily bread.* The unjust businessperson, the employer who cheats his employee by unjust wages, the employee who does not give a day's work for a day's pay, and the employer who denies a person the right to work because of a race or gender bias cannot pray this prayer.

B. *The prayer assumes a positive obligation on the part of the one praying to assist others to receive their daily bread.* It cannot be God's will that some have abundance while others starve. Our traditional viewpoint has been this: let a person work hard, save, and then live in old age on his or her savings. If one is strong and healthy, this is good, but suppose major sickness, mental illness, or the death of a spouse depletes a family's resources. It is the responsibility of the church to care for widows and orphans and those who through no fault of their own are unable to care for themselves. In a community of redeemed persons, the love of God constrains those who have material wealth to share with those who are less fortunate by providing food, clothing, shelter, hospitals, homes for the aging, orphanages, benevolence funds, and so on.

Conclusion

"Give us this day our daily bread" is a prayer of humility, of trust, and of faith to believe that God is concerned about the material needs of people. It is a prayer of Christian concern that cries out for social and economic justice.

Although "bread" is necessary and important, bread is not enough. Every person needs "the true bread from heaven" (John 6:32), "the bread of life" (v. 35). This bread is available to all. "Wherefore do ye spend money for that which is not bread? and your labour for that which satisfieth not? hearken diligently unto me, and eat ye that which is good, and let your soul delight itself in fatness" (Isa. 55:2).

WEDNESDAY EVENING, MAY 31

Title: The Great Woman of Proverbs

Text: "Charm is deceitful, and beauty is vain, but a woman who fears the LORD is to be praised" **(Prov. 31:30 RSV)**.

Scripture Reading: Proverbs 31:10–31

Introduction

Many books focusing on the role of women in modern society are being written today. The advice they contain is often contradictory and confusing. But the book of Proverbs has a timeless tribute to the role of a godly woman. Perhaps the description of this good woman came from the heart of a concerned mother who was eager that her son make a wise choice in a wife (Prov. 31:1).

In the ancient world, precious stones were highly valued as they are today. The good wife who fears the Lord and who faces life in a positive and responsible manner is said to be of far more value than the precious jewels people so greatly prize.

I. The great woman is described as being trustworthy (Prov. 31:11).

Dependability and reliability are virtues that have been recognized, appreciated, and prized from the dawn of human history. God needs people who can be trusted. Families need people who can be trusted. Society needs people who can be trusted. The good woman is described as one who is trustworthy.

II. The great woman is described as being benevolent (Prov. 31:12).

If both husbands and wives would seek to make a positive contribution toward the well-being of their companions, marriage and society would be much happier. The great woman is described as one who sees in her marriage an opportunity to contribute and to help.

III. The great woman is described as being industrious (Prov. 31:13–16, 21–22, 24–25, 27).

It is interesting to note in this description from the ancient world that while the great woman is a domestic, she is not restricted to the household in her interests or her activities. She has a career that extends outside the family circle. She is described as a producer and an achiever, as well as a contributor to the well-being of the family and to society.

IV. The great woman is described as having a good self-image (Prov. 31:17–19, 25).

Modern psychologists have emphasized that for us to be happy in life we must have a good self-image. A woman who holds herself in low esteem will not be able to relate positively and constructively to others. From the description of the great woman, we see that she properly evaluates herself and appreciates herself. She is no zero. Because she has a good sense of self-esteem, she is able to face the future without fear and with joyful confidence (Prov. 31:25).

V. The great woman is described as being compassionate (Prov. 31:20).

The great woman is described as one who does not limit her concern to her husband and to her household. Her eyes see the needs of the unfortunate and her ears hear their distress calls. She moves in compassion to meet the needs of the unfortunate and is a giver rather than a mere getter.

VI. The great woman identifies with her husband and rejoices in his recognition (Prov. 31:23).

This great woman is described as one who identifies with her husband and contributes to her husband's status and role in the community. She rejoices over the service he renders and the recognition he receives.

VII. The great woman is described as having the ability to make constructive use of her tongue (Prov. 31:26).

Proverbs has much to say about the manner in which we use our tongue. We can use it destructively and bring hurt comparable to a raging forest fire into the hearts and lives of others. Or we can use it as a soothing oil that brings help to those who have been hurt and inspiration to those who are in need of encouragement. The great woman is one who has mastered the art of using her tongue for the good of others.

Conclusion

From the ancient world we find a description of a liberated woman. She is free to worship God. She is free to be responsible and dependable. She is free to be a wife and a mother and a worker. She is free to be a helper and a builder. She does not define freedom in terms of license but in terms of liberty to be and to become, to do and to achieve. Great recognition comes to her because she is worthy of praise (Prov. 31:28–31).

JUNE

- ### Sunday Mornings

    Continue with the theme "The Living Christ and Our Home Life."

- ### Sunday Evenings

    Continue with expository messages from Jesus' Sermon on the Mount.

- ### Wednesday Evenings

    "Meeting Life's Crises" is the theme for the June and July messages. The experiences of various saints of God are considered that we might discover the best way for making a creative response to life's crises.

SUNDAY MORNING, JUNE 4

Title: Is Premarital Sex Wrong?

Text: "Keep thyself pure" (**1 Tim. 5:22**).

Scripture Reading: Matthew 5:1–16

Hymns: "Let Others See Jesus in You," McKinney
        "Footsteps of Jesus," Slade
        "Yield Not to Temptation," Palmer

Offertory Prayer: Our Father, we are grateful for every part of the worship experience. Now we have come to bring to you our tithes and offerings. Help us to understand this is as much a part of worship as the singing, the praying, and the preaching of the Word. Bless all the causes that we support as we give. Bless those who give. May they feel a part of your work around the world as they bring gifts this morning to be used in the preaching of the gospel both here and unto the uttermost part of the earth. We pray in Jesus' name. Amen.

Introduction

Any series of messages dealing with the home and related subjects should face frankly the matter of premarital sex. Actually, a broader subject is involved. Should sex be a part of any relationship outside of marriage? The two subjects are closely connected. Most of the rationale for one applies equally to the other.

On every hand we hear that the "times are changing." The white and black of right and wrong have faded into a dull gray of permissiveness. We are being told that Victorianism and Puritanism are "out" and that these days were actually harmful to us. Wise people, however, know better than to accept such statements as factual. Permissivism has been with us long enough now that we are beginning to see the results of it in sexually transmitted diseases including AIDS and in the huge percentage of babies brought into the world by teenage and single mothers. Let us examine the subjects this morning from several angles.

I. Biblical authority.

If one accepts the Bible as the Word of God and, therefore, as one's guide for life, he or she has the answer immediately concerning premarital sex. For one to consummate a marriage physically before the actual formal ceremony is a sin against God. God has made a people to have sexual desires, but he has also declared that these desires are to be fulfilled only within the framework of the marriage relationship. Both premarital and extramarital relations are sinful.

The term generally used for sexual relations between unmarried people is *fornication,* while the term used for extramarital relationships is *adultery.* The Bible—and therefore Christianity—condemns both specifically and severely. Although we have had varying viewpoints in many areas of life within Christian and so-called Christian groups, no accepted Christian interpretation of marriage has ever approved premarital sex activity. One old-timer expressed it succinctly when he said, "God said it; I believe it; that settles it." Another, however, improved on that statement when he said, "God said it; that settles it whether you believe it or not." Those of us who are Christians having been born again by the Spirit of God have our answer in God's Word—sex outside of marriage is wrong.

II. What about common sense?

Let's look at the subject from another standpoint. Many psychologists and psychiatrists are coming to the Christian viewpoint on sexual morality, not because they believe the Bible, but because they have come to see that what the Bible teaches is right. Non-Christian psychologists recognize that having sex before a real relationship has been established prevents a man and a woman from becoming acquainted with each other.

Many secular authorities today are coming to believe that an important part of love is the inhibition of sexual expression and that the unfulfilled sexual feelings add strength to love. Marriage then becomes "frosting on the cake" added after love has been built on many psychic fronts. Many of our accepted convictions arise out of centuries of experience as to what people have discovered is best for both individuals and society. Those who are fair and honest have come to the conclusion that even from a practical stand-point engaging in sexual intimacy before marriage is an unwise decision.

Regardless of how enlightened people claim to have become or how blasé society is or how sophisticated our attitudes, certain mores are ingrained within us, and we cannot change them. One of these is that to engage in sexual activity before marriage takes something away from the marriage experience. Whether sophisticated women will admit it or not, they experience a sense of guilt when they engage in sexual intimacy before marriage. This guilt will destroy much delight in the marriage experience. Also, no matter how liberally intellectual a person feels himself or herself to be, there will always be an erosive feeling that the woman who permitted intimacy before marriage is a sinful woman. We'll have to move farther down the road to paganism before we eliminate this feeling even from secular society.

III. The answer is Jesus.

As with most of our problems, the solution comes by accepting Jesus Christ as our Savior and Lord. Of course there are other helpful suggestions. We should be careful about the kind of literature we read and the kind of company we keep. The wrong friends can place temptations across our path that are difficult to overcome. When we feel our courtship is deteriorating to nothing more than a physical relationship, we should make haste to find an alternative to the places we are going and the things we are doing.

The only thing, however, that will guarantee us that we will not fall prey to this sin is for us to determine beforehand some standards for living and decide once and for all that we will not forsake our convictions. A dating couple would do well to talk frankly about the matter before it becomes a problem. With cool common sense, they should resolve that each will help the other.

Most of all, however, one should hide God's Word in his or her heart as fortification against sin. No one is strong enough to fight sexual temptation in one's own power. Jesus is more than a Savior from the guilt of sin. He is the one who will be with us day by day to help us over the bumpy roads that can ruin our lives.

Conclusion

Each person must make his or her own choice regarding the matter of conduct during the dating years. Some boys and girls will receive home training or religious teaching or both that is so effective that they never question the fact of whether sex before marriage is right or wrong. They know they should "save themselves" for marriage. This does not mean, of course, that they will not struggle with their own feelings or desires. From time to time they may have a tremendous battle on their hands, but deep in their hearts they know the outcome.

Sexual appetite can exist without love. Often people are deceived into thinking that physical desire is love. The truth is that love is something far deeper and more meaningful. It involves the desire for physical union, but this is by no means all of it. One who truly loves another person will not ask him or her to do that which will blight life for years to come by putting guilt feelings in the conscience that perhaps can never be overcome.

Yes, premarital sex is wrong! It is against everything God has taught. Save your sex life for marriage. You will always be glad you did!

SUNDAY EVENING, JUNE 4

Title: Forgive Us Our Debts

Text: "And forgive us our debts, as we forgive our debtors. . . . For if ye forgive men their trespasses, your heavenly Father will also forgive you: but if you forgive not men their trespasses, neither will your Father forgive your trespasses" **(Matt. 6:12, 14–15)**.

Scripture Reading: Matthew 18:21–35

Introduction

"As bread for the body so forgiveness for the soul" is a universal need. This petition, "Forgive us our debts," acknowledges the grace of God, which makes forgiveness possible. This is the central theme of Scripture as, for example, in John 3:16; Luke 19:10; Titus 2:11–14; and numerous other passages.

I. This petition points out the nature of sin.

In the petition in Matthew 6:12, Jesus used the word *debts*. In the commentary in Matthew 6:14–15, Jesus used the word *trespasses*. In the account in Luke 11:4 of Jesus' second giving of the model prayer, he used the word *sins*. Let us take a good look at the point he was making by using these terms.

Trespasses are sins of commission. They are sins of being or doing that which God has forbidden. "Thou shalt have no other gods before me" (Ex. 20:3), and one does. "Thou shalt not make unto thee any graven image" (v. 4), and one does. "Thou shalt not take the name of the LORD thy God in vain" (v. 7), and one does. "Thou shalt not kill" (v. 13), and one does. "Thou shalt not commit adultery" (v. 15), and one does. "Thou shalt not bear false witness" (v. 16), and one lies. "Thou shalt not covet" (v. 17), and one does. These are trespasses. According to John, "sin is the transgression of the law" (1 John 3:4). Now if law is defined in the ultimate sense as the will of God, then a sin of trespass is anything one does that is contrary to God's will.

Debts are obligations unfulfilled. They are sins of omission. James wrote, "To him that knoweth to do good, and doeth it not, to him it is sin" (James 4:17). Note some of the great commandments: "Thou shalt worship the Lord thy God, and him only shalt thou serve" (Matt. 4:10); "Thou shalt love" (Matt. 22:37); "Ye shall be witnesses unto me" (Acts 1:8). Failure to obey these and other positive commands is a sin of omission, a debt unpaid. After concluding the parable of the good Samaritan, Jesus commanded, "Go, and do thou likewise" (Luke 10:37). In this parable the robbers sinned by commission. They did that which they ought not. The priest and the Levite sinned by omission. They failed to do what they ought to have done.

In the parable of the talents, the man with one talent hid it safely in the earth. His master called him a "wicked and slothful servant" (Matt. 25:26). He had not stolen his master's money. His sin was that he had omitted to do with it what his master desired. An unmet obligation to one's fellowman is sin. It is not only a sin against the person, but also against God, for, said Jesus, "Inasmuch as ye did it not to one of the least of these, ye did it not to me" (Matt. 25:45).

Sins, *the word used in Luke 11:4, means missing the mark or goal.* It may be illustrated by one shooting arrows at a target. The goal or target in life is God's will. Shooting over, falling short, or going around that target is sin. Any want of conformity to God's will is sin. Sins may be of commission, of omission, or of disposition.

II. This petition acknowledges that we are sinners needing the forgiveness for which we pray.

Sin is a breach of personal relationships.

Only people sin. Material things do not sin. Animals do not sin. Since only people sin, it follows that only people can forgive or ask for forgiveness, or be held morally accountable for their deeds.

"Sin is not imputed when there is no law" (Rom. 5:13). Infants and children, as well as people who are mentally incompetent, will not be charged with guilt for their wrongdoings.

Guilt implies a measure of light and of willfulness. The Bible addresses itself to people with moral accountability.

All sin is against God.

Sin may be against another person, but it is primarily against God. When Potiphar's wife tempted Joseph, he replied, "How then can I do this great wickedness, and sin against God?" (Gen. 39:9). The immoral act she proposed would have been a sin against Potiphar, but primarily it would have been a sin against God.

Sin may be against oneself, but it is primarily a sin against God. One may foolishly assert, "If I want to get drunk or use drugs, it's my business, isn't it?" The answer is no. It is not God's will that you do this harm to yourself. In sinning against yourself, you are sinning against God.

Sin's guilt depends on willfulness. When we come to the years of accountability and know that life should be yielded to God but we refuse to do so, we become sinners by choice. Every day we delay to repent adds guilt to our account. We repent when we come to think about sin as God thinks about it and turn from it as a way of life. If we confess the Lord Jesus Christ, God justifies and regenerates us. The sin penalty is removed. We have new life, eternal life, and we will purpose to do God's will.

III. The nature of forgiveness.

God forgives.

When a debt is paid, it is canceled. One cannot collect on a debt that has been paid. When God forgives our sin debt, he cancels our obligation. It is paid in full. The forgiven sin ceases to be a barrier to fellowship with God.

God forgives sin in such a manner that he does not compromise his character. He does not wink at sin. He hates it. It is worthy of death. The death penalty has been paid by Jesus on the cross. God through Christ has done whatever was necessary "that he might be just, and the justifier of him which believeth in Jesus" (Rom. 3:26).

God regenerates the one who is forgiven.

God so changes the forgiven person that he or she is a "new creature: old things are passed away; behold, all things are become new" (2 Cor. 5:17). It would be unfair for God to take away the sin penalty from sinners without changing their sinful nature. This is the one petition in the model prayer on which our Lord comments (see Matt. 6:14–15). The forgiveness of others is not the ground on which God owes forgiveness, but it is the necessary condition. It is an evidence of repentance. It is folly to speak of forgiving a person who is not repentant. Jesus commanded, "If thy brother trespass against thee, rebuke him; and if he repent, forgive him" (Luke 17:3). God wants to forgive all people. It is not his will that any should perish, but even God cannot forgive an unrepentant person. Christians are to bear no malice; they are to be willing to forgive others. They desire to forgive others, but they cannot forgive except on evidence of repentance.

The parable of the unmerciful servant in Matthew 18:23–35 illustrates. A man who owed ten thousand talents—an impossibly large sum—besought his creditor, the king, to forgive the debt. The king did. The servant, however, refused to forgive a fellow servant who owed him a paltry hundred pence. This was reported to the king. "Then his lord, after that he had called him, said unto him, O thou wicked servant, I forgave thee all that debt, because thou desiredst me: Shouldest not thou also have had compassion on thy fellow-servant, even as I had pity on thee? And his lord was wroth, and delivered him to the tormentors, till he should pay all that was due unto him. So likewise shall my heavenly Father do also unto you, if ye from your hearts forgive not every one his brother their trespasses" (Matt. 18:32–35). The king had forgiven the servant on the assumption that his repentance was genuine. The servant's attitude to a fellow debtor showed that it was not. God knows the heart. He makes no mistakes. One forgiven of God has a forgiving attitude toward others.

Conclusion

"Forgive us our debts." "Forgive us our sins." To pray this prayer sincerely, we must dedicate ourselves to being and doing what God would have us to be and do. When we do this, God says, "Thy sins stand forgiven; go in peace; my peace I give unto you."

If God has forgiven you, forgive yourself also, and start living for God.

WEDNESDAY EVENING, JUNE 7

Title: Seeing beyond Today

Text: "Now the LORD had said unto Abram, Get thee out of thy country . . . unto a land that I will shew thee: . . . And Abram journeyed, going on still toward the south" **(Gen. 12:1, 9)**.

Scripture Reading: Genesis 12:1–9

Introduction

"Meeting Life's Crises" is the theme for the next eight devotional studies for the midweek services. The problems to be considered are common to all people. Sometimes it is a surprising discovery to find that men and women who lived in biblical times grappled with the same problems and faced the same crises as we do today.

One of the greatest frustrations people have faced from the dawn of time is the inability to see beyond today. When God made people, he chose to give them memory, the power to retain knowledge of the past. But he did not give them the power to see beyond what God has told them about the future in the Holy Scriptures. God compensates for this lack of knowledge, however, by giving the gift of faith to those who will receive it. Faith is a moment-by-moment fusion of our will and purpose into God's will and purpose.

No human being ever faced a future with more blind uncertainty than did Abraham. Yet we have demonstrated in his life perhaps the finest example of faith and commitment the world has ever known.

I. Abraham's call was a unique preparation for an unknown future.

The initiative for Abraham's move came from God. As far as we can tell, Abraham had been content with the status quo in Ur of the Chaldees. God broke into Abraham's life as he does into the life of every person who is born into the kingdom of God. There is nothing noble in humans that causes them to seek after God; rather, God mercifully seeks after humans.

Abraham's call was positive. God said to Abraham, "Get thee out. . . ." This is always the pattern of God's first call to an individual. He calls people away from the world, away from sin, away from the old life. Abraham had to leave three things: his country, his kindred, and his father's house. Jesus said, "He that loveth father or mother more than me is not worthy of me" (Matt. 10:37). Jesus was saying that the thing or person closest to one's heart must take second place to his lordship!

II. Abraham's commitment to God's call demonstrated his willingness to trust his tomorrows into God's hands.

In his defense before the Jewish Sanhedrin, Stephen said, "The God of glory appeared unto our father Abraham" (Acts 7:2). Literally Stephen said, "The God of the glory," which means that it was a glory peculiar to God. We do not know how God appeared to Abraham, but it was in such glory and power that he once and for all eclipsed the Babylonian gods Abraham had worshiped all of his life. From that day forward, there was one God, and his glory filled Abraham's life. Abraham still could not "see beyond today," but God was there, and that was sufficient.

Abraham's commitment to God's call did not assure a smooth and unchallenged pathway for him, however. He made errors in judgment (see Gen. 20), but each experience strengthened his faith and brought him nearer to the point of total commitment.

III. Abraham's final challenge proved that his faith had prepared him for whatever lay within his tomorrows.

There was one last test for Abraham. It had to do with the instrument God had chosen to implement the promise concerning the acquisition of the Promised Land. In Abraham and Sarah's old age, Sarah had miraculously given birth to Isaac. Then, out of the blue, God said to Abraham, "Take now thy son, thine only son Isaac . . . and offer him . . . for a burnt offering" (Gen. 22:2). Not until this moment in his spiritual growth was Abraham ready for this test.

As Abraham and Isaac approached the place of sacrifice, the personal agony of this spiritual giant must have reached the ultimate point of human endurance. He built the altar, laid the wood in order, bound Isaac and laid him on the altar, and then "took the knife to slay his son." At the last possible moment, God intervened. Abraham's faith was strong enough to know that God controlled both the present and the future.

Conclusion

"If we could see beyond today, as God can see." But we cannot. Yet God's compensation is more than adequate; he has made faith available. He has told us in his Word how to live so that faith can be developed in our lives. Further, he has provided periodic tests and trials to aid us in the development of our faith. With each victory, faith is made stronger, and the anxieties about our tomorrows become less and less paralyzing. We find increasing courage to walk confidently with God one day at a time.

SUNDAY MORNING, JUNE 11

Title: Train Up a Child

Text: "Train up a child in the way he should go: and when he is old, he will not depart from it" **(Prov. 22:6)**.

Scripture Reading: Proverbs 22:1–11

Hymns: "There Is a Name I Love to Hear," Whitfield
"Make Me a Channel of Blessing," Smyth
"The Solid Rock," Mote

Offertory Prayer: Our Father, we remember that Jesus cautioned his followers that when they came to bring their offering, they should pause and reflect on whether they had any broken relationships with fellow Christians. May we pause for a moment and ponder this question. It is important to bring money for the work of God, and every Christian should feel this obligation. First, however, we should always be reconciled to our brothers and sisters. Make this worship with our offerings a vital part of the service this morning, and if there is need to mend broken relationships with others, may we do it before this day ends. We pray in Jesus' name. Amen.

Introduction

When we tell others how to raise children, we do so with great fear and extreme self-consciousness. Those who are parents know that the job is not easy and that there is no sure formula for rearing children. When we speak too boldly on the subject, we may be told by others, "Physician, heal thyself." Michelangelo had a favorite saying: *"Ancora imparo,"* "Still I am learning." Anyone who has raised or is raising children probably shares the problems and frustrations common to most families. However, some observations and suggestions may be made without one feeling that the "advice giver" is walking with the presumptuous step of a know-it-all.

I. To want children is normal.

The supreme manifestation of one's growth as a person is the desire to bring others into the world through the creative process God has ordained. Regardless of feminist opinion, the bearing and rearing of children is unquestionably a female's greatest achievement. It brings women the greatest joy and gives them the greatest power.

Daddies are parents too. Some men seem to be nonchalant or even hostile toward the idea of having children, yet deep in their hearts they are thrilled when they become fathers. Unfortunately, men too often leave child raising to women and miss the joy of spending time with their children.

The excuse that some give for not bringing children into the world is that they do not want their children to have to live in such a wicked world.

Times have always been bad! And they always will be until Jesus comes again! Unless there are some strong reasons for it, no couple should enter marriage with the deliberate intention of permanently avoiding parenthood. No higher privilege exists than that of sharing with God in the ability to create life through the processes he has ordained.

II. A child needs love.

Ancient Jews placed a great value on bearing children. For one thing, developing the land required a number of "hands in the field," and children, especially males, produced this labor force. Armies, too, were important for defense. Also, until Jesus came and arose from the dead, there was no clear-cut understanding on the part of Jews as to the nature of life after death. Jews therefore found a sense of immortality through their children. Thus Old Testament writers placed a great value on parents loving their children.

Modern psychology is in full agreement with the importance of loving and nurturing children. Many psychiatrists tell us that emotional scars received in childhood are never permanently erased from one's character. Those who feel that they were not loved in childhood may spend the rest of their lives taking it out on society. Those who have had good childhoods filled with love and affection go forth with security to bless the world.

III. Love means discipline.

In our day, parents often forget that to show love they must sometimes place restrictions on their children. Parents may be reluctant to be firm with a child for fear of losing that child's love, but in reality, discipline properly applied will cause a child to love the parent more. Many stories appear in newspapers today in which children complain because their parents did not love them enough to discipline them. In Hosea 12 the prophet pictures God as both loving and chastising his child, the young nation Israel. Parents must be willing to run the risk of short-term rejection by their children in order to develop their character and thus win long-term approval.

IV. Bearing the yoke in one's youth.

Hidden away in the seldom-read book of Lamentations is a striking truth. The prophet says, "It is good for a man that he bear the yoke in his youth" (Lam. 3:27). Parents stand in the place of God to discipline their young children. Such training is the best possible preparation for the discipline God will put on them in the years to come. The wiser the earthly parents are in correcting their children during the formative years, the less likely they will need corrective discipline from their heavenly Father later on.

When children become accustomed to yielding to the will of a good father, they will not find it hard to obey God's will. They will grow up seeking to merge their will with someone who is wiser, and they will not consider it an irksome task to do so. The yoke of discipline should be borne early in one's life, and parents are those responsible for this corrective action. When one trains a vine in the field, he does not let it put forth its branches where it wishes. Rather, he uses a pruning knife to dress the vine. Likewise, parents are guilty of cruel neglect when they allow children to do anything they wish during their early years. The tendency to go the wrong way is strengthened by the indulgence of permissive parents. Every year this occurs, the path of obedience to God looks less inviting and becomes more difficult.

V. The way he should go.

This verse has received several interpretations. First of all, we think of the moral commandment that we should train a child according to the demands of righteousness. Those who give this interpretation point out that great emphasis should be placed on "when he is old," since sometimes children do go astray even when they have been trained properly in their youth. Those who hold this interpretation say that even though children may wander in their youth, after proper training, when they become older and wiser, they will return to the original teaching of their parents. This has much merit, and many hold tenaciously to this interpretation.

Others have suggested that the verse means that parents should train children according to their chosen goals in life. This means that parents should help their children achieve the ambitions they have set for themselves or even that parents have set for them.

A third interpretation, and a very practical one, is that the writer meant to train children according to their own natural characteristics of style and manner. In other words, train them up according to the bent of their personalities. Those who have reared children know that no two children are alike. Parents with as many as five or six children testify that each one is different. Some children can be reasoned with logically. Others must be conquered, even by force. Wise parents will study the personalities of their children and in light of their personalities seek to train them to love God and hold high standards. This latter interpretation offers much practical wisdom.

Conclusion

Parents have a tremendous obligation. Thinking of the responsibilities that go with rearing children is enough to frighten a young couple. Yet if Jesus lives in our hearts and therefore is a part of our home life, we can be successful parents. We cannot ignore the demands of parenthood, but we can seek help daily through prayer, Bible study, family worship, and regular church attendance. Even then things can go wrong. Good parents have been disappointed in their children. In the long run, however, if we are faithful in our duty and remain true to God's Word for our lives, God will overrule any adversity, and we will eventually find a blessing in it.

Love your children! Enjoy them while they are children! Don't force them to become adults before they are ready to be grown people. On the other hand, lead them early to recognize that life has certain responsibilities and the sooner they prepare themselves to meet them, the more effectively they will face life and the more victorious they will be. Most of all, lead your children to become Christians early in life!

SUNDAY EVENING, JUNE 11

Title: Lead Us Not into Temptation

Text: "And lead us not into temptation" (**Matt. 6:13**).

Scripture Reading: Luke 4:1–15

Introduction

One of the surest evidences that a person has been forgiven of his or her sins and is a child of God is the desire to avoid sin and all that leads to it. Now that the sins of the past have been forgiven, the new creation in Christ is eager to pray, "And lead us not into temptation, but deliver us from evil" (Matt. 6:13).

I. What is temptation?

God does not lead his children into temptation. "Let no man say when he is tempted, I am tempted of God: for God cannot be tempted with evil, neither tempteth he any man" (James 1:13). Temptation is a solicitation to do evil. Surely God does not solicit to do evil. Yet why the petition "Lead us not into temptation"? The answer to this apparent contradiction—which really is no contradiction at all—is that the same Greek word means both "tempt" and "test." The context will determine whether the test is for the purpose of tempting to evil or for the purpose of building character. In this petition the translation should be "test," as many modern translations recognize, for example, "Do not bring us to this test" (Matt. 6:13 NEB). Other translators who retain the word *temptation* phrase it in such manner that in allowing us to be tempted of the evil one, God's purpose is that we may gain the victory, for example, "And do not subject us to temptation, But save us from the evil one" (Matt. 6:13 Goodspeed).

Temptation can come from without. In the Genesis account of the entrance of sin into human experience, Eve is tempted by the serpent. The serpent is generally understood to have been an instrument of, if not a manifestation of, Satan. Satan can also use sinful people to tempt others. "If sinners entice thee, consent thou not" (Prov. 1:10).

Temptation can come from within. After warning that temptation does not come from God, James added, "But every man is tempted, when he is drawn away of his own lust, and enticed" (James 1:14).

God does allow us to be tested, as, for example, "God tested Abraham" (Gen. 22:1 RSV).

The test is meant for our good. A teacher who gives a test does not do it for the purpose of failing members of the class, although it is given with the knowledge that some may fail. A test pilot does not test the plane for the purpose of wrecking it, although the hard tests may wreck the plane. God did not test Abraham for the purpose of delivering him to Satan, but with the purpose that his faith might prove steadfast. Luke records: "And Jesus being full of the Holy Ghost returned from Jordan, and was led by the Spirit into the wilderness, being forty days tempted of the devil" (Luke 4:1–2). After the forty days of temptation in which Jesus gained the victory, Luke wrote, "And Jesus returned in the power of the Spirit into Galilee" (Luke 4:14). The author of Hebrews comments, "Wherefore in all things it behooved him to be made like unto his brethren, that he might be a merciful and faithful high priest in things pertaining to God, to make reconciliation for the sins of the people. For in that he himself hath suffered being tempted, he is able to succour them that are tempted" (Heb. 2:17–18).

No great character can be developed without tests. One would never become a great mathematician by working only the easy problems. The musician is developed by playing the hard pieces. Storms help make sturdy oaks. There can be no heroism without risk. There would be no patience nor endurance without trials. "My brethren, count it all joy when ye fall into divers temptations: knowing this, that the trying of your faith worketh patience. But let patience have her perfect work, that ye may be perfect and entire, wanting nothing" (James 1:2–4). "Blessed is the man that endureth temptation: for when he is tried, he shall receive the crown of life, which the Lord hath promised to them that love him" (James 1:12). Recall also the final beatitude in Matthew 5:10–12.

II. "Lead us not into temptation" is a prayer for every Christian.

No Christian progresses beyond temptation. Perhaps the only person who does not feel temptation is the one who has surrendered to Satan.

Often the nearer to the Lord one is, the more severely he or she is tempted. Jesus "was in all points tempted like as we are, yet without sin" (Heb. 4:15). He was also tempted in some ways that we are not. To know the temptations of Jesus, one would have to be Jesus. How can we possibly know the power of Satan's temptation of Jesus to avoid the cross?

One who knows government secrets would be tempted to sell them, whereas others who do not have access to classified material would not be tempted. The more one is like Jesus, the severer the temptations. Satan's arrows seek a shining mark.

III. How shall we prepare to meet temptation?

Determine to say no to Satan and yes to Jesus no matter how great the enticement to wrong. Jesus did not hesitate. He said, "Get three behind me, Satan: thou art an offence unto me" (Matt. 16:23). On the contrary, Judas said, "What will ye give me, and I will deliver him unto you?" (Matt. 26:15).

Determine to tell the truth or you will lie; to be honest or you will cheat; to be true to Christian morality or you will yield. One who does not decide on Saturday to be in church on Sunday will sleep in on Sunday morning.

Flee from sin. Courting temptation is foolish. A pastor and a small group of church friends were assembled at the parsonage following a revival service. The pastor received a call from a distraught woman. She said her husband had not come from work. She thought perhaps he had cashed his paycheck and would be found at the tavern. The pastor and a layman did find the man at the tavern inebriated and short most of his pay. One of the laymen who was a recovering alcoholic had declined to go. He said that the smell of alcohol was almost more than he could resist. He was very wise in refusing to go near the tavern. Sparks falling on the ocean and sparks falling on gunpowder are quite different situations.

No one has the right to put a boat in above the falls and then pray, "Lord, save me." One has no right to presume on God by stirring up the passions with erotic books or pictures and then pray, "Keep me moral." No one ought to handle large sums of money for others without an accounting. He or she cannot juggle the books a little bit and then pray, "Lord, keep me honest."

Dr. Robert J. Hastings illustrated as follows:

> Mary, age four, is playing in the backyard on her tricycle. Her mother comes outside to burn wastepaper then goes inside. At first Mary pays no attention. Then she gets off her tricycle, walks shyly toward the fire, close enough to feel its warmth. She wonders if she could make it burn bigger and brighter. Yes, she gathers up scrap paper and dry leaves and makes a huge bonfire. She wonders what would happen if she poked the fire with a stick. Yes! Sparks fly, and the smoke forms exciting patterns. Caught up in an ecstasy, she moves dangerously close until a spark ignites her dress, and she runs screaming to her mother, a living, burning torch. When did Mary's dress catch fire? With a stopwatch, you could have told the time to the fraction of a second. But from a moral perspective, she was afire the minute she started toward the fire. ("Proclaim" [Nashville: Sunday School Board of the Southern Baptist Convention], April–June 1972, 47–48)

Be diligent to keep one's Christian life healthy. The best defense is a good offense. There is no defense against a home run. Spiritual health demands the following:

Food. Feed on God's Word. "Thy word have I hid in mine heart, that I might not sin against thee" (Ps. 119:11). Note how Jesus answered Satan by quoting Scripture in Luke 4:1–15.

Breath. Prayer is the Christian's vital breath. It is communion with the living God under the leadership of the Holy Spirit. Thomas Chalmers, in his notable sermon "The Expulsive Power of a New Affection," had as his theme that the constraint of Christ's love will overcome love of sin. A mother with a live baby in her arms does not care to play with dolls. The so-called pleasures of sin have little appeal for one who has true riches.

Exercise. "Therefore we ought to give the more earnest heed to the things which we have heard, lest at any time we should let them slip" (Heb. 2:1). "Wherefore take unto you the whole armour of God, that ye may be able to withstand in the evil day, and having done all, to stand" (Eph. 6:13).

Fellowship with good people. In your church you will find good Christian people with high ideals and Christian standards. Your fellowship with them and your participation in the worship, teaching, and training programs of your church will be a powerful help in overcoming temptation.

Conclusion

Jesus promised, "Lo, I am with you alway, even unto the end of the world" (Matt. 28:20). The Holy Spirit is the advocate who comes to give us strength. "There hath no temptation taken you but such as is common to man: but God is faithful, who will not suffer you to be tempted above that ye are able; but will with the temptation also make a way to escape, that ye may be able to bear it" (1 Cor. 10:13).

Make no provision for sinning, but if you fall, fall toward Jesus. "If we confess our sins, he is faithful and just to forgive us our sins, and to cleanse us from all unrighteousness" (1 John 1:9). Make every defeat a stepping-stone to complete victory.

We pray, "Lead us not into testing," but if the test must come, then the urgent prayer is "but deliver us from evil."

WEDNESDAY EVENING, JUNE 14

Title: Knowing Where to Run

Text: "And he built there an altar, and called the place El-bethel: because there God appeared unto him, when he fled from the face of his brother" **(Gen. 35:7).**

Scripture Reading: Genesis 35:1–15

Introduction

Seasons of spiritual regression are common among Christians. Another malady that often accompanies these arid stretches in our Christian lives is what John Bunyan called the "Slough of Despond." We find ourselves in the dilemma of not knowing where to run.

To illustrate this crisis in a Christian's life, let us examine the life of

Jacob, who became Israel, the immediate father of God's chosen people. Jacob had an enviable heritage. He was the son of Isaac and the grandson of Abraham. A study of his life, however, reveals much human weakness, periods of wandering, of slipping away from God. At times Jacob did not know where to run. But with God's gracious intervention, he found out that there is a haven in which the child of God is welcome, whatever the reason for his or her wandering.

I. A pattern began to develop early in Jacob's life that affected his relationship with God and created a climate for running.

Jacob and Esau, twin sons of Isaac and Rebekah, were born struggling together. From the beginning, they were inclined in opposite directions. Esau became a hunter, a man of the fields, and lived a rugged life. But Jacob showed a quieter and more even temperament. He loved home, listened to his mother's dreams of the future, learned to control his appetites and passions, and cultivated the art of patience in working toward the realization of his ambitions. He was ready also to take advantage of Esau's weakness and turn it to his own profit.

The climax of Jacob's deceit came when he allowed Esau to sell him his birthright for "a mess of pottage." Jacob's scheming was wrong, but Esau "despised" his birthright, meaning that he counted it lightly, as of no real consequence to him. Jacob's sin was compounded as, in collusion with his mother, he deceived his blind and dying father into giving the parting patriarchal blessing to him instead of to Esau. With hatred and vengeance, Esau began to plot Jacob's death. So began Jacob's running—to Mesopotamia, to find a wife among the daughters of Rebekah's brother.

II. A picture of God's omniscience in regard to Jacob, his patient and tender care, became apparent almost immediately.

God is the all-seeing and all-knowing God. Even though many years were to pass before Jacob found the right pathway, God waited, because Jacob belonged to him, and he had plans for Jacob's life. Jacob reached Bethel, and with a stone for his pillow, he fell into a fitful sleep. Jacob had a dream in which he saw a ladder connecting heaven with earth, with angels ascending and descending on it. God spoke to Jacob, assuring him that he would go with him and keep him, and bring him back to his homeland, which he would give to him for a possession. Jacob's assessment of the experience was fitting: "Surely [Jehovah] is in this place; and I knew it not" (Gen. 28:16).

Jacob's first visit to Bethel was a turning point in his life. He had come with a great burden of sin, but he left with a consciousness of having been forgiven. Bethel remains to this day a symbol of the place of encounter, where one stops running long enough to face God, and, consequently, to face oneself. The road back was yet a lengthy one for Jacob, but he was on the way! God indeed forgives sin completely; he casts our sins away from us as far as the east is from the west.

III. A plan for bringing Jacob to his divinely appointed destination is revealed at the proper time.

Approximately thirty years had passed since Jacob's first visit to Bethel, and his experience with God at Bethel doubtlessly had become vague. He left his Uncle Laban's home a wealthy man. Then came Peniel, where he wrestled all night with an angel and had his name changed to Israel. Because of this experience, he was lame for the rest of his life. Though materially successful, Jacob was a weary and broken man.

Then God stepped in. The divine instructions were that Jacob was to go "back to Bethel" and tarry there in prayer and worship. He was to build an altar, a place of sacrifice. He was to "put away the strange gods," he was to "be clean," and he was to "change his garments." Jacob ran to Bethel. And from that day forward, the pieces of the puzzle of Jacob's life began to fall into place. He had truly made the Lord God central in his life.

Conclusion

It is good to know where to run! For the unbeliever, the road is marked "repentance," and the destination is the cross. For the disobedient Christian who has lost the joy of his or her salvation, it is "back to Bethel," back to where God began a work in that person's life, so that the person can "take up again where the interruption came" and commence afresh the molding and fashioning of his or her life into a vessel of honor for God's glory.

SUNDAY MORNING, JUNE 18

Title: God, Give Us Men

Text: "Run ye to and fro through the streets of Jerusalem, and see now, and know, and seek in the broad places thereof, if ye can find a man" **(Jer. 5:1)**.

Scripture Reading: Psalm 1:1–6

Hymns: "Stand Up, Stand Up for Jesus," Duffield
"Rise Up, O Men of God," Merrill
"The Church's One Foundation," Stone

Offertory Prayer: Our Father, help us not to worry about things. Our Master has told us to seek God's kingdom first. May we have faith enough in him to know that he will provide for every need we have and that only the life yielded to his purposes is the truly happy one. May this part of the service when we bring our offerings remind us afresh of your goodness and our responsibilities. Bless all who have a part in this offering and also all who will receive blessings from the expending of the money that is given. We pray in Jesus' name. Amen.

Introduction

Every home needs a strong symbol of authority. When the father is willing to accept this challenge and, at the same time, be compassionate and tender in dealing with every member of the family, the home has a solid human anchor. The father actually cannot be all he ought to be as a father and as a man unless he knows Jesus Christ as Savior. This message is twofold. First, it is an appeal for men to be godly. Second, it is an urgent plea for every father to be, in Christ, the head of the home and family.

I. Men of conviction.

As we look at our world, we see deterioration on every hand. We see that people who once had deep convictions concerning right and wrong have yielded to compromise and sacrificed principles. Years ago an ancient philosopher was walking throughout the streets of his city with a lantern. Someone asked him what he was doing. He replied, "I am looking for an honest man." The situation in Jeremiah's day was similar. He was urging the people to run throughout the streets of Jerusalem and see if they could find any man who practiced justice and sought the truth. Jeremiah's conclusion was that God would spare the entire city if only one such man could be found.

Christian people in our land have become discouraged because they have looked to leaders and have been disappointed. Instead of integrity, we have seen dishonesty. We need today, people with character who will not be swayed by the desire for gain or glory. In our homes we need fathers who have convictions concerning the great issues of life and who are willing to practice these virtues in daily living. When our homes have this kind of husbands and fathers, families will grow up in the nurture and admonition of the Lord.

II. Men of compassion.

To be strong and uncompromising is not enough, however, to make an ideal man or father. We need men who are tender and compassionate. Far too often a man thinks he has to put on a strong front or people will think him effeminate. Actually, the opposite is true. It takes strength of character to be kind and unselfish. Jesus was the manliest person who ever lived, and yet he also knew how to enter into the sorrows of others and share their griefs. Edward Young once said, "Shun the proud that is ashamed to weep." Edmund Burke said that "next to love, sympathy is the divinest passion of the human heart." When we are able to feel with people, we develop a tender heart and a compassionate disposition that is perhaps the manliest of qualities. One outstanding preacher said, "How long, oh, how long will it take us to learn that there are only two things in life that really count—one is character and the other is human sympathy."

III. Men who are open-minded.

One of the saddest sights to behold is a man who thinks he knows everything and has no need to learn anything. Such men are prisoners within the walls of their own ignorance. A real man is always willing to consider the possibility that there is some truth he has not yet discovered. It takes a great man to say, "I was wrong," and this is one of the noblest statements to ever fall from a person's lips. After all, when we admit that we were wrong, we are actually saying that we are smarter today than we were yesterday.

IV. Men who love their families.

A family is the most profound of all human relationships. A man who genuinely cares for his family is investing his affection in that which will pay the greatest dividends. Many changes have taken place in the family structure during the past decade. More and more fathers are having a part in duties that once were considered altogether the woman's role. When men can help their wives in such areas, it adds "icing to the cake" in their marriage relationship. This, however, is not the basic idea involved in loving one's family.

Most important, if a man loves his family, he will be faithful and true to the marriage vows. We can never be certain as to how accurate the polls are concerning marital infidelity in the nation. We do know, however, that an increasing number of men are unfaithful to their wives. Unfaithfulness also affects their children in a striking way. Often we hear men urged to love their children. This is important, but it is *more important* for men who want to show genuine love for their children to love their children's mother.

For children to know that Daddy loves Mama and is true to her in every relationship of life, produces stabler mental and emotional health than for the child to have Daddy pour out love in the form of extra gifts. All of the fishing trips and ball games will not suffice to bring love to a child if that father has been unfaithful to the mother. We shall never be able to measure accurately the emotional instability present in children because of parental bickering and fighting. Many children have been deeply scarred because of this. We need men today who love their families by showing loyalty in every way to the women they have chosen as their life companions.

Conclusion

God wants people who are willing to be responsible. Since people are made in God's image, they have power to do what God requires of them. God did not create people to be robots, but rather free moral agents. The capacity to choose makes people accountable for their choices. And God is the Judge of our use or misuse of the talents he has given to us.

Glorifying God involves total commitment to him. This means dying to self and to our own ambitions and cleverness. Such people must say with Paul, "Lord, what will you have me to do?" People God can use are those who will accept their blessings from God as opportunities for service. Knowing that God can be depended on to take care of our necessities, we must rest in this confidence and serve with steadfastness. In this world of uncertainty and turbulence, we can radiate peace and confidence if God lives in our hearts through Jesus Christ. Such people will obey God at all costs, realizing that they can do nothing in their own strength. We need people today who will walk with God continually and will consistently seek to know his will and then do it with all their might.

SUNDAY EVENING, JUNE 18

Title: Deliver Us from Evil

Text: "But deliver us from evil" **(Matt. 6:13).**

Scripture Reading: Luke 11:1–4

Introduction

A young, inexperienced preacher, in one of his sermons, attributed the quotations "God helps those who help themselves" and "Every tub stands on its own bottom" to the apostle Paul. When challenged after the service to cite the Scripture references, he was, of course, unable to find them; but he responded with considerable spirit, "Well, they are good enough to be from Paul."

One who has been accustomed to reading only the King James Version may be surprised to learn that the familiar ending to the model prayer, "For thine is the kingdom, and the power, and the glory, forever. Amen," is not found in the earliest manuscripts and is not a part of the prayer as spoken by Jesus. It was almost certainly a liturgical addition. That it seems good enough to be from Jesus does not change the fact that it is not. The early Christians, as we do, thought that the prayer ended rather abruptly with the petition "Deliver us from evil" and added various closings. Further contemplation, however, will reveal that the petition "Deliver us from evil" is a fitting climax to the prayer.

I. This prayer reveals:

Evil is a reality. In the parable of the tares, the householder says with reference to the one who sowed tares in the wheat, "An enemy hath done this" (Matt. 13:28). Jesus, during his explanation of the parable to his disciples, said, "The enemy that sowed them is the devil" (Matt. 13:39). Genesis 3 gives an account of Eve being tempted by the serpent to distrust God. She used her power of choice to choose her own way rather than God's way. The Bible does not explain the origin of evil, but neither does it explain it away. Evil is a reality, and Satan is an enemy. Someone has said, "A world where man would not sin would be heaven; a world where man could not sin would be hell." Moral choice is a reality. God with great courage has made human-kind in his own image. This power of moral choice is one's most precious and perilous possession. If evil is anything contrary to the will of God, then the supreme end of life is to be delivered from evil.

Evil is universal. "Deliver us from evil" is a prayer for all. "There is none righteous, no, not one" (Rom. 3:10). "For all have sinned, and come short of the glory of God" (Rom. 3:23). "All we like sheep have gone astray; we have turned every one to his own way; and the LORD hath laid on him the iniquity of us all" (Isa. 53:6). By the time we come to an age of accountability, we know by experience that we have sinned. Our salvation must be effected by the grace of God, because it can never be on the basis of our sinlessness. "For God has consigned all men to disobedience, that he may have mercy upon all" (Rom. 11:32 RSV).

God is able to deliver from evil and from the evil one. Paul cries out under con-viction for the weight of the penalty of his sins. "O wretched man that I am! who shall deliver me from the body of this death?" (Rom. 7:24). He knows the answer: "I thank God through Jesus Christ our Lord" (v. 25). This is the heart of the gospel. When sin first appeared, God promised a Savior from sin. The seed of the woman would crush Satan's head (see Gen. 3:15). God drove Adam and Eve from Eden, but at the east of the garden he provided a way—a symbolic altar guarded by the cherubim—by which they could come back to the tree of life (see Gen. 3:22–23).

The promises to provide a Savior from sin, which were given to sinners before Christ came, were fulfilled in Jesus, the Son of God, the Messiah, concerning whom John the Baptist testified, "Behold, the lamb of God, who takes away the sin of the world!" (John 1:29 RSV). "For God so loved the world, that he gave his only begotten Son, that whosoever believeth in him should not perish, but have everlasting life" (John 3:16). Satan is doomed. A part of the convicting work of the Holy Spirit in this age is to convict "of judgment, because the prince of this world is judged" (John 16:11).

God will not be defeated in his own universe. Jesus will be triumphant. "For he must reign, till he hath put all enemies under his feet" (1 Cor. 15:25). We can throw ourselves into the fight against sin with full assurance that we are on the winning side. "If God be for us, who can be against us?" (Rom. 8:31). "Therefore, my beloved brethren, be ye stedfast, unmoveable, always abounding in the work of the Lord, forasmuch as ye know that your labour is not in vain in the Lord" (1 Cor. 15:58).

II. How does God deliver us from evil?

God delivers from the penalty of sin by justification. "Therefore being justified by faith, we have peace with God through our Lord Jesus Christ" (Rom. 5:1). "For the wages of sin is death; but the gift of God is eternal life through Jesus Christ our Lord" (Rom. 6:23). "Who gave himself for us to redeem us from all iniquity and to purify for himself a people of his own who are zealous for good deeds" (Titus 2:14 RSV). "For the Son of man is come to seek and to save that which was lost" (Luke 19:10). "For this is my blood of the new testament, which is shed for many for the remission of sins" (Matt. 26:28). "There is therefore now no condemnation to them which are in Christ Jesus, who walk not after the flesh, but after the Spirit. For the law of the Spirit of life in Christ Jesus hath made me free from the law of sin and death" (Rom. 8:1–2).

God delivers by regeneration from the love of sin. "Therefore if any man be in Christ, he is a new creature: old things are passed away; behold, all things are become new" (2 Cor. 5:17). David in genuine repentance prayed, "Create in me a clean heart, O God; and renew a right spirit within me" (Ps. 51:10). God does both. When he justifies, he regenerates.

God adopts, claims as his own, and gives eternal life to the one who is justified and regenerated. "But as many as received him, to them gave he power to become the sons of God, even to them that believe on his name" (John 1:12). "My sheep hear my voice, and I know them, and they follow me: and I give unto them eternal life; and they shall never perish, neither shall any man pluck them out of my hand" (John 10:27–28).

God progressively delivers his children from the power of sin during this earthly life. Children of God cooperate with the Holy Spirit in growing more like Jesus. Paul wrote, "Brethren, I count not myself to have apprehended; but this one thing I do, forgetting those things which are behind, and reaching forth unto those things which are before, I press toward the mark for the prize of the high calling of God in Christ Jesus" (Phil. 3:13–14). "But grow in grace, and in the knowledge of our Lord and Saviour Jesus Christ" (2 Peter 3:18).

From the presence of sin, God will deliver us by glorification in heaven. "We shall be like him; for we shall see him as he is" (1 John 3:2).

Conclusion

This is a great missionary petition, for we are praying not only for our own deliverance, but also for the salvation of others. This certainly obligates us to proclaim the gospel by which persons are delivered from evil. "But deliver us from evil" *is* an appropriate climax to this great prayer.

WEDNESDAY EVENING, JUNE 21

Title: Loving Those Hard to Love

Text: "And Joseph saw his brethren, and he knew them, but made himself strange unto them, and spoke roughly unto them; . . . And he turned himself about from them, and wept" (**Gen. 42:7, 24**).

Scripture Reading: Genesis 42:1–25

Introduction

What is love? To start with basics, we might say that love is an emotion, an affection for or an attachment to someone. Love means to delight in, to take pleasure in. A popular song of the mid-1900s declared that "Love makes the world go 'round," and another insisted that "What the world needs now is love." How true that is in our day when jealousy, greed, and hate abound.

One kind of love, alien to natural man, describes the essence of God's character and enables Christians to love the unlovable, those who are "hard to love." All of us periodically encounter those who fit into this category. As children of God, we must love them. The Bible character whose life is an example of one who demonstrated the ability to love those hard to love is Joseph.

I. The seeds of conflict between Joseph and his brothers were sown early in his life.

Joseph was born in Padan-aram, the first son of Jacob and Rachel. After the death of his mother, Joseph experienced ten years of intimate and happy association with his father. During this time he became the errand boy of the family, taking messages back and forth between Jacob and the older sons working out in the fields. The first cloud across the relationship between Joseph and his brothers appeared when he "brought unto his father their evil report" (Gen. 37:2). Joseph was a tattler and soon incurred the contempt of his brothers.

The bad situation became intensified when Jacob showed partiality to Joseph by giving him a "coat of many colors." With its flowing sleeves and rich color, it was an obvious indication of Jacob's feeling toward Joseph. This fed the flame of hatred in the hearts of the brothers. To make matters worse, Joseph began to dream, and in his dreams he was the chief personality, and his brothers were doing obeisance to him. This served only to ignite the flames of hostility.

II. The seething hatred in the hearts of Joseph's brothers erupted, overwhelming Joseph and changing the course of his life.

Suddenly Joseph, who had enjoyed privilege and power in the family, found himself being jostled along to Egypt to be sold by the Ishmaelites. Joseph no doubt began to develop a deep hatred for his brothers. We can imagine the total frustration of this sheltered young man, wrested from the loving protection of his father's domain and deposited in an alien land! Things went from bad to worse: first he was victimized by a cunning and seductive woman; then he was imprisoned on false charges, where his life hung in the balance. But Joseph's genteel character kept him true, and the harsh discipline of his trials began to temper his life for the unique role God had prepared for him.

Maturity came quickly to young Joseph. In prison he prayed much and contented himself in humble service. He proved himself to the jailer and was soon put in charge of the other prisoners. Finally, Joseph found himself before Pharaoh, having been called on to interpret two dreams the king had dreamed. Joseph said, "I cannot do it, but God will give Pharaoh the answer he desires" (Gen. 41:16 NIV). The result of this encounter with Pharaoh was Joseph's elevation to the second highest position in Egypt.

III. Joseph's submission opened the way for God's love to flow through him to his brothers in their crisis.

Through all of these experiences, God was preparing Joseph for something special: he was to be God's instrument in the development of his chosen people, Israel. The climactic moment came when Joseph's brothers stood before him (although they did not recognize him) to appeal for grain, for Canaan had been stricken with famine. This was Joseph's moment for vengeance! Twenty-one years had passed since that infamous day they had sold him into slavery. Now was the time to get even! But such was not in Joseph's heart. When he saw them, "he turned himself about from them, and wept" (Gen. 42:24).

The story of Joseph's treatment of his brothers is one of the greatest stories in all literature. It is the story of love overcoming hatred and vengeance. Yet this happened in Joseph's life only after a long chain of events, during which time God had proved his love for Joseph.

Conclusion

"Loving those hard to love" is one of the most difficult experiences that can come in one's life. We find it exceedingly difficult to love those who have dealt viciously or treacherously with us. Yet God will teach us to love all people if we will allow ourselves to become teachable students in his university of discipline. Perhaps the best place to begin is to remember that "while we were yet sinners, Christ died for us" (Rom. 5:8).

SUNDAY MORNING, JUNE 25

Title: Don't Act Like a Baby

Text: "Let no man despise thy youth" (**1 Tim. 4:12**).

Scripture Reading: 1 Timothy 4:1–16

Hymns: "Give of Your Best to the Master," Grose
             "When I Survey the Wondrous Cross," Watts
             "Loyalty to Christ," Cassel

Offertory Prayer: Our Father, we remember that the Macedonia Christians were described as people who "first gave themselves to the Lord." As we are about to bring our gifts of money, may we take inventory of our own lives to see whether we have given you, first of all, the complete dedication of our lives. You have done so much for us! We recall the words of the psalmist who said, "What shall I render unto the Lord in exchange for all his benefits?" One of the answers was that we should "pay our vows" to you. Make us responsible stewards in every area of life's abilities. At this particular moment, help us to concentrate on our financial obligations and privileges in serving God. We pray for Christ's sake. Amen.

Introduction

In this series of sermons, we have sought to deal with all phases of family life: Today we deal specifically with young people. When we say young people, we include any child who is still in the home and still subject to parental discipline and dependent on parental support. As long as young people receive their livelihood from their parents, they have certain obligations to their parents, and this message seeks to examine these responsibilities.

I. An interesting command.

Paul was writing to his young preacher "son," Timothy. He was giving him many words of wisdom since he realized his own days were limited.

Young people do well to listen to experienced soldiers of the cross. They have much to tell us, and we can avoid many pitfalls along the way if we will heed the advice of those who have gone before us.

This command to Timothy to "let no man despise thy youth" is similar to an exhortation Paul gave to Titus when he said, "Let no man despise thee!" (Titus 2:15). The words Paul used in the original language, however, show a marked difference in the two commands. In both commands, Paul used the Greek word for "think" with a preposition in front of it. In the command to Timothy the preposition is "down," which has the force of "let no man think down upon you." This means that Timothy is not to act in such a way that people will think less of him than they ought to think.

In the words to Titus, Paul places a preposition meaning "around" in front of the verb. The prefix is the word from which we get our English word *perimeter*. Thus Paul was saying to Titus, "Don't let any man 'encircle you with his thoughts' or 'outthink you.'" Both of these injunctions are worthwhile for a young person to consider. Paul's command to Timothy, however, is perhaps a bit more forceful and urgent. Timothy was probably more than thirty years of age by this time, but Paul still thought of him as a young person. Sons never grow up as far as their parents are concerned, and Timothy was Paul's "son in the ministry." He cautioned him always to be firm in the faith, but here, in a very special way, he was commanding him to act like a grown man and not have the characteristics of a child.

II. The need for maturity.

Someone has said that there is no such thing as a "mature person." Rather, we should speak of a "maturing person" since we never completely arrive in this life. Although Jesus told us to "be ye therefore perfect" (Matt. 5:48), he used a word that indicated fullness or maturity rather than sinlessness or blamelessness. As long as we live in this body, we shall still continue to do some things that are wrong.

There is, however, a great need for Christian growth! One writer says, "We must grow up or blow up!" Nothing is quite so tragic as a Christian young man who fails to take advantage of opportunities for personal growth and move forward in his Christian life.

The supreme need for today's world is for us to learn how to live with one another. Modern means for travel and communication have placed us so close together that we must learn how to act as neighbors. Of course, we who are Christians know that the experience with Jesus Christ is the foundation stone for all Christian growth. Yet many Christians fail to grow as they should. Hostility between people comes because they have no inner resources to give them understanding that comes with maturity. Secular writers speak of maturity in terms of "a unifying philosophy of life." This phrase contains an element of truth but not enough for a Christian.

That unifying philosophy must be based on one having adopted Christianity as one's goal through receiving Jesus Christ as personal Savior. The true base of maturity is a Christian faith, because only this has sufficient resources and power to enable one to grow toward Jesus, the most mature person who ever lived.

III. Some helps for maturity.

When we look at psychology's definition of maturity and then examine our Bible, we will find that God's Word contains that which is necessary for us to realize every goal of growth. Too many people think of books written a long time ago as being out of date and largely in error. Thus they place the Bible in this category.

The truth is, however, that people who lived many years ago faced the same problems we are facing today. The principles of the Bible are true today because the writers, inspired of God, dealt with issues that have affected and always will affect people as long as life goes on in this world. The basic problems of life are still greed, pride, and the appeal to fleshly lusts. Immature people feel that every whim must be satisfied immediately. The Bible teaches that the long-range solution is always the best. If we sell our birthright for temporary satisfaction of a whim, we will soon regret the decision. If, on the other hand, we feast on God's Word and instill the principles laid down in it in our lives, we will come to the latter part of life with happiness and joy.

As we read the Bible and absorb its message, our values change. First, we cannot read God's Word long without meeting Jesus. When he comes into our life and challenges our best, things become different. We no longer act like a child wanting every whim satisfied immediately. We are willing to wait for his will to be worked out in our lives. The Bible teaches us also that suffering is not always a bad thing. Indeed, it may lead to some of life's greatest insights. One who has never been disappointed has never learned much about the true meaning of life. The spoiled child doesn't want anything to interfere with what he or she wants. The mature Christian is willing to wait for God's own time.

Conclusion

Put your Christianity to work! Learn to trust Jesus and then relax concerning the other needs of life. He will bring us everything we need. When we engage in prayer, sincere and frequent worship, and regular confession of sins, and we are willing to work with others, we will find real joy. Childlike trust in God's power will do more to keep us emotionally healthy than most people realize. There is a great difference in being childlike and being childish in our attitudes. To trust God and be certain he will provide for our needs is the simple message Jesus taught. To think the world should revolve around us and immediately gratify our desires is immature and displeasing to God. Paul was eager for Timothy to "grow up" in the gospel. This, too, is also one of our greatest needs.

SUNDAY EVENING, JUNE 25

Title: Fasting That Glorifies God

Text: "When you fast, do not look somber as the hypocrites do, for they disfigure their faces to show men they are fasting. I tell you the truth, they have received their reward in full. But when you fast, put oil on your head and wash your face, so that it will not be obvious to men that you are fasting, but only to your Father, who is unseen; and your Father, who sees what is done in secret, will reward you" **(Matt. 6:16–18 NIV)**.

Scripture Reading: Luke 9:23–27

Introduction

Christian motive for worship and service (Matt. 6:1–18) is the second major division of the Sermon on the Mount. The emphasis is on doing religious acts for God's glory rather than for the praise of men. Verse 1 issues the warning, "Beware of practicing your piety before men in order to be seen of them; for then you will have no reward from your Father who is in heaven" (Matt. 6:1 RSV). This warning is illustrated with reference to: religious acts toward others (Matt. 6:2–4), religious acts toward God (Matt. 6:5–15), and religious acts toward oneself (Matt. 6:16–18), which is the text for this message.

Note in this section the value of repetition: "be not as the hypocrites" in verses 2, 5, and 16; "They have their reward" in verses, 2, 5, and 16; "seeth in secret" in verses 4, 6, and 18; and "thy Father shall reward thee" in verses 4, 6, and 18.

The principle involved with fasting refers to every type of religious observance. God is concerned about the why as well as the what of religious acts. The late Dr. Ellis Fuller said, "If the devil cannot get you to do wrong, he will try to get you to do right for the wrong motive."

I. Fasting in Bible times.

Fasting is the abstinence from food for a religious purpose. God gives no command to fast either in the Old or the New Testament. It was widely practiced in Old Testament times, as one can discover by running the following references: Judges 20:26; 1 Samuel 7:6; 31:13; 2 Samuel 1:12; 12:22–23; 1 Kings 21:27; 1 Chronicles 10:12: Ezra 8:23; Nehemiah 1:4; Esther 4:16; Psalms 35:13; 69:10; 109:24; Isaiah 58:3–4; Jeremiah 14:12; Daniel 9:3; Joel 2:12; and Zechariah 7:5.

The scribes and Pharisees and the disciples of John the Baptist fasted often. They all condemned Jesus and his disciples for not fasting (see Luke 5:33–35 and Matt. 9:14–15). Jesus' reply indicates that fasting has no value unless it is a voluntary accompaniment to one's state of mind. It would have been as inappropriate for his disciples to fast as for a wedding party to fast. Jesus said that days of sorrow would come when fasting would be appropriate. Jesus had fasted forty days at the time of his temptation by Satan in the wilderness (see Matt. 4:2). His assertion, "Moreover, when ye fast" in our text seems to assume that his disciples will fast, but his emphasis is on the perversion of fasting for the wrong motive.

The religious leaders of Jesus' day had reduced fasting to a system. In addition to the half dozen fasts generally observed by the nation, they had adopted fasting twice a week, Thursday and Monday, the traditional days on which Moses ascended and descended Mount Sinai. The proud Pharisee in Jesus' parable boasts, "I fast twice in the week" (Luke 18:12).

The excessive merit attached to fasting in that day is illustrated by the way scribes inserted it in the early manuscripts and versions of the Scripture. A comparison of the King James Version and the Revised Standard Version shows that "and fasting" was added in Mark 9:29; the whole verse of Matthew 17:21 was added; "I was fasting," was added in Acts 10:30; and "and fasting" was added in 1 Corinthians 7:5. The word is genuine, however, in Matthew 9:15; Luke 2:37; Acts 13:3; and 14:23.

Fasting does not seem to be very popular among modern Christians. Yet some have found it a valuable aid to devotion. William Barclay, in his popular commentary *The Gospel of Matthew* (1:239–40), gives five reasons why he considers that "a wise fasting is an excellent thing."

II. The larger principle is that one should put God and his glory first.

Discipleship means saying no to self and yes to God. Jesus said, "If any man will come after me, let him deny himself, and take up his cross daily, and follow me" (Luke 9:23). Note that Jesus calls for denial of self rather than self-denial. One is called on to renounce the old unregenerate nature and to "seek first the kingdom of God, and his righteousness" (Matt. 6:33). *Cross* in the Scripture stands for death. "Let him . . . take up his cross daily" means to put self on the cross, and "Let him . . . follow me" means to put Christ on the throne. Since God is holy and loving, it is a wonderful paradox that one gains life by giving himself away. "For whosoever will save his life shall lose it: but whosoever will lose his life for my sake, the same shall save it" (Luke 9:24).

Denial of self may issue in apparent self-denial, for no one can really outgive God (see Matt. 19:27–29). For example, if it seems God's will that you abstain from food as an aid to devotion, as an aid to health, or for some other good reason, then do so as a matter of obedience to God's will and not with the idea of gaining merit. No religious act brings one merit with God. Even a profession of faith in Jesus as Lord is a sin rather than a virtue if the heart is not in it, as Jesus emphasizes later in this sermon (see Matt. 7:21–23). Paul informed the Corinthians that in coming together to partake of the Lord's Supper, their observance was for the worse rather than the better because of their divisions and other excesses (see 1 Cor. 11:18–22).

What do you think of this as an example of fasting? A fine Christian layman is a barber. He closes his shop at 6:30 p.m., but in accord with custom he services all of the customers who are in his shop at closing time. On Wednesday nights this does not usually leave him time to go home and eat before attending the midweek prayer service at his church. For more than thirty years, he has missed supper with regularity. It is not too surprising that a dedicated Christian layman would consider attending prayer meeting more important than having supper, but it is surprising that no one has ever heard him mention that he must fast in order to attend the service.

III. Beware of hypocrisy.

Hypocrisy of the scribes and Pharisees was evidenced by their desire to convey the impression to their fellowmen that they were religious. Fasting was popular. Religious men were venerated. They put on sad countenances, disfigured their faces, and made sure that all noticed they were fasting. They were seen of men, and that is all the reward they received. "They have their reward" is a translation of the term "paid in full," which is found on many receipts, especially grain receipts, written in the koine Greek of the New Testament. They can write "paid in full" on that religious effort, for they cannot expect favorable consideration from God for a religious effort designed to elicit people's approval.

Sincerity of the Christian is to result in religious acts done with an eye to God's approval rather than people's. Far from dressing and acting in such manner as to attract the attention of others, Christians who fast will be groomed neatly as usual and not give any outward indication of fasting. They know that the heavenly Father sees them and will reward them accordingly.

Conclusion

It is easy to recognize that it is hypocritical for people to advertise piety that they really don't have. Ananias and Sapphira, for example, wanted credit for a generosity they did not possess (see Acts 5:1–10). However, Jesus warned that even when our religious acts are genuine, we are not to seek personal glory by advertising them nor praise by letting it be known that we did not advertise them.

We must have faith to believe that God sees and responds. Jesus taught that the heavenly Father will recompense sincere hearts for every act of obedience to his will. It may be now; it will certainly be at the judgment and throughout eternity. "Your Father who sees in secret will reward you" (Matt. 6:18 RSV). "You will be repaid at the resurrection of the just" (Luke 14:14 RSV). "For whosoever shall give you a cup of water to drink in my name, because ye belong to Christ, verily I say unto you, he shall not lose his reward" (Mark 9:41).

WEDNESDAY EVENING, JUNE 28

Title: Finding God Unexpectedly

Text: "The angel of the LORD appeared unto him in a flame of fire out of the midst of a bush; and he looked, and, behold, the bush burned with fire, and the bush was not consumed. And Moses said, I will now turn aside, and see this great sight, why the bush is not burnt" **(Ex. 3:2–3)**.

Scripture Reading: Exodus 3:1–14

Introduction

Almost all of us can look back over our lives and discover that many of the unusual things that have happened, both good and bad, have been unexpected. Without warning they have simply "exploded" in our lives. Some unexpected happenings have to do with the confrontation between God and man. Usually these experiences come at crisis points in our lives. They are "corners" that we turn in our spiritual growth and development. A biblical event illustrating such an experience is Moses' unexpected meeting with God at the burning bush in the Midian desert. Perhaps a close examination of this unique encounter will help prepare us for the unexpected confrontations that may come in our lives.

I. There was a careful preparation for this encounter.

However "unexpected" or spontaneous this confrontation appeared to be, there was meticulous preparation on God's part. It began, historically, when Moses was set afloat on the Nile, watched over by his sister Miriam, and found by Pharaoh's daughter. As a prince of Egypt, Moses was trained in all the wisdom of the Egyptians. But he also was an integral part of God's plan, and the sovereign election of God began to operate. As a young adult, Moses began to make excursions among his suffering people, slaves of the Egyptians. He became convicted that he must identify with his people. Then, in a flash of indignation and anger, he killed an Egyptian taskmaster who had been brutally mistreating a Hebrew slave.

Moses' hasty act made it necessary for him to flee Egypt. God did not will that Moses kill the Egyptian, but he used the unfortunate incident to get Moses out of Egypt so that he could commence "phase two" of the preparatory period. Moses obviously needed forty years of seasoning, for that is how long God allowed the evil Pharaoh to remain on Egypt's throne! When Ramses died, the obstacle that had kept Moses from returning to Egypt was removed. Likewise, God's hand is on everything that concerns his children, and particularly as it relates to his plan and purpose.

II. There was a split-second timing for the moment of breakthrough.

Moses had received no advance notices concerning what was about to happen in his life. He had gone from prince of Egypt to shepherd, considered by the Egyptians to be the lowliest of all occupations. On this particular day, he was at the "backside" of the Midian desert, at Mount Horeb, a place of extreme solitude.

The instrument God used to manifest his presence to Moses was as unique as the location. A scrubby acacia bush, seared and blistered by the hot desert winds, was enveloped by a strange fire, and yet it was not consumed! And the angel of the Lord appeared in the fire with a startling command to Moses. Why this spectacular experience? Moses was about to embark on the most important mission of his life. Before he could represent God to the Hebrew people, he had to receive a vision of the ineffable glory of God in his own soul.

III. Moses' life was changed as a result of this unforgettable meeting.

God told Moses to remove his shoes, "for the place whereon thou standest is holy ground" (Ex. 3:5). Moses learned that he could not "stroll into God's presence" and expect to meet him there in fellowship and in power without personal preparation. Likewise, we cannot serve God haphazardly. Certainly there is a deep and pervasive joy, but all true worship and service must be prepared for.

Furthermore, God reminded Moses that as the God of Abraham, he was the sovereign elector; as the God of Isaac, he was the quickener, the giver of life, for Isaac was born to Sarah when she was dead insofar as childbearing was concerned; as the God of Jacob, he was the longsuffering God who demonstrated his patience repeatedly with a disobedient Jacob. Every provision necessary for Moses to become an effective deliverer was made by God. All God needed at this point was Moses' submission.

Conclusion

Moses was prepared by God. When each step of the preparation was completed, God confronted Moses. Though the encounter was shocking for Moses, the careful preparation God had made in Moses' life enabled him to have a life-changing experience.

Are you ready for God to prepare you in whatever ways he considers necessary for a truly life-changing encounter? Are you willing for God to make of you a unique vessel for useful and fruitful service? Answer carefully, for "meeting God unexpectedly" may change the entire course of your life!

JULY

■ Sunday Mornings

Our Lord provides us with a pattern to follow as we face the great issues of life. The theme for the July and August morning sermons is "Christ Sets the Pattern."

■ Sunday Evenings

Continue with expository messages from Jesus' Sermon on the Mount.

■ Wednesday Evenings

Continue with the theme "Meeting Life's Crises," by examining the responses made by men of faith in the past. We worship the same God they did. We can benefit by letting them speak to us in the present.

SUNDAY MORNING, JULY 2

Title: Boldness in Prayer

Text: "Let us then with confidence draw near to the throne of grace, that we may receive mercy and find grace to help in time of need" **(Heb. 4:16)**.

Scripture Reading: Hebrews 4:14–16

Hymns: "Come, Thou Almighty King," Anonymous
"I Need Thee Every Hour," Hawks
"Teach Me to Pray," Reitz

Offertory Prayer: Loving Father, we thank you for all of the privileges that you have granted to us as your children. We thank you for the privilege of reading your Holy Word and for the communications that come to us from your throne of grace through your Word. We thank you for the privilege of coming to this house of prayer and worship where we can meet with your people and experience the presence of the living Christ. We thank you for the continuing leadership of your Holy Spirit who is always seeking to enrich, to uplift, and to enlarge our lives. We thank you for the opportunity and the privilege to be givers. Accept these tithes and offerings and bless them to the end that others will come to know of your love, your grace, and your power for their lives. We pray in Jesus' name. Amen.

Introduction

Have you ever needed the help of another person as you faced the opportunities and responsibilities of life? Have you ever made an appeal for help in a time of need?

If you need medical attention and treatment, do you approach a physician with an attitude of hesitancy or with a spirit of confidence and boldness?

If you need a loan, do you approach your banker with fear and trembling, with great hesitation, or with a degree of confidence and boldness?

On what basis do you make your appeal to others for their assistance? Do you try to purchase their favor? Do you seek to bargain with them? Have you ever tried to intimidate someone into assisting you?

What kind of an attitude do you have when you approach God in prayer in your time of need? With feelings of unworthiness? With great hesitancy? Do you seek to bargain with God? Do you give up in despair and make no attempt to communicate with God?

The writer of the book of Hebrews tells us to practice confident boldness when we come before God's throne of grace in prayer. This may be shocking at first glance. How bold are you in your prayer life? How confident are you that God is going to hear and answer your prayer?

I. The practice of bold praying.

Our Lord was bold in his prayer life. He was in constant communication with the heavenly Father, and there was no friction between his will and God the Father's will.

A study of Christian history will reveal that great men and women of God have always been bold in their prayer lives. Without hesitancy they entered into the throne room of the eternal, bringing their praises, petitions, and expressions of thanks.

Yet others have practiced bold praying that has proved to be ineffective. We need to avoid this type of bold praying.

Let us avoid a bold prayer life like that of the proud Pharisee who recited complimentary things concerning himself (Luke 18:9–12).

Let us avoid the bold praying of the hypocrite who gave himself to public prayer to impress others with his piety (Matt. 6:1–2, 5). Jesus is not prohibiting praying in public. Rather, he is declaring that people who pray in public to imprcss others are merely putting on a performance that will not bring the blessings of God into their lives.

Let us avoid the long and persuasive prayers of the pagan who labors under the impression that by beautiful, empty phrases and constant repetition, God's reluctance can finally be worn down (Matt. 6:7–8). If we pray in God's will, he is not reluctant to answer our prayers.

II. The basis of bold praying.

The inspired writer encourages us to come boldly before the throne of grace because of Christ's nature. It is through Christ that both Jewish and Gentile converts have access into the presence of our Father God (Eph. 2:18). Christ, as our High Priest, has entered into the heavens, where he has been given a position of sovereignty at the right hand of the Father. It is through him and in him that we have the privilege of prayer. Christ, having worn the garments of human flesh and having experienced the trials and tribulations and pressures due all humanity, is declared to be a very sympathetic High Priest. On the basis of his sympathy and his sinlessness, we are encouraged to come boldly to the throne of grace that we may find mercy and grace to help in time of need.

Many words of encouragement toward being bold in prayer can be found in the teachings of our precious Lord.

Jesus made the assumption that we would want to communicate with our Father God (Matt. 6:6). He simply said, "When you pray. . . ."

Jesus invited his disciples to pray (Matt. 7:7–8). He made the observation that those who asked received. He affirmed that the Father God is generous and good and wise. He illustrated this with the example of a human father responding to the needs of his children (Matt. 7:9–11).

The example of Jesus should encourage us to pray. Our Lord made much of prayer in his personal life. Something about his prayer experience caused his apostles to hunger for a similar experience with God. When they requested his help, he responded by teaching them how to pray effectively (Luke 11:1–4).

The promise of Jesus concerning the results of prayer should encourage us to be bold in prayer (Luke 11:13). Jesus made observations concerning the rewards that come from God to those who make it a practice of coming into his presence in their times of need. Jesus never promised that God would grant the selfish and petty requests of people who view God as some kind of celestial Santa Claus.

The nature of our Lord himself should be the greatest encouragement for boldness in our prayer life (Heb. 4:14–16). He understands and suffers with us in our needs, and he is able to help us.

The leadership of the Holy Spirit should also be a basis for practicing boldness in our prayer life (Rom. 8:26). The indwelling Spirit will not only lead us into the closet of prayer, but he also will help us to pray according to God's will.

III. The need for boldness in prayer.

All of us need to pray with more confidence and more assurance that God is a prayer-hearing and a prayer-answering God.

Each of us stands in constant need of mercy and grace from day to day (Heb. 4:16).

There is never a day when we do not stand in need of the cleansing grace of God concerning our imperfections and shortcomings (1 John 1:9). All children of God need the constant cleansing that comes as a result of genuine confession so that they can enjoy unhindered fellowship with God and maintain proper fellowship with others.

The nature of our enemy the devil should cause all of us to stay close to the closet of prayer (James 4:7–8; 1 Peter 5:8). We must resist the devil if we would have him flee from us, and we need to draw near to God for the strength we need to overcome evil.

The immensity and the complexity of our task of witnessing demands that we stay close to the source of spiritual power (Matt. 9:38).

We should pray specifically for the leaders of the church that they might be able to overcome Satan and have victory in their lives and in their work.

We should also pray day by day for world leaders who are responsible for making significant decisions that affect us all. We are to be persistent in our prayer life.

Conclusion

As Christians we are to make much of the privilege and the responsibility of prayer. We are to pray all kinds of prayer and to pray on all occasions. We should pray in the power of the Holy Spirit. We should pray for all the saints, asking God to give us all we need to stand against Satan; and having done all, we must stand. Surely we will see that God answers prayer.

SUNDAY EVENING, JULY 2

Title: You Can Take It with You

Text: "Lay not up for yourselves treasures upon earth, where moth and rust doth corrupt, and where thieves break through and steal: but lay up for yourselves treasures in heaven, where neither moth nor rust doth corrupt, and where thieves do not break through nor steal: for where your treasure is, there will your heart be also" **(Matt. 6:19–21).**

Scripture Reading: Luke 12:13–21

Introduction

A cartoon depicted a wife asking her husband about the will of a prominent man who had recently died. "How much did he leave?" she asked. "He left it all," was his laconic reply. His reply will hold true for all of us, for we brought no material possessions into this world and can carry none out.

I. You can't take it with you.

In ancient days people were buried with articles they had used in this life, in the hope that they could use them in the next life. One notable twentieth-century discovery was that in 1922 of the tomb of young King Tutankhamen, who ruled Egypt about 1358–1346 BC. The royal tomb was filled with beautiful ornaments and furniture of many kinds, including the royal throne. Other royal tombs had been discovered by archaeologists, but only after their contents had been plundered by robbers. Obviously, the way to heavenly treasure is not to bury it with the deceased.

In the parable of the rich fool (Luke 12:16–21), "God said unto him, Thou fool, this night thy soul shall be required of thee: then whose shall those things be, which thou hast provided?" (Luke 12:20). The riches he had amassed would be passed to others because "you can't take it with you."

Material goods are important for this life. We all need food, clothes, shelter, tools, and transportation, as well as government, education, recreation, religion, art, health care, and so on—all of which cost money. Jesus would not have taught us to pray, "Give us this day our daily bread," if he had not considered material things important.

Because material things are important, Jesus' statement in our text is all the more emphatic: "Lay not up for yourselves treasure upon earth, where moth and rust doth corrupt, and where thieves break through and steal: but lay up for yourselves treasures in heaven, where neither moth nor rust doth corrupt, and where thieves do not break through nor steal: for where your treasure is, there will your heart be also" (Matt. 6:19–21). This is one of many Scripture passages that is stated absolutely but is meant to be understood relatively. (For other examples, see Matt. 11:25–26; Luke 14:12–14; 14:26.) As important as earthly treasure is, Jesus affirmed that laying up heavenly treasure is a much more important consideration. We do not understand Jesus to prohibit savings, life insurance, annuities, purchase of a house, and the like. We do understand him to say that one who makes the chief end of life the amassing of material things is a fool.

If this were the only world, the principle would still stand that one who made the chief end of life the gain of material things would be foolish. We would miss the joy of making and spending money as a good steward of that which God provides. However, this world is not the end. Another life lies ahead, and we can send heavenly treasure on before us.

II. You can take it with you.

Jesus commands you to "lay up for yourselves treasures in heaven." How? By using this earthly life, including material things, in accord with God's will. The late Pat Neff, former governor of Texas and president of Baylor University, said, "The way to lay up treasure in heaven is to invest it in someone who is going there." In the parable of the unjust steward, Jesus advised, "Use worldly wealth to gain friends for yourselves, so that when it is gone, you will be welcomed into eternal dwellings" (Luke 16:9 NIV). How wonderful to be welcomed by those whom you have never met in this life who were won through missionaries supported by your prayers and gifts!

An Italian, following shipwreck at sea, was picked up by a vessel bound for Rio de Janeiro, Brazil. A gospel tract written by a Baptist missionary fell into his hands. Encouraged by the tract and by the appealing music, he slipped into the First Baptist Church of Rio de Janeiro for the worship. After repeated conferences with the pastor, he became a Christian and a missionary to the Italian-speaking people of the United States. During a missionary tour in Missouri, he told of his conversion. A Missouri farm woman who heard his story questioned him carefully about the gospel tract. Then she said, "I gave money to help print that gospel tract." How wonderful that in this life she could see some results of her investment in the extension of the gospel. Think how many times in heaven that such a scene as this will be multiplied as the redeemed meet those who have been won through their gifts.

When a person travels from one country to another, it usually is necessary to exchange one's currency into that of the country to which one goes. "You can't take it with you," but by God's wonderful grace, what you do here for Jesus is turned into the currency of heaven and is laid up as heavenly treasure for you. Earthly treasure is subject to deterioration and decay. Robbers may steal it. At death you leave it. Treasure in heaven is secure, "where neither moth nor rust doth corrupt, and where thieves do not break through nor steal." At death you inherit it, and enjoy it forever.

III. Laying up heavenly treasure is right.

Self-interest is not selfishness. You lay up heavenly treasure by doing good to others in Jesus' name. The more good you do to others, the more heavenly treasure you will have. The more good others do to you, the more heavenly treasure they will have. The better Christian one is, the better the whole world is for it. The second commandment, "Thou shalt love thy neighbour as thyself" (Matt. 22:38), assumes that one loves oneself.

Would Jesus command what is selfish and wrong? Certainly not. Why have Christian people been so slow to follow our Lord when again and again he commands us to "lay up for yourselves treasure in heaven"? Jesus spoke repeatedly about rewards in heaven: "Otherwise ye have no reward of your Father which is in heaven" (Matt. 6:1); "Your Father who sees in secret will reward you" (Matt. 6:4 RSV); "Rejoice, and be exceeding glad: for great is your reward in heaven" (Matt. 5:12); "His lord said unto him, Well done, good and faithful servant; thou hast been faithful over a few things, I will make thee ruler over many things: enter thou into the joy of thy lord" (Matt. 25:23). (See also Matt. 10:40–42; 16:24–27; 19:27–30; Mark 10:21.)

Conclusion

"For where your treasure is, there will your heart be also" (Matt. 6:21) is a companion truth to the passage we have been studying. Jesus affirms that if we send on treasure to heaven, we will find our hearts rejoicing in the investment.

Life yielded to God is heavenly treasure. People helped to God are heavenly treasure. Food, clothing, education, comfort in sickness and bereavement, respect for others' rights, attempts to meet other's needs— these all are heavenly treasure. Heavenly treasure won't grow mildew, and moths can't eat it. Nor can anyone steal it. God wants you to be wealthy and happy in heaven. Those who lay up treasure in heaven are happier here on earth also. How can you know unless you try it?

Hear Jesus: "Take heed, and beware of covetousness: for a man's life consisteth not in the abundance of the things which he possesseth" (Luke 12:15). A fool, said Jesus, is "he that layeth up treasure for himself, and is not rich toward God" (Luke 12:21).

WEDNESDAY EVENING, JULY 5

Title: Listening for the Big Noise

Text: "And after the earthquake a fire; but the LORD was not in the fire: and after the fire a still small voice" **(1 Kings 19:12)**.

Scripture Reading: 1 Kings 19:1–18

Introduction

Discouragement is one of the most sinister and damaging states into which a Christian can fall. It carries its own kind of paralysis; it lays us low and takes away the song in our hearts and the joy from our souls. At least momentarily it takes us out of the race and puts us on the sidelines. What do we do when the crisis of discouragement arises? Does God provide resources and strength whereby we can overcome this spiritual malady?

The biblical event we will study to illustrate this crisis involves a man whose personality and record of achievement as a prophet of God leads one to say, "Discouraged? Surely not *this* man!" His very name is synonymous with strength and victory. Elijah! He was the prophet-giant of the Old Testament, the fiery and relentless voice of God's judgment, the hero of the Hebrews! Yet James describes him as a man "subject to like passions as we are" (James 5:17).

I. In our text story we discover Elijah riding perhaps the highest crest of victory in his life.

Elijah had stood fearlessly before King Ahab, confronting him with the idolatry of God's people. He called for a showdown, and the king ordered all the people and the prophets of Baal to assemble on Mount Carmel. Elijah's call to the people was, "How long halt ye between two opinions? if the LORD be God, follow him: but if Baal, then follow him" (1 Kings 18:21). The contest was begun, the Baal prophets prepared their sacrifice, and all day they called on their god to send fire and consume it, but no fire came.

Elijah's turn came, and following a quiet, simple prayer to God, the fire fell and consumed the sacrifice. A national revival broke out in Israel, and the story of this victory closes with this declaration: "And the hand of the LORD was on Elijah" (1 Kings 18:46).

II. Then we find our prophet walking the dark valley of discouragement.

"But [Elijah] . . . requested for himself that he might die; and said, It is enough; now, O LORD, take away my life" (1 Kings 19:4). Why did this giant of God come to this point of exasperation while the taste of Carmel's victory was still in his mouth and the people's cries of repentance were still ringing in his ears? How could Jezebel, a mere woman, strike such fear in Elijah's heart? Perhaps Elijah forgot that in the aftermath of victory there comes the moment when we are most vulnerable to temptation. While we celebrate our victories, we must not forget to keep in touch with the God who made them possible.

Elijah, in his own mind, did not allow God to keep his rightful place in this situation. He decided that the victory was a farce, and he gave way to fear. Cowardice whiplashed him down to the wilderness, where he dropped, physically and spiritually spent, under a juniper tree.

Elijah not only lost faith in himself, but in others as well. He decided that there was not a God-fearing person left in Israel. So, with his faith in God shaken, his faith in himself and in his people gone, what was left for him but to ask to die?

III. The story doesn't end on that sad note: Elijah was yet to find the Solid Rock of faith.

How did God cure Elijah's discouragement? First, he put him to sleep; he taught him how to "be still." God has many ways of making us "stop," causing us to be still and know that we are his sheep and he is our God. David said, "He maketh me to lie down in green pastures" (Ps. 23:2).

Second, God showed Elijah his sin and brought him to repentance. He instructed the prophet to go into the mountain, where a strong wind came that split the mountain and broke the rocks. There followed an earthquake and a blinding fire—and Elijah was awed by this fantastic display of power! But after all the noise and bluster were gone, there was "a still small voice," with which God spoke clearly and plainly to Elijah. Elijah listened, and the discouragement drained out of him. He was ready to be God's man again.

Conclusion

Are you discouraged? Do you feel like giving up? Are you waiting for some "big noise," some spectacular thing to happen to catapult you into some mountain-peak experience? Perhaps God wants you to be still and let him speak. Stop waiting for the big noise. When God speaks, "the sound of his voice is so sweet, the birds hush their singing." God will sustain his people through the valleys as well as on the mountaintops.

SUNDAY MORNING, JULY 9

Title: The Practice of Forgiveness—How to Handle Mistreatment

Text: "And Jesus said, 'Father, forgive them; for they know not what they do'" **(Luke 23:34 RSV)**.

Scripture Reading: Matthew 6:14–15; 18:21–22

Hymns: "Christ Receiveth Sinful Men," Neumeister
        "My Faith Looks Up to Thee," Palmer
        "Though Your Sins Be as Scarlet," Crosby

Offertory Prayer: Our heavenly Father, we come thanking you for laying our sins on Jesus Christ and for his being willing to die on the cross in our place. Today we take up our cross and bear it for him and for a needy world. Help each of us to share in the burden of carrying the good news of your love to those who are still in darkness and in spiritual death. Help us to be the light of the world that points them to faith in Jesus Christ. Bless these tithes and offerings to the end that those who have not yet been saved will receive Jesus Christ as Lord and Savior. In his name we pray. Amen.

Introduction

In living the Christian life, we do not find our pattern in a set of laws. Rather, the character and actions of Jesus Christ provide us with a wonderful example to follow with the help of his Holy Spirit.

Today we begin looking at the pattern set by our Savior as he faced the great crises of his suffering and his death on the cross. What can the words of the Savior from the cross say to modern humanity concerning the manner in which we should face the crises, the struggles, and the hurts of life? Can we agree that we are to make a serious and concerted effort to face life with its crises, responsibilities, and opportunities as our Lord did?

Let us listen to our Lord's words from the cross to discover his manner of facing the unpleasant things of life. We will find that our Lord faced, met, and conquered mistreatment by practicing forgiveness. How do you react to mistreatment?

Do you resort to personal revenge and retaliation in word or deed?

Do you respond by developing an attitude of resentment that eventually leads to self-pity and then to despair within your heart?

Do you respond with an attitude of hostility that develops into deep bitterness and hurtful hate? This can proceed to an attitude of anger that leads to murder.

Our text reveals that Jesus reacted with forgiveness to mistreatment by his apostles, by the Jewish officials, by the Roman authorities, by Roman soldiers, and by the crowds. A poet said, "To err is human and to forgive is divine." All of us can agree with this truth.

In the Old Testament, forgiveness is divine, for there is little human forgiveness to be found in it. To forgive meant "to cover up, to blot out, to lift up a burden, to send away." But in the New Testament some new elements are added to forgiveness. In the teachings of our Lord, to forgive means to repudiate the right to retaliate, to restore a ruptured relationship, to return good for evil, and to heal broken fellowship.

I. Jesus insisted that his disciples practice forgiveness.

Jesus taught that forgiveness of others is a condition for receiving forgiveness from God (Matt. 6:14–15; Mark 11:25). It is only when we grant forgiveness to others that we can receive forgiveness into our own heart and life. When we refuse to forgive, we destroy our capacity to receive forgiveness.

Forgiveness is to be granted as an act of grace on the part of the injured person (Luke 17:3–4). We cannot wait until the one who injures us deserves forgiveness for us to bestow the gift. It must be an act of grace on our part.

Forgiveness must not be limited (Matt. 18:21–22). God is eager to forgive all our sins, and we must be willing to forgive all the sins and injuries that are inflicted on us.

II. The importance of a spirit of forgiveness.

The primary benefit that comes as a result of forgiveness is experienced in the heart of the person who does the forgiving.

The practice of granting forgiveness is essential for a healthy emotional life on the part of the injured person. The unhealthiest thing a person can do is to harbor hate and hostility. Forgiveness purges this destructive emotion from the thought processes and from the emotional life of the person who has been injured.

The practice of granting forgiveness is essential for a successful marriage and for a wholesome home life. Even the most loving husband and wife will occasionally mistreat each other in some manner. Children have been known to mistreat parents, and parents have been known to mistreat children. The practice of forgiveness is the only thing that can heal broken relationships from day to day.

The practice of granting forgiveness is essential for effective Christian witness. People can believe in the forgiveness of God only when they see it practiced and when they feel the results of it in personal experience.

The practice of granting forgiveness is essential for maintaining the fellowship of the church. The church is made up of sinners who are mistake makers. They say and do unkind things from time to time. The church is a community of the forgiven and the forgiving.

The practice of granting forgiveness is essential for power in prayer. This is emphasized by the words that follow the model prayer found in the Sermon on the Mount (Matt. 6:14–15). If we harden our hearts with an attitude of hostility, we shut out God's grace as a benevolent power in our lives. Jesus was not declaring that forgiveness was a price we must pay in order to have power in prayer. He was affirming that it is a condition we must meet for power in prayer. There is a difference.

III. How can we develop a spirit of forgiveness?

To forgive has never been easy, because it is incompatible with our earthly nature. In fact, forgiveness is usually not even expected. It seems more reasonable that we should react with hate than with love when we are mistreated.

While on the cross our Lord demonstrated the possibility of our being able to grant forgiveness toward those who mistreat us. Do you need help in granting forgiveness to those who have mistreated you? Are you willing to develop a habit of being forgiving toward those who are unkind and at times even cruel toward you? Several things can be done to find this help and to develop the habit of being forgiving rather than giving way to hate and retaliation.

Recognize and acknowledge that an unforgiving spirit is contrary to the will of God. It goes against the mind of Christ and is contradictory to the spirit and to the pattern of our Savior.

Recognize and decide that forgiveness is the only sane way to deal with painful experiences.

Recognize that forgiveness is God's divinely ordained method by which we purge hate from our hearts. To harbor hate and to carry a grudge is to face life with a self-destructive approach. No one wins when hate rules.

Recognize that a spirit of forgiveness can be a strong creative force for good. This is significant for the forgiven and even more significant for the forgiver.

Recognize that our Lord's forgiving us of our sins is the basis on which we are to practice forgiveness toward others (Col. 3:13).

Conclusion

Unwillingness to grant forgiveness to another can keep a person out of heaven and create a little hell in that person's heart in the here and now. If you want to go to heaven when this life is over, and if you want to experience the joy of heaven in the here and now, then look to Jesus' pattern in granting forgiveness to those who mistreat you. With God's help in practicing forgiveness, you will become a medium through whom others will experience forgiveness, both human and divine.

SUNDAY EVENING, JULY 9

Title: What Is Important?

Text: "But seek ye first the kingdom of God, and his righteousness; and all these things shall be added unto you" **(Matt. 6:33).**

Scripture Reading: Matthew 6:24–34

Introduction

Every person must make choices. As Harry Emerson Fosdick stated so succinctly, "You can postpone making up your mind, but you cannot postpone making up your life."

Every person makes mutually exclusive choices. A child with a quarter to spend at the store must make choices. He cannot both spend the quarter and keep it. If he buys this, he cannot buy that. One cannot be doctor, lawyer, engineer, farmer, preacher, and geologist all at one time. One cannot be married and single at the same time. One cannot lie and be truthful. One cannot steal and be honest. One cannot be immoral and moral. One cannot be pagan and Christian. Each person has only one life; no one is granted several lives with which to experiment. The late George W. Truett said, "If I had a thousand lives, I would want every one of them to be lived for Jesus Christ." One precious life—and only one—is entrusted to each of us.

I. In every person's life something is most important.

Something comes first. Whether calculated or not there will be a principle around which life revolves. There will be one principal affection, to which all others are subordinate. The dominating principle may be:

What you consider best for yourself, what you want, what you like.

Obsession to possess worldly goods. "For the love of money is a root of all kinds of evil. Some people, eager for money, have wandered away from the faith and pierced themselves with many griefs" (1 Tim. 6:10 NIV).

Desire to be popular with one's peer group; willingness to please others even at the expense of right. Evangelist Chester Swor said, "Some mothers would give permission for their daughters to spend a weekend in hell if they could be sure they would be popular there." A little girl prayed, "Lord, help me to do what you want me to do and what everyone else wants me to do." That was an impossible prayer for God to answer.

Compromise—honest to a limit; truthful to a degree. A pastor had given a dollar to a man begging for money to buy food. The preacher admonished the man that it would be a breach of confidence to use the money for liquor instead of for food. The beggar replied, "Reverend, I wouldn't lie for a little amount like that. For a hundred thousand dollars I might lie, but not for that."

II. There are only two choices, and they are mutually exclusive.

One can "seek first the kingdom of God, and his righteousness" or one can settle for something less than that. The admonition is to put God's will and work before all else.

Note well the Scripture reading: "The light of the body is the eye; if therefore thine eye be single, thy whole body shall be full of light. But if thine eye be evil, thy whole body shall be full of darkness. If therefore the light that is in thee be darkness, how great is that darkness" (Matt. 6:22–23).

224

"If thine eye be single" means if your eye is healthy and can focus on one object with all else falling into proper perspective. The image transmitted by the eye to the brain is in conformity to outward reality so that "thy whole body is full of light."

"If thine eye be evil" means if your eye is diseased and cannot focus properly on one object and the sight is blurred so that the image the eye conveys to the brain is distorted and does not conform to reality. In that case the light that is in you is darkness. Just as a good eye cannot focus on two objects, so "no one can serve two masters. Either you will hate the one and love the other, or you will be devoted to the one and despise the other. You cannot serve both God and money" (Matt. 6:24 NIV). No more than one can draw a circle around two centers, can one serve God and also serve anyone or anything else.

III. What is important? What did Jesus put first?

Loyalty to God was first in the Savior's scale of values. His life stands as a perfect example of love and allegiance to the heavenly Father. A few examples will suffice.

At his baptism, Jesus dedicated himself to his messianic task, which he knew would culminate in his death and resurrection, with the statement, "Suffer it to be so now: for thus it becometh us to fulfil all righteousness" (Matt. 3:15). He would accept the Father's will even if it led to death on a cross. Note the Father's reply designating Jesus as "my beloved Son," a quotation from Psalm 2, a messianic psalm designating him the Servant of Jehovah, or Messiah, and from Isaiah 42:1: "This is my beloved Son, in whom I am well pleased" (Matt. 3:17).

Immediately following his baptism, Jesus was tempted by the devil to go some way other than the cross. "If thou be the Son of God" (Matt. 4:3) in our English translation sounds as if the devil doubted that Jesus was the Son of God. The Greek makes it clear, however, that the devil assumed Jesus' status as the Son of God to be true. "If you are the Son of God," the devil said in effect, "and I know you are because God so designated you at your baptism, then instead of going to the cross, use your miraculous power to make bread of stones, cast yourself down from the pinnacle of the temple before the multitudes, and fall down and worship me." Jesus replied by using Scripture and remained loyal to God.

Early in his ministry in Samaria, Jesus rejoiced over the salvation of a Samaritan woman. To the disciple who brought food to him, Jesus replied, "I have meat to eat that ye know not of. . . . My meat is to do the will of him that sent me, and to finish his work" (John 4:32, 34).

At the establishment of the Lord's Supper, Jesus gave thanks for the bread and the cup. He was thanking God for the privilege of dying on the cross in order to be the Savior.

Later that evening in Gethsemane, Jesus "fell on his face and prayed,

225

saying, O my Father, if it be possible, let this cup pass from me: nevertheless not as I will, but as thou wilt" (Matt. 26:39).

Correctly did the author of Hebrews apply to him the Scripture, "Lo, I come (in the volume of the book it is written of me), to do thy will, O God" (Heb. 10:7).

Conclusion

Don't cheat yourself of life's true riches by failure to "seek first the kingdom of God and his righteousness." Give your heart to Jesus Christ and live in obedience to his commands. A great missionary said, "I will value nothing except in relation to the kingdom of God."

Few deliberately say, "I will not be a Christian." Many are so preoccupied with the affairs of this world, which are means to the end of a good life, that they miss the good life itself. The parable of the gospel feast, recorded in Luke 14:16–20, pictured persons so busy buying oxen, buying land, and getting married that they missed the feast. Cars, land, boats, houses, recreation, sports, amusements, and so on, all good in themselves, are not the chief end of life and become positively evil when they keep one from the Savior. "All that is good is from God; but unjustly is anything loved that is from him if he be forsaken for it," wrote Augustine many centuries ago.

Be sure to live with an eye single to God's glory, then you will come to understand that there is not a joy that loyalty to God in Christ does not enhance; there is not a sorrow that loyalty to God does not mitigate.

WEDNESDAY EVENING, JULY 12

Title: Looking in the Mirror

Text: "Then said I, Woe is me! for I am undone; because I am a man of unclean lips, and I dwell in the midst of a people of unclean lips: for mine eyes have seen the King, the LORD of hosts" **(Isa. 6:5)**.

Scripture Reading: Isaiah 6:1–13

Introduction

Mirrors reflect the image before them. God's Word is a spiritual mirror that reflects the inner person, enabling one to see oneself as he or she really is. When one approaches this mirror with honesty, there are no distortions of the reflected image; it provides a true picture of the person before it.

There came a point in the life of Isaiah, the brilliant, aristocratic prince of Old Testament prophets, when he stood before God's mirror, the glory of God's presence. It was one of the more cataclysmic experiences of his life, for in that moment he realized that he had never truly seen himself before, and what he saw was not pleasant. The result of the experience was life changing.

I. For the first time in his life, Isaiah received a true conception of God—what his divine nature is really like.

Isaiah dated his experience as "the year that King Uzziah died." This marked the close of a significant epoch for the children of Israel. For fifty-two years Uzziah had reigned, and the people had been blessed. But now Uzziah was to die—and to die a leper! The name Uzziah means "the power of Jehovah." But the power of Jehovah to approve, to bless, to save the nation was under the covenant of the law, which was conditional. The people had transgressed the law, and there was no alternative but for judgment to fall.

Then Isaiah described his experience: "I saw also the LORD. . . ." The word for "LORD" is Adonai, a name for God that means sovereign master, owner, and controller. Isaiah saw God in that moment as the absolute disposer of all events, the master of men. Perhaps Isaiah had been willing to acknowledge God as Elohim, the majestic creator, but not as Adonai. God as Adonai becomes *involved in* one's life. Isaiah saw the Lord "on a throne, high and exalted." There is no throne higher than his (see Rom. 9:5). His raiment filled the temple so that there was no room left for any flesh to glory.

II. After receiving a true conception of God, Isaiah received a cleansing he had not experienced before.

His reaction was, Then said I, woe is me! for I am undone . . ." (Isa 6:5). When Isaiah found himself in the revealing, holy light of God's presence, his instinctive response was, "I am *lost.*" The first thing one sees concerning oneself in God's mirror is that all is chaos, "waste and desolate," just as God saw the world before he began the creative process in Genesis 1. Both Job and Daniel had similar experiences (see Job 42:5–6; Dan. 10:7–8).

Isaiah realized his own lips, and not merely those of his neighbors, were unclean. Until one is able to see oneself in the light of God's glory, it is much easier to detect the unclean life of one's neighbors. Isaiah realized a New Testament truth: "There is no difference, for all have sinned, and come short of the glory of God" (Rom. 3:22–23). Isaiah's lips are the external symbol of what people really are (see Matt. 12:37). The coal with fire in it, taken from the altar, symbolizes God's cleansing presence.

III. After Isaiah received his new conception of God and the cleansing of his soul, God commissioned him.

"And I heard the voice of the Lord, saying, Whom shall I send, and who will go for us? Then said I, Here am I; send me" (v. 8). God's question was not addressed to the host of seraphim or other heavenly creatures, but to a man who had been unclean and was now purged and fit for the Master's use. He could say to the unclean about him, "I know how you hurt, because I have hurt too!" Who can speak more convincingly of redemption than one who has experienced it?

Perhaps this is why God leaves his redeemed people on earth; else would he not,

227

after saving our souls, whisk us, as with Enoch and Elijah, into the perfect bliss of his presence? Rather, we too are people "of unclean lips," who have been touched by God. We, like Isaiah, know the despair and distress of uncleanness; and we also know the joy and the glory of God's cleansing presence—for we have looked in his mirror, his Word. We have seen our need, and we have accepted his salvation.

Conclusion

Because God's mirror reflects our lives exactly as they are in his sight, it is much more pleasant to turn away and find our own mirrors—those that flatter us in the deceptive, complimenting light of selfish pride. But when we look in God's mirror and let God do for us what he will, then there comes the cleansing, restoring touch of God, bringing "peace like a river" to our souls.

SUNDAY MORNING, JULY 16

Title: The Promise of Paradise

Text: "And he said to him, 'Truly, I say to you, today you will be with me in Paradise'" **(Luke 23:43 RSV)**.

Scripture Reading: Luke 23:39–43

Hymns: "Great Redeemer, We Adore Thee," Harris
"We Have Heard the Joyful Sound," Owens
"He Included Me," Oatman

Offertory Prayer: Holy Father, we thank you for all of the gifts you have so freely bestowed on us. Today we thank you not only for spiritual gifts but also for material gifts. We thank you for the privilege of being able to work and to produce, to earn and to have. Today we thank you for the privilege you have granted us of sharing that with which you have blessed us. We pray your blessings on these tithes and offerings. Bless the thoughts of our mind and the work of our hands. Bless these gifts that others might come to know Jesus Christ as Savior and Lord. In Jesus' name we pray. Amen.

Introduction

What can seven statements from the dying Christ on the cross communicate to modern people?

Our Lord's prayer for the forgiveness of those who crucified him provides us with a pattern to follow when we are mistreated. And Jesus' promise of paradise for the penitent thief provides us with hope and with a number of truths that can have real meaning for us today.

I. This promise of Christ reveals that salvation is by the grace of God.

The gracious words of promise from our Lord to an undeserving thief who was dying for his crime provide us with a vivid illustration of the unmerited love of God for sinners. Just as the thief was a sinner, you and I are sinners. We have not sinned in exactly the same manner as the thief, but we are sinners. God loves sinners.

The experience reveals that forgiveness is a free gift. The thief could not earn or purchase or deserve forgiveness. Forgiveness is always free.

Sonship to God is a free gift. We cannot buy or earn our way into the family of God. It is a free gift to those who put faith in Jesus Christ (John 1:12; Gal. 3:26).

Eternal life is the free gift of God (Rom. 6:23).

Heaven, the paradise our Lord promised to the thief, is a free gift. Heaven is not a reward given to those who demonstrate unusual piety and unexpected loyalty or generosity. Heaven holds rewards for those who have lived a life of faithfulness, obedience, and service. Heaven itself is the gift of God to those who receive Jesus Christ as Lord of life.

II. This promise of Christ reveals how God answers the prayer of an honest sinner.

To the thief's credit, he was honest in his admission of sin. He said to the other criminal who was being crucified, "We received the due rewards of our deeds" (Luke 23:41 RSV). People have a natural tendency to pass the buck and blame someone else. We rationalize our actions and try to put the responsibility on someone else.

Some blame their parents for everything that goes wrong.

Others try to hold society responsible for the situation in which they find themselves.

We need to honestly face our own personal responsibility for the situation in which we find ourselves. Only when we do so will we begin to make progress in life. We need to be honest with ourselves and with God. We need to quit blaming others for our failures, our shortcomings, our mistakes. Let's follow the pattern of the thief and admit our own shortcomings and failures and trust God for mercy and forgiveness.

III. This promise from Christ to the thief reveals encouragement and hope for all sinners.

Christ took time out of the agony of dying to save a helpless thief.

God will save to the uttermost all who come to him through Christ Jesus asking for forgiveness and help.

The Bible teaches us that we are the property of God by right of creation and by right of his providential care. Those of us who have trusted Christ belong to God also by right of our great redemption. In spite of the fact that we are God's property, many of us have stolen from him and robbed him, and

229

we fall into the category of being thieves. Our Lord would pray, "Father, forgive them." He would give us the joy of forgiveness and the promise of paradise.

IV. This promise of Christ to the thief reveals what death can mean to a believer.

Through faith in Jesus Christ, we can claim the promise that he made to the thief when he said, "Today thou shalt be with me in Paradise."

For the believer to be away from the body is to be at home with the Lord (2 Cor. 5:8).

Paul believed and affirmed that life for the Christian should be centered totally in Jesus Christ, but to die is to experience gain (Phil. 1:21).

The psalmist spoke of the death of the saints of God as being precious in the sight of the Lord (Ps. 116:15). It is through death that the children of God go home to be with God.

V. This promise of Christ reveals the nearness of heaven for the believer—"Today."

For the thief, heaven began on the day of his crucifixion. Heaven began on the day he made his plea to Jesus Christ for divine consideration.

Conclusion

Today the gates of the kingdom of God are still open. Today you can still confess your sins to God and ask him to forgive you and to grant you the gift of eternal life. Today the Savior stands at your heart's door gently knocking and pleading to come in to be your Redeemer, Savior, Friend, Guide, and Helper. Today the Savior listens for your plea just as he listened for the plea of the thief. Today the Lord will hear you if you will but pray as did the thief, and he will meet the deepest need of your heart and life.

One of the thieves waited until it was too late. One of the thieves waited until it was almost too late. What about you? Make your plea to the Savior today.

SUNDAY EVENING, JULY 16

Title: Why Worry?

Text: "So do not worry, saying, 'What shall we eat?' or 'What shall we drink?' or 'What shall we wear?' For the pagans run after all these things, and your heavenly Father knows that you need them" **(Matt. 6:31–32 NIV)**.

Scripture Reading: Matthew 6:25–34

Introduction

The powerful beauty of Matthew 6:25–34 has been praised by many persons. It concludes the third major division of the Sermon on the Mount that began in Matthew 6:19 on the Christian's relation to material things.

Due to the change in meaning of words, the King James Version of our Scripture text is not accurate today. A much better translation is found in the Revised Standard Version: "Therefore I tell you, do not be anxious about your life, what you shall eat or what you shall drink, nor about your body, what ye shall put on" (Matt. 6:25 RSV). Better yet is the New International Version's "Do not worry." The passage means don't be distracted, don't let your mind be divided, don't be torn apart. The context confirms that this is what Jesus was emphasizing: do not be turned aside from the goal of God's glory to be concerned for the body and its needs.

I. What Jesus did not mean.

Jesus certainly was not forbidding prudent forethought in preparing for the future. He repeatedly appealed to the outcome as a motive for personal action; as, for example, "Lay up for yourselves treasures in heaven" (Matt. 6:20); "Great is your reward in heaven" (Matt. 5:12); and count the cost of discipleship (Luke 7:27–33).

Jesus did not espouse the Pollyanna view that you can do nothing and God will provide: "If God wants to give me food, clothes, and shelter, he will; I do not need to plan or work. If God wants to give me health, he will; I do not need to see the doctor or take preventative health measures." Jesus warned against worry, not against work. The birds do not worry, but they certainly work. Jesus worked. He said, "I must work the works of him that sent me" (John 9:4), and "My Father worketh hitherto, and I work" (John 5:17).

Jesus was not saying that if you trust God enough you will have no problems. Far from what he was saying is the nonsense that it shows lack of faith for one to see a doctor or for a farmer to irrigate his crops. Joseph, Jesus' stepfather, died probably not long after Jesus was twelve years of age. Jesus' widowed mother seems to have known poverty. At least Jesus knew, probably by experience, about patching old garments, looking earnestly for a lost coin, and coping with the oppression of those who robbed widows of their houses. If piety would prevent all problems, surely Mary would not have had any problems.

II. What did Jesus say?

"Therefore" is always an important word. "Therefore" in verse 25 points back to the important statements in verse 19–24. In verses 19–21 Jesus said that one cannot make the amassing of both heavenly treasure and earthly treasure life's goal, because that person would be double-minded. Verses 22–23 illustrate and further emphasize that an eye single to God's glory cannot be an eye single to material comforts. Verse 24 concludes that the

master of one's life cannot be both God and Mammon (money). Therefore, Jesus continued in verse 25, don't be distracted, don't be divided in your minds, don't be separated from the true purpose of life by worry about food and clothing.

Luke 10:38–41 preserves for each of us an interesting illustration. Martha was so worried about preparing dinner for Jesus that she could not enjoy him. The dinner was important, but it was not most important.

If God has made each of us an immortal soul in his own image and has given to each of us a body, surely he will provide a way to feed and clothe us.

Verse 26. Consider the birds. God has a plan for them. They have continued from generation to generation. They do not sow, reap, or gather food into barns. They are cared for by the heavenly Father. As you are much more important to God than is a bird, surely you can trust him to provide a way for you to obtain food.

Verses 28–30. Consider the flowers. Their life is short, yet God clothes them more beautifully than King Solomon in all his glory could clothe himself. As you, a person, are more important than a flower, the heavenly Father will provide a way for you to be clothed.

III. Loyalty to God rather than distraction.

Concerning the past. Worry accomplishes nothing. The past is past. "What I have written, I have written," said Pilate. Tears, remorse, and anxiety accomplish nothing except to distract from the present opportunity and responsibility. Surely God does not want you to sacrifice the present and future by worry about the past. Confess your sins of the past fully, and God will forgive freely. The past will not be a barrier to your present and future fellowship with God. Hear Jesus say, "Thy sins are forgiven. . . . Thy faith hath saved thee; go in peace" (Luke 7:48, 50).

Concerning the present (v. 27).

Worry is useless. One cannot increase one's stature nor lengthen one's life by worry. The word used here may mean either "add one cubit unto his stature" (KJV) or "add one cubit to his span of life" (RSV). The context does not make clear which is correct. Both usages are true.

Worry is pagan (vv. 31–33). Heathen spend their energies in the pursuit of material things. You are not to be distracted from life's central purpose, which is to "seek first the kingdom of God and his righteousness." "Your heavenly Father knows that you have need of all these things," and he promises that when you put his kingdom first, all the material goods you need will be supplied. This will not be without work and forethought and perhaps not without the help of others. Do your best and leave the results to God.

Worry about the future is useless (v. 34). Many of the feared disasters will fail to materialize. "Don't cross the bridge before you get to it" is a popular way of saying what Jesus said: "Do not worry about tomorrow, for tomorrow will worry about itself. Each day has enough trouble of its own" (Matt. 6:34 NIV).

The future will probably bring sickness and death. Distraction from present opportunities to worry about it does no good. Loyalty to the heavenly Father is the best preparation one can make.

Conclusion

Here are some important points to remember:

Nothing can come to you in this world or in the next apart from God's permissive providence.

God will not allow any test beyond your ability to bear it. "There hath no temptation taken you but such as is common to man: but God is faithful, who will not suffer you to be tempted above that ye are able; but will with the temptation also make a way to escape, that ye may be able to bear it" (1 Cor. 10:13).

God's presence will abide. His grace will be sufficient. "And he said unto me, My grace is sufficient for thee: for my strength is made perfect in weakness. Most gladly therefore will I rather glory in my infirmities, that the power of Christ may rest upon me" (2 Cor. 12:9).

"We know that in all things God works for the good of those who love him, who have been called according to his purpose" (Rom. 8:28 NIV).

God grows great Christians through great trials.

Death holds no fear for Christians (see John 14:1–3). The important concern is that nothing distracts us from loyalty to the Lord. "For whether we live, we live unto the Lord; and whether we die, we die unto the Lord: whether we live therefore, or die, we are the Lord's. For to this end Christ both died, and rose, and revived, that he might be Lord both of the dead and living" (Rom. 14:8–9).

We do not know what the future holds, but we know that the heavenly Father holds the future. Let us be loyal to him and leave the results in his hands.

WEDNESDAY EVENING, JULY 19

Title: In the Shadow of Loneliness

Text: "Behold, the hour cometh, yea, is now come, that ye shall be scattered, every man to his own, and shall leave me alone: and yet I am not alone, because the Father is with me" **(John 16:32)**.

Scripture Reading: John 16:16–33

Introduction

One day the great frontiersman Daniel Boone walked into his log cabin and said to his wife, "Pack your things, dear; we're moving on. This area is getting too crowded with people!" The nearest neighbor had moved to within ten miles of the Boone home. Those days are past. There aren't

233

many vast and empty frontiers anymore. Our cities are crowded. And yet there are more lonely people who live pointless, purposeless lives than ever before. Why?

The answer is simple: humans are spiritual creatures. We are made in the image of God. And because of this, there is within us a thirst for communication. We were made for involvement with God and other people. Yet with so many people, this spiritual hunger and thirst are never satisfied. In the words of the songwriter, they are "blowin' in the wind." Out of their despair, they cry, "My God, why hast thou forsaken me?" Loneliness is a crisis of life that periodically affects all people, even Christians. Christianity speaks to the crisis of loneliness.

I. First, let us explore the cause of the loneliness that often plagues people.

Most who live in the twilight of loneliness do so because they think they are not wanted, loved, or accepted. They blame their loved ones, friends, and even the church for the rejection they feel. Many things can build this wall of loneliness around a person. Fear, suspicion, and resentment, resulting in overwhelming feelings of insecurity, are often factors.

Yet, whatever the symptom of one's loneliness may be, the cause is almost always a refusal to accept one's reason for being. Moses wrote, "And the LORD God formed man of the dust of the ground, and breathed into his nostrils the breath of life; and man became a living soul" (Gen. 2:7). God did not "speak" man into existence; he became personally involved in man's creation. Then he "breathed" *his* life into man, which made man unique among all creation. Man came to possess what no other creature could claim: a consciousness of God. Not only could man know that there is a God, but he could also communicate with him.

The great interruption in this communication and fellowship between God and man came when man sinned. Man became spiritually dead. He ceased to be able to recognize his reason for being. Man's life is something like a triangle: he is the base, from which a line ascends toward God, establishing communication there. Then the line descends toward one's fellow humans. Thus, man's reason for being is somewhat twofold: it involves communication with God *and* with man. When people have a right relationship with God through Christ, they come to possess a new sense of values regarding their fellow humans.

II. Second, let us examine the cure for this distressing malady of loneliness.

How can this communication between man and God be restored?

Jesus said, "He that findeth his life shall lose it: and he that loseth his life for my sake shall find it" (Matt. 10:39). Jesus meant more here than just giving one's life as a martyr for the gospel. The elder brother in the parable of the prodigal son lived a lonely life. Though he never left home and squandered his possessions as did his prodigal brother, he was guilty of greater sins. He refused to recognize his brotherhood; he did not care that his brother had repented; and consequently he would not welcome him home. His was probably the "I-told-you-so" attitude. Who was lonely in the end? Not the prodigal, for he had repented of his sins, and the communication lines between him and his father were restored. But the older brother saw no need for repentance. His communication with God and with his family was dissolved, and he was outside in the darkness of loneliness.

Paul said that man is "not to think of himself more highly than he ought to think" (Rom. 12:3). The quickest way to unpopularity and thus to loneliness is *conceit.* Phillips Brooks said, "The true way to be humble is to stand at your full height against someone who is taller."

Second, Paul said, "We, being many, are one body" (Rom. 12:5). Once a pen remarked, "I am writing a book." But the ink replied, "*I* am writing the book. You could not make a mark without me." Then the paper interjected, "But what could either of you do without *me*?" And the dictionary said, "If *I* did not supply the words, no book could be written!" And all during the argument, the *author* just smiled. It takes every one of us, in his or her place, fulfilling his or her role, to carry out God's plan.

Third, Paul said, "Abhor that which is evil; cleave to that which is good" (Rom. 12:9). Whoever refuses to stand for the good and against the evil has neither self-respect nor the respect of others.

Finally, Paul said that we must be "patient in tribulation" (Rom. 12:12). Constant complaining and sympathy-seeking never win friends.

Through all these admonitions, Paul was suggesting that one take the spotlight off self, focus on God, and then on one's fellow humans. That is the way to deal a death blow to loneliness.

Conclusion

Loneliness is a symptom of broken communication lines. How can they be restored? One must first focus on God, and through repentance and faith, reestablish "God-consciousness." Then the breath of God's Spirit, like a gentle zephyr, will dispel the swirling fog of loneliness. The mirror in which one has beheld only oneself will be removed, allowing for a clear view whereby one can behold others. Then there will be no more loneliness.

SUNDAY MORNING, JULY 23

Title: The Christian and Family Concerns

Text: "Standing by the cross of Jesus were his mother, and his mother's sister, Mary the wife of Clopas, and Mary Magdalene" **(John 19:25 RSV)**.

Scripture Reading: John 19:25–27; 20:10

Hymns: "Love Is the Theme," Fisher
"At Calvary," Newell
"When I Survey the Wondrous Cross," Watts

Offertory Prayer: Father, we thank you today for your rich blessings on us in the form of our Christian heritage. We thank you for the saints of old who suffered and struggled to be your messengers and to be our examples. We thank you for parents and for teachers and pastors and for all who have been your instruments to enrich and to uplift our lives. We thank you for every noble, uplifting influence that has made our lives better. In this time of worship when we bring our offerings to you, we also bring our lives and place them on the altar of service that we might be used by your love and by your power that others might be blessed and brought into a knowledge of Jesus Christ as Lord and Savior. Help us to recognize that all we are and all we have belong to our Creator and Redeemer and that we are but managers and overseers. Help us to be faithful in using what you have placed under our care. We pray in Jesus' name. Amen.

Introduction

In the words of our Scripture reading, our Lord and Savior has given us an example of how we should care for our mothers and for all the elder members of the human family. As we read the account of the crucifixion of our precious Lord, we should look for something more than a historical account of what happened two millennia ago. We should listen to his words to gain insight for living today, for Jesus is our example, and we can learn from the manner in which he cared for his mother in a time of great personal crisis.

In the words of our text, we can see that there were at least four women standing by the cross during Jesus' suffering. Of the wife of Clopas, we know nothing for certain. Concerning Mary the mother of our Lord, we see here demonstrated the eternal love of motherhood. Rudyard Kipling tried to put this quality of love in his beautiful poem *Mother o' Mine.*

> *If I were hanged on the highest hill,*
> *Mother o' mine, O mother o' mine!*
> *I know whose love would follow me still,*
> *Mother o' mine, O mother o' mine!*
>
> *If I were drowned in the deepest sea,*
> *Mother o' mine, O mother o' mine!*
> *I know whose tears would come down to me,*
> *Mother o' mine, O mother o' mine!*
>
> *If I were damned of body and soul,*
> *Mother o' mine, O mother o' mine!*
> *I know whose prayers would make me whole,*
> *Mother o' mine, O mother o' mine!*

The third woman spoken of in our text was Mary's sister, identified elsewhere as Salome, the mother of Zebedee's children (Matt. 27:56; Mark 15:40). This woman had received a stern rebuke from our Lord on one occasion (Matt. 20:20–23), yet she continued to love Jesus. Perhaps this indicates the manner in which our Lord could rebuke and yet reveal love at the same time. We can learn a lesson here about being able to give and receive a warning or rebuke.

The fourth woman who stood at the cross was Mary Magdalene. Our Lord had cast seven demons out of her (Luke 8:2), and it was to her that he appeared first following his resurrection (Mark 16:9).

In the record of this incident that took place while our Lord was suffering for our sins, we see a supreme demonstration of a mother's love, and we see also a supreme demonstration of the love and care of a son. In their mutual suffering, they sustained each other. We have here an illustration of filial love and maternal devotion.

I. Now there stood by the cross of Jesus his mother.

Mary was chosen by God for a unique mission (Luke 1:26–35).

Remarkable faith, devotion, and courage were evident in her submission to God's will (Luke 1:38).

Mary's mission for God involved her in much suffering and hardship.

The Christ was born in the most unfavorable of circumstances, and his crib was a manger.

He became the object of kingly hatred, and Mary and Joseph were compelled to flee as exiles into Egypt.

As a child, Jesus returned with Mary and Joseph to Nazareth as a fugitive, and Mary pondered all these things in her heart.

Later, when our Lord began his earthly ministry, Mary must have experienced both joy and bewilderment (cf. Mark 3:20–35).

The greatest test of Mary's faith and love came in connection with the horror of his shameful death on a cross. While the crowds were mocking, the thieves were taunting, the priests were jeering, and the Savior was dying, his mother stood by his cross.

II. The beloved apostle by the cross.

Our Lord needed friends. He developed close, intimate relationships with those whom he called friends and who later were his apostles.

John had been a fisherman until he heard Jesus' invitation and forsook all to follow him (Matt. 4:21). John became one of the chosen Twelve. At times we see him listed in an inner circle of three, and many people believe that he is the one who leaned on the bosom of our Lord at the Last Supper.

It is interesting to note that Matthew tells us that during the agony of Jesus' passion, "all the disciples forsook him and fled" (Matt. 26:56).

Sometime later John returned. Let it be said to his credit that he returned to be near the cross in a time of great danger. Love, gratitude, and concern brought him back. While standing by the cross, John was to receive a unique commission from our Lord.

III. The Savior on the cross.

On the cross we see the supreme demonstration of the love of God for a lost and needy world (John 3.16; Rom. 5:8) and of the love of Christ for his Father (John 14:31). We also see that while on the cross suffering for the sins of a guilty world, our Lord continued to demonstrate care, concern, and a sense of responsibility toward his mother.

Our Lord cared for his mother even while he was dying to save the entire world. From this we can conclude that there is no conflict between providing proper care for parents and at the same time giving of ourselves unreservedly to the will and purpose of God for us.

Jesus provided for his mother. He put the will of God first and foremost in his life. He died on the cross to do God's will. There is no question that God's will had top priority, but even with this being first on his list of priorities, our Lord still cared for his mother.

When Jesus could no longer care for his mother personally, he placed her in the most capable hands available. At this time, seemingly his half brothers and half sisters were alienated from him and certainly were not sympathetic with what he was doing.

Our Lord's care for his mother while dying on the cross reveals that it is not essential that we ignore the needs of family members who are dependent on us as we seek to do God's will.

Conclusion

Our Lord is tremendously concerned about family relationships. He wants us to relate to each other in love and helpfulness. He encourages us to practice love, demonstrate forgiveness, and manifest the fruit of the Spirit in our relationships with those who are nearest and dearest to us.

Christ also wants each of you to be a part of God's family. He died that you might have forgiveness of sins. He arose from the dead to give you the gift of life. He has sent the Holy Spirit into the world and into our hearts to make his presence real to all who receive him.

Our Lord gave John a task, and he will give you a task that will be meaningful and will bring joy to you and to others. Come to this Christ today and let him become to you that which you need.

SUNDAY EVENING, JULY 23

Title: A Judge Who Condemns Himself

Text: "Judge not, that ye be not judged" (**Matt. 7:1**).

Scripture Reading: Matthew 7:1–5; Romans 14:4, 10–13

Introduction

Matthew and Luke, in recording the Sermon on the Mount, obviously abbreviated their accounts. They probably dropped some of the transitional paragraphs so that this portion of the sermon is not as clear as the original. Matthew 7:1–12 appears to be another major division around the theme "The Christian's Relation to Other Persons."

Matthew 7:1–2 warns against censorious judgment. Matthew 7:4–5 warns against hypocritical judgment. Matthew 7:6 warns against indiscriminate judgment. In this most difficult area, Christians need God's help. Matthew 7:7–11 encourages them to pray for assistance. Matthew 7:12 concludes the division by summing up the Christian's relations to others in a principle universally recognized as the Golden Rule.

Tonight you are invited to consider carefully the Lord's warnings about censorious and hypocritical judgment of others as recorded in Matthew 7:1–5.

I. "Judge not"—prohibition of censorious judgment (Matt. 7:1–2).

The prohibition is not against forming tentative opinions and evaluating facts as the following Scriptures show: "Wherefore by their fruits ye shall know them" (Matt. 7:20). "Judge not according to the appearance, but judge righteous judgment" (John 7:24). "Yea, and why even of yourselves judge ye not what is right?" (Luke 12:57). "Beware of false prophets" (Matt. 7:15). "Prove all things; hold fast that which is good" (1 Thess. 5:21). "Therefore put away from among yourselves that wicked person" (1 Cor. 5:13).

The prohibition (as determined from the context) is against censorious judgment and against usurping God's place as final judge.

Prohibited is hasty and rash judgment that does not get all of the facts. "He that answereth a matter before he heareth it, it is folly and shame unto him" (Prov. 18:13). It was reported that J. C. Penney would not hire a man who salted his food before he tasted it.

When former Senator Inouye of Hawaii and others took their oaths of office, the picture appeared on television. A viewer wrote, "Senator Inouye does not know his right hand from his left." The viewer had been observant enough to note that Senator Inouye took the oath with his left hand uplifted. Had he obtained all the facts, he never would have written the letter, because the senator had lost his right hand serving in the US military.

A church hastily excluded from its membership a young woman who had been observed coming from a house of prostitution. When the facts came to light, it was revealed that she had gone in because she thought that her brother was there. Her motives were entirely honorable. Let a gossip start a rumor, and it is amazing how many people will believe it without getting all the facts.

Communication at best is a difficult art. One may understand the exact word as illustrated by this story. A woman was depositing the Ladies' Aid money. The hard-of-hearing bank teller thought she said "egg money" when she said "aid money," and commented that the old hens must be doing quite well to make that much money.

Ambiguous speech is always a possibility. A pastor, commenting about his plan to take a vacation, said, "It is good for the pastor to get away occasionally." One of the women responded, "It is good for the members also."

Prohibited is unmerciful judgment—thinking the worst rather than the best about another. Job 1:8–11 represents Satan as making that kind of judgment about Job when Satan asked, "Doth Job fear God for nought?" (Job 1:9). Second Samuel 10 records how King Hanun of Ammon mistook peaceful messengers from King David as spies.

One can do some mighty stupid things from a good motive. A pastor, when asked why he left his former pastorate, replied, "It is like the man who jumped through a plate glass window. When asked, 'Why did you do it?' he replied, 'I don't exactly remember, but at the time it seemed like a good idea.'"

Christians want to believe the best. They do not want to build themselves up by putting others down. They will go straight to the source to gather information before making a judgment.

Prohibited is hypocritical judgment. The delightful word cartoon in Matthew 7:3–5 represents a person with a beam in his own eye trying to get a speck out of his brother's eye. One with glaring faults who is busy condemning lesser faults in others stands condemned. A good illustration is that of David condemning the man who stole his neighbor's lamb while David had stolen his neighbor's wife (see 2 Sam. 12:1–7). Other examples are Judas, a thief who complained about the prodigality of Mary of Bethany; the unchurched man who hides behind the hypocrite; or anyone excusing oneself from responsibility because of the failure of others.

Prohibited is final judgment. No person knows enough to be the final judge. God is the Judge. No person can know the motives of others. Only God can. Judge not, for the moral quality of any act depends on the motive. Paul asked, "Why dost thou judge thy brother? or why dost thou set at nought thy brother? for we shall all stand before the judgment seat of Christ" (Rom. 14:10). It is not our business to separate the wheat from the tares. We do not know enough, nor are we good enough to do it. This is God's business (see Matt. 13:24–30, 36–43). Any theory of soteriology that places the eternal destinies of others in the hands of humans is in error. The command to humans is "Judge not." "Let us not therefore judge one another any more: but judge this rather, that no man put a stumbling-block or an occasion to fall in his brother's way" (Rom. 14:13).

II. Motives to enforce this prohibition (Matt. 7:2).

The one who judges will be judged.

We will be judged by people. Censure is like a boomerang: "For with what judgment ye judge, ye shall be judged: and with what measure ye mete, it shall be measured to you again." If you want friends, be friendly. If you want enemies, judge censoriously.

We will be judged by God. Just as our judgment of others is partial and faulty, so will be their judgment of us; but God's judgment will be final and just. "So then every one of us shall give account of himself to God" (Rom. 14:12).

Judging others establishes the basis on which God can judge us. If you should say, "He is a hypocrite," you by that statement acknowledge that you know he ought not to be a hypocrite and that you also ought not to be a hypocrite. If you have knowledge enough to judge another, you establish the basis on which God can judge you. Read carefully Romans 2:1–2 as you contemplate this solemn truth.

Conclusion

Final judgment belongs to God. Human judgment must be partial and tentative. "Cast the beam out of thine own eye" (Matt. 7:5) by repentance, faith, confession, and obedience. Have basic goodwill. Think the best, hope the best, desire the best for others as well as for yourself. Be willing to change your tentative opinions of others for the better. Your final accounting is to God as is everyone's. God is more interested that both you and your brothers and sisters be Christian than he is that you be punished. Be sure that your concern is for others' salvation rather than their condemnation.

WEDNESDAY EVENING, JULY 26

Title: Dealing with Despair

Text: "My God, my God, why hast thou forsaken me? why art thou so far from helping me, and from the words of my roaring?" **(Ps. 22:1)**.

Scripture Reading: Psalm 22

Introduction

In all of the Bible, there is found only one question Jesus ever asked his Father. In phrasing his question, he borrowed the words of David in Psalm 22:1: "My God, my God, why hast thou forsaken me?" They contained all the agony he experienced during the dark hours on Calvary. In the abysmal darkness of separation from God for the only time in eternity, Jesus cried out of the depths of his despair.

Because Jesus experienced this total agony, he is able to identify with the feelings of despair that invade people's lives. All of us experience times when we cannot seem to find a reason or purpose for living, and everything connected with the ongoing of life is blurred and indefinable. Psalm 22, which describes a period in David's life, can be divided into three sections for study.

I. First, the predicament in which the psalmist finds himself.

What is the implication of David's question in verse 1? First, it indicates a sense of forsakenness. Here the same individual who wrote the incomparable Twenty-Third Psalm, expressing the closest relationship with God, is now plumbing the depths of despair. He had come to a moment in his life when he felt totally alone in the world. This teaches us that there is nothing illusory about suffering.

David's cry also indicates perplexity. It is not true that "faith asks no questions." Rather, a sound faith in God will help a Christian ask profitable questions in the hour of distress. David's question springs from his *belief,* not his *unbelief.* In spite of the acuteness of David's despair, he did not lose sight of God. He could still cry, "My God, my God, . . ." It is the triumph of faith when one realizes, even in the darkness of the deepest anguish, that God is still there, and that he is the God "with whom is no variableness, neither shadow of turning" (James 1:17).

II. Second, David's plea for help.

In Psalm 22:19 David prayed, "Be not thou far from me, O Lord: O my strength, haste thee to help me." In *The Problem of Pain,* C. S. Lewis said, "God whispers to us in our pleasures, speaks to us in our conscience, but shouts in our pains: it is His megaphone to rouse a deaf world." Perhaps it is not so much that God "shouts," but that self is silenced and the voice of God sounds so clearly in our souls when a great crisis comes. Trouble is a blessing when it drives us nearer to God. At the lowest point of his suffering, Job cried, "Though he slay me, yet will I trust in him" (Job 13:15). That was not an expression of blind faith or stoicism, but of a child of God holding to his heavenly Father with the tenacity that only love can make possible.

David's despair drove him to God instead of away from him, because past experiences had taught him that God was merciful and gracious. His conditioning refused to allow him to believe that God was unconcerned with his suffering. He was perplexed; nonetheless, he bared his soul before God.

III. Finally, David's praise to God for deliverance from sorrow and suffering.

Verse 22 reveals David's abrupt change in mood, followed by his admonition to all to praise God. It is as if some holy quietness had settled on the turbulent soul of David. Now he was prepared to rejoice before the Lord. How often have we agonized through a long night over some problem, some unresolved heartache, only, with the dawning of a new day, to experience a rest in the Lord, a calm and sweet peace that defies description! God promises, "Weeping may endure for a night, but joy cometh in the morning" (Ps. 30:5). This is often the way of God's providence as he works out his will in us.

The psalm closes with the shout of deliverance. Instead of forsakenness, the psalmist found fulfillment; instead of question, the answer was at hand.

In spite of the bleak and doleful beginning of the psalm, the unbreakable strand of faith runs throughout. We can liken it to a communications cable that runs from the shore and dips down, out of sight, beneath the waves of the sea, and emerges on the other side—it is "out of sight," but it is intact, and the message is going through.

Conclusion

Paul said, "For now we see through a glass darkly; but then face to face: now I know in part; but then shall I know even as also I am known" (1 Cor. 13:12). Christians accept the reality of suffering in the light of their faith and confidence in God's redemptive purpose. There are many things we do not and cannot know about suffering and sorrow. We do not share omniscience with God, but we do know that beyond this vale of tears is a brighter day. Christians can deal with despair when they are able to look in retrospect at God's sustaining grace during heart-crushing experiences.

SUNDAY MORNING, JULY 30

Title: The Problem of Loneliness

Text: "And about the ninth hour Jesus cried with a loud voice, 'Eli, Eli, lama sabach-tha-ni?' that is, 'My God, my God, why hast thou forsaken me?'" **(Matt. 27:46 RSV)**.

Scripture Reading: Matthew 27:33–50; Hebrews 4:14–16

Hymns: "To God be the Glory," Crosby
"The Old Rugged Cross," Bennard
"Rock of Ages," Toplady

Offertory Prayer: Heavenly Father, you are the giver of every good and perfect gift. We thank you for the rich gifts of your love. We thank you for the pardon of our sins and the cleansing that comes through forgiveness. We thank you for the gift of eternal life. We thank you for opportunities and responsibilities. We thank you for the gifts of your Spirit. We come thanking you for the fruit of our labors. We come bringing offerings to express our love and gifts that we might participate with you in your work of redeeming people from the tyranny of sin. Bless these gifts to your glory and to the good of others. We pray in Christ's name. Amen.

Introduction

To walk the street of any major city in the world and to look in the faces of those you meet, is to be impressed with the look of loneliness that fills people's eyes even while they are in the midst of a multitude.

Do you have periods of extreme loneliness when you are forsaken, cut off, abandoned, isolated, and very alone? The desire for fellowship, a sense of belonging, and the assurance of acceptance are basic human needs.

I. Why do we have a problem with loneliness?

We can experience loneliness because we are lost in the crowd. Merely being in the midst of people does not guarantee that we won't be lonely.

We can experience loneliness when we feel that we are misunderstood by family members or by the circle of people whose acceptance is important to us.

We can feel lonely because of mistreatment at the hands of someone else. This is a perennial problem because we are always subject to mistreatment by others.

We can experience loneliness as a result of frustration in our work or in relationships that are important to us.

We can experience loneliness because of weariness of body and mind. The body and mind must have rest from the burdens and stresses of life.

We can experience loneliness because of a position of leadership. Bearing the weight of responsibility or standing at the top of an organization can be a very lonely position.

We can experience loneliness because of physical or emotional suffering. Pain can be so intense that it can cause us to feel we are alone in the midst of our agony.

We can feel lonely because of a negative and critical attitude toward self. This is one of the major contributing causes to a feeling of loneliness. Many of us developed a negative way of thinking early in life and have never been able to replace our negative thoughts with a positive mental attitude.

Many experience loneliness because of known, unconfessed, and unforsaken sin. This is true particularly among Christians. To tolerate known sin is to create a feeling of guilt and disharmony with God. The restoration of fellowship and the joy of association comes only when the sin has been confessed and forsaken. To truly make confession is to "agree with God" concerning the sin.

Many experience loneliness because of inadequate and incorrect understanding of God's nature. Many of us have accepted fragments of God's great self-revelation as being the complete revelation of his nature and purpose. To overcome the problem of loneliness, we need to have a proper understanding of God's nature and a life in harmony with his purpose.

Loneliness is often the result of our permitting ourselves to live on the level of our emotions rather than letting our intellect determine the way we are going to feel and react to the various situations of life.

II. Jesus and the problem of loneliness.

Would you be surprised to know that Jesus suffered the agony of feeling lonely? Because he has experienced the pain of loneliness, we are assured that he is able to sympathize with us and to assist us with this painful problem (Heb. 2:17–18).

Jesus, who suffered in all ways, can provide us with a pattern for dealing with life's painful problems. The words of our text are words of appalling woe, for we hear the Savior crying out, "My God, my God, why hast thou forsaken me?" The Savior felt utterly forsaken and very lonely. It seemed as if he were completely cut off from God. On many different occasions Jesus must have experienced the pain of loneliness.

Jesus was misunderstood by the members of his own family (Matt. 12:46–50).

Jesus was misunderstood and rejected by the people of his own city (Luke 4:24–30).

Jesus was betrayed by one of his twelve intimate friends.

In a time of great stress when Jesus needed the prayer support of his closest friends, they went to sleep, leaving him alone in his agony (Luke 22:45–46).

When Jesus was seized by wicked men, all of his apostles forsook him, though one did follow afar off.

The words of our text come from the lips of the lonely Savior while he was impaled on a cross. In the midst of Jesus' physical anguish, his greatest suffering was the feeling of having been forsaken by his God. The words, "My God, my God, why hast thou forsaken me?" are words of profound solemnity. The mystery behind these words and behind the event that was taking place is beyond human power to fully comprehend.

III. Was Jesus really forsaken?

There can be absolutely no question concerning the agony of Jesus' loneliness as he bore the burden of human guilt and condemnation. Jesus had taken on himself the sin and guilt of a rebellious creation and was dying under the penalty of human sin.

Jesus felt himself to be utterly forsaken. He felt the awful loneliness of being cut off from God and forsaken by his friends. There is no more intense agony than Jesus experienced as he died to redeem us from the awful penalty of sin.

Jesus' cry of utter pathos reveals the genuineness of his agony on our behalf. This was no farce, no mere drama. Jesus was "smitten by God, and afflicted." He suffered the wrath of a holy God against the malignancy of evil.

IV. What can we do to solve the problem of loneliness?

We need to admit that we cannot make ourselves totally immune from loneliness. It is a problem with which we will have to deal as time goes by, and Jesus provides us with a pattern to follow.

Jesus responded to the problem of loneliness by crying out to God in his time of need.

First and foremost, when we feel lonely we should look to the Lord for grace, guidance, and help. It is not the will of our Father God that any of us experience the painful agony of loneliness. It is his will that each of us be members of his family and that we dwell together and relate to each other with warm, generous love. It is his desire that we enjoy the delight of spiritual fellowship with other members of the family at all times.

Developing a positive mental attitude based on faith in God will aid us greatly in overcoming loneliness.

Accepting the humanity of others so as not to be knocked off balance by their misunderstanding or by mistreatment can help us overcome loneliness. Continuously forgiving others will assist us greatly in overcoming the loneliness that comes as a result of misunderstanding and mistreatment.

Securing proper rest and following good health habits will go a long way toward helping us overcome loneliness.

If unconfessed and unforsaken sin is causing us to feel lonely, we need to recognize the cause for our feeling of isolation and unhappiness and confess and forsake that attitude or action that has set up a vicious, destructive cycle in our life. Not to do so is to add to our problem of feeling lonely and forsaken.

We aren't so apt to be lonely if we define our reason for being in terms of living a life of giving rather than of getting. Jesus could endure the agony and loneliness of the cross because of the joy set before him (Heb. 12:2). He was strengthened and sustained because he knew that what he was doing was going to please the Father God and be most productive in its benefits for others.

Conclusion

Let the Lord Jesus Christ become your Savior if this is the great need of your life. If you have already trusted him as your Savior, then trust in his promise to be with you at all times and under all circumstances. He has promised, "I will never fail you nor forsake you" (Heb. 13:5).

SUNDAY EVENING, JULY 30

Title: Casting Pearls before Swine

Text: "Give not that which is holy unto the dogs, neither cast ye your pearls before swine, lest they trample them under their feet, and turn again and rend you" **(Matt. 7:6).**

Scripture Reading: Proverbs 9:1–10

Introduction

The general theme in Matthew 7:1–12 is "The Christian's Relation to Other Persons." In Matthew's condensed account, the relationship of our text with the preceding and following verses is not made clear. Some expositors think that the text is an apothegm standing in splendid isolation. Before examining the text's relation to the context, let us probe its meaning.

I. Meaning of the text.

Dogs and hogs were both considered differently in first-century Palestine than they are in the twentieth century. Dogs were mostly wild and ran in packs much as wolves in frontier areas do today. They were scavengers who often fought viciously over their food. *Dog* throughout the Old Testament was a term of reproach.

Dogs and hogs were both ceremonially unclean and unfit for food. The prodigal son sank about as low as one could in the eyes of his contemporaries when he hired out to a Gentile to feed hogs.

"Holy" probably refers to the food that had been offered on the altar, especially the flesh offered in sacrifice. Flesh torn by beasts was fit only for dogs (see Ex. 22:31), but every Jew would consider giving "holy flesh" (see Hag. 2:12) to the dogs as a horrid profanation. Their response to this impropriety was somewhat akin to that of a church member who saw a minister's son systematically drink the juice from the glasses remaining after the observance of the Lord's Supper.

Many years ago Bible scholars noted that the Aramaic word for "holy" had the same consonants as the Aramaic word for "earring." Since there were no vowels in the original manuscripts, this is a possible variant reading that is appealing since earrings cast before dogs would parallel pearls cast before hogs.

Pearls in the ancient world were valued much as diamonds are today. This is illustrated in Jesus' parable of the pearl of great price.

The meaning is this: Pearls—things that are holy—cast to vicious dogs or charging boars would not deter them at all. Dogs and hogs would have no appreciation of their value. Jesus is not calling people dogs or hogs. He is speaking about relations with people. A Christian can be as foolish in dealing with some people as one who casts pearls to swine.

Relation to Matthew 7:1–5. In Matthew 7:1–2 Jesus warned his disciples against censorious judgment. Only God can render final judgment, because he alone knows all of the facts, including motives. In Matthew 7:3–5, Jesus warned his disciples against hypocritical judgment. The picture of the man with a beam in his eye attempting to pick a speck of dust from his brother's eye is very effective. Although Christians are not to judge censoriously or hypocritically, they do need to use discretion and discrimination when dealing with others, lest they be harmed or, more importantly, the truth be disparaged. Some people have no more understanding of the value of the gospel than dogs and hogs have of the value of pearls. Christians must deal with them accordingly.

II. What Jesus did is a good commentary on what he meant.

Examples.

The high priest Caiaphas allowed Jesus to be condemned by witnesses whom he knew to be false. "And the high priest arose, and said unto him, Answerest thou nothing? what is it which these witness against thee? But Jesus held his peace" (Matt. 26:62–63). An answer to false charges before a corrupt high priest would have been like casting pearls before swine.

Jesus would not reply to the soldiers who spat on him, buffeted him, and made sport of him (see Matt. 26:66–68 and Luke 22:63–65).

Pilate, the Roman procurator, knew Jesus was an innocent man. He was willing, albeit reluctantly, to allow an innocent man to die rather than risk losing his office. When he asked cynically, "What is truth?" Jesus did not preach to him (see John 18:28–38).

King Herod hoped to see Jesus work a miracle. "He plied him with many questions, but Jesus gave him no answer. The chief priests and the teachers of the law were standing there, vehemently accusing him. Then Herod and his soldiers ridiculed and mocked him. Dressing him in an elegant robe, they sent him back to Pilate" (Luke 23:9–11 NIV).

Teaching. When Jesus sent out the Twelve, he instructed them to turn from those who refused to hear to those who would (see Matt. 10:11–15). The apostle Paul followed this same strategy, as illustrated by his turning to the Gentiles at Corinth (see Acts 18:4–6).

III. Conclusion

The Christian is under no obligation to argue with one who treats the truth as a dog or a hog treats jewels or pearls.

A navy chaplain in Honolulu was accosted by a group of men who had been drinking. They used obscene language, ridiculed him, then sportingly demanded, "Preach to us, Chappy. See if you can convert us." The chaplain followed the Lord's example and remained silent.

Since Christians are more tempted to extreme caution than to excessive zeal, it is wise to note that some hard cases were responsive to the gospel. The woman of Samaria, Zacchaeus, the harlot who came to Simon's supper, and the thief on the cross all received the gospel. Perhaps Christians should make the approach and then proceed or desist on the basis of the response.

While avoiding censorious judgment and hypocritical judgment, one must make tentative judgments on the basis of the facts and act accordingly. "Wherefore by their fruits ye shall know them" (Matt. 7:20).

Christians must make clear the distinction between saved and lost. We are not to welcome into the church those who are unrepentant.

Standards for pastors, deacons, and church officers are to be held high. Persons without understanding of the value of truth will be poor leaders no matter how much wealth or secular wisdom they have.

When people depart from their true humanity and act toward others as dogs that bite and boars that rend, then some measure other than speaking to them the pearls of the gospel must be used. A young preacher was murdered at the very time he was sharing the gospel with the gunman.

We have a right to defend ourselves, our homes, our property, and our rights against those who bite and rend like dogs and hogs. It is not Christian for us to allow ourselves or our loved ones to be robbed, raped, murdered, or mistreated. It is incumbent on Christians to join with all citizens of goodwill to support the authorities in combating crime.

It is no virtue for Christians to be so naive that they allow themselves to be cheated and defrauded, and especially by some racket posing as a

Christian benevolence or by some confidence man posing as a Christian. Just a few sentences later in the sermon, Jesus warns, "Beware of false prophets, which come to you in sheep's clothing, but inwardly are ravening wolves" (Matt. 7:15).

When people reject the truth (as dogs and hogs trample pearls) we must continue to love them and to care about them, interceding in prayer for them. In the Old Testament, the prophet Samuel said to the rebellious people of Israel, "God forbid that I should sin against the LORD in ceasing to pray for you" (1 Sam. 12:23). We can also witness to those who reject the truth by consistent Christian living. We must never fail in love and compassion even toward those who trample the pearls of the gospel under their feet.

AUGUST

- ## Sunday Mornings

    Continue with the theme "Christ Sets the Pattern."

- ## Sunday Evenings

    Continue with expository messages from Jesus' Sermon on the Mount.

- ## Wednesday Evenings

    Christianity is the only faith whose founder has conquered death and the grave. "Where Does Christ Live?" is the theme for these devotions.

WEDNESDAY EVENING, AUGUST 2

Title: Our Living Savior

Text: "Consequently he is able for all time to save those who draw near to God through him, since he always lives to make intercession for them" **(Heb. 7:25 RSV)**.

Scripture Reading: Hebrews 7:20–28

Introduction

Christianity is the result of the early disciples' faith that Jesus Christ had conquered death and the grave and was alive forevermore. Christianity has continued as a dynamic faith because those who have put their faith and trust in Jesus Christ have found him to be a living presence and a continuing power in their lives. While the words of the poet are relatively recent, the faith that he expresses has characterized the children of God since the days of Jesus' resurrection:

> He lives, He lives, Christ Jesus lives today!
> He walks with me and talks with me along life's narrow way.
> He lives, He lives, salvation to impart!
> You ask me how I know He lives: He lives within my heart.

I. Christ lives to be our Savior from the penalty of sin (Rom. 1:4; 4:24–25).

Only after Jesus' resurrection were the apostles capable of beginning to understand the nature of his shameful and terrifying death on the cross. In the days between his resurrection and his ascension back to the Father, the living Lord ministered to his disciples. He opened up their minds to understand the Old Testament Scriptures that pointed out the necessity for his death on the cross for the sins of a guilty humanity (Luke 24:44).

The apostolic preaching of the early church was characterized by a proclamation of Christ's substitutionary death on a cross and his victorious resurrection from the dead as the proof that God had been providing a way for humankind's salvation (Acts 10:39–43). By raising Jesus from the dead, God was assuring a needy humanity that their problem of sin had been dealt with radically and adequately.

II. Christ lives to be our Savior from the power of sin.

Jesus Christ came into this world to do more than die for our sins on a cross. He came also to save us from the bent toward evil that has plagued humans ever since Adam. The living Christ enters the hearts and the lives of believers in the moment when they express faith in him (Rev. 3:20). By his Holy Spirit, he lives within those of us who look to him in faith, enabling us to crucify our old lives and become new creatures in him (Gal. 2:20). The indwelling Christ provides us with a basis for hope in the present and in the future that we might become truly mature in him, living victoriously over evil (Col. 1:27–29).

As Paul faced the perplexities and difficulties of life, he expressed the confidence that he would be able to make all necessary adjustments and bear all essential burdens through the strength that Jesus Christ would provide (Phil. 4:13).

III. Christ lives to save us from the very presence of sin.

One of the greatest joys that comes as a result of receiving Jesus Christ as Lord and Savior is the gift of a new nature (2 Cor. 5:17). God grants us a nature like his own, and Peter proclaims that we become "partakers of the divine nature" (2 Peter 1:4). This new nature that is received in the miracle of the new birth causes us to have an appetite for the things of God and an aversion for the things that are evil. We begin to hunger and thirst after righteousness and for a perfect purity of heart (Matt. 5:6–8).

While our Lord holds up before us a standard of perfection, and while he places within us a holy discontent with anything less than perfection, at the same time he teaches us to pray, "Forgive us our sins; for we also forgive every one that is indebted to us" (Luke 11:4). In some instances in the New Testament, our salvation is spoken of in the future tense as a future prospect (Rom. 13:11; Heb. 9:28).

When salvation is spoken of in the future tense, it is not referring to a salvation from the penalty of sin, but rather from the presence of sin. We will be plagued with the problem of sin as long as we are in our flesh. When our physical bodies die, we will leave sin behind and receive new bodies suitable for heaven (1 Cor. 15:51–56).

Conclusion

Ours is a living Savior. Only a Savior who conquered sin and death can save us from the penalty of sin, which is death. The Savior lives within us to save us from the penalty, power, and presence of sin. The Savior who is alive forevermore and who intercedes for us before the Father will one day come to claim us for his own and take us to heaven.

SUNDAY MORNING, AUGUST 6

Title: The Thirst of Our Lord

Text: "After this Jesus, knowing that all was now finished, said (to fulfill the scripture), 'I thirst'" **(John 19:28 RSV)**.

Scripture Reading: John 19:17–30

Hymns: "Great Redeemer, We Adore Thee," Harris
"At the Cross," Watts
"The Banner of the Cross," Whittle

Offertory Prayer: Father, because you are the great giver, we come to you with petitions. We come praying that you will give us understanding hearts that we might understand more perfectly your great love for a needy world. We pray that you will give us more understanding concerning our stewardship. Help us to see ourselves as your servants, your ministers, your helpers. Accept not only these tithes and offerings, but help us to give ourselves totally into your service and into ministries of mercy. We pray in Jesus' name. Amen.

Introduction

As the followers of Jesus Christ, we are to continually focus our eyes on him as our example. He is to be our guide and leader as we face the crises of life (Heb. 12:2).

We have been studying Christ's words from the cross to better understand what God was doing when he gave his Son to die. We have been seeking to let the great sacrifice of Jesus stir our emotions that we might love God more and be more grateful to him for his magnificent gift to us in the person of Jesus Christ. May Jesus' giving of himself on the cross motivate us and move us not only to worship God more sincerely, but also to give ourselves in service to him that his kingdom might come in the hearts and lives of people here in our own community and to the uttermost parts of the earth. Today let us listen to the suffering Lord as he cries out in the midst of his sufferings, "I thirst."

I. "I thirst" for water because of intense physical suffering.

It is natural for one who has suffered great pain to be thirsty. Significantly, the apostle John interprets this thirst for water coming only after Jesus was assured that his work on the cross was finished. Here we have a supreme demonstration of Jesus' concentration on his primary goal and a profound illustration of his total lack of selfishness.

Jesus had suffered terribly in the garden of Gethsemane, being betrayed with a kiss and seized by wicked hands. He had appeared before Caiaphas and Annas, Pilate and Herod, and then had been returned to the court of Pilate. He had been scourged by soldiers and had fainted under the burden of the cross. For three hours he had hung on the cross. Only after all of this did he cry out of intense physical agony, "I thirst."

Because Jesus experienced the awful pain of suffering, he is able to sympathize and come to the assistance of those who suffer today (Heb. 2:18).

II. "I thirst" for full restoration of fellowship with the Father.

We cannot begin to understand the mystery of God's marvelous grace in which Christ took our sins on himself and suffered as a sinner. Paul spoke of it in his second epistle to the Corinthians: "For our sake he made him to be sin who knew no sin, so that in him we might become the righteousness of God" (5:21 RSV). Jesus had experienced the awful poverty of being deprived of a conscious awareness of both the favor and the presence of God while on the cross. He experienced the poverty of this loneliness that we might experience the riches of the assurance of God's love and abiding presence (2 Cor. 8:9).

No doubt Jesus thirsted for the full restoration of fellowship with the Father that he had known before creation and before the beginning of his redemptive mission (John 17:5). Jesus did not begin to be when he was born in Bethlehem. His birth was but the beginning of his earthly mission that would lead to his crucifixion. He yearned for the time when he would ascend back into heaven to be with his Father.

In his Sermon on the Mount, Jesus described the ideal characteristics of the citizens of his kingdom. One of these characteristics is a hunger and a thirst for righteousness (Matt. 5:6). Do you encourage the thirst of your soul for God through Bible study and prayer? You could increase the thirst of your soul for fellowship with God by improving both your public and private worship habits. The absence of an intense thirst for God indicates that you are either spiritually dead or are a spiritually unhealthy Christian.

III. "I thirst" for the salvation of an unsaved world.

Jesus also thirsted for the salvation of a needy world. He was so hungry and thirsty to lead people out of the darkness of spiritual death and into the sunlight of fellowship with God that he was willing to come and to give his life as a ransom for us (Mark 10:45). On another occasion Jesus had described himself as a seeker who had come to save the lost (Luke 19:10).

IV. "I thirst" for partnership in redemptive service.

During Jesus' ministry he selected 12 disciples to be with him. They became his friends, coworkers, and partners in the greatest business enterprise on earth, that of sharing the good news of God's love with every man, woman, boy, and girl in the world. Later the number was increased to 70. Then, on the Day of Pentecost, 120 were assembled as his partners and coworkers.

The number has continued to increase to this day. Jesus hungers and thirsts for your partnership with him in the work of bringing the good news of God's love to those who are in spiritual death and in great need. He not only wants you as a servant, but he also wants you as a friend. He needs your help as a partner. The only way by which he can carry on his work today is through us.

Conclusion

Jesus is thirsty for the privilege of bringing the blessings of God into your heart and life. One of the most beautiful pictures of his continuing thirst and desire to bring the blessings of God to you is verbalized in Revelation 3:20: "Here I am! I stand at the door and knock. If anyone hears my voice and opens the door, I will come in and eat with that person, and they with me" (NIV). He does not wait for you to take the initiative. He comes seeking you and offers the gifts of God to you. You can satisfy the thirst of Jesus today by opening the door of your heart and letting him come in as Lord and Savior, leader, guide, and helper.

SUNDAY EVENING, AUGUST 6

Title: Encouragement to Prayer

Text: "If ye then, being evil, know how to give good gifts unto your children, how much more shall your Father which is in heaven give good things to them that ask him?" (**Matt. 7:11**).

Scripture Reading: Matthew 7:7–11; Luke 11:1–13

Introduction

It is encouraging to preachers to note that Jesus repeated his messages to different audiences. Luke 11 records an occasion when Jesus replied to the disciples' request to teach them how to pray by repeating the model prayer. He added the parable of the friend at midnight and then repeated almost exactly the words about prayer spoken in the Sermon on the Mount as recorded in Matthew 7:7–11 (see Luke 11:9–13).

Jesus may have used some connecting material between his teachings about duties to others in Matthew 7:1–6 and his encouragement to prayer in 7:7–11 that does not appear in the gospel. The tremendous responsibility of right relations to others is enough to cause any responsible person to seek God's leadership and strength.

Prayer is fellowship with God. Wherever there are people there will be communication. Between people the medium is usually conversation. Between a person and God the medium is prayer. Prayer is a more perfect medium, for it is not subject to misunderstanding, because God knows the heart. Everyone prays whether he or she knows it or not. One's prayer is what one really desires—spoken or unspoken.

I. Assurance in prayer is based on faith in God as the heavenly Father.

Earlier in the sermon, Jesus had said, "After this manner therefore pray ye: Our Father which art in heaven" (Matt. 6:9). God is the personal, loving, wise Father. He knows all about us and purposes good for us. He will do no harm to us though ten thousand demons ask him to do so.

How forceful is Jesus' argument for answered prayer! No father—even though the best father is evil compared to the holy God—would give his child a stone when he asks for a biscuit; nor would he give him a snake when he asks for a fish. "If ye then, being evil, know how to give good gifts unto your children, how much more shall your Father which is in heaven give good things to them that ask him?" (Matt. 7:11).

Belief in God's providence does not mean that he manipulates the answer on request, but that we can have assurance that everything that ultimately matters is safe in his keeping. "For he that cometh to God must believe that he is, and that he is a rewarder of them that diligently seek him" (Heb. 11:6).

II. God answers every prayer.

His answer may be yes, no, or wait, or he may grant something better than one asks. He will not deliberately give a stone to one who asks for bread. It is an encouragement to prayer to know that God will not say yes to all of our petitions.

God would cease to be God if he said yes to all of our petitions. In that case, we, rather than the Almighty, would be running the universe.

There is a popular misunderstanding of Jesus' promise: "And whatsoever ye shall ask in my name, that will I do, that the Father may be glorified in the Son. If ye shall ask any thing in my name, I will do it" (John 14:13–14). This is not an invitation for a disciple to pray any prayer and expect God to answer because he concludes it by saying, "in Jesus' name." To pray in Jesus' name would be a prayer to which Jesus could sign his name because it is in accord with God's will and for his glory.

Another erroneous popular view is that if one is good enough, earnest enough, and believes enough, God will grant whatever he or she asks. Jesus, the perfectly good person, prayed earnestly in Gethsemane, "O my Father, if it be possible, let this cup pass from me" (Matt. 26:39). Although this was the earnest prayer of a perfect person in perfect faith, God did not say yes to Jesus' petition. It was not in his will. He did say yes to the greater petition, "Nevertheless not as I will, but as thou wilt" (v. 39). This leads to the truth that the purpose of prayer is not to get God to do our will, but rather to get God's will done through us.

All of us have prayed some foolish prayers in which we were thoroughly sincere and felt that the prayers were in the Lord's will. Two stories, which I expect are apocryphal, will illustrate.

A mother said to the new babysitter, "Give the child anything he wants." She returned to find the child with a badly swollen hand and in awful pain. "He wanted a bumblebee," the nurse explained.

A young lady prayed earnestly that her boyfriend would propose. He did—but to another girl. Ten years later, after she was married to a much better man, she thanked God that he had not granted her petition.

III. Some errors to be avoided.

The error of lack of earnestness. In the earlier part of the sermon, Jesus had warned against the hypocrisy of the Pharisees who pray "that they may be seen of men" (Matt. 6:5) and against the ignorance of the heathen who use vain repetitions and "think that they shall be heard for their much speaking" (Matt. 6:7). He now encourages to earnestness by inviting us to "keep on asking," "keep on seeking," "keep on knocking." "For every one that asketh receiveth; and he that seeketh findeth; and to him that knocketh it shall be opened" (Matt. 7:8).

The emphasis of the verb form is on repeated, continuous action. This is not "vain repetition," but earnestness that is exhorted. Jesus prayed three times in Gethsemane, but it was not vain repetition. Likewise, Paul besought the Lord thrice for the removal of the thorn, but it was not vain repetition. The parable of the friend at midnight in Luke 11:5–13 expressly illustrates this passage, and the twin parable of the widow and the judge in Luke 18:1–8 was spoken "to this end, that men ought always to pray, and not to faint" (Luke 18:1). God sometimes cannot give his children his best gifts until they are in earnest.

The errors that one should pray through some person, or use some material object, or be in a certain place, are to be avoided. Only God is to be worshiped. As God the Father, God the Son, and God the Holy Spirit, he receives worship. Satan is not to be worshiped. "Then saith Jesus unto him, Get thee hence, Satan: for it is written, Thou shalt worship the Lord thy God, and him only shalt thou serve" (Matt. 4:10). Angels are not to be worshiped. "And I John saw these things, and heard them. And when I had heard and seen, I fell down to worship before the feet of the angel which shewed me these things. Then saith he unto me, See thou do it not: for I am thy fellow servant, and of thy brethren the prophets, and of them which keep the sayings of this book: worship God" (Rev. 22:8–9). Men are not to be worshiped. "And as Peter was coming in, Cornelius met him, and fell down at his feet, and worshipped him. But Peter took him up, saying, Stand up; I myself also am a man" (Acts 10:25–26; see also 14:11–18).

Jesus' conversation with the Samaritan woman, recorded in John 4, makes it clear that one does not have to go to Mount Gerizim nor to Jerusalem to worship. "God is a Spirit: and they that worship him must worship him in spirit and in truth" (John 4:24). At the death of Jesus "the veil of the, temple was rent in twain from the top to the bottom" (Mark 15:38), symbolizing that the way to come directly to God is open to the humblest believer.

Conclusion

Prayer is primarily a fellowship. It is personal. It is as a child sharing with his or her parent. Anyone can pray for the forgiveness of sins and for salvation. An unsaved person can pray, "God, be merciful to me a sinner." When one prays that prayer sincerely, God answers and saves that person. From that time on, the person is in union with Christ and bases his or her prayer life on yielding to God's will.

WEDNESDAY EVENING, AUGUST 9

Title: Christ Lives within His Church

Text: "For where two or three are gathered in my name, there am I in the midst of them" **(Matt. 18:20 RSV).**

Scripture Reading: Ephesians 1:22–23

Introduction

Christianity is a religion of people who worship the Lord who has conquered death and the grave and who is alive forevermore. Because Christ lives in our hearts, he lives in his church.

By our irreverence, our lack of faith, and our lack of responsiveness to the Holy Spirit, we may from time to time shut our Lord out of his church (Rev. 3:20). The result of ignoring the promise and the presence of the living Christ is tragic for individuals and congregations, for Christ cannot manifest his wonderful works where there is no faith.

Jesus promised that when his disciples would come together in his name, he would bless them with his presence (Matt. 18:20). It is significant that in a time when the very existence of the church was threatened by persecution and it appeared that Christianity would be eradicated from the face of the earth, John, while in exile, was given a vision of the glorified Christ walking "in the midst of the lampstands" (Rev. 1:13). The word that John used to describe Jesus walking in the midst of the seven churches of Asia Minor is the same word our Lord used in promising his presence to those who would come together in his name.

I. Christ lives in the church to communicate the love of God.

Christ came into this world as an expression of God's love. He came to communicate God's love to a needy world. Christ continues to use the church as a living vehicle through which he communicates the grace, love, and mercy of God in a world of hate, selfishness, and despair.

II. Christ lives in the church to cleanse us from sin.

The Lord instructed John to write to the seven churches of Asia Minor. He gave the churches words of rebuke as well as of commendation. He insisted that they correct their ways and experience the cleansing of forgiveness.

From Sunday to Sunday, from service to service, as we come to God's house and meet with God's people, we should confess our sin to our loving God. We should go forth from the presence of God's people and from the experience of worship, having experienced the cleansing of forgiveness.

III. Christ lives in the church to counsel us and to commission us.

When we meet together as God's people for worship, we come not to worship a dead Christ or to pay tribute to the memory of one who lived in the past. We come to listen for the voice of God's Spirit as he speaks to the innermost part of our being.

Let us pray for eyes that can see spiritual reality.
Let us pray for ears that can hear the still, small voice of God.
Let us open our hearts with an attitude of eagerness to know God's will.

IV. Christ lives in his church to commend us and to comfort us.

Some people think of our Lord as a critic, and some neglect the church because they feel "put down" by coming to meet with the people of God. Jesus welcomes all with grace, and so should the members of his church.

Christ is eager to approve that which is good. It is interesting to note in the seven letters to the churches in Asia Minor that following Jesus' personal address, he issued words of commendation where it was due. Our Lord is more eager to see the good than he is to see the bad.

Christ gives the comfort that contains courage and hope. He wants to build within us a proper and appropriate sense of self-esteem. He wants us to believe that we are of supreme worth to God.

Conclusion

When we meet with God's people, we should listen for the voice of our living Lord. He will communicate to us God's love for us. He will cleanse us from our sins and remove our guilt. He will give us counsel concerning life's problems and issues. He will commend us and comfort us so as to encourage us. He will call us and commission us to render service in his name to those in need. The living Christ will call us to repentance and faith if we have not yet come to know him as personal Savior.

SUNDAY MORNING, AUGUST 13

Title: Mission Impossible—Accomplished

Text: "When Jesus had received the vinegar, he said, 'It is finished'" **(John 19:30 RSV)**.

Hymns: "Holy, Holy, Holy," Heber
            "Down at the Cross," Hoffman
            "What a Wonderful Saviour!" Hoffman

Offertory Prayer: Father in heaven, we come to you today because you are the great giver. You have given us your love and mercy, kindness and generosity. You have given to us our talents and abilities, our life and our strength. We are taught in your Word that if we would be your sons and daughters, we must also become givers. Help us to give ourselves to you fully and completely. Help us to give ourselves in ministries of mercy and helpfulness to others. Accept these tithes and offerings, and bless them to the end that others might come to know your love. In Christ's name we pray. Amen.

Introduction

The words that fell from Jesus' lips while he suffered on the cross provide us with insight into how Jesus dealt with the struggles, pains, problems, and purposes for his life.

Jesus' first word from the cross suggests that we should study his prayer life. There was something fresh and vital about his prayer life that caused the disciples to request that he teach them to pray as John had taught his disciples to pray.

Jesus' promise to the thief reveals that he came to lift people from a life of sin to a life of fellowship with God. This word reveals the marvelous grace of God and also that heaven is but a heartbeat away.

Jesus' word to his mother reveals that it is possible for a person to give his or her life totally to God's purpose and yet still have room to provide for the basic necessities of those who are near and dear.

Jesus' cry of pathos and loneliness reveals the awful price he paid for our redemption. As he suffered under the penalty of our sin, he revealed to us that when we feel lonely and cut off from God, we should come to him in prayer with hope and faith.

Jesus' cry of thirst reveals that he understands our human agony. He is a sympathetic Savior.

Let us listen today to Jesus' shout of triumph and victory as he comes to the conclusion of his redemptive mission. We hear him cry out, "It is finished!" From the words of the victim who was suffering intense agony, we now listen to the words of the Victor. Jesus made this proclamation to two worlds—heaven and earth. It was infinitely more than an expression of satisfaction with the termination of his physical sufferings. He was proclaiming that he had now completed his redemptive mission. He had experienced the opposition of the imperial authority of the king, for in Christ's infancy, the king had sought to put him to death. Satan, with all the forces of the underworld, had opposed and tempted Jesus in an effort to thwart his redemptive mission. His family and those in his community did not understand him. The citizens among whom he grew up, along with the religious and civil authorities, sought to bring about his death because of their misunderstanding of him. Worse yet, Satan even influenced the apostle Peter to try to keep Jesus from his redemptive mission (Matt. 16:23).

Holman Hunt painted a picture of the youthful Christ in which it is near sunset, and the weary, working Christ stands by his workshop with arms extended. The sun casts the shadow of a cross on the wall behind him. Jesus lived under the shadow of the cross from the beginning of his ministry. At age twelve he was aware of the Father's business (Luke 2:49), and from then on he worked diligently to accomplish God's work (John 9:4). In Jesus' great High Priestly Prayer, he rejoiced that he had finished the work for which the Father had sent him into the world (John 17:4).

I. It is finished—all that was needed to reveal God's great love has been done.

The cross reveals the greatness of the love of Jesus Christ for God the Father (John 14:31).

The cross reveals the greatness of God's love for sinners (Rom. 5:8). We can discover God's love by studying botany or astronomy or other areas of science, but we can experience his love for sinners only when we come to the cross.

II. It is finished—the penalty for a broken law has been paid.

All of us are lawbreakers and are under the penalty of sin, which is death. Christ fulfilled the requirements of a holy law perfectly. No sin was found in him. He met the demands of a holy law on behalf of guilty sinners. He died under the penalty of our sin that we might receive the gift of eternal life (Rom. 6:23).

III. It is finished—the power of the devil has been broken (Heb. 2:14).

By dying under the penalty of sin, Jesus was to destroy the power of sin and to take the sting out of death (Heb. 2:14). It is said that when a honeybee stings a person, it loses its stinger and becomes a harmless creature. Jesus

Christ took the stinger out of sin and out of death by forgiving our sin and giving us the assurance of victory over death and the grave.

IV. It is finished—the way to heaven has been provided and completed (John 14:6).

Jesus bore the guilt of the sin of all who lived before him and of those who were to live after him. The way to forgiveness and life was now available through his death and future resurrection.

Conclusion

Salvation has been provided for you through Jesus Christ. He has finished the work of paying the ransom for us (Mark 10:45). The impossible mission has been finished. The eternal God clothed himself in human flesh that he might become our Savior. The Christ became a son of man in order that we might become the sons and daughters of God through faith in him.

Put your trust and faith in the finished work of Christ, that he might finish his work in you. He wants to do the good work of God in you. He will begin when you invite him to become your Savior. He will continue his good work in you by the gift of the Holy Spirit as Teacher, Guide, and Helper.

SUNDAY EVENING, AUGUST 13

Title: The Golden Rule

Text: "Therefore all things whatsoever ye would that men should do to you, do ye even so to them: for this is the law and the prophets" (**Matt. 7:12**).

Scripture Reading: Romans 12

Introduction

The Golden Rule may be the best-known saying of Jesus. Jesus was original in stating the principle positively. Others, including Confucius, stated it negatively. Our Lord did not undervalue the thoughts of Jewish or secular thinkers, but rather he fulfilled their statements by his positive principle.

I. The foundation of the Golden Rule.

"Therefore" is an especially important word in our text. It is an arrow pointing back to all that our Lord had said on the meaning of Christian discipleship. It points back to the characteristics of a Christian in the Beatitudes; to the higher standard of righteousness in Christ, especially with reference to others; to the model prayer petitions, "Hallowed be thy name, Thy kingdom come, Thy will be done in earth, as it is in heaven"; and to the admonition, "But seek ye first the kingdom of God and his righteousness." More immediately it points to the words against censorious, hypocritical judgment, and to the call for discernment and discrimination in dealing with others. It points forward to this great summary statement of all that the Law and the Prophets have to say to disciples about relationship to their fellow humans, so succinct that it is called the Golden Rule. This is a misnomer, however, for Jesus did not speak in rules but in principles. It would better be named the Golden Principle.

II. The Golden Rule is not for everyone.

For the unsaved, the Golden Rule would be folly. A pagan with unregenerate desires would erroneously use the Golden Rule to justify doing wrong. An alcoholic who would like for someone to buy him a drink might use the Golden Rule to justify buying a drink for another. The criminal before the bar of justice might say, "Judge, remember the Golden Rule." The boy about to receive a needed whipping might say, "Father, if you were in my place you would not want to get whipped, would you? Remember the Golden Rule."

The Golden Rule is for saved people, children of God who are dedicated to being and doing what the heavenly Father wants them to be and to do. The Sermon on the Mount is a sermon for disciples. Recall Matthew 5:1: "And seeing the multitudes, he went up into a mountain: and when he was set, his disciples came unto him: And he opened his mouth, and taught them saying. . . ."

When we overlook this fact, we open the door to grievous misapplication.

III. The Golden Rule and royal law.

"For this is the law and the prophets" proclaims that the summary principle of all that the Old Testament had to say about relations to others is in the Golden Rule. On another occasion, Scripture records, "Then one of them, which was a lawyer, asked him a question, tempting him, and saying, Master, which is the great commandment in the law? Jesus said unto him, Thou shalt love the Lord thy God with all thy heart, and with all thy soul, and with all thy mind. This is the first and great commandment. And the second is like unto it, Thou shalt love thy neighbour as thyself. On these two commandments hang all the law and the prophets" (Matt. 22:35–40).

How can the Golden Rule and these quotations from Deuteronomy 6:5 and Leviticus 19:18 epitomize "all the law and the prophets"? The answer is apparent: things equal to the same thing are equal to each other. "Thou shalt love thy neighbour as thyself," which James so aptly called the Royal Law (see James 2:8), means exactly the same as the Golden Rule. The love commanded is agape love, which is goodwill accompanied by the appropriate action, which is equivalent to God's will.

The command "Thou shalt love the Lord thy God" is a command to have toward God the attitude he desires, accompanied by the right actions. This is exactly what Jesus expounded in the Sermon on the Mount, to which the "therefore" of the text points. To the one who loves God, the second and corollary command is, "Thou shalt love thy neighbour as thyself." The assumption is that one loves himself—that is, that one has toward himself the attitude God wants him to have. He then is ready to love his neighbor as himself, which would mean to have the attitude toward his neighbor that God wills for him to have. The Royal Law and the Golden Rule thus express what the Christian attitude ought to be.

IV. Corollary assumptions of the Golden Rule.

The dignity and worth of every person. Will Rogers said, "I never met a man I didn't like." You have probably seen some people who were not very likable, but every Christian disciple ought to say, "I never met a person I didn't love." We cannot by an act of our will make ourselves like someone, but we can have God's attitude of goodwill toward others, which is agape love.

The personhood and rights of others are to be equal to our own. The Lord commands, "Love thy neighbour as thyself." He does not command, "Love thy neighbour more than thyself." The Golden Rule commands, "Therefore all things whatsoever ye would that men should do to you, do ye even so to them." Christ does not command us to do more for others than we would wish them to do for us.

Consider of all the circumstances. Recall the warning given in Matthew 7:1–2 against censorious judgment. Only God knows all of the facts; only he can be the final Judge. Believe the best until the worst is proved. Recall Jesus' warning in Matthew 7:3–4 against looking for small flaws in others while great flaws are in oneself. Be discerning and discriminating.

A warmhearted, dedicated Christian preacher said that when he approached a man about his salvation, he imagined him to be his own father in order to increase his earnestness and compassion. A pastor, on meeting people for counseling would often breathe a prayer, "God, help me to treat this person as if he were my father or son [or as if she were my mother or daughter]." Jesus, however, bids us to identify with others so completely that we put ourselves in their place.

Conclusion

Role playing is a popular and useful aid that counselors use. Find a quiet place and try it. If you are a married man, imagine that you are your wife. Think through her day. What are her responsibilities? Her resources? Her desires? What would she like from her husband that she is not receiving? If you were your wife, what would you want your husband to do? Then do it. If you are a married woman, follow the same steps, putting yourself in your husband's place. Anyone can take on the role of father, mother, elderly parent, child, teenager, and so on. Ask what, if you were in their circumstances, you would want most that is in accord with God's will.

What if you were the employee? Would you be justified in wanting the boss to get off your back? To show a bit of understanding? To have concern for your working conditions? Put yourself in your employer's place. Is he worried about taxes? The slow economy?

Every area of personal relationships, in home, school, church, neighborhood, business, politics, race, and nation could be improved by people becoming Christians and practicing the Golden Rule.

WEDNESDAY EVENING, AUGUST 16

Title: The Living Christ in Your Home

Text: "He came to his own, and his own people received him not. But to all who received him, who believed in his name, he gave power to become children of God; who were born, not of blood nor of the will of the flesh nor of the will of man, but of God" **(John 1:11–13 RSV)**.

Scripture Reading: Revelation 3:1–20

Introduction

The inspired writer of the book of Hebrews proclaims that "Jesus Christ is the same yesterday and today and forever" (Heb. 13:8). He thus proclaims that in Jesus' essential nature, he continues to be in the present what he was yesterday and that we can depend on his continuing to be tomorrow what he has been in the past and what he is now. This great truth makes the New Testament a living record of what Jesus Christ wants to do rather than being a dusty, historical record of what happened two millennia ago.

We want to see how the Christ who loved us, who died for us, who conquered death and the grave, will minister to us and through us in our home if we will let him. A casual reading of the Gospels may leave one with the impression that Jesus rendered his ministries primarily in the temple area, or by the seaside, or on the mountaintop, or along the wayside as he went from one place to another. Mark's gospel in a unique way makes repeated references to the ministry of Jesus inside people's homes. While Christ has promised to meet with his people as they come together for worship (Matt. 18:20), we can rest assured that he wants to come into our homes to minister in our times of need.

I. Welcome the living Christ in times of illness (Mark 1:29–34).

Our Lord is the Great Physician. During his earthly ministry, he brought healing to a great number of people. We can rest assured that our Lord is against disease and illness and pain and that he is for health and physical well-being. We can be assured of his compassion and his desire to minister to us through family members, doctors, and medicine. We are encouraged to pray in faith for the sick that they may be healed (James 5:13–15).

We must understand divine healing in the context of our earthly situation. Healing is provided in the atonement, but we cannot tell God how to heal us. Sometimes he heals instantly, sometimes he heals over time with or without physicians and medicine, and sometimes he allows us to be sick. In any case, he promises that his grace will be sufficient for us. Our responsibility is to pray and patiently trust in him.

II. Welcome the living Christ as a divine teacher (Mark 2:1–12).

Our Lord used the home in which he lived as a classroom for teaching the family members and their guests great truths about God. The most effective teaching does not take place in school or church classrooms. It takes place in the home. We should have more conversations about spiritual things within the family circle instead of letting the television and other electronic devices monopolize the family's time and attention.

III. Welcome the living Christ in order to witness to others (Mark 2:14–15).

Levi, better known as Matthew the apostle, gave proof immediately following his conversion of his joy in knowing Jesus Christ as Lord and Savior. He was so eager that others became acquainted with Jesus that he held a banquet in his home and invited many other tax collectors and sinners to come and get acquainted with his Lord.

One of the most effective ways by which we can serve Christ is to use our home to entertain guests who do not yet know him as Lord and Savior. By inviting these people into our homes or taking them out to dinner, or doing whatever we can within the context of home life, we can develop friendships and relationships with them and demonstrate the difference that Jesus Christ makes in the home. This is a form of ministry that has been greatly neglected.

Jesus Christ, who conquered death for you and who lives within your heart, would like to come into your home and help you win not only the other members of your family to faith, but also neighbors, friends, relatives, and business associates.

IV. Welcome the living Christ in times of sorrow (Mark 5:35–42).

Many New Testament passages illustrate how our Lord came into the homes of those who grieved and brought comfort to their hearts. John's gospel relates Jesus' visit to the house of Mary and Martha in Bethany following Lazarus' death (John 11). There Jesus demonstrated his authority over death and the abode of the dead.

"Jesus wept" (John 11:35) is one of the most beautiful pictures of Jesus Christ to be found in the Scriptures. If he is the same yesterday, today, and forever, this verse indicates that he weeps with us in our sorrow and suffers with us in our griefs. Be sure to let Jesus Christ come into your home when sorrow touches the life of any member of your family.

V. Welcome the living Christ in times of joy.

Our Lord enjoyed eating and received many invitations to banquets (Mark 14:3–9; Luke 7:36–50; John 12:1–3). He wants us to share our homes, our hearts, and our lives with him in times of joy and happiness as well as in times of sorrow. We should thank him every day when we are enjoying health and prosperity and are able to work and serve. We should thank him for a happy marriage, for the birth of children and for their growth and development, and for a peaceful home.

Conclusion

Let us welcome Christ into our homes to minister to us in our times of need and through us to others in their times of need.

SUNDAY MORNING, AUGUST 20

Title: The Commitment of Faith

Text: "Then Jesus, crying with a loud voice, said, 'Father, into thy hands I commit my spirit!' And having said this he breathed his last" **(Luke 23:46 RSV)**.

Scripture Reading: Luke 23:44–49

Hymns: "Praise to the Lord, the Almighty," Neander
"Faith Is the Victory," Yates
"All the Way My Saviour Leads Me," Crosby

Offertory Prayer: Holy Father, thank you for the living presence of Jesus Christ in this worship service. Thank you for your abiding presence with us during the past week. We thank you for your blessings on the labor of our hands and the thoughts of our minds. Thank you for the fruits of nature and for the products of industry. Thank you for the gift of your Spirit. We come now to give ourselves to you. Accept these tithes and offerings and add your blessings to the end that your kingdom might come into the hearts and lives of people everywhere. In Jesus' name we pray. Amen.

Introduction

We are to focus our eyes on Jesus as the "author and finisher" of our faith (Heb. 12:2). It was by faith that Jesus came on a redemptive mission to earth. It was by a commitment of faith to his redemptive ministry that he submitted to the baptism of John the Baptist. It was because of faith that Jesus rejected Satan's suggestions concerning how he should accomplish his redemptive purpose. We can assume that it was because of faith in God's purpose that Jesus persisted in his redemptive mission when he was misunderstood by his family and rejected not only by the citizens of his own town but also by the religious leaders of the nation. It was as the pioneer and perfector of our faith that Jesus set his face toward Jerusalem, and "for the joy that was set before him endured the cross, despising the shame" (Heb. 12:2 RSV).

I. Faith in the Father led to prayer—"Father, into thy hands I commit my spirit!"

In his lowest moment of agony, feeling smitten by God, Jesus cried out, "My God, my God, why hast thou forsaken me?" In this moment of extreme agony, he was suffering as if he were a sinner. Having accomplished all things essential for the salvation of a lost humanity, we hear him giving voice to his faith in the Father. His faith led him to talk to God in his time of need. One indication of genuine faith is a continuing dialogue with God. At times in Jesus' life, his Father spoke to him as clearly and as forcefully as he talked to his Father.

Jesus' faith led him to talk to the Father as he came to the end of his earthly pilgrimage. His prayer was no desperate plea of a frightened soul. It was a calm, confident expression of genuine faith.

II. Jesus' faith was nourished by the Scriptures.

Jesus regularly attended the synagogue where the Scriptures were taught and studied (Luke 4:16).

Jesus used Scripture to conquer Satan's temptations (Luke 4:1–12).

Several of Jesus' statements from the cross were quotations from Scripture. Paul tells us that faith comes by hearing and hearing by the Word of God (Rom. 10:17). If we want to grow a great faith and face life's crises and responsibilities sustained by faith, we need to make much of the Holy Scriptures in our daily devotional life.

III. Jesus' faith focused on the need of the moment.

Many of us are very general in our prayer efforts, leaving out specifics. We need to come to the point of our need when we pray, and we need to pray in faith.

Jesus was at the end of his incarnation experience. He had finished his redemptive mission by dying for a guilty humanity, and he was now ready to return to the Father. Now he was not praying for the sick or for his disciples; he was praying for his own spirit. Jesus had been committed to God and to humanity from the beginning and had never failed in his commitment, so it was only natural that he commit his spirit into his Father's hands.

IV. Jesus' faith gave him a positive view toward death.

Jesus tasted death for us (Heb. 2:14–15). He came to earth to deliver us from the tyranny of sin and death. He came to make us victors rather than victims of death. Jesus visualized the experience that we call death as a departure to be with the Father. He speaks of the destiny of the redeemed as entering into the Father's many mansions (John 14:1–3).

Jesus teaches us that death is not the end of our existence.

Jesus wants us to know that God has something better for us than this life has to offer.

Jesus came and clothed himself in human flesh and lived his redemptive life, ultimately dying on the cross for our sin, that we might receive forgiveness of sin and eternal life. Jesus lived a life of faith and faithfulness. He faced death and eternity with faith in the Father God. He offers himself to you as the object of your faith that you might receive the forgiveness of sin and the gift of a life that exists on both sides of the experience that people call death. Jesus conquered death and the grave and came forth as a living Savior. In Spirit he has walked through the corridors of time to this hour, offering himself to you as the one whom God has appointed to be your Savior and Lord.

Conclusion

In the same manner in which Jesus faced life with its opportunities, responsibilities, and its crises, you are encouraged to face it with faith in this wonderful Savior. As he committed his Spirit into the hands of God, commit your life—past, present, and future—into the hands of the Father God.

SUNDAY EVENING, AUGUST 20

Title: The Road to Life

Text: "Enter through the narrow gate. For wide is the gate and broad is the road that leads to destruction, and many enter through it. But small is the gate and narrow the road that leads to life, and only a few find it" (**Matt. 7:13–14 NIV**).

Scripture Reading: Luke 13:23–30; Psalm 1

Introduction

The Sermon on the Mount is now drawing to an end. The major themes have been presented. These concluding verses from Matthew 7:13–23 contain exhortations and warnings: (1) Don't miss the way to life (vv. 13–14), (2) beware of false prophets (vv. 15–20), and (3) beware of self-deception (vv. 22–23).

The first of these exhortations is the text for today's message. Two roads are pictured: one is entered through a wide gate; it is a broad road; the destination is destruction. The other is entered through a small gate; the way is narrow; the end is life. The exhortation is: "Enter through the narrow gate" (Matt. 7:13 NIV). Luke's account is even stronger, "Make every effort to enter through the narrow door" (Luke 13:24 NIV).

Why would Jesus warn about the danger of missing the way to life in a sermon to disciples? Of the twelve apostles whom Jesus had chosen, one—Judas—had not entered the way to life. In the larger multitude listening there were doubtless many others. Preachers need to follow Jesus' example in this regard and always make clear the way to life. Most of Jesus' contemporaries thought that the descendants of Abraham were all in God's kingdom. The way to life is not entered by birth—no matter how fortunate one's birth—nor by church membership, nor by any ceremony. One who has been baptized, confirmed, and admitted to the church is not per se in the way to life. It is always possible that even among professed disciples some may be deceived about their true condition.

Another reason Jesus may have warned his disciples about the danger of missing the way to life is that his exhortation is not limited to a call to enter the door to life but also to continue to walk in that way to the destination. After the new birth one has new life that is eternal. This is synonymous with living as a citizen of the kingdom of God. The call is to yield to God's reign or rule. "And this is life eternal, that they might know thee the only true God, and Jesus Christ, whom thou hast sent" (John 17:3).

I. Jesus calls for decision.

Jesus has proclaimed these great truths in the sermon as the basis for a decision by each person about his or her life. They have not been presented as simply a basis for dialogue. His aim is very practical. He wants people to miss destruction and to find life. He calls for decision: "Enter," "Strive to enter. . . ."

Jesus addresses his call to persons who have moral responsibility. Every mentally competent person is morally responsible. Since God is just and will take into account all of the facts, I do not believe he will hold little children or mentally incompetent persons to account; but when a person's thinking is clear, that person is responsible to God for what he does, for what he does not do, and for what he purpose purposed to do. There is no escape from moral responsibility in alcohol, drugs, or suicide. There is no escape in willful ignorance nor in blaming others or God. There is nowhere to run from responsibility. "So then every one of us shall give account of himself to God" (Rom. 14:12).

II. The Two Roads

Only two roads: one leads to life, the other to destruction. They run in opposite directions, so one cannot be on both roads at the same time. Even though you may deceive others and even yourself, God knows which road you are on.

A person can easily drift into the road to destruction. The gate is broad. The road is wide. It is filled with people who are doing what comes naturally—drifting. And as one drifting is always moving to a lower level, so those on the broad road are going down all the way.

You will never get to life as long as you are on the road to destruction. One good news/bad news joke goes like this: "This is the captain speaking. First, the good news: We are making six hundred miles an hour. The engines are all functioning well. Now, the bad news: The guidance systems are out. We have no idea which way we are going." One can be certain that the plane unless guided will never reach the planned destination. It might reach a thousand other places, but only one destination is the right one. If a pilot neglects to chart the right course, then he is on the wrong course. There is only one right course—the will of God. Every other course is wrong.

To delay making a decision is to make a wrong decision. Postponing entering the door and road to life means you are taking the wide road toward destruction. If you have not given your heart to God, then you have thus far decided against him.

A pastor was making a night trip with a car full of people going to a distant assembly. They were making good time when he noticed that the highway sign was not the right number. A check of the map indicated that they had taken the wrong road about fifty miles back. There was no connecting road, and continuing on the wrong road would never get them to the assembly. There was nothing to do but go back and get on the right road if they were to reach their destination.

Neglect will never get you on the right road. You are not just preparing to live; you are living now.

III. How to get on the road to life.

Take the first turn to the right.

Anywhere, anytime, you can get on the road to life. Jesus' command is "Enter through the narrow gate." One enters by turning one's back on the broad road—an act called repentance—and entering the new road by yielding to the lordship of Jesus Christ. The directions are plain (see John 3:16; 5:24; Acts 16:31). The act of turning from the broad road that leads to death to the narrow road that leads to life is called conversion.

"Make every effort to enter through the narrow door" (Luke 13:24 NIV) is a command. One who says, "If God wants me on the road to life, he will put me there," has overlooked Jesus' command to "make every effort."

Conviction usually precedes conversion. Jesus said that the Holy Spirit is in the world to convict those in the broad way "of sin, because they believe not on me; of righteousness, because I go to my Father, and ye see me no more; of judgment, because the prince of this world is judged" (John 16:9–11). He does this by revealing the truth as it is in Jesus. Jesus is the Word of God. As speech is the expression of ideas, Jesus is the visible expression of what God has to say to humankind. The record of the revelation God has given concerning the preparation for the advent of Jesus, his incarnation, his life, death, resurrection, ascension, and continued intercession are recorded in the Bible. Paul in Ephesians 6:17 calls the Word of God the sword that the Holy Spirit uses. The author of Hebrews writes, "For the word of God is quick, and powerful, and sharper than any two-edged sword, piercing even to the dividing asunder of soul and spirit, and of the joints and marrow, and is a discerner of the thoughts and intents of the heart" (Heb. 4:12).

Those who are concerned about the way to life ought to read the Bible and call on God to show them the way. They will do well to counsel with Christians in whom they have confidence. God promises that the person who is in earnest will find the way: "And ye shall seek me, and find me, when ye shall search for me with all your heart. And I will be found of you, saith the LORD" (Jer. 29:13–14). "Blessed are they which do hunger and thirst after righteousness: for they shall be filled" (Matt. 5:6). "If any man will do his will, he shall know of the doctrine, whether it be of God, or whether I speak of myself" (John 7:17).

God does wonderful things for those who enter the door to the road that leads to life. Those who repent of sin and believe in Jesus, God regenerates and justifies, taking away their penalty for sin. They are born from above and are adopted into God's family as God's children. They receive the Holy Spirit to abide in their hearts as their companion and helper on the road of life. And ultimately they live in heaven with Jesus.

Conclusion

The road to life is restricted, disciplined, and narrow, but it is not hard. It is as narrow as the will of God. It is restricted to truth, goodness, beauty, love, light, honesty, and respect for people. Jesus said, "Come unto me, all ye that labour and are heavy laden, and I will give you rest. Take my yoke upon you, and learn of me; for I am meek and lowly in heart: and ye shall find rest unto your souls. For my yoke is easy, and my burden is light" (Matt. 11:28–30). Jesus says his "yoke is easy." Satan lies when he makes you believe the way is hard.

Hear the psalmist: "For the LORD God is a sun and shield: the LORD will give grace and glory: no good thing will he withhold from them that walk uprightly" (Ps. 84:11). In Romans 12:1–2 Paul affirms that those who give themselves without reservation to God will find that God's will is good, acceptable, and perfect. Jesus said, "I am come that they might have life, and that they might have it more abundantly" (John 10:10). So don't let Satan keep you from life. Enter the narrow door that leads to life now.

WEDNESDAY EVENING, AUGUST 23

Title: Servants to/for the Living Lord

Text: "Then he will answer them, 'Truly, I say to you, as you did it not to one of the least of these, you did it not to me'" **(Matt. 25:45 RSV)**.

Scripture Reading: Matthew 25:31–46

Introduction

Christianity is the result of Christ dying on a cross and rising from the dead. To be a Christian is to have a vital living relationship with Christ who lives and continues to love humankind on the basis of God's love and humanity's need for that love. Christ lives in the hearts of believers. Christ lives in his church. Christ lives on high in heaven, and one day he will come again.

The Scripture passage under consideration is not a parable but a picture, a vision of the future. The primary purpose of this description of this great future event is to encourage people to be ready for Christ's second coming. We see in this passage the literal Son of God in his literal person at his literal return, coming as a literal judge. Let us note several significant truths we can learn from this prophetic picture.

I. Our Lord is alive from the dead (Phil. 2:5–11).

The apostle Paul confronts us with the coming of Jesus Christ who came out of eternity into time to be our Savior. He not only became a man; he also became a servant. He not only took the place of a servant; he also endured the humiliation of death on a cross. As a result of Jesus' redemptive humiliation, he has been exalted to a position of highest authority. And the day will come when every knee shall bow and every tongue shall confess that Jesus Christ is Lord.

II. Our living Lord will return to claim his own (John 14:1–3).

Our Lord promised a personal and visible return. Time and time again he repeated this promise. The apostles proclaimed their faith that Jesus Christ would return. The last chapter of the last book of the Bible contains three specific promises from the living Lord that one day he will return for his own (Rev. 22:7, 12, 20).

Those who have put faith in Jesus Christ as Lord and Savior have made the necessary preparation for being ready when the Lord does return.

Those who have not yet received Jesus Christ as Lord and Savior are unprepared for this event. Where would you stand today if the heavens should roll back as a scroll and the Lord should descend to consummate history?

III. Our living Lord has been appointed as the final Judge of all people (Acts 17:30–31).

Death has been defeated, and all people will be held responsible for their choices when they stand before God at the end of history. Jesus Christ, who now wants to be the Savior of people, will one day serve as the Judge of people.

Our living Lord's judgment will be universal in scope. "Before him will be gathered all the nations" (Matt. 25:32 RSV).

Our living Lord's judgment will reveal that a life of ministry is the real proof of a vital saving relationship. "Come, O blessed of my Father, inherit the kingdom prepared for you from the foundation of the world" (Matt. 25:34 RSV). The significant word in this text is *inherit.* We do not enter into God's presence by buying our way in, by doing good works, or by breaking in. We enter into the home of the heavenly Father because we are his children who have received his nature. Jesus Christ provided the way by dying on the cross. We are therefore the heirs of God.

As Jesus spoke about the final judgment, he declared and explained "the manner in which a child of God acts" in the presence of human need. Acts of mercy, kindness, and helpfulness are the natural and spontaneous acts of those in whom the love of God dwells.

Dr. Frank Stagg said, "Place a mouse before a cat and one sees what a cat is; place a person in need before a true child of God and one sees what a child of God is" (*The Broadman Bible Commentary* [Nashville: Broadman, 1969], 8:227).

Our Lord's judgment will reveal that the living Christ identifies himself with the needy and the suffering.

Our living Lord's judgment will reveal the emptiness of a negative religion.

What is your response to the cry of human need?

How do you respond to opportunities where help is needed? Sins of omission bring the greatest condemnation (Matt. 25:45–46).

Conclusion

A lack of faith in Christ's work on the cross signifies that a person does not belong in God's family. The omission of obedience reveals an absence of love and the absence of a relationship with God. The omission of faithfulness and helpfulness to those who are suffering indicates that one has never come to know Jesus Christ in the pardon and forgiveness of sin. When we give ourselves in service to the suffering, in reality we are serving Christ and continuing his ministry in the world.

SUNDAY MORNING, AUGUST 27

Title: Getting Sinners to the Savior

Text: "And they came, bringing to him a paralytic carried by four men" (**Mark 2:3 RSV**).

Scripture Reading: Mark 2:1–12

Hymns: "Joyful, Joyful, We Adore Thee," Van Dyke
"Wonderful, Wonderful Jesus," Russell
"Make Me a Channel of Blessing," Smyth

Offertory Prayer: Holy Father, we thank you today for granting to us the many privileges, joys, and responsibilities of life. We thank you for putting within us a hunger for you. We thank you for spiritual food that comes to us through the reading of your Word. We thank you for strength of soul that comes through prayer and worship. We thank you for the privilege of bringing tithes and offerings as expressions of love. Help us to overcome our every tendency toward greed, and encourage us to be generous and charitable in all our dealings with others. In Jesus' name we pray. Amen.

Introduction

Our Savior came into the world to be the Savior of sinners. The church's task in today's world is to proclaim Christ as Savior and to put forth efforts to bring sinners to him. The incident described in our Scripture reading illustrates how we can work together to bring sinners to Jesus, and it dramatizes the importance of communicating the fact of Jesus' presence (Mark 2:1). People must be made aware of the presence and purpose of Jesus Christ and of his work in and through the church.

This incident also illustrates the helplessness of those who are in sin (Mark 2:3). Unsaved people are spiritually dead. They are confused about the real purpose for life. And they are as helpless as the paralytic when it comes to finding the path that leads to abundant life.

Further, we see in this story the role that each of us can play in getting sinners and the Savior together.

I. We notice the crowd of people (Mark 2:2).

When Jesus is present in the midst of his people, people will be attracted. Therefore the church should make certain that it allows Jesus Christ to live within its fellowship. Christ will serve as a magnet to attract people.

Crowds can be a great help but can also be a hindrance, as was the case in this incident.

II. We observe the concern of four men for a helpless paralytic who was a sinner.

Perhaps one of these men took the initiative in enlisting three others to assist him. Why should we not follow his example?

Perhaps one or more of these four were relatives. As such, they would have a special concern for bringing him to Christ.

Perhaps these four men were neighbors of the helpless man. Neighbors should be concerned for others.

Perhaps this man was an employee of one of the four, or perhaps a fellow employee. The significant truth is that they banded together and cooperated to get a helpless man into the presence of the Great Helper, Jesus Christ.

III. We should recognize the confidence of these men (Mark 2:5).

These men had faith in Jesus Christ. They believed that Jesus Christ could meet the deepest need of this helpless man whom they brought to him.

The four who brought the paralytic had faith in his competency to receive what Jesus Christ had to offer. They believed he could be healed, that he was not beyond hope.

IV. We see evidence of a redemptive conspiracy in this experience.

Conspiracy is a word that does not have the best connotations. By using it to describe this incident, we would suggest that compassionate concern compelled one man to enlist the assistance of at least three others to bring a helpless man to Jesus Christ.

Have you ever entered into a redemptive covenant, a spiritual conspiracy, to work with others to help bring a sinner to the Savior? Under the guidance of the Holy Spirit and in a spirit of prayer, let us imitate the example of these four men, and let us decide that we will enlist others in order that redemption might take place in the heart of a person who desperately needs to know Jesus Christ as Lord and Savior.

V. We see real cooperation demonstrated.

Four men found a helpless man and designed a program by which they could bring the sinner to the Savior. They not only conceived the plan, but they cooperated together to accomplish their goal for the glory of God and for the good of the man.

Nothing is said concerning the distance and time involved in accomplishing their purpose. We see four men working together in harmony, bearing a burden, carrying a load so that the Savior might be able to do his wonderful work in the life of a helpless sinner.

VI. Courage and creativity were required for the achievement of their goal.

The crowd was the first big obstacle the men faced when they came to where Christ was. They resorted to an unusual strategy to bring their friend into Jesus' presence.

Are you willing to use creative methods to bring sinners to the Savior? Are you willing to put forth some courage and be brave? These men were, and they experienced glorious success.

Conclusion

When Christ and the helpless man got together, Christ revealed his grace, his power, and his glory, and the paralytic man received forgiveness of his sins. This was our Lord's greatest gift to him. The paralytic was then made well. Perhaps his illness was due to his sin. We cannot be certain. It is interesting to note that Jesus forgave his sin first—this was his primary need—and then healed his body.

You and I have the privilege of cooperating with the Holy Spirit in bringing sinners to the Savior. To do so is to bring the highest honor and glory to God, to make life's greatest benefits available to those saved, and to experience the greatest possible joy as a Christian.

Let us follow the example of these four men in bringing sinners to the Savior. The Savior is seeking to save them.

SUNDAY EVENING, AUGUST 27

Title: The Folly of Hypocrisy

Text: "You must not be like the hypocrites" **(Matt. 6:5 RSV)**.

Scripture Reading: Matthew 23

Introduction

"You must not be like the hypocrites." The assumption is that you are not a hypocrite. If you are not a hypocrite, then do not act like one. A hypocrite is a person who intends to deceive with the hope of some selfish gain by the deception. The Greek word for hypocrite means an actor, a stage player. It was customary in ancient plays for actors to wear masks. They were in reality not what their faces said they were. An actor in a play, however, is not considered a hypocrite because the audience knows of the deception.

Similarly, much that passes for good manners involves deception. When you meet a friend and exchange greetings, his or her "How are you today?" does not anticipate your giving a list of symptoms and the medicine you have taken. When you reply, "Fine," even though you have a splitting headache, the deception can hardly be considered hypocrisy. The hypocrisy condemned in our Scripture passage has the purpose of benefiting personally from deception.

I. Hypocrites in Jesus' day and in ours.

Hypocrites want praise they don't deserve. You will recall the hypocrites delineated by Jesus in Matthew 6:1–18. They did their religious acts before people for the purpose of being applauded. One gave ostentatiously. Another managed to be at a public place at the hour for prayer. Another made sure that people knew he was fasting.

Acts 5:1–11 records the sad experience of Ananias and Sapphira, who wanted credit for a generosity they did not have, so much that they lied about their gift. "You must not be like the hypocrites."

Hypocrites are usually quite adept at picking out flaws in others while overlooking their own glaring defects. By putting down others, they hope to elevate their own image. Jesus pictures such a hypocrite in Matthew 7:3–5 by his word cartoon of the mote and the beam: "You must not be like the hypocrites."

Hypocrites are morally dishonest. They ask questions for which they do not desire answers. Their questions may be designed to embarrass the teacher. "And, behold, a certain lawyer stood up, and tempted [Jesus], saying, Master, what shall I do to inherit eternal life?" (Luke 10:25). Jesus answered him better than he deserved. "Then went the Pharisees, and took counsel how they might entangle him in his talk" (Matt. 22:15). They joined forces with the Herodians, and after a flattering salutation, they presented their trick question about the tribute money. "But Jesus perceived their wickedness" (Matt. 22:18) and did not allow himself to be trapped.

Hypocrites seek to deceive others.

Cheaters are hypocrites. Business is operated on the basis that goods will be as advertised, weights and measures will be honest, contracts will be fulfilled as agreed. School is operated on the assumption that everyone will do his or her own work. Sports are conducted on the assumption that the teams will play by the rules. Those who cheat seek an advantage to which they are not entitled while leaving the impression that they are following the rules.

Liars are hypocrites. Society is built on the assumption that people speak truth.

Thieves are hypocrites. People living in a community expect others to respect property rights. Those who steal are not only guilty of stealing but also of the hypocrisy of appearing innocent when guilty.

Marriage is built on mutual confidence. A wife expects her husband to be faithful; a husband expects his wife to be faithful. Adultery is hypocrisy. "You must not be like the hypocrites."

II. What are the results of hypocrisy?

Hypocrites may fool people enough to get some temporary gain. For a time, they may receive applause of people and use money gained by stealing, lying, and deceit. They enjoy the pleasures of sin for a season—usually a very short season, for sin has a way of finding one out.

Hypocrites (unless they repent and are saved and hence cease to be hypocrites) are going to hell. Jesus' solemn denunciation of the hypocrites in Matthew 23 climaxes in these powerful words: "Ye serpents, ye generation of vipers, how can ye escape the damnation of hell?" (Matt. 23:33). How much bigger fool could a person be than to think he or she can fool God?

III. Unsaved people who hide behind hypocrites are in many ways like a hypocrite.

Like a hypocrite, he or she is not earnestly seeking God's will. As children playing hide and seek, we learned that in order to hide behind a tree, we must be smaller than the tree. One who hides behind a hypocrite must be smaller than the hypocrite. Let the unsaved person who is honest forget about the hypocrite and approach God sincerely for himself or herself.

Like a hypocrite, he or she is acting on the assumption that God can be fooled. "Be not deceived; God is not mocked: for whatsoever a man soweth, that shall he also reap" (Gal. 6:7).

Like a hypocrite, his or her influence is against God. Badness avowed does not make it goodness. Because one is not a hypocrite, it does not excuse that person from other sins that need God's forgiveness.

Like a hypocrite, the unsaved person is going to hell. Consider the parable of the unfaithful servant in Matthew 24:42–51, which concludes, "The lord of that servant shall come in a day when he looketh not for him, and in an hour that he is not aware of, and shall cut him asunder, and appoint him his portion with the hypocrites: there shall be weeping and gnashing of teeth" (Matt. 24:50–51). How strange that some people refuse to come to Christ because they do not want to be with the hypocrites forever.

Like a hypocrite, the unsaved person is the object of God's love and concern. Jesus died to save sinners. "For the Son of Man is come to seek and to save that which was lost" (Luke 19:10).

Conclusion

If you are not a hypocrite, don't act like one. If you are a hypocrite, stop pretending and become a Christian. The blood of Jesus Christ cleanses from all sin, including the sin of hypocrisy.

WEDNESDAY EVENING, AUGUST 30

Title: The Promise of Christ's Abiding Presence

Text: "Where two or three are gathered together in my name, there am I in the midst of them" **(Matt. 18:20).**

Scripture Reading: Matthew 18:19–20

Introduction

Dr. A. J. Gordon, a famous nineteenth-century preacher, wrote his spiritual autobiography and gave it the title *How Christ Came to Church.* In the introduction to this autobiography, Dr. Gordon relates how that on a Saturday night, wearied from the work of preparing the next day's sermon, he fell asleep and had a dream. He was in the pulpit before a large congregation, ready to begin his sermon, when a stranger entered and passed slowly up the left aisle of the church, looking first to one side and then to the other as though silently asking with his eyes for a seat. He made a mental note of the presence of the visitor and determined that at the conclusion of the service he wanted to meet him. After the benediction had been given, the departing congregation filled the aisles and soon were gone. The stranger disappeared with them.

Dr. Gordon approached the man by whom the stranger had sat and, with genuine interest, asked, "Can you tell me who that stranger was who sat in your pew this morning?" In the most matter-of-course way, he replied, "Why, do you not know that man? It was Jesus of Nazareth." With a sense of keenest disappointment, he said, "My dear sir, why did you let him go without introducing me to him? I was so desirous to speak with him." And with the same nonchalant air, the gentlemen replied, "Oh, do not be troubled. He has been here today, and no doubt he will come again."

The rest of the book explains and applies the tremendous truth that dawned on the mind and heart of the dreaming pastor. For the first time in his life, he realized that if the promise of the Son of God, "Where two or three are gathered together in my name, there am I in the midst of them," means what it says, then Jesus of Nazareth was present every Sunday morning when his disciples assembled for worship.

The ministry of Dr. Gordon experienced a spiritual revolution. He was made vividly aware that Christ would be present to assist and that he should preach with one supreme motive: that of pleasing his living Lord.

Do you come to the house of God with the expectation of having an experience with the Christ who has promised to be present with his disciples always? As the Savior gave his missionary mandate, he promised those who were obedient, "I am with you always." The apostles experienced his living presence. John said of his experience with the living Lord on the isle of Patmos, "I saw seven golden lampstands, and among the lampstands was someone like a son of man" (Rev. 1:12–13).

I. Christ is always present to commend.

The epistles to the seven churches of Asia Minor contain words of commendation. Christ commends those things that are worthy in our lives and work if we will but make ourselves sensitive to his presence when we come to worship.

What could he commend in your life? Could he commend your attitudes and actions in the home? Could he commend your ambitions in the business world?

II. Christ is always present to convict.

We shy away from conviction. Many people think of God only in terms of his being a killjoy. They see him as a policeman who is wanting to apprehend them and punish them for wrongdoing.

God hates sin but loves sinners. God hates sin because by its very nature sin is destructive. God is against sin because of what it does to people. Peace-loving people are against war because war is evil. Doctors are the sworn foes of disease. God would not be God if he were not against evil.

When God forbids something, he does so with our best interest at heart. When God requires us to do something, it is always for our good and for the good of others. Only a hopeless egotist would be so conceited as to say that he had already eliminated all evil from his life and had arrived at the highest possible moral excellence. Christ will convict us of attitudes and actions that are destructive to either ourselves or to others.

III. Christ is always present to counsel.

A refrain throughout these epistles to the church is, "He that hath an ear, let him hear what the spirit saith unto the churches." Throughout these epistles specific instructions are given to individual churches concerning changes that should be made. As we come together for worship and witness, for prayer and praise, the living Lord who is always present will not only speak to us collectively but also individually.

He will counsel us concerning our character.

He will counsel us concerning our companions and family opportunities and responsibilities.

He will counsel us concerning the choice and conduct of our professional career.

IV. Christ is present to comfort and to cheer.

Over and over our Lord counseled his disciples to have faith rather than to surrender to their fears. He convinced them that the life of faith was the life of victory.

Not only did our Savior bring courage, confidence, and cheer into the hearts of the disciples as they faced life, but he also gave them comfort and hope as they faced death. By his resurrection from the dead, he assured them that death was not the end. He gave them a demonstration of the reality of eternal life.

Conclusion

Jesus is with us always to guide us in the way we should go. Sometimes he commends us and sometimes he rebukes us—but all is done in love. He has promised to be with us in all of our ways throughout all of our days. He will be with us in days of sunshine and in days of shadow. He will be with us in days of strength and days of weakness. He will be with us in the day of battle and in the day of victory.

The precious promise of Jesus' abiding presence was not designed as a sedative to create a complacent conscience. It was given to provide us with an incentive to give ourselves without reservation in worship and service to God.

SEPTEMBER

■ **Sunday Mornings**

The theme for the morning messages is "The Power to Cope with Life." Our Father God makes available to us the resources that we need to face life with faith, courage, and unselfishness, depending on the Holy Spirit for assistance.

■ **Sunday Evenings**

Complete the series of expository messages from Jesus' Sermon on the Mount.

■ **Wednesday Evenings**

The theme for the midweek services is "Ugly Attitudes and Actions to Avoid." Four negative characteristics will be spotlighted. May the God of grace help us not to be characterized by these destructive ways of life.

SUNDAY MORNING, SEPTEMBER 3

Title: Putting on the Christian's Uniform
Text: "Put on then, as God's chosen ones, holy and beloved . . ."
(Col. 3:12 RSV).
Scripture Reading: Colossians 3:5–17
Hymns: "All Creatures of Our God and King," Francis of Assisi
"We Praise Thee, O God," MacKay
"More about Jesus," Hewitt

Offertory Prayer: Holy Father, for your gift of another day in which to live, to serve, to worship, and to proclaim your goodness, we thank you. We recognize every good gift as coming from your bountiful hand. We praise you with our lives and with our lips. We praise you with tithes and offerings to the end that others might come to know your love and share in your grace. Bless those persons and those causes that will be assisted by these offerings. In Jesus' name we pray. Amen.

Introduction

Many people in a variety of occupations, such as athletes, medical personnel, service technicians, police officers, flight attendants, and many others, are required to wear uniforms. Some are required to wear one uniform when they are training, but after they have attained professional status, they are given another uniform. When people join the military, they are required to wear a uniform that indicates the branch of service in which they serve and the rank they occupy.

The old adage that "clothes make the man" probably is an oversimplification. However, what you wear says something about you. It indicates your evaluation of yourself and the role you are seeking to follow at the time you are so dressed. When you dress nicely, it usually means that you feel better and that you will perform better than if you dress yourself in a slipshod manner. In many instances, the manner in which you dress yourself indicates both the type and the quality of the service you will render.

When people dress in the uniform of their profession, they are communicating something.

By the uniform they wear, they speak to themselves concerning the path they have chosen or the role that has befallen them.

By putting on a uniform, they speak to their family members.

By wearing a uniform, they speak to their friends and associates.

By accepting and wearing a uniform, a student says something to the faculty of a school or to the coaching staff of an athletic team.

Nurses and doctors communicate to themselves, to each other, and to the public by the uniforms they wear.

A similar experience should characterize the life of every disciple of Jesus Christ. When people become followers of Jesus, they should publicly proclaim their inward spiritual experience. Following this decisive and significant experience of commitment to Jesus Christ, believers should request and submit to baptism. In the act of being baptized, people formally declare their desire to put off the attitudes, ambitions, and actions of the old life. In the same experience, they should express their desire to begin walking in newness of life (Rom. 6:1–4).

While baptism may picture in symbol the putting away of the old and the beginning of the new, in reality the task of putting away the old and putting on the new is a lifelong process. The writer of the book of Hebrews strongly urges believers to lay aside every weight and sin so that they might run the race of life with persistence and productiveness (cf. Heb. 12:1–2).

In his words of warning and encouragement to the Ephesian Christians, Paul describes the conflict we face when overcoming our enemy, the devil. He declares in graphic terms the necessity of putting on the whole armor of God so that we can resist the persistent and malicious attacks of our spiritual foe (Eph. 6:10–20).

To the Colossians the apostle proclaims the absolute necessity of Christians discarding inappropriate attire—unbecoming attitudes and unworthy ambitions and actions that would discredit anything they might say concerning a vital relationship with Jesus Christ. After telling his readers what they need to take off, he tells them what proper moral and spiritual clothes are fitting for Christians to put on.

I. We must discard garments that characterize paganism.

It would be highly inappropriate for a nurse to wear dirty blue jeans, an old sweatshirt, and ragged tennis shoes while assisting a surgeon. It would be inappropriate for an automobile service technician to adorn himself in his finest dress suit to work on greasy motors in a garage. Inappropriate clothing must be discarded if we are going to serve effectively and render the service that God wants us to render as his children and as his servants.

Grasping greed is an attitude that is inappropriate for the Christian (Col. 3:5). Covetousness, which is an overpowering desire for and seeking after material things, must be recognized for what it really is—idolatry. In a materialistic and highly commercial and competitive society in which success often is judged in terms of the things that people, possess, the follower of Jesus Christ must beware lest he or she be capture by the same secular scale of values.

The garment of an evil disposition must he eliminated as a filthy garment (Col. 3:8). Christ Jesus came into the world to do more than save our souls from going to hell. By the gift of his Holy Spirit, he seeks to Christianize our disposition (Gal. 5:22–23). It is necessary that we be willing and eager to forsake all harmful traits and attitudes. Many who for years have professed to believe in Jesus Christ have vast areas of their lives that need to be redeemed. They need to let Jesus perform a miracle of transformation in their hearts and minds.

All dirty language and lying speech must be cast aside as unworthy garments (Col. 3:8–10). There is no place in a Christian's conversation for profanity, filthy jokes, or falsehoods. With God's help we need to be pure and truthful in speech at all times.

All unworthy garments that would leave the impression that we are pagans must be cast aside so that we might be recognized as followers of Jesus Christ, members of his team, and servants of his cause.

II. The pieces of the Christian's uniform.

Paul calls the Colossian Christians and each one of us to put on the virtues appropriate for followers of Jesus Christ. He calls us to put on attitudes and follow courses of action that affect our relationships with those about us. Each of these virtues mentioned as essentials of the Christian's uniform will either eliminate or reduce friction in personal relationships. Those who wear these garments will not be abrasive, difficult, unpleasant, or unlovely people. Each portion of the Christian's uniform must be put on internally, in the mind and heart, rather than externally where it is expressed.

Put on the character of Christ (Col. 3:12). A verbal picture of the character of Jesus Christ is presented for our admiration and imitation. These gracious attitudes and actions are made possible by the presence of the Holy Spirit as he seeks to reproduce within us the mind and personality of Jesus Christ.

Put on the example of Christ (Col. 3:13). There are many unpleasant things with which we must somehow learn to cope if we want to enjoy peace and serve God effectively. Not everyone will treat us kindly, so we must learn to cope with those who make life painful or difficult for us. Jesus handled unkindness, not by developing an attitude of hostility and resorting to unkindness, but by the practice of granting forgiveness to them.

Forgiveness is not something that is granted only to those who deserve it. Forgiveness is the gift of one who chooses not to respond to hostility with an attitude of hate. To be a true follower of Jesus Christ requires that we repudiate the right to retaliate in a vindictive manner toward those who mistreat us. The motive for our practicing forgiveness is the example of Jesus Christ. We are to let Christ be our pattern, and we are to imitate him.

Put on the love of Christ (Col. 3:14). The love of Christ must not be identified with the shallow, cheap, shoddy, emotional thing that often is called love today. The love of Christ is a persistent, unbreakable spirit of goodwill. He expresses love in terms of kindness, thoughtfulness, helpfulness, and self-sacrifice. When on earth, he practiced a persistent, unbreakable spirit of goodwill even toward those who crucified him. With the help of the Holy Spirit, we too can love in this manner (Rom. 5:5).

Put on the peace of Christ (Col. 3:15). The peace of Christ is not merely the absence of war and tension. In reality peace is the result of harmonious relationships. Jesus seeks to bring people into a right relationship with God, with others, and within themselves. In putting on the peace of Christ, we seek persistently to establish and maintain harmonious relationships with others.

Put on the Word of Christ (Col. 3:16). We are encouraged to let the words of Jesus Christ dwell in us. To do this we must read the Bible and meditate on and memorize the Word. We should recognize the truths that Jesus spoke as being absolute truth for governing our lives. We should respond to his teachings and his commandments as being authoritative over us. He overcame temptation through the power of the Word of God. He was strengthened while on the cross by giving voice to the great truths of the Old Testament. If we would live the abundant life, we must plant his words in our innermost being and let them bear heavenly fruit.

Put on the thankfulness of Christ (cf. Col. 3:15–17). Three times in these short verses, Paul emphasizes the importance of being grateful and giving expression to that attitude of gratitude. Christ gave thanks on many different occasions. He was a grateful person. The attitude of gratitude is not instinctual. It must be developed. Thankfulness is a habit to be cultivated and practiced. To be grateful to God and to others continuously is one of the traits of a true follower of Jesus Christ.

Put on the name of Christ (Col. 3:17). To be baptized into the name of Jesus Christ is to acknowledge his ownership and to respond to his authority. We are to do all that we do as if we are in his presence and as a service for him.

Conclusion

Putting off the uniform of the old life calls for a continual forsaking of the sins that so easily beset us. We will find it necessary to give attention to this as long as we live. To put on the new uniform of a Christian is our glorious opportunity, and it is a continuous necessity. Because we receive a new nature when we are born again and because the Holy Spirit comes to dwell in us, it is possible for each of us to wear the new uniform. And it is absolutely essential if are to be true to our Lord and a blessing to those about us.

SUNDAY EVENING, SEPTEMBER 3

Title: The Test of Deeds

Text: "Wherefore by their fruits ye shall know them" **(Matt. 7:20)**.

Scripture Reading: Matthew 7:15–20

Introduction

One who enters the narrow gate and walks the restricted path that leads to life is now exhorted to beware of further dangers: (1) Beware of false prophets (Matt. 7:15–20), (2) beware of self-deception (Matt. 7:21–23), and (3) beware of building life on a foundation of sand (Matt. 7:24–27). The first of these warnings is tonight's theme.

I. You sheep beware of false prophets who are wolves in sheep's clothing (Matt. 7:15).

The Christian is concerned with truth and sincerity.

John has preserved for us the account of Jesus' ministry in Samaria before the preaching of the Sermon on the Mount. Jesus explained to the Samaritan woman that "the hour cometh, and now is, when the true worshippers shall worship the Father in spirit and in truth: for the Father seeketh such to worship him. God is a Spirit: and they that worship him must worship him in spirit and in truth" (John 4:23–24).

Jesus often heard persons whose understanding of the truth was faulty. The woman who superstitiously thought that she would be healed if she could but touch the hem of his garment was healed in spite of her superstition rather than because of it. Her faith was genuine (see Matt. 9:20–22).

The repentant robber on the cross who dared to appeal to Jesus directly had a faulty theology. His appeal, "Lord, remember me when thou comest into thy kingdom," did not evidence any faith in Jesus' ability to help until the end of the age. Jesus answered him by affirming, "Verily I say unto thee, To-day shalt thou be with me in paradise" (Luke 23:43).

Every Christian has to mature in his or her grasp of truth. How beautiful is the story of Aquila and Priscilla who recognized some deficiencies in the preaching of young Apollos. With wonderful Christian spirit, "they took him unto them, and expounded unto him the way of God more perfectly" (Acts 18:26).

Jesus' express warning is not against the immature person who has not come to full truth, but rather is against the hypocrite.

The illustration of the people of God as sheep and the enemy as a wolf was readily understood by those who heard Jesus. It was accepted Old Testament usage, as in Psalm 23 and Isaiah 40:11. Jesus developed the idea considerably as John 10:1–18 illustrates.

Paul in his address at Miletus to the elders of the church of Ephesus issued the same warning as did Jesus: "For I know this, that after my departing shall grievous wolves enter in among you, not sparing the flock. Also of your own selves shall men arise, speaking perverse things, to draw away disciples after them" (Acts 20:29–30).

II. How can the Christian recognize the hypocrites?

God knows who the hypocrites are. He will not be fooled. Christ, not Christians, will be their Judge, for only he has full knowledge.

"Ye shall know them by their fruits" (Matt. 7:16). One is to apply the observable laws of nature to this problem. Thorn bushes do not bear grapes. Thistles do not bear figs. One may tie grapes on thorn bushes and figs on thistles, but they do not grow there. The corrupt tree of verses 17 and 18 does not refer to a diseased tree, but rather to one whose fruit has no value. In the parable of the net in Matthew 13:47–50, the bad fish the disciples cast away were the fish that were inedible. So in our Scripture reading, the bad fruit is that which is inedible.

Christian pretenders may deceive for a time. They speak the language of Zion; they pray long prayers; they act very pious. "For such are false apostles, deceitful workers, transforming themselves into the apostles of Christ. And no marvel; for Satan himself is transformed into an angel of light" (2 Cor. 11:13–14). Eventually the sheep will know that the wolf is a wolf by his deeds, just as one knows a tree by its fruits.

III. Applying the test.

The sermon Jesus is now concluding has been on the meaning of Christian discipleship. It is a good guide as to whether one is a sheep or a wolf in sheep's clothing. Does he show the qualities of the Christian that are stated in the Beatitudes: repentance, faith, submission to God's will, hungering and thirsting after righteousness? Is he a peacemaker between God and people? Between people? Does he stand on the side of Jesus when it is not to his personal advantage to do so? Does he have the qualities of salt and light? Do people glorify God for what they hear him say and see him do? Does he follow the will of God as revealed in Jesus as the ethical rule of his life? Does he evidence goodwill toward others? Does he call people names? Is he willing to forgive and to ask forgiveness? Is his yes, yes, and his no, no? Does he go beyond what is ordinarily expected in his relations with others? Does he show evidence of goodwill—even for his enemies? Does he seem genuinely to serve God in his acts of worship and good deeds? When he gives and when he prays, do you think about what a good man he is or about how great God is?

A wolf is interested in his own gain. Does this man serve with an eye single to God's glory? Is he a good steward of his possessions? Does he seek first the kingdom of God and his righteousness? Does he point out little faults in others while proudly proclaiming his own virtues? Are there evidences that he loves God and his fellow humans? Does he keep the Royal Law and the Golden Rule? These are all indicators of the good fruit produced by a regenerated person.

Conclusion

When people join the church, they affirm that they are Christians. They enter into a covenant relationship with other members in the church. An unsaved person in the church membership is either deceived about his or her salvation or is deceiving others. If deceived, he or she needs to become a Christian. If a hypocrite, he or she also needs to become a Christian; but let the sheep heed our Lord's warning. Beware! Don't let a wolf covered by a sheep's skin destroy the flock. "By their fruits ye shall know them" (Matt. 7:20). The wolf is not a sheep. He is a predator. The sheep need to warn each other and if possible pull off the wolf's disguise and reveal him for what he is.

WEDNESDAY EVENING, SEPTEMBER 6

Title: Anger

Text: "Be ye angry, and sin not: let not the sun go down upon your wrath: Neither give place to the devil" **(Eph. 4:26–27)**.

Scripture Reading: Ephesians 4:25–32

Introduction

Anger is a strong feeling of displeasure usually brought on by antagonism. Anger is strong passion, or emotion of the mind, exalted by a real or imaginary injury or the intent to injure oneself or another. We have all experienced anger at one time or another, for we have all been hurt or thought we were. It matters not if the injury was intentional and real or just imaginary, the effects were the same: we became angry.

In the Old Testament several words are translated as anger. These words occur 45 times to express human anger and 177 times to express God's anger. The words denoting God's anger refer to his holy response to sin. When God takes action against sin, his anger become his wrath.

I. What causes anger?

One cause of anger is antagonism. The word *anger* itself means a strong feeling of displeasure and usually of antagonism. The antagonism may be real or imaginary. The writer of Proverbs said, "The discretion of a man deferreth his anger; and it is his glory to pass over a transgression" (Prov. 19:11).

Another cause of anger is grievous words. "A soft answer turneth away wrath: but grievous words stir up anger" (Prov. 15:1). A word that causes vexation of spirit causes anger to rise higher and higher. Saying the wrong thing at the wrong time causes anger.

Still another cause of anger is foolishness, or weakness. The writer of Proverbs said: "He that is soon angry dealeth foolishly: and a man of wicked devices is hated" (Prov. 14:17).

II. What are some of the excesses of anger?

Harm to our physical self is one of the excesses of anger. When we become angry definite hurtful reactions are set off in our bodies. People often cry or turn red when they become angry. These outward signs are caused by a chemical reaction set up in the body. Anger can also cause sleepless nights, digestive disorders, and nervous problems.

Another excess of anger is remorse, deep regrets. It is not until reason has been restored and we recover our poise and think things over, realizing what we have said and done, that we can measure the terrible excesses of losing our temper.

Still another excess of anger is emotional instability, a form of insanity. When people are excessively angry, they say and do things they would not say or do if they were not inflamed by anger. When people are inflamed by anger, their reason often is dethroned and they cannot think clearly. They lose their poise and balance. They are bent on destroying whatever or whoever inflicted their hurt. The Bible warns, "Make no friendship with an angry man; and with a furious man thou shalt not go: Let thou learn his ways, and get a snare to thy soul" (Prov. 22:24–25).

Still another excess of anger is unhappiness. We cannot be happy and angry at the same time.

III. Should we ever get angry?

Are we ever justified in being angry? The answer to this question is found in God's Word: "Be ye angry, and sin not: let not the sun go down upon your wrath" (Eph. 4:26). There are some things against which Christians are justified in being angry and should register their anger. At times it is proper for a whole community to rise up in anger and move in indignation against those things that threaten to inflict injury on the community.

At times we have a cause to be angry. Jesus said, "Whosoever is angry with his brother without a cause shall be in danger of the judgment" (Matt. 5:22). All about us, in many places, there are things going on against which we should be moved with anger. People become cowards when they fail to act against evil.

God, the Holy One, often is moved to anger. He sometimes acts as a foe of people and of nations. He cannot excuse, pass over, or condone wrong. He can forgive sin when confessed, but he will not condone evil. He is moved by his righteous anger or wrath to punish, to correct, to discipline the disobedient.

IV. How can we control our anger?

One way of controlling anger is to settle our differences before the sun goes down (Eph. 4:26).

Another way of controlling our anger is to exercise self-control over our spirit, soul, and flesh. The Bible says: "He that is slow to anger is better than the mighty; and he that ruleth his spirit than he that taketh a city" (Prov. 16:32).

Another way of controlling anger is meekness. "A soft answer turneth away wrath" (Prov. 15:1). If you are prone to anger try being meek.

Another way of controlling anger is to stop being sensitive. Are you quick to feel slighted or hurt? Do you carry your feelings on your sleeve? Do you blow your top easily? Are you given to emotional flare-ups? Be ashamed of yourself and stop being sensitive.

Still another way of controlling anger is to use wisdom and common sense. The Bible says, "Scornful men bring a city into a snare: but wise men turn away wrath" (Prov. 29:8).

Conclusion

Few of us are able to get angry and sin not. Let us heed the words of the apostle Paul: "Let all bitterness, and wrath, and anger, and clamour, and evil speaking, be put away from you, with all malice" (Eph. 4:31). Again the Bible says, "But now ye also put off all these: anger, wrath, malice, blasphemy, filthy communication out of your mouth" (Col. 3:8).

Either let us put off anger or be angry and sin not. This is the admonition of God's Word!

SUNDAY MORNING, SEPTEMBER 10

Title: The Way of Faith

Text: "O Lord of Hosts, blessed is the man who trusts in thee!" **(Ps. 84:12 RSV).**

Scripture Reading: Psalm 84:1–12

Hymns: "O Worship the King," Grant
"I Need Thee Every Hour," Hawks
"Faith Is the Victory," Yates

Offertory Prayer: Holy Father, thank you for the gift of another week and for the goodness of this day. We recognize you as the giver of every good and perfect gift. We respond to the encouragement of our Savior and look upon ourselves as being givers rather than mere receivers. We come today to give to you the affection of our heart and the praise of our lips. Help us to receive the blessings that you have for us today that we might go forth to be channels for your mercy and grace and help to others. Receive and add your blessing to the tithes and offerings that we bring for the work of your kingdom. In Jesus' name we pray. Amen.

Introduction

Simple but genuine trust in God is the heart of true religion. Faith in, trust in, and dependence on God are the keys to being right with God. Paul declared to the Christians in Galatia that "a man is not justified by works of the law but through faith in Jesus Christ . . . because by works of the law shall no one be justified" (Gal. 2:16 RSV). We become the children of God as a result of faith in Jesus Christ (Gal. 3:26). Faith in God as he has revealed himself in Jesus Christ is the basis on which we let God come into our lives. It is through faith that we let God do wonders in us, to us, and through us.

Genuine faith needs better definition and understanding. The writer of the book of Proverbs encouraged faith and at the same time explained the nature of the walk of faith in these words: "Trust in the LORD with all your heart, and do not rely on your own insight. In all your ways acknowledge him, and he will make straight your paths" (Prov. 3:5–6 RSV). Those who put faith in God do not walk with the presumptuous step of a know-it-all. They keep themselves open for divine direction and seek daily to do God's will.

The writer of the book of Hebrews defined faith: "Now faith is the substance of things hoped for, the evidence of things not seen" (Heb. 11:1). To walk by faith is not to walk by sight; risk is involved. The walk of faith is based on the conviction of great truths that are both invisible and intangible yet very real. The same writer described faith in terms of a deep conviction that God exists and that he is a rewarder of those who diligently seek him (Heb. 11:6). Our Lord encouraged people to "have faith in God" at all times (Mark 11:22).

There are at least three elements in genuine faith. The first is knowledge of God. The second is intellectual assent. One must acknowledge with one's mind that the knowledge he or she has is true. The third element is trust, putting confidence in that which one has accepted with one's mind as truth. Many people believe they have faith when in reality there is not much evidence that they walk in the way of faith.

I. The way of faith focuses our worship on God (Ps. 84:1–2).

Genuine faith in God focuses people's minds, hearts, and energies on God as being the supreme value in their lives. Genuine faith in God leads people to commit all their ways to God.

Married people may worship their mates by putting them first and foremost in all of life's relationships.

Parents may worship a child and give to the child the status of an idol.

People may worship their work and live only for their work.

People may worship insignificant goals and spend their lives in mediocrity. To worship anything less than the true and living God is to be guilty of idolatry. Genuine faith causes a person to let God be God. Have you let the God and Father of our Lord Jesus Christ have first place in your scale of values?

II. The way of faith finds its security in God (Ps. 84:3–4).

The psalmist had been in the temple area and had observed the sparrows building their nests and raising their young. Evidently this was a very secure place for the sparrows. This scene reminded him of the security that comes to those who trust implicitly in God for grace and guidance.

Friends can aid in bringing to us a feeling of security.

Many people seek security through the purchase of property or through the building of an insurance program.

The only real security people can experience is in the realm of the spiritual. God wants to forgive our sins and remove destructive guilt. He wants to assure us of his abiding presence and his purposes of love in order to relieve our fears and our anxieties. He wants to give us courage as we face the struggles and crises of life.

The psalmist was able to face tomorrow with all of its uncertainties with confidence because he was assured of the abiding presence of his Shepherd Lord (Ps. 23:4).

III. The way of faith finds fulfillment in helpfulness (Ps. 84:6).

The valley of Baca was a desolate desert area. The psalmist saw people of faith as having the capacity and the disposition to transform the deserts of life into oases that bring refreshment and joy to others.

There will be many times of difficulty and disappointment along the road of life. There will be times of serious disagreements with others. Life can be a very unpleasant experience unless someone serves as a change agent and works for the good of all.

The first deacons were problem solvers who brought harmony into the fellowship and peace among those who felt they were being mistreated. The result of the ministry of these first deacons was that the Word of God increased and the number of disciples multiplied greatly in Jerusalem and a great many of the priests were obedient to the faith (Acts 6:7).

One of the traits of being an ideal follower of Jesus Christ is that of being a peacemaker (Matt. 5:9). To be a true follower of Jesus Christ means that we work for harmonious relationships with and among those about us.

Jesus told the story of a good Samaritan who illustrates the thought of this passage in Psalms. The Samaritan found a man in the most difficult of circumstances, and out of a loving heart he ministered to the man's needs and cared for his future. The good Samaritan is a beautiful illustration of the way in which faith finds fulfillment in helpfulness. Is your faith expressing itself in deeds of kindness and helpfulness to others?

IV. The way of faith is a life of dialogue with God (Ps. 84:8–9).

People were made to walk and talk with God. Prayer is not a pious pose we must assume. Prayer is not a burdensome duty we must perform. Prayer is the joyful privilege of communicating to a loving Father all of our questions, problems, and needs.

God is always present. God is everywhere present and on the job for good to those who love him (Rom. 8:28). The life of faith will reveal itself in a constant openness to divine direction.

V. The way of faith is a way of joy that excels all others (Ps. 84:10–12).

One day with God is better than a thousand days away from him. The psalmist would agree with the poet who said, "Every day with Jesus is sweeter than the day before."

To be a humble doorkeeper in the house of the Lord brings more joy than to dwell on high in the tents of wickedness.

Conclusion

Jesus speaks of the importance of faith in saying, "If you have faith as a grain of mustard seed, you will say to this mountain, 'Move from here to there,' and it will move; and nothing will be impossible to you" (Matt. 17:20 RSV). A mustard seed was one of the smallest objects known to Jesus' disciples. A mustard seed was a living, growing thing. Jesus was saying to use the faith you have.

To have faith, we need to read God's Word daily and listen to the Lord as he speaks to us. We also need to claim his promises. To grow a greater faith, we must give ourselves not only to private worship but also to regular public worship. To walk the way of faith, we need to give ourselves to something outside ourselves that is bigger than ourselves and trust God to help us accomplish it.

SUNDAY EVENING, SEPTEMBER 10

Title: Warning against Self-Deception

Text: "Not every one that saith unto me, Lord, Lord, shall enter into the kingdom of heaven; but he that doeth the will of my Father which is in heaven" **(Matt. 7:21)**.

Scripture Reading: Matthew 7:21–23

Introduction

This text contains one of the most solemn warnings in God's Word. It warns that active church members, even preachers—even those whose ministries appear successful—may not be saved. The solemn warning must have been needed, else our Lord would not have spoken of it.

We cannot always know the facts about wolves in sheep's clothing; but we can know the facts about our own relationship with the Savior. A person who is self-deceived is without excuse.

I. Not everyone professing faith in Jesus Christ as Lord will be saved.

"Not every one that saith unto me, Lord, Lord, shall enter into the kingdom of heaven" (Matt. 7:21).

There are no magic words we can say to assure us of salvation. "Lord, Lord," spoken in sincerity would be a good confession. Paul affirmed, "Wherefore I give you to understand, that no man speaking by the Spirit of God calleth Jesus accursed: and that no man can say that Jesus is the Lord, but by the Holy Ghost" (1 Cor. 12:3). One may *profess* either truth or falsehood. One *confesses* only the truth. The Greek word translated *confess* means "to say the same thing" as God says. Paul is not denying that some profess the Lord in falsehood. He is affirming that one cannot confess the Lord apart from the help of the Holy Spirit. Jesus asked, "Why call ye me Lord, Lord, and do not the things which I say?" (Luke 6:46). Words are not enough. There is no magic in the words. Only pagans such as the seven sons of Sceva (see Acts 19:13–16) would think that there is power in the mere calling of the name of Jesus.

There are no deeds that we can do to assure our salvation. Matthew 7:22–23 indicates that many persons who had prophesied in Jesus' name, who had cast out demons, and had done many mighty works in the name of Jesus, would in the day of judgment hear Jesus say, "I never knew you: depart from me, ye that work iniquity" (Matt. 7:23).

Salvation does not depend on words or works but on "doing the will of my Father who is in heaven." There are appropriate words to speak and works to do once we accept Jesus, but apart from the acceptance of God's will, no words and no deeds can avail to make us right with God.

Isn't this what Paul was affirming in 1 Corinthians 13? "Charity" or "love" is a translation of the Greek word *agape,* which means a right heart attitude accompanied by the right deeds. The right heart attitude is goodwill, which is to be equated with God's will. "Love" in 1 Corinthians 13 is the same as "doing the will of my Father which is in heaven." In this light, how much more meaningful Paul's words become. Speech, learning, miracle working, faith, and martyrdom are nothing unless a person has a heart yielded to God's will. Jesus in our Scripture reading and Paul in 1 Corinthians 13 are using different words to state the same truth.

Judas was an example of the person described in our text. He preached and worked miracles in the name of Jesus as did the other apostles. If there had been any distinction, surely the fact would have been recorded; yet apparently this man was never saved, for Jesus said of him, "Woe to that man by whom the Son of man is betrayed! good were it for that man if he had never been born" (Mark 14:21).

II. The Judge's sentence.

"I never knew you: depart from me, ye that work iniquity" (Matt. 7:23). The knowledge of which Jesus the righteous Judge speaks is a knowledge that implies approval and acceptance. "For the LORD knoweth the way of the righteous: but the way of the ungodly shall perish" (Ps. 1:6). "My sheep hear my voice, and I know them, and they follow me: And I give unto them eternal life; and they shall never perish, neither shall any man pluck them out of my hand" (John 10:27–28). Note that the Judge did not say, "I once knew you but now I do not know you." He said, "I never knew you." They had been doing the works of God without being citizens of the kingdom of God. People judge by words and deeds, but God judges by the heart.

Being in the will of God comes before doing the works of God. These who are commanded to depart are described as "ye who work iniquity." The New American Standard Bible correctly translates, "Depart from Me, you who practice lawlessness" (Matt. 7:23). God's law for any person or thing is God's will for that person or thing. Anything contrary to or other than God's will is sin, "for sin is the transgression of the law" (1 John 3:4). Earnest, sincere Christians have nothing to fear at the judgment. The pseudo-Christian, however, no matter how successful he or she may appear to be, who is not doing the will of the Father in heaven, should beware and repent.

III. The one doing the will of the Father in heaven is known of Jesus and will enter the kingdom of heaven.

The phrase "in that day" (Matt. 7:22) indicates that Jesus was speaking of the day of judgment at the end of the gospel age when eternal states will be fixed and the righteous judgments of God will be manifest to all. It is the day of which Jesus said, "When the Son of man shall come in his glory, and all the holy angels with him, then shall he sit upon the throne of his glory: and before him shall be gathered all nations; and he shall separate them one from another, as a shepherd divideth his sheep from the goats" (Matt. 25:31–32). [Read on through the entire chapter.]

One who does "the will of the Father in heaven" will be acknowledged by Jesus as his own. Jesus said, "I am the good shepherd, and know my sheep" (John 10:14). "Then shall the King say unto them on his right hand, Come, ye blessed of my Father, inherit the kingdom prepared for you from the foundation of the world" (Matt. 25:34). To the faithful servant he will say, "Well done, thou good and faithful servant: thou hast been faithful over a few things, I will make thee ruler over many things: enter thou into the joy of the Lord" (Matt. 25:21).

When Jesus desired to inform the disciples about the eternal joys that awaited them in the blessed fellowship of heaven, he used the illustration of a home. The nearest thing to heaven on earth is a home in which love abides. It was a compliment to his mother, Mary, and to his stepfather, Joseph, that he used this illustration. "You must not let yourselves be distressed—you must hold on to your faith in God and to your faith in me. There are many rooms in my Father's house. If there were not, should I have told you that I am going away to prepare a place for you? It is true that I am going away to prepare a place for you, but it is just as true that I am coming again to welcome you into my own home, so that you may be where I am" (John 14:1–3 Phillips).

One who does the will of God is blessed.

One day a woman piously cried out, "Blessed is the mother who gave you birth and nursed you." [Jesus] replied, "Blessed rather are those who hear the word of God and obey it" (Luke 11:27–28 NIV).

On another occasion, "there came . . . his brethren and his mother, and, standing without, sent unto him, calling him. And the multitude sat about him, and they said unto him, Behold, thy mother and thy brethren without seek for thee. And he answered them, saying, Who is my mother, or my brethren? And he looked round about on them which sat about him, and said, Behold my mother and my brethren! For whosoever shall do the will of God, the same is my brother, and my sister, and mother" (Mark 3:31–35).

Conclusion

"The world passeth away, and the lust thereof; but he that doeth the will of God abideth forever" (1 John 2:17). If our hearts are yielded to God's will, then we are children of God through the new birth, and the heavenly Father will forgive and discipline us but will never forsake us. If our hearts are not right, nothing we say or do will make us right with God. Are you in God's will? If yes, rejoice! If no, repent while the door to repentance is open.

WEDNESDAY EVENING, SEPTEMBER 13

Title: Backbiting

Text: "Wherefore laying aside all malice, and all guile, and hypocrisies, and envies, and all evil speaking, as newborn babes, desire the sincere milk of the word, that ye may grow thereby" **(1 Peter 2:1–2)**.

Scripture Reading: 1 Peter 1:22–2:3

Introduction

The word *backbiting* means to say negative things about another person behind his or her back. It means to harm another person by slander or libel. The sin of backbiting is the sin of evil speaking so as to condemn, to lower or disgrace the reputation of another, to malign another. Thus the backbiter is a defamer, an evil speaker, a slanderer. Let us examine the teachings of God's Word in regard to backbiting.

I. The sin of backbiting is a serious and gross sin.

The sin of backbiting is a common and accepted sin today. All sin is serious, but when we examine God's Word we find that the sin of backbiting is a horrible sin. It is listed with other serious and gross sins (Rom. 1:29–32). Peter classifies the sin of backbiting with malice, guilt, hypocrisies, envies, and evil speaking (1 Peter 2:1). Backbiting is listed with the sins of a generation that practiced every vice that could be conceived of by the wicked imagination of a degenerate and depraved people. It is listed with adultery, murder, disobedience, idolatry, unrighteousness, and envy. It is with this unholy company that all backbiters belong and are associated. Backbiting is a serious and grievous sin.

II. The sin of backbiting is the sin of a reprobate mind.

In Romans 1 Paul described the sinners of his day as those who did not like to retain God in their knowledge and as those whom God gave over to a reprobate mind (Rom. 1:28). Those with reprobate minds are those who have no distinction of right and wrong. A person with a reprobate mind is one who acts the fool in moral matters.

The vast majority of men and women in churches would not knowingly associate with a company of adulterers, murderers, and idolaters unless it was to win them to Christ. However, these same church members are found with gossips and backbiters, and they will indulge with them in cheap scandal. It is a well-known fact that many committee meetings, class meetings, and women's meetings held in the church break up afterward into little groups of backbiting cliques who slander others.

III. The sin of backbiting is a sin of untruth or half-truths.

Nearly every case of backbiting is based on falsehoods, untruths, or half-truths. Usually backbiting is based on half-truths manipulated to slander a person. If you should ever quote the person who told the lie, that person would deny it or tell you that you misunderstood him or her. Let your truths pass three gates of gold:

> If you are tempted to reveal a tale that someone has told you about another, make it pass before you speak, three gates of gold:
>
> Three narrow gates. First, "Is it true?" Then, "Is it needful?" In your mind give truthful answer. And the next is last and narrowest, "Is it kind?"
>
> And if to reach your lips at last it passes through these gateways three, then you may tell the tale, not fear what the result of speech may be.

One pastor recommended following the four rules of conduct of Rotary International before saying anything about another person: Is it the truth? Is it fair to all concerned? Will it build goodwill and better friendships? Will it be beneficial to all concerned? Let us not be guilty of telling untruths, half-truths, doctored truth, or outright falsehoods.

IV. The sin of backbiting is the sin of character assassination.

Backbiters have no respect or regard for others. They will break up husband and wife, separate parents and children, tear up communities, divide churches, assassinate the character of young girls, besmirch the reputation of young men, and impugn the motives of innocent people. These backbiters will be dealt with by a just God who will mete out justice in that day when people's deeds shall be revealed.

Paul wrote to the Corinthian church that he was afraid that when he came he would find them debating, envying, striving, backbiting, whispering, and swelling with conceit. Such a condition would be bad anywhere but all the more so among people claiming to be Christians.

V. The sin of backbiting is the sin of cowardice.

The sin of backbiting involves talking about another when he or she is absent. It means criticizing people behind their backs. It means assigning motives to and interpreting the acts of people without any knowledge of the circumstances. Backbiting is a cowardly crime. It is base, mean, ungodly, and unwarranted.

Dr. John Huff once said: "Brother and Sister Backbiter live in Gossip Town, on Hearsay Street, just off Telltale Avenue, near Cut-Throat and Character-Assassin Alley. Their neighbors are Mr. and Mrs. Hearsay, Sister Have You Heard?, Mr. and Mrs. Don't Repeat, Brother Whisper, and Mr. and Mrs. I Do Declare. It is a terrible section of the city in which to live and rear your children. No one is safe, day or night, from the vicious attacks of these backbiting hounds, common curs of society." Yes, backbiters are scandalmongers who are cowards.

Conclusion

How can we overcome backbiting? Let us resist it; let us vow here and now not to be guilty of this great sin (James 4:11–12).

What can a victim of backbiting do? The Word of God has the answer to this question: "Having a good conscience: that, whereas they speak evil of you, as of evildoers, they may be ashamed that falsely accuse your good conversation in Christ. For it is better, if the will of God be so, that ye suffer for well-doing, than for evildoing" (1 Peter 3:16–17). "Having your conversation honest among the Gentiles: that, whereas they speak against you as evildoers, they may by your good works, which they shall behold, glorify God in the day of visitation" (1 Peter 2:12).

SUNDAY MORNING, SEPTEMBER 17

Title: An Ambassador in Chains

Text: ". . . that utterance may be given me in opening my mouth boldly to proclaim the mystery of the gospel, for which I am an ambassador in chains; that I may declare it boldly, as I ought to speak" **(Eph. 6:19–20 RSV)**.

Scripture Reading: Philippians 1:12–14

Hymns: "When Morning Gilds the Skies," Caswall
"God Will Take Care of You," Martin
"I Know Whom I Have Believed," Whittle

Offertory Prayer: Holy heavenly Father, help us to recognize that you are the giver of every good and perfect gift, and that all your purposes toward us are purposes of grace and love and power. Help us to see the evidences of your redemptive work in all the events that take place about us. Help us to cooperate with you in making known the message of your grace so that your redemptive power can be experienced in all the relationships of life. Today we come bringing tithes and offerings for the work of your kingdom. Thank you for the privilege of being able to work so we may acquire these resources to share with others. Add your grace and blessings to these gifts and multiply them for the good of others. We pray in Christ's name. Amen.

Introduction

Paul, the missionary evangelist and writer of Holy Scripture, uses the role of the ambassador to describe the function of the followers of Jesus Christ, "So we are ambassadors for Christ, God making his appeal through us. We beseech you on behalf of Christ, be reconciled to God" (2 Cor. 5:20

RSV). It is our joyful privilege to communicate a message of reconciliation to a world in rebellion against God, to announce that in Jesus Christ, God has reconciled a sinful world to himself (2 Cor. 5:19). The news of reconciliation is not merely good news but urgent news that the world needs to know.

We are the ambassadors of Christ and for Christ. An ambassador is one who represents one's government at the court of another government and communicates the wishes of his or her government. As ambassadors for Christ, we are his spiritual brothers and sisters. He called his apostles friends, and we are his friends if we love and obey him. We are also his ambassadors to a world in rebellion against God.

In Paul's epistle to the Ephesians, he described himself as "an ambassador in chains." For some time Paul had been wearing chains that imprisoned him (see Acts 21:33). Instead of being hostile or depressed, Paul magnified his office and responded positively to his responsibility in the midst of his unpleasant circumstances. Instead of bewailing his sad lot, he described himself as "an ambassador in chains," a high-ranking diplomat of Jesus Christ.

I. Ambassadors in chains speak of obstacles.

Ambassadors of Jesus Christ must not wait until all circumstances are favorable before they begin to fulfill their function as servants of Jesus Christ. Obstacles, handicaps, difficulties, and disappointments will always abound.

The world—society organized in rebellion against God—will always be against the person who seeks to live sincerely for Jesus Christ. We must expect this as an obstacle.

The flesh—that part of our lower nature that does not welcome the presence of a holy God and the work of the Holy Spirit—will continue to be open to temptation and to the lure of sin.

Until the end of this age, the devil will walk about as a roaring lion seeking whom he may devour. Paul, as an ambassador of Christ, did a number of things to overcome Satan's tricks. He kept his eyes on God, prayed continually, obeyed Christ in all circumstances, focused on evangelism, and lived for eternity rather than for time.

II. Ambassadors in chains speak of obligations.

Paul did not throw in the towel and quit when he found himself bound with chains, and neither should you and I give up simply because the way is difficult.

Paul wore a chain that had been created by the grace of God. He was primarily the prisoner of Jesus Christ rather than the prisoner of the Romans. He had permitted a loving Lord to put his chain upon his heart, and he was a prisoner of the grace of God.

Paul wore a chain created by joy. He had come to know the joys of forgiveness, sonship, God's presence, and eternal life. He had a great desire that others might come to know this same joy, and he felt obligated to share the good news that he had discovered in Jesus Christ.

Paul wore a chain created by compassion. The Holy Spirit had poured out the love of God for others in his heart, and he was eager to share this with a lost world.

III. Ambassadors in chains speak of opportunity.

It was through Paul's limitations and handicaps that he received his most prominent opportunities.

Because of his imprisonment, Paul was permitted to address the Sanhedrin, the highest court of the Jewish nation (Acts 23:1–10).

Because of his imprisonment, Paul gave his witness to the Roman governor, Felix (Acts 24).

Because of his imprisonment, Paul was able to give his witness to the Roman governor, Festus, and to King Agrippa (Acts 25–26).

Because of his imprisonment, Paul was sent to Rome to appear before Caesar (Acts 27–28).

The ambassador in chains conquered circumstances and transformed obstacles into opportunities, tragedies into triumphs. You and I can do the same if we will respond positively with faith to our Lord.

IV. Ambassadors in chains speak of optimism.

Paul faced his situation with a positive mental attitude based on his faith in Jesus Christ.

Paul could have reacted to his circumstances in a negative manner.

He could have given way to self-pity.

He could have permitted himself to be filled with hostility.

He could have surrendered to an attitude of depression that could have led to utter despair.

Paul could have been intimidated by his circumstances.

This could have led to a compromise of his message.

He could have just waited silently, hoping that his circumstances would improve.

Paul believed that God was at work in love and power to redeem people from emptiness, waste, weakness, and loneliness.

The apostle in chains could not and would not permit himself to do anything except be a true servant of Jesus Christ in the midst of the most unpleasant of circumstances.

Conclusion

God in Christ seeks to make peace with people. He wants people to come into a harmonious relationship with himself and with those in their families, communities, and world. We are the ambassadors of Christ, God's spokespersons. He is depending on us to take his Good News to those who desperately need to hear it. Let us follow the example of the ambassador in chains.

SUNDAY EVENING, SEPTEMBER 17

Title: Why Be Foolish?

Text: "Therefore whosoever heareth these sayings of mine, and doeth them, I will liken him unto a wise man, which built his house upon a rock" **(Matt. 7:24)**.

Scripture Reading: Matthew 7:24–27; Luke 6:46–49

Introduction

The Sermon on the Mount closes with the parable of the wise and foolish builders. The story may well have been the account of an actual occurrence. This is the substance of the story: Two men built houses. One "dug down deep and laid the foundation on rock" (Luke 6:48 NIV). The other "built a house on the ground without a foundation" (v. 49 NIV), or according to Matthew, on sand. The sandy ground was probably a location convenient to water and more level than other lots. "And the rain descended, and the floods came, and the winds blew" and beat on both houses. The house built on the rock remained standing, but the house built on the sand collapsed. The man who built his house on the rock was wise. The man who built his house on the sand was foolish.

Jesus applied the story to the building of one's life. "Therefore, whosoever heareth these sayings of mine and doeth them," said Jesus, "I will liken him unto a wise man, which built his house upon a rock. And every one that heareth these sayings of mine, and doeth them not, shall be likened unto a foolish man, which built his house upon the sand."

I. All of us are building the house of our lives.

We cannot postpone living until some more convenient time. Every moment we are building our lives.

II. All of us are either building on rock or on sand.

Rock represents whatever Jesus said to build on. Building on rock means obeying Jesus' instructions. "These sayings of mine" to which Jesus referred would naturally refer to the words he had just spoken. They need not, however, be limited to the sayings in the Sermon on the Mount, but would apply to every word of the Lord. The whole burden of the sermon has been, "But seek ye first the kingdom of God, and his righteousness" (Matt. 6:33). In every area of life, we are to seek the rule of God and what God reveals as

301

right. Jesus has made it clear that the will of God is that every person love God, neighbor, and self (see again Matt. 22:38–40).

As pointed out many times in this series of sermons, love *(agape)* is synonymous with doing God's will. It includes being the kind of people God desires as well as saying and doing what he wants us to say and do. It is synonymous with repentance, faith, conversion, regeneration, and sanctification. It means to accept Jesus' invitation extended in Matthew 11:28–30 to become his disciple and to keep on learning in his school. It means to accept Jesus as Savior and Lord.

Sand represents any other foundation than the rock. The person who is not building on the rock is building on sand. As in the former parable (Matt. 7:13–14), the person who did not enter the narrow door and walk in the straightened way was already on the broad road leading to destruction, so one not building on the rock is building on a foundation that will not stand.

Many are the unworthy foundations on which people build their lives. Some build life on the search for glory from people. Jesus addressed this error in Matthew 6:1–18. Some build life on gaining material riches. Jesus condemned this folly in Matthew 6:18–34. In Luke 12:16–21, Jesus pictured a man who laid up treasure for himself and was not rich toward God. Jesus called him a fool. Some try to build life on the condemnation of others. Jesus condemned this hypocrisy and sin in Matthew 7:1–6. Others build on the foundation of doing good deeds without being a Christian. These, said Jesus in Matthew 7:21–23, will not stand in the judgment.

Note the beautiful words of Edward Mote's familiar hymn "The Solid Rock," which is based on this parable.

III. Every life will be tested.

"Therefore," the word introducing this parable, points back to verses 21–23, which picture the separation at the final Judgment Day. Jesus said that the separation would be between those who do "the will of my Father which is in heaven" on the one hand, and those who "work iniquity" on the other. Those who do the Father's will correspond to the wise man who built his house on the rock, and those who work iniquity correspond to the foolish man who built his house on the ground. The house of one's life must pass final inspection.

Jesus will be the Judge. Note how easily and naturally Jesus claimed his rightful place as Lord and Judge. Earlier in the sermon he had equated "for righteousness' sake" and "for my sake" (see Matt. 5:10–11). He assumed a position of authority above the sacred Scriptures. In Matthew 5 he repeatedly quoted from them and fulfilled them with his own authoritative teaching, saying, 'Ye have heard that it was said by them of old time . . . but I say unto you. . . ." He fulfilled the good, but he also judged the bad.

Now in this concluding parable, he made clear that eternal destiny will be based on doing the will of the Father in heaven as revealed in his sayings. These claims to authority on the lips of any other person would be blasphemy.

One who claims to live by the Sermon on the Mount but rejects Jesus as the Son of God must come face-to-face with Jesus' claim to be the rightful Lord of life and to speak the authoritative truth by which all people will be judged.

Life built on obedience to Jesus stands up well before the floods and winds of this life. Every person must face the fact of sin, the probability of sickness, and the certainty of death. The sorrows and adversities of life overwhelm even the strongest who don't know God.

A young wife whose husband had just left for overseas duty during the last war said to her pastor, "What do people do in a time like this who do not have faith in God?" The pastor replied, "I don't know." Is there any other adequate foundation?

Conclusion

Usually the appeal to yield one's heart to God's love as revealed in Jesus by repenting of sin is made on the basis that it is the right thing to do. This is a correct basis of appeal. However, note that Jesus made the appeal on the basis of wisdom. A person who gives his or her heart to Christ is wise. A person who fails to do so is foolish. Why be foolish?

WEDNESDAY EVENING, SEPTEMBER 20

Title: Boasting

Text: "For men shall be lovers of their own selves, covetous, boasters, proud, blasphemers, disobedient to parents, unthankful, unholy" (**2 Tim. 3:2**).

Scripture Reading: 2 Timothy 3:1–5; Romans 1:28–32

Introduction

As strange as it may seem, the word *boast* means to praise. It is used in the Bible in a good sense and in a bad sense. It may be used to praise God, to praise others, or to vaunt oneself. Other words that belong in the same general category with boasting are *conceit, pride,* and *vanity.* These words describe a spirit that is repulsive to the Lord, and none of these words should characterize a Christian. They are the opposite of humility, meekness, sincerity, and truth.

I. Who is guilty of boasting?

Religious leaders often are guilty of boasting. Religious bigotry was pronounced in Jesus' day, and it still is today. The people of the nation of Israel, before Jesus came, were among the chief offenders. Because they were the chosen of God and the beneficiaries of his special covenant blessings, they considered themselves above others. In their vain conceit, they became proud, boastful, and exclusive in their self-centeredness, and they failed to represent God to the nations. God sent his prophets to plead with them and warn them against the spirit of boasting, but to no avail. As a result of their self-centeredness, they were oppressed by foreign governments.

When Jesus came he found boasting especially among the religious leaders. He warned the people: "Beware of the scribes, which desire to walk in long robes, and love greetings in the markets, and the highest seats in the synagogues, and the chief rooms at feasts; who devour widows' houses, and for a shew make long prayers: the same shall receive greater damnation" (Luke 20:46–47).

Jesus told a parable that has to do with boasting, conceit, and self-righteousness:

> Two men went up into the temple to pray; the one a Pharisee, and the other a publican. The Pharisee stood and prayed thus with himself, God, I thank thee, that I am not as other men are, extortioners, unjust, adulterers, or even as this publican. I fast twice in the week, I give tithes of all that I possess. And the publican, standing afar off, would not lift up so much as his eyes unto heaven, but smote upon his breast, saying, God be merciful to me a sinner. I tell you, this man went down to his house justified rather than the other: for every one that exalteth himself shall be abased; and he that humbleth himself shall be exalted. (Luke 18:10–14)

The spirit of boasting is repulsive to our Lord.

The wealthy and the famous often are guilty of boasting. A few wealthy, famous, and successful people are given to boasting, pride, bigotry, and vain conceit. They usually are those who have fame and success thrust upon them. People who have earned their wealth, fame, and success usually are humble about it, and there are no traces of conceit or of boasting in them.

Hear what the Bible says about boasting in riches:

> When the Lord your God brings you into the land he swore to your fathers, to Abraham, Isaac and Jacob, to give you—a land with large, flourishing cities you did not build, houses filled with all kinds of good things you did not provide, wells you did not dig, and vineyards and olive groves you did not plant—then when you eat and are satisfied, be careful that you do not forget the Lord, who brought you out of Egypt, out of the land of slavery. (Deut. 6:10–12 NIV)

> Go to now, ye that say, To-day or to-morrow we will go into such a city, and continue there a year, and buy and sell, and get gain; Whereas ye know not what shall be on the morrow. For what is your life? It is even a vapour that appeareth for a little time, and then vanisheth away. For ye ought to say, If the Lord will, we shall live, and do this, or that. But now ye rejoice in your boastings; all such rejoicing is evil. (James 4:13–16)

There is real danger in riches, fame, and success, lest a man forget his Lord, his friends, the poor, and the causes of Christ, and shut himself up and off from others to live too exclusively a life of self-indulgence.

Foolish sinners are guilty of boasting. There is little or no hope for proud, boastful sinners. "The fool hath said in his heart, There is no God" (Ps. 14:1). "The way of a fool is right in his own eyes" (Prov. 12:15). "Answer a fool according to his folly, lest he be wise in his own conceit" (Prov. 26:5). "Do you see a person wise in their own eyes? There is more hope for a fool than for them" (Prov. 26:12 NIV).

The psalmist said, "How long, LORD, will the wicked, how long will the wicked be jubilant? They pour out arrogant words; all the evildoers are full of boasting" (Ps. 94:3–4 NIV). "He boasts about the cravings of his heart; he blesses the greedy and reviles the LORD" (Ps. 10:3 NIV).

There isn't much hope for the boastful sinners unless they repent of their sins and turn to Christ for forgiveness and salvation.

II. Should Christians boast?

There are times when Christians should not boast.

Christians should not boast because they are saved by grace through faith in the Lord Jesus Christ. "For by grace are ye saved through faith; and that not of yourselves; it is the gift of God: not of works, lest any man should boast" (Eph. 2:8–9).

Christians should not boast, because they do not know what tomorrow shall bring. "Boast not thyself of tomorrow; for thou knowest not what a day may bring forth" (Prov. 27:1).

At other times Christians should boast—in the Lord. "My soul shall make her boast in the LORD; the humble shall hear thereof, and be glad" (Ps. 34:2). "In God we boast all the day long, and praise thy name for ever" (Ps. 44:8).

Conclusion

Let us beware of boasting unless it is in God, who has redeemed us, provides for us, and strengthens us from day to day. Let us guard against conceit, pride, bigotry, and vanity.

True Christianity "vaunteth not itself, is not puffed up, doth not behave itself unseemly" (1 Cor. 13:4–5). "Blessed are the meek: for they shall inherit the earth" (Matt. 5:5).

SUNDAY MORNING, SEPTEMBER 24

Title: The Highest Joy of Living

Text: "It is more blessed to give than to receive" (**Acts 20:35**).

Scripture Reading: Acts 4:32–37

Hymns: "O for a Thousand Tongues," Wesley
"I Gave My Life for Thee," Havergal
"Trust, Try, and Prove Me," Leech

Offertory Prayer: Holy heavenly Father, we come today to give you the worship of our hearts and the praise of our lips. We would let your presence be recognized at all times and in every area of our activity. We come believing that you are the giver of every good and perfect gift. We remind ourselves that we are the channels through which your blessings are to reach the needy. We bring tithes and offerings that are but the fruits of the power you have given us to work and to get wealth. Please receive these gifts and bless them to the end that men and women, boys and girls around the world will come to know Jesus Christ as Lord and Savior. In his name we pray. Amen.

Introduction

William Barclay told of the prominent notice given in the London Central YMCA to the death, funeral, and memorial service of a man named Basil Oliver who had lived at the Y for thirty years, serving as an errand boy, and died at the age of eighty-five *(In the Hands of God* [New York: Harper and Row, 1966], 11–13). Basil collected papers, went for stamps, ran errands, did all kinds of odd jobs, brought the Sunday papers, served tea and coffee, and was always willing and glad to help. Only after he died did people find out all that he did.

Barclay made three significant observations about this man. One, he was exceedingly happy. Two, he was supremely useful. And three, he was exceptionally kind. The man whose death was being announced had provided a brilliant example of a person who found both joy for himself and love from others by simply doing the little things that came to his hand in the place where life had set him. He had come to know the highest joy of living. If you would know the highest joy of living, you must discover the joy of giving.

Where do you search for the highest joy in life? What do you do to overcome despair and depression? In what do you find meaning and purpose and fulfillment?

Some say that you find the highest joy in what you eat. All of us must admit that many of the most pleasant experiences of life take place around the dining table.

Some say that you find the highest joy of life in what you feel. These concentrate on the dynamics that surround the emotional nature of people. This way of thinking leaves one wide open to letting alcohol, drugs, and sex play prominent roles in their lives.

Some say that you find the highest joy of life through what you believe. It is said, "You become what you believe." There is a great deal of truth in this concept. We cannot overemphasize how much what we believe contributes to a meaningful life.

Some insist that you find the highest joy through what you think. These seek to find strength in the realm of the intellect and through the rational processes of the mind.

Some insist that you find the highest joy of life through what you do. And these would emphasize a goal-orientated purpose for life in which success is measured in terms of achievements. One of the benefits of this way of life is that it is highly measurable and that one can mark off the areas of success in life.

Jesus says that the highest joy in life is found in a life of devoted, unselfish, persistent giving. The apostle Paul had this great truth in mind when he wrote to the Corinthians, "The point is this: he who sows sparingly will also reap sparingly, and he who sows bountifully will also reap bountifully. Each one must do as he has made up his mind, not reluctantly or under compulsion, for God loves a cheerful giver" (2 Cor. 9:6–7 RSV). Paul was seemingly indicating that something has happened to a man that makes it possible for him to be a cheerful giver, and because he has become a cheerful giver, he is precious to God, for God loves him in a special way.

To be cheerful in our giving indicates that great progress has been made from the mind of the flesh to the mind of the spirit, from our natural state toward becoming more like Jesus Christ in thought and deed. While God loves all of us, he loves and responds to those who are making progress toward spiritual maturity and competency.

I. God loves the cheerful giver.

The cheerful giver has found security in the grace and goodness of God's bounty. A psychologist has said that it is impossible for the insecure person to be cheerful in his or her giving. Cheerfulness in giving is possible only to the person who feels secure. The greatest security we have is not in the piling up of material things but in responding to the grace and goodness of God. God loves the cheerful giver because cheerful giving is an indication that one has come to a position of feeling secure in God's grace and goodness.

The cheerful giver has become a channel through which God can give abundantly. The cheerful giver is not a reservoir but rather a channel through which God can send his blessings into the hearts and lives of others.

The cheerful giver has become a producer rather than remaining a parasite. An unborn baby is totally dependent on his or her mother. Tragic indeed is the fact that some remain parasites on their parents, on society, and on God as long as they live. They are always demanding that others do for them. They never seek to be givers and doers on behalf of others. God loves cheerful givers because they are no longer parasites.

The cheerful giver has discovered the highest joy of being. God wants his children to have fullness of joy. The highest joy comes not to the one who gets but to the one who becomes a giver.

The cheerful giver has reached a plateau of maturity rather than remaining in infancy.

The cheerful giver has discovered the joy of Jesus. Jesus said, "Give, and it will be given to you; good measure, pressed down, shaken together, running over, will be put into your lap. For the measure you give will be the measure you get back" (Luke 6:38 RSV). These words from the Lord contain one word of command—"give." The balance of this statement is a promise and an observation of what happens in life. Jesus is the greatest giver. On earth he lived a life full of joy and prayed for his disciples that they likewise might have fullness of joy. This joy comes only to those who live to be givers.

God rejoices and loves the cheerful giver because of the harvest that will come. The farmer must plant sufficient seed to reap a full harvest. The same law rules in the relationships of life. Only those who give of themselves will be able to receive all that God has for them. Jesus spoke of the significance even of little gifts, "And whoever gives to one of these little ones even a cup of cold water because he is a disciple, truly, I say to you, he shall not lose his reward" (Matt. 10:42 RSV). To know the highest joy of living, you must discover the joy of giving.

II. Cheerful giving is not easy.

To be a giver is not instinctive. People are born as getters rather than givers. We have an acquisitive instinct rather than a sharing instinct.

Giving is a habit that must be learned. It does not come easy, and it is not a natural development of life. It is a difficult habit to form and to maintain.

The joy of giving must be experienced to be believed. At first glance and at first impression, Jesus' saying "It is more blessed to give than to receive" will be rejected by most.

To become a cheerful giver, you must begin giving what you have. You cannot give what you do not have. When Jesus spoke of giving a cup of cold water, he was speaking of a readily available gift that is needed by all.

You can give a friendly greeting to strangers. You can give good citizenship to your community. You can give understanding and sympathy to the members of your family. You can give words of appreciation and praise to those with whom you come in contact day by day. You can give daily thanks to God for all the blessings that come to you from him. You can give a good day's work for your salary. You can give service and helpfulness to those about you. The secret to success is to be found and developed within your inner attitude toward your purpose for being.

III. How to become a cheerful giver.

You first must find your greatest security in God's grace, forgiveness, and love. Until you feel secure with God, you will never be able to be a persistently cheerful giver.

You should seek to see your life as a channel for the blessings of God rather than a reservoir into which the blessings of God flow to be stored up. The more you give to others, the more God will give to you. You must let God's blessings flow through you if you want to receive greater blessings from him.

You should visualize yourself as a producer instead of a parasite. Even those who are totally dependent on others for everything, if they have a cheerful inward attitude, can sow cheer and joy into the hearts and lives of others.

You should see yourself as the recipient of many unearned resources. It is true that we work and earn a living and perhaps reap a profit. Some come to the place where they possess a good portion of this world's goods. Yet the greatest things that we have are free. God has freely given us the sun, the oxygen we breathe, our health, and many other things that we take for granted.

To be a cheerful giver, you must see the eternal significance of the present. We are more than intelligent animals. We are creatures made in the image of God. We are passengers through time toward eternity. Death is not the end. The grave is not the goal of this life. There is a place called heaven, and there will be a time when God will reward his children for their faithful service and for their deeds of kindness. All that we do in this life is of eternal significance. If you would know the highest joy of living in the present, you must discover the joy of giving.

Conclusion

God gave his Son to die for our sins. Christ Jesus gave his life on a cross as a substitute for each of us. God, through the Holy Spirit, offers to us the rich gifts of forgiveness, new life, and help to live an abundant life. God is a great giver, and you and I will discover the highest joy of living when we discover the joy of being a giver in every area of life.

SUNDAY EVENING, SEPTEMBER 24

Title: Where Is Religious Authority?

Text: "And it came to pass, when Jesus had ended these sayings, the people were astonished at his doctrine: For he taught them as one having authority, and not as the scribes" **(Matt. 7:28–29)**.

Scripture Reading: Matthew 28:18–20; Mark 9:2–10

Introduction

When asked, "What is your religion?" a woman replied, "Episcopal." When asked about a specific congregation, she answered, "I am not a member. I really don't have religion. What I meant was that if I were going to have religion, I would go there to have it." She had her religion. A man who says, "There is no God," has his religion. Those who say, "I don't know" or "I don't care," have their religion just as surely as those who are Christians, Jews, Muslims, or Buddhists.

No one can be content living in spiritual darkness. At some point, everyone asks such questions as, Why am I here? Who am I? What is life's purpose? Is there a God? If so, what is he like, and why do I yearn to know him? If not, how did I get here? What is ultimate reality? What is the truth about God? What we believe about God and his will for us is the ultimate authority. How can we know about God and his will?

I. Some alleged authorities.

For a few years, a child believes on the basis of parental authority. But the guise of parental infallibility is hard to maintain, as illustrated by the following story. A little boy said, "Father, the teacher knows you helped me with my homework. She said, 'I don't see how one boy could make so many mistakes!'" As a child matures, his or her faith must also mature. A child's "Why? Why? Why?" must be answered by more than "Because I say so."

Some governments have claimed to speak for God and have tried to establish their authority by force. They say, "This you must believe upon the penalty of the law." Force may coerce the body, but it cannot enlighten the mind nor convince the conscience. A mature man who was not a church member asked an evangelist, "How many religious denominations are there?" The evangelist replied, "About 260, but they can be classified in about 20 main groups." "They cannot all be right, can they?" he asked. The evangelist agreed. The man replied, "Then why doesn't the government pass a law telling us which one is right?" The evangelist told him that the support of the government for a religious view would not make it the correct view. The vote of Congress would be about as valuable in determining ultimate religious authority as was the vote of the little children in determining whether the little chicken was a "boy" or a "girl."

Some churches claim religious authority. They claim that their heads are the representatives of God and that when they speak on morals or doctrine they speak infallibly and must be believed on penalty of mortal sin. Some even claim that the power to forgive sin or to refuse to forgive has been delegated to their clergy.

Most of us are not willing to allow any church to be our authority. The records of the pronouncements of those who claim infallibility do not justify the claim. Human inconsistencies show through clearly. It just does not seem right that certain people should be given power over the souls and consciences of others. We do not believe that God has given the power to any person or group to act for him. He is God, and he deals directly with all people without a human mediator. Those who hold a contrary view have misinterpreted Jesus' teaching.

"The Bible is our religious authority," many millions of devout Christians will affirm. The Bible is unique. It is a true revelation of God not found elsewhere. It is preeminently the book about Jesus Christ. The Old Testament prophesies the coming of the Messiah, and the New Testament records his advent, life, teaching, death, resurrection, ascension, and promised return. It also records the advent of the Holy Spirit and the early growth of Christianity.

II. God's revelation in Jesus Christ.

Jesus claimed religious authority. He said, "All authority in heaven and on earth has been given to me" (Matt. 28:18 RSV). He preexisted with the Father before Creation and came to earth as God incarnate. He was sinless, and he revealed God in word and in deed. He fulfilled all that God had spoken through Moses, the Psalms, and the prophets about the Messiah. He died a vicarious death; arose from the dead on the third day; and after instructing his disciples for forty days, ascended to heaven, from whence he will return at the end of the age to judge the world. In the person of the Holy Spirit, he now abides on this earth, giving guidance and strength to those who believe on him.

Assuming that Jesus is who and what he claimed to be, he is the ultimate religious authority. The voice of God from heaven said, "This is my beloved Son: hear him" (Mark 9:7).

When Jesus ended the Sermon on the Mount, "the people were astonished at his doctrine: For he taught them as one having authority, and not as the scribes" (Matt. 7:28–29). As we learn from John 1, the disciples of Jesus believed he was the Messiah (v. 41), the Lamb of God (v. 36), "him, of whom Moses in the law, and the prophets, did write, Jesus of Nazareth, the son of Joseph" (v. 45), and "the Son of God" and "the King of Israel" (v. 49). The multitudes, however, could not have been expected to hold this view. The authority of Jesus for them must have been that of the impact of truth as well as the power of his person.

Conclusion

The ultimate authority is the truth, conformity to fact. God is truth and light. God reveals his truth in nature (see Ps. 19; Rom. 1:18–20), in a person's spiritual nature (see Rom. 2:14–16; John 1:9), through various persons and providences, but finally and fully through Jesus Christ (see John 1:1–5, 9–18; Heb. 1:1–3).

Jesus revealed God by what he did and said. He spoke in principles rather than in laws. Any statement of Jesus that is so applied as to conflict with love and righteousness is misinterpreted. He is present in the Holy Spirit to guide earnest seekers to the truth (see John 16:7–14).

No one person can be your religious authority. You must find the truth for yourself. The truth in Jesus brings a revelation of a God of love, righteousness, forgiveness, and purpose, who satisfies both the mind and the heart. Do not be content until you know him personally. Find the personal authority the Samaritans found when they said to the woman who had witnessed to them about Jesus, "Now we believe, not because of thy saying: for we have heard him ourselves, and know that this is indeed the Christ, the Saviour of the world" (John 4:42).

WEDNESDAY EVENING, SEPTEMBER 27

Title: Envy

Text: "A sound heart is the life of the flesh; but envy the rottenness of the bones" **(Prov. 14:30).**

Scripture Reading: Proverbs 14:30; 27:4; Matthew 27:18; Romans 1:29–30; Galatians 5:21

Introduction

One of the great common sins of society is envy, a base and contemptible sin. Webster defines envy as the "painful or resentful awareness of an advantage enjoyed by another with the desire to possess the same advantage."

Envy has a twin sister named jealousy. They have a strong affinity for each other and seldom are separated. However, envy and jealousy can be distinguished from each other. We are jealous of our own; we are envious of another person's possessions. Jealousy fears to lose what it has; envy is pained at seeing what others have.

Envy is not confined to any one group of people. It is amazing to notice this deadly sin in the hearts of men and women in all walks of life. This monster evil shows itself in preachers, doctors, lawyers, politicians, bankers, merchants, teachers, musicians, athletes, social climbers, church officials, and church members. If envy could only serve to make one ambitious to excel, to achieve, to reach a higher goal, then it would be commendable, but the opposite usually is true.

The Bible has much to say against the sin of envy. It is classified with the unholy company of unrighteousness, fornication, wickedness, covetousness, murder, debate, deceit, backbiting, God hating, disobedience, and lying (Rom. 1:29–30). What are some of the effects of the sin of envy?

I. Envy causes people to fail to appreciate and enjoy what they have.

Numerous people do not appreciate and enjoy what they have because they are envious of what others have. Envy is the root sin that produces covetousness. The Bible plainly says, "Thou shalt not covet" (Ex. 20:17).

To covet what another has or to be envious of what one has results in unhappiness. It causes a person to fail to appreciate and enjoy what he or she has. The Bible says, "Let us not be desirous of vain glory, provoking one another, envying one another" (Gal. 5:26). "Fret not thyself because of evildoers, neither be thou envious against the workers of iniquity" (Ps. 37:1). "Let not thine heart envy sinners; but be thou in the fear of the Lord all the day long" (Prov. 23:17).

II. Envy causes littleness.

To be envious is a sign of littleness, narrowness of soul. To be envious is a frank admission that you neither have the ability nor the winsomeness to compete with those who excel.

Envy keeps one from rejoicing at the success of others, from applauding winners and honoring those who excel. Why should one suffer pain, uneasiness, or fear at another's success? Why should one be depressed and seek to discredit and depreciate another's victories?

Paul said to the Corinthians: "For ye are yet carnal; for whereas there is among you envying, and strife, and divisions, are ye not carnal, and walk as men? For while one saith, I am of Paul; and another, I am of Apollos; are ye not carnal?" (1 Cor. 3:3–4). Those who envy are little and carnal.

III. Envy causes people to dislike others.

When people see what others have or enjoy, they are prone to be envious. This envy can produce dislike or even hatred. Envy breeds contempt for superiors, and there is no limit to which envy will go to discredit and depreciate others who may excel. Paul said of the envious: "They are conceited and understand nothing. They have an unhealthy interest in controversies and quarrels about words that result in envy, strife, malicious talk, evil suspicions and constant friction" (1 Tim. 6:4–5 NIV).

IV. Envy causes destruction.

It was envy that brought about the death of our Lord Jesus Christ: "For he knew that for envy they had delivered him" (Matt. 27:18). "For he knew that the chief priests had delivered him for envy" (Mark 15:10).

Envy will destroy people. "For wrath killeth the foolish man, and envy slayeth the silly one" (Job 5:2). "A sound heart is the life of the flesh; but envy, the rottenness of the bones" (Prov. 14:30). "Wrath is cruel, and anger is outrageous; but who is able to stand before envy?" (Prov. 27:4).

Envy is so destructive that it will keep people from going to heaven. Paul said, "The acts of the sinful nature are obvious: . . . envy; drunkenness, orgies, and the like. I warn you, as I did before, that those who live like this will not inherit the kingdom of God" (Gal. 5:19–21 NIV).

Conclusion

Biblical warnings against envy are numerous. David said: "Truly God is good to Israel, even to such as are of a clean heart. But as for me, my feet were almost gone; my steps had well nigh slipped. For I was envious at the foolish, when I saw the prosperity of the wicked" (Ps. 73:1–3). Solomon said, "Envy thou not the oppressor, and choose none of his ways" (Prov. 3:31), and "Let not thine heart envy sinners: but be thou in the fear of the LORD all the day long" (23:17). Paul said in Romans, "Let us walk honestly, as in the day; not in rioting and drunkenness, not in chambering and wantonness, not in strife and envying" (13:13). Peter said, "[Lay] aside all malice, and all guile, and hypocrisies, and envies, and all evil speakings" (1 Peter 2:1).

If you are given to envy, ask the Lord to drive it out of your heart. Determine with the Lord's help to be big in soul, charitable in attitude, and Christian in spirit, for Jesus' sake.

SUGGESTED PREACHING PROGRAM FOR THE MONTH OF
OCTOBER

■ **Sunday Mornings**

The church should always be involved in the ministry of evangelism—proclaiming the good news of God's love for sinners. "Proclaiming the Good News" is the suggested theme for five evangelistic sermons.

■ **Sunday Evenings**

"Responding Positively to the Holy Spirit" is the suggested theme for five messages based on great imperatives found in the book of Ephesians.

■ **Wednesday Evenings**

The Wednesday evening messages for the rest of the year form a series based on Jesus' parables titled "Jesus Continues to Speak."

SUNDAY MORNING, OCTOBER 1

Title: Did God Make a Mess?

Text: "As it is, we do not yet see everything in subjection to him. But we see Jesus . . ." **(Heb. 2:8–9 RSV)**.

Scripture Reading: Psalm 8:3–8

Hymns: "O Love That Wilt Not Let Me Go," Matheson
           "Jesus Paid It All," Hall
           "Breathe on Me," Hatch

Offertory Prayer: Father, we praise your name because we are made in your image and after your likeness. Even in our sins you have made us perfect in Christ Jesus. Now, as we bring our gifts, the fruits of our labors, we are bringing a part of ourselves. May we surrender all we are and have to you in Jesus' name. Amen.

Introduction

Did God make a mess when he made humans? Historical accounts and the daily news may cause us to think that God did make a mess. But can we really blame God? Let us discover the answer by studying three topics: What we are meant to be, what we are, and how we can be what we are meant to be.

I. What we are meant to be.

The writer of Hebrews said, "'Thou didst make him for a little while lower than the angels, thou hast crowned him with glory and honor, putting everything in subjection under his feet.' Now in putting everything in subjection to him, he left nothing outside his control" (2:7–8 RSV). This sounds very much like the Genesis account: "So God created man in his own image, in the image of God he created him; male and female he created them. And God blessed them, and God said to them, 'Be fruitful and multiply, and fill the earth and subdue it; and have dominion over the fish of the sea and over the birds of the air and over every living thing that moves upon the earth'" (1:27–28 RSV).

Humanity at its best demonstrates that we are this kind of creation. In our aspirations and ambitions, we are always trying to climb higher. In our dreams and desires, we are always reaching out. Philosophies have been developed and governments have been organized with a view of attaining goals "out of this world." There seems to be a built-in belief among the ambitious young that they can correct the mistakes of the past and make a better world. They are made that way. Thank God! What a mess we would be in without it. Because of this God-given, built-in capacity to make dreams come true, discoveries have been made and civilizations have been born.

People keep trying to be what they are meant to be. They persist in gaining glory and honor. They make a noble effort to bring everything in subjection to themselves, leaving nothing out of their control.

Humankind, forgetting their God, and trying to act like gods, keep seeking control militarily, politically, economically, physically, sexually, intellectually, and even religiously. Since the building of the Tower of Babel, people have said, "Come, let us build ourselves a city, and the tower with its top in the heavens, and let us make a name for ourselves." Some have been noble and altruistic while others have been self-serving and destructive.

II. What we are.

God made man in his own image, a little less than divine. He "crowned him with glory and honor, putting everything in subjection under his feet. Now in putting everything in subjection to him, he left nothing outside his control." The trouble is that "we do not yet see everything in subjection to him" (Heb. 2:7–8 RSV). You see, God made man right, but man went wrong. God made Adam perfect, but Adam fell, and all since him are fallen. As soon as people are old enough to begin making choices, they begin making wrong choices.

In Psalm 53:3 we read, "Every one of them has gone back: they are altogether become filthy; there is none that doeth good, no, not one." In Isaiah 53:6 we read, "All we like sheep have gone astray; we have turned every one to his own way." In Isaiah 64:6 we read that all our righteous acts are like filthy rags. In Romans 3:23 we read, "All have sinned, and come

315

short of the glory of God." In 1 John 1:8 we read, "If we say that we have no sin, we deceive ourselves, and the truth is not in us." Even after we become Christians, this sinful nature is still there.

Paul said, "I do not understand my own actions. For I do not do what I want, but I do the very thing I hate. Now if I do what I do not want, I agree that the law is good. So then it is no longer I that do it, but sin which dwells within me. For I know that nothing good dwells within me, that is, in my flesh. I can will what is right, but I cannot do it. For I do not do the good I want, but the evil I do not want is what I do. Now if I do what I do not want, it is no longer I that do it, but sin which dwells within me" (Rom. 7:15–20 RSV).

You ask, "Why didn't God just make man so he couldn't sin?" If he had, man would not be in the likeness of God with freedom. There is no glory and honor in being a robot without choice. Man was given freedom and became a slave. He was made a king and became a servant. The image of God has been defaced.

Our passage says that God put everything in subjection to man, but it adds, "We do not yet see everything in subjection to him." About the time man seems to be subduing nature, nature subdues man. Man is able to make rain for his crops, then the floods destroy his crops. He harnesses nuclear energy and then becomes scared to death he will destroy himself. Solomon is not the only man who reached his goals and then concluded the foolishness of it all.

Carefully laid foundations often tumble. A man accumulates wealth and loses it. He gets training, and it becomes obsolete. He attains political fame and loses it in one day. He is in a constant struggle to reach his potential. It seems as though for every two steps forward he takes one step back. Paul summed up his consternation and frustration in Romans 7:24: "Wretched man that I am! Who will deliver me from this body of death?" Then he answers the question: "Thanks be to God through Jesus Christ our Lord." In Romans 8 he continues, "There is therefore now no condemnation for those who are in Christ Jesus" (RSV). In the verses that follow, he shows that the only answer is Christ in us.

III. How to be what you are meant to be.

The answer to being what you are meant to be is to have "Christ in you, the hope of glory" (Col. 1:27). Paul was so convinced of this truth that he was always talking about it. He said, "For me to live is Christ" and "It is no longer I who live, but Christ who lives in me."

Do you see how it works? God created man to be someone, but he blew it. With Christ in us, we can become the people we are meant to be. Is that an oversimplification? Listen to Paul. He was not given to oversimplification: "For as in Adam all die, so also in Christ shall all be made alive" (1 Cor. 15:22 RSV).

Jesus said, "I am the vine, you are the branches" (John 15:5 RSV). You become who God wants you to be by abiding in Jesus. The branch can never be what the branch is meant to be without the vine. Man was made like God, but he isn't like God. But Jesus in him makes him who he is supposed to be in relationship to the vine.

Conclusion

You carefully select and buy a new automobile. But do you know what? It is not really an automobile. The word *automobile* suggests that it mobilizes itself. It will not do this. The only way the automobile can be what it is supposed to be is for you to take over the controls. The only way you can be the person you are meant to be is for Jesus to take over the controls.

God didn't make a mess. We have made a mess, and God invites us to allow him to come in and make us what we are supposed to be.

SUNDAY EVENING, OCTOBER 1

Title: Maintaining the Unity of the Spirit

Text: "Maintain the unity of the Spirit in the bond of peace" **(Eph. 4:3 RSV)**.

Scripture Reading: Ephesians 4:1–6

Introduction

Each disciple of the Lord Jesus Christ needs to recognize and respond to the indwelling presence of the Holy Spirit (1 Cor. 3:16; 6:19–20; 12:1). The book of Ephesians gives at least five great imperatives to each believer concerning a proper response to the Holy Spirit. The first of these encourages us to be eager to maintain the unity of the Spirit (Eph. 4:3). There is a sevenfold basis for this unity:

There is one body.

There is one Spirit.

There is one hope.

There is one Lord.

There is one faith.

There is one baptism.

There is one God and Father of us all (Eph. 4:4–6).

Paul urges Christ's followers in Ephesus to put forth an earnest effort to promote and maintain this unity of the Spirit within the family of God. He would encourage us to learn how to get along with the other members of God's family and to maintain a spirit of agreement and unanimity that avoids division and strife. Paul makes some suggestions for maintaining the unity of the Spirit.

I. We should hear and heed the high call of God to our hearts (Eph. 4:1).

The high call of God is not limited to those who receive a divine constraint to enter the ministry or to volunteer for missionary service. Every child of God receives God's call to devotion to Christ and ministry to others. Ours is a high and holy calling because it comes from God. He requires us to walk in harmony with each other.

II. To maintain the unity of the Spirit, we need to face life with an attitude of humility (Eph. 4:2).

If we are to promote a spirit of unity within the family of God, human pride must go. We must avoid the peacock complex that causes some people to strut. We should follow the encouragement of Paul as he wrote to the Romans, "Outdo one another in showing honor" (Rom. 12:10 RSV). We are to have a modest view of self rather than an exaggerated sense of our importance. Many conflicts in the fellowship come as a result of someone desiring more credit than he or she has received. It is tremendously important that we avoid this kind of strife.

III. To maintain the unity of the Spirit, we need to face life with an attitude of meekness (Eph. 4:2).

Meekness is not weakness. Moses was said to be the meekest man of his generation, and there was nothing weak about Moses. Our Lord was described as meek and lowly in heart, and there was nothing weak about Jesus Christ. Meekness is an attitude of openness to God. Meekness means to be gentle and sensitive and responsive to God's will and to others' needs.

IV. To maintain the unity of the Spirit, we need to face life with patience (Eph. 4:2).

This trait is often described as being longsuffering. It means to be willing to suffer long with something that is inconvenient or difficult or even painful. It means to be long-tempered rather than short-tempered. It means to cool your anger rather than adding fuel to the fire.

We need to practice patience with respect to things over which we have no control.

We need to practice patience with respect to people. Sometimes this is exceedingly difficult. To be patient means to bear up under the burdens of life and not to lose courage.

V. To maintain the unity of the Spirit, we must relate to each other in terms of genuine love.

The love referred to here is the God kind of love demonstrated by his giving his only Son to die for us on Calvary. Likewise, Christ demonstrated his love for God and his love for us by being willing to die on the cross. This kind of love toward people is a persistent, unbreakable spirit of goodwill not dependent on the loveliness of the recipients. Its source is the Holy Spirit of God in the heart of believers. The badge of Christian discipleship is the Calvary kind of love (John 13:34–35), and it is the kind of love the world needs today.

VI. If we are to maintain the unity of the Spirit, we must not break the bonds of peace (Eph. 4:3).

Peace is the gift of God that comes to those who put faith in Jesus Christ as Lord and Savior. It is a by-product of right relationships between a believer and God and a believer and those about him or her. The Holy Spirit works within us to keep us always in a right relationship with God and with others. To maintain the unity of the Spirit, we must guard against anything that ruptures proper relationships between ourselves and others.

Conclusion

How wonderful it is for God's children to live in unity! The Holy Spirit creates and maintains that unity, and we the church have the privilege of cooperating with him. Let us make those responses to the Holy Spirit that will maintain this precious, wonderful unity that God wants us to have.

WEDNESDAY EVENING, OCTOBER 4

Title: Forgiveness

Text: "Wherefore I say unto thee, Her sins, which are many, are forgiven; for she loved much: but to whom little is forgiven, the same loveth little" **(Luke 7:47).**

Scripture Reading: Luke 7:41–50; Matthew 18:23–35

Introduction

More than one-third of our Lord's teachings are parables. They comprise 16 percent of the gospel of Mark, 43 percent of Matthew, and 52 percent of Luke. An understanding of these parables is absolutely essential to an understanding of the kind of persons we should be.

The parables of Christ wrestle with real life problems. The first parable recorded by Luke deals with that difficult problem of forgiveness. The word *forgiveness* is used sixty-two times in the Bible. Twenty-two times it refers to our forgiving one another, and the other forty times it refers to God's forgiveness of us. Both of these aspects of forgiveness are dealt with by Christ's parables of the two debtors in Luke 7 and the unmerciful servant in Matthew 18.

I. The liberality with which forgiveness is granted (Luke 7:41–42).

Forgiveness is never stingy. It never says, "Small debts I will forgive but not large ones." Real forgiveness grants pardons indiscriminately, whether the offense is major or minor. In Christ's story one main character was a Pharisee and the other a prostitute, but both were sinners and both were forgiven.

Verse 42 tells us "they had nothing to pay." Both were debtors even if one owed only a tenth of what the other owed. Incapable of paying their debts, they both stood in the same relation to their creditor—bankrupt! This is exactly our relationship to God. One may be a "great" sinner and the other a "moderate" sinner, but all are sinners and as such all are spiritually bankrupt. And the liberality with which forgiveness is granted is extended to all alike. God expects us to forgive others no matter how great or small their offenses.

II. The response that forgiveness evokes (Luke 7:44–47).

Not the relation between forgiveness and salvation, but the relation between forgiveness and love is the main thrust of this story. Christ seems to be saying that there is a direct ratio between how much one is forgiven by God and how much one loves God.

Consciousness of sin and the need of forgiveness has everything to do with our response. The woman who lived a sinful life had an overwhelming sense of guilt and need, but Simon had no such sense of need. Thus, since he considered his need small, he responded with a small measure of love. Doubtless Simon had been forgiven, but his forgiveness had failed to evoke from him a response of love.

The failure of Christians to acknowledge that they are sinners accounts for much of the coldness in the church. This failure prevents them from trusting Christ to forgive much, and thus, "to whom little is forgiven, the same loveth little" (Luke 7:47).

III. The avenue through which forgiveness is obtained (Luke 7:50).

Each of us wants to know how to receive forgiveness. The answer is found in Luke 7:50: "Thy *faith* hath saved thee; go in peace." You simply must trust in God's goodness and in his faithfulness to keep his promise to forgive and impart peace. He who has yet to lose his first star surely will not lose you. He asks only one thing of you as his child—wait on him! Believe and keep on believing God's promises of forgiveness. No matter what happens, no matter what complications may develop, and no matter how adverse the circumstances, keep on believing! When you relax in the assurance that God is honest and will keep his promises of forgiveness, you too will hear your Savior say, "Go in peace."

IV. The obligation that forgiveness imparts (Matt. 18:23–35).

This obligation is clearly spelled out in Matthew 18:33, "Shouldest not thou also have had compassion on thy fellow-servant, even as I had pity on thee?"

It is an obligation you owe yourself. Medical doctors tell us that often the least important factor in an illness may be that part of the body affected, and the most important factor may be emotional tension. Hatred, resentment, guilt, anxiety, and unforgiveness have been identified as some of the most destructive emotions.

When we fail to forgive another, something happens inside us. We may not be able to sleep or digest our food, or we may develop ulcers, headaches, or muscle tension. For your own good, you must forgive. You owe it to yourself!

It is an obligation you owe others. The father confessor asked Narvaez, a Spanish patriot, as he lay dying, if he had forgiven all his enemies. Narvaez replied, "I have no enemies—I shot them all!" That may be one way to deal with your enemies, but the Christian way of forgiveness is far better! Get rid of your enemies by getting rid of the enmity within yourself.

It is an obligation you owe God. Why did Jesus use "ten thousand talents" in this parable? A lesser sum would have served the purpose as well and would have been more within our comprehension. He used this vast sum to illustrate our tremendous obligation to God. Thus, since God, to whom we are so hopelessly in debt, keeps on extending to us the credit of forgiveness, we are obligated to him to forgive others.

Conclusion

In God's sight, how big is your debt—$50, $500, $2,000, or $10 million? It makes no difference to him, for the liberality with which God's forgiveness is granted knows no limit. Realizing there is no way you can ever pay that debt, either in this life or in the life to come, in simple faith believe that God through Christ can and will forgive, and forgiveness is yours today!

SUNDAY MORNING, OCTOBER 8

Title: God on a Campground

Text: "And the Word became flesh and dwelt among us, full of grace and truth; we have beheld his glory, glory as of the only Son from the Father" **(John 1:14 RSV).**

Scripture Reading: John 1:1–14

Hymns: "Crown Him with Many Crowns," Bridges
"Glorious Is Thy Name," McKinney
"I've Found a Friend," Small

Offertory Prayer: Father, we know you desire not our possessions but ourselves. Nevertheless, we know we cannot bring ourselves to you without including our possessions. So now we pray that we may worship in truth as we bring a portion of that which is already yours. We pray that you will be so real in our lives that the portion we use for physical sustenance will be as spiritual as the part we place in the offering today. In Jesus' name. Amen.

Introduction

Mike, an eight-year-old, attended church services with his grandmother. He wouldn't leave the church until he shook hands with me. One Sunday he said, "Pastor, I would like to talk with you."

I said, "Fine, Mike, when would you like to talk with me?" His grandmother tried to rush him on, insisting that the pastor was busy. I said, "Mike, do you want to see me today or at some later time?"

He answered, "I would like to see you today."

His grandmother apologized, but I explained that if Mike wanted to talk with me, this was as important as anything else for the day.

I asked, "Do you want to talk with me here in the corridor, Mike, or would you like to go up to my office?"

Mike said that he would like to go up to the office. When we got to the outer office, Mike said, "Pastor, I would like to talk with you privately." With some embarrassment, the grandmother took a seat in the outer office.

When we got inside my private office, Mike said, "Pastor, I want to ask you a question."

I said, "Don't make it too hard."

Mike did. He said, "Was God born, or was he always?"

How do you answer this question for an eight-year-old, or for anyone else for that matter? I began discussing the birth of Jesus.

Mike said, "I know about the baby Jesus, but I want to know was God born or was he always?"

In the conversation, I learned that Mike really wanted to be sure that he belonged to Jesus. There were two significant spinoffs from the conversation: both of his parents came into the church also.

I will discuss Mike's question this morning, looking at three things in our passage: (1) Christ before he was born; (2) Christ on a campground; and (3) Christ in us. It will be helpful if you keep the Scripture passage before you.

Suppose a child—or an adult—came to you with his Bible open at John 1 and asked, "What does it mean when it says, 'In the beginning was the Word'?" Of course you would say, "That means Jesus." But why would Jesus be called "the Word"?

What is a word? A word is a means of communication. It is defined in the dictionary as a representation or symbol that communicates a meaning. There were some additional meanings for the philosophers in John's day as there are today. One of the reasons Jesus is called "the Word" is that he came to speak for God. In the book of Revelation, he said, "I am the Alpha and the Omega." Alpha is the first letter of the Greek alphabet, and omega is the last. Alphabets are used to form words. So Jesus was saying in essence that he was God's alphabet. The first two verses of the book of Hebrews convey the same idea: "In the past God spoke to our ancestors through the prophets at many times and in various ways, but in these last days he has spoken to us by his Son" (NIV).

I. Christ before he was born.

There is a sense in which the message in this passage is even older than the Old Testament. The book of Genesis begins with the creation of the world, but the gospel of John begins with God before the world began. John is saying that Jesus lived before he was born. In fact, he took part in Creation. Before the world was created, the Word already existed.

We are also reminded in this passage that the Word was always with God. The word used here indicates separate but equal personalities. It means they were not only together but they also saw things eye to eye. Some Bible teachers have implied that Jesus came to patch things up for God. This passages declares that Jesus came to make God known.

Further, our text declares that "the Word was God." When Jesus walked among people, God was walking among them. Our passage says not only that Jesus lived before he was born, but also that he participated in bringing the world into being. Jesus is more than a man, even an unusual and good man. He is God.

A medical doctor in Taiwan said to me, "I couldn't understand how somebody dying for me two thousand years ago could get rid of my sins until I learned that the one who died for me was God. Since he never sinned, his death could atone for my sins."

II. Christ on a campground.

My wife and I spend a lot of time living in a motor home. My work takes me to a lot of different places, and we have found that a motor home is a convenient and practical way to live. Most of the time we are parked on some church parking lot where we happen to be working. Sometimes while en route we stop at a state park or other campground. In either case, the campground is a temporary dwelling place.

John 1:14 says, "The Word became flesh and dwelt among us." The word used here is similar to our word *tent* or *tabernacle*. It means that Jesus left heaven and came to this world to live here temporarily. God went "camping" so that we might have a permanent home. We call this the incarnation. Scripture says that God became flesh and pitched his tent with us and became one of us. Why? It was the only way we could know and understand God.

I recall a story about a man who loved birds and enjoyed watching them. A friend said to him one day, "As much time as you spend watching birds, it seems that they would know now that you would not harm them. Why do they fly away as you approach them?"

His response was that the only way the birds could trust him would be for him to speak their language, and the only way he could speak their language would be to become one of them. That is exactly what God did. The Word came to this world to speak our language.

III. Christ in our lives.

Paul wrote to the Colossians, "God has chosen to make known among the Gentiles the glorious riches of this mystery, which is Christ in you, the hope of glory" (Col. 1:27 NIV). God's Son lived before the world began and long before he was born to Mary as Jesus of Nazareth. He came and lived in this world for more than thirty years. Before he left, he assured his disciples that he would continue to be with them and in them in the person of the Holy Spirit. We enjoy this privilege today.

Several years ago I awakened in the early morning hours thinking about some exceedingly pressing problems. To be sure I would not forget any of them, I turned on the light and wrote down a number of things that needed my urgent attention. My anxiety intensified during the next hour, and I soon saw that I was not about to sleep anymore.

Suddenly I remembered a passage of Scripture. Jesus was speaking: "Behold, I stand at the door, and knock; if any one hears my voice, and open the door, I will come in to him, and will sup with him, and he with me" (Rev. 3:20). The message of the passage was so clear that it was as if Jesus were actually speaking to me right there in the darkness. It occurred to me that the Holy Spirit was bringing this to my memory in order to say to me, "I know everything you have written on that piece of paper. I know it is too much for you, but it is not too much for me. I am knocking on your door to say to you that if you will open the door and let me come in, I will spend the day with you and lift those loads, guide you through those decisions, and do for you what you cannot do for yourself."

I took the Lord at his word (I have not always done so) and went back to sleep. At about the usual time, I awoke refreshed and immediately remembered the Lord's promise. I prayed for reassurance and began the day trusting Jesus. I have learned from that experience that the greatest need among those who have trusted Jesus is that they do trust him. The victories of that day still live in the lives of several different people.

Conclusion

When you receive Christ as Savior, he comes into your life. He desires to live in you to make you the person you are meant to be. Is the Lord knocking on your door? The latch is on your side. He will not force his way in. Your feeling of need and the desire to let him come in is his Spirit knocking on the door. He may have been waiting there a long time. Are you going to keep him waiting? Why not open the door right now and let him come in?

SUNDAY EVENING, OCTOBER 8

Title: Do Not Grieve the Holy Spirit

Text: "And do not grieve the Holy Spirit of God, in whom you were sealed for the day of redemption" **(Eph. 4:30 RSV)**.

Scripture Reading: Ephesians 4:22–5:2

Introduction

We look at another of the great imperatives with regard to our personal response to the Holy Spirit found in Paul's epistle to the Ephesians. Paul was encouraging the believers who lived in the city of Ephesus to make a proper response to God's presence in their hearts. He described this response in terms of a walk. They were to walk worthily (4:1–16), differently (4:17–24), in love (4:25–5:2), in the light (5:3–14), and carefully, or in wisdom (5:15–20).

These recent converts continued to have areas in their lives that needed to experience the redemption of Christ Jesus. To experience this full redemption, Paul urged them to make a positive response to the indwelling Spirit. In our text, he urged them to "bring to an end those practices which grieve the Holy Spirit." He emphasized that the Holy Spirit had come to dwell within them to make saints out of sinners. The Holy Spirit was eager to Christianize their disposition as well as bring their souls into a secure relationship with God.

I. The Holy Spirit is a person.

The Holy Spirit can be grieved. Only a person can experience grief. The Holy Spirit is not an "it." The Holy Spirit is more than a power or an influence. The Holy Spirit is the divine person who has come to dwell within the heart of each believer.

That the Holy Spirit is a person is indicated by the use of the personal masculine pronoun in many references to him. He is described as having a will and as giving gifts to equip believers for service. The Holy Spirit is the spiritual presence of Jesus Christ who comes to dwell in believers.

II. The Holy Spirit dwells within and is to be treated as a person.

It is at this point that we see the tenderness of the heart of our God who has come to dwell within us. Paul said that we must avoid offending, distressing, hurting, and grieving the Holy Spirit of God by neglecting to make any response or by making an improper response to God's work in us.

We need to recognize and respond to the indwelling Holy Spirit.

We need to accept by faith the gift of the Holy Spirit and recognize that he has already arrived within us to do God's work. He comes not as a reward for performance but as a gift of God through faith (Gal. 3:5).

We need to respond to the Holy Spirit with trust. We need to put confidence in him. The divine purposes toward us are benevolent and redemptive.

We need to cooperate with the Holy Spirit as he seeks to accomplish God's purpose within us. Only as we make a positive and continuous response to the Holy Spirit of God can we avoid bringing grief and sorrow to the divine heart.

III. Conditions that grieve the Holy Spirit and responses that please him.

By studying the context, we can discover the conditions, attitudes, and activities that bring grief to the Holy Spirit.

If we would avoid grieving the Holy Spirit, and if we would please him, we must replace falsehood with absolute honesty (Eph. 4:25). The recent converts to whom Paul wrote needed to be encouraged to follow a policy of being honest rather than dishonest. If we would please the Holy Spirit, we must be honest, dependable, reliable people. We bring grief to him when we tolerate dishonesty and falsehood in our lives.

If we would avoid grieving the Holy Spirit, and if we would please him, we need to control anger (Eph. 4:26). There is a time and a place when anger is appropriate. There is a time when the mind should revolt against that which is dishonest, unjust, and evil. Anger is an attitude of displeasure against evil. However, anger is a very dangerous emotion. When we allow it to control us, we give the devil an opportunity to do harm in us and through us to others. Paul was suggesting that if we ever get hot about something, we need to cool off and control our anger. We must avoid pouring fuel on the fire of anger, recognizing that it can lead to hate and murder.

If we would avoid grieving the Holy Spirit, and if we would please him, we must cease being parasites and thieves and become producers and givers (Eph. 4:28). Some recent Ephesian converts had come from a pagan and evil way of life and had made their living at the expense of others. They were parasites rather than producers. They were out to get rather than to give. They saw themselves as reservoirs rather than channels. Paul says that the Holy Spirit is pleased when a person is a worker and becomes a producer and a giver, a contributor and a helper.

If we would avoid grieving the Holy Spirit, and if we would please him, we must cut off all evil talk and communicate constructively (Eph. 4:29). Literally, we are to "put to silence all evil talk." We are to cut off all filthy conversations and avoid that which is destructive, hurtful, and slanderous. We grieve the Holy Spirit when we do not control our thoughts and our conversation.

If we would avoid grieving the Holy Spirit, and if we would please him, we must cooperate with him in the matter of converting a bad disposition (Eph. 4:31–32). The focus here is on sins of attitude that lead to sins of action.

The Holy Spirit is eager to redeem our emotional life and to so affect our feelings that we will relate to others in terms of kindness, tenderheartedness, and forgiveness rather than living with an attitude of bitterness, wrath, anger, and slander concerning others. The Holy Spirit is not pleased when we harbor bitterness and hate. He experiences sorrow when we shout at one another and use abusive language. The Holy Spirit wants us to be helpful and merciful and great-hearted as we seek to establish harmonious relationships with others.

The Holy Spirit would enable us to become instruments of God's grace and mercy, love and power. God has given the Holy Spirit to each believer so that the Holy Spirit might assist us in our pilgrimage toward becoming Christlike. If we tolerate sins of the flesh or sins of the spirit, attitude, or disposition, we bring grief to the Holy Spirit.

Conclusion

The words of our text challenge us to bring to a halt any attitude, ambition, action, or appearance that brings sorrow to the heart of the precious Holy Spirit who wants to reproduce within us the beauty of Jesus Christ. It is our individual responsibility to quit grieving the Holy Spirit and to bring joy to the heart of our Father God.

WEDNESDAY EVENING, OCTOBER 11

Title: Rejected Love

Text: "And have ye not read this scripture; The stone which the builders rejected is become the head of the corner" (**Mark 12:10**).

Scripture Reading: Mark 12:1–12

Introduction

If we would survey all of Jesus' parables, we would see something remarkable. All of the parables that deal with nature, such as the lilies of the field, the birds of the air, and the shepherd and his sheep, speak of peace, safety, and order. But whenever humans are in the center—no matter whether it be the unmerciful servant, the unjust judge, the rich man, or another—there is always an element of dramatic tension, conflict, doom, and/or disaster.

And so it is in this parable of rejected love. Here Christ does not appear in the attitude of blessing, nor as a kind shepherd with warmth and security. This is the story of a conflict between God and man. It is like a drama divided into individual acts. And the main scenes in the drama are indicated by a series of woodcut-like pictures through which runs the theme of rejected love.

I. The goodness of God (v. 1).

He provides our needs. The vineyard was deliberately planted on a fertile hillside. It was not a child of chance. It was an expression of the goodness of the owner. Every provision had been made for the renters to have a comfortable and profitable enterprise. Jesus was saying, "God is like that." He has provided lavishly for all our needs.

He grants our freedom. The renters were treated as free men. They could operate the vineyard as they pleased. The only requirement was payment for the use of the vineyard. Such freedom is an expression of God's love. You are free to spit in God's face or to live each day as a trustworthy steward of your Master's blessings.

He reveals his character. This parable reveals that God is generous, trusting, and patient. All the goodness should have evoked a gracious and thankful response. But instead, notice the following:

II. The ingratitude of man (vv. 2–5).

The immediate point that Christ was making is that God planted Israel as his "garden." He hedged and protected it. He sent his servants, or messengers, to it. But like these ungrateful renters, Israel rejected and abused God's messengers. The vinedressers were ingrates in the face of all their master had done for them. And as such they portray the ingratitude of people who reject God's love.

The owner keeps on sending messengers beyond the point of all reason, but the exaggeration in this story is deliberate, for the purpose is to illustrate the incomprehensible love of God for people regardless of their ingratitude. This parable of God's rejected love tells us not only of God's goodness and humankind's ingratitude, but also of the following:

III. The gift of the Son (vv. 6–8).

When servant after servant was driven away, beaten, or killed, the owner reasoned, "Surely they will honor my only son and accept the claims he makes on them." And so "he sent him also last unto them."

What was the response of those renters? They rejected the son and his claims, and they killed him, reasoning that then all would be theirs. Could we be guilty of this same offense? Could we too be caught up in the spirit of a materialistic society?

And what is this materialism that rejects the gift of the Son? It is the belief that humans can find emotional fulfillment in things. If you are bored, go buy something. Are you guilty? Give a gift or flowers to make amends. Are you insecure? Put better locks on your doors or perhaps purchase a gun. So reasons the materialist.

Christianity is not an antimaterialistic religion. C. S. Lewis said that God must love material things since he made so many of them. But preoccupation with things is wrong. The materialist, Christian or non-Christian, is guilty of rejecting God's love by rejecting the gift of his Son. Like the farmers in Christ's story, the materialist says, "If the Son comes into my life making claims on my vineyard, then I too will cast him out of the vineyard, that I might be lord of all."

IV. The gravity of sin (v. 9).

Christ used this story to stress that we take sin too lightly. God does not! Anytime we reject and replace Christ with our puny selves and seek to own and control our lives and destinies, God considers it a grave matter! And this is exactly what the farmers were doing. They claimed everything as their own. When this is our attitude, the gravity of our sin moves God to discipline us as the owner disciplined his renters by giving the vineyard to others.

V. The guilt of the offenders (vv. 10–12).

Christ is saying that Israel is guilty of rejecting God's love by rejecting God's Son. Christ is either the foundation stone on which you build your life or the stumbling block over which you fall and destroy yourself. But how did the renters' guilt affect them? And how does our guilt affect us?

Guilt caused them to reject Christ (v. 10). They had a choice to make. Either get rid of the son or get rid of their guilt by accepting him and his claims. But the problem is that when we get rid of the Son by excluding him from our lives, we don't really get rid of our guilt—we only compound it.

Guilt convicted them of their sin (v. 12). "They knew that he had spoken the parable against them." No one needs to tell you when you have done wrong or when God has spoken to you. You know it, for guilt convicts of sin.

Guilt drove them from Christ (v. 12). Guilt will either draw you to Christ or drive you from him. It all depends on how you have handled your guilt. God never intends for guilt to be destructive, but rather redemptive.

Conclusion

How will you respond to Christ? Will you accept his love and his claims on your life, or will you be like the ungrateful tenants who rejected and killed the son? As the parable makes evident, the penalty for rejecting God's Son is eternal damnation. Receive him today so that you might live an abundant life here and in eternity.

SUNDAY MORNING, OCTOBER 15

Title: People Need Help

Text: "And a leper came to him beseeching him, and kneeling said to him, 'If you will, you can make me clean.' Moved with pity, he stretched out his hand and touched him, and said to him, 'I will; be clean.' And immediately the leprosy left him, and he was made clean" **(Mark 1:40–42 RSV)**.

Scripture Reading: Philippians 4:13, 19

Hymns: "Guide Me, O Thou Great Jehovah," Williams
"O for a Thousand Tongues," Wesley
"Make Me a Blessing," Wilson

Offertory Prayer: Our Father, we pray this morning that your name may be honored and your kingdom a reality in our lives as we worship in giving. We thank you for meeting our needs of daily bread, deliverance from temptation, and forgiveness of sin. Be especially near to any with special needs today. Bless both the givers and recipients of these gifts. In Jesus' name. Amen.

Introduction

People need help, and our Lord is in the help-giving business. Jesus explained his coming into the world by saying, "I have come that they may have life, and have it abundantly." He said he came not to be ministered to but to minister. People everywhere need Jesus. I need him, my family needs him, and you need him.

Several months ago I spoke to a meeting of pastors and other religious leaders. Following the meeting, a pastor came to me and said, "I want to talk to you." He began to tell me about his teenage daughter. She was away from home, in the streets, involved in narcotics and drinking. He asked, "Will you pray for her?" As a parent, I could easily identify. I said, "Let's pray right now."

We went to a quiet spot where we could have privacy. We prayed that God would forgive us as parents, and we prayed for the girl. About four months later, we were opening an evangelism conference in another city about two hundred miles away. Just before the session was to begin, I felt a tap on my shoulder. Turning around, I recognized that pastor. He pointed to the young lady by his side and said, "I want you to meet the answer to your prayer." People everywhere need the Lord.

I. Some people need the Lord and don't know it.

Five years ago we knew our son-in-law was in the hospital in a distant city for what we supposed was minor surgery. During the day, our daughter called and said, "Lon has cancer." Over and over we thank God for what he has done for Lon and the family throughout this experience. But you know he probably had cancer for a long time, and it perhaps would have been better if he could have had the surgery earlier. He had cancer and didn't know it. Many people need the Lord and are totally unaware of it.

A deacon friend and I were out making evangelistic calls one evening. We were in a new subdivision, and the only information we had was a list of names we had gotten from the utilities company. So we visited Catholics, Methodists, Baptists, and a few who admitted they did not know the Lord. Finally, we had called on every name we had but one. We couldn't even find the street. I had given up when the deacon said, "Let's make one more circle down this street that doesn't have a name on it. There is one house about midway." As we drove in front of the house, a young man and young woman were standing in front looking at the new house. You could just see as they stood there, arm in arm, that they were enjoying that wonderful moment of looking at their first new house. The deacon stuck his head out the window and said, "We are looking for such and such a street." The fellow said, "Who are you looking for?" When the deacon told him, the young fellow said, "You are looking at him."

We got out of the car, and they invited us inside the house. The young man had grown up in a Baptist home, and the young woman said hers was Catholic. Within thirty minutes, both of these young people had trusted Jesus as their Savior. As we left, she said, "Isn't it marvelous? Less than an hour ago we were standing there in the front yard thinking we had everything in the world. Now we have found something that we needed more than anything else in the world."

Saul of Tarsus gave every indication of having everything he needed religiously, politically, educationally, and in every other way, but one day he discovered his greatest need had not been met.

II. Some people need the Lord and are only subconsciously aware of it.

Nicodemus gave no outward evidence of having any religious needs. He was a religious leader and was well educated and politically oriented. He was the kind of person who would seem to have just about everything. He came to Jesus one night to say something like, "You have impressed me, young man. I know you have not gone to the theological seminary, and your background in Galilee is not outstanding. However, I would have to say that God must be in what you are doing or you couldn't do these great things."

It is likely that the real issue that brought him to Jesus was the tugging he had felt in his own soul as he had heard about or watched Jesus in his ministry. Many people need the Lord and are only subconsciously aware of it. They are all around us: in our homes, schools, and workplaces. About 90 percent of them are "church-connected." They are poor connections, and some of them have even blown a fuse, but we must not pass them by because they are not classified as "church prospects."

Some people are only subconsciously aware that they need the Lord; they have never been exposed to his message enough to feel conviction. They know something is wrong and need help in identifying it. I shall never forget the young medical doctor in Taiwan who told me, "Always I knew there was something wrong inside me. Before I ever heard of Jesus or read a Bible, I knew I had some need." He thanked me for helping him see that sin was his problem and that Jesus could meet the need.

Some people are at least subconsciously aware that they need the Lord but do not know how to find him because once they were closer to him and they do not know how to find their way back. A man said to me on the citizens' band radio, "I used to modulate with Jesus, but I guess I have been off the channel lately." Jesus is interested in helping people find their way back to the Lord.

III. Some people need help and never expect to find it.

Zacchaeus, I am sure, was this kind of person. He was a crooked businessman and corrupt politician. He probably had not started out that way. He just wanted to provide well for his family with maybe a hope of getting things straightened out later on. He likely felt that he had reached the point of no return. He was despised by his own people and was not respected by those for whom he worked. He had been intrigued by what he had seen and heard of Jesus, but certainly no religious leader would have anything to do with him. He had enough sense of need to want to see this exciting, revolutionary, young teacher, but not enough self-respect to believe he could be helped. Demonstrating more curiosity than pride, he climbed up in a tree to see Jesus. The important thing is that Jesus saw him.

The Samaritan woman never expected help—and certainly not from a Jewish religious leader. We do not know her past life, but we have no reason to doubt that she started out with high ambitions and good intentions. Her first marriage could have been a model marriage, the kind about which every parent in the community would say, "They seem exactly suited for each other." For some reason the marriage failed, and another, and another, until finally she had been married five times.

You can understand why she would now say, "What's the use? What is the value of a piece of paper? Why go and stand in front of a preacher? I have blown my life in the eyes of the religious leaders." She was now living with a man to whom she was not married, and every encounter was defensive and protective. She didn't expect help because she did not know about Jesus.

IV. Some people need help and sincerely seek it.

A woman was making a "people search" by telephone. The purpose was to gather names for future church visits. A young man answered the phone in response to one of her calls and began to pour out to her how bad the world was and especially how badly it had treated him. He told about his drug and alcohol abuse and of how he had considered suicide. As he poured out his soul, she thought of a Christian coach who could help the young man. She also thought of calling the pastor. But do you know what she did? She invited the young man to come to her house. As a result, she led him to know Jesus as his Savior and Lord.

Two weeks later, my wife and I were leading a lay evangelism school in the Baton Rouge church where this woman was a member and this young man had just joined. During the school, this young man witnessed to a sixty-year-old man and his son. They both, by the testimony of this young man, invited the Lord into their lives.

Conclusion

Will you bring your needs to the Lord right now? Do you have friends who need Jesus? Jesus says, "Come to me, all who labor and are heavy laden, and I will give you rest" (Matt. 11:28 RSV).

SUNDAY EVENING, OCTOBER 15

Title: The Command to Be Filled with the Holy Spirit

Text: "And do not get drunk with wine, for that is debauchery; but be filled with the Spirit" **(Eph. 5:18 RSV)**.

Scripture Reading: Acts 4:31–33

Introduction

The Spirit-filled life is the plan of God for each of his children. It is only when a child of God lives under the control of the Holy Spirit that he or she is able to produce the fruit of the Spirit and labor in the power of the Spirit. To better understand this thrilling truth, we need to be aware of several great assumptions.

Every sincere baptized believer has received the gift of the Holy Spirit (Acts 2:38).

Every believer has been baptized into the body of Christ by the Holy Spirit (1 Cor. 12:13).

Every believer has received the seal of the Holy Spirit, which indicates God's ownership and identifies us as the children of God (Eph. 1:13).

Every believer is commanded to be continuously filled with the Holy Spirit (Eph. 5:18).

From before his birth, John the Baptist was declared to be one who would be filled with the Spirit (Luke 1:15). Elizabeth, the mother of John the Baptist, was filled with the Spirit (v. 41). Our Lord was filled with the Holy Spirit continuously (4:1). The 120 in the upper room were filled with the Spirit on the day of Pentecost (Acts 2:3–4). Peter was filled with the Holy Spirit (4:8). The early church experienced the fullness of the Holy Spirit as they gave themselves to prayer (4:31). The first deacons in the early church were to be men "full of the Spirit" (6:3). Stephen labored in the fullness of the power of the Holy Spirit (6:8). Paul wrote this tremendous letter to the Ephesian church, commanding them to be filled with the Spirit.

There was a religious group in the city of Ephesus known as the cult of Dionysius who believed that deliverance or salvation was to be found through the use of alcohol. They sought to escape depression, disappointment, grief, failure, monotony, and drabness through an artificial "life for the spirit." They believed that salvation came through escape and flight. They have many descendants in the present who are seeking to solve the problems of life through intoxication.

Paul said to seek for the power to live life through the Holy Spirit.

I. This is an all-inclusive command, "Be filled with the Spirit."

The Spirit-filled life is not just for a select few.

The Spirit-filled life was not limited to the apostles or to the clergy.

The Spirit-filled life is for all believers.

Each believer has the responsibility to experience fullness of the Holy Spirit.

II. The command to be filled with the Spirit contains a promise or provision.

When God issues a command, the fulfillment of that command is always possible. If it were impossible for us to live the Spirit-filled life, he would not have commanded us to do so.

To be filled with the Spirit enables one to walk in wisdom rather than in foolishness (Eph. 5:15). All of us want to walk in wisdom. The Holy Spirit will give us surefootedness as we walk through a dangerous world.

To be filled with the Spirit is to recognize and see spiritual opportunities (Eph. 5:15). To be filled with the Spirit enables one to recognize open doors of opportunity for spiritual service and makes one sensitive to the heart hungers of others.

To be filled with the Spirit is to understand and to find the will of God (Eph. 5:17). If you would discover and do God's will, let the Holy Spirit be your leader.

To be filled with the Spirit is to experience an inward joy that issues in praise to God (Eph. 5:19). The Spirit-filled life is a joy-filled life. It is joy in the Lord rather than the superficial happiness that comes as a result of happenings.

To be filled with the Spirit is to be grateful and thankful (Eph. 5:20). A Spirit-filled person is never a negative, critical, fault-finding person. The Holy Spirit enables one to have a positive mental attitude in all of the circumstances that come in life.

To be filled with the Spirit is to be mutually helpful to each other (Eph. 5:21). It is God's will that we build each other up and adjust to each other in a creative relationship. This is made possible by the fullness of the Holy Spirit.

III. What is the filling of the Holy Spirit?

We are not empty containers, and the Holy Spirit is not a substance like water or gravel or sand. The Holy Spirit is a divine person. And to be full of the Spirit means to be controlled by the Spirit. He is the coach who calls the plays, and we are the players who play the game. We are the instruments, but he is the instrumentalist. We are the tools, and he is the craftsman.

To be filled with the Spirit is to be empowered by the Spirit (Acts 1:8).

To be filled with the Spirit is to be taught by the Spirit (John 14:26).

To be filled with the Spirit is to be guided by the Spirit (John 16:13).

To be filled with the Spirit is to reap the harvest of the Spirit (Gal. 5:22–23).

To be filled with the Spirit is to properly use the gifts of the Holy Spirit (1 Cor. 12–14).

IV. How can we experience the Spirit-filled life?

We are to accept the fullness of the Spirit by faith (Gal. 3:14). The response we make to receiving Jesus Christ as Lord and Savior is the same response we make to the Holy Spirit. The fullness of the Spirit does not come to us as some kind of a reward for spiritual excellence. The fullness of the Spirit does not come as a result of a long program of self-denial and self-discipline. One can do these things and not experiencing the fullness of the Spirit.

To experience the fullness of the Spirit, we need to present our bodies to the Lord as living sacrifices (Rom. 12:1–2). We are to recognize and respond fully to the truth that the Holy Spirit has come to dwell within these bodies in which we live. We are to present them as holy dwelling places—wholly given over to the purposes of God for our lives.

If we would maintain the fullness of the Spirit, we need to confess and forsake every sin the Holy Spirit reveals to us. As time goes by, the Holy Spirit will give us spiritual x-ray images of our motives and actions, revealing to us those facets or characteristics that are not acceptable to the Father God. As we "agree with God," we will experience cleansing and forgiveness and a deeper understanding of the nature and purpose of God.

The Spirit-filled life is a life in which we deliberately abide in God's will and let him fill us with his fullness and use us for his glory (1 John 3:24).

Conclusion

The fullness of the Spirit within us may be lost if we fail to nurture our spiritual lives. The fullness of the Spirit may be regained as we exercise faith, yield ourselves joyfully to God's purposes, and let him accomplish his will through us.

It is God's will that you not only be saved but that you also be filled with the Spirit. Not to be filled with the Spirit is a sin against God, yourself, and others. The Spirit-filled life is a part of your birthright as a child of God. It is your privilege and responsibility to be filled with the Spirit.

WEDNESDAY EVENING, OCTOBER 18

Title: The Four Who Were Lost

Text: "I say unto you, that likewise joy shall be in heaven over one sinner that repenteth, more than over ninety and nine just persons, which need no repentance" **(Luke 15:7).**

Scripture Reading: Luke 15

Introduction

One of the most cherished chapters of the Bible is Luke 15. I like the way it begins: "Then drew near unto him all the publicans and sinners for to hear him." Much is said about Christ in those words. They mean that those who failed realized that in Christ they would find help instead of condemnation. The publicans and sinners found that he was "a friend of sinners," that he liked to eat with them, and that he gave most of his time to them.

Jesus had hard words for self-righteous people, but he always spoke kindly to those who had missed the way. In fact, the word *sinner* was seldom on his lips. He thought of them as "lost." So when the people "murmured" because he received sinners, he told them four stories. In these stories we see four ways of getting lost, four consequences of being lost, and a fourfold quest for the lost.

I. Four ways of getting lost.

Lost through heedlessness—the sheep (v. 4). The one sheep that was lost was not a bad sheep. He was perhaps no worse than the rest of the flock. His love for the shepherd was as great as any other member of the fold.

He just kept drifting away from the flock in quest for better grass and greener pastures. Then when darkness fell, he realized he was all alone. Through failing to give heed to the shepherd's call, this sheep got lost.

And this is the way many people get lost. Busy with the pressing affairs of life, they gradually drift from God, his church, and his people. Then in the darkness of some tragic hour they discover they are all alone—all because of heedlessness!

Lost through idleness—the coin (v. 8). The coin was the same coin before and after it was lost. That which was silver did not turn to brass. And being lost does not mean that a person has no value or character.

The coin was out of circulation and thus "lost." The coin may represent service. When we remove our lives from service to God, we are out of circulation and thus lost.

Lost through willfulness—the prodigal (vv. 12–13). This younger son was lost because he willed to be lost. He was basically a good son, but he chafed under the rules and expectations of home. He thought only of the moment, ignored his duty to family and society, and deliberately took off on his own. In an effort to prove and exercise his "freedom," he became a slave to sin and a slave to a strange man in a distant land. He was lost through his own willfulness.

Lost through haughtiness—the elder brother (vv. 25–26). This conscientious and honest young man stayed at home and still got lost. He was lost through pride and haughtiness. Being satisfied with himself, he became intolerant toward others and lost to the purpose of his father.

It has been said that if the prodigal had seen his brother before he saw his father, he might have returned to the pigpen! I wonder how your lifestyle and attitude affects others. Does it attract people to Christ or drive them away?

II. Four consequences of being lost.

The consequence of helpless distress—the sheep (v. 4). The sheep was lost not because it had been destroyed. It was very much alive. It was lost because it had wandered away from the shepherd and the flock and now found itself in a state of helpless distress.

The aimless multitudes with no sense of purpose in life, no laws to follow, and no God to worship, suffer the same consequences of helpless distress.

The consequence of uselessness—the coin (v. 8). The lost coin still had its value, and it still had the image of the emperor stamped on it, but because it was lost, it was useless. Although the coin was still the property of its owner, it was of no value.

If you have lost touch with God, you have not lost your value, but you are useless to him and his service.

The consequence of degradation—the prodigal (v. 16). The clean-cut, well-dressed young man was now living in filth and poverty and was clothed in rags. Friends, wealth, self-respect, and virtue were now all gone. This is the consequence of willfully choosing to leave the Father. Degradation awaits each one who decides to walk away from God.

The consequence of joylessness—the elder brother (vv. 28–30). Whatever else may be said about this son, he was not a happy person! The consequence of his sin of haughtiness was joylessness.

III. A fourfold quest for the lost.

The quest of Christ (vv. 5–7). Surely with ninety-nine sheep in the fold a shepherd would be both content and thankful. But not Christ. If one sheep is lost from the fold, he will search "until" he finds it. And when he finds the lost sheep, he will not beat or upbraid it. He will lovingly lift it to his shoulders and carry it to the safety of the fold.

The quest of the Holy Spirit (v. 8). The Holy Spirit sweeps through our lives, removing the dirt of sin until we find ourselves like bright and precious coins restored to useful service.

The quest of the heavenly Father (vv. 20, 28). The Father always takes the initiative. "We love him because he first loved us." And "God so loved the world, that he [taking the initiative] gave his only begotten Son."

The quest of the church (Luke 14:23). "As my Father hath sent me, even so send I you," Christ said (John 20:21). Just as Christ was sent on a quest for souls, so are we sent.

Conclusion

However you may be lost—through heedlessness, idleness, willfulness, or haughtiness, you can be assured that there is a Father in heaven who loves you, a Savior who died for you, and a Holy Spirit who seeks to bring you into the fold of safety.

SUNDAY MORNING, OCTOBER 22

Title: How to Get Help

Text: "The man believed the word that Jesus spoke to him and went his way" **(John 4:50).**

Scripture Reading: John 4:46–53

Hymns: "A Mighty Fortress," Luther
"Have Faith in God," McKinney
"Christ Receiveth Sinful Men," Neumeister

Offertory Prayer: Lord, we come to you with thanksgiving because you have heard our prayers and met our needs. We thank you that you meet all our needs according to your riches in glory by Christ Jesus. We therefore bring ourselves to you as we bring our tithes and offerings, through Jesus Christ our Lord. Amen.

Introduction

During his lifetime, Jesus worked with all kinds of people and met many different kinds of needs. Sometimes he worked with the very poor and deprived, and it is easy to get the impression that this was almost exclusively true, but a careful study of the Gospels will reveal the contrary. We need only to be reminded that Nicodemus, Zacchaeus, Lazarus, and the rich young ruler were all privileged people in their day. You see, all kinds of people need Jesus. All of us always need him for the forgiveness of our sins and the daily direction of our lives. The man we have just read about was a Roman official, possibly of blood relation to royalty.

The moving story we have read is dramatic and exciting. As the curtain is raised, Jesus is coming into Cana of Galilee, where he earlier had turned water into wine. The scene then changes to Capernaum, where this official sits by the bedside of his sick son. Word has likely gone from Cana to Capernaum about Jesus performing the wedding miracle of turning water into wine. Perhaps also word has come up from Jerusalem about the miracles he recently performed there. People all over Galilee are excited about Jesus' return.

Every parent here can identify with the father of a sick child who needs help. This morning I want us to look for four things in the story: (1) the man knew he needed help, (2) the man came to Jesus for help, (3) the man took Jesus at his word, and (4) the man found out Jesus had already met his need.

I. The man knew he needed help.

Do you recognize a need in your life that you have not been able to meet? If so, you have already taken the first step in finding help. Maybe you have a child with a physical, mental, or spiritual need. I am thinking of a father whose adult daughter has serious needs in all three areas. For you it may be the need of some other family member, or it may be your own personal need, but whatever the need, the first step in finding help is recognition of the need. Certainly if the need is spiritual, you cannot receive help from Jesus until you know you need it, for Jesus does not force himself on us. But if we know we need him, his help is available.

Since forgiveness of sin is a universal need, suppose we use that as an example. If there are other needs, they will be met by the same general conditions. If you say to me, "I have not sinned," I must say to you that there is no help for you in your sins. If you say to me, "I have sinned and need forgiveness and cleansing," I am happy to say to you that help is readily available. "If we confess our sins, he is faithful and just, and will forgive our sins and cleanse us from all unrighteousness" (1 John 1:9).

The Bible is clear in saying that we all have sinned. You may open your Bible almost at random and find a reminder wherever you read. Not only do we begin with the story of the sin of Adam and Eve, but sin shows up in the lives of such spiritual giants as Abraham, Sarah, Samuel, David, and all the rest. Read the Ten Commandments and you will find a reminder of your own failure. We then have those clear-cut passages like, "All have sinned, and come short of the glory of God" (Rom. 3:23); "All we like sheep have gone astray; we have turned every one to his own way" (Isa. 53:6); and "There is none that doeth good, no, not one" (Rom. 3:12). We may not sin as much as some other person, but all of us have sinned, and if we have sinned at all, we need Jesus because "there is none other name under heaven given among men, whereby we must be saved" (Acts 4:12).

The closer you come to God, the more you recognize your sin. Isaiah tells of a vision he had of God in the temple. When Isaiah came face-to-face with God's glory, holiness, and power, he saw himself as a sinner. If you are conscious of the words of the songs you sing in worship, you are reminded of your sin. If you listen to the preacher or Sunday school teacher, you are reminded of your sin. Just to be reminded of God is to be reminded of sin. A young man recently confessed, "I thought I was a pretty nice guy until I started attending services with my family. The more I came, the more I realized I was not a good guy, but in reality a bad guy."

The Holy Spirit convinces you of sin even if you have never seen a Bible or heard a sermon. A man who was brought up in the Buddhist faith told me, "Always I knew there was something wrong inside, even before I ever saw a Bible or heard of Jesus." Of the Holy Spirit, Jesus said, "When he is come, he will reprove the world of sin, and of righteousness, and of judgment" (John 16:8).

What do you do about the sin in your life? You really can't do anything about it yourself. You can no more get rid of your sin by your own determination and effort than you can perform a heart transplant on yourself. The Bible makes this clear. It is "not by works of righteousness which we have done, but according to his mercy he saved us by the washing of regeneration, and renewing of the Holy Ghost" (Titus 3:5). Can Jesus do anything about your sin? He not only hears us when we ask for forgiveness, he not only forgives us, but he also cleanses us. "Though your sins be as scarlet, they shall be as white as snow; though they be red like crimson, they shall be as wool" (Isa. 1:18). When Jesus cleanses you, you are clean. You are just as if you had never sinned. His only requirement is that you desire to be delivered from sin, recognize that you cannot do it yourself, and trust him to do it for you. If you know you need him, you have already taken the first step in finding help.

If you believe, he will also meet other needs in your life. Jesus says, "Have faith in God. Truly I tell you, if anyone says to this mountain, 'Go, throw yourself into the sea,' and does not doubt in their heart but believes that what they say will happen, it will be done for them. Therefore, I tell you, whatever you ask for in prayer, believe that you have received it, and it will be yours" (Mark 11:23–24 NIV).

The man in the story knew he needed Jesus' help. His son was sick and at the point of death. He likely had sought medical aid and had not been able to find it. He had heard about Jesus and, therefore, the next step was reasonable.

II. The man came to Jesus for help.

He acted decisively and immediately. This is necessary if your need is to be met. If you are not capable of making a decision, you are not capable of becoming a Christian. God's Word says that "whosoever shall call on the name of the Lord shall be saved" (Acts 2:21).

Because the man had a need and he felt that Jesus could meet his need, he immediately came to Cana, sought Jesus out, and prayed for help. Are you willing to take that step?

There does seem to be one weakness in the man's request. He insisted, "Sir, come down before my child dies" (John 4:49 NIV). He knew he needed Jesus' help, but he was trying to tell Jesus how to do it. Many people know they need Jesus to forgive their sins, but they have not yet had their sins forgiven because they are trying to tell Jesus how to do it. Perhaps you have not been willing to let Jesus do it his way. He may not answer your prayer exactly as you expect him to. When you go to the doctor for treatment, you do not try to write out your own prescription; you let the doctor do it. You must trust Jesus enough to leave your sin need entirely in his hands.

Long ago I heard the story of a young man who was eager to be a Christian. When someone told him to "let God," he went back to his room, cut out the letters LET GOD and fastened them up on the wall where every time he looked up from his study table or walked into the room he saw them. He still had difficulty "letting GOD." One day the letter D came loose from the wall and fell to the floor. The next time he looked up, it said, "LET GO." This made it easier for him to make the decision to "let go and let God."

This principle not only applies in the matter of becoming a Christian but also in enjoying the abundant life. A person recently told me that for a long time he made the mistake of trying to accomplish the abundant life by serving Jesus dutifully, yet he found only failure. He then discovered what Paul revealed in Colossians 1:27, "Christ in you, the hope of glory."

III. The man took Jesus at his word.

Faith is believing, taking Jesus at his word, and leaving your situation in his hands. "God so loved the world that he gave his one and only Son, that whoever believes in him shall not perish but have eternal life" (John 3:16 NIV). "To all who did receive him, to those who believed in his name, he gave the right to become children of God" (John 1:12 NIV).

Jesus said to this official, "Go, your son will live!" (John 4:50 NIV).The man believed Jesus' words and went. He took Jesus at his word then and there. You become a Christian the moment you take Jesus at his word. Your prayers are answered the moment you take Jesus at his word.

I first trusted Jesus as my Savior when I was alone one day in a field. I think that if someone had come along in fifteen minutes and asked, "Are you a Christian?" I would have answered yes. I would not have given this affirmative answer because of some peculiar feeling or outward manifestation, but because I was assured that Jesus would keep his word. This is what belief is.

IV. The man discovered that Jesus had already met his need.

On his way home, the man's servants met him and told him his son was living. He asked them the hour when he began to get better, and they told him, "Yesterday, at one in the afternoon, the fever left him" (John 4:52 NIV). The father knew it was the same time Jesus had made him the promise. He had already trusted Jesus, and this was a confirmation.

Recently I talked with a banker about becoming a Christian. As we sat alone and talked, I explained to him the necessity of complete surrender to Jesus. I read him some passages of Scripture and invited him to join me in prayer. When I finished praying, I said to him, "Do you think you can now place your faith and trust fully in Jesus to get rid of your sins, come into your life, and make you the person you are meant to be?" He extended his hand to me and said, "I just now have." We walked back in the room where his wife was waiting, and he said, "Honey, your prayers have been answered. I have just now trusted Jesus."

Conclusion

Do you need Jesus? Will you right now ask Jesus for help? Will you right now take Jesus at his word and believe he has heard and answered your prayer? Do you believe it strongly enough that you are willing to make a full commitment to him right now and confess before people that you have trusted him?

SUNDAY EVENING, OCTOBER 22

Title: The Holy Spirit's Use of the Word of God

Text: "And take . . . the sword of the Spirit, which is the word of God" **(Eph. 6:17 RSV).**

Scripture Reading: Psalm 119:9–16

Introduction

While Paul was always magnifying Jesus Christ, he did not neglect to emphasize the role of the Holy Spirit in the believer's life. In Ephesians he declares that the believer is "sealed with the promised Holy Spirit" (1:13). The readers of this epistle were aware that a seal indicated ownership. Paul declared that each believer has received the Holy Spirit as an indication of God's divine ownership.

The apostle Paul also spoke of the Holy Spirit as being "the guarantee of our inheritance until we acquire possession of it, to the praise of his glory" (Eph. 1:14 RSV). The Holy Spirit is God's down payment guaranteeing that he will complete the great redemption begun in one's conversion experience.

Throughout this epistle there are five positive responses with an imperative note issued to the believer. Tonight we look at the fourth of these, the commandment to take "the sword of the Spirit, which is the Word of God." Paul was declaring that the Word of God as used by the Holy Spirit performs the function of a sword. While the Holy Spirit uses the Word of God in the mouth and life of the believer to overcome external spiritual enemies, the Holy Spirit also uses the Word of God to perform surgery within the believer. For us to ignore this truth is to miss a part of the emphasis that is being made in this call to victorious Christian living.

I. The Holy Spirit uses the Word of God to cut through our sinful defenses and bring conviction of sin (cf. John 16:7–14).

A Bible scholar tried to illustrate the difference the Holy Spirit makes by comparing Peter's use of a sword in an attack on the servant of the high priest (John 18:10) with his use of the sword of the Spirit when he preached on the day of Pentecost (Acts 2:37). In the first instance, Peter used the sword to cut off the ear of the high priest's servant. Following the coming of the Holy Spirit, Peter preached with the sword of the Spirit, and his hearers experienced heart surgery.

Average unbelievers are self-righteous and on the defensive if anyone speaks to them concerning their need of Jesus Christ. Only the Holy Spirit can open people's eyes to their need for the perfect righteousness of Jesus Christ and convince them that they are sinners in God's sight.

Each of us experienced this spiritual surgery before we were aware of what was really happening. God was at work through the Holy Spirit using the Word of God to cut off the blindfolds that blind people's minds lest the light of the gospel should shine in on them.

II. The Holy Spirit uses the Word of God to pierce through and reveal our innermost thoughts and motives.

"For the word of God is living and active, sharper than any two-edged sword, piercing to the division of soul and spirit, of joints and marrow, and discerning the thoughts and intentions of the heart" (Heb. 4:12 RSV). After we have been saved, the Holy Spirit continues to use the Word of God to do God's work within us. As a surgeon uses a scalpel to open up and reveal a hidden abscess within the body, so the Holy Spirit uses the Scriptures as we read them and study them to take an x-ray of our innermost beings. The Scriptures sit in judgment on our secret thoughts and motives, revealing to us that which needs to be removed from the center of our thought processes and emotional makeup.

Perhaps this is one of the reasons why many do not study the Scriptures as intently and as regularly as they should. It can be a very painful experience if we are harboring attitudes and ambitions that are contradictory to the mind of Jesus Christ.

III. The Holy Spirit uses the Word of God to cleanse and prune unproductive branches from the vine (John 15:2–3).

In this great passage in which our Lord identifies himself as the true vine of God, he honors each believer by declaring that we have the privilege of being branches on the vine. He reveals that the Father God is the gardener and that the gardener prunes off from the vine the branches that are nonproductive and serve as parasites. The pruning process cleanses the vine. Jesus affirmed that his apostle had been pruned by the words he had spoken to them. Does it not follow that God wants us to let the Word of God cleanse us and prune off of us those things that are displeasing to the Father God?

The Word of God is the sword of the Spirit. The sword was used in both offensive and defensive battle. The Holy Spirit wants to use the Word of God to help us purge out and slough off those attitudes, ambitions, or activities that are nonproductive and destructive.

IV. The Holy Spirit uses the Word of God to call us out from and to sever us from that which contaminates and compromises (2 Cor. 6:14).

Paul is not suggesting that recent converts from paganism separate from a marriage partner who continues to be an unbeliever (1 Cor. 7:12–16). He is calling us to forsake and separate ourselves from any relationship with the business or social world that would compromise and contaminate our faith and faithfulness. The Word of God calls us to sever relationships that would lure us away from faithfulness to our God and his will for our lives (2 Cor. 6:15–18).

Conclusion

The Holy Spirit wants to use the Word of God as a sword with which we can overcome the enemy and as a scalpel with which surgery can be performed on our innermost beings so that we can live healthy, wholesome, productive lives. Let us give ourselves consistently and with real devotion to a careful study of God's Word that the Holy Spirit might be able to use the Word to fulfill God's good purpose in our lives.

WEDNESDAY EVENING, OCTOBER 25

Title: The Religion of Resourcefulness

Text: "And I say unto you, Make to yourselves friends of the mammon of unrighteousness; that, when ye fail, they may receive you into everlasting habitations" **(Luke 16:9)**.

Scripture Reading: Luke 16:1–14

Introduction

Jesus told a story of a man who had been looking after the wealth of another man who became suspicious of him and called for an accounting. The employee said to himself, "What shall I do?" He was face-to-face with a crisis, for he was losing his job and his security. Being resourceful, he began to work out a plan. As dishonest as it was, we must confess that he was most resourceful. Jesus did not commend this man's deeds, but he did commend his resourcefulness. He challenged Christians to be as resourceful in the right way as this man was in the wrong way.

Jesus had more to say about money than any other subject. One-third of all his parables and one-sixth of all the verses in the four Gospels are about money. Christ is teaching that within the Christian faith is a place for the religion of resourcefulness.

I. The religion of resourcefulness faces reality (v. 3).

This parable is a challenge to face reality. The dishonest steward faced the cold, hard facts of his situation. As bad as he was, he at least was honest with himself. He said, "I'm not strong enough to dig, and I'm ashamed to beg" (v. 3 NIV).

How often as Christians and as the church, we close our eyes to reality! We refuse to face the fact that only in the gospel of Christ is there really any hope for our world, and that for the gospel to reach people where they live, we must give of ourselves as well as our means. What facts must we face? And what facts did the manager in our parable have to face?

344

The wealth he had been using did not belong to him.

His possession was temporary even though he had complete possession of it. Only a few years earlier another person managed it, and in a brief time it would fall into the hands of yet another.

How he used his possessions now would determine his wealth tomorrow.

II. The religion of resourcefulness practices foresight (v. 4).

Christ commends the man's foresight and resourcefulness, not his dishonesty. All at once the man realized how important other people were to him. Before he was independent and friends were objects to be used. But the fact that he would soon lose money, position, and everything else made him aware of how dependent he was on others. Using foresight, he went out and helped as many people as he could. Why? So that when he was in desperate need, they in turn would help him!

His motives were selfish, but even so he was resourceful enough to use a little foresight. And that is something too few Christians and churches do. Tomorrow will have enough difficulties of its own without our generation adding to them through shortsightedness and failure to be resourceful stewards.

III. The religion of resourcefulness dares to act (vv. 5–7).

The manager could not afford to waste time with regrets. What he had done was wrong, and he knew it. But it could not be undone. Now was the time to act, and he dared to do just that. "I am resolved what to do," he said (v. 4). Unlike certain churches as well as individual Christians, he had enough courage to commit himself to a definite line of action.

Christ was saying, "As wrong as this man was, at least he had the resourcefulness to act. He was not frightened into a state of immobility!"

We are called on to act, not to react. Instead of reacting, we should take the initiative and *act* by going out into the "highways and hedges" and compelling people before a crisis compels us to react.

Many are this way in their stewardship. The only appeal that will motivate them is the "empty pockets," "we have a crisis" appeal. Christ admonished us to use our heads, to practice both good stewardship in giving and good management in spending his money. He expects us to dare to act as good stewards before some crisis compels us to react.

IV. The religion of resourcefulness receives a commendation (vv. 8–9).

"The master commended the dishonest manager because he had acted shrewdly. For the people of this world are more shrewd in dealing with their own kind than are the people of the light. I tell you, use worldly wealth to gain friends for yourselves, so that when it is gone, you will be welcomed into eternal dwellings" (NIV). Did Christ actually commend this man? He did indeed—not for his dishonesty, but for his resourcefulness.

In verse 9 Christ was saying, "Those who through the prudent use of money enrich the lives of others may well be greeted by these very people in heaven." The deceitful accountant took money and changed it into friends. In doing this he provided friends and homes into which he would be welcome in the future. The point Christ was making in verse 9 is that through the proper use of money you can convert it into treasures in heaven (cf. Matt. 6:19–20).

V. The religion of resourcefulness opens the door to greater opportunities (vv. 10–14).

"He that is faithful in that which is least is faithful also in much" (v. 10). The right kind of resourcefulness in managing small matters opens the door to the greater opportunity of being entrusted with weightier matters. In these verses four *D*'s are seen.

A *doctrine (v. 10)*. "For unless you are honest in small matters, you won't be in large ones. If you cheat even a little, you won't be honest with greater responsibilities" (TLB).

A *decree (v. 11)*. "And if you are untrustworthy about worldly wealth, who will trust you with the true riches of heaven?" (TLB).

Trustworthiness in financial matters qualifies you for being trusted in spiritual matters. If you will not be a good and honest steward when sheer money is involved, then there is no reason to wonder why God cannot trust you with "the true riches of heaven"—spiritual power, effectiveness in his work, power in prayer, and so on—riches that deal with human souls.

A *decision (v. 13)*. "For neither you nor anyone else can serve two masters. You will hate one and show loyalty to the other, or else the other way around—you will be enthusiastic about one and despise the other. You cannot serve both God and money" (TLB).

Those who choose to serve money soon become its slaves through credit and indebtedness! Indebtedness is one of Satan's most treacherous traps. He uses it to cripple believers and to diminish their effectiveness. Those who can't see their way out of the financial trap often worry to the point of despair.

A *derision (v. 14)*. "The Pharisees, who dearly loved their money, naturally scoffed at all this" (TLB). When the claims of Christ in the area of money are mentioned, what is your response? With what group do you classify yourself? With the Pharisees "who dearly loved their money" or with resourceful and responsible Christian stewards who dearly love their Lord?

Conclusion

The real question facing every one of us is this: "Can we survive our extravagances?" The question is not rhetorical. Egypt, Babylon, Persia, Greece, and Rome rise up to answer no. Our answer is being written by our decision now.

SUNDAY MORNING, OCTOBER 29

Title: The Word of God

Text: "For the word of God is living and active, sharper than any two-edged sword, piercing to the division of soul and spirit, of joints and marrow, and discerning the thoughts and intentions of the heart" **(Heb. 4:12 RSV)**.

Scripture Reading: 2 Timothy 3:14–17

Hymns: "Break Thou the Bread of Life," Lathbury
"Wonderful Words of Life," Bliss
"Tell Me the Old, Old Story," Hankey

Offertory Prayer: Lord, we gather in your name to worship, praise, and serve. We give thanks for the Word of God and for your personal direction for our lives by the Holy Spirit. Today we bring special praise to you and thanksgiving because of the Bible. Help us to recognize and accept it emotionally, reverently, and obediently. In Jesus' name. Amen.

Introduction

It is easy for us to forget that people have not always had access to the Bible. Today it is important to remember that millions still do not have it. On this day when we are praising God for the privilege of opening its pages and feeding our own souls, we ought to resolve to make it available to the peoples of the world.

I. The revolutionary nature of the Bible.

When people seriously read the Bible, revolutionary things happen. Isn't it interesting that one year Erasmus published his Greek New Testament and the next year Martin Luther posted his Ninety-Five Theses in Wittenberg? Luther's own translation of the New Testament into German resulted in people calling themselves "Protestants." A similar response followed Tyndale's English translation and Olivetan's French translation.

Peter Waldo was translating and his followers were distributing the Scriptures at the beginning of the thirteenth century. Another renewal period was stimulated in the fourteenth century as John Wycliffe translated the Bible into English. He taught the Bible to his followers, called Lollards. These simple people were prototypes of Wesley's lay renewal movement four hundred years later. Savonarola was a Catholic evangelist who taught the Scriptures as a means of renewal in the church in the fifteenth century. Martin Luther's life was changed, and the Reformation began as the result of Bible study.

The Anabaptists, though condemned by Luther, used his New Testament and claimed the Bible alone to be authoritative in matters of faith. The revival they led out-reformed the Reformers. The Pietistic movement of the seventeenth century kept the Bible open for the revival movements of the eighteenth century.

II. What people say about the Bible.

Halley's Bible Handbook lists testimonies about the Bible from internationally known personalities. Here are abbreviated statements from some of them:

Abraham Lincoln: "I believe the Bible is the best gift God has ever given to man."

W. E. Gladstone: "I have known ninety-five of the world's great men in my time, and of these eighty-seven were followers of the Bible."

Daniel Webster: "If there is anything in my thoughts or style to commend, the credit is due to my parents for instilling in me an early love of the Scriptures."

Thomas Carlyle: "The Bible is the truest utterance that ever came by alphabetic letters from the soul of man."

Robert E. Lee: "In all my perplexities and distresses, the Bible has never failed to give me light and strength."

John Quincy Adams: "I have for many years made it a practice to read through the Bible once every year."

Charles Dickens: "The New Testament is the very best book that ever was or ever will be known in the world."

Sir Isaac Newton: "There are more sure marks of authenticity in the Bible than in any profane history."

Johann Wolfgang von Goethe: "Let mental culture go on advancing, let the natural sciences progress in ever greater extent and depth, and the human mind widen itself as much as it desires; beyond the elevation and moral culture of Christianity, as it shines forth in the Gospels, it will not go."

III. What the Bible says about itself.

It is everlasting. "For ever, O LORD, thy word is firmly fixed in the heavens" (Ps. 119:89). "The grass withers, the flower fades; but the word of our God will stand for ever" (Isa. 40:8). "Heaven and earth will pass away, but my words will not pass away" (Matt. 24:35 RSV). "'But the word of the Lord abides for ever.' That word is the good news which was preached to you" (1 Peter 1:25).

It is divinely inspired. "All scripture is inspired by God and profitable for teaching, for reproof, for correction, and for training in righteousness" (2 Tim. 3:16 RSV). "No prophecy ever came by the impulse of man, but men moved by the Holy Spirit spoke from God" (2 Peter 1:21 RSV).

It is profitable for instruction. "And you shall teach [God's words] to your children, talking of them when you are sitting in your house, and when you are walking by the way, and when you lie down, and when you rise" (Deut. 11:19 RSV). "For whatever was written in former days was written for our instruction, that by steadfastness and encouragement of the scriptures we might have hope" (Rom. 15:4 RSV).

It is powerful. "Is not my word like fire, says the LORD, and like a hammer which breaks the rock in pieces?" (Jer. 23:29 RSV). "For I am not ashamed of the gospel: it is the power of God for salvation to every one who has faith, to the Jew first and also to the Greek" (Rom. 1:16 RSV). "For the word of God is living and active, sharper than any two-edged sword, piercing to the division of soul and spirit, of joints and marrow, and discerning the thoughts and intentions of the heart" (Heb. 4:12 RSV).

It gives life. "But these are written that you may believe that Jesus is the Christ, the Son of God, and that believing you may have life in his name" (John 20:31 RSV). "Therefore put away all filthiness and rank growth of wickedness and receive with meekness the implanted word, which is able to save your souls" (James 1:21 RSV). "Truly, truly, I say to you, he who hears my word and believes him who sent me, has eternal life; he does not come into judgment, but has passed from death to life" (John 5:24 RSV).

IV. The Bible and evangelism.

The very genius of evangelism is announcing the Good News. It is always an announcement with enthusiasm and excitement. The announcer is a herald. Christians "gossip" or "chatter" the Good News. The Bible is the sourcebook of the Good News.

Jesus, in his teaching, appealed to the Old Testament Scriptures, the only Bible he had. Peter, Stephen, and Paul quoted the Old Testament in their preaching.

How do you instruct a person about becoming a Christian? Your opinion will not suffice. The real prescription must be found in the Bible, whether you are speaking to one person or ten thousand.

During citywide crusades, we have sometimes gone to the streets with the gospel. The police department has roped off the downtown streets for forty-five minutes at noontime. Using a public address system, we would sing a couple songs or choruses and preach for about fifteen minutes. Those messages would consist of about 80 percent Scripture quotations. In terms of time invested and conversions reported, those were the most profitable meetings of the crusades.

Before speaking to an audience of several thousand in a municipal auditorium in Taipei, my interpreter called to say he would like to have a copy of my message to work on ahead of time. I told him if he would get his Chinese Bible and review the Scripture passages I would give him, he would have no trouble. Of course he was an excellent preacher. For thirty minutes I did almost exactly the same thing I had done in street services in the United States; I quoted the Bible and related the passages to each other. The Holy Spirit used the Scriptures and the prayers of the people, and about five hundred people responded to the invitation to receive Jesus as Lord and Savior. During the week following this service, we heard of nearly 150 of them voluntarily reporting to churches and asking for membership.

Conclusion

This book, which has survived more criticism than any other book, is still "alive and active. Sharper than any double-edged sword, it penetrates even to dividing soul and spirit, joints and marrow; it judges the thoughts and attitudes of the heart" (Heb. 4:12 NIV).

SUNDAY EVENING, OCTOBER 29

Title: Praying in the Spirit

Text: "Pray at all times in the Spirit, with all prayer and supplication" **(Eph. 6:18 RSV).**

Scripture Reading: Romans 8:26–28

Introduction

What personal response have you made to God's precious gift of the Holy Spirit who came to you in your conversion experience? Is it possible that you have not recognized that you are the recipient of this priceless, personal gift (1 Cor. 3:16)? Is it not true that many of us have either ignored or neglected this precious gift of God's Spirit abiding within us?

In Paul's epistle to the Ephesians, he emphasized the urgency of a personal response to the indwelling Spirit if we would live a joyful life in Christ and a productive life for Christ. The words of our text emphasize the necessity of being persistent in our prayer lives. Such persistence characterized the life and ministry of our Lord (Luke 18:1). In addition to his emphasis on persistence, the apostle also declared that we should pray "in the Spirit." To recognize the role the Holy Spirit wants to play in our prayer lives can be encouraging and helpful.

It is interesting to note that when our Lord prayed, his disciples were eager to learn to pray (Luke 11:1). Jesus responded to this interest by teaching his disciples "how" to pray. He described the attitude, the manner, and the content that should characterize the prayer of a disciple.

James spoke of the fact that many offer petitions for which there is no affirmative answer because they are selfish in nature (James 4:3). Paul also spoke of difficulty concerning the substance, the purpose, and the manner of effective praying (Rom. 8:26). All of us could use divine assistance in praying effectively. Some great scriptural truths can stimulate and assist us in praying.

I. Our risen and exalted Christ intercedes for us (Heb. 7:25).

Some may be shocked to learn that our Lord did not ascend to the right hand of the Father merely to rest and wait. The inspired writer described the present activity of the risen Lord as being a ministry of intercession on behalf of those who trust in him as Savior. If the Savior ministers to us in the present through prayer, it follows that he is vitally concerned about our praying effectively as we live and labor as his servants.

II. The Holy Spirit intercedes for us.

"The Spirit himself intercedes for us with sighs too deep for words" (Rom. 8:26 RSV). The Holy Spirit is urgently concerned about our well-being as the children of God and as the servants of Jesus Christ. The sincerity and the urgency of his ministry of intercession is emphasized in those words from the apostle Paul.

Someone has suggested that every prayer experience we have is the result of an invitation planted in our minds and hearts by the indwelling Spirit. The hunger to pray is in reality a divine invitation to enter into the throne room of the eternal Father God.

III. The Holy Spirit assists us in our prayers relating to God's will.

"And he who searches the hearts of men knows what is the mind of the Spirit, because the Spirit intercedes for the saints according to the will of God" (Rom. 8:27 RSV). It is not always easy to know God's will concerning the choices and the complexities we face in life. When the option is between something that is absolutely evil or absolutely good, it usually is fairly easy to arrive at a conclusion. Often we face a more complex set of choices, as between the better of two goods or the lesser of two evils. The Holy Spirit of God has come to live within believers to create a hunger to know and do God's will. And he will teach us and guide us in carrying out God's will.

IV. The Holy Spirit will assist us in our prayers with regard to spiritual gifts that are needed in Christian service (I Cor. 12–14).

We cannot do the work of God without God's help. We are not to depend on human talent and abilities alone. The New Testament teaches that the Holy Spirit gives gifts as they are needed and according to the divine will (1 Cor. 12:4–11).

V. The Holy Spirit will assist us in our prayers regarding our cultivating the fruit of the Spirit (Gal. 5:22–23).

We are to walk in the Spirit and be led by the Spirit. We are to live by the Spirit and pray in the Spirit. The Holy Spirit comes to live in us to create a determination to do God's will (Phil. 2:12–13). The Holy Spirit wants each of us to experience the fruit of his indwelling presence.

Conclusion

We must not think of our prayer efforts as being the strivings of our own human soul to come into the presence of God. Instead, every hunger for God, every impulse to come into his presence, is in reality the work of the Holy Spirit. When we kneel to pray, let us remind ourselves that the Holy Spirit has come to live in us and that our highest thoughts, our deepest and most sincere aspirations, are conceived by him. Let us cooperate with the Spirit instead of ignoring him when we kneel to pray. We are to "pray at all times in the Spirit."

NOVEMBER

■ **Sunday Mornings**

This month's series is based on stewardship and is titled "The Response of a Grateful Heart." Only when we live life in partnership with God can we experience it abundantly.

■ **Sunday Evenings**

The evening messages for November are based on the theme "Overcoming Our Spiritual Enemy."

■ **Wednesday Evenings**

Continue with the studies of the parables, using the theme "Jesus Continues to Speak."

WEDNESDAY EVENING, NOVEMBER 1

Title: The Optimism of Jesus

Text: "Another parable put he forth unto them, saying, The kingdom of heaven is like to a grain of mustard seed, which a man took, and sowed in his field: which indeed is the least of all seeds: but when it is grown, it is the greatest among herbs, and becometh a tree, so that the birds of the air come and lodge in the branches thereof" **(Matt. 13:31–32)**.

Scripture Reading: Matthew 13:31–33, 44–46

Introduction

Jesus is an optimist! His attitude expressed through his teachings is a contradiction of the dismal, pessimistic, forlorn, defeated spirit so often expressed in the name of Christianity. Were he here in person today, Christ would have little in common with many who bear his name.

From within and without the church there are prophets of doom who have pronounced the death of the kingdom of God and have (to their satisfaction) conducted its final rites. But the church is not dead, for the kingdom of heaven is alive and well and continues to march on as the church triumphant!

So much did our Lord believe in the cause of his kingdom that he gave us four parables that express his optimism concerning it.

The optimism of Jesus is based on the following:

I. The phenomenal growth of the kingdom of heaven (Matt. 13:31–32).

Jesus uses the mustard seed as an analogy because of the contrast between the smallness of the seed and the immensity of the plant that comes from it. Christ encourages his followers by setting before them the phenomenal growth of the kingdom of heaven.

It had a humble beginning: "the least of all seeds" (v. 32). Often Jesus talked about small and unnoticed things—for example, the widow's mite, the one lost coin, the one talent, the cup of cold water, and now the single grain of mustard seed. Smallness and humble beginnings never meant weakness or insignificance to Christ. We should recall that his was a humble beginning, and so was the beginning of his kingdom.

A little church was organized here and another sprung up there. Christians were persecuted, and their numbers were small, but in fleeing their enemies, Christians spread the kingdom around the world.

It has survived many trials: "when it is grown" (v. 32). "When"—there was no question in Christ's mind but that his kingdom would survive and that it would grow despite its trials. None of the trials of the early church could keep the kingdom of God from marching on. And as it marched, it marched not with the force of the sword but with the power of God!

It has reached unbelievable proportions: "it is the greatest among herbs, and becometh a tree" (v. 32). From the eleven followers of Christ after his ascension have come innumerable people who have borne his name. Though Christ was not teaching that Christianity would conquer the entire world, he was teaching that it would have a phenomenal growth that would reach amazing proportions—and it has!

II. The permeating influence of the kingdom of heaven.

"The Kingdom of Heaven can be compared to a woman making bread. She takes a measure of flour and mixes in the yeast until it permeates every part of the dough" (Matt. 13:33 TLB). Jesus' optimism was not based on a flamboyant, explosive display of power by the kingdom of heaven but rather on the quiet, unpretentious yet relentless and undeniable influence it would have on millions of lives and countless civilizations through untold ages yet to come.

It begins from within. This parable does not speak of the visible outward increase of the kingdom as does the mustard seed parable. Rather, the parable of the leaven speaks of the invisible inward change the kingdom would effect. It is an illustration of salvation or regeneration. As the leaven is placed in the dough but once and yet continues to change the entire loaf, so regeneration is a one-time experience, the influence of which is progressive and continual. And it always begins within.

It works quietly yet relentlessly. Yeast is silent as it does its work, and so is the kingdom of heaven. No one has ever yet heard yeast at work or a seed breaking forth into life. Likewise the kingdom works not in the noisy affairs of our feverish efforts, but in the quiet and yet relentless manner of God.

It brings about moral and spiritual change "till the whole [is] leavened" (v. 33). Even as yeast subdues the dough, so the kingdom of heaven permeates, transforms, and conquers people's lives. Christ has placed Christians as bits of leaven hidden in their own parts of the world. Small and insignificant as Christians may think they are, they must never underestimate their potential. They can be used of God, not to change all of society into the kingdom of heaven, but to make the influence of that kingdom felt wherever they go.

III. The infinite worth of the kingdom of heaven (Matt. 13:44–46).

Jesus was an optimist not only because of the phenomenal growth and the permeating influence of the kingdom, but also because of its infinite worth. The thrust of both of these stories is the great worth of the kingdom of heaven.

Many are unaware of it. How many had walked over the treasure hidden in the field without the least idea of its presence or worth? How many had given the pearl of great price only a passing glance, never detecting its real worth?

It far exceeds all we have or are (vv. 44, 46). The climax of Christ's stories of the man finding the buried treasure and of the merchant finding the pearl of great price is the eagerness with which they gained possession of their discoveries. Each man, when he made the discovery, "went and sold all that he hath." Neither felt he was making any real sacrifice because the treasure he was possessing was worth so much more than what he had to offer for it.

It is not beyond our grasp (vv. 44, 46). Both men were able to possess their prizes regardless of their great worth. And you can possess the kingdom of heaven—its infinite worth does not remove it from your grasp! Though many treasures of this world are beyond your grasp, the treasure of God's kingdom with all the riches and joy it brings is well within your reach today.

Conclusion

The optimism of Jesus speaks of the infinite worth of the kingdom of heaven. And joyfully he offers it to you today. Christ asks for your unconditional surrender. When you give all, he gives all, and you will find the kingdom in no other way.

SUNDAY MORNING, NOVEMBER 5

Title: The Vows of God

Text: "I will pay my vows to the LORD in the presence of all his people" **(Ps. 116:14 RSV).**

Scripture Reading: Psalm 116:12–19

Hymns:　"Great Is Thy Faithfulness," Chisholm
　　　　"The King of Love My Shepherd Is," Baker
　　　　"Standing on the Promises," Carter

Offertory Prayer: Holy Father, we come into your presence in the faith that you are the giver of every good and perfect gift. Please grant to each of us a mind open to the truth you want to reveal to us. Give each of us a responsive heart that will yield to your will. Help each of us to give our bodies into your service that we might be your servants and that we might be a blessing to others. Accept our tithes and offerings and add your blessings to the end that others may come to experience your love and your goodness. Through Jesus Christ we pray. Amen.

Introduction

We are the receivers of many vows, some written and some unwritten. The stability of society is dependent on vows made and received with integrity. For example, the medical profession vows to treat us with the best medical know-how. Most hospitals vow to be available twenty-four hours per day every day of the week for medical emergencies. Police departments vow to put forth an honest and consistent effort to protect the innocent against lawbreakers. Fire departments remain on alert around the clock to protect our property from fires. Those who serve in the military vow to be under the authority of their commanding officers to protect our country from invasion from without or anarchy within. In marriage a man and a woman make vows designed to enrich their lives together and to offer security and strength to each other. Vows, both written and unwritten, in the business world give stability to the economy and create trust between buyers and sellers.

If suddenly all vows were made void and nullified, the result would be utter chaos in every area of life. It is by vows that we establish our identity and give evidence of our integrity. By vows we make commitments concerning what we will do and what we will not do. By vows we make announcements concerning our position, and we let others know what to expect from us. The vows we make are recorded and accepted by others.

Because some people make vows without any intention of fulfilling their commitment, we need to be cautious about receiving the vows of others and also in making vows. There is always a risk involved when we accept the vow of another.

The life of faith is a life of discovering the vows of God and putting our confidence in his faithfulness.

I. Our God has vowed to love us with an eternal love (Rom. 8:35–39).

You can depend on it. God will deal with you in terms of his eternal purpose of love and grace.

II. Our God has vowed to forgive and to cleanse us from our sins (Isa. 1:18; 1 John 1:7).

Our God is not primarily in the sin-punishing business; rather, he is in the sin-solving business. When we are willing to recognize the self-destructive nature of evil and bring our inward attitude into conformity with the mind of Christ, we will experience the cleansing of forgiveness, which is full, free, and forever.

III. Our God has vowed to save all who come to Jesus Christ (Matt. 11:28–30).

Our Lord receives all comers. He is not selective in the sense that some are considered beyond hope. The rich, the poor, the high, the low, the well educated, and the illiterate are all included in this invitation. If a person has not yet come to know God in a loving relationship, it is because he or she has not come to Jesus Christ in faith.

IV. Our God has vowed to work for good in all of those who love him (Rom. 8:28).

There is much that is sad and tragic and disappointing in life. There are times when it seems as if the heavens have caved in on us and the earth has collapsed beneath our feet. The pain of suffering often causes people to question the love and the power of God. The inspired writer does not solve the problem of suffering for us, but he does assure us that our loving God will be at work in all situations to bring about good for those who love God and who trust in his gracious care.

V. Our Lord has vowed rich blessings to those who trust him enough to be tithers (Mal. 3:10).

Our God is no pauper. He is no beggar. He is no thief. In the final analysis, our God is not dependent on us for anything. If that is true, why does God command us to bring the tithe into the storehouse? Is it possible that God is leading us to discover the highest joy of living—the joy that comes as a result of giving? Is it possible by means of this command that God is seeking to lift us to a level above the material as a reason for being?

If we come to the place where we can trust God on a physical and economic level, then we can trust him more fully in the spiritual realm. When we cooperate with God, he will pour out his blessings on us.

VI. Our Father has vowed to reward those who pray (Matt. 6:6).

It has been declared that prayer is a science to be learned and that Jesus Christ is the teacher. This section of the Sermon on the Mount illustrates this truth in a powerful manner (Matt. 6:5–13). We rob ourselves of the rich treasures of God when we neglect to follow our Lord's teachings in the matter of praying properly.

VII. Our Lord has vowed to reward his faithful servants after we come into our eternal home (John 14:1–3; Rev. 22:12).

Eternal life is the gift of God. Heaven is not a reward; it is the gift of our Father God to those who receive Jesus Christ as Lord and Savior. Once we have entered the heavenly home at the end of the way, our Lord will bestow on us rewards for faithful service rendered on earth.

Conclusion

God has made many vows to us. It is time for us to make some vows to him. Let us vow to trust our Lord at all times and under all circumstances to bring good out of every situation. Let us vow to make much of the Word of God in our daily lives. Let's feast on the Bread of Life through Bible study each day. Let's vow to give priority to public worship and to the ministry and work of our church. Let's vow to give God control of our finances and let him be Lord of all areas of our lives. The God who has made vows to us will help us as we make the vows that will lift our lives into conformity with his will.

SUNDAY EVENING, NOVEMBER 5

Title: The Wiles of the Devil

Text: "And the serpent said unto the woman, Ye shall not surely die: for God doth know that in the day ye eat thereof, then your eyes shall be opened, and ye shall be as gods, knowing good and evil" **(Gen. 3:4–5)**.

Scripture Reading: Genesis 3:1–13

Introduction

Our chief concern with this Genesis record is to see the amazing subtlety of the devil who tricked Adam and Eve into disobedience, causing them to fall from the state of innocence in which they were created into shame, sorrow, and death.

Jesus called the devil "a liar, and the father of lies" (John 8:44 NIV). Paul wrote of "the wiles of the devil" (Eph. 6:11) and of the devil's ability to transform himself into "an angel of light" (2 Cor. 11:14). The devil continues to deceive men and women and entice them to sin. He has not changed.

Eve clearly stated God's prohibition: "We may eat of the fruit of the trees of the garden: but of the fruit of the tree which is in the midst of the garden, God hath said, Ye shall not eat of it, neither shall ye touch it, lest ye die" (Gen. 3:2–3). In his reply (vv. 4–5), the devil did three things that he still does in dealing with us.

I. The devil denied God's truthfulness.

God said, "Ye shall not eat of it . . . lest ye die" (v. 3), but the devil said, "Ye shall not surely die" (v. 4). This was a contradiction. The word *devil* means "slanderer." He does not hesitate to slander God or to call God a liar. When Paul advised that deacons' wives (or deaconesses) not be "slanderers" (1 Tim. 3:11), he used the feminine plural for the word *devil*, so literally, they shall not be "she devils."

The man and the woman knew their instructions, the boundaries of their freedom, and the penalty for disobedience, but they believed the tempter's lie that instead of death the forbidden fruit would bring a new thrill, a new knowledge, and a new freedom. God's warning is that you cannot win the game of sin. The devil's lie is that you can win.

In counseling sessions I have asked young people who have dabbled with drugs, "Why did you do this?" "Oh," they replied, "I thought I would experience a new thrill." I replied, "Why not try the game of Russian roulette with a six-shooter, with only one bullet, held against your head? When you pull the trigger, if it doesn't blow your head off, that is a tremendous thrill. But if you keep on pulling the trigger, you can't win. Sooner or later you will find that one bullet and blow out your brains. One game is as sensible as the other. You can't win." Sin never brings about a winning situation.

Sin is an attempt to violate God's laws and get away with it. It cannot be done! The soul that sins dies (Ezek. 18:4). When we live in sin, we die spiritually; and if we don't repent, we will experience eternal punishment when we die physically. The bloom of life withers, something within snaps, and the machinery of life, in trying to work against itself, destroys itself. "Ye shall not surely die," said Satan, but something within Adam and Eve did die. Their souls died, and their bodies became mortal. They were driven from the garden where "the tree of life" bloomed. Physical death, Paul told the Romans, is the result of sin (5:12).

II. The devil questioned God's goodness.

The devil said, "God doth know that in the day ye eat thereof, then your eyes shall be opened" (v. 5). The tempter was saying, "God is concealing something from you. He is withholding something good to which you are entitled." The subtlety here is that what the devil said was technically true in words but false in fact. Their eyes were opened to know good and evil, but not in the way in which God knows good and evil. God knows evil objectively; he has no personal experience with it. On the other hand, Adam and Eve came to know evil by experience, tasting its bitter gall and becoming defiled and polluted by it. This kind of knowledge of evil, gained by disobedience, was not desirable, as the devil suggested, but exactly the opposite. He said they would get a blessing; they actually came under a curse.

The devil always ignores God's ample provision for his creatures. The man and woman lacked nothing. Their happiness lay in enjoying what God had permitted and abstaining from what he had forbidden. Both his provision and his prohibition issued from sheer goodness and love. But the devil twisted this, making the permitted things seem drab and dull and the prohibited things seem desirable. He denied the goodness of God, and Eve believed him. She was convinced that the fruit was "to be desired to make one wise" (v. 6). She believed that the devil was kinder in offering her the fruit than God was in forbidding it. And she found out too late that her disobedience brought her not gain, as the devil promised, but irreparable loss as God had warned.

Even today the devil questions God's goodness by seeking to make sin attractive. He tries to deceive us by making God's permitted things seem dull and the prohibited things pleasant and exciting. He coats his bitter pill with the sweetest sugar and allures us with "the pleasures of sin" (Heb. 11:25).

III. The devil repudiated God's otherness.

The devil said to Eve, "and ye shall be as gods, knowing good and evil" (v. 5). In this temptation of all temptations—man's desire to become like God—we have the essence of sin laid bare. Man was not content simply to be God's creature; he wanted to be like God himself. Man is made in the image of God but was never intended to become God. The attempt to become God is the central sin of religion.

George Cornell, a well-known feature writer in the religious field, put this choice clearly when he said, "We believe in the 'god' of our own making, of the scientific laboratory, of the senses and natural phenomena, or in a super-natural God. We worship our own minds and capacities (just as Adam and Even chose the tree of superior knowledge in Eden), or we worship a greater supersensible power. According to our faith, we consider ourselves 'god'—or we know there is Another. We are orphans, or God's children" (George W. Cornell, *The Way and Its Ways* [New York: Association Press, 1963], 30).

The fundamental way in which man is unlike God is that God is man's Creator and Lord. Man is under the authority of God and dependent on him as his Creator and subordinate to him as his Lord. It was against this that our first parents rebelled. The devil repudiated God's "otherness" in that he refused to honor God as God. Every time we sin, we do the same thing, for every sin is an unwillingness to let God be God. It is to rebel against his authority and to claim an independence we can never have.

Conclusion

How shall we resist "the wiles of the devil"? We will learn obedience to God only if we turn a deaf ear to the devil's lies and only if we see through his clever devices. But also, we need constantly to remind ourselves that God's threatened penalties are true; that his purpose in his prohibitions is wholly good and loving; and that God is God, our Creator and our Lord, who has a right to issue commands, expect obedience, and threaten penalties.

The devil does not persecute Christianity now; he professes it. He does not fight churches today; he joins them. This is the strategy of this evil angel disguised as an angel of light. Remember, the devil takes no holidays.

WEDNESDAY EVENING, NOVEMBER 8

Title: God's Wage and Hour Law

Text: "So the last shall be first, and the first last: for many be called, but few chosen" **(Matt. 20:16)**.

Scripture Reading: Matthew 20:1–16

Introduction

The main character of this parable is the owner of the vineyard. He operated his business in a most unorthodox manner. Whether employees came to work at six in the morning or at noon or even at five in the evening, each received the same wage at the end of the day. He was far more concerned with men's needs and motives than he was with the amount of work they produced. A modern business management consultant surely would have been baffled by his procedures!

Christ used this man to illustrate how God deals with people. It is important to remember that this story is not an economic treatise. Jesus was not attempting to establish principles by which the business world is to operate, but he was illustrating "God's wage and hour law."

God's wage and hour law:

I. Reveals that God is concerned not only with what we can do for him but also with what he can do for us (Matt. 20:3–7).

The owner hires men both at the normal time (6:00 a.m.) and also at much later hours in the day. And he hires them, not for his own personal gain, but for the benefit of those poor souls who are unemployed. Christ was saying, "God's wage and hour law may be out of step with man's, but it nevertheless reveals that God is concerned not only with what man can do for God, but also with what God can do for man." And that's an encouraging thought!

II. Provides compensation not only for work done but also for work that would be done (Matt. 20:8–9).

The word *idle,* referring to the men in verse 6, does not mean "lazy" or "loafing"; it means "workless." The reason they were not working is not because they did not want to work, but because they could not find an opportunity to work. The fact that they were in the marketplace is proof that they were seeking employment. If they were not seeking employment, they would have stayed home.

These men never gave up. Imagine waiting eleven hours, hoping for an opportunity to work. The waiting took more determination than the working. And finally, when an opportunity did come, though only one hour was left, they did not say, "Well, it's too late to start now." Instead, they went and did their best in the time left. Here is the important lesson of Christ's parable: the men were compensated not only for the work done, but also for the work they would have done had they had the opportunity. Jesus said this is how God deals with us.

Whether we get to do all that our hearts long to do or not, we rest assured that God's wage and hour law provides compensation not only for work done but also for work that would be done if only the opportunity came!

III. Warns against mercenary motives (Matt. 20:10–15).

The owner is more concerned with the motive behind the work than the amount of work. He seems to delight in the attitude of thankful devotion. On the other hand, he abhors selfishness, envy, and cold mercenary calculation. "You who are complaining about my generosity toward others today may not be hired at all tomorrow unless your attitudes and motives are changed," the employer says.

God's wage and hour law deals with us according to our motives. If you want to drive a hard bargain with God for one denarius a day, you will be paid your denarius—but no more! You shall have "received your reward." But if you are willing simply to work in faith, trusting the goodness of God, you will be rewarded with "good measure, pressed down and running over." So Jesus warns us that in spite of all we may do, if our motives are wrong, we will miss the real blessing!

IV. Guarantees that we shall be paid (Matt. 20:8).

In Christ's story, every laborer was paid. Not one went home without being paid for the work done. We should be thankful that God alone is in charge of life's payday.

The good substitute is always ready whenever the coach calls. It seems that God keeps a lot of people waiting in the great game of life, but you can be assured that God does not forget us. We must remain free of bitterness. We must do our best under the circumstances and leave the rewards to him. But we can be sure the love and justice of God guarantee that we shall be paid. "For in due season we shall reap, if we faint not" (Gal. 6:9).

Conclusion

God's wage and hour law gives expression to his love toward us, and God's love cannot be portioned out in quantities neatly adjusted to the merits of individuals. Rather, it is offered on the basis of divine grace, and this grace is extended to you today.

SUNDAY MORNING, NOVEMBER 12

Title: Channels of God's Grace

Text: "As every man hath received the gift, even so minister the same one to another, as good stewards of the manifold grace of God" **(1 Peter 4:10)**.

Scripture Reading: 1 Peter 4:7–11

Hymns: "Make Me a Channel of Blessing," Smyth
           "Take My Life and Let It Be," Havergal
           "Give of Your Best to the Master," Grose

Offertory Prayer: Dear Lord, thank you for the trust you have placed in us in giving us these manifold blessings. Help us to know that you have blessed us that we might be a blessing and that we are responsible for ministering these blessings to others. Grant that we shall this day be channels of your grace. In the name of Jesus, we pray. Amen.

Introduction

A pastor preached a sermon on missions and gave the church an opportunity to make an offering. Among those who responded was a very poor widow who pledged one dollar.

That afternoon the deacons met to count the money and sort the pledges. On finding the widow's pledge, one deacon said, "I know that woman. She washes for my wife. She is not able to pay this money." The deacon took a dollar from his pocket, put it in the envelope, and marked her pledge paid.

After two weeks the woman came to the church to pay the pledge. The pastor informed her that her pledge was already paid. The widow insisted that it was not paid, because she still had the money. She stated that she had saved ten cents out of each washing and that now she had the money to pay the pledge. Finally, the pastor told her about the deacon who had paid her pledge.

Tears came into her eyes, and she said, "The work of the Lord goes forward, the gospel is preached, souls are saved, but I have no part in it!"

That woman had a right to have a part. Every saved man, woman, and child should have a part every week in the Lord's work. That's what stewardship is all about.

Paul had an important word for us: "Be strong in the grace that is in Christ Jesus. And the things that thou hast heard of me among many witnesses, the same commit thou to faithful men, who shall be able to teach others also" (2 Tim. 2:1–2). Peter admonished: "As every man hath received the gift, even so minister the same one to another, as good stewards of the manifold grace of God" (1 Peter 4:10).

I. The Lord has given you the resources to be a blessing—"As every man hath received the gift."

You have something to offer in God's service. The word for "gift" means a "gift of grace." It is used here as endowment on the believer by the operation of the Holy Spirit (cf. Rom. 12:6; 1 Cor. 12:4, 9, 28, 30, 31; 1 Tim. 4:14; 2 Tim. 1:6). Your abilities are God-given. "This is not your own doing, it is the gift of God" (Eph. 2:8 RSV). God does not give his grace for the sole enjoyment of the recipient. He expects the recipient to pass it on to others.

The basic frailty of human nature is that too often we wish to do as little as possible and to get as much as possible. The genuine Christian spirit is to put more into life than you take out—to serve others so that your life becomes a channel through which God's grace flows to bless others.

Peter indicated that we are responsible for ministering these blessings to others. It is significant that the word translated "minister" is *diakone[amo]*. This word is akin to *diakonoa* (deacon), which signifies a servant or minister.

II. The Lord expects you to be a channel of his grace—"even so minister."

Paul stated our case when he wrote, "I long to see you, that I may impart unto you some spiritual gift" (Rom. 1:11). When you bear witness to the gospel, whether by personal proclamation, Christlike service, or tithing, you are a channel of God's grace. Concerning our responsibility of being channels of grace, Paul said, "God was in Christ, reconciling the world unto himself, not imputing their trespasses unto them, and hath committed unto us the word of reconciliation. Now then we are ambassadors for Christ, as though God did beseech you by us: we pray you in Christ's stead, be ye reconciled to God" (2 Cor. 5:19–20).

Jesus said, "As my Father hath sent me, even so send I you" (John 20:21). The fact that we have been "allowed of God to be put in trust with the gospel" (1 Thess. 2:4) makes us responsible for the spiritual needs of the world. Let us remember that we will one day give an account of how we have lived our lives in God's service. "Let a man so account of us, as of the ministers of Christ, and stewards of the mysteries of God. Moreover it is required of stewards, that a man be found faithful" (1 Cor. 4:1–2).

III. The Lord wants you to be a good steward—"as good stewards."

As Christians we are to be examples of good stewards. *Kalos* (good) means that which is intrinsically good, fair, and beautiful. This *kalos*-type goodness is born only out of fellowship with and dedication to Christ. It grows out of an encounter with God and a continuing relationship with him until one becomes possessed with the mind and spirit of Christ.

Stewardship understood in its broadest sense cannot be limited to the responsible management of your material possessions. The wise and dedicated stewardship of possessions, however, is a verification of your

SUNDAY EVENING, NOVEMBER 12

acknowledgment of such total stewardship. If we really believed that we are stewards—not owners—the whole face of Christianity would be changed. There would be people and money for all causes, and the world would be bright with unselfish and varied ministries worthily representing "the manifold grace of God."

Conclusion

When the Nazis were at the height of their power in Germany, in 1939, this poem appeared in a Berlin newspaper:

> We have captured all the positions
> And on the heights we have planted
> The banners.
> You had imagined
> That was all
> That we wanted.
> We want more.
> We want all!
> Your hearts are our goal.
> It is your soul we want!

The struggle for people's hearts is still alive—materialism, whose god is things, seeks your all. Jesus, too, seeks your life. He says:

> Your heart is my goal,
> It's your soul I want.

SUNDAY EVENING, NOVEMBER 12

Title: Tempted of the Devil

Text: "Then was Jesus led up of the Spirit into the wilderness to be tempted of the devil" **(Matt. 4:1)**.

Scripture Reading: Matthew 4:1–11

Introduction

Jesus' temptations by the devil were an inward spiritual struggle. Whether the devil appeared in bodily form, whether the devil had control over our Lord's person and took him through the air from place to place, or whether anything was seen by the eye or heard by the ear—these are moot questions. His temptations, like ours, constituted an inner spiritual struggle. If it had been otherwise, how could he be touched with "the feeling of our infirmities" (Heb. 4:15)? How could he be "able to succour them that are tempted" (Heb. 2:18)?

Jesus' temptations fixed the path and spirit and method of his ministry. He refused to act out of selfish concern, or to try to force sensational support from God, or to seek apparent advantage by a surrender to the devil. Had he compromised on any point, he would have defeated the Father's purpose for him.

In analyzing these three temptations, I will make four affirmations.

I. Jesus' temptations by the devil were real.

This needs to be said emphatically, for many people are sure Jesus' temptations were not and could not have been real, at least not as real as our own. While this idea springs from the praiseworthy motive of seeking to glorify Jesus by saying he won his victory over sin always without effort, would it not glorify him far more to say he marched to it through an agony of sweat and blood? And indeed the whole gospel and our own hope of salvation are bound up with a Christ who was "in all points tempted"—not just here and there, but in all points—"like as we are" (Heb. 4:15).

As we see Jesus in this desert experience, we see him quite alone. He is sitting on a spur of rock with his head bowed and his hands clenched. He falls on his knees and then on his face, with a cry breaking from his lips that sounds like "If it be possible, let this cup pass from me" (Matt. 26:39). So his ministry begins and so it ends. The writer of Hebrews settled this question once and for all with the words, "He himself hath suffered being tempted" (Heb. 2:18).

II. Jesus' temptations by the devil were personal.

This experience was not shadow boxing or a sham. At the outset two personal influences on Jesus are clearly indicated: Jesus was led up by the *Spirit* to be tempted by the *devil*.

On the one hand, Jesus' temptations were a personal encounter with the devil. It is rash to assert that the devil is only a generic name for impersonal evil impulses. The teaching of our Lord and the apostles is clear on this point. Jesus plainly designated his struggle with the empire of Satan as a personal one. In the New Testament the existence of the devil and demons is everywhere taken for granted.

The apostle John said, "To this purpose the Son of God was manifested, that he might destroy the works of the devil" (1 John 3:8). That battle was joined in the wilderness long ago, and it is still going on.

On the other hand, Jesus' temptations were personal in the sense that they struck at his relationship with the Father. His principles of action were rooted in the inner life of his relationship with God. Think of each temptation in this light.

The temptation to turn stones into bread was a test of faith in God. If he was the Son of God, he had divine power. Would this not be a good chance to test that power, to see if it actually worked, to prove whether it was something more than his imagination or a dream? "Son of God"—but was he Son of God? "Try it!" said the devil. "Put it to the test."

Was Jesus prepared to trust God to the uttermost even when desperate with hunger and physically exhausted? Could he hold on to await God's time? Jesus knew that to use his divine power for personal ends would be an act of distrust, so he put the temptation aside.

The temptation to leap from the pinnacle of the temple was a temptation to turn from the law of reason as the guide and ally of faith. Faith may hold firm under physical suffering yet fail through disregard of reason. In the first temptation, Jesus was to be freed from a peril that already existed; in the second, he was to create a peril for himself and expect God to free him from it. This would be to force sensational support from God as Moses had done (Num. 20:7–12).

There is only a step between faith and fanaticism. When Jesus rejected the temptation to cast himself down, he turned from the way of fanaticism and chose the law of reason as the guide and ally of faith. He refused a sensational messiahship and chose the way of love.

The temptation to bow his knee to the devil was a temptation for Jesus to modify his principles on the plea of reason. Reason brings its own special temptations. Nothing is more common than to think we must modify our principles under the plea of what the world calls "reasonable." It is to debase the noble gift of reason into mere clever diplomacy, following a path of expediency and compromise with evil on the pleas that high ends justify low means. Jesus rejected this with indignation and rebuke.

III. Jesus' temptations by the devil were vocational.

This is to say each temptation struck him along the line of his life's work. "Do this and this and this," the devil said, "and you will advance your work."

Notice the sublime restraint of the gospel writer concerning the first temptation, "he was afterward an hungered" (v. 2). Jesus was near death from starvation. Should he win the world by using his power for self-preservation, and thus for the saving of his cause? If he died out there in the desert, what then? Would he not be defeating God? Would he not be robbing the world of its Messiah and humanity of salvation? Was it not his duty to save himself?

Notice that the temptation to leap from the pinnacle of the temple also had its appeal through Jesus' life's work and the methods he would follow. He was sent to save the world. What was the best way to do it? Should he confine himself to preaching? Would they listen? This seemed doubtful, to say the least. Then the tempter struck, suggesting another way: "Why confine yourself to the simple gospel? Why not do something startling, dramatic, spectacular, something that would bring the world to its feet?" So the wild idea of leaping from the temple was born.

Notice that the third temptation, the temptation to compromise with Satan, also had Christ's life's work at issue. The passion and goal of his life was to win the whole world for God. What the tempter now suggested was that the easiest, quickest, surest way to do it would be to lower his demands, to lower the flag of faith ever so little, to come to terms with the world powers. "One moment kneeling at my feet," the devil said, "and your dream will be realized." But Jesus rejected the compromise because he knew it would be the death of Christianity to ask anything less than the whole.

IV. Jesus' temptations by the devil were conclusive.

On every score, Jesus was completely victorious.

Suppose Jesus had consented to the suggestion to turn stones into bread. Then Christ the brother and comrade, who is one with us in our sufferings and sorrows, would have been lost to us forever. But our Lord did not consent. He defeated the tempter and threw his suggestion back with scorn.

Suppose Jesus had accepted the devil's suggestion to cast himself from the pinnacle of the temple? Would this have affected his purpose? Would this have saved a single soul? It would have had a sensational immediate effect. People acclaim something that stirs their imaginations, but they are saved only by something that touches their hearts. Jesus is not going to force people into the kingdom by miracles and magic. His method is this: "Behold, I stand at the door, and knock . . ." (Rev. 3:20). And he wins.

Suppose Jesus had compromised with the devil and had bowed his knee? This would have been the death of true religion, for Christ asks a person for all or nothing. This decision made Calvary inevitable, for such a demand always means a cross.

The early church would not bow the knee to Caesar, and Rome hunted them down, threw them to the lions, and flung their bodies outside the camp to bear Christ's reproach. Because Christ's church was obedient, it was also crucified, dead, and buried; and because it was obedient, it was also raised from the dead and has gone forth conquering and to conquer.

Conclusion

The night before his death, Jesus said, "The prince of this world is judged" (John 16:11). And he had been long since. Satan was defeated in the desert. Now it is true that "the kingdoms of this world are become the kingdoms of our Lord, and of his Christ; and he shall reign for ever and ever" (Rev. 11:15).

WEDNESDAY EVENING, NOVEMBER 15

Title: Making the Most of What You Have

Text: "Wherefore then gavest not thou my money into the bank, that at my coming I might have required mine own with usury?" **(Luke 19:23)**.

Scripture Reading: Luke 19:11–27

Introduction

This is one of the most unusual parables Christ ever told. Its structure is totally different from any other parable. Actually it is composed of two parables—one set within the other. The parable that is the frame of this story concerns a king and his subjects. The canvas that is set within this frame is the parable of the pounds.

Though the immediate purpose of the story as stated in verse 11 is to correct the impression that the kingdom of God would physically begin right away, there is also contained in it a lesson on "making the most of what you have." It is to this lesson that we direct our attention today.

What do the "pounds" represent? The gospel, "the faith" once delivered to the saints (Jude 3). What was rejected by the citizens in this story? The gospel of Christ, with all its privileges offered to every person and entrusted to every believer. This is our "treasure in earthen vessels" (2 Cor. 4:7). The gospel is our capital with which we are to trade until Christ returns as the King of his kingdom. But there are four responses you may make to the gospel of Christ.

I. You may refuse to have any part of it (Luke 19:14).

"They cried out, 'Away with him, away with him, crucify him. . . . We have no king but Caesar'" (John 19:15). The background of this story was set in Archelaus's palace at Jericho. He went to Rome, leaving his palace and the business of his kingdom to his servants. He left Philippus in charge of his revenue while he was away. Fifty Jews were sent after him to make a protest against his becoming king. When they arrived in Rome, they were joined by eight thousand Jews who joined their protest.

In time the emperor divided the kingdom, and Archelaus received Judea (Matt. 2:22). When he returned he took vengeance on those who had supported the appeal against him.

Christ therefore took a common incident and applied it in a remarkable way to himself to show that what they were expecting would not then take place. He was going away to receive a kingdom, and he was leaving responsibility with his servants while he was away.

II. You may make the most of it (Luke 19:13, 16–17).

No Christian man or woman is without that pound. We may say we do not have ten talents, but that is another matter. The pound is something quite different than the gift. The pound is a deposit; it is the gospel. We are witnesses to that gospel, and our duty in this world is to do business with that deposit until the King returns.

Our Lord said that there are different ways of using the deposit. One is to make the most of it. One man at the reckoning said, "Thy pound hath made ten pounds more." Notice he did not say, "I have been very successful and have managed to make your pound into ten." He had simply fulfilled the responsibility of trading with it, and in time there were ten. The pound, the gospel of the grace of God, has the power of increase!

John Vassar of Boston approached a woman on the street and spoke to her about her soul. At dinner that evening she told her husband about her encounter. He said, "If I had been there, I would have told him to mind his own business." "But if you had been there," she replied, "you would have known that he was minding his own business." You have the pound, the gospel, so make the most of it, for this is your business!

III. You may make something of it (Luke 19:18–19).

This man did not make the most of his pound, but he did make something of it! He gave it neither his best nor his worst. He simply chose to handle his responsibility in a mediocre manner.

Notice in verse 19 that the master withholds any expressions of praise in addressing this second servant. He is not said to have done "well," and he is not called "good," as was the first servant who had made the most of his trust.

This is no oversight on Christ's part. He withholds praise deliberately, because in his judgment this servant had not earned it. What does this imply? That the second servant had not done all that was possible for him to do. This man was given exactly the same amount as the first man, but the difference was that he was content simply to make something of it.

The gospel is given equally to all of us. Some make the most of the opportunity to spread the gospel while others do not put their hearts into their work; they do not take their stewardship of the gospel seriously. This is the person who says, "I'll teach in your department, but don't expect me to attend teachers' and officers' meetings, or visit, or be regular. . . ."

IV. You may make nothing of it (Luke 19:20–26).

This servant's reply is typical of the self-righteous Pharisee who hoarded the truth God had entrusted to him and kept for himself what God had meant to be shared with all humankind. Such selfishness produces no profit to God on his investment in us. It is the same as stealing from God, for it is to prevent his gospel from bearing the fruit it normally would have borne.

In all fairness we must realize that this man did not misappropriate or "skim off" his employer's money. He simply did not do anything with it. He is like the Christian whose wickedness is found not in his misuse but in his disuse of the gospel committed to him. He does not renounce the gospel; he simply does not invest it in the lives of others.

The plain truth of this parable is that being good, moral, honest, and religious is not enough. Christ expects us to trade with the gospel and by so doing show a profit for him. What happened to the second man? Nothing—except that he lost his pound. He was saved "so as by fire." He represents Christians who are content to let the rest of the world go to hell so long as they are saved!

Conclusion

You have only two choices when you really take something seriously. You either risk your all for it or you repudiate it. You value it and trade with it, or you discard it. No other viable alternative exists.

The gospel is entrusted to you. You may hide it because of shame or fear, or you may share it. Allow Christ to be the controlling power of your life. Take him and his claims in dead earnest. But don't wrap the gospel up and hide it. It is your divine trust, so "make the most of what you have"!

SUNDAY MORNING, NOVEMBER 19

Title: The Shape of Our Thanksgiving

Text: "O give thanks to the LORD, for he is good; for his steadfast love endures for ever!" **(Ps. 107:1 RSV).**

Scripture Reading: Psalm 92:1–4

Hymns: "We Gather Together," Baker
           "Thanksgiving Hymn," McNeely
           "Saviour, Like a Shepherd Lead Us," Thrupp

Offertory Prayer: Holy Father, today we offer to you the thanks of our hearts. We thank you for your greatness and goodness. We thank you for the gift of your Son. We thank you for the abiding presence of your Holy Spirit. We thank you for the church. We thank you for the Bible. We thank you for the privilege of being able to communicate with you in prayer. We come now thanking you with our gifts. Accept these gifts as tokens of our gratitude, and bless them to the end that others might come to know your grace through Jesus Christ. Amen.

Introduction

The psalmist observed that the habit of giving thanks to the Lord is good. For us to be thankful brings joy to the heart of our Father God. For us to develop the habit of being thankful will enable us to overcome our negative inclinations and will lead us to face life with a positive and benevolent attitude. For us to be thankful will be a blessing to others. It is indeed a good thing to give thanks to the Lord.

It is good for us to give thanks to God for being the kind of God he is. We should be thankful for the Father who revealed his love in the Son and who abides with us at all times as the Holy Spirit. We should be thankful to God for the fellowship of the church. Through the church we have heard the good news of God's love. In the fellowship of the church we receive the strength we need for living a victorious life. We should give thanks to God for our country and for all good men and women who live and work to make it a better country. We should give thanks to God for the members of our family who have sustained us and who now help to give us a reason for being. It is a good thing to give thanks to God for all the good things in life.

If it is a good thing to give thanks to God, what is the proper form for the expression of our gratitude? It is interesting to note the various forms of thanksgiving revealed in the lives of the great characters of the Bible.

I. The three mighty men of David (2 Sam. 23:13–17).

David, the future king of Israel, was weary in body and perhaps faint in mind as he fought the Philistines. He probably was both hungry and thirsty, and in this condition he expressed appreciation for the water of the well in Bethlehem where he grew up as a boy. Three of his mighty men decided that if their leader wanted water from the well of Bethlehem, it would be given to him. They broke through the enemy line at the risk of their lives and returned to the camp of David with water from the well. We can only imagine the pleasure that flooded the heart of David as he recognized the devotion of these men. He responded to their generosity and bravery with an act of gratitude and thanksgiving that reveals something about the heart of this great leader. He refused to drink the water that had been secured at the risk of the lives of his men. Instead of consuming it, he poured it out as a sacrifice to the Lord.

In this incident we have a most beautiful expression of the thanksgiving of men for their leader and of the leader for those who loved him.

II. The thanksgiving of the sinful woman (Luke 7:36–50).

In this description of the incident that took place in the house of the Pharisee, we have a condensed account of what happened.

In some unexplained manner, our Lord had revealed his divine compassion for the sinful woman who was an outcast. She perceived that God's attitude toward her was one of compassion rather than condemnation.

This sinful woman approached our Lord in such a manner that she was granted the gift of forgiveness. She was assured that God would not be vindictive toward her and that she was cleansed and accepted.

She expressed her thanksgiving to the Lord by bringing an alabaster flask of ointment to anoint the Savior's feet. While this may seem strange in today's Western world, it was a common courtesy extended to those who walked either barefooted or with sandals in those days. The Pharisee had not extended this common courtesy to our Lord, but the sinful woman came to express her thanksgiving and her gratitude. The service she rendered was normally rendered by a servant. As she anointed Jesus' feet, her emotions of gratitude and thanksgiving overflowed, and she found herself weeping, her tears falling on Jesus' feet. In desperation and devotion, she wiped these tears away with her hair. It is a beautiful scene of sincere devotion and thanksgiving.

III. The thanksgiving of the Samaritan leper (Luke 17:11–19).

In this incident from the life of our Savior, we can see a reflection of the attitude of many of us.

The response of the nine. All ten lepers who pled for mercy received cleansing. Nine out of the ten did not return to the Lord to give him thanks for the miracle he had performed in their lives. This is a picture of the response we all sometimes make.

The thanksgiving of the Samaritan, a leper. When one of the ten discovered the wonderful healing he had received, he immediately turned back to express his gratitude. He praised God with a loud voice and fell on his face at Jesus' feet, giving him thanks.

The Scriptures tell us that every good gift and every perfect gift is from above and comes down from our Father God. How long has it been since your gratitude took the form of falling on your face before God in the private place of prayer to thank him and praise him and rejoice in his goodness to you? And how long has it been since you lifted your voice in the presence of others to give thanks and praise to God for his goodness to you?

IV. The thanksgiving of Zacchaeus (Luke 19:8).

Zacchaeus was despised by the people of his community because of his profession. He experienced the loving concern of God in Jesus Christ and experienced forgiveness and acceptance. As an indication of the genuineness of his experience, Zacchaeus changed the course of his life and the manner of his conduct. What have you given to indicate your gratitude?

I think of a story of a new convert from the continent of Africa. She was attending a worship service in which a mission offering was taken. She had no money. When the offering plate came to where she was, she placed it on the ground and then stood in the center of it as an indication that she wanted to give herself totally to the mission of her Lord.

V. Paul wrote an epistle to express his thanksgiving (Phil. 1:3–5).

Philippians has been called Paul's epistle of joy. The occasion for his writing this epistle was the gratitude of his heart for a gift received from his beloved friends in the church at Philippi (Phil. 4:10–13). How long has it been since you have written a letter to express gratitude to your parents, companion, or children, or to people who have rendered you a great personal service?

Conclusion

How do you say thank you? With words? With your face? With your deeds? By the service you render to others? The thankful heart will find a proper way to express gratitude.

SUNDAY EVENING, NOVEMBER 19

Title: The Enemy of the Kingdom—the Devil

Text: "An enemy hath done this" **(Matt. 13:28).**
"The enemy that sowed them is the devil" **(Matt. 13:39).**

Scripture Reading: Matthew 13:24–30, 36–43

Introduction

Who did it? "From whence then hath it tares?" (v. 27). This is the question at the heart of the parable. The answer is simple: "An enemy hath done this" (v. 28). In his interpretation of the parable in a private session with his disciples, Jesus left no doubt as to the identity of this malicious sower: "The enemy that sowed them is the devil" (v. 39). Note well the term *enemy*. This means an adversary, one who wills ill toward us, one who would destroy us.

No one can look out on our world and deny the presence of the tares. They are here. "An enemy hath done this." There's no doubt about that! "The enemy that sowed them is the devil." This parable teaches us that evil in the world is something more than the failure of good seed. Evil is alive, propagating itself in the world, the result of the havoc some sinister and aggressive personal power has wrought in humankind. Evil has been sown by an evil being, and it is growing, spreading, and producing a harvest. The enemy who planted all these tares, who sowed all this evil is the devil. Always his purpose and design is to delay, destroy, and defeat the coming of the kingdom of righteousness.

What about this great and mysterious enemy? The Bible tells us a great deal about him, but we will confine ourselves to what this parable teaches.

I. The enemy's character is fully revealed.

The devil is real. He is a deadly, sinister, and inescapable factor in our lives. In this parable, Jesus drags him out of his hiding place and holds him up to the light of day that we may see him.

Our enemy is a person. It would have been easy for Jesus to represent the weed seeds as having been sown by the wind. But he didn't! They were not! Just as in the parable of the sower Jesus makes the birds, who take up the seeds sown by the wayside, represent not impersonal forces but "the evil one" (Matt. 13:4, 19), so here he makes these evil seeds to be sown by a personal, evil agent, the devil. Jesus believed in a personal devil.

To discuss the personality of our enemy, other than to note the fact, is beyond the limits of this message, but the name *devil* is suggestive. This is our English translation of the Greek word *diabolos*, which means "the slanderer par excellence," and hence, an enemy.

Our enemy is aggressive and subtle in opposing the kingdom. "While men slept, his enemy came and sowed tares" (v. 25). The point is not to rebuke the servants for sleeping, for farm laborers need to rest, but to show the aggressive and subtle way the enemy did his evil work. He took every advantage in order to sow his evil seed. He still does.

The devil is active and versatile. A young minister in his first pastorate was upset when his wife bought an expensive new dress. "Honey," he said in desperation, "why did you do it? You know we can't afford it." She replied meekly, "I guess it was the devil tempting me." "Then why," he asked, "didn't you say, 'Get thee behind me, Satan'?" "I did," she said, "but then he whispered over my shoulder, 'It fits you perfectly in back too.'" This happens every day.

Our enemy is a trespasser. For all his aggressiveness and subtlety the devil has no right in the field where he sows his evil seed. The parable begins, "The kingdom of heaven is likened unto a man which sowed good seed in his field" (v. 24). Note the words, "his field." In his exposition, Jesus said, "He that soweth the good seed is the Son of man; the field is the world" (vv. 37–38). This is God's world. He has sown the good seed. He has created all things "very good" (Gen. 1:31).What about the evil we see about us every day? Jesus said, "An enemy hath done this. . . . The enemy is the devil." He is an intruder, trespassing in a domain where he has no right.

In his commentary on Matthew, Dr. G. Campbell Morgan said, "The devil is a squatter. . . . A squatter is a man who settles on land he has no right to, and works it for his own advantage" (G. Campbell Morgan, *Matthew*, 4th ed. [New York: Fleming Revell, 1939], 152). This is an apt descriptive term. We know the law about "squatter's rights." If someone settles on your property and you neither charge him rent nor drive him off, after a certain length of time he is there for keeps, and you can't dispossess him.

II. The enemy's method and design are clearly demonstrated.

The method is demonstrated in the type of seed sown by the enemy. Many versions say "tares," but more accurately the word is "darnel," a type of counterfeit, illegitimate wheat that cannot be distinguished from the genuine until the time of harvest (v. 26). The grains of the darnel are black and bitter and unfit for food.

The devil's method is plainly that of imitation, of substituting the counterfeit for the genuine, of mingling his illegitimate wheat with the real. That is his mission and method at the heart of the parable. The devil himself is a phony angel, a counterfeit saint. How widely and successfully has he sown his tares among the wheat.

The devil's purpose is to defeat the kingdom, to make it unfruitful. What did that malignant man in the parable hope to gain by sowing his neighbor's wheat with tares? He hoped only to destroy the harvest of good seed. This is the devil's purpose exactly. He works at it. The devil is never too busy to rock the cradle of a sleeping backslider. To defeat Christ's kingdom—that is his goal. Will he succeed?

III. The enemy's defeat is emphatically foretold.

"Why," someone asks, "are the wicked permitted to remain [vv. 28–30] and to prosper, materially at least, in a world ruled by a righteous God?" Not because God doesn't have the power to perceive and uproot the tares. He does have. Then why doesn't he?

God's world is a world of moral freedom. So long as this age shall last, God will respect this freedom, which includes persons' rights to choose to follow the devil if they will. And many have!

The precipitous uprooting of the tares might harm the wheat, the good and the genuine. I read the minutes of one church that, in nine business conferences out of ten, excluded from one to six members. One wonders how much wheat they uprooted in those meetings.

The counterfeit will not be fully manifest, at least not to us, until the harvesttime. Then the owner will say, "First collect the weeds and tie them in bundles to be burned; then gather the wheat and bring it into my barn" (v. 30 NIV). Jesus didn't leave us to guess at the result. "As the weeds are pulled up and burned in the fire, so it will be at the end of the age" (v. 40 NIV).

Conclusion

Is that all? No! Ten thousand times no! Thank God for the hope of the saints! "Then the righteous will shine like the sun in the kingdom of their Father" (v. 43 NIV). There will come a time when evil will be removed, the devil defeated, and the righteous vindicated. May God hasten the day!

WEDNESDAY EVENING, NOVEMBER 22

Title: Staying Out of God's Business

Text: "For the earth bringeth forth fruit of herself; first the blade, then the ear, after that the full corn in the ear" (**Mark 4:28**).

Scripture Reading: Matthew 13:3–8, 18–23, 24–30, 36–43, 47–50; Mark 4:26–29

Introduction

Jesus loved a good story. He told quite a few himself! But we have almost put a halo around them and lifted them out of the reach of the average person by calling them "parables," from the Greek word *parabola*. Yet all that word means is "a good story with a spiritual meaning"!

I would like for us to think of these particular teachings of Jesus as some good stories he told. They were always extemporaneous, dealing with real life and real people. Every story Jesus told was meant to evoke a response, call for a verdict, and bring about a change in the lives of his listeners. He used these little stories to make people think by putting truth in a vivid, challenging, and memorable way. And by doing this, he dealt with some real problems of life, including getting into other people's business!

Christ knew there is always a temptation to get into someone else's business—even God's business. And when this happens, we usually mess up things, both for ourselves and for God. So in four of his stories, Jesus suggested three ways we can stay out of God's business.

We can stay out of God's business:

I. By sticking to our own business—evangelization (Matt. 13:3–8, 18–23).

One of the best ways to stay out of someone else's business is to stick to our own business. Usually when we get involved in business that is none of our concern, it is not because we have nothing to do but rather because we are letting what we should be doing go undone.

Jesus was saying, "You have plenty to do in sharing your faith (sowing the seed). And you need not get into my business of evaluating others."

A sower went forth to sow. He did not go out as a soil conservation agent to test the soil, but to sow the seed. This man was hired by the farmer to plant the seed. And that is exactly what he did. He stuck to his own business. The owner knew some parts of the field were better than other parts, but he did not assign the job of judging the soil to the sower. He assigned him only the task of planting seed. That was the end of the sower's responsibility.

Once we learn that our business is to sow the seed and that when that is done our responsibility ends, much of our worry and anxiety over God's work will become a thing of the past. And sharing our faith will become a delightful experience!

In the face of discouraging response. All the sower is to do is to sow. It is beyond his power to make the seed grow. If all who witness were responsible for the effect of the gospel in the lives of others, theirs would be a sorry plight indeed! To illustrate this, Jesus mentioned three types of soil that hold little promise of response.

The closed mind—"wayside" (vv. 4, 19). In every church there are a number of "wayside" Christians. Their minds are closed, hard-packed soil indeed! Absolutely nothing, not even the truth, can penetrate their minds. Every question has been answered, and they do not want to be disturbed by the facts. New ideas are definitely out! They are hard-hearted souls who are destitute of the slightest trace of spiritual perception. They come to church, and they are religious enough, but the seed never penetrates their hardened souls.

It is when facing such characters as these that we tend to get over into God's business and assist him in moving people forward. But even in the face of such discouraging response, we must resist the temptation to get into God's business by sticking to our own business—sowing the seed.

The emotional mind—"stony places" (vv. 5, 20–21). There are many "stony soil" Christians. They get very enthusiastic and excited. They are superficial, and their faith is thin-surfaced. When temptations and persecution arise, they quickly drop out. We must use caution in classifying people as religious fanatics. Most pastors would rather try to restrain a fanatic than to resurrect a dead corpse. If some spiritual stirring of your soul should bring a tear to your eye or a word of praise to God, don't be ashamed. Real religion always begins with our emotions. The tragedy is when we let it end there.

The distracted mind—"among thorns" (vv. 7, 23). Some of our most capable people are represented by this analogy. They gladly accept the Word and get involved in serving God, and because they are so capable, they begin taking on many responsibilities, and slowly but surely God is crowded right out of their lives.

Three things are mentioned that will crowd God out if a person is not on guard: (1) "The cares of the world"—legitimate interests and duties that dominate one's life; (2) "the deceitfulness of riches"—being so distracted by wealth or the pursuit thereof that God is forgotten; and (3) "the lusts of other things"—enjoyments that prosperity makes possible and that ultimately can smother the seed.

Yet in the face of all these various forms of discouraging responses, we must stick to our own business and stay out of God's. He will handle these problems in his own way and in his own time.

In the knowledge that some will respond (vv. 8, 23). Paul has assured us that, "in due season we shall reap, if we faint not" (Gal. 6:9).

II. By trusting the Holy Spirit to do his business—salvation and sanctification (Mark 4:26–29).

There were those who wanted to speed the kingdom's progress by direct intervention. They wanted instant success. Jesus gently rebuked these eager and impatient souls by means of a little story.

This man could not make the rain fall, the sun shine, or the seed sprout. But he could plant the seed and leave the rest to God! Stage by stage, silently but surely, the seed grows to harvest.

Christ said, "Patience!" Leave the results to God. The seed has been sown, and a new divine energy has been released. Now stand back and trust the Holy Spirit to do his work!

Salvation. The "seed" is God's Word, and it has within itself the power to bring salvation. It is "the power of God unto salvation!" Once the Word is sown in a person's heart, the Holy Spirit alone can make it break forth into life.

Sanctification (Mark 4:28). "Of herself" means self-acting. The same word is used in Acts 12:10 to describe the city's gate opening of its "own accord." We get the word *automatic* from this Greek expression, *automate.* As the forces of nature continue to go on, so does the work of the Holy Spirit in the life of the Christian.

III. By allowing the angels to do their business—separation (Matt. 13:41, 49).

The temptation for good people to sit in judgment on others—to attempt to determine who is "saved" and who is "lost"—is ever present. They set out on the task of separating the "tares from the wheat" or the "bad fish from the good." Christ declares that this is the business of his angels at the end of time and thus is none of our concern today.

Once Socrates was asked to pass judgment on another. He said, "He who takes only a few things into account finds it easy to pass judgment." God will take care of his business in good time, and then we will know the wheat from the tares. Until then, people can be remade and lost souls can be saved. God is willing to wait and is willing to change the imperfect into the perfect, and that can happen only as we stick to our own business of evangelization, trust the Holy Spirit to do his business of salvation and sanctification, and allow the angels to do their business of separation.

Conclusion

If we have neglected our business of planting the seed, God's grace reclaims us into a life of productive service. If we have grown impatient with the work of the Holy Spirit or have run ahead of angels, by the grace of God we can get out of his business and back to our own.

SUNDAY MORNING, NOVEMBER 26

Title: What Is Your Heart's Desire?

Text: "Brethren, my heart's desire and prayer to God for them is that they may be saved" (**Rom. 10:1 RSV**).

Scripture Reading: Romans 9:1–3; 10:1–4

Hymns: "There's a Wideness in God's Mercy," Faber
"I Love to Tell the Story," Hankey
"Bring Them In," Thomas

Offertory Prayer: Our Father, you have given of yourself to us in the coming of Jesus Christ, who died on a cross for our sins and conquered death and the grave that we might have eternal life. You have bestowed on us the gift of your Holy Spirit as an abiding presence. You also have granted to us the privilege of cooperating with you in telling men and women, boys and girls of your saving love and your great life-changing power. Help us this day to give ourselves in cooperation with you in this purpose. Help us to dedicate time, talent, treasure, and testimony all to the end that your kingdom might come and your will be done in people's lives. In Jesus' name we pray. Amen.

Introduction

What is the deepest desire of your heart? I can remember that as a small boy, to be the owner of a bag of marbles was the height of my boyhood dreams. For some, life continues to be nothing more than a game of marbles.

I can remember when my dad would return from a trip to town bringing a sack of candy for us children. He was always met with joy and gratitude. Is the purpose behind your life the desire to enjoy a sack of candy?

I can remember when bringing a good report home to parents would bring happiness to my heart as well as to theirs. Have you defined your purpose for being in terms of securing an academic degree from some great university? Have you made knowledge your chief purpose for being?

I can remember moments when my greatest desire was to go to bed and find rest and sleep for the moment. The desire and the need for sleep cause some to define their purpose for being in terms of finding a bed and rest from the responsibilities of life.

Others have defined their purpose for being in terms of searching for a cushion on which to sit. For these, life is a search for comfort and ease.

All of us must admit that there are times when we look for a throne on which we can sit and have our wishes fulfilled. We must be on guard against building an empire with ourselves at the center.

Some have defined their purpose for being in terms of accumulating a pocketful of money. Our Lord pointedly warned against letting this be the purpose for our lives (Matt. 6:19–21). He warned against the seeking of wealth for wealth's sake. We must always be on guard against the peril of believing that in the accumulation of material things we will find our highest good and our greatest happiness (Luke 12:13–21). Our Lord offered some wise advice concerning our attitude toward earthly treasure: Earthly treasure is subject to decay from within and destruction from without. It is also subject to theft. It cannot satisfy the deepest longings of the human heart, and heaping up earthly treasure causes the heart to be distracted from the greater values of God's kingdom (Matt. 6:21). Our Lord strongly recommended that we labor for that which endures to everlasting life rather than investing our all in that which is going to perish (John 6:27).

It has been declared that mammon is the largest slaveholder in the world. Mammon will usurp the throne of the heart, which belongs only to Jesus Christ. Those who define their purpose for being in terms of securing a pocketful of money will spend life in anxiety.

Paul defined his purpose for being in terms of helping men and women experience God's great salvation (1 Cor. 9:19–23). All of us would be wise to identify with the apostle's heart's desire.

I. Paul's heart's desire grew out of the grace of God.

The apostle had experienced the forgiving grace of God. He had come to know Jesus Christ in the pardon and forgiveness of sin. He had received the precious gift of eternal life. The Holy Spirit was a permanent guest within him. He acknowledged that all he was, he was because of God's grace and mercy (1 Cor. 15:10). Paul's experience of the grace of God gave him an inward sense of obligation to help others come to experience that same grace (Rom. 1:14–15).

II. Paul's heart's desire arose out of an awareness of humankind's deepest need.

As we look over the world, we see many pressing and desperate needs—needs for better education, health care, housing, and employment opportunities. But humankind's greatest need is to know God. The greatest service that can be rendered to people is to help them come to know God in a relationship that brings peace and purpose to their lives.

III. Paul's heart's desire assisted him in determining the priorities for his life (Phil. 3:13).

Paul was a man with one great controlling purpose that determined his priority of values. One of the reasons why many of us go around in circles and arrive out of breath is that we do not have any clearly defined purpose for being. Once we determine our priorities, it is much easier to get from where we are to where we ought to be.

IV. Paul's heart's desire led him to a thorough self-inspection and a continuous dedication to his purpose (1 Cor. 9:24–27).

We must have more than a clearly defined objective for living. We need to properly evaluate ourselves and then dedicate ourselves without reservation to the accomplishment of our desired objective. The apostle Paul set for us a good example of self-inspection, self-discipline, and self-dedication.

Prayer for the apostle Paul was not a duty to be performed; it was a continuous dialogue with the Lord for guidance as he sought to make disciples in his going about from place to place. To the apostle, the indwelling Spirit was not to be ignored or neglected. Paul let the Holy Spirit work in him and through him to accomplish God's will in his life.

Conclusion

What is your heart's desire? Are you searching for a bag of marbles or a sack of candy? Are you searching for a report card or for a cushion on which to sit? All of us would be wise to define our purpose for being in terms of helping others come to know the great salvation that is available through Jesus Christ.

If we are to be good servants of Christ and good stewards of our opportunity, we will spend our time so as to please God and help others. We will give our testimony, both by the life we live and by the words we speak. We will utilize our talents for the glory of God and the good of others rather than for selfish purposes. We will not hesitate to share our finances to support spiritual services and kingdom enterprises for the glory of God and the good of others.

SUNDAY EVENING, NOVEMBER 26

Title: The Tricks of the Devil

Text: "Put on the whole armour of God, that ye may be able to stand against the wiles of the devil" **(Eph. 6:11)**.

Scripture Reading: Ephesians 6:10–20

Introduction

When I was a small boy, a magician of sorts came to our town and gave a performance in the schoolhouse. Everyone in town was there, including the village half-wit. Using members of his audience for his tricks, the magician provided amusement for many at the expense of a few, though everyone entered into the fun of the show.

No one had a better time than the village half-wit until the magician asked to borrow a watch. This poor boy loaned his. By a bit of sleight of hand, the magician put it in his pocket and slipped a piece of lead into a small leather pouch, though it appeared to the boy that his watch was in the pouch. The performer held the pouch to his ear and cried out: "This watch has stopped." He threw the pouch on the floor and stomped on it. Then he beat it with a hammer and squeezed it in a vice. All the while this poor boy was sweating profusely and pleading, "Don't break my watch." It was all so much fun until he became the victim of the magician's wiles.

Our text tells us of one who is a master trickster, a sleight-of-hand artist supreme, a magician without a peer. His purpose is not to entertain. He is our adversary, our enemy. He plays for keeps. He is bent on opposing God and destroying people's souls. Warning against this master trickster, Paul urged the Ephesians, "Put on the whole armour of God, that ye may be able to stand against the wiles of the devil" (v. 11).

I. What are some of the devil's tricks?

He has a bagful of them, and he knows all the latest methods.

One trick is to make sinning appear attractive by making it expensive. When people see how high priced a thing is in the marketplace, they think it must be good. So they indulge, pay a high price, and make fools of themselves.

Another trick is for the devil never to appear as the devil. "The most subtle form of evil," said theologian Reinhold Niebuhr, "is always good that pretends to be better than it is." The devil is hard to identify because he looks so distinguished, so intellectual, so successful, and sometimes so saintly. He moves in the best circles and is socially acceptable. He looks like a gentle-man and sometimes like a Christian.

The devil has a number of disguises. "The devil has an impressive wardrobe: he matches his wiles to our weaknesses, promising 'romance' to the teenager, academic preferment to the professor, money and a suburban house to the broker, a large church to the ambitious preacher, and continued youth to the man who is actually getting old. Ponder that list of disguises!" (George A. Buttrick, *God, Pain, and Evil* [Nashville: Abingdon, 1966], 65).

Another trick of the devil is to see to it that no one believes in him. Though opposing Scripture head-on, this is one of his choice tricks. He works under-ground and out of sight and, if possible, out of the human mind, but he works continually and effectively.

A little boy was annoyed because his grandmother, who lived in his home, always defended anyone who was criticized by saying something good about him or her. He heard about the devil for the first time in Sunday school one Sunday morning and could hardly wait to get home to challenge his grandmother. "Grandma," he said, "I know one you can't say anything good about—the devil, that's who." She eyed him calmly and said, "If you would attend to your business like he attends to his, you would get along a lot better." He does attend to his business.

The devil wants no credit for his work. Although there is abundant evi-dence to prove he exists, the devil sees to it that it is overlooked. He is the archdeceiver. He sees to it that people believe in their own intellect, their own power, their own skill, rather than the power of God.

Still another trick of the devil is to seduce people through something that is good. Humility is a good thing, but the devil can make people so proud of their humility that it is perverted into pride. He can make people so proud of their righteousness that they become self-righteous. He can make people think they are spiritual when actually they are just too lazy to commit some sins that require energy and hard work. The devil perverts and twists to his own ends the highest powers of people.

And still another trick of the devil is to try to get people to take him as a joke. Those who think of themselves as too enlightened to take the devil seriously are more enlightened than Paul, for he believed in a personal, invisible, pervasive spirit of evil, the enemy of goodness, with numberless other evil spirits at his command. He still wants people to laugh him off, to think of him as an outmoded superstition unrelated to modern life.

II. What is the devil's purpose in his subtlety?

This appears in three relationships.

As far as God and his kingdom's cause are concerned, the devil is the adversary, the deadly, age-long enemy.

He would deny the power, wisdom, truth, and purpose of God. Paul spoke of those "who changed the truth of God into a lie" (Rom. 1:25).

382

He would defeat the work of the kingdom if he could. He will cause turmoil among God's people if he can. He would rather start a church fuss than sell a barrel of whiskey. He trespasses in God's domain to plant his servants among the people of God.

As far as Christians' efforts to live for God are concerned, the devil's purpose is clear.

To trip them into falling, into committing sin in order to discredit them before the world. David was forgiven on the basis of repentance and confession, but God's prophet warned, "But because by doing this you have shown utter contempt for the LORD, the son born to you will die" (2 Sam. 12:14 NIV). The devil tries to defeat our witness and take us out of service.

To trick Christians to neglect. Jesus said, "Go . . . and make disciples" (Matt. 28:19). The devil has no objection to our going if we don't make disciples. The devil would trick Christians into neglecting the means of grace, the worship of God, and witness to the lost.

To trick Christians into complacency. That is the best and deadliest trick in the book.

As far as unsaved people are concerned, the devil's purpose is to destroy them body and soul. "Be alert and of sober mind. Your enemy the devil prowls around like a roaring lion looking for someone to devour" (1 Peter 5:8 NIV). The devil would oppose the resolve and defeat the purpose of a person who wants to be a Christian. Seldom does one see an unsaved person without an excuse for not being a Christian. As soon as he or she is converted, that person's eyes are opened to see that in the past Satan had deceived him or her and provided excuses.

III. Four suggestions for resisting Satan's deadly tricks.

We are to make sure we leave no vulnerable spots exposed. "Wherefore take unto you the whole armour of God, that ye may be able to withstand in the evil day, and having done all, to stand" (v. 13). Study that figure and you will see that the whole body is protected unless we turn our backs to run from the devil; and this we are not to do.

We are to resist his approaches. Peter said, "Resist him, standing firm in the faith" (1 Peter 5:9 NIV). James said that the devil is a coward: "Resist the devil, and he will flee from you" (James 4:7). The "shield of faith" (Eph. 6:16) is to be our strong defense.

We are to take up the fight. "And take . . . the sword of the Spirit, which is the word of God" (v. 17). The sword is a weapon for attack. In his first epistle, John said, "The reason the Son of God appeared was to destroy the devil's work" (3:8 NIV).

We are to make it clear whose side we are on. God is more powerful than the devil. When an old man was converted, a friend teased him, "Sam, I hear you've got the mastery of the devil." He replied, "No, but I've got the Master of the devil for my Friend."

Conclusion

Do we have Christ as our Friend, our Savior, our constant companion? Jesus said, "He that is not with me is against me; and he that gathereth not with me scattereth abroad" (Matt. 12:30).

WEDNESDAY EVENING, NOVEMBER 29

Title: When God Throws a Party

Text: "Then said he also to him that bade him, When thou makest a dinner or a supper, call not thy friends, nor thy brethren, neither thy kinsmen, nor thy rich neighbours; lest they also bid thee again, and a recompense be made thee. But when thou makest a feast, call the poor, the maimed, the lame, the blind: and thou shalt be blessed; for they cannot recompense thee: for thou shalt be recompensed at the resurrection of the just" **(Luke 14:12–14)**.

Scripture Reading: Luke 14:12–24

Introduction

Normally we do not think of turning to Jesus for advice on how to throw a party. We may turn to him for advice on how to pray, how to fix a broken heart, how to understand the Scriptures, or how to face death. But Jesus and parties do not seem to mix. We identify Jesus with good news but not with good times.

The problem is not his but ours. If we could rid ourselves from ascetic caricatures of Jesus, we would find that he was indeed a "party man." He performed his first miracle at a wedding party. At a dinner occasion he allowed a woman to anoint his feet. He was accused by his enemies of being a "winebibber and a glutton" (Matt. 11:19). The kingdom of heaven is like a festive banquet.

The gospel of Luke is our best guide to Jesus' social life. It takes us to one dinner party after another. It was at such a party that Jesus told this story about the kind of invitation God extends when he throws a party.

I. An invitation to divine food and fellowship (Luke 14:16).

"Supper" is a mealtime, but more than that it is a time for fellowship with those whom you love most. I remember the big kitchen we had as a child in our home in Louisiana. It had a fireplace in the corner, and a large round table sat in the center of the room with five chairs around it. Suppertime was the best time of the day. I think of how hungry we were as children and how good everything tasted. But supper was not only a time to eat; it was also a time to be with my mother, father, sister, and brother—those whom I loved most.

Supper is still the best time of the day around our house. It means food, yes, but it also means fellowship. It means laughter and joy. It means satisfying not only the body but also the soul. Jesus was saying that coming to God is like that. God invites us to divine food and divine fellowship.

II. An invitation—not a subpoena (Luke 14:17).

"Come" is the key word in the invitation. God's Word is full of divine invitations to people. Jesus said, "Whosoever will, let him take of the water of life freely" (Rev. 22:17). People are invited to be saved; they are not subpoenaed. We can go out and invite people, but we cannot make them come. They must decide for themselves. There are no captive members of the kingdom of God.

III. An invitation that can be declined (Luke 14:18–20).

The word here is "excuse," and there is a difference between an excuse and a reason. We give an excuse when we have no reason to offer. And why do we usually offer an excuse? Because we know that what we are doing is wrong.

That these were excuses offered is seen in the fact that land could not be inspected at night, oxen could not be proven in darkness, and nothing is said of the supper being a "stag party." Doubtless the guest could have brought his wife. It is always a dangerous thing to use your family as an excuse for failing to do what you know you ought to do!

The first two were courteous. They said, "I pray thee have me excused" (vv. 18–19). The third man was downright rude, for he said, "I cannot come" (v. 20). But it matters not how one declines; it is still saying no to God's invitation!

IV. An invitation to all who are hungry (Luke 14:21–22).

These were unfortunate people for whom life had been almost unbearable. They were hungry, and when good food and cordial fellowship were offered, they gladly accepted the invitation. There will always be those who do not hunger and thirst after righteousness, but it is equally true that there are always those who do, and they will respond.

Christ's emphasis seems to be on the invitation list. He is saying that when you have a dinner, do not restrict your invitation list to your own kind. Mix it up. Invite the "poor, maimed, lame and blind" (v. 13). Don't invite only those who will reciprocate by inviting you to their parties. Rather, follow God's example and extend your generosity to all who are hungry.

V. An invitation of urgency (Luke 14:23).

Christ said to "compel" them to come in. He strongly persuades us to come to his banquet. But why the note of urgency?

Because of the need of those invited. We have all sinned, and the wages (results) of our sin is death. We shall never be able to satisfy our own spiritual hunger. It is urgent that we respond quickly!

Because the invitation will not always be extended. God warns that his Spirit will not always strive with man. Isaiah 55:6 admonishes us, "Seek ye the Lord while he may be found, call ye upon him while he is near."

VI. An invitation to which you can become deaf (Luke 14:24).

God does not shut the door; people do. The three who offered excuses became so absorbed with their property, activities, and social life that they never thought of the invitation again. This happens time and again to those who refuse God's invitation. A person can decline God's invitation so long that eventually he or she ceases to hear God's call at all.

Conclusion

Do you still hear the voice of God, however faintly? Do you hear his invitation to join him at his banquet table? If you have a hunger in your heart, rejoice. Too many people can be satisfied by a night out, by getting drunk, by buying things, or by being applauded. So long as your heart is hungry, there is hope that you will give God a chance—that you will respond to his invitation.

SUGGESTED PREACHING PROGRAM FOR THE MONTH OF
DECEMBER

■ **Sunday Mornings**

With the coming of the month of December, we will focus primarily on preparation for the observance of Christmas. This time of the year provides an opportunity for ministers to interpret the meaning of the coming of Christ. "Responding Properly to the Coming of the Christ" is the suggested theme for these messages.

■ **Sunday Evenings**

The gospel is not good advice: it is good news. "Sharing the Good News of Christmas" is the suggested theme for missionary messages that encourage believers to join with the angels and the shepherds in proclaiming the coming of Christ.

■ **Wednesday Evenings**

The Wednesday evening sermons this month focus on living our lives in such a way that difficult life circumstances don't derail our faith. Use the theme "Be Prepared for What Life Throws Your Way."

SUNDAY MORNING, DECEMBER 3

Title: The First Christmas

Text: "Behold, a virgin shall be with child, and shall bring forth a son, and they shall call his name Emmanuel, which, being interpreted is, God with us" **(Matt. 1:23)**.

Scripture Reading: Matthew 1:18–25

Hymns: "Hark! The Herald Angels Sing," Wesley
"Joy to the World!" Watts
"Ye Servants of God," Wesley

Offertory Prayer: Gracious and loving Father, during this period of the year we are reminded over and over of the lavishness of your gift to us in your Son, Jesus Christ. Today we would bow down with the wise men and present to him the best gifts we have. We bring the gift of love, the gift of reverent worship, the gift of grateful hearts, and the gift of dedicated lives in his service. Bless our tithes and offerings that his name might be made known throughout all the world. In Jesus' name we pray. Amen.

Introduction

Who is the greatest person of all time? Who is the greatest teacher of all time? Who is the greatest leader of all time? Who lived the only perfect life ever lived? The answer to these questions is Jesus Christ. None other can compare with him. No other religion ever boasted of such a founder.

There is no question that the birth of Jesus Christ is the most meaningful birth in the annals of time. It changed the chronology of history and introduced on the stage of human existence the greatest one who ever blessed the world with his presence. He is the most unique character of all time.

Jesus' teachings, miracles, parables, precepts, example, life, death, resurrection, and purposes all reveal his uniqueness. However, his birth, the first Christmas, really reveals his uniqueness. Let us examine the first Christmas, the coming of Jesus Christ into this world.

I. The first Christmas was an advent.

The birth of our Lord Jesus Christ differs in one momentous respect from every other birth. His life did not begin with his birth, for he existed in the beginning with the Father God. His birth was an advent, a coming into this world from heaven on a special mission. "In the beginning was the Word, and the Word was with God, and the Word was God. The same was in the beginning with God" (John 1:1–2). "And the Word was made flesh, and dwelt among us" (John 1:14).

"But when the fullness of the time was come, God sent forth his Son, made of a woman, made under the law, to redeem them that were under the law, that we might receive the adoption of sons" (Gal. 4:4–5).

"For ye know the grace of our Lord Jesus Christ, that, though he was rich, yet for your sakes he became poor, that ye through his poverty might be rich" (2 Cor. 8:9).

"Let this mind be in you, which was also in Christ Jesus: who, being in the form of God, thought it not robbery to be equal with God, but made himself of no reputation, and took upon him the form of a servant, and was made in the likeness of men; and being found in fashion as a man, he humbled himself, and became obedient unto death, even the death of the cross" (Phil. 2:5–8).

Jesus did not come to be; he already was. Through his birth he came to earth as a man.

II. The first Christmas came about through the virgin birth of Christ.

The question of the virgin birth is a relevant question that has to do with miracles, for the virgin birth of Christ was a miracle. The virgin birth is the keystone of the arch of history. If Jesus was not born of a virgin, he is not God but man.

Both Matthew and Luke record the virgin birth. Christian tradition supports the virgin birth, and it is incorporated in the Apostles' Creed.

Roman Catholics and orthodox Christians believe it is a necessary article of faith.

The virgin birth reveals that Christ is God. The angel spoke to Mary: "The Holy Spirit shall come upon thee, and the power of the Highest shall overshadow thee; therefore also that holy thing which shall be born of thee shall be called the Son of God" (Luke 1:35).

The virgin birth displays the power of God. The birth of Jesus Christ was not accomplished through the normal human process but rather through the power of God. "[The angel said,] For with God nothing shall be impossible. And Mary said, Behold the handmaid of the Lord; be it unto me according to thy word. And the angel departed from her" (Luke 1:37–38).

The Virgin Birth declares the purpose of God. "For unto you is born this day in the city of David a Saviour, which is Christ the Lord" (Luke 2:11). "And she shall bring forth a son, and thou shalt call his name JESUS; for he shall save his people from their sins" (Matt. 1:21). Paul said, "For he hath made him to be sin for us, who knew no sin, that we might be made the righteousness of God in him" (2 Cor. 5:21). Jesus Christ was born of a virgin, lived without sin, and died on the cross that he might redeem us. What a blessed thought! What a glorious truth!

III. The first Christmas proclaims that God is with us.

Matthew quoted Isaiah as saying, "Behold, a virgin shall be with child, and shall bring forth a son, and they shall call his name Emmanuel, which being interpreted is, God with us" (Matt. 1:23). The great truth of Christmas is that God has come to be with us. In the Bible 256 titles are given to Jesus in an effort to reveal to us his majesty, deity, and humanity. Jesus Christ as God with us reveals some great truths:

Jesus Christ, the Incarnate One, is the greatest revelation ever made. "And the Word was made flesh and dwelt among us" (John 1:14). "God was manifest in the flesh" (1 Tim. 3:16).

Jesus Christ, the Incarnate One, embodies the greatest power ever known. "Emmanuel, which being interpreted is, God with us" (Matt. 1:23). The person who wants to experience the power of God must experience Jesus Christ as Savior.

Jesus Christ, the Incarnate One, came on the mightiest mission ever known to man. "That through death he might destroy him that had the power of death, that is, the devil, and deliver them who through fear of death, were all their lifetime subject to bondage" (Heb. 2:14–15).

Jesus Christ, the Incarnate One, is the bearer of the grandest gift ever bestowed. "I am come that they might have life, and that they might have it more abundantly" (John 10:10).

Jesus Christ, the Incarnate One, is the most potent force ever communicated. "Behold, this child is set for the fall and rising again of many in Israel" (Luke 2:34).

Conclusion

The first Christmas presents to us the Christ. Let us seek him, believe on him, and serve him.

SUNDAY EVENING, DECEMBER 3

Title: Sharing the Good News

Text: "We do not well: this day is a day of good tidings, and we hold our peace" (**2 Kings 7:9**).

Scripture Reading: 2 Kings 7:1–11

Introduction

One of the most distressing and desperate conditions in our world today is hunger. Millions die each year from starvation and related diseases. Most of these are children five years of age and under. Our Christian compassion constrains us not only to share the Bread of Life but also to share the bread from our tables.

Our text tells of a time when there was hunger and starvation in Samaria. Benhadad, king of Syria, surrounded the city with a vast army. His blockade was completely successful, and each day brought the whole population closer to a horrible end. Cannibalism was practiced. Mothers killed their children for food. The king looked upon the agony of his people and put on sackcloth beneath his royal robes.

In the open space between the walls of the city and the Syrian camp were four lepers. Their plight was even worse than those within the city. Samaria had evicted them. The Syrians would not associate with them. They had made their living by begging from the Samaritans. Now they were excluded from the Samaritans, who had nothing to give them anyway. They were starving to death, and they were also dying of leprosy. They were desperate.

They reasoned among themselves, "If we were allowed in the city, there is nothing for us there. If we go into the camp, the worst thing they could do to us is kill us, and we are going to die anyway."

As they approached the camp, they expected to be challenged by a sentry with the words, "Halt, who goes there?" but they heard no human sound. Benhadad and his army were frightened into fleeing by sounds that suggested that the Hittites from the north and the Egyptians from the south had come to the rescue of Samaria.

Fearing a trap, the lepers looked into the first tent. A table of food was spread, but there were no human occupants. They ate and drank from the provisions. They took the gold and silver and cloth and hid it. Entering a second tent, they repeated the process.

Then one of them remembered the famished people in Samaria. "We do not well: this is a day of good tidings, and we hold our peace," he said.

He knew they had no right to withhold this information from a starving city. The conscience of each leper was awakened. They reported to the king, who sent patrols to support their story. The famine was broken. The blockade was lifted. The lepers had made a wonderful discovery. When they were filled, they remembered the desperately hungry in the city. When their appetites were satisfied, they did not forget those who were starving. Out of the experience of these lepers we find lessons that apply to us.

I. People are hungry, and we have bread.

Bestseller lists almost always include a book on dieting or suggestions for losing weight. People in the deprived nations of the world do not have a problem with being overweight. While people in other countries are dying from malnutrition, many American families stuff themselves and throw enough into the garbage can to keep another family alive.

II. People in our world have never heard of Christ.

We also have the Bread of Life. Jesus said, "I am the bread of life: he that cometh to me shall never hunger" (John 6:35). We have found that Jesus satisfies our inner hunger. We have heard about him over and over again. We have several Bibles in our homes. In the Sunday school classroom and from the pulpit, we hear the message weekly. How can we be satisfied to hear the message over and over when some have not heard the message even once?

Conclusion

Jesus commands us to take the gospel to everyone in the world. The small band of first-century Christians took him seriously, and they came closer to winning their world than we have ever done since. And now we have the Internet, television, radio, printing presses, and skills and experience that early Christians did not have. We have means of swift transportation to any country of the world. Yet we lack their commitment and zeal.

Is it too much to dream that by the year 2020 every person in the world who consents to hear will have heard the message at least once? This is possible and practical if Christians join hearts, money, and lives in an all-out effort to take seriously the commission of our Lord to tell all for whom he died.

WEDNESDAY EVENING, DECEMBER 6

Title: The Danger of Delay

Text: "Afterward came also the other virgins, saying, Lord, Lord, open to us. But he answered and said, Verily I say unto you, I know you not. Watch therefore, for you know neither the day nor the hour wherein the Son of man cometh" (**Matt. 25:11–13**).

Scripture Reading: Matthew 25:1–13

Introduction

Delay has been the downfall of countless individuals and nations. An army delays its attack an hour and loses the battle. A patient delays an operation a year and loses his life. An aviator delays his point of descent fifty yards and loses his aircraft. A man delays his day of salvation one day and loses his soul. So the tragic story of man continues page after page and century after century.

Life at its fullest ends all too soon. One moment's delay may usher in an eternity of regret. Delay poses so serious a threat to man that Christ offers an entire parable on the danger of delay.

I. The danger of being foolish.

"Five of them were wise, and five were foolish. They that were foolish took their lamps, and took no oil with them" (Matt.25:2–3). The danger of delay is the danger of being foolish because of a failure to see your present need. The five foolish bridesmaids felt they had sufficient oil to last the rest of the night. Theirs was a present need, but they failed to see it.

Your present need may be overshadowed by other interests. The five foolish bridesmaids were so excited about the events of the night that they failed to see their own need. Your present need has eternal significance because of a failure to exercise any forethought. The bridesmaids did not anticipate possible future events. Their failure to consider the bridegroom's tarrying resulted in their lamps running out of oil. Forethought is a mark of wisdom. One may be like the man who fell from a fourteenth-story window. As he fell past the tenth floor, he waved at a friend and said, "Everything is all right so far." The greatest act of folly is to die without Christ. For this there is no excuse.

II. The danger of being wasteful.

"While the bridegroom tarried, they all slumbered and slept" (Matt 25:5). Precious time was wasted. Instead of using these moments for getting prepared, the five foolish bridesmaids slept and thus squandered what little time was left. The lost cannot afford to waste whatever time they may have left.

As theologian and poet Robert H. Smith (1932–82) wrote:

> *The clock of life is wound but once,*
> *And no man has the power*
> *To tell just when the hands will stop*
> *At late or early hour.*
> *To lose one's wealth is sad indeed,*
> *To lose one's health is more,*
> *To lose one's soul is such a loss*
> *As no man can restore.*

The present only is our own,
So Live, Love, toil with a will—
Place no faith in "Tomorrow"—
For the clock may then be still.

There was nothing wrong with the five wise ones sleeping, because they were prepared. But the five foolish ones could not afford to waste these valuable moments. These were moments in which the Lord should be sought. Isaiah admonishes us to: "Seek ye the LORD while he may be found, call ye upon him while he is near" (Isa. 55:6).

Delay wastes life itself. Every moment that is wasted is that much of life that is wasted. Christ said that a life is wasted when a person gains the whole world and loses his own soul. The sad fact is that such a life could be of great value to God.

What a waste of life it would have been if Paul had been converted at seventy instead of thirty-two. There was a Mathew Henry because he was converted at eleven and not seventy. There was a Jonathan Edwards because he was converted at eight and not eighty.

Perry Doss was saved during a revival at the First Baptist Church of Chickasha, Oklahoma, where I was pastor. He was seventy years old. After the service I was visiting with Perry. Tears began to flow down his cheeks. I asked him if he was not glad he was saved. He said," I am glad my soul is saved, but I am so sad my life is lost." He went on to explain, "None of my children will have any memory of my sitting with them in church, or hearing me pray, or seeing me read the Bible. Oh yes, I am glad my soul is saved but I am so sad my life is lost."

Delay wastes influence. If only one of the five foolish bridesmaids would have become concerned about her need and rushed to buy oil, undoubtedly the other four would have gone also. Delay not only affects you but others as well.

III. The danger of being unprepared.

"The foolish said unto the wise, 'Give us of your oil; for our lamps are gone out'" (Matt. 25:8). Some, like the five foolish bridesmaids, are unprepared because of a misplaced trust in an uncertain future. They are confident that there is plenty of time yet left in which to make preparation. Hell is filled with people who intended to trust Christ—tomorrow.

Some are trusting in the merits of others. Could it have been that these five foolish bridesmaids were actually planning to draw from the oil reserves of others?

It may be that some are trusting in the prayers of loved ones or in their own good works. This is misplaced trust. Christ says so in Matthew 7:22–23.

IV. The danger of being rejected.

"And when they went to buy, the bridegroom came; and they that were ready went in and the door was shut. Afterward came also the other virgins, saying, Lord, Lord, open to us. But he answered and said, Verily I say unto you, I know you not" (Matt. 25:10–12).

Some will be rejected because of the nature of Christ's coming. He will come to receive His own—those who are ready. "They that were ready went in" (Matt. 25:10). Those who were not ready were rejected. Christ's coming terminates all possibilities of being saved—"the door was shut." There is no second chance when Christ comes again.

Others will be rejected because of a failure to know the Lord. The bridegroom said, "I know you not." The Lord must be known other than his name. "Not every one that says unto me, Lord, Lord, shall enter into the kingdom of heaven; but he that doeth the will of my Father which is in heaven" (Matt. 7:21). And what is the will of the Father? Peter said that the Lord is "not willing that any should perish, but that all should come to repentance" (2 Peter 3:9). One must know the Lord as personal Savior.

There will be those who will be rejected because of the imminence of Christ's return. Christ commands us to "Watch therefore, for ye know neither the day nor the hour wherein the Son of man cometh" (Matt. 25:13). His coming will be like "a thief in the night" (1 Thess. 5:2). Two things end all chances of being saved: death and the return of Christ.

Conclusion

Nowhere is the danger of delay more clearly expressed than in an old hymn by Philip Bliss:

> *"Almost persuaded," harvest is past!*
> *"Almost persuaded," doom comes at last!*
> *"Almost" cannot avail; "Almost" is but to fail!*
> *Sad, sad that bitter wail–"Almost," but lost.*

SUNDAY MORNING, DECEMBER 10

Title: Is Christmas Too Costly?

Text: "And when they were departed, behold, the angel of the Lord appeareth to Joseph in a dream, saying, Arise, and take the young child and his mother, and flee into Egypt, and be thou there until I bring thee word: for Herod will seek the young child to destroy him" **(Matt. 2:13)**.

Scripture Reading: Matthew 2:13–23

Hymns: "Jesus Shall Reign Where'er the Sun," Watts
"Angels from the Realms of Glory," Montgomery
"Glory to His Name," Hoffman

Offertory Prayer: Our Father and our God, you are the author and giver of every good and perfect gift. Today we offer to you the sincere thanks of our hearts for your unspeakable gift to us in Jesus Christ. Today we come bringing ourselves as well as our substance in grateful worship. Bless these gifts to the honor and glory of your name and to the advancement of your kingdom. We pray in Jesus' name. Amen.

Introduction

One of the standard complaints heard at Christmastime is that the holiday is too costly. Is Christmas too costly? The answer to this question depends on each individual's viewpoint.

What about the first Christmas? Was it costly? It cost Mary and Joseph the comforts of home during a journey to Bethlehem and an angel-directed exile to Egypt to protect the Christ child from the wrath of Herod. It cost mothers and fathers in and around Bethlehem the massacre of their babies by the wicked Herod. It cost the shepherds the neglect of the shepherd's life for a journey to Bethlehem to see the thing the Lord had made known to them. The Bible says, "And they came with haste, and found Mary, and Joseph, and the babe lying in a manger" (Luke 2:16). It cost the wise men a long journey, expensive gifts of gold, frankincense, and myrrh. It also cost them changed lives and a journey home by another way. It cost the early apostles and the church persecution and sometimes martyrdom. It has cost missionaries untold suffering and privation to spread the gospel of Christ.

What did Christmas cost God the Father? It cost him more than all, for it cost the Father his only begotten Son. The Bible says, "For God so loved the world, that he gave his only begotten Son, that whosoever believeth in him should not perish, but have everlasting life" (John 3:16).

What did Christmas cost Jesus? It cost him a life of sacrifice and service, a cruel death that is unmatched in history.

Is Christmas costly? Yes. Is Christmas too costly? That is another question, and I want to discuss it with you.

I. Christmas is too costly if it does not mean hope.

The prophecies of the Old Testament had pointed to the coming of the Messiah, the great deliverer. The world had been looking and longing for his coming for more than four thousand years. The waiting time had been long, and the world was weary. It was to a world almost without hope that the angels had brought their message of hope. People since that day have not been without hope. Those who know the Christ of Christmas will never be without hope. Hopeless are all those who have not heard about Christ.

II. Christmas is too costly if we do not receive God's gift, if we do not experience God's love.

The greatest word of all for Christmas is, "For God so loved the world, that he gave his only begotten Son" (John 3:16). "But God commendeth his love toward us, in that, while we were sinners, Christ died for us" (Rom. 5:8). "Herein is love, not that we loved God, but that he loved us, and sent his Son to be the propitiation for our sins" (1 John 4:10).

No one understands the first Christmas until he experiences the love of God in Christ. Let our hearts be filled with love, the genuine love of God in Christ. And let us manifest that love to others.

III. Christmas is too costly if we do not experience the forgiveness of sins.

An angel said to Joseph, "And thou shalt call his name Jesus; for he shall save his people from their sins" (Matt. 1:21). To the shepherds an angel said, "For unto you is born this day in the city of David a Saviour which is Christ the Lord" (Luke 2:11). Paul spoke of the costly purpose of Jesus' coming: "In whom we have redemption through his blood, for forgiveness of sins, according to the riches of his grace" (Eph. 1:7).

W. Malcolm Fuller tells the story of a man who sat down after Christmas to "review the damage." He wrote to a friend, "The toys we bought are already broken, the tree has lost its freshness and has been thrown out. We have overeaten, overspent, and overlooked."

We would truly overlook the true meaning of Christmas if we forgot that Jesus' purpose for coming into the world was to seek and save the lost (Luke 19:10).

IV. Christmas is too costly if we do not radiate joy.

The angel of the Lord said to the shepherds, "Fear not, for, behold, I bring you good tidings of great joy, which shall be to all people" (Luke 2:10). Joy filled the hearts of the people who heard the good news from the hillside. Joy filled the hearts of Simeon and Anna in the temple as they realized the significance of the child for the world. Joy filled the hearts of the wise men when they saw his star, when they presented their gifts, and as they returned to their homes after worshiping the Christ. *Joy* is a Christmas word. Let joy fill your heart during this Christmas season.

V. Christmas is too costly if we do not manifest peace and goodwill among people.

The angel of the Lord said: "Glory to God in the highest, and on earth peace, good will toward men" (Luke 2:14). There is no room for bitterness at Christmas. Christmas is the time for peace and goodwill. If we have been recipients of God's goodwill, then we will have goodwill toward God and others.

Christmas means giving up unreasonable and stubborn attitudes. Christmas is the time to reexamine our attitudes in the light of the Christmas star. To have the true spirit of Christmas, we must have peace with all people.

VI. Christmas is too costly if we do not proclaim the Good News.

What is the good news of Christmas? "For unto you is born this day in the city of David a Saviour, which is Christ the Lord" (Luke 2:11).

The greatest privilege that can come to any of us is to share our knowledge of the Lord with those who do not know him. This can be done through our witnessing efforts, our soul-winning efforts, and our missionary program. We can link our lives to God's eternal purposes by proclaiming the Good News. Make this Christmas meaningful by sharing the Good News.

VII. Christmas is too costly if we do not exercise faith.

Faith is a word for Christmas. God's faith in man is revealed by the gift of his Son Jesus. Can anyone ever doubt that God cares for sinful people? God has provided the object of humankind's faith.

God's wonderful provision demands a response. Remove your doubts and questions by responding with faith in the Lord Jesus.

Conclusion

Christmas isn't too costly if we respond to our Lord. God loves us tremendously, and he wants to come and dwell with us. He can do this through the Christ of Christmas!

SUNDAY EVENING, DECEMBER 10

Title: The Great Commission and You

Text: "Go ye therefore and make disciples of all nations" **(Matt. 28:19 RSV).**

Scripture Reading: Matthew 28:16–20

Introduction

The Great Commission was addressed not only to missionaries but to all believers. We must accept three supreme missionary imperatives if we are to be a missionary people.

I. A Christian experience we wish to share.

Unless we have had a vital experience with Christ, we have no motivation to share him with others. But if we have yielded our hearts and lives to him and have felt the joy and peace of his forgiveness, we have a message to proclaim.

Dr. E. Stanley Jones wrote, "If a Christian says he does not believe in mission, he is really saying, 'Christ doesn't mean much to me, so I presume that he would not mean much to anyone else.'"

II. A Christian conviction that Christ is the only way.

A popular philosophy today is that it doesn't make any difference what you believe as long as you are sincere. If you believe that the false religions found in all countries around the world are as good as the Christian faith, you have no justification to support world missions. Jesus said, "I am the way . . . ; no man cometh unto the Father but by me" (John 14:6). Do you believe he is the only way, or just one of several ways? All who are not committed to Christ are outside the circle of the redeemed of God. That should make us zealous to work so that all may hear.

As the conviction that "there is none other name under heaven given among men whereby we must be saved" is softened and compromised in a denomination, their missionary zeal is diminished. As long as we believe there is no way to salvation except through Christ, the Holy Spirit can fire our hearts with missionary zeal.

III. A Christian compassion that responds lovingly to need.

Jesus looked at the multitudes and had compassion on them, for they were as sheep without a shepherd. He stood above the city of Jerusalem and wept over their refusal to hear and believe and repent. How much compassion do you have for a world without Christ?

Conclusion

"The night cometh when no man can work." That time may be closer than we think. What are we doing about it?

WEDNESDAY EVENING, DECEMBER 13

Title: Make the Most of Your Life

Text: "Let no man despise thy youth; but be thou an example of the believers, in word, in conversation, in charity, in spirit, in faith, in purity" **(1 Tim. 4:12)**.

Scripture Reading: 1 Timothy 4:12–16

Introduction

"Make the most of your life!" These are six power-packed words. And they are supported by a dynamic statement of the Bible also composed of six words. In 1 Timothy 4:12 Paul challenges every person with these words: "Be thou an example of the believers."

Sadly, most people have a low opinion of themselves and spend hours maximizing their weaknesses. The end result of such negative thinking is a failure to become what they are quite capable of being. Today I challenge you to make the most of your life. How does this come about?

I. Visualize your own potential.

"Where there is no vision, the people perish" (Prov. 29:18).

Author Grenville Kleiser said, "Success is your birthright." Do you ever take a long look into yourself and ask yourself, "Who really am I?"

Thomas Edison said, "If we would only do what we are capable of doing, we would absolutely be astounded."

When called to preach at age fifteen, I began to visualize my own potential. I ordered catalogs from colleges and seminaries. Then I adopted a plan that would take me from a high school diploma to a ThD in nine years. Because of this visualization, doors were opened that otherwise might have been closed. Like Timothy, I was challenged to make the most of my life. And like Timothy, I sought to do just that.

II. Recognize the possibility of the "impossible."

"The things that are impossible with men are possible with God" (Luke 19:17). Bob Jones pointed out that Zacchaeus had short legs, but he outran the crowd when Jesus passed through town. Short legs will get you there as fast as long legs when you recognize the possibility of the impossible.

I grew up with the great gospel songwriter and arranger W. Elmo Mercer in a small Louisiana town. He was never conquered by lack, loss, or limitation. He lived in a humble home with no piano, but he would come to the church and practice. Having a gift of music, he began to compose. My mother paid for Elmo's first copyright. As a high school senior, he preenrolled in Louisiana College. After his first semester, he had to drop out because of a lack of funding. He was hired by a bank, but he so much wanted a career in music. Recognizing the possibility of the impossible, he refused to give in. He kept practicing, composing music, and even teaching a few students.

Then one day Mr. John T. Benson, of the Benson Music Publishing Company in Nashville, phoned Elmo. He offered him a job and published several of Elmo's songs. Elmo worked hard and kept writing songs, believing he could succeed. In time he became the chief music editor for the Benson Company.

Elmo visualized his own potential, believed that nothing was impossible, and gave all he had to make the most of his life. He is now happily retired in Nashville.

III. Patronize a winning set of values.

"Set your affections on things above, not on things on the earth" (Col. 3:2). Don't be guided by a losing set of values. For years Paul patronized a losing set of values. What was important to others was, of necessity, important to him. He found himself pulled into the undertow of the popular current values.

But there came a pivotal point in his life when he discovered that they were not "values" at all. They were petty status symbols that did little more than feed his ego. As a much wiser man, he later said of this losing set of values, "What things were gain to me, those I counted loss for Christ" (Phil. 3:7).

People of this world say that greatness is having power over people, having power to influence others. The world says possessions make you great. The kind of car you drive, the kind of home you live in, and the kind of clothes you wear determine your degree of greatness. Others contend that popularity determines your greatness. But the real set of values is found in the Ten Commandments.

IV. Utilize your present opportunities.

Paul admonished Timothy, "Be sure to use the abilities God has given you" (1 Tim. 4:14 TLB). Opportunities are not reserved for the future. They are here for today! You will never have a future opportunity unless you utilize your present opportunity. Francis Bacon said, "A wise man will make more opportunities than he finds." James Oliver contended, "The fellow who does it now has time to do something else while the other fellow is still thinking about it."

The pessimist says, "It can't be done." The optimist says, "It can be done." The "peptimist" says, "I just did it!"

Bill Logan was a black boy born in a humble Alabama home. His family was dirt poor. He used to lie in bed at night listening to the great trucks bite into the grade of U.S. 31, and he would say to himself, "Someday I want to drive a great bus. I want to have a fleet of buses." He visualized his own potential, recognized the possibility of the impossible, and patronized a winning set of values. And then he utilized his present opportunity.

A vice president of the Brooklyn Chase Manhattan Bank believed in Bill and offered to loan the funds needed, to serve on Bill's board of directors, and to advise him. Today Bill has a fleet of fifteen beautiful charter buses. Sometimes when a driver is ill, Bill drives the bus. He says, "I still think a bus makes sweeter music than any orchestra in the world." He often thinks of his mother standing in the front of her Sunday school class, saying, "Children, you take that first step, and the Lord will help you the rest of the way."

Conclusion

Bill Logan is a perfect example of a person who responded to Paul's challenge, "Be thou an example of the believers."

You can make the most of your life. You can become that person of whom you will be proud for years to come when you visualize your own potential, recognize the possibility of the impossible, patronize a winning set of values, and utilize your present opportunities.

SUNDAY MORNING, DECEMBER 17

Title: What to Give for Christmas

Text: "And when they had opened their treasures, they presented unto him gifts: gold, and frankincense, and myrrh" **(Matt. 2:11)**.

Scripture Reading: Matthew 2:1–15

Hymns: "Majestic Sweetness Sits Enthroned," Stennett
"The Head That Once Was Crowned," Kelly
"Great Redeemer, We Adore Thee," Harris

Offertory Prayer: Eternal gracious Father, giver of eternal life and bestower of all good gifts, to you we come to offer the love of our hearts, the praise of our lips, and the fruit of our labors. As the wise men of old brought precious gifts of their substance, so today we bring tithes and offerings in sincere reverence to him whom you have appointed to be our King. Help us to give our lives fully and freely into his service. We pray in his saving name. Amen.

Introduction

The first Christmas was a time of giving, and so has been every Christmas since. When Jesus was an infant, the magi brought him gifts of gold, frankincense, and myrrh—the best money could buy. The shepherds did not bring material gifts, but they brought their faith in response to the angels' report. Joseph and Mary gave their lives. They committed themselves to God's plan even though they did not fully understand it. God the Father gave the greatest of all gifts, his only begotten Son. He gave the gift that cannot be described with words and cannot be duplicated.

What shall we give this Christmas? Here are some suggestions.

I. Let us give love.

The Pharisees asked Jesus this question to test him: "Master, which is the great commandment in the law?" (Matt. 22:36).

Jesus answered, "Thou shalt love the Lord thy God with all thy heart, and with all thy soul, and with all thy mind. This is the first and great commandment. And the second is like unto it. Thou shalt love thy neighbour as thyself. On these two commandments hang all the law and the prophets" (Matt. 22:37–40).

Love the Lord.
He comes before family (Matt. 10:34–38).
He comes before things (Matt. 6:33).
Love others (1 John 4:20–21).

II. Let us give forgiveness.

In the model prayer, Jesus said to pray, "Forgive us our debts, as we forgive our debtors" (Matt. 6:12). To forgive means "to bear away, to wipe off, to dismiss." When God forgives us, he considers the debt paid. He no longer holds it to our account, and reconciliation becomes possible.

Unforgiven sins or debts cause strife, bitterness, or jealousy. It is interesting to note that Jesus, knowing the hearts of people, felt constrained to explain this petition of the Lord's Prayer. He said, "For if ye forgive men their trespasses, your heavenly Father will also forgive you: But if ye forgive not men their trespasses, neither will your Father forgive your trespasses" (Matt. 6:14–15).

Forgiveness is a characteristic of one who is a member of God's kingdom. It requires great effort to be forgiving. It cost God his Son to forgive us, and we should be forgiving too!

III. Let us give a good example.

Simon Peter said, "For even hereunto were ye called: because Christ also suffered for us, leaving us an example, that ye should follow his steps" (1 Peter 2:21).

Paul said to Timothy: "Let no man despise thy youth; but be thou an example of the believers, in word, in conversation, in charity, in spirit, in faith, in purity" (1 Tim. 4:12).

The word *example* means "writing under." Children trace the writing of the writing master. Jesus Christ, our Lord and Savior, left his imprints in the steps he took while on earth. We are to walk in his steps. We are to be Christlike examples. Let us be godly examples, especially to children at Christmastime.

IV. Let us give the gospel to hungry souls.

What is the gospel? The gospel is the good news about Jesus Christ. It includes his coming, his death, and his resurrection (1 Cor. 15:1–5). We are to share the gospel with others.

Amos records, "Behold, the days come, saith the Lord GOD, that I will send a famine in the land, not a famine of bread, nor a thirst for water, but of hearing the words of the LORD; and they shall wander from sea to sea, and from the north even to the east, they shall run to and fro to seek the word of the LORD, and shall not find it" (Amos 8:11–12). There is indeed a famine in America and across the world. Men, women, boys, and girls are hungry to hear the gospel of the Lord Jesus Christ.

The angel of the Lord announced the birth of Christ to the shepherds with these words: "Fear not; for, behold, I bring you good tidings of great joy, which shall be to all people. For unto you is born this day in the city of David a Saviour, who is Christ the Lord" (Luke 2:10–11).

Let us give the gospel to the lost of our day. Let us proclaim Christ to all.

V. Let us give glory to God.

The multitude of heavenly host on the first Christmas day praised God, saying, "Glory to God in the highest, and on earth peace, good will toward men" (Luke 2:14). There are five good reasons why we ought to give glory to God:

It magnifies the right person. John the Baptist had it right when he said, "He must increase, but I must decrease" (John 3:30).

It acknowledges our stewardship. "Bless the LORD, O my soul: and all that is within me, bless his holy name. Bless the LORD, O my soul, and forget not all his benefits" (Ps. 103:1–2). Since God is the giver of every good and perfect gift, let us give glory to him.

It expresses humility and gratitude. The proud do not give glory to God. Base people do not express gratitude. God is praised by the humble and grateful. Glory to God warms the Christian's heart. Whose heart is not warmed by the singing of hymns of gratitude and praise?

It produces power. People are turned to our Lord when we give glory to him and praise his name.

Conclusion

In all our giving this Christmas, let us give the gift that will last for all eternity. God gave such a gift to us when Christ came.

For some years the *Chicago Daily News* printed on its front page each Christmas Eve a cartoon by the Nobel Prize winner Vaughan Shoemaker. It showed beneath a beautifully decorated Christmas tree an unopened package labeled "Eternal Life." The title of the cartoon was "The Untaken Gift." John 3:16 was quoted in the cartoon. God in goodness gave Christ to the world. Now he offers eternal life to all who will receive it: "And whosoever will, let him take the water of life freely" (Rev. 22:17).

SUNDAY EVENING, DECEMBER 17

Title: The Whole Gospel for the Whole World

Text: "Go ye therefore, and make disciples of all nations, baptizing them in the name of the Father and of the Son and of the Holy Spirit, teaching them to observe all that I have commanded you" **(Matt. 28:19–20 RSV)**.

Scripture Reading: Matthew 28:18–20

Introduction

Many countries have been born within the last few decades. New nations are struggling to move from the eighteenth century into the twenty-first century over a short period of time, thus presenting a challenge for Christian missions. What are the principles our missionaries are conveying to the people of these nations to help lead them in God's ways?

I. You are the object of God's love.

When we realize that God loves us, we take on a sense of dignity and self-respect that will no longer willingly endure the degrading practice of tyranny or paternalism. The mission message is that each person is important to God. God so loved each one of us that he sent his Son to die for our sins.

In days from the past the story is told of a poor African-American sharecropper family in Georgia. They barely eked out an existence and were always in debt. One year they had a good harvest and had a few dollars left over after their debts were paid. There was not enough money for a separate gift for each family member, so the mail order catalog was examined to find a modest gift all could share. They decided to order a mirror, for they had never had a mirror in their house. Ten days later the mailman brought them a package. They opened the box. The father looked in the mirror and frowned. The mother smiled. The baby giggled. Each saw his or her own likeness for the first time. Finally, the mirror was passed to little Willie. He did not know whether to cry or frown, for you see, Willie had been kicked in the face by a mule when he was a toddler. His face was scarred and twisted.

"Mom," he asked, "do I really look like this? Did you know it all the time? And you still loved me?"

"Yes, Willie," she replied, "I loved you."

This is the message from God to our world. No matter how scarred and twisted our lives, God loves us. "While we were yet sinners, Christ died for us."

II. Human nature can be changed.

We have seen this in our own lives since Christ came into our hearts. We have seen it in our family and our friends. We also have seen it in primitive lands when the message of Christ and God's love has been received.

Seventy-five years ago world missions was at a crossroads. It was considered a joke by many, even in high places. Missionaries were regarded as nosy meddlers or irrelevant dreamers, throwing their lives away as naive, ineffective do-gooders.

When World War II extended into the Southwest Pacific, American servicemen were apprehensive about falling into the hands of tribes on the islands. Sixty-five years before, on New Guinea, wild savages practiced witchcraft and sorcery and ate their enemies. One chief had thirty-five human jawbones hanging from his rafters.

One day a missionary appeared. They promptly killed him, roasted his flesh, and consumed him. Then they braced themselves for the appearance of armed troops to avenge his death. But another missionary came, unarmed and alone, and took up where the last missionary left off. Gradually the message sank in: "God loves us, and he can change our lives though his Son, Jesus Christ." When our men landed on the island, they were met by barefoot, dark-skinned men who looked like savages but turned out to be

Christians. They rescued our soldiers, fed them, nursed their wounds, protected them, and transported them to safety. The missionary message had transformed these people into happy Christian friends.

Conclusion

Human nature can be changed anywhere in the world. And your nature can be changed right now when you commit your heart and life to Jesus Christ.

WEDNESDAY EVENING, DECEMBER 20

Title: Don't Worry about Tomorrow

Text: "Take no thought of your life, what ye shall eat, or what ye shall drink; nor yet for your body, what ye shall put on" **(Matt. 6:25)**.

Scripture Reading: Matthew 6:25–34

Introduction

Albert Einstein said, "I never think of the future. It comes soon enough." Vance Havner, an evangelist of the past generation, said, "Worry is like a rocking chair. It will give you something to do, but it won't get you anywhere."

Rev. R. C. Trench, for years the Protestant archbishop of Dublin, Ireland, had a terrible fear of being paralyzed. At a party one evening, the lady sitting next to him heard him whispering to himself, "It has happened at last. I have lost all feeling in my right leg."

"Reverend," the lady said, "it might comfort you to know that it is my leg you are pinching and not yours!"

We make light of worry, yet we continue to worry. Christ was aware of the universal practice of worry, and in Matthew 6 we find an entire lesson he gave on the problem of worry. In this passage there is a command, a contrast, a comfort, and a calling.

I. A command.

Verse 25 is a command and a prohibition. When Jesus said, "Do not worry about your life" (NIV), he was using the Greek aorist tense that forbids continuing doing something. If God gave us life, surely we can trust him for lesser things. If God gave us bodies, surely we can trust him to give us clothes for these bodies. We can trust God not to be stingy or forgetful about our needs. Therefore, worry is wrong.

William Barclay, a British Bible expositor, said that we should use our past as a guide for better action in the future. The past should not be something that leads us to brood until we worry ourselves into emotional paralysis. When we come to Christ for forgiveness, God forgives and forgets our past, and so should we. Therefore, worry is useless.

A French soldier in World War I carried with him this quote about worry: "Of two things, one is certain. Either you are at the front, or you are behind the lines. If you are at the front, of two things one is certain. Either you are exposed to danger, or you are in a safe place. If you are exposed to danger, of two things one is certain. Either you are wounded or you are not wounded. If you are wounded, of two things one is certain. Either you will recover or you will die. If you recover, there is no need to worry. If you die, you can't worry. So why worry?" Worry is useless.

Worry is harmful. Worry wears out the body and the soul. Judgment, the ability to make decisions, and the power to deal with life are all hindered by worry. Let us do our best, for we cannot do more and God does not expect us to do more.

II. A contrast.

Christ strengthened his command "Do not worry" by drawing three contrasts. First, he drew a contrast between men and birds. Birds do not worry about their lives. They do not try to hoard food for the future. The lesson Jesus was teaching is not that birds do not work. No other creature works harder. The lesson is that though birds work, and work hard, they do not worry.

The Lord was not saying that we should sit like caged birds waiting to be fed. Rather, like the birds of the air, we are to work hard and yet remain free from worry. The contrast Christ made illustrates that God, who cares so much for the birds, cares even more for us.

Christ drew a contrast between men and flowers. Flowers bloom one day and soon wither and die. Yet they are clothed with a beauty that surpasses that of kings. When they die they are good only for fuel. When a woman wanted to increase the heat of her oven, she would grab a handful of dried grasses and wildflowers and fling them in the oven.

William Barclay said, "If God gives such beauty to a short-lived flower, how much more will he care for man?"

The third contrast drawn by Christ is between men and pagans. He admonished us not to worry like the pagans do. "So don't worry at all about having enough food and clothing. Why be like the heathen? For they take pride in all these things and are deeply concerned about them" (Matt. 6:31–32).

If you have trusted God with your soul, which will live forever, can't you trust God and the promises he has made? We can understand a pagan's distrusting God, but for a Christian to distrust him is beyond understanding!

III. A comfort.

Now that we have heard the command and seen the contrast, there is a comfort. It is awfully comforting to know that God knows all our needs—even those needs of which we are not aware. Even before we ask that our needs be met, God is aware of them. Do you believe in such a God? He is personal, he is all-powerful, and he is all-knowing. He understands us. He cares for us.

We stand on the threshold of a dark unknown. A lot of us are wondering what lies ahead. We may not know what tomorrow holds, but we know who holds tomorrow. With Paul we can say, "I know whom I have believed."

IV. A calling.

Jesus issued a calling, which if fulfilled, will defeat worry. "Seek ye first the kingdom of God, and his righteousness; and all these things shall be added unto you" (Matt. 6:33). He requires that we put God's kingdom first. It is his conviction that worry is banished when God becomes the dominating power in our lives.

Suppose your doctor tells you, "You are terminally ill." You plead, "Doctor, do something, an operation or medication, or some treatment. I want to live." The doctor asks, "Live for what?"

Quite frankly, it would be difficult for most of us to say without premeditation, "This is what I want to live for. This is my one overriding goal!" How would you answer the doctor's question? It should be, "For me to live is Christ." We are called to "seek first the kingdom of God."

Christ has called us to place tomorrow in God's hands. "Take therefore no thought for tomorrow: for the morrow shall take thought for the things of itself" (Matt. 6:34). Worry can be defeated when we place tomorrow in God's hands—when we live one day at a time. If each day is lived as it comes, if each task is done as it appears, then the sum of these days is certain to be good. The psalmist said, "Commit your way to the LORD; trust in him and he will do this: He will make your righteous reward shine like the dawn, your vindication like the noonday sun" (Ps. 37:5–6).

Conclusion

How do you place tomorrow in God's hands? It all begins with placing yourself, your past, your present, and your future in the hands of Jesus as your Savior and Lord.

SUNDAY MORNING, DECEMBER 24

Title: Why Is Jesus Coming Again?

Text: "I go to prepare a place for you. And if I go and prepare a place for you, I will come again, and receive you unto myself; that where I am, there ye may be also" (**John 14:2–3**).

Scripture Reading: John 14:1–6

Hymns: "Have Faith in God," McKinney
"O for a Thousand Tongues," Wesley
"Make Me a Blessing," Wilson

Offertory Prayer: We come to you this day, Father, with the sincere gratitude of our hearts and the praise of our lips. We come now to worship you with our gifts, the fruit of our labor. We thank you for the ability to work, to earn, and to save, and to have and to share. Add your blessings to these gifts that the good news of your love might be known in this community and to the uttermost parts of the earth. In Jesus' name we pray. Amen.

Introduction

The story of Christmas is incomplete without the second coming of Christ. Christianity had a historical incarnation, and it will have a historical consummation. Salvation, the purpose of Christ's first coming, would be incomplete without Christ's coming again. The second coming of Christ is the glorious event that will bring to fruition all the benefits and blessings of salvation.

Why is Christ coming again? Let us seek some answers to this great question.

I. Jesus is coming again to claim his own.

Jesus said, "I go to prepare a place for you. And if I go and prepare a place for you, I will come again, and receive you unto myself: that where I am, there ye may be also" (John 14:2–3). Christ returned to heaven from the earth to prepare a place for his people. He will gather his people to him.

He will resurrect the righteous dead at his coming. "And the dead in Christ shall rise first" (1 Thess. 4:16).

He will translate the righteous living at his coming. "Then we who are alive and remain shall be caught up together with them in the clouds, to meet the Lord in the air: and so shall we ever be with the Lord" (1 Thess. 4:17).

II. Jesus is coming again to judge.

The Bible makes it clear that Christ is coming to judge. His coming will be glory for the believer but disaster for the unsaved person.

> God is just: He will pay back trouble to those who trouble you and give relief to you who are troubled, and to us as well. This will happen when the Lord Jesus is revealed from heaven in blazing fire with his powerful angels. He will punish those who do not know God and do not obey the gospel of our Lord Jesus. They will be punished with everlasting destruction and shut out from the presence of the Lord and from the glory of his might on the day he comes to be glorified in his holy people and to be marveled at among all those who have believed. (2 Thess. 1:6–10 NIV)

One of the last things Jesus said in Revelation is, "Behold, I come quickly; and my reward is with me, to give every man according as his work shall be" (Rev. 22:12). When our Lord comes again, everyone will have to give an account of his or her life.

III. Jesus is coming again to reward the righteous.

At the second coming of Christ, the righteous will be rewarded for their faithfulness. He will send his angels out to gather the elect. The redeemed will be suited in white robes for eternity, and crowns will be placed on their worthy brows. The redeemed will enter Christ's kingdom, where nothing can ever molest or make afraid or cause unhappiness. When the Chief Shepherd appears, his people will receive crowns of glory that will not fade (1 Peter 5:4).

IV. Jesus is coming again to reject unbelievers.

The second coming of Christ will be tragic for unbelievers who reject Christ as Lord and Savior. It will be a devastating time for those who are not redeemed, for Jesus will say: "Depart from me, ye cursed, into everlasting fire, prepared for the devil and his angels. . . . And these shall go away into everlasting punishment: but the righteous into life eternal" (Matt. 25:41, 46).

Those who have refused his mercy, turned away from his truth, trampled on his law, neglected his church, persecuted his people, and despised his grace will meet their eternal fate at Christ's coming again.

V. Jesus is coming to make cosmic changes in the earth.

Bible passages that speak of cosmic changes at Christ's coming are found in several places, for example, Romans 8:19–23 and Revelation 21:1.

Peter asked, "Seeing then that all these things shall be dissolved, what manner of persons ought ye to be in all holy conversation and godliness, looking for and hasting unto the coming of the day of God, wherein the heavens being on fire shall be dissolved, and the elements shall melt with fervent heat? Nevertheless we, according to his promise, look for new heavens and a new earth, wherein dwelleth righteousness" (2 Peter 3:11–13).

The earth was cursed after Adam and Eve sinned in the garden of Eden. The harmony and the beauty will be restored. The second Adam will completely undo the works of the first Adam, and there will be a new heaven and a new earth.

VI. Jesus is coming again to usher in the eternal kingdom of God.

At the second coming of Christ, the work of redemption will be finished. He will then give the kingdom back to the Father. "Then cometh the end, when he shall have delivered up the kingdom to God, even the Father: when he shall have put down all rule and all authority and power" (1 Cor. 15:24).

VII. Jesus is coming again to manifest his glory.

Paul gave this charge to Timothy, and we do well to accept it as well:

> In the sight of God, who gives life to everything, and of Christ Jesus, who while testifying before Pontius Pilate made the good confession, I charge you to keep this command without spot or blame

until the appearing of our Lord Jesus Christ, which God will bring about in his own time—God, the blessed and only Ruler, the King of kings and Lord of lords, who alone is immortal and who lives in unapproachable light, whom no one has seen or can see. To him be honor and might forever. Amen. (1 Tim. 6:13–16 NIV)

Christ has been glorified with the glory he had with the Father "before the world was" (John 17:5). Christ also has been glorified in his death (John 12:23; 13:31).

Peter declared to the Jews that in the resurrection of Christ "the God of Abraham, and of Isaac, and of Jacob, the God of our fathers, hath glorified his Son Jesus" (Acts 3:13; cf. 1 Peter 1:21). Christ now has a glorified body (Phil. 3:21). He is glorified by the Holy Spirit (John 16:14) and is glorified in his redeemed (John 17:10), in the sufferings of his own (1 Peter 4:14), and in the gospel (2 Cor. 8:19). The very gospel now preached is the "gospel of the glory of Christ" (2 Cor. 4:4) and the "gospel of the glory of the blessed God" (1 Tim. 1:11).

VIII. Jesus is coming again to reign forever and ever.

Jesus is coming as King of Kings and Lord of Lords, to reign forever and ever. Hear John the apostle: "And I saw heaven opened, and behold a white horse; and he that sat upon him was called Faithful and True, and in righteousness he doth judge and make war . . . And he hath on his vesture and on his thigh a name written, KING OF KINGS, AND LORD OF LORDS" (Rev. 19:11, 16).

The kingdom over which our Lord will reign is an everlasting kingdom. The angel Gabriel said to Jesus' mother, Mary, "And he shall reign over the house of Jacob for ever; and of his kingdom there shall be no end" (Luke 1:33).

Daniel the prophet said, "And in the days of these kings shall the God of heaven set up a kingdom, which shall never be destroyed: and the kingdom shall not be left to other people, but it shall break in pieces and consume all these kingdoms, and it shall stand for ever" (Dan. 2:44).

Conclusion

The first coming of Christ brought hope. His coming again is the blessed hope. As we contemplate his coming again, our hearts cry out with the apostle John, "Come, Lord Jesus" (Rev. 22:20).

SUNDAY EVENING, DECEMBER 24

Title: The Song the Angels Sang

Text: "For behold, I bring you good tidings of great joy, which shall be to all people" **(Luke 2:10)**.

Scripture Reading: Luke 2:8–20

Introduction

The first Christmas service was celebrated at night. It was not observed in a church or synagogue or in the temple. It took place on the Judean hills. The meeting was not lighted by candles or lamps. The stars and the glory of God lighted the scene. The congregation was not composed of the rich, the famous, and the favored. A handful of lowly shepherds made up the assembly. The choir was a heavenly chorus.

It was night in Bethlehem. It was also night—the night of hopelessness and despair—all over the world. There was peace in the land, but it was the peace of the graveyard. Rome held God's chosen nation under its heel. People longed for a lasting peace. God sent them an eternal Prince of Peace.

God had a message of good news to deliver to the world. He didn't have the modern conveniences of the Internet and television, so how would he get out his message? Through an angel who visited a group of shepherds in the fields at night. The angel delivered the most electrifying announcement ever heard. A baby was born in Bethlehem, and his name was Jesus. He was the incarnate Son of God, the promised Messiah. He would save his people from their sins.

I. Jesus was the Savior.

Jesus came to save sinners from the greatest curse on the human race—sin that had alienated people from God. Jesus came to reconcile God and humans. Jesus did not come primarily as a reformer or as a miracle worker or as a prophet.

II. Jesus was the Christ.

Peter replied to Jesus' question as to his identity, "Thou art the Christ, the Son of the living God" (Matt. 16:16). Jesus was God's anointed. Israel longed for a Messiah and had been waiting for his appearance for a long time. Sadly, when he came they refused to acknowledge and receive him.

III. Jesus was the Lord.

Jesus came not only to serve but to be served. He came not just to die for our sins but to also live in our hearts. He rules in the hearts of his children by love, not by force.

Because Jesus humbled himself and became obedient to death on a cross, "God exalted him to the highest place and gave him the name that is above every name, that at the name of Jesus every knee should bow, in heaven and on earth and under the earth, and every tongue acknowledge that Jesus Christ is Lord" (Phil. 2:9–11 NIV). "For he must reign, till he hath put all enemies under his feet" (1 Cor. 15:25). "The Lord God omnipotent reigneth; Alleluia" (Rev. 19:6).

The Christmas message is a missionary message. It is good news for all people. Some news is good for one person and bad for another. Good news of a war won is bad news for the losers. Good news of a team victory is bad news for the losing team. Good news of an election won is bad news for the other candidates. The gospel is good news for everyone—for the poor as well as the prosperous, for the ignorant as well as the learned, for the child as well as the adult. It is good news for everyone in every nation.

"Go ye into all the world, and preach the gospel to every creature" (Mark 16:15), Christ commanded us. His farewell words were, "Go ye therefore, and [make disciples of] all nations" (Matt. 28:19).

Conclusion

The Christmas message is the missionary message. The missionary message is the Christmas message. Jesus was born, and he lived, died, rose again, and ascended to the Father. He will return, and it could be today. Let us be zealous to get the message out to all the world.

WEDNESDAY EVENING, DECEMBER 27

Title: When Life Hands You a Lemon

Text: "What? shall we receive good at the hand of God, and shall we not receive evil? In all this did not Job sin with his lips" **(Job 2:10)**.

Scripture: Job 2:7–10

Introduction

How do you react when life hands you a lemon? How should you react when adversity comes crashing into your life? I think we learn the answer from Job.

One of the most profound statements in all the Bible was made by Job when he asked, "Shall we accept good from God, and not trouble?" (Job 2:10 NIV).

Job, was right! It is wrong to accept the good things of life and then complain about the bad. This was Job's response to his wife's suggestion that he curse God and die. Job was a good man and did not deserve what was happening. If anyone knew that, it was his wife!

Job accepted the good of life with a thankful spirit. Now he would bear the bad of life with a thankful spirit. He would face his losses quietly and courageously. He would allow no bitterness to spoil his spirit. From Job we learn how to respond when life hands us a lemon.

Author and lecturer George Buttrick observed, "The same sun that hardens the clay melts the wax." Why does an identical cause produce opposite results? The answer is found in the response of the substance to the cause.

We can choose to be like the clay and respond to the hurt of life by allowing it to harden us and make us bitter. Or we can choose to be like wax and let what happens melt us and shape us into something new.

I. The options before us.

"Then said [Job's] wife unto him, Dost thou still retain thine integrity? Curse God, and die" (Job. 2:9).

One option is the clay response. I witnessed this response while visiting a terminally ill church member in the hospital. She was a faithful member of the church for years, always present and always willing to help. We visited for some time. Then I asked her if I could offer a prayer. Her response shocked me! I had never heard such a response before, and I have never heard one since. She said, "Yes, you can pray, but I can tell you right now it won't make any difference!" Hers was a clay response.

We have another option. Ours can be that of Job's: the wax response. "For I know that my redeemer liveth, and that he shall stand at the latter day upon the earth. And though after my skin worms destroy this body, yet in my flesh shall I see God" (Job 19:25–26).

Scripture and secular history are filled with examples of such positive responses to negative experiences.

II. The examples that challenge us.

David was a lemonade maker. He wrote, "I will bless the LORD at all times; his praise shall continually be in my mouth" (Ps. 34:1). King Saul sought to kill David. Even his own son Absalom turned against him. Yet his was a wax response.

Paul was a lemonade maker. Even though he suffered severely, his letters reveal a positive response to difficult circumstances. Never once in any of his writings did he complain about his life in prison. Paul found a way not just to endure prison but actually to utilize it. He did this by moving on with his goal in life. He found a way to make the most of a bad situation.

Jesus was a lemonade maker. Even when he died, he did not have a plaintive word on his lips. Rather, he gave a shout of victory: "It is finished!" He was not a stranger to hardship and disappointment. If anyone had a right to complain about injustice and to become cynical toward life, it was Jesus.

A list of other lemonade makers include John Bunyan, who in Bedford jail wrote *The Pilgrim's Progress*; Martin Luther, who, imprisoned in Wartburg Castle, translated the entire New Testament; and Dietrich Bonhoeffer, who in a Nazi prison wrote *The Cost of Discipleship*.

III. The secret that frees us.

How were all these people able to respond so positively and graciously to their hardships and disappointments? What is the secret of this resilience that enables some people to pick up the pieces and start anew rather than going to pieces under the impact of tragedy?

The secret lies in how we visualize God's relation to our lives. The problem with Job's wife was that she had a wrong view of God. She was spoiled by expecting a life free of difficulty. She felt that God was acting unfairly. In contrast, Job saw God as he is and not as his wife wanted him to be. God does not promise us a rose garden, and he is not to blame for every bad thing that comes our way. Some things come straight from God; others come straight from Satan.

The Bible teaches us that God is present with us regardless of what may come our way, be it good or bad, intentional or unintentional. It further asserts that God will not give us more than we can bear. In fact, we are told that good can come out of the worst experiences.

Myron Madden, the author of *The Power to Bless*, says, "The essence of despair is relegating God solely to the past." We must continue to believe that God is still at work in our world and in our lives today. We need to hold on to the fact that his sovereign purpose will, in time, be fulfilled.

When we feel abandoned by God, we must remind ourselves that feeling and fact are not the same. In times of difficulty when prayers are not being answered, do not despair. God is not hard of hearing, He has not abandoned us, and he is not powerless. He is still accomplishing his will and purpose quietly and relentlessly.

Conclusion

Paul Powell, author of *When the Hurt Won't Go Away*, admonishes us with these words: "So, when troubles come, don't give up in despair; don't become angry at God; don't feel sorry for yourself; don't syndicate your sorrows; don't let bitterness consume you. Fight these attitudes and temptations with all your heart."

Say with Job, "For I know that my redeemer liveth, and that he shall stand at the latter day upon the earth: and though after my skin worms destroy this body, yet in my flesh shall I see God" (Job 19:25–26).

SUNDAY MORNING, DECEMBER 31

Title: Retrospective and Perspective

Text: "Surely I am with you always" **(Matt. 28:20 NIV)**.

Scripture Reading: Matthew 28:18–20

Hymns: "O God, Our Help in Ages Past," Watts
"The Nail-Scarred Hand," McKinney
"Lead On, O King Eternal," Shurtleff

Offertory Prayer: Holy Father, you have blessed us in a bountiful way in the year that is about to come to a close. We thank you for each blessing. As we make our offering today, help us to particularly express our love and appreciation for the multiple blessings that have been ours. Then take the offering and use it to bring similar blessings to people all over the world. In Jesus' name we pray. Amen.

Introduction

This is the last Sunday in 2017. We cannot come to the end of a year without reflecting on the past. Neither can we project our thoughts into the incoming year without thinking what it holds for us.

Whether we reflect on the past or project into the future, we can be assured of God's presence with us. He is with each of his children always, even unto the end of the age.

I. The word *retrospective* is used to define looking backward on the year that is coming to a close.

There is a group of words that deals with the physical and psychological aspects of our lives. Paul used the word *forget* (Phil. 3:13). He said to forget those things which are behind. To make one's reflections on the past fruitful, forgetting must be thought of in two ways—positively and negatively. The thought here is to forget the things that are bad. Every person needs to forget the unpleasant and unhappy. Such experiences as defeat, disappointment, and guilt are things that should be forgotten. This can be done by an unconditional surrender to Jesus for forgiveness and cleansing (1 John 1:9).

Each person needs to forget the attitudes that make for pride and egotism. The Bible says that "pride goeth before destruction" (Prov. 16:18). The Bible also says that "every good gift and every perfect gift is from above, and cometh down from the Father of lights" (James 1:17).

The word *remember* is used many times in the Bible and is also helpful as we seek to be retrospective. To make the past productive, it is necessary to remember that we are dependent on God for all that he has and is. We also need to remember the blessings and opportunities of the past year.

Another word that ought to be prevalent in the mind of each person as we reflect on the past is *learn*. Most honest and/or intelligent persons learn from mistakes. They also learn from their achievements and use these lessons to build the future.

Look is another word that will aid the retrospective mind. We need to look at what has happened in the past and use that knowledge. A good hard look at the past and an intelligent analysis of it is profitable for every person. The same thing is true of what could have happened.

There is another group of words that applies to the spiritual aspects of our lives. Reflecting on God's past dealings with us will cause us to stand in *awe*. We are amazed when we come to realize how sinful we really are and how merciful and long-suffering the Lord is toward us.

Then the awe leads to repentance. Conscientious people will turn from their wicked ways after reflecting on the past. To behold our sinfulness and God's goodness in our past will provoke repentance.

One of the greatest words in the Christian's vocabulary is *forgiveness*. The Bible assures every sinner of forgiveness when we confess our sins. It is indeed a spiritually healthy experience to be retrospective and realize that we are forgiven of all our sins.

II. The word *perspective* is used to project one's thought into the future.

There are some helpful words that apply to the physical. The word *vision* looms high in our minds as we think of the future. Proverbs 29:18 says, "Where there is no vision, the people perish." This applies to individuals and churches. It applies to the physical as well as the spiritual.

One word that is prevalent in the minds of many on the eve of a new year is *resolution*. This word implies purpose. For adequate plans to be made and for motivation to expedite them, there must be purpose.

Closely related to resolution is the word *determination*. This puts firmness into resolutions. Before much can be accomplished in the incoming year, determination is necessary. This will involve planning, work, sacrifice, and dedication.

To be truly successful in the coming year, we must feed into our subconscious the thought of victory. The Christian religion is a triumphant, victorious religion. Jesus came to triumph over evil. He is victorious, and his followers have the same assurance.

There are some words that apply to the spiritual realm that are applicable to perspective attitude. Paul said, "Be filled with the Spirit" (Eph. 5:18). This means to be controlled by the Holy Spirit and is a must for great accomplishments in kingdom work and personal aggrandizement.

Paul also said, "Pray without ceasing" (1 Thess. 5:17). "Prayer is like a vast continent, the shores of which one can touch from many directions, but a lifetime of exploration will not reveal its secrets" (Bruce E. Mills, *Help in Troubled Times* [Valley Forge, PA: Judson, 1962], 139). Prayer takes on the aspects of eternity and is also a must to make the incoming year a fruitful one.

Obedience to God's will is the one greatest desire for next year. Whatever he says, do. Wherever he leads, follow. Complete obedience is our assurance of a full and meaningful life.

III. There is a word that stands between *retrospective* and *perspective*, and that word is *now*.

Now is between the past and future. To use the past and anticipate the future, we need to act now. The past is gone, and the future is yet to come. We must learn our lessons from the past and start preparing now to be ready for the future. God has spoken in the past and has worked in the past, but he also has plans for the future. Now is the time to respond to the voice of his Holy Spirit.

Conclusion

As you reflect on the past year and on God's goodness to you, give him your thanks. As you look forward to the year just ahead, surrender your life to him. Place your hand in his nail-scarred hand and say, "Lead on, O King eternal."

SUNDAY EVENING, DECEMBER 31

Title: You Can Take It from Here

Text: "Therefore go and make disciples of all nations, baptizing them in the name of the Father and of the Son and of the Holy Spirit, and teaching them to obey everything I have commanded you. And surely I am with you always, to the very end of the age" **(Matt. 28:19–20 NIV)**.

Scripture Reading: Matthew 28:16–20

Introduction

Very appropriate to the concluding Sunday service of a year is the scene in the last verses of Matthew's gospel. Jesus gathers his disciples closely about him, reviews for them their base of authority, and gives them their marching orders into the world. At no other place in the history of the world is it more obvious that our Lord has committed the gospel to his church. We have a fourfold account of the great commission of our Lord. Matthew declares that the content of the gospel is "good news" and instructs his disciples to cross the barriers of geography, socioeconomic disparities, cultural and racial differences, and interpersonal relationships by the good news of God in Christ Jesus.

It is further appropriate that in the concluding Sunday evening service of this year we be reminded of the three great missionary motives: the command of Christ to go; the inner compulsion of the spirit that says, "I must go"; and the voice from God that keeps saying, "Go!" The needs of the world are obvious. The mission task of the people of God is not a matter of emotion or feeling. It is not a work to be carried on at our convenience. We are under orders of the Lord. He said, "You take it from here!"

This command of our Lord has at least three characteristics.

I. The authority of the command.

A religion that has no authority is a worthless one. Some have emphasized the autonomy of the individual to ridiculous extremes. In the backdrop of this principle, we might conclude that things pertaining to the Christian life are arbitrary or optional. We can do them or not do them as our souls command. But the flip side of that record is the authority of Christ, and Jesus leaves no question. "All power is given unto me in heaven and in earth." These are the orders of our King. If the church asked you to do it, you might have wavered; if the preacher asked you to do it, you might have made a decision; if the only reason we had for our missionary enterprise was that other churches were doing it, we would question. But our Lord, whose authority is beyond question, has given this command. Forever the principle is established!

This is the authority of the King. The task of the church and the task of the minister is to show people who God is in Christ Jesus. The one who left the glory of heaven and came among humans, who lived as a man, who gave his life sacrificially on Calvary's cross, who demonstrated the power of God over death and the grave by his glorious resurrection—it is he who says, "The authority belongs to me." This is the one who so majestically and regally certifies his work. He is the one who so royally stands by his disciples and gives them marching orders. The cross was behind him, the resurrection was the sealing bond. He lived, he loved, he taught, he served, and he died for people of all time. He has a right to say to his church, "Go make disciples."

II. A steady task.

Our Lord has not merely given us something to believe but something to do. Here in a few sentences is the scope of our task. The command leaves no question. What is the business of the church, the business of the Christian? It is to bring people to God through Jesus Christ. It is to baptize those who are won; it is to teach the way and the work and the purposes of our Lord. It is written indelibly in the history of the church that a Christian thrives spiritually when passing on his or her faith to others.

Significant and appropriate for the needs of our world is an individual review of personal mission. The mission God gives us is expressed in personal terms. It is not meant to be done by professionals; it is meant to be an expression of the faith and hope and love of an individual found in personal relationship with Christ Jesus. It is the task of each Christian.

A church may have some admirable characteristics. It may be financially successful, physically attractive, and organizationally complete, but if it does not reflect a flame of missionary zeal, surely "the glory of the Lord" has departed from it.

In hundreds of metropolitan areas of our nation, individuals are groping, seeking, and longing for the filling of a spiritual vacuum. Personal face-to-face encounters by the people of God can provide the good news of God through Christ Jesus. These areas are full of domestic problems, youth dilemmas, economic anxieties, and social and cultural chaos. Great barriers exist in the minds and behavior patterns of tens of thousands of persons. Jesus himself said, "I am the way, the truth, and the life; no man cometh unto the Father, but by me" (John 14:6). On this concluding day of a year when we review our yesterdays, let us take a new look at tomorrow and understand that God is saying in Christ Jesus, "As you go, make disciples."

III. A divine presence.

Jesus expressed his authority for this mission, defined the continued and steady task of personal relationships with others, and concluded his commission with a promise: "Surely I am with you always, to the very end of the age."

One of the traumatic experiences of personal relationship is the moment in which you must say good-bye to a dear friend. It is difficult to express feelings in a moment like this. Sometimes we say, "I will be thinking of you." By this, we mean that in spirit we will be sharing our friend's experience, helping, sustaining, and encouraging our friend in his or her new venture though separated physically. Certainly it does help to know that we are not forgotten, and continuing relationships can be maintained by correspondence and phone calls.

But our Lord goes farther than that. He says, "I will go with you." The promise of the living Christ is not just a dream. It is the promise of a very real presence. John expresses this truth in chapters, 14, 15, and 16 of his gospel.

Always is the word that Jesus used. This means all the days of summer, winter, spring, and fall—the sunny days and the cloudy days, the days of storm and the days of joy, the days of faith and the days of doubt, the days of victory and the days of defeat, the days of strength and the days of weakness, the days of peace and the days of war, the days of youth when significant decisions are made and the days of midlife when decisions are being carried through, the days of life and, yes, even the days of death and the years of eternity. Jesus meant it when he said, "I will be with you *always.*"

Conclusion

Here then is the final word of our Lord to his people: "You take it from here." At the highest moment in Jesus' ministry, he expressed the royal authority of King. It is by the authority of heaven and the authority of the earth entrusted to him that he says to every Christian, "You take it from here."

MISCELLANEOUS HELPS

MESSAGES ON THE LORD'S SUPPER

Title: The Lord's Supper: Interpretations of It

Text: "And as they did eat, Jesus took bread, and blessed, and brake it, and gave to them, and said, Take, eat: this is my body. And he took the cup, and when he had given thanks, he gave it to them: and they all drank of it" **(Mark 14:22–23)**.

Scripture Reading: Mark 14:22–25

Introduction

To obey the Lord and observe the Lord's Supper is an outstanding privilege of every believer. Because of the importance of this ordinance, people have a variety of opinions about it. The purpose of this message is to explore these opinions.

I. There are four prominent historic views.

A. *The Roman Catholic view is known as* transubstantiation. *Trans* means "over," and *substantia* means "substance." Thus the meaning is "to change into another substance." The word applied to the doctrine of the Lord's Supper means that the elements—bread and wine— are changed into the body and blood of Jesus.

B. *The Lutheran view is known as* consubstantiation. The word *consubstantiate* means "to regard as, or make to be, united in one common substance or nature." Thus *consubstantiation* means "the actual substantial presence and combination of the body of Christ with the eucharistic bread and wine." This doctrine, then, holds to the idea that through some miraculous or mysterious way, when one partakes of the bread and wine, Christ's body and blood are actually present.

C. *The "*grace with*" view is that when a person takes the elements—bread and wine—he or she receives grace through the taking that is not available otherwise.*

D. *Many evangelicals endorse the* symbolic *view.* This is the concept that the elements are symbols of the broken body and shed blood of Christ.

II. This is a larger discussion of the symbolic view.

A. *The word* symbol *means "a sign by which one knows or infers a thing."* Applied to the ordinance of the Lord's Supper, it means the elements are placed in such a way that one may know.

B. *Synonyms such as* emblem, attribute, *or* type *help us better understand.* These words mean something visible standing for something invisible or intangible. The elements are outward signs of something spiritual. For example, a cross is a symbol of the death of Jesus, which wrought salvation, and so to some it is a symbol of their salvation.

Conclusion

Regardless of one's doctrine of the Lord's Supper, it is a wonderful means of worship. Each time a child of God worships in this way, the death of Jesus should take on greater meaning.

Title: The Lord's Supper from the Journalistic Point of View

Text: "And he took bread, and gave thanks, and brake it, and gave unto them, saying, This is my body which is given for you: this do in remembrance of me. Likewise also the cup after supper, saying, This cup is the new testament in my blood, which is shed for you" **(Luke 22:19–20)**.

Scripture Reading: Luke 22:14–20

Introduction

It has been said, "When you have good news that you know will interest an individual or group, follow the newspaper style and tell your reader Who, What, When, Where, and Why in the opening" (Lillian Doris and Besse May Miller, *Complete Secretary's Handbook* [Englewood Cliffs, NJ: Prentice-Hall, 1960], 192).

The death of Jesus Christ for sin is good news, and the journalistic technique to tell about his death and the Lord's Supper as it relates to it is used here.

I. Who is to observe the Lord's Supper?

A. *Each child of God, each person who knows Jesus as Savior, is to observe the Lord's Supper.* Only Christians can appreciate the significance of the bread and wine. They are aware of what the death of Jesus really means.

B. *The church as an aggregate is also to observe the ordinance.* Many church bodies call it a church ordinance. Therefore, the church gathered in worship is to observe the Lord's Supper.

II. What is the observance of the Lord's Supper?

It is partaking of bread and juice in obedience to Christ's command.

A. *It is an ordinance.* God ordained that his children obey this commandment.

B. *It is a memorial.* God's children are to partake of the elements in order to better remember the death of Jesus and what it means to each believer.

III. When are the believers told to observe the ordinance?

A. *First Corinthians 11:26 says, "as often as ye eat this bread, and drink this cup," but a specific time is not mentioned.*

B. *Acts 20:7 says, "Upon the first day of the week, when the disciples came together to break bread . . . ."* A logical interpretation of this passage is that they came together for this purpose. Some groups do this each Sunday, others once a quarter, and others at different times.

IV. Where is the Lord's Supper to be observed?

Most commonly in a church worship service. The majority of Christians hold to the opinion that this is not a private affair.

Sometimes privately. By so doing, the proper administrator goes to the individual—such as the sick or a confined person—and observes the ordinance.

V. Why should people observe the ordinance?

This already has been alluded to, but there are two points that explain the why.

A. *From God's standpoint, it is commanded.* This is not just a capricious act on God's part. It is done out of his knowledge of our needs. It is given to people by God for our good.

B. *From the human standpoint, it is a reminder.* Jesus said, "This do in remembrance of me." It is rather strange that we must be reminded of what Jesus did for us on the cross, but we must be.

Conclusion

A high and distinct privilege of every Christian is to partake of the Lord's Supper. It is truly good news.

Title: Taking the Bread and Cup

Text: "And as they were eating, Jesus took bread, and blessed it, and brake it and gave it to the disciples, and said, Take, eat, this is my body. And he took the cup, and gave thanks, and gave it to them, saying, Drink ye all of it" **(Matt. 26:26–27)**.

Scripture Reading: Matthew 26:26–29; 1 Corinthians 11:23–34

Introduction

A record of the Lord's Supper is found in four places in the Bible (Matt. 26:26–28; Mark 14:22–26; Luke 22:19–20; 1 Cor. 11:23–24). Christians believe that the Lord's Supper is a memorial to the death of Christ on the cross. The Lord's Supper is a prophecy for those who partake of it to "show the Lord's death till he come" (1 Cor. 11:26). The Lord's Supper is a fellowship with Christ and with other Christians. In fact, the words "till he come" was a frequently used phrase among early Christians that assured recognition, consideration, kindness, and fellowship.

Let us look at what it means to take the bread and the cup.

I. When we take the bread and the cup, we proclaim that Christ is the Savior of sinners (Matt. 26:28).

A. *Christ was born in fulfillment of prophecy (Mic. 5:2).*
B. *Christ was born of a virgin (Matt. 1:18—25).*
C. *Christ lived a sinless life (2 Cor. 5:21).*
D. *Christ died a vicarious death (1 Peter 2:21–25).* Christ is the Savior of sinners. The bread and wine of the Lord's Supper declares him so.

II. When we take the bread and the cup, we confess our need of Christ's atoning sacrifice (I Cor. 11:24–25).

The Bible teaches that all have sinned and come short of the glory of God. It teaches that the wages of sin is death. The Bible also teaches that Christ died on the cross for sinners. The death of Christ on the cross is necessary and sufficient for the sinner's salvation. When we become Christians, we receive Christ into our lives as Savior and Lord. When we as Christians take the bread and the cup, we confess our need of Christ's atoning sacrifice.

III. When we take the bread and the cup, we declare that heaven is our home (Matt. 26:29).

The Lord's Supper speaks of the Father's kingdom. In the new kingdom, Christ will meet his disciples and eat and drink with them there. All of us who have believed in him will be with him there.

IV. When we take the bread and the cup, we show forth the Lord's death till he comes (I Cor. 11:26).

The Lord's Supper teaches:

A. *Christ died for us (Rom. 5:8).*
B. *Christ is coming for us (1 Thess: 4:13–17).*
C. *Christ will take us to heaven to be with him forever (Matt. 26:29).*

Conclusion

When we partake of the Lord's Supper, we remember what Christ did for us on the cross and look forward to our future with him in heaven. Songwriter James M. Black had it right when he wrote:

> *When the trumpet of the Lord shall sound,*
> *And time shall be no more,*
> *And the morning breaks, eternal, bright and fair:*
> *When the saved of earth shall gather over on the other shore,*
> *And the roll is called up yonder,*
> *I'll be there.*

MESSAGES FOR CHILDREN AND YOUNG PEOPLE

Title: The Search for Happiness

Text: "Remember now thy Creator in the days of thy youth. Let us hear the conclusion of the whole matter: Fear God, and keep his commandments; for this is the whole duty of man" **(Eccl. 12:1, 13)**.

Scripture Reading: Ecclesiastes 12:1–14

Introduction

How to live in these tense days and be happy and useful is the deep concern of youth. The days in which we live are days of confusion, perplexity, bewilderment, uncertainty, and disillusionment. They are critical days for all of us. Let us discover how to live life at its highest.

King Solomon, the writer of the book of Ecclesiastes, traveled down many blind alleys in search of happiness. Life for him was full of many perplexing problems and disappointments. His theme is "vanity of vanities; all is vanity" (Eccl. 1:2). Dr. John Sampey, in his book *Syllabus for Old Testament Study* ([Nashville: Sunday School Board of the Southern Baptist Convention, 1924], 148–49), points out twenty-seven things that disturbed Solomon:

1. One event happens to the wise man and to the fool (2:14–17).
2. A man has to leave the fruits of his toil to another, and his heir may be a fool (2:18–23).
3. Man is under the decrees of God and cannot change them (3:1–15).
4. There is wickedness in the place of judgment (3:16–17).
5. Man dies like the beasts (3:18–22).
6. Oppressors are full of power (4:1–3).
7. Skill begets envy (4:4–6).
8. Wealth does not fulfill (4:7–12).
9. The old, even on a throne, are quickly forgotten (4:13–16).
10. Increase of goods brings an increase of those who consume them and loss of sleep to the owner (5:10–12).

11. Wealth can be lost suddenly (5:13–17).
12. Some possessors of wealth cannot enjoy their riches (6:1–6).
13. Appetite and desire are never permanently satisfied, and the future is unknown (6:7–12).
14. The laughter of fools is unfounded (7:5–6).
15. Women are not to be trusted (7:23–29).
16. Man knows not the day of his death and cannot avert it (8:6–8).
17. One man has power over another to his hurt (8:9–11).
18. The fate of the righteous and of the wicked often are identical (8:14).
19. Death is inevitable, and the dead are soon forgotten (9:2–6).
20. Chance renders everything uncertain (9:11–12).
21. Achievements of a poor wise man are unrewarded and forgotten (9:13–16).
22. A little folly outweighs wisdom and honor (10:1).
23. Fools are placed in distinguished positions (10:5–7).
24. The days of darkness shall be many (11:8).
25. Old age can be dreary and comfortless (12:1–7).
26. Much study is a weariness of the flesh (12:12).
27. We must give an account for all things at the judgment bar of God (11:9; 12:14).

Solomon wrote from a skeptical human viewpoint, but at the conclusion of the book, he came to the road that leads to happiness. "Let us hear the conclusion of the whole [duty of man]" (Eccl. 12:13).

I. If we are to find happiness, we must fear God.

We are taught in the Bible to fear God.

A. *The fear of God is life (Prov. 19:23).*
B. *The fear of God is wisdom (Job 28:28).*
C. *The fear of God is holiness (2 Cor. 7:1).*
D. *The fear of God causes one to hate evil (Prov. 8:13).*
E. *The fear of God causes one to depart from evil (Prov. 16:16).*
F. *The fear of God prolongs one's day (Prov. 10:27).*
G. *The fear of God produces great confidence (Prov. 14:26).*

II. If we are to find happiness, we must remember the Creator in the days of our youth (Eccl. 12:1).

A. *Responsible for your youth (Eccl. 11:9).*
B. *Rejoice in your youth (Eccl. 11:9; 1 Tim. 4:12).*

III. If we are to find happiness, we must keep God's commandments.

A. *What are God's commandments?*
   1. The first commandment (Matt. 22:36–38).
   2. The second commandment (Matt. 22:39–40).

B. *What is necessary for the keeping of God's commandments?*
   1. Reverence.
   2. Love for God (John 14:15; 15:10).
   3. Obedience to God (John 15:14).
   4. Walk as Jesus walked (1 John 2:3–6). How did Jesus walk?
      a. With purity of conduct.
      b. With divine purpose.
      c. With implicit faith.
      d. In humility and self-sacrifice.
      e. With compassion for others.

Conclusion

To leave God out of life is to miss the road to happiness. Let God take control of your life so that you may have happiness. He is the end of the search for happiness.

Title: God Is Looking

Text: "And I sought for a man among them, that should make up the hedge, and stand in the gap before me" **(Ezek. 22:30)**.

Scripture Reading: Ezekiel 22:23–31

Introduction

Jonathan Edwards once said, "Resolve: First; that every man should live at his highest and best for Christ always and everywhere, and Second; whether any other man in the world so lives or not, I shall strive with God's help so to live to the end of my day" (quoted in George W. Truett, *The Prophet's Mantle* [Grand Rapids: Baker, 1973], 197).

I. Each individual is an important person in God's sight (Isa. 45:4–5).

A. *God has a plan for each person's life.* Before a person was born into this world, he or she was planned by God. There is nothing that should be more encouraging than the thought that God made us and has a plan in accordance with the way we are made.

B. *The plan God has for a person makes it obvious that people don't become famous by accident.* God had a plan for Moses and provided for that plan. The Lord enabled Moses to be a mighty man for good. Neither was the apostle Paul an accident. The Lord made him and used him according to his plan. Moses and Paul are examples of greatness because they complied with God's plan for their lives.

C. *To be great, then, one must find God's plan for his or her life.* One is not to look for *a* plan or *some* plan, but *God's* plan.

427

II. God is looking for people who are willing to comply with his plan (Ezek. 22:30).

A. *The context of the passage found times similar to contemporary times.*
People in high places had thrown all standards of righteousness
into discord. But rather than compromising with such behavior,
God was looking for someone to change the conditions for good.

    The country was plunging into chaos. Such times are a chal-
lenge. God looks for people to stand tall for righteousness.

> *God give us men. A time like this demands*
> *Strong minds, great hearts, true faith, and ready hands,*
> *Men whom the lust of office does not kill,*
> *Men whom the spoils of office cannot buy,*
> *Men who possess opinions and a will,*
> *Men who have honor; men who will not lie.*
> *Men who can stand before a demagogue*
> *And damn his treacherous flattery without winking,*
> *Tall men, sun-crowned, who live above the fog*
> *In public duty and in private thinking.*
> *For while the rabble with their thumb-worn creeds,*
> *Their large professions and their little deeds,*
> *Mingle in selfish strife, lo freedom weeps,*
> *Wrong rules the land and justice sleeps.*
> —John G. Holland, in *The Prophet's Mantle*, 201

B. *A genuine test of a civilization is the kind of men and women it produces.*
The civilization is a miserable failure if it produces a generation of
people who ignore God, but it is a tremendous success when that
generation acknowledges God.

    A traveler from abroad mentioned four valuations of a person
in the United States: "How much does a man know?" "Who is his
father?" "Where does he come from?" and "How much does he
have?" But none of these are adequate. The real question is, "To
whom does he belong—to God or to something or someone else?"

III. We must ask three vital questions as we fit into God's plan.

A. *What is the most valuable life in the social order?* It is not the longest
or most famous. It is the one that seeks to live in harmony with
God's will.

B. *What is the greatest trait in human character?* Faithfulness. The
greatest epitaph one could have is "Faithful unto the end." There is
a need for faithfulness to the standards of right.

C. *What are the three greatest institutions?* Home, church, and state. They
all have their problems, but by all means, don't be a part of the
problem. Be a part of the solution.

Conclusion

We are never to think of ourselves as unimportant or insignificant. God knows each of us intimately. He knows us by character, talent, and opportunity. He is always out in front leading, encouraging, and helping us.

Title: An Abundant Life

Text: "I am come that they might have life, and that they might have it more abundantly" **(John 10:10)**.

Scripture Reading: John 10:7–18

Introduction

John 10:10 tells us that the Lord intends for us to have happy, useful, fruitful lives. This kind of life is the result of pure, clean, upright living. Young people search for this kind of life, but many search in the wrong direction. To have a full and meaningful life, people must be right, think right, and do right.

I. The abundant life is a life of healthy thoughts.

A. *We can learn by observing.* People who face surgery with a wholesome, positive attitude generally fare better than those who have a negative attitude. People who have a wholesome attitude generally get much more out of life than others. The reverse is also true: people who maintain a negative attitude are miserable.

B. *The Bible says a great deal about how people think.* Philippians 4:8–9 gives a series of good things to think about and a promise for those who think correctly. Colossians 3:2 says, "Set your minds on things above, not on earthly things" (NIV). Proverbs 23:7 is the classic passage that says, "For as he thinketh in his heart, so is he."

C. *Most illnesses are caused by stress from cares, difficulties, and troubles.* Casting our cares on Christ and developing a positive attitude will help us have an abundant life.

II. The abundant life is a life that has spiritual depth.

A. *Human beings are made by God to have fellowship with him.* To deny that we are created to have fellowship with God is to destroy the possibility of having a happy life. There is no way we can ignore God and have ultimate happiness. To defy this fact or to run from God is a sure way to be miserable.

B. *One of the greatest challenges young people can have before them is to be true spiritual children of God.* The initial act of becoming a child of God is to be born into God's family. John 3:3 calls it the new birth. After the new birth, by the help of the indwelling Holy Spirit, we must refrain from evil, draw close to God, and be purged from sin.

429

III. The abundant life is a life that has social wealth.

A. *Of all the choices young people make, one of the most important is choosing right friends.* Our associates can make or ruin us.

B. *It is of vital importance that we learn early in life how to choose friends.* We must be kind and courteous to all. No one can be a snob to some, ignore others, and be friendly to a select few and find the right kind of friends. Rather, we must have the mind of Christ toward everyone.

We must go to the right places and stay away from the wrong ones. Generally, the right kind of friends are found and made when a person goes to good, wholesome places.

We must respect the opinions and judgment of older, mature people, such as parents, pastors, and teachers, who love us and sincerely try to give the right kind of advice.

Conclusion

God has planned a happy, victorious life for everyone, and he has provided the means whereby we can have this life. Now each person in turn is to make a total commitment to him, walk in his Spirit, and have the abundant life.

FUNERAL MEDITATIONS

Title: The Lord Provides

Scripture Reading: Psalm 23

Introduction

Over the years, Psalm 23 has brought comfort to those in grief. When human minds are clouded with an emotional disturbance such as grief, they turn to the beautiful and familiar. This psalm fills both requirements. Understanding the psalm's background will enable us to draw even greater comfort from it. The psalmist was experiencing unrest, hostility, weariness, danger, and perplexing problems.

I. The first verse recognizes God as the one who supplies all needs.

A. *"The Lord is my shepherd."* The personal pronoun "my" makes God personal. He is claimed as one's own. Even though a statement of this nature seems audacious, it is true. In the time of grief, such a realization is of much comfort.

B. *Because he is the Shepherd, there is no want.* When the heart seems to be breaking because of grief, one may wonder where the truthfulness of this statement is. But the Lord is good to his word, and his promise applies to every need of mind and body.

II. The second verse promises rest and refreshment.

A. *"Green pastures" and "still waters" are symbols of sustenance and nourishment.* David's circumstances as a fugitive dictated the value of such needs being supplied. Grief is a similar circumstance, and the promise is good here too.

B. *Helplessness is what makes one realize the need.* So long as all people can go in their own strength, they do not recognize the need for help. But when a loved one is taken in death, there is a crying need for strength that comes only from God.

III. The third verse speaks of restoration.

A. *David had been guilty of gross sin.* During the time of carrying his guilt around, he felt that the hand of God was heavy on him (Ps. 32:4). When he confessed his sin, he found the guilt gone, the shame removed, and the burden lifted.

B. *David's experience with sin has a parallel with each person who is sorrowing because of the death of a loved one.* The soul becomes burdened with emotional disturbance, the heart grows weary with sorrow, and the Lord restores.

IV. Verses 3 and 4 tell about God guiding, protecting, and leading.

A. *To be a guide, one must be out in front.* Prior to anyone's death, the Lord Jesus has already been there. He is able to lead through it. He also is out in front of those in sorrow, ever ready to comfort.

B. *The "paths of righteousness" denote right living.* God leads us away from evil. He also leads us away from sorrow beyond which we can bear. He leads to wholesome thoughts and actions of faith. Only through faith and dependability on God can we bear the burden of grief gracefully.

C. *"Thou art with me."* No person or word is able to supply the deep need of the innermost being like the presence of God.

V. Verses 5 and 6 picture a loving host welcoming the guest.

This is a change from the shepherd scene. It is a beautiful picture of an elaborate banquet.

A. *"Preparest a table before me."* All through life we experience hunger of one sort or another. In the presence of the Lord, our needs are totally supplied.

B. *"Anointest my head with oil."* This is a picture of someone welcoming a loved one home. As we read this passage, we can almost hear the voice of God welcoming by name his child who has passed on. The remaining loved ones find comfort here.

VI. "I will dwell in the house of the Lord forever."

This is a picture of the end of the journey and home at last.

Conclusion

Beautiful literature is of much help to many. Divinely inspired literature is even more helpful. Combine the two, and help is at its best. Psalm 23 is both.

Title: Victory over Death

Text: "So when this corruptible shall have put on incorruption, and this mortal shall have put on immortality, then shall be brought to pass the saying that is written, Death is swallowed up in victory" **(1 Cor. 15:54).**

Scripture Reading: 1 Corinthians 15:42–58

Introduction

The Bible speaks of death as an enemy. It is an enemy of both the person who dies and of the loved ones who are left behind. All people need comfort and help in such a crisis.

The passage of Scripture used in this discussion points out the positive side of death. When Christians die, it is victory for them and not defeat.

I. For many, it is a victory over the immediate past.

This is referring to a recent illness that takes life away.

A. *The word "victory" implies struggle.* Loved ones struggle with killer diseases such as cancer, heart disease, and the like. Sometimes even though we obtain all the medical help we can, the end is death.

B. *At the moment of seeming defeat, there is the greatest victory.* When the human body is at its weakest, God's grace is at its greatest. When all human instruments are defeated, the great Victor steps in and the Christian's coronation service takes place.

II. For others, death is victory over the past.

A. *From birth, life is a struggle.* Struggle is a way of life. It is not necessarily bad. Athletic events are contest and struggle. However, the body does grow tired and the game must come to an end.

B. *All games have an element of frustration.* There are errors and mistakes. The competition is keen and inabilities loom high. Victory is truly a rewarding experience. Death is swallowed up in victory.

III. Death is victory because of the destiny to which it leads.

    A.   *Again, reference is made to the athletic contest and the locker room after victory.* One of the most exciting times a television viewer has in watching an athletic event is the locker room celebration. It is a great time of hilarity and celebration. There is no way the human mind can grasp the celebration of those who die in the Lord and enter the portals of heaven.

    B.   *Because of the victory of a loved one in death, those who are left behind want only to mourn the separation of a loved one.* By the same token, when a Christian loses a Christian loved one in death, the ones left behind need to rejoice over the victory of the dead in Christ.

Conclusion

Death is grievous from the human standpoint, but Jesus Christ conquered it when he arose from the grave. Therefore, all who die in him are victorious. Death is swallowed up in victory.

Title: Quality Living

Text: "I therefore, the prisoner of the Lord, beseech you that ye walk worthy of the vocation wherewith ye are called" **(Eph. 4:1).**

Scripture Reading: Ephesians 4:1–10

Introduction

The title of this sermon, "Quality Living," may seem unusual for a funeral message. However, a scriptural study of the subject will bring comfort to those who grieve over the death of a loved one who died in the Lord.

I. Quality living starts with a new birth.

    A.   *The image of God is restored in a person when he or she becomes a Christian.* A person who is spiritually dead can never live the life that is intended apart from the restoration of the divine image. Sin has marred that image.

    B.   *When a person is born again, the Holy Spirit comes to live in that person and to provide supernatural strength to walk worthy of his or her earthly vocation.* Since the earthly life is plagued with heartache, troubles, temptation, and the like, everyone needs more than human strength to cope with it.

II. Quality living is realized during the earthly life.

    A.   *Each Christian has a divinely chosen vocation.* For people to have the quality of life that the Lord has ordained for them, they must follow that vocation. Anything other than that is less than the best and does not bring fulfillment.

B. *Service to humankind is the supreme test of quality living.* Even though some may frown upon eulogizing at a funeral service, there are some lives that deserve such, and when done in good taste, a eulogy becomes an inspiration to others. It also is a means of comfort to the bereaved in attendance at the service.

III. Quality living makes for victory in dying.

A. *People are never ready to die until they have been born again.* The Bible emphasizes the necessity of the new birth to enter the kingdom of God. The opposite of this is also stressed. If people are not born again, their eternal destiny is separation from God.

B. *A good life is not what takes a person to heaven, but a personal relationship with God through Jesus Christ makes for quality earthly living.* Such a relation to God makes for assurance and peace of mind as death approaches. It is truly a sense of personal satisfaction when a person is about to draw his or her last breath, to be able to look back on life with no regrets.

IV. Quality living is at its best in the life beyond earth.

A. *In heaven, life is perfected.* The heavenly life excludes any negatives the human mind can conceive. The Bible assures us that "God shall wipe away all tears . . . ; and there shall be no more death, neither sorrow, nor crying, neither shall there be any more pain" (Rev. 21:4). What a triumphant victory for extended illness, pain, and dread of separation.

B. *In heaven, service is at its best.* All children of God go to heaven when they die. In heaven there will be no limitations to service and no weaknesses to hinder service. Service there will be perfected and glorified.

Conclusion

The gift of God is eternal life through Christ Jesus. When one receives eternal life, he or she begins a pilgrimage of living that lasts forever in heaven. This quality living is what God wants for us.

WEDDINGS

Title: Marriage Service

Organist: "Aria," Peters

Instrumentalists: "Adagio," Bach
"Prelude," Couperin
"Siciliene," Couperin
"Fantasy Piece," Schumann
"Jesu, Joy of Man's Desiring," Bach

Soloist: "The Greatest of These Is Love," Bitgood

Congregational: "Rejoice, Ye Pure in Heart," Plumptre

Processional: "Variations on a Theme by Haydn, Opus 56B," Brahms

Scripture: Ephesians 5:22–33

Benediction: "O Perfect Love," Barnaby

Recessional: "Joyful, Joyful, We Adore Thee," Beethoven

Ceremony

Beloved friends, we are gathered here in this place, hallowed by the presence of God, and illumined by the smile of his approval, to join in holy wedlock _____ (groom) and _____ (bride). This joyous occasion is associated in our thoughts with all that is nearest and dearest to the most sacred relation of life. It is an honorable estate designed by God for the happiness of humankind and the perpetuity of the human race.

Who gives this woman to be married to this man?

(Prayer)

Marriage is the culmination of the miracle of love that two people born a whole world apart can come together one day and read the deeper meaning of life in one another.

The union into which you two are about to enter is the closest and tenderest into which human beings can come. It is a chief moment in life when two people are drawn together by an irresistible attraction so that their souls cannot thenceforth be divided by time or space; when one sees in a single woman that dream of purity and sweetness which has ever haunted his soul; when in a single man she finds that rest and satisfaction her heart has been unconsciously seeking. It is a revelation from above and makes all things new. It is an act of utter faith, believing in one another to the end.

If you wish your new estate to be touched with perennial beauty, cherish those gracious visions that have brought spring to your hearts during the days of your courtship. Make real this ideal in your united lives, and your home will be a place of contentment and abiding joy.

_____ (groom), the highest ideal you can have before you is that which is presented in God's holy Word: "Husbands, love your wives, even as Christ also loved the church and gave himself for it." That love is pure, tender, and constant, and a love even unto death.

_____ (bride), God's Word also says, "And let the wife see that she reverence her husband." It becomes you to promote his happiness to the utmost of your power; by sympathy, genial consideration, and by constant kindness and care to do all of which you are capable to insure the completeness and happiness of his life.

You have been taught from childhood to love God. Live in the sunshine of that love, and look for the blessings he gives that secures true and abiding felicity.

In the hope and with the prayer that it may be so with you, let us proceed with the vows. Please join your right hands.

_____ (groom), in taking the woman whose hand you hold to be your lawful wedded wife, I require you to promise to love and cherish her, to honor and sustain her, in sickness as in health, in poverty as in wealth, in adversity as in prosperity, to be true to her and cleave to her and her only until death alone do you part. Do you so promise?

(Groom responds: I do.)

_____ (bride), in taking the man who holds you by the hand to be your lawful and wedded husband, I require you to promise to love and cherish him, to honor and sustain him in sickness as in health, in poverty as in wealth, in adversity as in prosperity, to be true to him and to cleave to him and him only until death do you part. Do you so promise?

(Bride responds: I do.)

Then you are mutually pledged.

_____ (groom), what token do you bring as a pledge that you will faithfully perform these vows?

(Groom responds: A ring.)

Let this ring be the sacred symbol of your unchanging love and a ceaseless reminder of this hour and of the vows you have taken. Place it on the hand of _____ (bride) and repeat after me:

_____ (bride), I give thee this ring in token and pledge of our constant faith and abiding love.

_____ (bride), what token do you bring as a pledge that you will faithfully perform these vows?

(Bride responds: A ring.)

May this ring likewise be a symbol of your unchanging love and a ceaseless reminder of this hour and of the vows you have taken. Place it on the hand of _____ (groom) and repeat after me:

_____ (groom), I give thee this ring in token and pledge of our constant faith and abiding love.

Let us pray.

(After prayer) And now by the authority that is given me as a minister of the gospel by the State of _____, I pronounce you husband and wife.

Remember, that which God has joined together, let no man put asunder.

SENTENCE SERMONETTES

Prayer is the key to the day and the lock to the night.

If you live a Christless life, you will die a Christless death.

Time will not tarry.

The life of a Christian is like breathing in and out: in for strength and training, out for ministry and service.

Walk your talk.

To step out of God's will is to step down, never up, in quality of life.

Does your walk match your talk as a Christian?

Grace is divine love in action.

The choice to rejoice leads to an attitude of gratitude.

Make every decision carefully and prayerfully.

Faith that does not call for sacrifice will never experience victory.

You do not solve a problem by destroying it.

People remain restless until they rest in the arms of God.

A faith that saves produces a faithful person.

God can take a nobody and make of that person a somebody.

You cannot lose with Jesus, and you cannot win without him.

The devil can only take as much ground as the Christian will give him.

Do not trifle two minutes of pleasure for a lifetime of tragedy.

A better world begins with me.

Age is a matter of mind. If you don't mind, it doesn't matter.

Some people are discovered; others are found out.

By failing to prepare, you prepare to fail.

A mistake not corrected is another mistake.

To stay youthful, stay useful.

Give without remembering; take without forgetting.

There is no right way to do the wrong thing.

Hope is the anchor of the soul made possible by our acceptance of God's grace.

He who aims at nothing usually hits it.

Don't be caught dead without Jesus, because you will need him.

People who know go to people who need to know.

A fault recognized is half corrected.

Only when we fill our existence with an aim do we make it a life.

To belittle is to be little.

Spiritual results do not come apart from spiritual discipline.

Faith is the eyesight of the soul.

God is only a prayer away.

The greatest of faults is to be conscious of none.

He who has no cross will have no crown.

Subject Index

This index includes main sermon topics and references that appear in bold subheadings. It is not an index that compiles every page reference for a word or phrase.

Abraham, 187-88
Anger, 287-89
Armor of God, 21-23
Attitudes, 50, 318; in crisis, 96-98
Authority, 124, 144, 182, 309-11, 417-18

Backbiting, 296-98
Bible, as Word of God, 347
Boasting, 303-5

Children, 73-74, 189-92, 199, 425-30
Christ. *See* Jesus
Christian life, 119, 235, 281, 433; in crisis, 195; in the home, 72, 167; struggle of, 67
Christmas, 387-90, 394-97, 401-3, 410
Church, 82, 96, 107, 257; early, 91

Danger, 391-94
David, 241-43, 371
Death, victory over, 432-33
Deliverance, 81, 242, 273
Depression, 139-40; of disciples, 238-41, 272, 294
Despair, 241-43
Devil, 357, 373; temptations of, 364; tricks of, 381
Dorcas, 173-74

Elijah, 219-20
Envy, 311-13
Evil, deliverance from, 273

Faith, 51-54, 154, 171, 188, 220, 255, 266-68, 293, 397; the way of, 289-92

Faithfulness, 357
Family, 51-54; concerns of, 235
Fasting, 207-10
Folly, 301
Forgiveness, 26, 48, 100, 128, 184-87, 221-23, 319-21

Glory, 57-59, 140-43, 208-9, 403, 409-10
Golden Rule, 261-64
Grace, 229, 362-64, 379

Hannah, 159-62
Happiness, 68; the search for, 425-27
Healing, 80-82, 106
Holy Spirit, 13-16, 28, 129, 144, 325-27, 333-35; use of the Word, 342-44
Hope, 57-59, 66, 229, 395
Hunger, 38-41, 385, 390-91, 402
Hypocrisy, 209, 276-278

Integrity, 118-21
Isaiah, 226-28

Jacob, 195-97
Jesus, 123, 250-52, 264, 271, 278-80; death of, 259-61; optimism of, 352-54; purpose, 410; resurrection of, 130, 145, 152-54; second coming of, 407-10; temptations of, 364-67
Joseph, 202-4
Joy, 44, 116-18, 128, 129, 144, 266, 292, 312, 396; of giving, 305-9
Judgment, 238-41, 272, 294

Kingdom of God, 34, 162-65, 409

Law of God, 102, 119, 125, 134, 260, 262, 360-61
Light of the World, 85-88
Loneliness, 233-35, 243-46
Lord's Prayer, 155-57
Lord's Supper, interpretations of, 421-25
Love, 27, 73, 120, 144, 190, 199, 258, 260, 307, 318, 355, 356, 396, 401-5, 435-36; of Jesus, 165-67, 327-29

Marriage ceremony, 434-36
Martha and Mary, 165-67
Maturity, 204-7
Meekness, 31-33
Men, 197-200
Mercy, 46-48, 142
Moses, 210-12
Motives, 140-43, 143-45, 240, 343, 361

Paul, 298-301, 378-80
Peace, 43-46; making, 62-65
Persecution, 69-72, 144
Poverty, of spirit, 16-19
Prayer, 34-35, 41-43, 74-77, 90-93, 100, 106, 129, 159-62, 193, 229, 254-57, 267, 436; boldness in, 213-16; difficulties of, 19-21; models of, 148-50, 155-57, 162-65, 170-72, 177-79, 184-87, 200-201; in the Spirit, 350-51; for spiritual prosperity, 49-51
Promises, 172, 228-30, 431
Purity, 54-57

Religion, resourcefulness of, 344-46
Righteousness, 35-38, 39, 40, 44-45, 93-96,

Ruth, 151-52

Salt of the earth, 77-79
Salvation, 59-62, 229, 253, 377
Self-deception, 293-95
Sermon on the Mount, 16-19, 23-26, 31-33, 38-41, 124; *see also* Lord's Prayer, *and look up all sermons based on Matthew 5-7.*
Sex, premarital, 181-84
Sickness, 28, 80-82, 105-6, 264; visiting the sick, 113-15
Sinners, converting, 273-75
Solace, 88-90
Solomon, 100, 425-27
Sorrow, 23-26, 241-43, 265; of Holy Spirit, 325-27
Strength, 13-15, 27, 50

Temptation, 27, 192-95, 364-67
Testifying, 121-23, 128-30, 132, 136-38, 143-45,
Thanksgiving, 42, 370-72
Thirst, 38, 40; of Jesus, 252-54
Truth, 28-31, 297, 357

Unity of the Spirit, 317-19

Victory, 433, 454; over Satan, 22, 68, 219
Vows, of God, 354-57

Wealth, 216-19
Witnessing, 107-10, 143-45; kinds of, 121-23, 128-30, 136-38
Women of the Bible, 151-52, 159-62, 165-67, 179-80
Worry, 230-33, 405-7

Index of Scripture Texts

Genesis
3:4–5 357
12:1–9 187
35:7 195
42:7, 24 .202

Exodus
3:2–3 210

Joshua
24:15 174

Ruth
1:18 151

1 Samuel
1:10–11 159

1 Kings
19:12 219

2 Kings
7:9 390

2 Chronicles
7:14 98

Job
3:10 412

Psalms
22:1 241
23. 430
84:12 289
102:1–2 41
107:1 370
116:14 354
127:1 167

Proverbs
14:30 311
22:6 189
31:30 179

Ecclesiastes
12:1, 13 425

Isaiah
6:5 226

Jeremiah
5:1 196

Ezekiel
22:30 427

Zechariah
9:9 123

Matthew
1:23 387
2:11 401
2:13 394
4:1 364
5:3 16
5:4 23
5:5 31
5:6 38
5:7 46
5:8 54
5:9 62
5:10–12 69
5:13 77
5:16 85
5:20 93
5:23–24 102
5:37 118
5:41 125
6:5 276
6:9 . . . . .148, 154
6:10 . . . . .162, 170
6:11 177
6:12, 14–15 184
6:13 . . . . .192, 200

6:16–18 207
6:19–21 216
6:25 405
6:31–32 230
6:33 223
6:44–45 133
7:1 238
7:6 246
7:7 26
7:11 254
7:12 261
7:13–14 268
7:20 285
7:21 293
7:24 301
7:28–29 309
13:28 373
13:31–32 .352
13:39 373
16:18–19 82
18:20 . . . . .257, 278
19:4–6 110
20:16 360
25:11-13 .391
25:45 271
26:26–27 .423
27:46 243
28:19 397
28:19–20 . . . . .403, 417
28:20 414

Mark

1:40–42 329
2:3 273
4:28 375
12:10 327
14:22–23 .421

Luke

2:10 410
7:47 319
8:50 96
11:1 34
14:12–14 .384
15:7 335

16:9 344
19:23 367
22:19-20 .422
23:34 219
23:43 228
23:46 266
24:11 130
24:32 138
24:48 121

John

1:11–13 264
1:14 321
1:32–34 128
4:13–14 157
4:47 105
4:50 338
5:2 80
10:10 429
11:5 165
11:35 88
14:2–3 407
16:32 233
19:25 235
19:28 252
19:30 259
20:20 152

Acts

4:20 107
8:4 143
9:36 173
10:43 136
12:5 90
20:35 . . . . .140, 305

Romans

10:1 378

1 Corinthians

14:40 113
15:3–4 145
15:54 432

Ephesians

4:1 433
4:3 317

4:26–27 287
4:30 325
5:18 333
6:10 13
6:11 . . . . .21, 381
6:14 . . . . .28, 35
6:15 43
6:16 51
6:17 . . . . .59, 67, 342
6:18 350
6:19–20 298

Philippians
4:6 19

Colossians
1:9 49
1:27 57
3:11 65

3:12 281
3:17 72

1 Timothy
4:12 . . . . 204, 398
5:22 181

2 Timothy
3:2 303

Hebrews
2:8–9 314
4:12 347
4:16 213
7:25 250
12:2 116

1 Peter
2:1–2 296
4:10 362